Letters and Homilies *for* Hellenized Christians

VOLUME II

A Socio-Rhetorical Commentary on 1-2 Peter

BEN WITHERINGTON III

IVP Academic
An imprint of InterVarsity Press
Downers Grove, Illinois

Apollos
Nottingham, England

InterVarsity Press, USA
P.O. Box 1400, Downers Grove, IL 60515-1426, USA
World Wide Web: www.ivpress.com
Email: email@ivpress.com

APOLLOS (an imprint of Inter-Varsity Press, England)
Norton Street, Nottingham NG7 3HR, England
Website: www.ivpbooks.com
Email: ivp@ivpbooks.com

InterVarsity Press®, USA, is the book-publishing division of InterVarsity Christian Fellowship/USA®, a student movement active on campus at hundreds of universities, colleges and schools of nursing in the United States of America, and a member movement of the International Fellowship of Evangelical Students. For information about local and regional activities, write Public Relations Dept., InterVarsity Christian Fellowship/USA, 6400 Schroeder Rd., P.O. Box 7895, Madison, WI 53707-7895, or visit the IVCF website at <www.intervarsity.org>.

Inter-Varsity Press, England, is closely linked with the Universities and Colleges Christian Fellowship, a student movement connecting Christian Unions throughout Great Britain, and a member movement of the International Fellowship of Evangelical Students. Website: www.uccf.org.uk.

Design: Cindy Kiple
Images: Camperaphoto Arte, Venice/Art Resource, NY

USA ISBN: 978-0-8308-2933-0
UK ISBN: 978-1-84474-215-8

Printed in the United States of America ∞

Library of Congress Cataloging-in-Publication Data

Witherington, Ben, 1951-
Letters and homilies for Hellenized Christians/Ben Witherington III.
v. cm.
Includes bibliographical references and indexes.
Contents: v. 1. A socio-rhetorical commentary on Titus, 1-2 Timothy, and 1-3 John.
ISBN-13: 978-0-8308-2931-6 (cloth: v. 1: alk. paper)
ISBN-10: 0-8308-2931-8 (cloth: v. 1: alk. paper)
1. Bible N.T. Pastoral Epistles—Commentaries. 2. Bible N.T. Pastoral Epistles—Socio-rhetorical criticism. 3. Bible N.T. Epistles of John—Commentaries. 4. Bible N.T. Epistles of John—Socio-rhetorical criticism. I. Title. BS2735.53.W58 2006
227'.077—dc22

2006020866

British Library Cataloguing in Publication Data
A catalogue record for this book is available from the British Library.

P 18 17 16 15 14 13 12 11 10 9 8 7 6 5 4 3 2 1
Y 22 21 20 19 18 17 16 15 14 13 12 11 10 09 08 07

This volume is dedicated to my friend and fellow New Testament scholar **Richard Bauckham** on the occasion of his early retirement. May God bless you with good health and energy as you live out your days in Cambridge so you may finish all those wonderful writing projects you still have in mind.

Pentecost 2007

Contents

2 Peter

Abbreviations

Ancient Works

Apoc. Mos.	*Apocalypse of Moses*
Apos. Con.	*Apostolic Constitutions*
2 Bar.	*2 Baruch*
4 Bar.	*4 Baruch* (= *Paraleipomena Jeremiou*)
Barn.	*Barnabas*
b. Sanh.	Babylonian Talmud, *Sanhedrin*
1-2 Clem.	*1-2 Clement*
CD	Cairo Genizah copy of the *Damascus Document*
Did.	*Didache*
1 En.	*1 Enoch (Ethiopic Apocalypse)*
2 En.	*2 Enoch (Slavonic Apocalypse)*
1 Esd	1 Esdras
2 Esd	2 Esdras = *4 Ezra*
Herm. *Mand.*	Shepherd of Hermas, *Mandate*
Herm. *Vis.*	Shepherd of Hermas, *Vision*
Ign. *Eph.*	Ignatius, *To the Ephesians*
Ign. *Magn.*	Ignatius, *To the Magnesians*
Ign. *Phld.*	Ignatius, *To the Philadelphians*
Ign. *Pol.*	Ignatius, *To Polycarp*
Ign. *Rom.*	Ignatius, *To the Romans*
Ign. *Smyrn.*	Ignatius, *To the Smyrnans*
Ign. *Trall.*	Ignatius, *To the Trallians*
Jdt	Judith
Jub.	*Jubilees*
LXX	Septuagint
1-4 Macc	1-4 Maccabees
m. Soṭ.	Mishnah, *Soṭah*
MT	Masoretic Text
NT	New Testament
OT	Old Testament
Pol. *Phil.*	Polycarp, *Letter to the Philippians*
Pss. Sol.	*Psalms of Solomon*
1QH	*1QHodayot*

1QpHab	*1QPesher to Habakkuk*
4QpHos	*4QPesher to Hosea*
4QpNah	*4QPesher to Nahum*
1QS	*1QRule of the Community*
Sib. Or.	*Sibylline Oracles*
Sir	Sirach
Sym.	Greek translation of Hebrew Bible (ca. AD 170) by Symmachus
T. Ab.	*Testament of Abraham*
T. Ash.	*Testament of Asher*
T. Benj.	*Testament of Benjamin*
T. Dan	*Testament of Dan*
T. Job	*Testament of Job*
T. Jud.	*Testament of Judah*
T. Levi	*Testament of Levi*
T. Mos.	*Testament of Moses*
T. Naph.	*Testament of Naphtali*
T. Reu.	*Testament of Reuben*
T. Zeb.	*Testament of Zebulun*
Tg. Ps.-J.	*Targum Pseudo-Jonathan*
Tob	Tobit
Wis	Wisdom of Solomon

Anaximenes of Lampsacus (Pseudo-Aristotle)

Rhet. Alex.	*Rhetorica ad Alexandrum (Ars rhetorica)*

Aristides

Or.	*Orationes*

Aristotle

Eth. Nic.	*Ethica Nicomachea*
Oec.	*Oeconomica*
Rhet.	*Rhetorica*

Augustine of Hippo

Conf.	*Confessions*

Cicero

Att.	*Epistulae ad Atticum*
Brut.	*Brutus or De claris oratoribus*
De or.	*De oratore*
Inv.	*De inventione rhetorica*
Nat. d.	*De natura deorum*

Part. or.	*Partitiones oratoriae*
Top.	*Topica*
Clement of Alexandria	
Paed.	*Paedagogus*
Quis Div.	*Quis dives salvetur*
Strom.	*Stromata*
Cyprian	
Hab. virg.	*De habitu virginum*
Demetrius	
Eloc.	*De elocutione*
Demosthenes	
Or.	*Orationes*
Diogenes Laertius	
Lives	*Lives and Opinions of Eminent Philosophers*
Epictetus	
Disc.	*Discourses*
Epiphanius	
Pan.	*Panarion (Adversus haereses)*
Eusebius	
Hist. eccl.	*Historia ecclesiastica*
Fronto	
Ep.	*Epistulae*
Herodotus	
Hist.	*Historiae*
Hesiod	
Theog.	*Theogony*
Irenaeus	
Haer.	*Adversus haereses*
Isocrates	
Ep.	*Epistulae*
Or.	*Orationes*
Jerome	
Epist.	*Epistulae*
Josephus	
Ag. Ap.	*Against Apion*
Ant.	*Jewish Antiquities*
J. W.	*Jewish War*
Life	*The Life*

Justin Martyr
  1 Apol. *Apologia i*
  Dial. *Dialogus cum Tryphone*
Lucretius
  Nat. *De rerum natura*
Minucius Felix
  Oct. *Octavius*
Philo
  Abr. *De Abrahamo*
  Conf. *De confusione linguarum*
  Flacc. *In Flaccum*
  Fug. *De fuga et inventione*
  Her. *Quis rerum divinarum heres sit*
  Legat. *Legatio ad Gaium*
  Mos. *De vita Mosis*
  Praem. *De praemiis et poenis*
  Sobr. *De sobrietate*
  Spec. *De specialibus legibus*
  Virt. *De virtutibus*
Philostratus
  Her. *Heroicus*
Plato
  Ep. *Epistulae*
  Pol. *Politicus*
Pliny the Younger
  Ep. *Epistulae*
Plutarch
  Arist. *Aristides*
  Demetr. *Demetrius*
  Mor. *Moralia*
Polybius
  Hist. *Universal History*
Quintilian
  Inst. *Institutio oratoria*
Rhet. Her. *Rhetorica ad Herennium*
Seneca
  Ep. *Epistulae morales*
Strabo
  Geogr. *Geographica*

Tertullian

Cult. fem.	*De cultu feminarum*
Marc.	*Adversus Marcionem*
Or.	*De oratione*

Theophilus of Antioch

Autol.	*Ad Autolycum*

Xenophon

Mem.	*Memorabilia*

Modern Works

AB	Anchor Bible
ABD	Anchor Bible Dictionary. Edited by D. N. Freedman. 6 vols. New York, 1992
ACCS	Ancient Christian Commentary on Scripture. Edited by Thomas C. Oden et al. Downers Grove, Ill.: InterVarsity Press, 1998-
AnBib	Analecta biblica
ATJ	*Ashland Theological Journal*
BBR	*Bulletin for Biblical Research*
BDF	Blass, F., A. Debrunner, and R. W. Funk. *A Greek Grammar of the New Testament and Other Early Christian Literature*. Chicago, 1961
BECNT	Baker Exegetical Commentary on the New Testament
BGU	*Aegyptische Urkunden aus den Königlichen Staatlichen Museen zu Berlin, Griechische Urkunden*. 15 vols. Berlin, 1895-1983
Bib	*Biblica*
BNTC	Black's New Testament Commentaries
BSac	*Bibliotheca sacra*
BT	*The Bible Translator*
BTB	*Biblical Theology Bulletin*
BZ	*Biblische Zeitschrift*
CBQ	*Catholic Biblical Quarterly*
CEC	*Catena in Epistolas Catholicas*. Edited by J. A. Cramer. Oxford, 1840
CNT	Commentaire du Nouveau Testament
ConBNT	Coniectanea biblica: New Testament Series
CPR	*Corpus Papyrorum Rainerii*. 24 vols. to 2002. Vienna, 1895-
CTJ	*Calvin Theological Journal*

CTM	*Concordia Theological Monthly*
EKKNT	Evangelisch-katholischer Kommentar zum Neuen Testament
ET	English translation
EvQ	*Evangelical Quarterly*
ExAud	*Ex auditu*
ExpTim	*Expository Times*
FN	*Filologia neotestamentica*
FRC	Families, Religion, and Culture
Hermeneia	Hermeneia—A Critical and Historical Commentary on the Bible
HTR	*Harvard Theological Review*
HUCA	*Hebrew Union College Annual*
IBC	Interpretation: A Bible Commentary for Teaching and Preaching
IBS	*Irish Biblical Studies*
ICC	International Critical Commentary
IGUR	*Inscriptiones Graecae urbis Romae*. Edited by L. Moretti, custodian of the epigraphical database. Rome, 1968-
Int	*Interpretation*
IVPNTC	The IVP New Testament Commentary Series
JBL	*Journal of Biblical Literature*
JETS	*Journal of the Evangelical Theological Society*
JSNT	Journal for the Study of the New Testament
JSNTSup	Journal for the Study of the New Testament: Supplement Series
JTS	*Journal of Theological Studies*
KEK	Kritisch-exegetischer Kommentar über das Neue Testament (Meyer-Kommentar)
KJV	King James (Authorized) Version
Metzger, *TC*	Bruce M. Metzger. *A Textual Commentary on the Greek New Testament*. London: United Bible Societies, 1971
MHT	Moulton, James Hope, Wilbert Francis Howard, and Nigel Turner. *A Grammar of New Testament Greek*. 4 vols. Edinburgh: T & T Clark, 1906-1976
MNTC	Moffatt New Testament Commentary
NAC	New American Commentary
NCB	New Century Bible
NCBC	New Cambridge Bible Commentary
Nestle-Aland	*Novum Testamentum Graece*. Edited by Eberhard and Erwin Nestle, Barbara and Kurt Aland, et al. 27th ed. 8th corrected printing. Stuttgart: Deutsche Bibelgesellschaft, 2006

NEB	New English Bible
NewDocs	*New Documents Illustrating Early Christianity*. Edited by G. H. R. Horsley and S. Lewelyn. North Ryde, N.S.W., 1981-
NIBCNT	New International Biblical Commentary on the New Testament
NICNT	New International Commentary on the New Testament
NIV	New International Version
NIVAC	NIV Application Commentary
Notes	*Notes on Translation*
NovT	*Novum Testamentum*
NovTSup	Novum Testamentum Supplements
NRSV	New Revised Standard Version
NTD	Das Neue Testament Deutsch
NTS	*New Testament Studies*
P.Cair.Preis.	*Griechische Urkunden des Aegyptischen Museums zu Kairo*. Edited by F. Preisigke. Strassburg, 1911
P.Flor.	*Papiri greco-egizii: Papiri Fiorentini*. 3 vols. Milan, 1906-1915
P.Mich.	*Michigan Papyri*. 19 vols. to 1999. Ann Arbor, MI, et al., 1931-
P.Oxy.	*The Oxyrhynchus Papyri*. 68 vols. to 2003. London, 1898-
PG	Patrologia Graeca [= Patrologiae cursus completes: Series Graeca]. Edited by J.-P. Migne. 162 vols. Paris, 1857-1886
PL	Patrologia Latina [= Patrologiae cursus completus: Series Latina]. Edited by J.-P. Migne. 221 vols. Paris, 1844-1865
RB	*Revue biblique*
RevExp	*Review and Expositor*
ResQ	*Restoration Quarterly*
RHPR	Revue d'histoire et de philosophie religieuses
RSV	Revised Standard Version
RV	Revised Version (1885)
SB	Sources bibliques
SBFLA	*Studii biblici Franciscani liber annus*
SBLDS	Society of Biblical Literature Dissertation Series
SBLMS	Society of Biblical Literature Monograph Series
SBLSP	Society of Biblical Literature Seminar Papers
SBS	Stuttgarter Bibelstudien
SBT	Studies in Biblical Theology
ScrB	*Scripture Bulletin*
SecCent	*Second Century*
SMTSMS	Society for New Testament Studies Monograph Series
SP	Sacra pagina

SwJT	*Southwestern Journal of Theology*
TBT	*The Bible Today*
THKNT	Theologische Handkommentar zum Neuen Testament
TNTC	Tyndale New Testament Commentaries
TynBul	*Tyndale Bulletin*
UBS	*The Greek New Testament*. Edited by Kurt Aland et al. 4th rev. ed. 4th printing. Stuttgart: German Bible Society / United Bible Societies, 1998
WBC	Word Biblical Commentary
WTJ	*Westminster Theological Journal*
WUNT	Wissenschaftliche Untersuchungen zum Neuen Testament
ZB	Zürcher Bibelkommentare
ZNW	*Zeitschrift für die neutestamentliche Wissenschaft und dieKunde der älteren Kirche*

General Introduction to 1 and 2 Peter

In this last of the three volumes in this series, we will be dealing with two quite different documents: 1 and 2 Peter. We will be arguing that the early church fathers were right that 1 Peter is written by Peter to Jewish Christians, much as the Johannine Epistles were written to these same sorts of folks in the neighboring region of Asia Minor. Our assumption, as argued in the first two volumes, will be that the Jewish Christian congregations founded by persons like the Beloved Disciple, Peter, Jude, emissaries of James, and the author of Hebrews basically had a life of their own, when compared to the Pauline churches. Often these churches were in the same regions as various churches founded by Paul and his coworkers, and they may well have had considerable interaction with the Pauline churches. There is no evidence that the Jewish and Pauline churches would have regarded each other as heterodox, but nonetheless they each had their own existence. The Jewish Christian churches were not amalgamated with or incorporated into the Pauline ones before the late first century or early second century, and many of these Jewish Christian churches actually appear to have continued to have their own existence well beyond the era in which the New Testament itself was written.

The ongoing viability and vibrancy of Jewish Christianity is shown not just by the existence of the Ebionites, or documents like the Hebrew Gospel of Matthew, which continued to support and educate these groups, but also by the continued warnings of some of the church fathers well into the fourth century about "Judaizing." In other words, we have done a disservice to Jewish Christianity if we think that it quickly disappeared due to the rising tide of Pauline and Gentile Christianity even as early as the first century A.D. This is simply not so, and the very number of documents in the New Testament canon originally addressing groups that were largely if not wholly composed of Jewish Christians eloquently testifies to their ongoing existence.

Some of these Jewish Christian groups, particularly the ones located in or near the Holy Land, were more traditionally Jewish (e.g., the audience of Matthew or Jude); some were more Hellenized (e.g. the audience of 1 Peter or the Johannine Epistles); but it is certainly something of an irony that documents like Hebrews, James, Jude, the Johannine Epistles, and 1 Peter were lumped together under the heading of the "Catholic Epistles." Nothing could be further from the truth than the suggestion that these documents were a bunch of general encyclicals written to all Christians everywhere in the Roman Empire. The label "Catholic Epistles," by which was meant universally directed epistles, was not placed on these diverse documents until long after they were written. It does not reflect how the original authors or audiences viewed these documents.[1] Apparently Eusebius first called seven of these letters the "general epistles" (Eusebius *Hist. eccl.* 2.23.35). Hebrews was not included in the General or Catholic Epistles group since it was thought to be by Paul and fairly early was grouped with the Pauline corpus.

But what about 2 Peter? In many ways this is the most enigmatic book to make it into the canon, arriving with some considerable doubts. We will reserve most of our analysis of it for later. Here it is enough to say that in my view it is clearly a composite document based on earlier resources—resources that go back to Peter and Jude. But it is also a document promulgated in a time when a collection of Pauline letters is circulating, as the last chapter of 2 Peter attests. As such it appears to have been compiled and composed at the very end of the New Testament period. It is a sermon more than it is a letter, lacking all personalia, and even the audience seems to be of a broad and generic sort. Here finally then, we may have a general encyclical trying to preserve and pass on some of the apostolic legacy to another generation. Later in this volume we will say more on this matter.

For now it is enough to say that 2 Peter appears neither to be written by Peter nor to be a pure pseudepigraphon, not least because we do not have a falsely attributed audience in this document. The compiler of 2 Peter clearly knew 1 Peter (see 2 Pet 3:1) as well as other apostolic literature, and the epistle raises various issues of intertextuality. It is something of an anthology of a general sort, and as such it deserves to be treated as the final addition to the documents that came to be called the General Epistles, and chronologically the latest canonical document to be written. It is the only more "general" epistle among the General Epistles. In it we glimpse not only the dying of the apostolic light but also the

[1]See Ben Witherington III, *Letters and Homilies for Jewish Christians: A Socio-Rhetorical Commentary on Hebrews, James and Jude* (Downers Grove, Ill.: InterVarsity Press, 2007).

willingness and concern to consolidate and preserve the apostolic legacy and begin to treat it not merely as wise words, but also as sacred texts. Significantly, by the time we come to Ignatius of Antioch in the early second century, church leaders, though they might see themselves even as monarchial bishops, were well aware that the apostolic era was over. For example, in a letter Ignatius says, "I do not address you as Peter and Paul. They were apostles . . ." (Ign. *Rom.* 4.3; cf. Ign. *Trall.* 3.3). Similarly Polycarp (*Phil.* 6.3) sees apostles, like Old Testament prophets, as being figures of a bygone era and having just as much authority as those prophets of old. What then was the church to do when it recognized it was beyond the apostolic era? As we shall see, 2 Peter gives some guidance on this matter.

Introduction to 1 Peter

It has been said that in the first century Christianity was a social world in the making.[1] This is certainly true, but questions remain: What sort of social world was being constructed by the external evangelistic program, and by the internal ordering of Christian communities based in house churches? Was it an ordering that baptized various forms of the social status quo and called it good? Was the aim to make clear that Christianity was not a revolutionary new religious sect in the Roman Empire? Was it an attempt to extend largely Jewish values and beliefs to a wider audience? And what role was 1 Peter meant to play in this social constructing of a "new world" or at least a new Christian society and subculture? These are germane and crucial questions to address as we study 1 Peter, which has in some circles been taken to be the least revolutionary and most socially conservative of all New Testament documents.

Often missed in such a sociological study of 1 Peter is the fact that the author is also busily constructing a rhetorical world, a world of advice and consent, of persuasion or dissuasion, inculcating certain beliefs and behaviors not merely for social reasons but also for theological or ideological ones. When we analyze 1 Peter as rhetoric, what do we learn about the aims and purposes of this document, broadly speaking? Is it meant to steel the audience for persecution by persuading them about the value of Christlikeness? Is there some considerable rhetorical exigency or problem this discourse is meant to overcome? And what do we make of the intertextual echoes in this document, not only of the Old Testament but also of material from Jesus' rhetoric, James's rhetoric, and Paul's rhetoric as well?

Carl R. Holladay remarks: "For all its Pauline echoes, however, 1 Peter also has close affinities with the synoptic tradition and to a lesser extent with the

---

[1]See Elliott, *Home for the Homeless,* p. 2.

Gospel of John, Hebrews, and James. There are remarkable convergences with Peter's speeches in Acts. Since 1 Peter resonates with such a wide spectrum of early Christian witnesses, some scholars have suggested, only half jokingly, that its author knew the whole New Testament! . . . Part of 1 Peter's enduring appeal stems from the breadth and depth of common tradition on which it draws and its appropriation of the earlier, apostolic consensus in giving authority to its distinctive voice."[2] Where was our author placed, geographically, socially, temporally, rhetorically that he would have known all of this material, and does such evidence provide clues to the authorship of this document? Could 1 Peter really be the masterpiece and last grand act of the great apostle who had personally known Jesus, James and Paul, including their rhetoric, and now was making their contributions serviceable for his own audience? Was our author at the font from which the apostolic tributaries flowed forth, and so in touch with the origins of Jewish and Gentile Christianity and its leaders, or was he at the place where all those tributaries came back together at the end of the first century and the beginning of the second? All of these sorts of questions are intertwined in a study of 1 Peter, and an orienting discussion is required at the outset to see the lay of the land. For now it is interesting to recognize that though 2 Peter is a composite document deeply indebted to its predecessors, this sort of indebtedness to previous Christian sources also characterizes 1 Peter, though in a quite different way. The Petrine legacy in the canon is tradition rich.

READING 1 PETER IN ITS SOCIAL MILIEU

The sociological study of 1 Peter has in fact been going on longer than the modern rhetorical discussion of this document, and so not surprisingly has borne more fruit. We may attribute the real impetus to examine 1 Peter in terms of social history and sociological theory to the stimulating and at times provocative work of John H. Elliott, who wrote his classic work *A Home for the Homeless* in 1979 (published in 1981). This led the study of 1 Peter down various productive roads, which are still being traveled and analyzed today, not least because of Elliott's massive commentary on 1 Peter, published in 2000. Elliott was right that a document like 1 Peter should not in the first instance be given a history of ideas treatment, as if its main focus, concern, purpose was to attack wrongheaded ideologies at odds with the author's own thought.[3] Much less is 1 Peter a purely theological message for Christian pilgrims and strangers in this world,

[2]Carl R. Holladay, *A Critical Introduction to the New Testament* (Nashville: Abingdon Press, 2005), p. 485.
[3]See Elliott, *Home for the Homeless,* pp. 3-4.

inculcating an otherworldly attitude and approach to life. To the contrary, this document is an ad hoc pastoral document, and even the theological discussions present serve as the undergirding for the ethics, values, virtues, practices being inculcated by the author.

The paraenesis is not an afterthought or an add-on to the discourse in 1 Peter. On the contrary it is at the heart of the socially formative purposes of the author, who is constructing the ethos of a community under fire and enduring some persecution and suffering, with the possibility of more on the way. The advice about rulers, masters, wives, husbands, elders, young men is the outworking of the theology and ideology of the author. He is not interested in merely endorsing a conservative household code; he is interested in constructing the Christian household and individual Christian behavior in a more Christlike manner. We need to be asking questions about what sort of social networks and social relationships the author envisions Christians being involved in, and how their faith affects their behavior in these relationships. Understanding the social context of a persecuted minority religious sect is paramount to understanding the response this document gives to the social situation. But there is more.

First Peter itself is part of an ongoing social relationship between the author and the audience. As such, it has a certain social dynamic to it. We may ask what it tells us about the state of the relationship between the author and the audience. Does he see them as peers ("fellow elders"), as followers, as friends, as converts? Does he view them as largely Jews, largely Gentiles, or a balanced mixture of the two ethnic groups? What is the social level of the author and the audience? Is it commensurate? Is there disparity? What is the social strategy of our author to help the audience cope with its now alien world, from which they are increasingly alienated by their faith? As Leonhard Goppelt stresses in his 1 Peter commentary, this can be said to be the only New Testament document that systematically addresses the issue of Christians being resident aliens within the macrostructures of the larger society.[4] Why does 1 Peter have this character and peculiar distinction within the canon? These sorts of questions lead to a deeper understanding of the social dimensions of this document, particularly its ethical and practical content, but also its theology.

As one of Elliott's real contributions to our study of 1 Peter, he has demonstrated that the language in this document about being resident aliens and visiting strangers should not be treated in a purely spiritual sense. He is arguing that the terminology has a clear social and political sense in 1 Peter, whatever else we may want to say in addition. He points out that all the uses of the term

[4]Goppelt, *Commentary on 1 Peter,* pp. 3-41.

paroikos and its cognates in the New Testament (with one possible exception: Eph 2:19) do refer to actual social conditions, indicating that the persons in question have legal status of something less than a full citizen; indeed, the noun means a resident alien who has some limited legal rights (cf. Lk 24:18; Acts 7:6, 29; 13:17; Heb 11:19; 1 Pet 1:17; 2:11), and can be contrasted with the term *xenos,* which refers to a foreigner who has no legal status or rights. The Latin equivalent is *peregrinus,* which strangely enough is the origin of the word *pilgrim,* but *paroikos/peregrinus* does not mean either "exile" or "pilgrim" and should not be so translated. It literally refers to someone who lives beside or outside the house. In other words, it refers to someone who is not part of the in-group in that particular social locale. The usage of *paroikos* to refer to an actual resident alien status of Jews in exile from Israel is prevalent in the LXX (cf. 1 Chron 29:15; Ps 119:19, where the proper rendering is "I am a resident alien in the land," not "a stranger on the earth"; cf. Ps 119:53-54).

This usage to refer to literal exiles in a foreign land, in particular in Babylon, we find in the postexilic literature as well (LXX: Jdt 5:7-10; Wis 19:10; 1 Esd 5:7; 2 Esd 8:35 [= Ezra 8:35 ET]). In some cases the term *paroikia* is a virtual synonym for the term *diaspora*.[5] Furthermore, twelve times in the LXX *diaspora* is the rendering of the Hebrew *gôlâ,* and notably there is an instance where *paroikia* is also translated *gôlâ,* (2 Esd 8:35). In light of the highly Jewish character of 1 Peter anyway, it seems logical to conclude that, since in all the above references it is *Jews* who are called resident aliens, we should surely conclude that this is likely in 1 Peter as well. And there is further good reason to do so.

The superscript in 1 Peter 1:1 refers to God's elect, who are then called *parepidēmois,* or visiting strangers in the world, scattered throughout the western part of Asia Minor, in what we call Turkey. The language of the Jewish Dispersion is used here, in similar fashion to what we found in James 1:1 in our previous study.[6] The term *parepidēmois* as well should not be translated either "exile" or "pilgrim." Furthermore, our author, writing from a foreign capital where there is a pagan ruler, calls his locale Babylon (1 Pet 5:13), coded language that alludes to the exilic status of Jews. The author, then, is indicating to his audience that he shares their resident alien and exilic condition where he is. Indeed, he is at the epicenter of the Diaspora in his day, for it was the Romans who displaced so many of the Jews living in Asia Minor and its neighboring regions. One can even say that the social function of this discourse is to encourage the sense of alienation from the macroculture and thereby aid the integration

[5] See Elliott, *Home for the Homeless,* p. 30 and the notes.

[6] See Witherington, *Letters and Homilies for Jewish Christians,* pp. 417-18.

with the microculture of early Christianity. Their dual identity is that they are resident aliens in the Roman Empire, but they are "in Christ" in God's kingdom!

Look closely at the language of 1 Peter 2:12. The audience is to live Christian lives among the *ethnesin*. Literally this means the "nations," more specifically the Gentile nations. Notice that here Peter does not use religious language (e.g., the term "pagans" or "idolaters"); he simply uses ethnic language. It would be rather strange to say to an audience of Gentiles, or largely Gentiles, to live like Christians among the "Gentiles." Gentiles do not talk about themselves as "the other nations."[7] This is Jewish language, and it best suits the theory that the audience itself is Jewish, in this case Jewish Christian. The Jewish Christians are to live as resident aliens or visiting stranger Christians among the overwhelmingly Gentile majority in each of these regions. Are there other reasons to affirm the sociological conclusion that these terms should not be spiritualized, and that they refer to actual Jews in the Dispersion?

Few scholars today doubt that, in the first and second centuries of the common era, there was a quite sizable Jewish population in the provinces listed at the beginning of 1 Peter (Pontus, Galatia, Cappadocia, Asia, Bithynia). One estimate says that of a population of about 4 million in Asia Minor in the 60s A.D. , some 300,000 or so were Jews, and there were perhaps 5,000 or so Christians as well.[8] The evidence is equally clear that the Jewish Diaspora in Asia Minor dates from at least the third century B.C., when Antiochus III sent some 2,000 Jews from Babylon to colonize various places in the region, including the kingdoms of Lydia and Phrygia.[9] Paul Trebilco has shown just how sizable and indeed influential this population had become in many cities in the region by the early part of the first century A.D.[10] The evidence we have, both literary and archaeological, suggests as well that Jews, perhaps particularly in Asia Minor, were well integrated into the social ethos of the region, having become quite Hellenized. This is particularly evident in a place like Sardis, where we have a remarkable Diaspora synagogue built next to the gymnasium at the center of

[7]One could counter that in 1 Cor 5:1; 1 Thess 4:5; and Eph 4:17, Paul, speaking to Gentiles, does refer to the audience in distinction from the *ethnesin*. However, Paul's use of the word there is not merely ethnic; it is also religious and is rightly translated "pagan" in these places.

[8]See Elliott, *Home for the Homeless,* p. 45.

[9]See Stephen Mitchell, *Anatolia,* 2 vols. (Oxford: Clarendon Press, 1993-1995), 2:32. One could point to Obadiah 1:20 as referring already to Jews in the exile in Asia as early as 580 B.C. or so, but this depends on assuming that Sepharad is in fact Sardis, which is unlikely. The Jews of Spain came to call their new home Sepharad probably based on the Aramaic word Sephar, meaning further limits of the coast, in this case the Mediterranean coast. Sardis, whatever else one says about it, is nowhere near the coast. The further suggestion that Jews who moved to Spain took the name Sepharad with them referring to Sardis is probably pure conjecture.

[10]Trebilco, *Jewish Communities in Asia Minor,* p. 32.

the town, and also abutting a series of shops where Jewish merchants sold their wares. Just how Hellenized some Jews could become in such an environment is shown by reports of Jewish athletes' attempts to remove evidence of their circumcision, so they could work out in the gymnasium and compete in Olympic style games as well.[11]

At length and in several studies, Martin Hengel has showed the degree to which Hellenization had affected Jews even in the Holy Land long before the spread of Christianity across the empire.[12] In a volume collected and edited by Martin Goodman, a variety of scholars have recently further demonstrated this. The various studies demonstrate that, although Jews lived to some extent apart from others and kept distinctive customs, in many ways they showed the same cultural presuppositions and preoccupations of their Gentile contemporaries.[13] Even more recently Rodney Stark concludes that many Jews of the Diaspora were indistinguishable from Gentiles unless one sought them out in the synagogue or in the home.[14] For Hellenized Jews long living in the Hellenistic milieu of Anatolia, accepting invitations to dinner parties, sometimes held in dining rooms attached to Greek or Roman temples, must have seemed far less problematic than for Jews in Judea. Though still wanting to be part of the Jewish subculture, such Hellenized Jews nevertheless sought to have the sort of business and personal relationships with non-Jews that were cemented at such dinner parties.

Having spent considerable time at archaeological sites in Asia Minor over the last several years, I have come to see more and more clearly that we must not imagine Jews in cities of Asia Minor and the neighboring regions as living in some Jewish cultural ghetto. To the contrary: the picture of Saul and his family, for example, being citizens of a great city like Tarsus (Acts 21:39) is by no means uncommon. This means that they were thought to model some of the civic virtues and participate as fully as they could in the life of the city, presumably without, in their own minds, crossing the line into idolatry and obvious violations of something like the Ten Commandments.[15]

[11] See Ben Witherington III, *Acts of the Apostles* (Grand Rapids: Eerdmans, 1998), pp. 210-13.

[12] See Martin Hengel's classic study *Judaism and Hellenism,* 2 vols. (Minneapolis: Fortress, 1998); and idem, *Jews, Greeks, and Barbarians* (Philadelphia: Fortress, 1980); and Martin Hengel in collaboration with Christoph Markschies, *The "Hellenization" of Judaea in the First Century after Christ* (Harrisburg, Penn.: Trinity Press International, 1990).

[13] Martin Goodman, ed. *Jews in a Graeco-Roman World* (Oxford: Oxford University Press, 2006).

[14] Stark, *Cities of God,* p. 78.

[15] At least for many Jews, eating unclean food was a rather normal problem in the Diaspora, which could be remedied after the fact by going through rites of purification. Many Jews apparently would not have seen such eating as some major violation of their Jewish faith and practice.

The degree of Hellenization of such Jews would no doubt have been dismaying to some Jews who lived in Judea or Galilee, but that it was a fact of life for perhaps the majority of Jews in Asia Minor should no longer be disputed. When it comes to a document like 1 Peter, we should adjudicate questions of audience and also of authorship against this sort of highly Hellenized backdrop of Diaspora Jews in this particular region. Lest we think it unlikely that our author would consider Jews outside of Christ as just as lost as Gentiles, I point to Ephesians 2:3, which says of both groups: "At one time all of us also lived among them [the powers and principalities and the devil], gratifying the desires of our sinful inclinations and following its cravings and thoughts. Like the rest we were by nature objects of wrath." In other words, our author takes a sectarian view of all his contemporaries outside of Christ; whether they are Jews or Gentiles, they are lost.[16]

On these matters we must pay close attention to the recent work of Rodney Stark. Here is his important and telling conclusion, which supports what we have been saying thus far:

> Another link between Hellenism and early Christianity was through the Jews of the Diaspora, who like the early Christians also worshipped in Greek. Many of them chafed at the ethnic barrier their religion placed between them and their full participation in Hellenic society—the Law made it difficult for them even to eat with their Gentile associates. . . . When Paul stripped the Jewish prerequisite from Christianity, he not only made the faith open to Gentiles, but offered the Hellenized Jews an attractive religious option, which many of them took.[17]

This is exactly right; in my view Peter in his missionary work simply followed Paul's lead and offered Hellenized Jews the same Gospel of salvation by grace through faith without the restrictions of the law that hindered their fuller participation in society in some respects. Christianity offered such Hellenized Jews a form of ethical monotheism that did not set up the same barriers to participation in the wider culture that came from the full practice of Judaism itself. The result is what we find in 1 Peter—Peter writing largely to Hellenized Jewish Christians.

By way of reminder, all the earliest commentators on 1 Peter, including the Greek Fathers in general, concluded that 1 Peter was written to an audience

---

[16]His attitudes about the patriarchs and OT prophets would be different, and indeed 1 Peter hints at what he thinks when he talks about OT prophets having the spirit of Christ within them. Clearly enough, from his use of the OT, our author should not be seen as a Marcionite before his time either. Like Paul, however, our author does think that persons outside the body of Christ are not directly part of the people of God or in continuity with the OT prophetic and religious heritage.

[17]Stark, *Cities of God,* p. 78.

largely, if not entirely, made up of Jewish Christians. In the West, Jerome and Augustine were exceptions to this rule, as were Luther and Tyndale among the later classic commentators. Wycliffe, Calvin, Bengel and Wesley all followed Eusebius and the early Greek Fathers, who saw the audience as Jewish. How, then, has it happened that the general consensus of modern commentators is that the audience of 1 Peter is mostly Gentiles, if not entirely so? This is because certain passages in 1 Peter itself, despite the way the document begins, seem to point in this direction. In my view, these passages have been misunderstood, and so I want to briefly review the internal evidence once more.

First we must note that it is not just the superscript that gives the impression that the audience is largely Jewish. First Peter 1:17 refers to "your time living as resident aliens." Whatever else one may say about Gentiles living in these regions, they certainly would not have seen themselves as living in some sort of exile presently *or in the past*, even if they had become Christians, nor would they see themselves as resident aliens. They were living in their own native provinces and regions. The Jewish character of the audience seems further supported by what the author says about the audience in 1 Peter 2:9, where he reminds them that they are a chosen race, a royal priesthood, a holy nation, God's own people and the like. This is a direct echo of the Pentateuch's report of what God said to Israel. In some early Christian contexts such language did in due course come to be applied to all Christians, including Gentile believers, but we should not simply assume that this is the case here in 1 Peter. That conclusion needs to be demonstrated.

Let us consider now the texts thought to make the case for a largely or entirely Gentile audience in 1 Peter. Peter H. Davids, for example, argues that 1 Peter 1:14, 18; 2:9-10; and 4:3-4 "could hardly have been used of Jews" (and he points as well to 2:25 and 3:6, which he takes as more naturally addressed to Gentile Christians).[18] We will begin with the two texts that have come to be seen as the smoking guns in this argument.

First Peter 2:10 is frequently seen to be a clear proof that the audience must be Gentiles. Here we have an intertextual echo or partial quotation of Hosea 1:9-10. Could our author really have been referring to Jews by phrases like "once you were not a people" or "once you had received no mercy"? This in some ways is a very odd question when one reads the original text of Hosea in its own context, where Hosea is clearly speaking of and about *Jews*, and offering a prophetic critique of their behavior. The prophet is indeed talking about Israel being temporally rejected and then restored. Thus there is no good reason why

[18]Davids, *First Peter*, p. 8.

the author of 1 Peter could not be using this language *in the same way* as some of his own Jewish contemporaries. The key perhaps is to recognize that our author, himself a Jew, reflects the view of over-Hellenized Diaspora Jews that was not uncommon among more Torah-true Jews, who had been raised and lived in a more conservative environment in the Holy Land. For instance, consider the reaction of Qumranic Jews to Hellenized Jews in Jerusalem and elsewhere.

Various scholars, however, have found 1 Peter 4:3-4 to be even more decisive in determining the audience of 1 Peter. In this text we hear: "You have already spent enough time in doing what the Gentiles like to do—living in licentiousness, passions, drunkenness, revels, carousing and lawless idolatry. They are surprised that you no longer join them in the same excesses." But we must pay close attention to what is said here.

In the first place the term "Gentiles" here *(ethnōn)* refers not to the audience themselves, but to non-Christian Gentiles, to whom the next verse refers as "them," a group that the audience of this discourse is no longer joining. In other words, none of the audience is directly called Gentiles here. Rather, we are told that the audience is no longer joining them in what the author views as acts of idolatry and immorality.

I suggest that this is fairly typical Jewish polemical rhetoric, often used by various Jewish Christians in the New Testament era to stigmatize what went on at pagan temple feasts. These feasts were viewed as the occasions where one found the convergence of all that was worst about pagan culture—both idolatry and immorality.[19] The horror of devout Jews about others attending such feasts can be seen not only in the long discussion in 1 Corinthians 8—10, where Paul discusses eating at such a feast and even calls it dining at the table of demons, but also in other places where the discussion of *eidōlothyton* crops up (the eating of meat sacrificed to idols in their very presence), we have the same polemic (see, e.g., Acts 15:20, 29; Rev 2:14). Thus, our author is saying that the audience has left such compromising behavior behind.

If we ask whether Jews, particularly those of higher social status who were more thoroughly Hellenized and indigenized into the local milieu, might have participated in temple feasts in some of these cities, the answer is certainly yes. They would have done so as they participated in various existing signs of civic virtue and cooperation in that era. Eating such a meal, perhaps with business partners, would not necessarily have been seen as an act of idolatry by a highly Hellenized Jew, who sat loosely with some of the Torah's dietary requirements.

---

[19]I have demonstrated this at length elsewhere. See Ben Witherington III, "Not so Idle Thoughts about *eidōlothyton*," *TynBul* 44, no. 2 (1993): 237-54.

Participating in a temple feast did not necessarily require being present for the prior worship act of pagan sacrifice, and temples after all were the major restaurants where socially more elite persons, or those who were climbing the social ladder, would often dine to cultivate their business and personal relationships. If they needed to go home and wash in a ritual bath thereafter to divest themselves of ritual impurity, they would see this as no big deal. The point here is that our author is not decrying these Jews for not keeping kosher.

Peter, then, is warning these Jewish Christians against having any longings to go back to their past *Gentile-like* behavior, and in particular he wants them, just as he would want Gentile converts, to stay away from even the appearance of idolatry or immorality. It would ruin their Christian witness. If we ask what social situations would have led Jews in Anatolia to participate in temple meals, one obvious answer is guild meetings and their banquets. There is clear evidence of Jews in this region being in guilds for various sorts of artisans. Paul himself was apparently part of the tentmaker's guild, which is probably the basis for his initial association with Priscilla and Aquila.[20]

Another text sometimes thought to demonstrate that the audience is largely if not entirely Gentile is 1 Peter 1:14, perhaps coupled with 1 Peter 1:18. In the former text the author speaks of the desires "you formerly had in ignorance." This theme of ignorance, however, is found elsewhere in the New Testament applied quite specifically to Jews in Luke-Acts (e.g., cf. Lk 23:34; Acts 3:17; 13:27). There is no reason why this notion could not be applied to highly Hellenized Jews in the Diaspora as well.

Our author writes with a conversionist and sectarian mentality, assuming that those who are outside the Christian circle are to one degree or another religiously in the dark, whether they are formerly Jews or formerly Gentiles. But even more to the point, if we look at 1 Peter 1:14-16 carefully, we note the following points: (1) our author is quoting from Leviticus 11:44-45, which is directed quite specifically to Jews alone; and (2) in this context we hear about the audience of that Leviticus passage being God's chosen children. Again, this is most naturally taken to be a reference to Jews in 1 Peter as well. We need to remember that the Levitical rules were originally given to Israel so that they would not slip back into their old sinful, wilderness-wandering ways, before God revealed himself to them on Sinai with the Ten Commandments and the ensuing legislation. Thus, when our author in 1 Peter 1:14-16 says, "Don't slip back into your old ways," and quotes Leviticus, he is thinking that his present

[20]See Ramsay MacMullen, *Enemies of the Roman Order: Treason, Unrest, and Alienation in the Empire* (Cambridge: Harvard University Press, 1966), pp. 173-79, 341-44, 347, n. 24.

Hellenized audience is rather like the Jews of old before the Holiness Code and indeed all of Leviticus was given, and like them, the present audience is called to go forward into holiness, not to give way to backsliding into their old Hellenized ways.

But what about the statement about being "ransomed from the futile ways of your ancestors"? This, to be sure, could be a reference to the audience having a Gentile background; yet this is not necessarily the right conclusion. Much depends on whether we regard the author of this document as thinking that before Christ came, Jews were engaged in inefficacious or inadequate sacrificial practices (like the author of Hebrews) or not, and whether he might be thinking of the futile ways of the wilderness-wandering generation or those who were carted off to Babylonian exile. If our author views the audience as being in some ways like many of the exilic Jews of the Babylonian period, this language then becomes understandable.

Thus the question becomes whether our author has something of a completionist or supersessionist reading of the earlier history of Israel or not. I do not think that such a view can be lightly dismissed since other New Testament authors seem to reflect it. I even suggest that this is precisely how our author thinks. For example, in 1 Peter 2:5 he exhorts his audience to let themselves be built into a new spiritual house, to be a new holy priesthood, to offer new spiritual sacrifices acceptable to God through Jesus Christ. Here he is certainly taking up the language of the Hebrew Scriptures and applying it now to Christians engaged in a very different sort of worship, the worship of Jesus as Lord. Whether we call this completionist or supersessionist rhetoric, clearly enough our author feels that he can make such a hermeneutical leap in the way he handles the Hebrew Scriptures, and he is comfortable in applying terms previously reserved for non-Christian Israel to his audience.

There are other texts sometimes also thought to suggest a non-Jewish audience for this document. For example 1 Peter 2:25 speaks of the audience having previously gone astray but now turning back to the shepherd and guardian of their souls. But once more one can easily argue that our author has adopted the language of the prophetic critique of Israel, and surely the reference to "returning" or "turning back" ***(epestraphēte)*** to the shepherd favors the conclusion that they had once been united with the shepherd God of Israel and then had strayed. In short, it suggests the audience could certainly be Jews viewed as having gone astray but now having returned to the one who had always been their shepherd.

What about 1 Peter 3:6, which refers to the female part of the audience having become Sarah's daughters as long as they do what is good? On first blush this appears strange if it is written to Jews, until one realizes that our author may well share the view we find in Paul in regard to a "righteous remnant." He may well have shared the view that not all those who are "of Israel" are true Israel, only those who follow the positive examples of the past, in this case of Sarah. Behavior and spiritual orientation, not mere ethnicity, are viewed as finally determining who is a daughter (or son) of Sarah. In light of the extensive use of the Old Testament, even John H. Elliott has to admit that there must have been Jewish Christians in the audience to justify the appeal for imitating venerable Old Testament figures like Sarah, and the use of biblically loaded terms like *exodus, Babylon,* the *elect of God.*[21]

In addition Paul J. Achtemeier has argued that the reference to the audience's shock in persecution (cf. 1 Pet 1:6; 4:12; 5:6-9) is surely more likely to reflect the reaction of Gentiles to persecution than Jews.[22] This argument may have some force to it, but not as much as he seems to think. In the first place, Jews in the provinces mentioned, from all the literary and archaeological evidence we have, were able to be quite thoroughly integrated into the existing society, becoming citizens in various of these cities; and since they practiced what was regarded as a *religio licita,* a legitimate ancient religion rather than a superstition, they could certainly normally expect to be exempt from actual religious persecution. One must not make the mistake of simply amalgamating the notions of prejudice and persecution. To be sure, there was plenty of anti-Semitism in the Roman Empire in this period. This in itself, however, did not necessarily lead to the sort of religious persecution that our author is talking about in 1 Peter.

It is no accident that our author uses the term *Christianos* in 1 Peter 4:16. Christians were now distinguishable from Jews in general, and if they were thought not to be Jews, they did not have the umbrella of being part of a licit religion. They were now subject to even more marginalization as "resident aliens" who were part of a superstition. This subjected them to legal abuse, especially when they refused to worship the emperor. I suspect that Peter adds this warning in light of what has just happened in Rome: the emperor Nero had named the Christians as responsible for the horrible fire in A.D. 64, which gutted whole areas in Rome. Peter thus is anticipating that this sort of persecution may well happen in Asia Minor as well. The Greek construction (*ei* plus an assumed present imperative verb) implies a possible condition, not one already necessarily transpiring for the audience.

Let me be clear here. Elliott is right when he stresses that the social up-

---

[21]Elliott, *Home for the Homeless,* pp. 55-56.
[22]Achtemeier, *1 Peter,* p. 51.

heaval described in the document must correlate with something going on, or potentially happening soon where the audience is. It cannot simply be a description of what is happening where the author is, in Rome. And as Elliott also says, "All the pertinent terms refer to verbal rather than physical abuse or legal action: *katalaloun,* 2:12; 3:16; *epērazein,* 3:16; *oneidizein,* 4:14; and similarly *kakoun,* 3:13."[23] These terms refer to social pressure and persecution, not yet ending in governmentally inaugurated legal action. This surely makes it more likely that this document was written *before* the Neronian persecution had reached its zenith, resulting in the martyrdoms of Peter and Paul. If it had been written after that time, it is hard to imagine why there are no clear references to martyrdoms, as there are in Revelation, especially considering how much emphasis there is on suffering in 1 Peter, along with the various allusions to the Suffering Servant of Isaiah in this discourse. Peter is still urging respect for governing authorities, whereas Revelation sees the central government as an instrument of Satan (cf. 1 Pet 2:13-17). As in the book of Hebrews, in this document we see a social situation where the audience (and the author, of course) has not yet suffered to the point of loss of life, but there has been abuse of various sorts.[24]

As our second volume in this series pointed out, and we need to reiterate here, it is a mistake to underestimate the size or spread of Jewish Christianity well into the second century A.D. In his landmark study, Rodney Stark puts it this way: "Jewish Christianity played a central role until much later in the rise of Christianity; . . . not only was it the Jews of the Diaspora who provided the initial basis for church growth during the first and early second centuries but [also] . . . Jews continued as a significant source of Christian converts until at least as late as the fourth century."[25]

In our second volume we also saw that the division of labor between largely Gentile missionaries (the Pauline circle) and largely Jewish missionaries (the Petrine and Jamesian and Johannine circles) led to basically separate communities of Christians in various cities in the empire, including cities in Asia Minor and its surrounding provinces. Peter is writing to churches some of which are in areas where Paul has set up house churches, and some of which are not. And yet Peter is exercising authority over the churches to which he is writing. The obvious conclusion to be drawn from this is that the division of missionary labor

[23]Elliott, *Home for the Homeless,* p. 80.

[24]My explanation of this matter is that these documents are both written at about the same point in time—the mid-60s.

[25]Rodney Stark, *The Rise of Christianity: A Sociologist Reconsiders History* (Princeton: Princeton University Press, 1996), p. 49.

had to do with the ethnic target audience, not regions of the empire, and that Peter is addressing largely Jewish Christians (perhaps with some God-fearers) in this discourse, not addressing communities founded by Paul or his coworkers.[26] I thus concur with Elliott when he suggests the "letter's geographical destination offers neither evidence nor reason for regarding 1 Peter as intended for Pauline churches or for areas of the Pauline mission field; . . . 1 Peter is best read on its own terms, as an independent though complementary witness to the diversified growth of early Christianity in Asia Minor."[27] Indeed, as Colin Hemer points out, several of these provinces were so huge that he is able to envision Peter being involved in eastern Galatia on his way north to Pontus, while Paul is involved in southern Galatia.[28]

Here is where we observe that the order of the regions mentioned in the beginning of the document (1 Pet 1:1), Pontus, Galatia, Cappadocia, Asia and Bithynia, suggests the planned route through which this encyclical would be taken.[29] Notice that though Pontus and Bithynia had long since been made into one Roman province by the time this document was written (in fact it had happen in about 65 B.C.), our author does not mention the two regions together. This is because he is thinking of the route the document would travel. In other words this document, like Revelation, mentions cities or regions in the order in which the circular document will reach them. We may envision Peter setting out from Antioch (where we find him in the late 40s—see Gal 1—2) to reach these destinations. Edward Gordon Selwyn puts it this way: "An excellent road ran from the Cilician Gates northwards through Cappadocia and Galatia to Amisus on the Euxine [i.e., in Pontus], probably the first city on that coast to receive the Gospel; and at Mazaca [in Cappadocia] it crossed another fine route which the enterprise of Ephesian traders had utilized so effectively as to direct the commerce of Cappadocia from Sinope to their Levantine seaboard. Syrian Antioch occupied a key position in relation to both routes."[30] It is entirely possible that Paul, who knew these roads from his own early evangelistic work in Syria-Cilicia, had advised Peter in Antioch on the best ways to reach these regions, where the Jewish pilgrims lived.

One aspect of Elliott's social analysis that simply does not work is his assumption that the audience of 1 Peter is likely to be primarily rural and are to be viewed as the sharecroppers or migrant agrarian workers of antiquity, though

---

[26]See Witherington, *Letters and Homilies for Jewish Christians.*

[27]Elliott, *Home for the Homeless,* pp. 64-65.

[28]Hemer, "Address of 1 Peter," pp. 239-43, here p. 241, and see his map on p. 239.

[29]Ibid., pp. 239-43.

[30]Selwyn, *First Peter,* p. 48.

he allows that merchants and artisans may also be meant.[31] There are various problems with this analysis. First, there is the linguistic one. This document assumes that the audiences know Greek, and indeed know it well. The letter would have been read out to them for their aural consumption. First Peter represents some of the better Greek in the New Testament, and indeed it is a rhetorically adept use of Greek as well. This does not fit the profile of the audience Elliott thinks is being addressed. Nor, for that matter, does the actual social description of the audience as registered in the document. You don't need to warn either female migrant workers or artisan's wives against wearing gold jewelry and fine clothes (1 Pet 3:3).

Second, as Bruce W. Winter has pointed out at length, the call to seek the good or welfare of the city in 1 Peter simply does not comport with either the notion that the audience is basically rural or with the argument that they are overwhelmingly poor. You do not ask people to do "the good" and so silence criticisms of the city, indeed even of the rulers, unless indeed there is some public good that they are capable of doing and ought to do. Winter concludes, "There must have been Christians of very considerable means to warrant [the injunction] . . . of 1 Pet 2:15."[32] These sorts of clues suggest that there are some socially elite or pretentious members of these Christian communities who need some correction and prodding. Winter is also exactly right when he points out that this document is not at all trying to inculcate an isolationist sectarian ethos, but rather is trying to prod a Christian community to overcome abuse and persecution through doing good to the neighbor as well as the community. In this way Christians could be seen as good citizens of their cities and thereby subvert charges that they are subversive. Notice the emphasis in 1 Pet 2:11-12 on the believers being "seen" to do good works. Obviously the public witness is of concern to our author.[33]

Third, this document's use of the Jewish traditions and the importance of intertextual echoes for this discourse's rhetorical effectiveness positively rule out the audience being illiterate Jewish workers, who have little or no background not only in the Scriptures but also in early Christian traditions. Fourth, it is simply untrue that resident aliens could not own things, including land in these regions. They made up a considerable portion of the population of most of these

[31]See Elliott, *Home for the Homeless,* p. 63.

[32]Bruce W. Winter, *Seek the Welfare of the City* (Grand Rapids: Eerdmans, 1994), pp. 12-40, esp. 37.

[33]The one aspect of Winter's study (ibid.) that is unconvincing is the attempt to suggest that the language about resident aliens and visitors in the land has no social significance, only a theological one. This seems quite out of keeping with the rest of his argument.

cities; although they did not have the same rights as full citizens, they could be quite prosperous, as could freedmen, for that matter. First Peter presupposes and addresses Christian households, which means he presupposes Christian household owners. As elsewhere in early Christianity, here we must assume that the spectrum of social level in these Petrine churches was considerable, ranging from slaves and poor freedmen at the low end of the spectrum, to socially rather elite and well-to-do persons at the other end. There could have been considerable status inconsistency for the latter group, being educated and having money and property on the one hand, but not being full citizens on the other and having to deal with Gentile anti-Semitic prejudice as well.

If one were to characterize the social makeup of the population of these regions, there was in fact an enormous diversity of cultures, minor languages, ethnic groups, customs, religious and political histories of those who lived in these areas.[34] There are about 129,000 square miles of territory encompassed by these regions, and it is diverse and often rugged territory at that. And yet our author thinks he can address the audience as if this hardly matters. This is far more believable if he is addressing a more homogeneous group of persons in those regions—Jewish Christians. It is also far more believable if he is addressing city dwellers. The sorts of behaviors our author is critiquing are behaviors that must be directly associated with Hellenization, which was largely an urban phenomenon in these regions. Jews in general, when they began to live in these regions, were placed in cities, and they remained there, where they were subject to the vicissitudes of Hellenization. Remember—their history in this region goes back at least to Antiochus III and the last wave of Hellenization, which was more than two centuries before the writing of this document. In short, the social evidence of the document itself suggests that the addressees live in urban settings in these regions and are a reasonably homogeneous group, being Hellenized enough to know Greek and Greco-Roman cultures, but Jewish enough to recognize, appreciate and feel indebted to Jewish religious traditions and sacred texts. If this is not the case, then the rhetorical strategy of our author is not very effective.

In sum, it appears to me that it is possible, indeed likely correct, to read 1 Peter as a document written to an audience the majority of whom are Jewish Christians, with some God-fearers perhaps included. As such, this makes far better sense of the attribution of this document to Peter (see Gal 2:7), whether the attribution is genuine or contrived. At a minimum, it seems to me, one should not simply assume, without sufficient argumentation, that the audience of this letter was Gentiles. There are some good reasons to think otherwise. Finally, we

---

[34]As writes Elliott, *Home for the Homeless,* p. 61.

can now say that the social resonance of the resident alien language not only comports with this conclusion; it also further strengthens it. Peter is telling the audience that not only are they resident aliens in the sense of being Jews in the Diaspora; in addition, now that they are estranged from their Hellenized ways, they are also no longer fitting in with their Gentile neighbors. Hence, they are double aliens from both non-Christian Jews and from Gentiles. Thus, the sectarian nature of this discourse becomes even more clear, as Peter seeks to carve out a unique niche for his Jewish Christian audience in their social settings.

The discussion thus far naturally leads to a discussion of what can be said about this document's social situation and indeed of its author's identity. That he is a Jew, few if any scholars would dispute, and a Jew who has a special affinity for the Psalms and some Isaianic material as well. That he is in addition a Jewish Christian is clear enough from the content of the document as well, and again this is rarely disputed. The next question of import is how one should take the reference to Babylon in 1 Peter 5:13. Today few would dispute that it is coded language. The actual region of Babylon went by another name during the Greco-Roman era. It is natural to compare this usage to Rev 18, where we have a woe oracle about the fall of Babylon, and the reference there is clearly enough to Rome.[35] But now we must ask: If Babylon = Rome in 1 Peter 5, what does it tell us about the social situation of the author that he would use such language?[36] The most reasonable answer is that he is in a marginalized condition, as a Jewish follower of Jesus, and he views his locale as the source and center of the oppression and persecution. One has to ask—Why?

If you take the time to read Romans carefully, a very different ethos is conveyed in that document when it comes to Rome. Why, in addition, does the author of 1 Peter speak of a king *(basileus)* rather than the emperor when he talks about governing authorities (1 Pet 2:13)? I suggest: (1) The document was written during a period of persecution, hence needing the coded language both

[35]See Ben Witherington III, *Revelation,* NCBC (Cambridge: Cambridge University Press, 2003).

[36]Unconvincing is the argument of Elliott (*Home for the Homeless,* p. 272) that the use of the term "Babylon" must point to a time after 70 A.D., which is to say after the fall of the temple in Jerusalem. In the first place, there is no reason why 1 Peter could not be the first to use the term for Rome, followed by the usage in Revelation and various Jewish sources such as *2 Baruch, 4 Ezra,* or the *Sibylline Oracles.* In the second place, the use of the terminology could be produced by the beginnings of the Neronian persecution. This letter is concerned about Christians suffering. It is not in any way interested in the cultus in Jerusalem. Indeed, it is interested in promulgating a very different sort of priesthood, which focuses on a one-time sacrifice made in A.D. 30 outside the walls of Jerusalem. Still, the absence of the reference to the fall of the temple is telling in a document written to Jewish Christians. See the discussion about Hebrews in Witherington, *Letters and Homilies for Jewish Christians,* pp. 27-28.

about the city and the emperor (though the author may in addition be thinking of client kings elsewhere in the empire). (2) Only two periods best suit that description, during the latter years of the reign of Nero (contrast Romans written in about A.D. 57, during the early Neronian period), or during the time of Domitian, thus either in the mid-60s or the early to mid 90s. Our author expects the persecution to go on and to affect Christians both where he is, and perhaps where the audience is as well. This helps to explain the strong stress on the language about resident aliens. Obviously, whoever is persecuted feels alienated from the existing governance and social structures in your region. Clearly too, our author is some major religious authority figure: he calls himself an apostle and an elder in relationship to the audience.

Another piece of the puzzle comes together in realizing the implications of the echoes of earlier Pauline material (e.g., the phrase "in Christ"), earlier material from the homily of James, some of the sayings of Jesus, and finally perhaps some of the material in the Pastorals as well. In my view, 2 Timothy was written from Rome by Paul and a cowriter, Luke, in the mid-60s, after the fire and likely before Paul's death. I suggest that 1 Peter is a document that comes from the very same place and likely during the very same time period, though for a very different audience: Jewish Christians. It does not seem to me to be an option to suggest that 1 Peter was written in the 70s or 80s, due to the reference to persecution and even suffering unto death, following the example of Christ. It is either a pseudonymous document written in the 90s, or it actually is by Peter, with the help of Silvanus (= Silas) and in the 60s. Since there are severe problems with the notion of first-century Christian pseudepigraphic letters,[37] the burden of proof must be on those who want to maintain that this document is an example of such literature. I remind them that they must not only come up with a falsely attributed author but also a falsely attributed audience, and presumably one not so close in time to the end of the first century A.D. that they would recognize that this is a forgery. There are more problems with accepting that hypothesis than with accepting the traditional ascription of authorship of this document to Peter himself. And as N. Hillyer has rightly stressed, the early church without question accepted 1 Peter as authentically from Peter, while they had doubts about 2 Peter, and it rejected a whole series of other later documents supposedly penned by Peter, including the *Gospel of Peter*, the *Acts of Peter*, and the *Apocalypse of Peter*, all seen as unsuitable for inclusion in a collection of sa-

[37]On which see Ben Witherington III, *Letters and Homilies for Hellenized Christians*, vol. 1, *A Socio-Rhetorical Commentary on Titus, 1-2 Timothy and 1-3 John* (Downers Grove, Ill.: InterVarsity Press, 2006), introduction.

cred Christian writings that came to be called the New Testament.[38] Edward Gordon Selwyn is quite right that the reception of this document as authentic, and indeed as a sacred text, is early, clear, and widespread.[39] It and 1 John are the only documents from among the so-called Catholic Epistles whose authenticity was uncontested in either the Eastern or Western part of the church.

The character of the discourse favors the suggestion that these congregations have been founded for some time. In my view, it is likely that Peter began evangelizing these regions in the 40s, and after the Jerusalem Council in A.D. 50 returned to these areas again. This means he certainly covered a lot of ground, and he and his coworkers had considerable success with the Jews in these areas. Among other things, this also suggests a date not earlier than the 60s for this document. My suggestion would be, based on Acts 2:9-11, that Peter followed up on the initial success he had with Diaspora Jews at Pentecost by literally following them to their home regions in due course and building on those social networks. Notice the mention of both Pontus and Cappadocia in the list in Acts 2.

Finally, at this juncture we may also stress that it is a mistake to underplay the potential danger Christians were in, in the regions addressed, once we recognize that they were not simply Jews. From the *Letters* of Pliny the Younger to Trajan, speaking about experiences in the first decade or two of the second century in Bithynia, we can see that Christians in this region did in due course suffer persecution and prosecution and even torture and martyrdom. Pliny in addition refers to defections from Christianity that had happened in the very same region some twenty-five years earlier (i.e., apparently in the 80s; see Pliny *Ep.* 10.96). Peter was right to be concerned about the effect of pressure, persecution, and prosecution and the resultant suffering on Christians in this region he had evangelized.

The Greek Style and Rhetoric of 1 Peter

It will be well if we discuss the Greek of 1 Peter before turning to its use of rhetoric. Happily, the Greek text of 1 Peter is rather well preserved. There are three very important papyrus witnesses to this document—𝔓[72] from the third or fourth century, which contains the full text of both 1 Peter and 2 Peter as well as other documents canonical and otherwise (e.g., Jude and the *Odes of Solomon*). For our purposes it is important to note that 𝔓[72] stands in the textual

[38]Hillyer, *1 and 2 Peter, Jude,* p. 9. The usual objections to 1 Peter coming from Peter mostly have to do either with the echoes of other early Christian literature or the rather good Greek of the document. We have addressed the former issue to some extent, but the latter we will deal with below in our discussion of the Greek and rhetoric of 1 Peter.

[39]Selwyn, *First Peter,* p. 38.

tradition of uncials like A and B. Then $\mathfrak{P}^{72}$ dates to the fourth century and unfortunately only contains 1 Peter 2:20—3:1 and 3:4-12. Also, $\mathfrak{P}^{72}$ dates to the sixth-seventh century and contains parts of the first three chapters. The great uncials Aleph (ℵ, Codex Sinaiticus) and B (Codex Vaticanus), both from the fourth century, contain the whole text of 1 Peter, as do A, C and P from the fifth-sixth centuries. There are more than 550 minuscules as well dating from the ninth and following centuries that include our document as well. Since it is well represented, we may not be entirely surprised to discover that 70 of the 105 verses lack any significant textual variants at all. There are only about thirty-eight notable variants in the remaining 35 verses, and none of them significantly affect the wording or meaning of the text. This suggests that this text was widely accepted as it was, and scribes thus felt no need or especial inclination to fiddle with the text to adjust it to one or another sort of agenda. The influence of this text on other early Christian literature can hardly be doubted. It appears that the compiler of 2 Peter knows this document (see 2 Pet 3:1), and later in this volume we will have occasion to comment on the possible influence of 1 Peter on 2 Peter, though on the whole 2 Peter seems far more indebted to Jude.[40]

First Peter has a total of 1,675 words and a vocabulary of 547 different terms, of which 61 occur nowhere else in the New Testament, but 34 of those words do occur in the LXX, which certainly shapes the diction of this discourse in various respects. There are also seventy-four terms in 1 Peter that occur only twice in the New Testament. As Elliott points out, relative to its length we have the most frequent use of *paschō* in the New Testament (some 12 times), and also the most frequent use of the verb *hypotassō*. This is telling since suffering and submission are indeed two major themes of this discourse. Notable for its absence is the Pauline use of the term *ekklēsia* or the phrase "body of Christ," though we do have the use of the phrase "in Christ."[41] Importantly, *1 Clement*, written somewhere around 95-96 A.D., is indebted to all of the chapters in 1 Peter. What is especially telling is not merely that 1 Clement shares some 327 words with 1 Peter, but also that some of the rare words found only in 1 Peter in the New Testament are also found in *1 Clement* (e.g. *agathopoiia, adelphotēs, hypogrammos, ktistēs* [of God], *tapeinophrōn*). It seems clear enough as well that Polycarp's *Letter to the Philippians*, written before 140 A.D., is also indebted to our 1 Peter.[42]

---

[40]See the introduction to 2 Peter later in this volume.

[41]See Elliott, *1 Peter,* pp. 41-80, giving complete lists of the unique or distinctive vocabulary in 1 Peter.

[42]See ibid., pp. 134-48.

It has sometimes been argued that the Greek of 1 Peter is too good for a Galilean fishermen. This argument has some merit, but it may be vitiated by the fact that the document itself tells us that this discourse was composed "with the help of [or 'through'] Silvanus" (1 Pet 5:12).[43] The question then becomes, How much help? Did Peter dictate the letter and Silvanus compose? Did Peter tell Silvanus in general what to say and leave it to him to draft the specifics? On the whole, the former seems more likely when we actually look at the grammar, syntax, and vocabulary used.

The Greek of this document is better than some other New Testament documents (e.g., Revelation) but not as good as we for instance find in Hebrews. It is somewhere in the middle. And as Karen H. Jobes shows, the author does not have the mastery of prepositions, the use of the genitival personal pronoun, the position of the attributive adjective, and the use of the dative case with *en* that we would expect from a person for whom Greek is their first language.[44] The use of participles as imperatives is also hardly an example of literary Greek. As Jobes shows in detail, in this document there is rather clear evidence of Semitic interference: the author is thinking in one language and writing in another such that it affects his grammar and syntax.[45] This is all the more telling since our author chooses to use the LXX when quoting the Old Testament, rather than directly translating the Hebrew. This is easily explained if the author feels his Greek is not as good as the translation of the Old Testament. Jobes is also able to show that the Semitic interference and quality of Greek in 1 Peter is comparable to what we find in 1 Thessalonians on the whole. This is especially interesting since Silvanus may well have been involved in the composition of that document as well.[46]

But even if the Greek of 1 Peter is seen as possible for Peter himself, with help from Silvanus as his scribe, some scholars have found the degree of rhetorical sophistication of 1 Peter beyond the reach of Peter. Before commenting on the rhetoric of 1 Peter, I need to mention that a person's oral skills with Greek, particularly in using it for rhetorical purposes, is one thing; perfection in grammar and syntax is quite another. There are plenty of excellent preachers then and now who are skilled rhetoricians, but they do not necessarily write the most seamless prose. Paul J. Achtemeier reminds us that there were three sorts of styles of Greek in this era—Koine, Atticistic and Asiatic. In view of the audi-

[43]On the meaning of this phrase, see the discussion of 1 Pet 5:12 below.

[44]Jobes, *1 Peter*, p. 7.

[45]See ibid., pp. 328-32.

[46]On which now see Ben Witherington III, *1 and 2 Thessalonians: A Socio-Rhetorical Commentary* (Grand Rapids: Eerdmans. 2006).

ence addressed in this document, it should not surprise us that the style of Greek in this letter is not Koine but rather Asiatic, and furthermore we are dealing with deliberative Asiatic rhetoric here. Peter will have heard this style of rhetoric for years during his time of making converts in Asia and the surrounding regions. At this juncture we need to recognize Greek style and Asianism, which was so popular in this area during the 150 or so years between the time of Julius Caesar and the end of Domitian's reign.

GREEK STYLE AND ASIANISM

Koine, or common Greek, could be called the lowest common denominator and was the most basic style of Greek that ordinary people were capable of and apt to use. It was used as a "medium of communication throughout the Near East by persons without deep roots in Greek culture."[47] Too often people assume that the New Testament reflects only this unvarnished approach to Greek. How often have we been told that the New Testament is simply written in Koine Greek? This however is not entirely true, as we should have realized once we admit that some authors' Greek style and ability go well beyond ordinary or basic communication style Greek (e.g., Hebrews, 1 Peter). In other words, some portions of the New Testament reflect a more self-conscious and literary quality of Greek.

When it comes to the self-conscious adaptation of a style of Greek that goes beyond Koine, there were basically two options: (1) to take up an Asiatic style, or (2) to take up an Atticizing style of Greek. Using Atticizing Greek was a deliberate attempt to emulate classical Greek style, and it is not a surprise that some Christian writers of the second century A.D. did strive to do this. When they try to do apologetics in a Greek vein, they do sometimes adopt such a style. This is not what we find in 1 Peter. Instead, what we find is the more refined or mild form of the Asiatic style.

What did Asiatic style look like? George Kennedy suggests: "Asianism is a highly artificial, self-conscious search for striking expression in diction, sentence structure and rhythm. It deliberately goes to almost any possible extreme."[48] Nevertheless, there seem to have been two kinds of Asianism. Cicero (*Brut.* 325) says that one kind of Asian style is epigrammatic and brilliant (called smooth, sententious and euphonious), with a focus on offering utterances that are neat

---

[47]George A. Kennedy, *New Testament Interpretation Through Rhetorical Criticism* (Chapel Hill: University of North Carolina Press, 1984), p. 32. Kennedy calls Koine a simplified form of Attic Greek. See his *Classical Rhetoric and its Christian and Secular Tradition from Ancient to Modern Times* (Chapel Hill: University of North Carolina Press, 1980), p. 86.

[48]Ibid.

and charming. This was sometimes the less substantive form of Asiatic rhetoric. The other form of Asiatic rhetoric was noted for a torrent of speech, full of ornamentation, redundancy and fine language. This style was called swift and impetuous.

Cicero says that the latter style was especially prevalent in his day, when he went to Asia to study this form of rhetorical expression. He cites two first-century B.C. orators from Asia who modeled this style, Aeschylus of Cnidus and Aeschines of Miletus.[49] Asiatic style was noted for a particular kind of singsong rhythm—the dichoree or double trochee was regarded as the favorite Asianist rhythm (Cicero *De or.* 212). We see Asiatic style quite clearly in Asian Christian writers of a slightly later period, for example in the work of Melito of Sardis.

Cicero himself, it seems, adopted the second of these two Asiatic styles, to the lament of his detractors who favored a more Attic style of Greek and rhetorical delivery.[50] Notice the summary by Ann Vasaly: "The hallmarks of Ciceronian style, most of which have been identified with 'Asianism,' appear in the [Ciceronian] speeches of all periods, early and late. Among these we might mention: complex periodicity, often making elaborate use of parallelism; the presence of rhythm, both in the sense of the employment of clauses within periods that are carefully balanced in length and sound, as well as the employment of favored combination of long and short syllables at the end of periods . . . ; constant use of a wide variety of *ornamenta*, involving both word and phrase, aimed at artistic expression and often privileging sound and general impression of precision of meaning; recourse to wit, irony, wordplay, and humor; employment of *variatio* at all levels, including within the period, between periods, between parts of speech, as well as in the styles employed in different types of speech; and the constant appeal to the emotions, especially in the opening and closing sections of the speech."[51]

So many of these stylistic features and techniques occur in 1 Peter that it is hard to understand why this discourse has not more readily been recognized as

---

[49] See the analysis in George A. Kennedy, *The Art of Rhetoric in the Roman World 300 B.C.-A.D. 300* (Princeton: Princeton University Press, 1972), pp. 97-100. Kennedy points out that many Romans like Cicero went to Asia to study rhetoric because there were so many famous rhetoricians and schools in this region.

[50] The first of these two styles strives for sophisticated sentences, full of wordplay and metaphors, arranged in artificial rhythmic patterns; the second style is characterized as less flamboyant but still involving a flow of colorful words, often involving redundancy (e.g., "the strength of his might"), alliteration, assonance, and digressions, all of which we find in the Petrine corpus.

[51] Ann Vasaly, "Cicero's Early Speeches," in *Brill's Companion to Cicero,* ed. J. M. May (Leiden: Brill, 2002), pp. 71-111, esp. 86. I am indebted to Professor Christopher McDonough of Sewanee for pointing me to some of this material.

an exercise in an Asiatic style of grammar and rhetoric. Perhaps the reason is that while 1 Peter reflects the former of the two sorts of Asian style mentioned above, 2 Peter is more often associated with Asiatic style and reflects the latter more florid and torrential form that Cicero had originally adopted and adapted. For example, notice what Paul J. Achtemeier says about the style of 1 Peter:

> Written in a direct if somewhat studied style, the prose is marked by such characteristics as the frequent use of comparison (1:7, 14; 2:2, 16, 25; 3:4-5; 5:8) often introduced by the particle *hōs* (1:19; 2:2, 5, 25; 3:7; 5:8); series of words with similar sounds (1:4, 19; 3:18), the accumulation of synonyms (1:8, 10; 2:25; 3:4), the use of anaphora to introduce parallel phrases (4:11) or to organize a passage (*hypotassein*, 2:13—3:1), the use of antithetic (2:14; 3:18; 4:6) and synthetic (2:22-23; 4:11; 5:2-3) parallelism; coordinate parallel expressions, first negative, then positive underlining the same idea (1:14-15, 18-21, 23; 2:16; 5:2-3), rhythmic structure (1:3-12), the frequent use of the imperative; . . . the frequent use of conjunctive participles (e.g., 1:8. . .11, 23) and relative clauses, which can lead to long periods (e.g., 1:17-21). Peter, along with Luke, is also unique in the New Testament in the use of *ei* plus the optative (3:14, 17).[52]

What Achtemeier fails to note is that many of these features are characteristic of Asiatic style, especially the use of long periods and the piling up of comparisons, synonyms, words that involve alliteration and assonance, and the frequent use of highly emotive language. One problem we continually confront in New Testament scholarship is the failure to realize that New Testament documents like 1 Peter are oral documents: they are meant in the first place to be heard, not read, and to have their style evaluated on the basis of an oral performance. It is unfortunate that we have no recording of the "sound" of the Asiatic style because the oral dimensions of this sort of rhetoric were important: pitch, volume, speed, intonation, voice modulation and the like (not to mention the visual dimensions such as facial contortions and gestures) all contributed to this style.[53]

Asiatic rhetoric was noted for its emotion and even affectation. In contrasting it with Attic rhetoric, Cicero says: "The styles of Asiatic oratory are two—one epigrammatic and pointed, full of fine ideas which are not so weighty and serious as neat and graceful; the other with not so many sententious ideas, but voluble and hurried in its flow of language, and marked by an ornamented and elegant diction" (*Brut.* 95, 325). Both forms of the Asiatic style were also marked

---

[52]Achtemeier, *1 Peter,* pp. 3-4.

[53]See Anton Daniël Leeman, *Orationis Ratio: The Stylistic Theories and Practice of the Roman Orators Historians and Philosophers,* vol. 1 (Amsterdam: Adolf M. Hakkert, 1963), pp. 93-94. As Leeman says, reading Cicero's orations is but a poor shadow of hearing them properly delivered, particularly because of the histrionic Asiatic style of the material and its delivery.

by the use of repetition of various sorts to hammer home the main points, just as we find in 1 Peter. It appears that Asiatic oratory was a development of the highly ornamental style cultivated by Isocrates, who lived in 436-338 B.C. It thus had a long history before New Testament times. It was especially prized and often practiced in western Asia Minor by sophists and rhetors of various sorts.[54] This thoroughly Hellenized region of the Empire had long been a haven for the rhetoric of advice and consent as well as the rhetoric of praise and blame, a trend only exacerbated with the rise of the emperor cult.

When we begin to reflect more specifically on the rhetoric of 1 Peter, one of the primary questions immediately comes to mind: Is the author trying to inculcate new values and virtues, or is he simply commending and strengthening old ones? This is another way of asking, Is he using deliberative or epideictic rhetoric in this discourse? Is he trying to change behavior and belief in the near future, or merely praise certain extant forms of these things? Here we are helped by the detailed work of Barth L. Campbell, who points out that the injunctions introducing each major section of this discourse (1 Pet 1:13; 2:11; 3:14b-16b; 4:12-13) "are not for the continuation of present and acceptable behavior. Peter gives no indication whether the conduct that he enjoins is present to any degree among his readers. He writes as if it is not."[55] This document is thus best seen as an example of deliberative rhetoric in an Asiatic mode.[56] He is also right that the injunctions are general in character, not surprisingly since this is a circular letter. As such, it addresses topics of what is advantageous, expedient, profitable, necessary, honorable and their negative counterparts, and it will do this by using *synkrisis*—rhetorical comparisons and contrasts of various sorts as well as examples to persuade the audience to change their beliefs and behaviors.[57]

The Structure of 1 Peter

Both Campbell and Troy Martin have rightly pointed out the major flaws in a purely epistolary analysis of 1 Peter: "It can identify basic parts of the letter (prescript; body-opening, middle and closing, and postscript), . . . but it cannot account for the composition of the letter-body. Other analytical methods must be used to explain that part of the letter. . . . According to Martin, the paraenetic

[54]On the many sophists and rhetors in Western Asia, especially in Ephesus, Pergamum, Smyrna, and in the Lycus valley in Hierapolis, but also in the cities of Galatia, Cappadocia, and elsewhere in the region, see Glen Warren Bowersock, *Greek Sophists in the Roman Empire* (Oxford: Clarendon Press, 1969), pp. 17-29.

[55]Campbell, *Honor, Shame,* p. 25.

[56]Campbell (ibid.) thinks it is of mixed genre, with the exordium being an epideictic encomium. I will argue against this conclusion below. See "Structure of 1 Peter" below, pp. 56-58.

[57]See ibid., pp. 30-31.

genre exhibits *no fixed form and* "therefore, the identification of 1 Peter as paraenesis does not provide an explanation of its compositional structure."[58] This is as much as to admit that we cannot account for the majority of this document's form and structure through epistolary analysis at all. Here is where I say once more what I have stressed in the other two volumes in this series: epistolary analysis only helps us with analyzing some of the so-called Epistles of the New Testament, and even then it only helps with analyzing how they begin and end. These documents are mainly structured on the basis of rhetorical considerations, not epistolary ones, since they are oral documents, meant to be read aloud to their various audiences.

Martin is helpful in showing how various of the major images/metaphors/ideas in this discourse cohere with each other and show that the author was careful about his composition of this document. Martin suggests that the Diaspora is the overarching and indeed controlling metaphor of this discourse, which results in two different sorts of supporting images, some general, some specific. The author sees the audience as on an eschatological journey, beginning at the new birth and climaxing when they receive final salvation at the End (1 Pet 1:3-5). On this journey one must thus be concerned to stay on the right path; hence comes the emphasis on the audience's conduct. One of the things seen as possibly throwing the audience off track is reassimilation to the pagan environment, resulting in apostasy from the people of God. Thus the author inculcates steadfastness, hope, sobriety (see 1 Pet 1:13; 4:7; 5:8-9). Martin stresses that there are three specific metaphor clusters that unite the discourse: (1) the *oikos* cluster, referring to the elect household of God, and not surprisingly, then, household codes for behavior therein (1 Pet 1:14—2:20); (2) the cluster on resident aliens, visiting strangers (1 Pet 2:11—3:12); (3) cluster for sufferers of the Diaspora (1 Pet 3:13—5:11).[59] Notice the drift of the argument. The audience is alienated from both its homeland, Israel, and from its immediate environment, which is pagan. In such a situation their only "home" for now is the household of God, the community of Christ; but they can expect suffering, since association with that household makes them part of a minority sect that is both illegal and subject to persecution. Martin, however, does not go further to see how 1 Peter places this development of images within a rhetorically formed discourse. For example, it would have helped his case if he could have seen that the deeper emotions—involving pathos, love or hate, grief or euphoria—are

[58]See ibid, p. 20, with my emphasis; and Martin, *Metaphor and Composition,* p. 270. Here Campbell is quoting Martin.

[59]Martin, *Metaphor and Composition*, see pp. 271-73 and cf. pp. 144-61.

things to which 1 Peter appeals at the end of the discourse and particularly in the peroration. It is not an accident that suffering is the major image in that segment of the discourse, and its attendant emotions.

I take it as demonstrated by a whole battery of recent commentaries by Elliott, Achtemeier, Jobes, Senior and others that there is no serious case to be made for seeing 1 Peter as containing a baptismal liturgy that would then explain the form of our discourse. This older argument can be found in full in Edward Gordon Selwyn's commentary, but it has shown to be wanting by so many of these other recent commentaries that if interested, a reader may refer to them. There is actually only one direct reference to baptism in all of 1 Peter, and it is a brief and passing one. Further, we do not have any independent evidence that such Christian liturgies were already being created in the first century, or if they were, what they looked like. Second, baptismal liturgy is not a literary genre in itself, and as C. F. D. Moule long ago pointed out, it is hard to see how a baptismal liturgy could have been dressed up as a letter and hastily sent off.[60] Indeed, it is even harder to see why the rhetorical character and structure of 1 Peter has been so long ignored in favor of a later and more anachronistic explanation of the structure, such as via the baptismal liturgy theory. As we consider the rhetorical structure of 1 Peter, it will be useful for us first to put forward one of the nonrhetorical outlines that has been influential, that of J. N. D. Kelly:[61]

I. Non-Pauline Prescript (1 Pet 1:1-2 ; cf. Jas 1:1)

II. Doxology or Thanksgiving Section (1 Pet 1:3-12)
[Possibly a hymn or a baptismal thanksgiving combined with 1 Pet 1:6-12 on rejoicing in suffering. Note the switch from "us" to "you" in 1 Pet 1:4, and the addition "who are kept safe," indicating a source used.]

III. Call to Holiness (1 Pet 1:13—2:10)
A. Paraenesis of a Traditional Sort (1 Pet 1:13-19)
B. Hymn or Creed (1 Pet 1:20-21)
C. A Collage of Old Testament Illustrations (1 Pet 1:22—2:10)
[Kelly, *Peter and . . . Jude,* p. 23: "Indeed, what knits together all these disparate scraps, so diverse in their provenance, is this confident promise that, however harassing his experiences, the Christian who sets his hope on Christ will never be put to shame, since God has raised Him from the dead and given Him glory (e.g., 1:13, 21; 2:6)."]

---

[60]See rightly Moule, "Nature and Purpose of 1 Peter," p. 8.
[61]Kelly, *Peter and Jude,* 25.

IV. Social Code and Haustafel (1 Pet 2:11—3:12)
[Note the catchword connection at the end of Psalm 34 quote linking "harm" in the Psalm to what follows.]

V. Addressing the Audience's Problems of Persecution (1 Pet 3:13—4:19)
Closing Advice to Preserve Community Unity (1 Pet 5:1-5)
Typical Closing (1 Pet 5:6)
Eschatological Sanction (1 Pet 5:4, 6)
Call to Steadfastness (1 Pet 5:8-9)
Doxological Remarks (1 Pet 5:10-11)
Closing Greetings (1 Pet 5:12-14; cf. James and 1 John)

From the above we can see that the letter is largely practical in nature and ethical in content, though with much more theology than James or Jude. Kelly adds: "His correspondents' troubles are the ever-felt background of every paragraph, sometimes emerging into the open, but always determining his selection and manipulation of catechetical, liturgical and hortatory matter; and it is they, illuminated by the passion of Christ Himself, which inspire and give point to his paradoxical summons to exultation."[62]

Barth L. Campbell provides us with our first full-fledged rhetorical outline of 1 Peter:

Epistolary Prescript (1 Pet 1:1-2)
Exordium (1 Pet 1:3-12)
Argument 1 (1 Pet 1:13—2:10)
Argument 2 (1 Pet 2:11—3:12)
Argument 3 (1 Pet 3:13—4:11)
Peroratio (1 Pet 4:12—5:14)

Though broadly speaking this outline is helpful and correct, there are some problems. First Campbell wants to see the discourse as having each argument introduced by a proposition. So, for example, 1 Peter 1:13-16 and 1 Peter 2:11-12a and 1 Peter 3:13-16b are all seen as propositions.[63] This is not normally how a single discourse would structure things. Normally the proposition for the whole discourse would come at the end of the exordium and before all the arguments on behalf of the proposition. Second, 1 Peter 4:12—5:14 is surely much too long and diverse us to consider it as the peroration of this discourse. Surely

[62]Ibid.
[63]See Campbell, *Honor, Shame,* pp. 58-198.

1 Peter 5:12-14 is an epistolary closing like the ones we find in Paul's letters. It is far better to take 1 Peter 4:12—5:5 as giving further deliberative arguments about suffering and leadership, and count 1 Peter 5:6-9 as the peroration, with a concluding doxology in 1 Peter 5:10-11. Note how clearly this peroration in 1 Peter 5:6-9 echoes the initial proposition in 1 Peter 1:13-16, where the themes of self-control and hope for the future are also brought forth. This thus is a discourse that issues a call to holiness, which entails self-control, avoidance of old patterns of behavior and temptations, purification through obedience to the truth, endurance of suffering and following good examples like that of Christ and the author.[64]

I propose a more exact and helpful rhetorical outline:

Epistolary Prescript (1 Pet 1:1-2)
Exordium: Thanksgiving for So Great a Salvation (1 Pet 1:3-12)
Propositio: You Are Holy and Have a Hope, So Live Accordingly (1 Pet 1:13-16)
Argument 1: Living as Redeeming Resident Aliens (1 Pet 1:17—2:10)
Argument 2: Submission to Authority Figures (1 Pet 2:11—3:12)
Argument 3: Suffering and Self-Control (1 Pet 3:13—4:11)
Argument 4: Sharing the Sufferings of Christ (1 Pet 4:12-19)
Argument 5: Appeal to the Elders and the Youth (1 Pet 5:1-5)
Peroratio: Humility and Self-Control in Suffering (1 Pet 5:6-9)
Closing Doxology (1 Pet 5:10-11)
Epistolary Postscript (1 Pet 5:12-14

But whose rhetoric is this? Is Peter capable of such rhetoric? According to church tradition that goes back to Papias and is probably reliable, Mark wrote down the Petrine remembrances about Jesus in his Gospel,[65] and there is some evidence that there was an Aramaic original for some of that document.[66] If there is truth in this tradition, it suggests that Peter needed some help in communicating in Greek, at least in written form. Thus 1 Peter 5:12 becomes crucial.

Unlike in 1-2 Thessalonians, where Paul indeed is the speaker but wants to make known that two other authority figures involved in founding the church in Thessalonica (Silvanus and Timothy) are also standing behind him and are in

[64]See the discussion in Achtemeier, *1 Peter,* pp. 4-8.

[65]See the new study by Richard J. Bauckham, *Jesus and the Eyewitnesses: The Gospels as Eyewitness Testimony* (Grand Rapids: Eerdmans, 2006).

[66]See Ben Witherington III, *The Gospel of Mark: A Socio-Rhetorical Commentary* (Grand Rapids: Eerdmans, 2001).

agreement with what is said in the discourse, 1 Peter makes no such claims about the authority of Silvanus. He is not mentioned until the end of the document, and at its beginning stands Peter the apostle alone. In deliberative rhetoric the assertion of one's authority at the outset, establishing one's ethos and indeed the tenor of the document, was crucial. This discourse is presented as an authoritative word from Peter, presumably to his various converts.

What, then, was the role of Silvanus? It is true some scholars have attempted to see 1 Peter 5:12 as claiming that the letter was sent to these various churches through Silvanus the letter carrier. There is a problem with this conclusion. If one diagrams the Greek sentence in question, leaving out the subordinate clauses, it reads: "Through Silvanus . . . I wrote to you briefly." Silvanus may well have carried this document through these regions, just as he carried the letter from the Jerusalem Council meeting (see Acts 15), but this Greek sentence surely claims more. Notice that we do *not* have the verb "send/sent" in 1 Peter 5:12, unlike what we find in Acts 15:22-23, where it seems clear that the reference is to a letter carrier rather than a letter writer, as is also the case in Ignatius's letters (Ign. *Phld.* 11.2; Ign. *Smyrn.* 12.1). It was the normal practice for an author who used a scribe to take up the pen toward the end of the document and add a few words of his own. We see this in various Pauline letters (e.g., Rom 16:21-23; Gal 6:11; Col 4:18), and there is no reason to think the situation is different in this case, considering where Silvanus's name is mentioned. It is difficult to judge how much Silvanus contributed to what we have here, but since he is not claimed as an "author" *even at this juncture* (here Peter says, "I wrote . . ."), we may assume that at most he simply played the role of scribe or amanuensis so far as the composition of the document is concerned. He may in addition have been its deliverer and interpreter.[67]

Like Paul, Silvanus may well have received good training in Greek and in rhetoric in Jerusalem, a training that Peter will not have received while growing up in Galilee and before his conversion. Since there is some evidence of Semitic interference in 1 Peter, it may well be that Peter dictated in Aramaic and Silvanus wrote in Greek, looking at and transcribing from his own copy of the LXX when quoting the Old Testament; or perhaps Silvanus was himself bilingual but more literate that Peter and so he framed Peter's words in better Greek and better rhetorical style. Peter's spoken Greek may well have been better than his written Greek, as is so often the case in such oral multilingual cultures. This being the case, we may conclude that the voice is decidedly the voice of Peter if we trust the rhetorical claim of the document itself, even if the hands are the hands of

---

[67]On this latter point see E. Randolph Richards, *Paul and First-Century Letter Writing*.

Silvanus. Indeed, as we shall see, there are hints in the text that the author has a direct knowledge of the trial of Jesus (1 Pet 2:21-24), the transfiguration of Jesus (1 Pet 5:1), the specific command of the risen Jesus in John 21:17 (see 1 Pet 5:2), and the footwashing by Jesus (1 Pet 5:5). When we couple this with some ten echoes of Jesus' sayings, no author better fits these facts that Peter himself.[68] But up to this point we have said little about Peter the man. Once Petrine authorship seems reasonably likely, then one has to ask about the man himself.

The Peter of the New Testament and Early Christian History

Some 188 times the New Testament mentions Peter, and there can be no question that he is the most well known of all the original disciples of Jesus.[69] His proper Hebrew name was "Simeon" (Acts 15:14), with "Simon" being the Greek form of the same name, which he is called some twenty-two times in the New Testament. Since it was well known that Peter was not the man's proper name, some twenty-seven times we see the phrase "Simon, called Peter," and at 2 Peter 1:1 we even have the hybrid "Simeon Peter." Double names, or a name and a nickname, were not uncommon in this era and culture.[70] Before this time, neither *kephas* nor *petros* were ever proper names in Aramaic or Greek. According to John 1:43 and Matthew 16:18 (see also Mk 3:16), Jesus gave Simon the nickname "Cephas," meaning "rock" or "rocky." It obviously stuck because Paul is content to use only the nickname at 1 Corinthians 1:12; 3:22; 15:5; Galatians 2:9, 11, 14, or its rendering in Greek (Gal 2:7-8). Perhaps it is not accidental that Paul uses the Greek form first when writing to the Galatians, but he uses only the transliteration of the Aramaic in 1 Corinthians. He never uses both the Aramaic and the Greek form of the nickname together, since that would be redundant. It seems clear especially from Matthew 16 that the nickname is meant to imply something about Peter's character or career or both.

The name of Simon's father was Jonah (Mt 16:17), which apparently was rendered as John on some occasions (see Jn 1:42; 21:15-17). My theory as to why it is always "son of John" in the Fourth Gospel is that the author is not a Galilean disciple but rather a Judean one who has chosen to render the name more helpfully into sound-alike Greek for his audience in Asia Minor. From multiple sources we also know that Peter had a brother named Andrew (Mk 1:16, 29; Jn 1:40, 44; et al.), and that he had a wife as well (1 Cor 9:5; Eusebius *Hist. eccl.*

---

[68]See Harner, *What Are They Saying About the Catholic Epistles?* p. 30.

[69]In this excursus I am following the helpful synopsis of Elliott, *1 Peter,* pp. 323-27, and my own summary of what we can know about Peter in *What Have They Done with Jesus?*

[70]See G. H. R. Horsley, "Names, Double," ABD 1011-17.

3.30.1-2), though her name and the mother-in-law's name are unknown (cf. Mk 1:30 and par.). The Fourth Gospel properly identifies Simon's hometown as Bethsaida (Jn 1:44), and we know from Mark that his mother-in-law's house was in Capernaum, a house that seems to have become home base for Jesus and his disciples. Both houses in Bethsaida and Capernaum have been well excavated: in the former we have evidence of a fisherman's rather spacious home (complete with courtyard where fish hooks and other fishing paraphernalia were found); and in the latter we have evidence of the first Christian house church, complete with graffiti that goes back to at least the second century A.D., probably the locale of the house referred to in Mark 1:29 and Matthew 8:14. The archaeological evidence reminds us that fishermen were not illiterate peasants. Indeed, they could be rather well-to-do and as businessmen needed to be able to read and write, including in Greek.[71] What Acts 4:13 indicates is that Peter was not a scribe or Torah scholar, being untrained in the finer points of exegesis and oral tradition. He was not a man of "letters" *(agrammatos)*. This in no way suggests that he could not read or write, or even do these things well. Notice that Peter was not a cosmopolitan person. He was noted for speaking with a recognizable Galilean accent (Mk 14:70 and par.).

Peter was apparently the first of the called disciples (Mk 1:16-18; cf. John 1:40-42), and he is listed first in lists of the Twelve (Mk 3:16-19 and par.). He really is just about the only member of the Twelve for whom we can tell something about his personality. He is variously portrayed as dense about some things (cf. Mt 16:22-24; Mk 9:5-6; Jn 13:8-10; Acts 10:14; 12:9), vacillating (cf. Gal 2:11-14) or quixotic even to the point of being cowardly at times (Mk 14:31, 66-72), yet after Easter he was capable of being quite determined and loyal and courageous most of the time (cf. Jn 21:15-17; Acts 4:10; 5:1-10; 11:2-17; 15:6-17). We must as well bear in mind that Peter was not only the spokesman for the Twelve, but he was a pioneer as well in his public confession of Jesus' identity (Mk 8), his seeing of the risen Lord, apparently in isolation as well as with other disciples (cf. 1 Cor 15:5; Lk 24:34), and also in reaching out to Gentiles for the sake of the gospel (Acts 10; Gal 2:11-14).

What Peter did after Pentecost in A.D. 30 and until his death in about 66-67 is subject to debate and dispute. If in the early days he was the head of the Jerusalem Church (see Acts 1—4), this office seems to have been passed on to James when Peter went on the road as an evangelist to Jews (Acts 12). This event seems to date in the early 40s. We can probably date it to just before the death of Herod Agrippa in A.D. 44 (Acts 12:20-23; Josephus *Ant.* 19.343-352). In due course, and

[71]See Frederick M. Stickert, *Bethsaida: Home of the Apostles* (Collegeville, Minn.: Liturgical Press, 1989).

after some missionary work in Judea, Samaria, perhaps Galilee (Acts 1—12), then in Antioch (Gal 2) and on to Asia Minor, Peter eventually ended up in Rome. This seems clear not only from 1 Peter but also from *1 Clement* 5.1-4 and Ignatius *To the Romans* 4.3. There is substantial tradition that Peter preached in Rome and was the one whose memoirs ended up in a Gospel that John Mark wrote (according to Papias, Irenaeus, and Clement of Alexandria: see Eusebius *Hist. eccl.* 2.15; 3.11; 3.39.15; 5.8.2-3; 6.14.5-7). *First Clement* 5.4 indicates that Peter died in Rome at the end of the Neronian persecution (cf. Eusebius *Hist. eccl.* 2.25.4-8, citing Tertullian, Gaius, and Dionysius of Corinth as witnesses).

Nothing in this brief survey suggests either that Peter was the letter writer to match Paul, or that he was incapable of at least orally dictating a document like 1 Peter. What is perhaps most important is that we must take very seriously what Paul tells us in Galatians 2, that Peter was the major apostle to the Jews. That was the focus of his ministry. One assumes that in the Jewish Christian community in Rome (mentioned at length and by name in Rom 16), Peter made his final mark, and from that context wrote to his earlier Jewish Christian converts in western Turkey. In other words, the substance of the story of Peter supports the conclusion we have been reaching in this study: (1) Jewish Christianity had something of a life of its own, though there was cross-fertilization with more Gentile congregations started by the Pauline mission. (2) These congregations continued to exist well into the latter decades of the first century and beyond. (3) Apparently Peter, perhaps along with James and Jude, was in charge of these congregations and was their apostle until late in the 60s.

Peter was not the apostle of all Christians everywhere, much less the founder of the church in Rome, which arose long before Peter or Paul ever came there. He however was the most important of all the disciples of Jesus, with one foot in the ministry of Jesus and one foot in the early church, bridging and linking the two. He helped keep Jewish Christianity alive and growing even after the death of James the Just in A.D. 62. He helped spawn the first Gospel, and he wrote the crucially important letter we know as 1 Peter. Scot McKnight observes:

> We can discern in Peter an "about-face" over the question of Jesus' death: from outright rejection (Matt. 16:22) and denial (Luke 22:54-71), to restoration (John 21), to preach the death and vindication of Jesus (Acts 2), to finding in the death of Jesus the ultimate paradigm of Christian existence (1 Peter 2:18-25). . . . His name change included Jesus' prediction of his role in the development of the early church: Simon would be a "foundation," a "rock," . . . upon whom the church would be built. In light of this, Peter developed the metaphor of Christians as "living stones" (2:4-8).[72]

[72]McKnight, *1 Peter*, p. 45.

Accordingly, Peter's legacy loomed large after his demise in Rome, and 2 Peter is a fitting tribute to this legacy, seeking to extend it at the cusp of the second century A.D. We cannot call him the first bishop in Rome, but when it comes to evaluating who, humanly speaking, most shaped and contoured the movement known as early Christianity, other than Jesus himself, we can certainly call Peter one of the two most important disciples of Jesus in the first century, the other being Paul.

Bibliography for 1 Peter

Unfortunately, we are not well blessed with good introductory books about 1 Peter. There is Phillip B. Harner's slender volume *What Are They Saying About the Catholic Epistles?* (New York: Paulist, 2004), but there is not a lot of meat on that bone when it comes to 1 Peter since the author is covering too many documents in just 150 pages, with only seventeen pages for 1 Peter. Still, there is some good introductory information in those seventeen pages. This lack of a good introductory textbook on 1 Peter is in some ways odd since we have so many good commentaries on 1 Peter, not to mention numerous good monographs and articles. There is the volume edited by Charles Talbert, *Perspectives on 1 Peter* (Macon, Ga.: Mercer, 1986), but it is out of print and no longer than Harner's volume.

Commentaries on 1 Peter

Of the brief more-popular level commentaries on 1 Peter, I commend the following: (1) C. E. B. Cranfield, *The First Epistle of Peter* (London: SCM Press, 1950). (2) Wayne Grudem, *1 Peter* (Grand Rapids: Eerdmans, 1988). (3) Norman Hillyer, *1 and 2 Peter, Jude,* NIBCNT 16 (Peabody, Mass.: Hendrickson, 1992). (4) I. Howard Marshall, *1 Peter,* IVPNTC (Downers Grove, Ill.: InterVarsity Press, 1991). (5) Scot McKnight, *1 Peter,* NIVAC (Grand Rapids: Zondervan, 1996). (6) Donald P. Senior and Daniel J. Harrington, *1 Peter, Jude and 2 Peter,* SP 15 (Collegeville, Minn.: Liturgical Press, 2003). In terms of exegesis, the most substantive of these commentaries are Marshall and Senior, though Senior is mainly just following Elliott (see below). David L. Bartlett's "The First Letter of Peter," in *The New Interpreter's Bible,* vol. 12 (Nashville: Abingdon, 1998), pp. 229-319, packs a lot into ninety pages, but one wishes for a bit more.

Of the midlevel commentaries, four can be recommended: (1) Ernest Best, *1 Peter,* NCB (London: Oliphants, 1971). (2) Peter H. Davids, *The First Epistle of Peter,* NICNT (Grand Rapids: Eerdmans, 1990). (3) Leonhard Goppelt, *A Commentary on 1 Peter* (Grand Rapids: Eerdmans, 1993), an edited and translated edition of the 1978 German work, which is especially good on comparing 1 Peter to the Qumran material. (4) Karen Jobes, *1 Peter,* BECNT (Grand Rapids: Baker, 2005). All of these are useful, but the last two are more substantial and detailed.

There are several omnibus volumes that contain brief commentaries on 1 Peter. Of those we may commend John Calvin, *The Epistle of Paul the Apostle to the Hebrews, and the First and Second Epistles of St. Peter* (Grand Rapids: Eerdmans, 1963), J. N. D Kelly's *A Commentary on the Epistles of Peter and of Jude,* BNTC (London: Black, 1969), James Moffatt's *The General Epistles,* MNTC (London: Hodder & Stoughton, 1928), and Pheme Perkins's volume *First and Second Peter, James and Jude,* IBC (Louisville: John Knox Press, 1995).

Of the technical commentaries, pride of place should go to Paul J. Achtemeier, *1 Peter,* Hermeneia (Minneapolis: Fortress, 1996), for its clarity and scope. More detailed, and indeed too detailed, is John H. Elliott's massive tome *1 Peter,* AB 37B (New York: Doubleday, 2000), with 956 pages. Quite useful is J. Ramsey Michaels's *1 Peter,* WBC 49 (Waco: Word, 1988). The volume that shaped the discussion thereafter in the English-speaking world is the still useful work by Edward Gordon Selwyn, *The First Epistle of St. Peter* (London: Macmillan, 1946), which has gone through a massive number of reprints. See also Francis W. Beare, *The First Epistle of Peter,* 3rd ed. (Oxford: Blackwell, 1970).

Of the foreign language commentaries, certainly C. Spicq's *Les Épîtres de Saint Pierre,* SB (Paris: Gabalda, 1966) has been helpful, as has Eduard Schweizer's *Der erste Petrusbrief,* 3rd ed., ZB (Zurich: Theologischer Verlag, 1972). Influential in seeing 1 Peter as a pseudepigraphon has been Norbert Brox's *Der erste Petrusbrief,* EKKNT 21 (Zurich: Benziger, 1979), which is grounded in his earlier monograph *Falsche Verfasserangaben: Zur Erklärung der frühchristlichen Pseudepigraphie,* SBS 79 (Stuttgart: Katholisches Bibelwerk, 1975). One of the apparent effects of the general conclusion that 1 Peter is a late pseudepigrapha is that German scholars have not paid as much attention to this document as one might have expected when it comes to studying early Christianity in general, and Jewish Christianity in particular, which is unfortunate. Certainly one needs to consult the commentary by Reinhard Feldmeier, *Der erste Brief des Petrus,* THKNT 15/1 (Leipzig: Evangelische Verlag, 2005). Even though it is too brief, it is a rich resource.

Monographs on 1 Peter

There is a host of good monographs on 1 Peter of various sorts. We have already spoken of the influential work of John H. Elliott, *A Home for the Homeless: A Sociological Exegesis of 1 Peter, Its Situation and Strategy* (Philadelphia: Fortress, 1981), and we should also mention his earlier study *The Elect and Holy: An Exe-*

getical Examination of 1 Peter 2:4-10 and the Phrase Basileion hierateuma, NovTSup 12 (Leiden: Brill, 1966). Of a quite different nature but equally important has been David L. Balch's *Let Wives Be Submissive: The Domestic Code in 1 Peter,* SBLMS 26 (Chico, Calif.: Scholars Press, 1981), which came out in the same year as Elliott's monograph. Both of these works pioneered certain kinds of sociological approaches to 1 Peter. On ancient households and the family of faith, see now David L. Balch and Carolyn Osiek, *Families in the New Testament World: Households and House Churches,* FRC (Louisville: Westminster / John Knox, 1997); and Joseph H. Hellerman, *The Ancient Church as Family* (Minneapolis: Fortress, 2001). Still extremely valuable is the little monograph by Edwin Arthur Judge, *The Social Pattern of the Christian Groups of the First Century* (London: Tyndale, 1960). Powerful confirmation for my thesis about Hellenized Jewish Christians in Asia and the surrounding provinces can now be found in Rodney Stark's *Cities of God: The Real Story of How Christianity Became an Urban Movement and Conquered Rome* (San Francisco: HarperCollins, 2006). Also helpful in analyzing the contribution of ancient scribes to written documents authored by others is E. Randolph Richards, *Paul and First-Century Letter Writing: Secretaries, Composition, and Collection* (Downers Grove, Ill.: InterVarsity Press, 2004).

Of other monographs of importance and influence, we can commend the influential study of William Joseph Dalton, *Christ's Proclamation to the Spirits: A Study of 1 Peter 3.18—4.6,* 2nd ed., AnBib 23 (Rome: Pontificial Institute Press, 1989). Important from the rhetorical side of things are Steven Richard Bechtler, *Following in His Steps: Suffering, Community, and Christology,* SBLDS 162 (Atlanta: Scholars Press, 1998); especially Barth L. Campbell, *Honor, Shame, and the Rhetoric of 1 Peter,* SBLDS 160 (Atlanta: Scholars Press, 1998); and Troy W. Martin, *Metaphor and Composition in 1 Peter,* SBLDS 131 (Atlanta: Scholars Press, 1992). Lauri Thurén's two monographs are also of some importance in this area, both his *The Rhetorical Strategy of 1 Peter* (Åbo, Finland: Åbo Academis forlag, 1990) and more recently his *Argument and Theology in 1 Peter: The Origins of Christian Paraenesis,* JSNTSup 114 (Sheffield: Sheffield Academic Press, 1995). From a different literary angle is Philip L. Tite's *Compositional Transitions in 1 Peter: An Analysis of the Letter Opening* (San Francisco: International Scholars Publications, 1997). While not qualifying as a full monograph, Ralph P. Martin's little study of 1 Peter's theology in *The Theology of the Letters of James, Peter and Jude,* by Andrew Chester and Ralph P. Martin, New Testament Theology (Cambridge: Cambridge University Press, 1994), pp. 87-133, is quite helpful. A helpful volume in beginning to assess the impact of Is 53 on Jesus and his followers is William H. Bellinger Jr. and William R. Farmer, *Jesus and the Suffering Servant: Isaiah 53 and Christian Origins* (Harrisburg, Penn.:

Trinity Press, 1998); unfortunately, it offers little discussion of 1 Peter and the relevance of its data for the discussion.

Of the German monographs, the work of Reinhard Feldmeier, *Die Christen als Fremde: Die Metaphor der Fremde in der antiken Welt, im Urchristentum und im 1 Petrusbrief,* WUNT 64 (Tübingen: Mohr, 1992), has had a large impact. His commentary (2005) is equally useful. We may also note a monograph by William L. Schutter, published in English by a German company: *Hermeneutic and Composition in 1 Peter,* WUNT 30 (Tübingen: Mohr, 1989). Of general importance to this study is Paul R. Trebilco's *Jewish Communities in Asia Minor,* SMTSMS 69 (Cambridge: Cambridge University Press, 1991), which has the merit of framing the questions in the right manner, especially when it comes to trying to identify the audience of 1 Peter. Especially interesting is his discussion of how Noah became a local folk hero in Asia Minor, and even emperors issued coins with Noah's picture on it!

Studies on Peter Himself

There are too many studies to mention that deal at some length with Peter himself. The well-written though skeptical study by Michael Grant, *Saint Peter: A Biography* (New York: Scribner, 1994), is an interesting read. One may also profit from the essays written and edited by Raymond E. Brown, Karl P. Donfried, John Reumann et al., in *Peter in the New Testament* (Minneapolis: Augsburg, 1973), though some contributions are rather dated by now; what makes this study interesting is that it emerges from ecumenical discussions between Catholics and Lutherans. A helpful Catholic study by a fine New Testament scholar is that of Pheme Perkins, *Peter: Apostle for the Whole Church* (Columbia: University of South Carolina Press, 1994). Often overlooked though equally scholarly is Carsten Peter Thiede's *Simon Peter: From Galilee to Rome* (Grand Rapids: Academie / Zondervan, 1988). If we count Grant's approach as minimalist, then Thiede's is maximalist, and *Peter in the New Testament* stands somewhere in between. One may also now want to consult the relevant chapters in Ben Witherington III, *What Have They Done with Jesus?* (San Francisco: HarperSanFrancisco, 2006). An older study that still has some good data in it is Daniel William O'Connor's *Peter in Rome: The Literary, Liturgical, and Archaeological Evidence* (New York: Columbia University Press, 1969). On Peter and others as church elders, see now R. Alastair Campbell, *The Elders: Seniority within Earliest Christianity* (Edinburgh: T & T Clark, 1994).

Articles of Note on 1 Peter

Achtemeier, Paul J. "Newborn Babes and Living Stones: Literal and Figurative in

1 Peter." Pages 207-36 in *To Touch the Text: Biblical and Related Studies in Honor of Joseph A. Fitzmyer*. Edited by Maurya P. Horgan and Paul J. Kobelski. New York: Crossroad, 1989.

———. "Suffering Servant and Suffering Christ in 1 Peter." Pages 176-88 in *The Future of Christology: Essays in Honor of Leander E. Keck*. Edited by Abraham J. Malherbe and William A. Meeks. Minneapolis: Fortress, 1993.

Agnew, Francis H. "1 Peter 1.2—an Alternative Translation." *CBQ* 45 (1993): 68-73.

Applegate, Judith K. "The Co-Elect Woman of 1 Peter." *NTS* 38 (1992): 587-604.

Bammel, Ernst. "The Commands in 1 Peter." *NTS* 11 (1964-1965): 279-81.

Bandstra, Andrew J. "'Making Proclamation to the Spirits in Prison': Another Look at 1 Peter 3:19." *CTJ* 38 (2003): 120-24.

Barclay, John. "Conflict in Thessalonica." *CBQ* 55 (1993): 512-30.

Bauckham, Richard J. "James, 1 and 2 Peter, Jude." Pages 309-13 in *It Is Written: Scripture Citing Scripture; Essays in Honour of Barnabas Lindars*. Edited by D. A. Carson and H. G. M. Williamson. Cambridge: Cambridge University Press, 1988.

———. "Spirits in Prison." ABD 6:177-78.

Best, Ernest. "A First Century Sect." *IBS* 8 (1986): 115-21.

———. "I Peter II.4-10—a Reconsideration." *NovT* 11 (1969): 270-93.

———. "1 Peter and the Gospel Tradition." *NTS* 16 (1969-1970): 95-113.

Blevins, James L. "Introduction to 1 Peter." *RevExp* 79 (1982): 401-25.

Brooks, Oscar Stephenson. "1 Peter 3.21—The Clue to the Literary Structure of the Epistle." *NovT* 16 (1974): 290-305.

Brown, Jeannine K. "Just a Busybody? A Look at the Greco-Roman Topos of Meddling for Defining *allotriepiskopos* in 1 Pet. 4:15." *JBL* 125 (2006): 549-68.

Chin, Moses. "A Heavenly Home for the Homeless." *TynBul* 42 (1991): 96-112.

Cook, David. "1 Peter iii.20: An Unnecessary Problem." *JTS* 31 (1980): 72-78.

Dalton, William Joseph. "The Interpretation of 1 Peter 3.19 and 4.6: Light from 2 Peter." *Bib* 60 (1979): 547-55.

Danker, Frederick W. "1 Peter 1.24—2.17—a Consolatory Pericope." *ZNW* 58 (1967): 93-102.

Daube, David. "*Kerdainō* as a Missionary Term." *HTR* 40 (1947): 109-20.

DeSilva, David A. "1 Peter: Strategies for Counseling Individuals on the Way to a New Heritage." *ATJ* 32 (2000): 33-52.

Elliott, John H. "Ministry and Church Order in the New Testament: A Traditio-Historical Analysis (1 Pt. 5.1-5 and Parallels)." *CBQ* 32 (1970): 367-91.

Feinberg, John S. "1 Peter 3.18-20, Ancient Mythology, and the Intermediate State." *WTJ* 48 (1986): 303-36.

Gross, C. D. "Are the Wives in 1 Peter 3.7 Christians?" *JSNT* 35 (1989): 89-96.

Gundry, Robert H. "Further Verba on Verba Christi in First Peter." *Bib* 55 (1974): 211-32.

———. "Verba Christi in 1 Peter: Their Implications Concerning the Authorship of 1 Peter and the Authenticity of the Gospel Tradition." *NTS* 13 (1966-1967): 336-50.

Hemer, Colin J. "The Address of 1 Peter." *ExpTim* 89 (1977-1978): 239-43.

Hiebert, D. Edmond. "Living in the Light of Christ's Return: An Exposition of 1 Peter 4.7-11." *BSac* 139 (1982): 243-54.

Horrell, David G. "Whose Faith(fullness) Is It in 1 Peter 1:5?" *JTS* 48 (1997): 110-15.

Jobes, Karen H. "Got Milk: Septuagint Psalm 33 and the Interpretation of 1 Peter 2:1-3." *WTJ* 63 (2002): 1-14.

Johnson, Dennis E. "Fire in God's House: Imagery from Malachi 3 in Peter's Theology of Suffering (1 Pet. 4.12-19)." *JETS* 29 (1986): 285-94.

Johnson, Sherman E. "The Preaching to the Dead." *JBL* 79 (1960): 48-51.

Kiley, Mark. "Like Sara: The Tale of Terror behind 1 Peter 3:6." *JBL* 106 (1987): 689-92.

Kilpatrick, George D. "1 Peter 1.11 ΤΙΝΑ Η ΠΟΙΟΝ ΚΑΙΡΟΝ." *NovT* 28 (1986): 91-92.

Klassen, William. "The Sacred Kiss in the New Testament: An Example of Social Boundary Lines." *NTS* 39 (1993): 122-35.

Knox, John. "Pliny and 1 Peter: A Note on 1 Pet. 4:14-16 and 3:15." *JBL* 72 (1953): 187-89.

Lea, Thomas D. "How Peter Learned the Old Testament." *SwJT* 22 (1980): 96-102.

Manns, Frédéric. "La theologie de la nouvelle naissance dans la premiere letter de Pierre." *SBFLA* 45 (1995): 107-41.

Martin, Troy W. "The Present Indicative in the Eschatological Statements of 1 Peter 1.6, 8." *JBL* 111 (1992): 307-14.

———. "The TestAbr and the Background of 1 Pet. 3,6." *ZNW* 90 (1999): 139-46.

McCartney, D.G. "*Logikos* in 1 Peter 2,2." *ZNW* 82 (1999): 128-32.

McKelvey, R. J. "Christ the Cornerstone." *NTS* 8 (1961-1962): 352-59.

Michaels, J. Ramsey. "Eschatology in I Peter III.17." *NTS* 13 (1966-1967): 394-401.

Moule, Charles Francis D. "The Nature and Purpose of 1 Peter." *NTS* 3 (1955-1956): 1-11.

Omanson, Roger. "Suffering for Righteousness' Sake (1 Pet. 3.13—4.11)." *RevExp* 79 (1982): 439-50.

Osborne, T. P. "Guidelines for Christian Suffering: A Source-Critical and Theological Study of 1 Peter 2.21-25." *Bib* 64 (1983): 381-408.

Oss, Douglas A. "The Interpretation of the 'Stone' Passages by Peter and Paul: A Comparative Study." *JETS* 32 (1989): 181-200.

Parker, David C. "The Eschatology of 1 Peter." *BTB* 24 (1994): 27-32.

Pilch, John J. "Visiting Strangers and Resident Aliens." *TBT* 29 (1991): 357-61.

Piper, John. "Hope as the Motivation of Love." *NTS* 26 (1978-1979): 212-31.

Prigent, Pierre. "I Pierre 2,4-10." *RHPR* 72 (1992): 53-60.

Richards, E. Randolph. "Silvanus was Not Peter's Secretary: Theological Bias in Interpreting *dia Silouanou egrapsa*." *JETS* 43 (2000): 417-32.

Richard, G. C. "1 Pet. iii.21." *JTS* 32 (1930): 77

Rodgers, P. R. "The Longer Reading of 1 Peter 4.14." *CBQ* 43 (1981): 93-95.

Scharlemann, Martin H. "'He Descended into Hell': An Interpretation of 1 Peter 3:18-20." *CTM* 30 (1989): 352-56.

Schutter, William L. "1 Peter 4.17, Ezekiel 9.6 and Apocalyptic Hermeneutics." *SBLSP* (1987): 276-84.

Schweizer, Eduard. "The Priesthood of All Believers: 1 Peter 2.1-10." Pages 285-93 in *Worship, Theology, and Ministry in the Early Church: Essays in Honor of Ralph P. Martin*. Edited by M. J. Wilkins and T. Page. Sheffield: JSOT, 1992.

Seland, Torrey. "The 'Common Priesthood' of Philo and 1 Peter: A Philonic Reading of 1 Peter 2.5, 9." *JSNT* 57 (1995): 87-119.

———. "*Paroikos kai parepidēmos:* Proselyte Characterizations in 1 Peter?" *BBR* 11 (2001): 239-68.

Senior, Donald P. "The Conduct of Christians in the World (1 Pet 2.11—3.12)." *RevExp* 79 (1982): 427-38.

Sleeper, C. Freeman. "Political Responsibility According to I Peter." *NovT* 10 (1968): 270-86.

Sly, Dorothy I. "1 Peter 3:6b in the Light of Philo and Josephus." *JBL* 110 (1991): 126-29.

Snodgrass, Klyne R. "1 Peter 2.1-10: Its Formation and Literary Affinities." *NTS* 24 (1977-1978): 97-106.

Snyder Scot. "Participles and Imperatives in 1 Peter: A Re-examination in the Light of Recent Scholarly Trends." *FN* 8 (1995): 187-98.

Spencer, Aída Besançon. "Peter's Pedagogical Method in 1 Peter 3.6." *BBR* 10 (2000): 107-19.

Spicq, Ceslas. "La place ou le role des jeunes dans certaines communautes neotstamentaires." *RB* 76 (1969): 508-27.

Stewart-Sykes, Alistair. "The Function of 'Peter' in 1 Peter." *ScrB* 27 (1997): 8-21.

Sylva, Dennis D. "Translating and Interpreting 1 Peter 3.2." *BT* 34 (1983): 144-47.

Unnik, W. C. van. "The Critique of Paganism in 1 Peter 1.18." Pages 129-42 in *Neotestamentica et Semitica: Studies in Honour of Matthew Black*. Edited by E. E. Ellis and M. Wilcox. Edinburgh: T & T Clark, 1969.

———. "Le role de Noé dans les épîtres de Pierre." Pages 207-39 in *Noé, l'homme universel*. Colloquium of Louvain, 1978. Brussels: Institutum Judaicum, 1979.

———. "The Teaching of Good Works in 1 Peter." *NTS* 1 (1954-1955): 92-110.

Volf, Miroslav. "Soft Difference: Theological Reflections on the Relationship Between Church and Culture in 1 Peter." *ExAud* 10 (1994): 15-30.

Warden, Duane. "The Prophets of 1 Peter 1.10-12." *ResQ* 31 (1989): 1-12.

Wenham, John W. "Did Peter Go to Rome in A.D. 42?" *TynBul* 23 (1972): 94-102.

Westfall, Cynthia Long. "The Relationship Between the Resurrection, the Proclamation to the Spirits in Prison and Baptismal Regeneration: 1 Pet. 3.19-22." Pages 106-35 in *Resurrection*. Edited by Stanley E. Porter, Michael A. Hayes and David Tombs. JSNTSup 186. Sheffield: Sheffield Academic Press, 1999.

Witherington, Ben, III. "Not so Idle Thoughts about *eidōlothyton*." *TynBul* 44, no. 2 (1993): 237-54.

Bibliography for Rhetoric in 1 Peter

Achtemeier, Paul J. *1 Peter*. Hermeneia. Minneapolis: Fortress, 1996 (esp. pp. 4-6).

———. "Newborn Babes and Living Stones: Literal and Figurative in 1 Peter." Pages 207-36 in *To Touch the Text: Biblical and Related Studies in Honor of Joseph A. Fitzmyer*. Edited by Maurya P. Horgan and Paul J. Kobelski. New York: Crossroad, 1989.

Bowersock, Glen Warren. *Greek Sophists in the Roman Empire*. Oxford: Clarendon Press, 1969.

Campbell, Barth L. *Honor, Shame, and the Rhetoric of 1 Peter*. SBLDS 160. Atlanta: Scholars Press, 1998.

Ellul, Danielle. "Un exemple de cheminement rhétorique: 1 Pierre." *RHPR* 70 (1990): 17-34.

Kennedy, George A. *The Art of Rhetoric in the Roman World 300 B.C.-A.D. 300*. Princeton: Princeton University Press, 1972.

———. *Classical Rhetoric and its Christian and Secular Tradition from Ancient to Modern Times*. Chapel Hill: University of North Carolina Press, 1980.

———. *New Testament Interpretation Through Rhetorical Criticism*. Chapel Hill: University of North Carolina Press, 1984.

Leeman, Anton Daniël. *Orationis Ratio: The Stylistic Theories and Practice of the Roman Orators Historians and Philosophers*, vol. 1. Amsterdam: Adolf M. Hakkert, 1963.

Longenecker, Bruce W. *Rhetoric at the Boundaries: The Art and Theology of New Testament Chain-Link Transitions*. Waco: Baylor University Press, 2005.

Martin, Troy W. *Metaphor and Composition in 1 Peter*. SBLDS 131. Atlanta: Scholars Press, 1992.

Moore, Bruce R. "Rhetorical Questions in Second Corinthians and in Ephesians Through Revelation." *Notes* 97 (1983): 3-33.

Rousseau, Jacques. "A Multidimensional Approach Towards the Communication of an Ancient Canonized Text: Towards Determining the Thrust, Perspective, and Strategy of 1 Peter." D.D. thesis, University of Pretoria, 1986.

Thurén, Lauri. *Argument and Theology in 1 Peter: The Origins of Christian Paraenesis.* JSNTSup 114. Sheffield: Sheffield Academic Press, 1995.

———. *The Rhetorical Strategy of 1 Peter: With Special Regard to Ambiguous Expressions.* Åbo, Finland: Åbo Academis forlag, 1990.

———. "Style Never Goes Out of Fashion: 2 Peter Re-Evaluated." Pages 329-47 in *Rhetoric, Scripture and Theology: Essays from the 1994 Pretoria Conference.* Edited by Stanley E. Porter and Thomas H. Olbricht. JSNTSup 131. Sheffield: Sheffield Academic Press, 1996.

Thompson, James W. "The Rhetoric of 1 Peter." *ResQ* 36 (1994): 237-50.

Vasaly, Ann. "Cicero's Early Speeches." In *Brill's Companion to Cicero.* Edited by J. M. May. Leiden: Brill, 2002.

Von Lips, Hermann. "Die Haustafel als 'Topos' im Rahmen der urchristlichen Paränese: Beobachtungen Anhand des 1. Petrusbriefes und des Titusbriefes." *NTS* 40 (1994): 261-80.

1 Peter

1 Peter 1:1-2—Epistolary Prescript: Alien Nation

[1]*Peter, apostle of Jesus Christ, to the elect sojourners of the dispersion (in) Pontus, Galatia, Cappadocia, Asia and Bithynia, [2]according to the foreknowledge of God the Father in sanctification of the Spirit unto obedience and sprinkling of the blood of Jesus Christ. Grace to you and peace be multiplied.*

In **1 Peter 1:1-2** we have one of the richest salutations in all of the New Testament in terms of theological content, and we must comment on certain key words. First, in **1 Peter 1:1a** Peter calls himself an apostle, unlike James or Jude. The word "apostle" comes from the verb *apostellō,* meaning "to send." An apostle is thus, strictly speaking, a sent one, and in the New Testament one sent by Christ or his church to perform some specific task—usually evangelizing or related activities. The background of the term "apostle" probably lies in the Jewish concept of *šālîaḥ,* one who was an authorized agent or representative appointed to carry out a specific mission (cf. Mt 10:5-40; Mk 3:13-19; Jn 13:16; 2 Cor 8:23).

For Paul it appears that the qualification for being an apostle is "having seen the risen Lord" (cf. 1 Cor 9:1; 15:1-11). Luke, in Luke-Acts, seems to use the term more broadly (Lk 6:13, noting the *kai;* Lk 24:9-12, 34-36; Acts 1:2, 8; 14:4, 14; cf. 13:1-3). It can include such people as Barnabas. There may perhaps be a distinction between being an apostle of *a* church and sent on a specific mission (a sent one of a church), and an apostle of Jesus Christ and sent more broadly by him and the church to be involved in a wider and ongoing work. There is evidence to suggest that a *šālîaḥ* could not pass on his authority or commission in a Jewish context. Did this also apply to Christian apostles? C. K. Barrett has pointed out: "If they (Peter and his colleagues) had been appointed . . . *šālîḥîm* by the Lord, this naturally means that he regarded them as officials and administrators in his stead for the community, the eschatological Israel, that he had brought into being."[1] Now it must be said that if the Spirit plays a vital role in singling out people for church leadership since Pentecost (cf. 1 Cor 12), then the Twelve cannot be seen, at least by Luke, as paradigms of leadership for the Spirit-filled community after apostolic times. This is so because (1) the Twelve had a special task of helping to found the community of Christ in the world, and (2) they received their commission and recommission *before* the Spirit was given. Notice how the Twelve are filled up to count before Pentecost in Acts 1 and are *not* increased again thereafter. Therefore, we must distinguish between the Twelve as The Twelve, with their unique roles at the beginning and at the end of salvation history (cf. Mt 19:28; Lk 22:30, judging the Twelve tribes) and as apostles.

This does not mean that the Twelve are outmoded by Pentecost or are of no historical purpose after Acts 1:15-26. Indeed, it is Peter in Acts 2 who takes charge of matters at Pentecost and becomes the spokesman for the Christians. Further, it is the Twelve, as apostles, who must have been responsible for distributing charity until the responsibility became too much and they had to ordain seven others chosen by the people to assume this role (Acts 2:42-47; 4:32-37:6:1-7). Here we see the Twelve, especially Peter, in leadership roles during the transition period. They have one foot in the life of Jesus and the other in the life of the church; they are able to relate the one to the other. In Acts their witness has also changed from the days of the earthly ministry. Though in Luke they witness *for* Jesus *about* the kingdom, in Acts they witness *about* Jesus *and* the resurrection. After the early days of the community, the Twelve do not seem to have been in the forefront of church expansion, and Luke for the most part leaves them behind after Acts 6. This is undoubtedly good history and does not give the Twelve more prominence than they actually had. Still, there is surprisingly little about them in Acts.

We must conclude, however, that it is apostles as apostles who, if any leadership or guidance was given on choosing leaders, gave such guidance. Further, if Paul's definition of apostle is the one that prevailed (i.e., one who has seen and been commissioned by the risen Lord), then necessarily we cannot talk about apostolic succession, the passing on of the apostolic office. We can, however, talk about the passing on of the apostolic faith or traditions and also in some regard to the parceling out of various apostolic functions and later church leadership (deacons, elders, bishops; as apostles, the Twelve act even like deacons in distributing charity until it was necessary to ordain the seven: Acts 2:42-

[1]C. K. Barrett, *The Signs of an Apostle* (London: Epworth Press, 1968), pp. 7-8.

47). In view of other Pauline influences evident in 1 Peter, one may suspect that when we hear the phrase in 1 Pet 1:1 that Peter is an "apostle of Jesus Christ," he means the same thing as Paul does: an emissary commissioned by the risen Jesus; hence, this is an implicit claim to having seen the risen Lord after Easter. The author also identifies himself by his nickname, Peter, rather than as Simon (note the partial contrast with 2 Pet 1:1). As I. Howard Marshall puts it, Simon may have been the first person ever to have the nickname "Peter," which later became a proper name.[2]

In **1 Peter 1:1b** Peter calls his audience *parepidēmois,* "sojourners" (a foreigner currently staying in a place where one has little or no legal status),[3] which may imply both the transience of their life here on earth, but also suggest that their home lies elsewhere: in heaven; thus many have taken these words. They are God's vagabonds by election, with the election alienating them from their non-Christian neighbors, according to Leonhard Goppelt.[4] The problems with spiritualizing this language, however, are several: (1) This term had a social and legal meaning in its day, and there is nothing in this superscript to suggest that the term "elect" should carry more weight in meaning than the following word,[5] "Diaspora/Dispersion." Especially since we then have a list of actual locations in the Diaspora, it likely connotes both a physical place and a social condition. (2) Nothing at all is said here about heaven being the home of believers. The term "Diaspora" had a specific social sense for Jewish Christians: it didn't mean being on earth as opposed to being in heaven. It meant being outside of Israel as opposed to dwelling in the Holy Land. This is perfectly clear from observing its use in the LXX (cf. Deut 28:25; 30:4; Neh 1:9; Ps 146:2 [147:2 ET]; Is 49:6; Jer 15:7; 41:17 [34:17 ET]; Dan 12:2). (3) John H. Elliott has adequately demonstrated other problems with spiritualizing this language.[6] Here it is worth quoting John Calvin against spiritualizing and also against Elliott's form of socializing the terminology: "Those who think that all the godly are so called [foreigners] because they are strangers in the world, and are going on metaphorically towards the celestial country, are greatly mistaken, and this mistake can be refuted by the

[2]Marshall, *1 Peter,* p. 29.

[3]One can debate whether we have two substantives here, "elect" and "visitor" or whether one or the other of these terms is adjectival, meaning "the elect sojourners" or "the visiting elect." The former of these last two options seems more likely since the word "Diaspora" follows these two terms.

[4]Goppelt, *1 Peter,* p. 64, 67-68.

[5]See Pilch, "Visiting Strangers and Resident Aliens," pp. 357-61.

[6]See "Reading 1 Peter in Its Social Milieu," above. The one person who seems most clearly and wholeheartedly to follow Elliott in his reading of this terminology as referring specifically to lower-class and probably rural persons and slaves is McKnight, *1 Peter,* pp. 48-51.

word *dispersion* which immediately follows. This can apply only to the Jews."[7] W. C. van Unnik is equally clear and emphatic on this point about the term "Dispersion" signaling that the audience is Jews.[8]

Here we must say something about Karen H. Jobes's theory that Peter is in fact addressing Jews who have been expelled from Rome during one of the purges.[9] This is a possibility, but nothing in the document especially favors this theory. On the positive side such an event might explain why Peter would be calling them sojourners and resident aliens in these various regions; but then, just the fact of their being descended from transplanted Jews who were moved before the time of the empire could explain this terminology as well. More to the point, in this document Peter uses a style of rhetoric that suggests the audience is well familiar with Asiatic rhetoric. This is more likely to be true if they are longtime residents of these provinces. If Peter is actually writing to Jews who once lived in Rome, it is quite strange that he mentions no personal names of people in the audience and does no more than send a perfunctory greeting from the church in Rome to these churches (1 Pet 5:13). Furthermore, 1 Peter 2:11 says they are resident aliens and strangers "among the pagans." This strongly suggests that Peter is using this social terminology to describe their relationship with their immediate Gentile neighbors, not to suggest they have been recently exported from Rome to these regions. It is not strange at all that Peter should call Jewish Christians the "chosen of the Dispersion." Jews would quite naturally apply these terms to themselves if they lived outside the Holy Land; even more pertinent, Peter, Paul and other Jewish Christians were sectarians who thought such terminology applied quite specifically to Jewish Christians as the righteous remnant ("the saints," as Paul sometimes calls them), viewed as being in continuity with the legacy and heritage of the patriarchs, prophets and priests.

"Dispersion" here seems to mean the same as it did in James, those outside Palestine, but here even more narrowly defined to refer to certain provinces or regions in western Turkey. Josephus, quoting Strabo, notes the widespread perception that "this people has already made its way into every city, and it is not easy to find any place in the habitable world which has not received this nation" (Josephus *Ant.* 14.115). This did not mean that Jews were in the majority in most of these places; it only meant that the majority of these places had some Jews.

In the introduction we have observed that the provinces as listed possibly

[7]John Calvin, *The Epistle of Paul the Apostle to the Hebrews, and the First and Second Epistles of St. Peter* (Grand Rapids: Eerdmans, 1963), p. 230.

[8]W. C. van Unnik, *Sparsa Collecta: The Collected Essays of W. C. van Unnik*, vol. 2, *Peter, Canon, Corpus Hellenisticum, Generalia,* NovTSup 30 (Leiden: Brill, 1980), pp. 95-105.

[9]Jobes, *1 Peter,* pp. 63-64.

reflect the order in which this document was taken to them on Roman roads, but there is something odd about that suggestion. We might have expected a west-to-east listing of the provinces since this document is coming from Rome; but perhaps Peter is thinking of the order in which he visited these places.[10] Ancient letters had both an outside and an inside address: on the "verso" or reverse side of a papyrus letter, it was normal to identify the addressees. This becomes important in the case of a document like James, which is basically undeliverable if the only address is "the Twelve tribes in the Diaspora." There had to be an external address as well as this internal one. In 1 Peter, however, though we have an encyclical, it is for a specific group of churches in specified regions. The external address in this case may have only included reminders of which cities in those regions to visit.[11]

One may suggest that Peter, like Paul, began his evangelization of the region from Antioch. After all, this is where we find Peter in Galatians 2 in about A.D. 49-50. We may assume, then, that he went from Antioch overland, passed through the Cilician Gates, the pass in those formidable mountains in the province of Syria and Cilcia, and then began evangelizing the region, perhaps in Pontus. This region involves some 129,000 or more square miles, so we are talking about an enormous amount of territory. Following the route that ends in Bithynia may suggest that Peter kept heading west from Bithynia across the Hellespont (and perhaps south to Corinth in the early 50s (see 1 Cor 1:12; 9:5). From Corinth he perhaps went back east and did more work in the provinces mentioned in 1 Peter. This enormous amount of territory partly covered by Peter, but not by the Pauline mission, would certainly explain why Peter falls entirely off the Lukan radar after Peter's appearance at the Jerusalem Council in A.D. 50; indeed, Peter had already been mostly off Luke's radar since the early 40s (see Acts 12), when he escaped from jail in Jerusalem, said good-bye to the church there and "went to another place" (Acts 12:17 NRSV).[12] We thus may envision Peter's ministry in the listed provinces of Turkey in the 40s and perhaps

---

[10]Marshall, *1 Peter,* p. 31, sees a route suggested by the order of the provinces: the letter arrives with the boat from Rome, lands at Amisus, on the north coast of Asia Minor, and then is taken on a circular route from one place to another. But this suggestion does not explain why Pontus and Bithynia are separated and treated as separate places if the journey began and ended at Amisus.

[11]See the discussion in *NewDocs* 7:44.

[12]One wonders if Acts 16:6-7 preserves the memory that Paul went one way in this region and Peter a different way since there was plenty of ground to cover in Anatolia. Achtemeier, *1 Peter,* p. 85, is likely correct that the regions listed here deliberately avoid the Pauline mission territory. Paul went especially to Roman colony cities where there were lots of Gentiles. Peter on the other hand was going to places where colonies of Jews had been settled for 250 years, and perhaps where he knew some of the Pentecost pilgrims had returned to.

in the 50s as well. By A.D. 57, when Paul writes to the churches in Rome, Peter has not yet arrived. This may have transpired in the late 50s or more likely the early 60s. By then Mark is assisting Peter in Rome; 1 Peter does not mention Paul at all. This can be either because Paul has gone back east after being released from house arrest in Rome in A.D. 62, in which case this document is written sometime during A.D. 63-64, or more likely it is written after the fire in 64 but before Paul is dragged back to Rome in chains, and so perhaps about 65-66. This chronology of the later life of Peter is speculative, but it meets the facts that the New Testament and certain early church traditions about Peter and Paul being martyred in Rome present us with, and it has the added advantage of explaining the silences in both Acts and 1 Peter, as well as in the Pastorals.

Peter in **1 Peter 1:2** also calls them "the elect," or if you prefer "the chosen," and they are chosen according to the foreknowledge of God, which is a way of saying they were not chosen arbitrarily or without foresight and insight into how they would respond. The term *eklektos* was used of Israel or Jerusalem in the Old Testament (cf. Deut 31:11; Neh 1:9; Ps 134:4 LXX [135:4 ET]; 1QS 8.6; 11.16). He proceeds to state that God has chosen them, by means of or "in" the sanctifying work of the Spirit, and for obedience and sprinkling of the blood of Jesus Christ. In these three phrases about the choosing, Peter refers to Father, Spirit and Christ, in that order. The implication is clearly that all three are in some sense God, and involved in the divine choosing. The order of reference is interesting: Father, then Spirit, then Son. I suggest that this makes sense if the audience is Jews. As Jews, they already had a relationship with the Father, and indeed with the Spirit of God (see, e.g., 1 Pet 1:10-11), but the relationship with Jesus Christ came last. If the author had been addressing pagans here, we might have expected a reference to the sprinkling of the blood and the coming to faith in Christ first.

The concept of election and God's foreknowledge is certainly found also in Paul and in other early Jewish sources before that time. As elsewhere in the New Testament, this terminology functions here as a reassurance device for Christians under pressure: Don't worry; God has chosen you, and he will protect you even through your trials and sufferings. The concept entails the idea that no outside force such as suffering can separate a believer from Christ (cf. Rom 8:28-39). Peter is talking about the people who made up the churches in this area, the Christians. He is addressing an elect and select *group*, not an elect individual. The question thus becomes this: Is Peter talking about a choice made *before* the response of faith, *contemporary* with such a response or *following* such a response? It may well be the first of these, but if so, we need to remember that it was a choice made on the basis of foreknowledge of something about those who would be chosen, not an example of mere divine fiat.

It could for instance be argued that Peter (and Paul in Rom 8) is talking about God choosing a destiny and a way of living for Christians, not God electing individuals to *become* Christians. Clearly the focus here and in Romans 9 is on what Christians must do *after* they believe: persevere, and obey Christ until he returns. The term *prognōsin,* from which we get the word "prognosis," makes clear that God's choice is based on His foreknowledge (cf. the other uses in Acts 2:23 [compare the verbal cognate in Rom 8:29 and 11:2]; and only once in the LXX: Jdt 9:6). As Edward Gordon Selwyn says, "The preposition (*pro-*, "fore") in the compound denotes the fact that God's knowledge is part of his eternal counsel, . . . and the knowledge is with a view to choice and calling."[13] Notice that not just these Jewish Christians but also Christ himself is said to be the object of God's foreknowledge (1 Pet 1:20). This language stresses the divine initiative in choosing and the divine plan of salvation.

What is the content of God's foreknowledge? Strictly speaking, God simply knows all things; we call it foreknowledge because from our perspective in time, in relation to us, God knew it beforehand. If 2 Timothy 2:19 is a clue, it refers to God knowing the ones who are his, *in advance.* It is true that God knows everything *about them* as well, but the focus here and in Romans 8 seems to be on knowing *them,* knowing who would be his. We can thus conclude that though Peter does not explain, he does mean (1) that God's choosing is on the basis of his knowledge. God knew who would be his, and he chose them, even chose them before they responded and enabled them to respond through the prevenient work of the Spirit in them. (2) If, however, God's choice is based on God's knowledge, then it cannot be said to be arbitrary or capricious. God chose those whom God knew were and would be his, those he knew would respond. There is a clear contradiction to the idea that God's knowledge is based on what he first antecedently willed, in which case Peter would have said, "He (fore)knew them *because* he had first chosen them." Origen understood that the term *prognōsis* does not refer to predetermining something. He puts it this way: "Foreknowledge means no more that seeing what is inside a person. It is now no longer foreknowledge in effect, but knowledge of something real which has been foreseen. Those to whom Peter is writing were chosen according to foreknowledge."[14]

It is probably too narrowly constricting the sense of election to confine it to what is involved *after* one becomes a Christian: God chose Christians to obey rather than God choosing them to be Christians and obey. The question, how-

---

[13]Selwyn, *First Peter,* p. 119.
[14]Quoted in ACCS 11:69.

ever, can remain open as to whether Peter has in view the election of individuals or the church as a corporate entity. Probably he would have avoided saying "sojourners" (plural), however, if he had intended to speak only of the elect church. The point is to reassure all the individual believers that God has a destiny for them and will protect them, but they must respond in obedience. Indeed, they were saved in the first place due to their responding to the divine initiative. And they are only elect as part of the elect group, not in isolation. Peter is addressing a body of people as a group and assumes the collectivistic identity they share. Peter shares with Paul the notion that Christ was the foreknown and destined Savior, or as he will call in 1 Peter, the elect stone; if believers are joined to him by faith, they also can become living and elect stones. In other words, this election took place "in Christ," a phrase our author borrows from Paul as well (1 Pet 5:10).

Various commentators, including J. Ramsey Michaels and Leonhard Goppelt, have concluded that the language of being sojourners and resident aliens comes not from the actual social condition of the audience but as a somewhat negative reciprocal of the language about the audience being God's elect, thereby alienating them from the world.[15] While there perhaps is something to this suggestion, there is no reason why this language cannot be multivalent: Jews certainly viewed themselves in a theological light as God's chosen people, and this in various ways set them apart from their neighbors, due especially to their orthopraxy and also to their belief in only one God. But Diaspora Jews also experienced actually being resident aliens in these very regions mentioned in the prescript to this discourse.

It thus should not be a shock that Peter could speak of his audience of Jewish Christians in this same way, and that the discussion carries both a theological and a sociological referent. It is true enough that the two key terms *paroikos* and *parepidēmos* can be virtually interchangeable (cf. Gen 23:4; Ps 38:13 LXX [39:12 ET]) to refer to foreigners living in a foreign land, but the lack of technical specificity in 1 Peter should not lead us to think that there was no social significance to the terminology. The issue in the social usage is not the "homelessness" of the audience. They certainly had and could own homes as resident aliens (pace Elliott). The issue is whether they were treated as citizens by outsiders, and whether they viewed themselves as in some sense marginalized due to their Jewishness and Christian faith, or not. On both counts they were like foreigners in these provinces. Not only is Peter writing to Jews in real locations; we also have specific evidence from Philo about the Jewish presence in this part of Asia

[15] See Michaels, *1 Peter*, p. 7.

Minor north of the Taurus mountains (Philo *Legat.* 281). Josephus in fact tells us that some 2,000 Jewish families settled in western Asia Minor as early as 200 B.C. (Josephus *Ant.* 12.149); if we take normal reproductive rates for the period, this would lead to the conclusion that there were at least 100,000 Jews in this region by the mid-first century A.D.[16]

From 1 Peter 1:2 we notice that the purpose of the Spirit's sanctifying work is twofold, and the first half is easier to explain: obedience. This means we are not to see the Spirit's work in the believer as an end in itself, as if the experience were the whole purpose. Rather, the experience and cleansing work of the Spirit is to enable and equip the believer to respond positively and obey God. It is unlikely that this phrase refers to the consecration of the messengers who conveyed the gospel to the audience or even the consecration of the gospel message itself, since that is not the subject here: rather, "the chosen ones" of the audience is the subject. This becomes even more likely an interpretation when we notice that the second phrase, "and the sprinkling of blood of Jesus," seems to refer to Exodus 24:1-11, about which Vincent Taylor says:

> In this narrative (Ex. xxiv. 1-11) a distinction is drawn between the blood sprinkled upon the altar and that which is sprinkled upon the people. The former is the symbol of the people's obedience; it is their offering to God, confirmed by the words: "All the words which Yahweh hath spoken will we do" (cf. the "obedience" in St. Peter's phrase). The latter, the blood sprinkled upon them, is dedicated blood which Yahweh has accepted, and the sprinkling means that the people now share in the blessings and powers which it represents and conveys. It is this blood which is described as "the blood of the covenant."[17]

Thus, in this case, it means that the Spirit works in the believer for the purpose of applying the benefits of the sprinkled blood: presumably cleansing and perhaps forgiveness and reconciliation are in view. It may be that this is a reference to the "obedience of faith," the initial obedient response of faith, when one receives the benefits of Christ's shed and applied blood.[18] However, more likely it refers to the life of obedience and cleansing that begins at the initial response of faith.[19] Peter wishes these believers grace and peace in abundance, both of which they will definitely need in abundance to persevere and obey through suffering. It nevertheless is possible to read the Spirit clause as an in-

---

[16]See Davids, *First Peter,* p. 46.

[17]Vincent Taylor, *Jesus and His Sacrifice* (London: Hodder & Stoughton, 1943), p. 137.

[18]See Best, *1 Peter,* p. 71. He compares Rom 1:5; 6:16; 15:18; 2 Thess 1:8. The problem is that we do not have the phrase "the obedience of faith" here in 1 Peter.

[19]See Cranfield, *First Peter,* p. 17.

strumental dative, in which case the subject is not the experience of the believer (of sanctification), but rather the comment is being made about the Spirit being the agent by which believers are chosen.[20] The problem with this conclusion is that we must take these three phrases together: "chosen according to God's foreknowledge," "in the sanctifying Spirit" and "unto obedience and sprinkling." The last two phrases have a particularly close connection. Obedience is only possible due to the sanctifying work of the Spirit: this seems to be the drift of the sentence. As Goppelt points out, at Qumran we have language similar to what we find here: "For it is through the Spirit of true Counsel concerning the ways of humankind that all his sins shall be expiated. . . . He shall be cleansed from all his sins by the Spirit of holiness uniting him to his truth. . . . And when his flesh is sprinkled with purifying water and sanctified by cleansing water, it shall be made clean by the humble submission of his soul to all the precepts of God" (1QS 3.6-8).[21] The subject in both texts is sanctification by the Spirit, not consecration or predetermination. It is worth noting the differences as well. There is no mention of any water ritual in 1 Peter 1:2. The sprinkling is with blood, not water, and the allusion is to the act of covenanting, which produces both atonement and cleansing. I thus quite agree with Goppelt's translation here: "the sanctification accomplished by the Spirit" (thus internally, not by water sprinkled on the body).[22] We may compare a similar discussion in Hebrews 9:18-21; 12:24.[23]

As we have seen above, the third clause about Christ probably alludes to Exodus 24:7-8 and therefore has nothing to do with Christian baptism at all. It is referring to the establishment of the covenant, in this case the new covenant inaugurated by means of the shed blood of Jesus himself; we can also note here that the language about becoming a royal priesthood and a holy nation in 1 Peter 2:9 is also the language of covenanting (cf. Ex 19:5-6).[24] But we must stress here that the purpose of God's choosing, of the Spirit's sanctifying, and indeed of Jesus' shedding of blood—this purpose is not merely that believers may be saved, but also that they may obey God's commandments. He has been chosen, empowered and cleansed so that he can do so, says Peter. This hortatory emphasis at the end of the sentence sets up the following discourse, which is loaded with imperatives. The imperative clearly grows out of the indicative of what God has done for the believer, as 1 Peter 1:2 so aptly demonstrates.

[20]See Jobes, *1 Peter,* pp. 69-70.
[21]See Goppelt, *1 Peter,* p. 71.
[22]Ibid., p. 73.
[23]See Witherington, *Letters and Homilies for Jewish Christians,* pp. 273-74; 344-45.
[24]See Achtemeier, *1 Peter,* p. 89.

Some scholars have actually tried to take the last part of 1 Peter 1:2 to refer to the obedience and blood-shedding of Christ himself.[25] The problems with this view are several. First, we would have expected a *hoti* clause here rather than *eis* and the phrase that follows if the author wanted to say "because of the obedience . . ." Second, sprinkling is hardly an apt term if Jesus' shedding of blood on the cross is meant here. Here we should not ignore the allusion to Exodus 24, nor the fact that the author is describing what God has done for the audience: chosen, sanctified and cleansed them so they could both believe and obey God.

The final clause of this opening segment of the discourse involves the traditional Christian or at least Pauline greeting: "Grace and peace" (cf. Rom 1:7; 1 Cor 1:3; 2 Cor 1:2; Gal 1:3). The unique feature of this particular greeting is the addition of the verb *plēthyntheiē*, which means "be multiplied" (cf. Dan 4:37c LXX [not in MT]). There is some later Jewish evidence that Paul may be following a traditional form of greeting Jews in the Diaspora. In the Babylonian Talmud, for example, *Sanhedrin* 11b records the letters of Rabbi Gamaliel to "the sons of the Diaspora of Babel, . . . of Mede, . . . of Greece," and the greeting includes the words "May your peace be multiplied." One may wish to compare the normal Jewish greeting in 2 Maccabees 1:1. We may compare the close of the letter as well, where we find a peace wish at 1 Peter 5:14. Since this closing also mentions election and the term Babylon (1 Pet 5:13), there seems to be a deliberate attempt to begin and end the document with some rhetorical symmetry emphasizing the situation of Jews in the Diaspora.[26]

1 Peter 1:3-12—Exordium: Suffering Now, Salvation Later

An exordium in a deliberative discourse such as we have here in 1 Peter can serve a variety of purposes. In the prescript we have already noted that Peter, while stating his authority (as an apostle of Jesus Christ) does not have to argue for it: his ethos seems well established with this audience. Therefore, in the exordium Peter can focus on other aspects of setting up the arguments that will follow: establishing rapport with the audience and giving them a preview of coming attractions (cf. Cicero *De or.* 2.80.325; Quintilian *Inst.* 4.1.23-27). We can see this preview aspect immediately by comparing 1 Peter 1:6-7 with 1 Peter 4:12-13; 5:10.[27]

In terms of form, what follows in 1 Peter 1:3-12 can be said to be a blessing

---

[25]Elliott, *1 Peter*, p. 319.

[26]See Jobes, *1 Peter*, p. 74.

[27]See Dalton, *Christ's Proclamation to the Spirits*, pp. 95-96, who calls this an example of inclusio.

or thanksgiving prayer offered to God for his salvific works past, present and future. While it is true that there often were health wishes at the outset of Hellenistic letters, they were always brief and did not contain any attempts to preview what would follow in the letter, nor really to establish rapport with the audience. Such health wishes were about as perfunctory as the word "goodbye" is today in a modern letter. Even though "goodbye" is the shortened form of "God be with ye," the connotation today is no more than "farewell," just as the ancient health wish was simply a necessary element in the ancient letter that needed to be expressed at the outset to mark this as a "friendly" correspondence of some sort. For example, here is the opening of a Hellenistic letter: "Apion to Epimachus his father and lord, many greetings. Before all things I pray that you are in health, and that you prosper and fare well continually together with my sister and her daughter and my brother. I thank the Lord Serapis that when I was in peril on the sea he saved me immediately."[28] This in fact would qualify as an effusive health wish by the standards of pagan writing: it is more elaborate and emotional than most we find in the papyrus letters from Egypt and elsewhere. We can see at once that the Christian thanksgiving prayer/exordium has far more to it than the pagan parallels.

It is thus not the case that form follows function when it comes to these opening blessings or thanksgiving prayers. The form is like an expanded version of the Hellenistic health wish, but the function is purely rhetorical: establishing rapport with the audience and alerting them to upcoming themes in the discourse. Barth L. Campbell is absolutely right to identify 1 Peter 1:3-12 as the exordium of this discourse. He is also right that the major theme of this discourse is announced here: suffering for being a Christian and with Christ. This however is a delicate subject, and the whole issue of honor and shame is wrapped up with this concept. To suffer honorably for an honorable cause is one thing. To suffer unjustly can also be honorable. But to suffer in a way that the vast majority of the culture would see as shameful and humiliating, such as by dying on a cross, is a whole different matter. The word *paschō* and its cognates appears some sixteen times in these five chapters, making it the dominant theme of the discourse. There may be something to the old suggestion that since the text usually refers to Christ's suffering with the term *pathēmata* (1 Pet 1:11; 4:13; 5:1) and to the believer's suffering, first here, as *peirasmoi* (1 Pet 1:6), there is a difference in kind between the atoning suffering of Jesus and that endured by the believer. But Peter's main concern is to relate the two sorts of suffering as both for the same honorable cause, while still maintaining some distinctions.

[28]Quoted by Marshall, *1 Peter*, p. 33.

As Campbell notes, it is striking that in the first argument of the discourse (1 Pet 1:13—2:10) the believer's suffering receives only a passing mention after it has been announced here in the exordium, but later in the discourse between 1 Peter 2:11—4:11 it becomes a very prominent theme.[29] I suggest that the reason for this is because suffering is a delicate matter, and so Peter uses the method of *insinuatio*, postponing the discussion of the real bone of contention until later in the discourse, after he has established his audience's readiness to listen to his arguments.[30] Nevertheless, the exigence, the rhetorical problem that prompts the discourse, is clearly announced here in the exordium: that problem is suffering for one's faith, whether the suffering amounts to being shamed and enduring slander, or to absorbing more physical forms of suffering.

In this exordium Peter does not focus directly on himself or his own experiences, but he does indicate by the use of the first person plural in 1 Peter 1:3 that he and the audience worship the same God and share a common salvation through Jesus Christ. "The commonality of Lord and new birth serves to unify Peter and his readers."[31] He also enhances his authority and further establishes his ethos in 1 Peter 1:4-12 by implicitly associating himself with the Old Testament prophets and their inspired speech. This becomes especially clear in 1 Peter 1:12, where we are told that the preachers of the good news are in fact fulfilling what the prophets foresaw would happen, standing in the same line as the prophets and speaking for God by means of the same Holy Spirit. What is probably going on here is that Peter is claiming that the following discourse, like his initial preaching to the audience, is divinely inspired. As Quintilian stresses, the authority of a discourse is enhanced to the degree that it can be said to involve inspired speech, or even the quoting of the deity (cf. Quintilian *Inst.* 10.1.48).

One of the giveaways as to the rhetorical species of a discourse is whether or not the discourse focuses on the past, the present or the future. Clearly enough, this exordium signals that we are dealing with future-oriented rhetoric. Thus we hear about the living hope (1 Pet 1:3), the permanent inheritance (1 Pet 1:4), and most important, the salvation yet to be revealed (1 Pet 1:5-9). The future orientation of the discourse is also signaled in 1 Peter 1:10-12 by the discussion of the prophets looking forward and trying to peer into the future, to see when and where and how their prophecies would be fulfilled. As with all New Testament writers, Peter emphasizes the already-and-not-yet nature of that fulfillment. It has come in part already in the Christ event and in the current lives

---

[29]Campbell, *Honor, Shame,* p. 34.
[30]See rightly Thurén, *Rhetorical Strategy,* p. 132.
[31]Campbell, *Honor, Shame,* p. 35.

of his followers, but clearly the climax and conclusion of God's salvation plan is yet in the future.

In his rhetorical study, Campbell tries to argue that 1 Peter 1:3-12 is an encomium, involving issues of honor and praise in the present. The problem with this conclusion is that we find neither the language of honor and shame in this exordium, nor the language of praise and blame on the whole. What Peter mentions is that believers will receive praise and glory and honor at the eschaton. But this discourse is not written for those already basking in the light of the eschaton and hearing "Well done, good and faithful servant; inherit the kingdom" (cf. Mt 25:23; Lk 19:17). This discourse is meant to aid pressured and persecuted Christians to keep the eye on the prize, and to change in the near future any belief or behaviors that are out of line with living according to Christian hope and Christian virtues. There is a good deal of talk about joy and rejoicing amid suffering and distress, which is not the same as praising the audience for already modeling key virtues and avoiding vices. *Now* is the time for testing faith and perseverance through trials. *Later* is the time for praise and honor and glory at the eschaton. In short, this is the language of deliberative rhetoric.

What has confused Campbell is that this exordium contains effusive Asiatic rhetoric with long sentences, which he associates with epideictic oratory. But Asiatic style can be expressed in deliberative rhetoric as well.[32] Notice what Campbell admits: "Although in the main, the exordium in 1 Peter introduces deliberative speech, it is epideictic in nature and especially encomiastic."[33] If anyone is being praised here, it is God, who has regenerated the audience. There is nothing here at all about praising or blaming the audience's virtues or vices. Rather, there is a discussion about the eschatological outcomes of their faith, hope and love in action. The focus here is not on qualities they have but activities they need to engage in, especially amid their suffering. Like most deliberative discourses, Peter must show the "benefit" or "usefulness" of such behavior, and he does so by stressing the eschatological conclusion of things. In no way does Peter view the Father and Son as the audience's ancestors, nor describe their salvation as a list of their accomplishments or achievements. To the contrary, we are talking about God regenerating them and sustaining them.[34]

---

[32]But see ibid., pp. 38-41. Martin, *Metaphor and Composition,* admits on p. 39 that epideictic exordiums bear resemblance to deliberative ones. The question is whether Peter is trying to give advice to his audience so they may persevere through suffering. The answer: yes, he is. See Quintilian *Inst.* 3.7.28.

[33]Campbell, *Honor, Shame,* p. 41.

[34]It is especially a stretch to say that God and Christ are viewed as the "ancestors" of the believers, as in ibid., pp. 44-45. On the contrary, they are viewed as God, who regenerates people.

Campbell, however, is able to demonstrate some of the rhetorical finesse of this exordium. For example, notice the use of alliteration in 1 Peter 1:4 *(aphtharton, amianton, amaranton)* to describe the quality of the eternal inheritance coming in the future.[35] Here we especially see Asiatic rhetoric in play, the rhetoric of redundancy and repetition or use of near synonyms, for these three terms are basically three different ways to speak of the same thing. The ultralong period also supports the conclusion that we are dealing with Asiatic rhetoric, as does, for example, the use of multisyllable words when simpler ones would have done; and of pleonastic, excess verbiage in praise of joy to indicate its importance in 1 Peter 1:8 *(aneklalētō* and *dedoxasmenē)*. Notice as well the exact repetition of the form of the verb *agalliasthe* in 1 Peter 1:6, 8.

Inartificial proofs are the kind that the rhetor does not need to make up. It involves appeals to higher or earlier and well-recognized authorities, authorities that are accepted by both author and audience and thus are the stronger kinds of proofs (Aristotle *Rhet.* 1.2.1355b.2). Peter knows perfectly well that his message about suffering will in some respects be a hard sell, even if he is able to appeal to texts like Isaiah 53, which he will do. Therefore, here he reminds his audience that they live at a special time in history when they can see God's salvation plan being realized. Old Testament prophets and even angels could only dream of seeing such a day. Thus Peter trots out divine authority as the backing for what he will go on to say in this discourse. First Peter 1:9-12 serves the purpose of making the audience well disposed to receive the acts of persuasion that follow. Throughout the section, Peter is going back over ground he shares in common with the audience, things they should already know; in this section he avoids any imperatives as he establishes rapport with his audience, emphasizing the positive side of things such as the joy the audience can and does have, while introducing briefly the theme of the suffering righteous person.[36] As an apostle Peter could certainly simply send a letter with orders and commands in it; yet he would rather persuade the audience and build comradery, and in this he was following the example of his master. "Jesus did not choose to overwhelm his enemies with his power. Persuasion, love, and faith are very different realities. They leave the pathway for rejection or merely civilized disregard wide open."[37]

> [1:3] *Blessed be the God and Father of our Lord Jesus Christ, who according to his plentiful mercy caused us to be born again into a living hope through the resurrection of Jesus Christ from the dead* [4] *into an inheritance imperishable and undefiled and*

---

[35] Ibid., p. 45.

[36] See Thurén, *Rhetorical Strategy,* pp. 130-31.

[37] Perkins, *First Peter,* p. 32.

> *unfaded, having been kept in heaven for us, [5]who are guarded (shielded) by (in) the power of God through faith into (a) salvation ready to be revealed in the last days. [6]In this you rejoice (greatly) even if it is necessary that now for a while you be distressed in various trials [7]so that the tested part (or genuineness) of your faith, more valuable than gold that perishes through fire, being tested is found unto (your) praise and glory and honor in (at) the revelation of Jesus Christ. [8]You love (him) though you have not seen (him), whom though (even) now you do not see you believe; you rejoice with joy inexpressible and glorious; [9]you are receiving the goal (end) of your faith, the salvation of your very beings. [10]Concerning this salvation the prophets researched and examined, who prophesied about your grace, [11]trying (to find out) at what time or (in what) circumstances the Spirit of Christ within them declared, testifying beforehand about the sufferings in store for Christ and the glories after (with) them. [12]It was revealed to them that not for themselves, but for you they were serving these things, which now has been declared to you through the good news brought to you by the Holy Spirit sent from heaven, into which things even angels desire to peer.*

This paragraph is certainly convoluted and full of complex ideas, but then this is what one should expect from hyperbolic Asiatic rhetoric. Not only do we have long sentences, but also a series of subordinate clauses qualifying 1 Peter 1:3-5. The context is clearly eschatological. Peter is talking about a salvation that will be revealed in the last days, about the revelation of Jesus Christ, about an inheritance kept in heaven for believers but to be realized at the eschaton on earth, about the age which the prophets looked forward to and foretold. One thing that becomes especially clear, from examining this section and its immediate successor, is that Peter is convinced that salvation, or in this case the beginning of salvation called the new birth, is the basis of Christian ethics.[38] He must speak of the new birth here in the exordium, so he can then speak about ethics.

First Peter 1:3 speaks of Jesus' "Father" and Jesus' God. As Edward Gordon Selwyn points out, this phraseology is intended to indicate that the incarnation by no means exhausts the Godhead, so in a sense the Father could be called Jesus' God.[39] However, even if this phrase implies a certain subordination of the Son to the Father, the term Lord *(kyrios)* is used in the Old Testament for God as well as in pagan contexts. It says he is *our* Lord, in a special sense Lord over Christians. God causes a believer to be born again; this does not come from a self-help program. It is an act of his mercy and nothing God owes us.

This concept of "new birth" we find in John 3; Titus 3:5 (but not elsewhere

---

[38]See McKnight, *1 Peter,* p. 69.

[39]Selwyn, *First Peter,* p. 122.

in Paul); James 1:18; and here. The term used here, *anagennaō* (meaning "birth again"), occurs only in 1 Peter (here and at 1 Pet 1:23) and nowhere else in the New Testament, nor is it found in the LXX or in classical Greek.[40] Paul prefers the "new creation" language: the concept implies that outside activity caused the change. What needs to be said about the "new birth" idea is that we can no more cause ourselves to be born again than we can cause ourselves to be born the first time. Judaism used this terminology, but it may have been mostly a metaphor.[41] In early Christian literature, however, we seem to be talking about a real though not physical change, and not merely a change of mind either. We may call it an inward and spiritual change. Believers have a living hope based on a historical fact: the resurrection of Jesus. His resurrection is from the dead and thus not merely a resuscitation of one in a coma. Hence, it was a hope based in the past, but looking forward to the future.

The most striking characteristic that distinguished the early Christians from their pagan neighbors was their *hope*. God had begotten them again "unto a living hope." When Paul described the pagans as "having no hope" (1 Thess 4:13), it was plain truth, no mere rhetorical flourish. The world of ancient Greek and Roman civilization was a world of fascinating beauty. It could boast of splendid courage, high intellectual power, and superb loveliness of poetry and art; but in spite of all the grandeur and charm, it was a world without hope.[42]

Peter calls this a *living* hope, not dormant or dead, but very much alive. Notice how the clauses follow "born again": born again *into* a living hope, *into* an inheritance, *into* a salvation—all of which are conceived as essentially future, things waiting to be given or revealed on the last day. The inheritance is not gained at death, but rather at the eschaton. It is a mistake to see this discourse as being about a journey to a heavenly city from which Christians are presently in exile.[43]

In James "we" are kept; in **1 Peter 1:4** "our inheritance" is kept in heaven. Whoever becomes part of Jesus' family inherits what he has to give his own: salvation. It is said to be kept in heaven because Jesus is in heaven. With it being in heaven, there is no chance of it perishing or being corrupted: it is kept in a perfect place and is a perfect salvation to be brought to us by our perfect Lord on his Day. This inheritance is unlike that promised to Old Testament Israel: an imperfect land or generations of imperfect descendents. It is possible, as C. E. B.

[40]Goppelt, *1 Peter,* p. 81.
[41]See Best, *1 Peter,* p. 75.
[42]Cranfield, *First Peter,* p. 22.
[43]See Perkins, *First Peter,* p. 31. She rightly contrasts this expression with the idea of individualized inheritance at death, as in Wis 4:20—5:16.

Cranfield suggests, that *Jesus* is primarily our inheritance, and the rest of the blessings are by-products of receiving him (cf. Ps 16:5; 73:25-26; Lam 3:24).[44] In any case this inheritance is said to be "untouched by death, unstained by evil, unimpaired by time."[45] Here is possibly an echo of Matthew 8:19-21 or Luke 12:33, or at least it reflects knowledge of those sayings of Jesus.[46] Finally, nothing suggests that this inheritance is nonmaterial or purely spiritual in nature. This depends on what Peter thinks will happen at the eschaton, when Jesus returns. Since there is good reason to think he believes that resurrection is what will happen, it is likely that he envisions a permanent material condition free from disease, decay and death that would affect both Christians and the creation itself (see Rom 8). The fact that he does not limit this expectation to the return of the Holy Land to Jews as their inheritance does not mean he envisioned something nonmaterial.[47] Peter has surely heard the beatitude promising that the meek would inherit the earth, not just the Holy Land (Mt 5:5).

In the meantime **1 Peter 1:5** tells us that God is also active here on earth, protecting believers with his power. This protection does not mean a protection *from* suffering, not even suffering in the last days, but a protection from *falling out of the faith* due to suffering. The believers' salvation is ready and waiting for them. It is not that God has not finished preparing salvation for them, but rather that God has more persons to prepare for salvation, and this sentence suggests that Peter does not yet see believers as being in the very last days. Notice that 1 Peter 1:20 uses a different expression: Jesus "was revealed in the last age *[ep' eschatou tōn chronōn]*." Here in 1 Peter 1:5 we have *en kairō eschatō,* "at the last," or "in the last time" (days). He is likely making a distinction of some sort here: one refers to a past event, the other to a future one. In one sense, salvation and the last age came when Christ first came. In another sense salvation is future, to be finally given when Christ returns; those days will be the climax of the eschatological period, the real last days.

First Peter 1:6 tells us that Christians can already rejoice greatly because of the *partial* receiving and future *certainty* of this blessing. The "now" indicates that Peter's audience's trials are present or are about to happen, though his *even if* seems to hint they may not yet be suffering. Perhaps he has heard that some of them to whom he is writing are suffering in some areas, but not in others. Notice the word *oligon,* "small" or "little," and also the qualifier *ei deon,* "if nec-

[44] Cranfield, *First Peter,* p. 23.

[45] Francis W. Beare, *The First Epistle of Peter,* 3rd ed. (Oxford: Blackwell, 1970), pp. 83-84.

[46] See Jobes, *1 Peter,* p. 86.

[47] Against Elliott, *1 Peter,* pp. 334-35.

essary" or as we might put it, "if God wills." Peter is not minimizing their suffering, but in comparison to the greatness of salvation, it appears small (cf. 2 Cor 4:7-18).

According to **1 Peter 1:7**, however, this suffering is seen as a means of refining their faith and proving its genuine part. This verse may reflect a knowledge of James 1:12, but here the reference is not to a process of testing, as in James. It appears here that *to dokimion* means something "tested," *not* the testing process,[48] and this leads as well to the conclusion that *periasmos* must surely be translated "testing" rather than "temptation" in 1 Peter 1:6, though in itself the word can have either meaning.[49] The tested part, by which is meant the genuine part of their faith, will be tested and refined. Even gold perishes (in part) through fire, but not even so valuable a metal is as valuable or durable as faith under fire. A faith that has passed the test will result in praise and glory and honor for the faithful one at the day Christ returns (here the term "revelation" refers to the event of his second coming, not to an oral or written revelation of Jesus; cf. Rom 8:19; 1 Cor 1:7; 2 Thess 1:7).[50] It seems possible that the author of the Shepherd of Hermas knew 1 Peter, for he says: "Just as gold is tried by fire and becomes useful, so also you who live in the world are tried in it. So then, you who remain in it and pass through the flames will be purified. For just as gold casts off its impurity, so also you will cast off all sorrow and tribulation, becoming pure and useful" (Herm. *Vis.* 4.3).[51] More important, there are hints in this document that Peter, like Jesus knows some of the earlier Jewish sapiential literature. Here we may cite Sirach 2:1-6, which has much the same language as we find here: "My child, when you come to serve the Lord prepare yourself for testing *[peirasmon]*. Set your heart right and be steadfast, and do not be impetuous in time of calamity. Cling to him and do not depart, so that your last days may be prosperous. Accept whatever befalls you, and in times of humiliation be patient. For gold is tested *[dokimazetai]* in the fire, and those found acceptable in the furnace of humiliation. Trust in him, and he will help you; make your ways straight, and hope in him" (NRSV).[52] Wisdom of Solomon 3:5-6 is quite similar as well.

First Peter 1:8 implies the strength of the audience's faith: they have loved

---

[48]Nigel Turner, *Grammatical Insights into the New Testament* (Edinburgh: T & T Clark, 1965), pp. 168-69.

[49]See Marshall, *1 Peter,* pp. 40-41.

[50]Elliott, *1 Peter,* p. 342.

[51]Or one could argue he knew the Sirach passage instead, but it is closer to the 1 Peter text.

[52]See the discussion of this in Jobes, *1 Peter,* p. 95. On Jesus' and various NT writers' indebtedness to the Jewish sapiential tradition, see Ben Witherington III, *Jesus the Sage* (Minneapolis: Fortress, 2000).

Christ even though they did not and do not now see him, but nonetheless believe him. Here we may have a contrast between Peter's own position, who has seen Jesus, and that of his audience.[53] Oddly enough, the New Testament Epistles speak little about believers loving Christ, but this passage is eloquent.[54] Knowing and being in Christ now is inexpressible joy, even in the midst of suffering—a glorious experience.[55] As Michaels stresses, there is no claim here that suffering in itself is a cause for rejoicing or that it is redemptive. The audience is to rejoice because they have the honor of suffering for Christ's sake and thus are sharing the experience of Christ (see 1 Pet 4:13-14), and they are to rejoice because the outcome of their faith will be final salvation at the eschaton.[56]

In **1 Peter 1:9** *komizomenoi* literally means "carrying off for yourself" = "winning for yourself" or possibly "receiving for themselves." Here is tension between present and future. The receiving is present, but the goal or end of salvation is future. Thus we perhaps should translate "winning for yourselves." They are winning the prize but have yet to receive the trophy because they are still in the process of winning it. They must persevere to win. *To telos* could mean "end" here, but more likely means "goal" or "consummation": the end of a process, its consummation or goal. Obviously the goal of our faith is salvation. *Psychē* here means "being, self," probably not "the soul" (cf. 1 Pet 1:22; 2:25; 3:20; 4:19): salvation of the self = your salvation. Ernest Best says:

> Soul [Greek: *psychē*]: This is not a special part of man's physical or mental structure, or a divine spark within him, or his higher nature, but man as a whole; it is a Jewish rather than a Greek or modern usage of the word. In 1 Peter it is used in a somewhat different way from Paul, who tends to apply it to the natural and not the redeemed man. It is almost the equivalent of the personal pronoun (it can be so replaced at 1:9, 22; 2:25; 4:19); it is the man himself (at 3:20 the plural is translated "persons"), the whole man, who is saved (cf. Mk 8:35-37, where "life" is the translation of the same word).[57]

First Peter 1:10 begins another sentence; however, it is linked to 1 Peter 1:9 by the word "salvation." We must immediately ask, Who are these proph-

---

[53]Selwyn, *First Peter,* p. 131.

[54]See Senior, *1 Peter,* p. 37.

[55]See Martin, "Present Indicative in the Eschatological Statements," pp. 307-12.

[56]Michaels, *1 Peter,* p. 36. I am not however persuaded that Peter is merely saying "Then you will rejoice" (i.e., at the eschaton), though that is true as well. This would require taking the verb "rejoice" in 1 Pet 1:6, which is in the present tense, as if it were a future verb. I am unconvinced. Peter is thinking of present and future joy, not just one or the other, and not even the repetition of the verb in 1 Pet 1:8 was likely originally a future tense verb. Achtemeier, *1 Peter,* pp. 100-101, has the better of this argument.

[57]Best, *1 Peter,* p. 80. See also rightly Elliott, *1 Peter,* p. 344.

ets? Are they (1) Old Testament prophets? (2) New Testament prophets? or (3) all prophets, including Christian prophets, perhaps especially New Testament prophets?

Now against Selwyn and others and thus against (2) and (3), it appears that the author is distinguishing his audience's time from that of the prophets. These prophets had to research to find out about the when and manner of this salvation. New Testament prophets very well knew at least the means, and in part they knew the when: it began when Jesus came and died and rose. The two verbs here, referring to seeking out and inquiring carefully (cf. Ps 118:2 LXX [119:2 ET]; cf. Josephus *J.W.* 4.654, referring to a house-to-house search), which indicates that the answers to their questions were not immediately apparent to them. This certainly better suits Old Testament prophets than New Testament ones. If there is anything to the argument that Peter frequently alludes to Jesus' sayings (and I think there is), then Matthew 13:17 may be relevant to this discussion: "Many prophets and saints longed to see what you now see; yet never saw it."[58]

Second, Selwyn's view requires us to see New Testament prophets as studying the Old Testament Scriptures (together?) and communicating the results to the church (by missionaries?).[59] I. Howard Marshall is surely correct in saying: "We do not need to envisage God as actually describing the Christian church to the prophets; it is sufficient that they were told that their prophecies would be fulfilled in the future 'in those days and at that time' (Joel 3:1)."[60] In other words, Peter is using Christian language (Spirit of Christ = Holy Spirit) to describe the experience of Old Testament prophets.[61] It nevertheless is interesting that he envisages the prophets as having a dialogue with God about the meaning of what they were predicting. This seems most like what we hear at Jeremiah 12:1-6; 14:11-16; 15:15-21. The prophets are seen not merely as FedEx, delivering others' messages, or as mere mouthpieces for God, but rather as those who have a personal relationship with God and a stake in and concern about the message they proclaim. The work and words of the prophets are seen as a "service" *(diēkonoun)* or ministry to the audience (1 Pet 1:12).

First Peter 1:11 is making the point that the Old Testament prophets foretold or "prewitnessed to" the sufferings of Christ and the glory that would fol-

[58]Gundry, "Verba Christi in 1 Peter," pp. 336-50.

[59]Cf. Best, *1 Peter,* pp. 83-84; Selwyn, *First Peter,* pp. 135-36.

[60]Marshall, *1 Peter,* p. 46.

[61]Though it is not impossible that Peter is envisioning Christ as the preexistent inspirer of these prophecies, he does not make this clear here. But see Senior, *1 Peter,* p. 34. If the Peter who experienced Pentecost wrote this, it is easy to see why he would call the Holy Spirit "the Spirit of Christ." It was Christ who promised and then sent the Spirit when he ascended on high.

low.[62] Peter implies they did *not* know the when or what circumstances by inspiration, but studied, trying to find out.[63] In particular they tried to find out the when and nature of Messiah's sufferings and the glories (note the plural) that followed. Peter also says that these prophets prophesied by means of the Spirit of Christ. The plural of "sufferings" would presumably not refer to Christ's death, or not to it alone, but also to those that preceded the execution by crucifixion. The glories likely include Christ's glorious resurrection but perhaps also the glorious things that have happened to believers and are yet to happen to believers (cf. 1 Pet 1:7-8). The reference to the Spirit of Christ may be a reference to Christ's preexistence rather than the Holy Spirit.[64] However, it is more likely that this is simply a reference to the Holy Spirit, which Christians, since they believe Christ sent the Spirit, can call the Spirit of Christ; or perhaps it means the Spirit, who knows about and reveals Christ (see 1 Pet 1:12c).[65]

Various Old Testament phrases or names for God were applied to Christ, and also various New Testament ideas and phrases were used to see the Old Testament "in light of Christ." This passage is an example of the latter: **1 Peter 1:12** shows how Christians believe that the Old Testament prophets were indeed acting in service of Christ. Christians received the fulfillment of all that the prophets spoke in preparing his way, even if they did not know the precise timing or nature of this Coming One and coming age. Yet Peter does not try, nor should we, to retroject the whole gospel into the mouths of the prophets. They saw a coming Messiah and some of what he would do (cf. Is 53 and messianic psalms). There is no indication they knew this coming one would be Jesus of Nazareth, who was born between 6 and 2 B.C.

Notice how Peter distinguishes the Old Testament prophets from those who *now* have announced the good news, sent by the same Holy Spirit (the Spirit in a sense being the chief "sent one," the chief apostle, the messenger of God's good news about Jesus). The word "now" is a refrain throughout this epistle as Peter tries to show how much God has now already given and done and is now

---

[62]The Greek reads literally, "the prewitnessing to the sufferings of Christ and the glorious events that would follow." See Michaels, *1 Peter,* p. 44; Elliott, *1 Peter,* p. 346.

[63]Michaels, *1 Peter,* p. 42, points out that the use of *tina ē poion* is redundant, meaning "what time or what sort of time." What he does not note is that Asiatic rhetoric is characterized by slight redundancy, or repetition with slight variation or amplification, to emphasize a point, which is what we have here. Kilpatrick, "1 Peter 1.11," pp. 91-92, not only misses the rhetorical point but also the way such language is used in apocalyptic literature where there is inquiry about times and seasons of things (cf. 1 Thess 5:1; Mk 13:32). See Achtemeier, *1 Peter,* p. 109; cf. Dan 12:6.

[64]See Best, *1 Peter,* p. 81.

[65]Ibid., pp. 80-81. Also Acts 16:7; Rom 8:9, 16; Gal 4:6; Phil 1:19.

announcing that he will yet do to encourage his suffering audience. This good news is such an exciting, tremendous, earth-shattering, late-breaking story that even the angels in heaven desire to peer down from above and watch the climax of the salvation history drama (cf. Lk 15:10, which Peter may have in mind here). Probably he implies that they are allowed to see this drama.[66] Ernest Best says:

> "Things into which angels long to look": it is not clear whether the angels succeed in seeing the salvation offered to the church, or whether their desire to look arises from a wrong curiosity or a true desire for spiritual insight. Although angels are commonly regarded as possessing supernatural knowledge of salvation, there is much in the New Testament which implies their inferiority to believers (1 Cor. 6:1ff.); Heb. 1:14; 2:16); their knowledge may be limited (1 Cor 2:8; Eph 3:10; cf. *1 En.* 16:3; Ign. *Eph.* 10:1); at 1 Peter 3:22 they are subordinated to Christ in a way that Christians are not. The desire of the angels to understand God's salvation serves to emphasize in the eyes of the letter's readers the greatness of what God has done for them. The references to the Old Testament and to angels thus fitly round off 1:3-12 in building up the wonder of God's salvation.[67]

Certainly the reference to inquiring angels intrigued the church fathers. Clement of Alexandria, for example, combined what is said here with 1 Corinthians 2:9 to come up with "which eye has not seen nor ear heard, nor have they entered into the heart of a human being, which angels desire to look into and to see what good things God has prepared for the saints and for his children that love him" (Clement of Alexandria *Quis Div.* 23).

A CLOSER LOOK

The Theologizing of Peter

One of the things that all too frequently happens when one is dealing with scholarly commentaries on one or another portion of the so-called General Epistles is that there is an implicit judgment made that they have little to teach us by way of theology. Sometimes this judgment arises because the document has already been deemed a pseudepigraphon, and scholars therefore expect that the level of creativity or even consistent and coherent thinking must be less than what we find in Paul's letters or Hebrews. In the case of 1 Peter, this is unfortunate in the extreme: it has much to teach us about early Christian eschatology, Christology, ecclesiology, anthropology and other related subjects. The theologizing found in 1 Peter needs to be evaluated on its own mer-

[66]It also implies that even angels have limited knowledge. Cf. Mk 13:32; Lk 15:10; Rom 16:25; Rom 8:19; 1 Cor 2:6-9.

[67]Best, *1 Peter*, pp. 82-83.

its, and not on the basis of some pejorative comparison, not least because 1 Peter is probably not at all a pseudepigraphon by a would-be admirer or imitator of Peter. No, here we are actually in touch with the mature thinking of the original paradigmatic disciple of Jesus, the leader of the Twelve, and it is about time we give him proper respect. We will attend to the particulars of Peter's theologizing at the appropriate points in the exegetical discussion, but here it is crucial to say that Peter has not received his just due as a theologian. It will not do to write him off as a merely moralizing pastor.

First a word about the term "theologizing," which I prefer over theology. First Peter, like much of the New Testament, is an ad hoc document. It is not written in a vacuum; indeed, it is written into specific situations that existed in the early part of the second half of the first century A.D. Specifically, it is written into situations that involve abuse, persecution, suffering, and potential martyrdom. The situation is serious, and we should see 1 Peter as a warning shot fired across the bow: the apostle serves notice to his charges that they must be ready to give "the last full measure" for their faith. No estimation of the theologizing in this letter can ignore the context of hostility and persecution and actual suffering envisioned. This is not a letter written by an armchair theologian, reflecting in the abstract about a series of topics. Instead, our author is bringing his theological arsenal to bear on specific situations in a pastoral way. Since the discourse is a word on target, there are ever so many theological topics (and their interrelationships) that are not addressed in this document, even though we might wish our author to be more forthcoming. Instead, we must be content with what he has decided to give us. This document is not an exercise in systematic theology. It is nearer the mark to say that it is an exercise in pastoral care, offered from one sufferer to the fellowship of sufferers abroad. And standing in the shadows is the towering figure of the suffering servant Jesus, whose teaching and life pattern colors our author's remarks over and over again. There is a poignancy to the theologizing in this document that is not adequately captured by a technical description of the theologizing. And one more thing: The whole is greater than the sum of the parts, greater than the sources of his substance. We have not adequately analyzed the import and character of what is said by being able to decipher where he obtained his source material. In some ways the rhetorical use he puts the material to is more important than the source of his material.

In another monograph I have dealt at some length with the Christology of 1 Peter, and here I can only review a few things that were stressed there.[68]

[68]See Ben Witherington III, *The Many Faces of the Christ: The Christologies of the New Testament and Beyond* (New York: Crossroad, 1998), esp. pp. 207-13.

Commentators have often stressed that 1 Peter is more of a theocentric than christocentric discourse, but if we ask what has caused the reconfiguration of Peter's thought world, there can be no doubt that it is what he thinks about Christ that has caused the shift. When it comes to Peter's handling of the Old Testament (see, e.g., 1 Pet 1:10-12), he operates with a christocentric or christotelic[69] hermeneutic, by no means unique in the New Testament (cf. Lk 24:25-26, 45-47): not only does the teaching of Christ echo in his words, and the figure of Christ entirely shape his theology of sacrifice and atonement; Christ also provides the ethical pattern set forth for his audience to emulate. This brings us to a further critical point. The longer I work with the New Testament, the less and less satisfactory it seems to me to divide theology and ethics from one another as if they were discrete subjects. After all, the figure and pattern of Christ binds the two together and grounds both the indicative (what Christ was and did) and the imperative (what his followers should do and be). In one sense the ethics of 1 Peter is just a playing out of what it means to be like and to follow Christ. In some sense they participate in the sufferings of Christ, and they look forward to an exaltation like Christ's as the *V* pattern (humbling self and being exalted) is repeated in the life of the disciple (cf. 1 Pet 4:13; 5:1-6).[70]

Let us consider several features of 1 Peter's Christology. Many have observed the use of the Pauline phrase "in Christ" in 1 Peter 3:16; 5:10, 14, but what has been less often commented on is the fact that this phrase is used in spite of the fact that we also have the term *Christianos* in this document (1 Pet 4:14-16). *Christianos* appears originally to have been a pejorative term applied to Christians by outsiders, but the phrase "in Christ" seems to come from Paul and is still Peter's preferred self-designation. This is telling. Discipleship happens "in Christ," not merely in the context of Christ's body of followers, but especially also in the context of one's relationship to and emulation of Christ. The term *Christianos* is not the preferred self-designation, but rather is a term spoken of in the context of Christian public witness and consequent suffering; this is all the more striking since in 1 Peter we have the phrase "Jesus Christ" (with "Christ" now almost a second name) some eight times, and even more tellingly we have just the term "Christ" as a name used an additional twelve times in this discourse. To this we may add the use of the phrase Lord Jesus Christ once in 1 Peter. Clearly our author knows that *Christos* is a title, but just as clearly he is comfortable in using it as a virtual name for Jesus. So wrapped up in the identity of Jesus is his Jewish messianic role for our author that the

---

[69]"Christotelic," a term I borrow from my friend Richard Hays, refers to how Scripture is seen as pointing to Christ or having Christ as its goal or fulfillment.

[70]I will say more on this subject in my forthcoming volumes to be titled *The Indelible Image*, a study of both the theology and the ethics of the NT.

two cannot be completely separated. It thus is no surprise that nowhere in the New Testament is there a more profound reflection on how Christ should be seen as the fulfillment of Isaiah 53 than here in 1 Peter. It is a great shame, and indeed a great oversight, that a recent volume dedicated entirely to Isaiah 53 and Christian origins treats the use of Isaiah 53 in 1 Peter as if it deserves scant mention. This is all the more strange when one of its contributors, David A. Sapp warns: "Allusions to the Hebrew text of Isaiah 53:10-11 in the above New Testament passages [Mt 20:28; Mk 10:45; 14:24; Acts 3:13; Rom 5:15, 19; Phil 2:7; first part of 1 Jn 3:5] would call into question the view that atonement theology based on Isaiah 53 arose in a late stage of New Testament teaching *represented by 1 Peter 2:24*."[71] Indeed, what would call such thinking even more into question is the fact that 1 Peter is likely written right at the end of Paul's lifetime, in the mid-60s, and formulated by Peter himself! Here is a person in direct contact with both Jesus and his original teaching. Even if his authorship was only likely rather than "very probable," as I think, it could hardly fail to be important to the discussion of "Isaiah 53 and Christian origins" that Isaiah 53 makes a large imprint on the thinking of the author of 1 Peter about Jesus. If I am right about this, the import is great: it means that what we are dealing with in 1 Peter to some degree is a reflection of the Christology of Jesus himself, how he viewed himself and his life mission and death.[72]

If we pause to reflect for a moment on the use of the *kyrios* language in 1 Peter, we discover the interesting phenomenon, also known from Paul's epistles, where this title is applied to both Christ and to God with equal ease. In some texts it is difficult to actually decipher which is meant (cf. 1 Pet 1:25; 2:3; 3:12), though twice "Lord" is used as a clear-cut form of address for Jesus, including in a variation on the primitive (Pauline?) Christian confession formula "Jesus is Lord" or "Jesus Christ is Lord" (Rom 10:9; Phil 2:11); only here it is "Christ is Lord" (see 1 Pet 3:15). The term "Christ" is used more frequently than "Lord" in this discourse, which may be a small indicator not only of the primitive character of the Christology here but also of the Jewish character of the audience, for whom Jesus being the fulfillment of early Jewish messianic expectations was of paramount importance.

The christological language, indeed the whole theological language set, is suffused with the eschatological and apocalyptic worldview of our author. It thus is no surprise that 1 Peter refers to Jesus' second coming as a "revealing" or "unveiling," with the same language being applied to the day of judgment that comes at and with and by means of the return of Christ (cf. 1 Pet 1:3-7,

[71]David A. Sapp, "The LXX, 1QIsa, and MT Versions of Isaiah 53," in Bellinger and Farmer, *Jesus and the Suffering Servant,* pp. 170-92, esp. 187.

[72]See my older study, *The Christology of Jesus* (Minneapolis: Fortress, 1990).

13 with 1 Pet 1:5; 4:13; 5:4). Christ is exalted, having entered heaven, and so now is hidden, but one day will be revealed, at which juncture believers will see him once more (1 Pet 1:8; 4:13b). Peter is even prepared to call the first coming of Christ an "appearance" (1 Pet 1:20). That appearing set the eschatological clock ticking, and our author lives in the exciting atmosphere of expectation about the return of Christ, possibly his near return, though expectation never degenerates into calculation in 1 Peter.

The evidence that Peter views Jesus as in some sense divine is by no means limited to his use of divine titles like "Lord" for Christ. In addition there is the evidence that Peter possibly speaks about the preexistence of Christ in the reference to the pretemporal choosing of Christ (1 Pet 1:20). We must remember that 1 Peter 1:20 is a discussion about a person, a person chosen in advance, not merely about a preexistent plan or purpose. Paul J. Achtemeier suggests that 1 Peter 1:11 refers to the idea of Christ being present with the Old Testament prophets and inspiring them and supports the idea by showing how common this idea was in the early postapostolic era.[13] What gives this some plausibility is that in this ad hoc document, Peter has little to say about the Holy Spirit (contrast Acts 2), though certainly he has a robust pneumatology (see 1 Pet 1:2, 12; 4:14), which includes an understanding of the sanctifying work of the Spirit in and after conversion, a Spirit of glory that is said to rest on the believer.

Much has and should be been made about the intersection of Christology and atonement thinking in 1 Peter. In 1 Peter 1:19 we hear about the precious blood of Jesus "as of a lamb" chosen before all worlds as a sacrifice for sin, a possible allusion to Is 53:7. The sprinkled and thus atoning blood of Jesus has already been mentioned in 1 Peter 1:2, with allusion to Exodus 24:3-8. To this we must add 1 Peter 2:24, where Christ is said to be sin bearer or carrier for others in his body, thus applying the scapegoat concept to Jesus. We cannot stress enough that Peter envisions the sacrifice of Christ as both substitutionary and penal in character. It is a death endured as a punishment for sins, and it is a death undertaken in our stead or place. Thus 1 Peter 2:21-22 can speak of Jesus suffering "for you" (the audience). Christ carries the consequences of those sins to the cross on behalf of others and does away with those consequences (cf. 1 Pet 2:24; 3:18; 4:1). Christ's death is once for all time and persons, and he is the representative sacrifice and simply the Representative for all sinners as a result (1 Pet 3:18-22).

---

[13] Achtemeier, "Suffering Servant and Suffering Christ," pp. 176-88, esp. 186-87. Note that the phrase "chosen according to the foreknowledge" in 1 Pet 1:2 in reference to human beings does not by any means necessarily imply the preexistence of human beings in general. Foreknowing happens pretemporally, but the clause does not tell us when the choosing happened.

While the death of Jesus is likely viewed in the light of Isaiah 53 as a crucial eschatological turning point, so also is the resurrection of Jesus, for it is by the raising of Jesus that God gave Christians both new birth and a living hope (1 Pet 1:3). It is by the resurrection and not by magical means that baptism is said to save (1 Pet 3:21). And it is the resurrection of Jesus that leads to believers placing their faith and hope in God the Father (1 Pet 1:21). J. Ramsey Michaels puts it this way: "If the cross is the basis of Christian ethics [for Peter], the resurrection is the basis of Christian experience. . . . It is quite apparent that Peter's interpretation of the death and resurrection of Jesus Christ in relation to Christian experience is neither a perfect carbon copy nor a pale shadow of Paul's interpretation of these saving events. It is a theology of Christian salvation in its own right, worthy of attention alongside of the other major witnesses of the New Testament canon to the meaning and significance of Christ's saving work."[74] In addition, there is a narrative arc to Peter's Christology that reflects the early Christian pattern found in Philippians 2:5-11, charting the career of a Christ who was preexistent, existed on earth, was exalted, and will come again to judge "the quick and the dead" (1 Pet 4:5 KJV). The possible use of creedal fragments in 1 Peter 1:20; 2:21-24; 3:18-22 point us in this direction.[75] And clearly from texts like 1 Peter 4:1 no one could claim that the Christology of Peter is docetic in the least. Christ's sufferings in the body are not only just as real as the sufferings of the audience. There is also a sense in which the audience's visceral sufferings participate in those of Christ!

There are some distinctive christological ideas in 1 Peter that show the author's creativity. Though the image of Jesus as the Shepherd of the sheep is not novel,[76] the notion of Jesus being the "overseer" and chief shepherd and guardian of the flock (1 Pet 2:25), relating him to the undershepherds and elders, is an interesting and pregnant idea and image. Equally striking is the image of the risen and exalted Jesus as the Living Stone, with disciples being a copy of that stone, or a chip off the old block. The notion of the stone that the builders rejected becoming the head of the corner provides us with an interesting combination of ideas from Isaiah 53 and from the psalms. I do not think it is accidental that Peter is portrayed as using Psalm 118:22 in Acts 4:11, just as we see it used here in 1 Peter 2 as well. This is because the summaries of speeches in Acts have been carefully crafted by Luke after interviewing the eyewitnesses and early preachers of the word, including probably Peter.

[74]Michaels, *1 Peter,* p. lxxii.

[75]See E. Randolph Richards, "The Functional Christology of First Peter," in *Perspectives on First Peter,* ed. Charles H. Talbert (Macon, Ga.: Mercer University Press, 1986), pp. 121-39, esp. 127-33.

[76]On Jesus as the Shepherd, see the discussion of 1 Pet 2:25.

The detailed discussion of the theology of 1 Peter by Ralph P. Martin can be commended as a good jumping-off point for evaluating the larger significance of this theology and its contribution to the wider realm of New Testament thought, and we will draw on his work briefly here in the rest of this excursus.[77] Martin is quite right to stress that 1 Peter has a strong theocentric flavor. From the outset God is portrayed as the Father of the Lord Jesus Christ (1 Pet 1:3) and right to the end of the discourse as the one from whom grace ultimately comes (1 Pet 5:12). The term *theos* refers to God the Father in this discourse, not to Jesus the Son. We should see this in itself as one more piece of evidence that the author and the audience share a Jewish background as well as a Christian foreground. God is depicted as the one who raised Jesus from the dead (1 Pet 1:3; 3:21), enthroned him at God's right hand and crowned him with glory (1 Pet 1:21; 3:22). Repeatedly in this discourse we hear about how God has called the audience and called them to follow Christ, who was also called by God to a vocation of suffering (1 Pet 2:20-21), and called them to reverence or "fear" God throughout and by means of every aspect of their lives (1 Pet 2:17). Jesus is indeed the Christ, the Elect One of God, and human beings only become part of the Chosen by being "in Christ" (1 Pet 1:2; 2:4, 7). The theology of election is christocentric and corporate, and nothing is said about lost individuals being destined to be "in Christ." The means of entry is described as involving both grace and a faithful response to it. Even just true belief in God is now said to come about through Christ (1 Pet 1:21; 5:14). Likewise, God is depicted as the Father who protects and looks after his children, all the while judging their works (1 Pet 1:17; 2:25), but this is done in tandem with Christ, who is also the overseer and shepherd of the flock. The christological reformulation of monotheism is in full evidence in 1 Peter, but this does not lead to the eclipse of traditional Jewish God talk about the Father.

It would be a mistake not to discuss Peter's rather robust ecclesiology, which has its distinctive elements. The audience is not merely actually resident aliens and sojourners in Asia Minor; they also have an inherent alien and alienated character just because they are Christians. Unlike in Hebrews, our author does not much reflect on the journey or pilgrimage notion as a description of the Christian life (cf. Heb 11). Yet it is fair to say that this discourse is eschatologically focused to such a degree that we would not expect much language about heaven, much less of dying and going to heaven. It is rather resisting the devil while enduring suffering, with one eye on the horizon for the future return of Christ, which our author exhorts the audience to focus on. To that

[77]Martin, "1 Peter," in Chester and Martin, *Theology of the Letters*, pp. 87-133, esp. 104-33.

end he talks about the audience being built into a holy building, indeed being the house of God and also priests within it (1 Pet 2) instead of talking about "the assembly" or assemblies *(ekklēsiai)*. Here he departs from Paul in an important way. And here we need to stress an important point. Peter is suggesting that his converts need not be looking for a home, heavenly or otherwise. They need to be getting on with being a home, a house of God, a hospitable place for all sorts of people, including especially the suffering ones. The members of the audience are, like Christ, living stones being shaped and fitted into the household of God (again a reference to the Father).

This reinforces the discourse's insistent paraenetic thrust, calling the audience to a holy life; it also gives them a sense of well-being, of having arrived, of their calling to a priesthood of all believers. Peter is equally comfortable talking about the worldwide brotherhood and using family language to describe believers. These two images, household of God and brotherhood, coinhere ideologically (families live in and make up households), thus comporting with the actual social praxis of the early church, which met in people's homes and not in churches, synagogues or other purpose-built structures. Rather, the audience is God's purpose-built dwelling place, which is constantly under construction. It is a surprise to me that Martin did not say more about the ecclesiology of 1 Peter in his detailed study. Like all other facets of Peter's thinking, the church has been galvanized and transformed by what he believes to be true of Christ—the mediator, the model, the mentor, the Shepherd, the overseer, the Living Stone, the head of the corner, the head of the household.

Though Peter lived in the shade of towering figures like Paul, and was indebted to significant leaders like James, he nevertheless cast his own distinctive theological shadow, which we have still not taken the full measure of. We must do so, for no one more profoundly reflects on the sufferings of the Christ or Christians in the New Testament than Peter, and no one is likely to be more directly indebted to the teaching and impact of the Christ himself than Peter. As such, he needs to be appreciated as the living link to the Living Stone. And that is no small contribution to early Christianity.

1 PETER 1:13-16—PROPOSITIO: YOU HAVE A HOPE, SO BE HOLY

Though some might be tempted to pronounce the benediction after 1 Peter 1:12 and go home, Peter intends to say a great deal more on a practical note, which follows from what he has previously said. All this hope and salvation has been revealed to the audience for a reason: they are called to respond. Notice the link to the paraenesis: "Therefore *[dio]* do the following. . . ." Certain key words are used here that Peter will stress, such as obedience (1 Pet 1:2, 14, 22). His advice is similar to that given to the young man in Psalm 119. Another key word is "holy" (1 Pet 1:15, 16; cf. 1 Pet 1:22) as is "fear" (1 Pet 2:17, 18; 3:2, 14). There is a reason why certain major terms and themes appear here. We have arrived at the proposition of this entire discourse, a proposition that makes clear that the discourse has fundamentally hortatory aims and that the theme of this entire discourse will be holiness of heart and life, as the quotation from Leviticus 19:2 LXX in 1 Peter 1:16 shows.

In deliberative rhetoric, unlike in forensic rhetoric, it was not required to have a narration of pertinent facts leading up to the proposition, though one could read 1 Peter 1:3-12 as containing both an exordium and a *narratio*. The function of the proposition was to make a smooth transition from what had come before, and to set up the thesis statement for what comes after and will be argued for thereafter. This aptly describes 1 Peter 1:13-16, which is connected directly with what comes before by the word "therefore" and thus draws a conclusion based on the exordium that precedes; at the same time it announces the theme of holiness while believers remain strangers in a strange land, which will be unpacked in what follows (see Cicero *Inv.* 1.22.32).

Perhaps what is most notable about Peter's proposition here is that it is so clear and succinct in comparison to the more expansive rhetoric that precedes and follows it. There is a reason for this. Quintilian says: "The proposition, whether single or multiple, must, on every occasion when it can be employed with profit, be clear and lucid; for what could be more discreditable than the portion of the speech whose sole purpose is to prevent obscurity elsewhere, should itself be obscure?" (Quintilian *Inst.* 4.5.26). He adds that brevity is important here, without superfluous words, because one is not yet explaining what he is saying, but identifying what he is going to say. It thus is not a shock that 1 Peter 1:13-16 is the least Asiatic in character in the whole discourse when it comes to the matter of redundancy, though 1 Peter 1:21-23 are in fact one continuous sentence. And yet there are still some hints of Asianism, as in the love for mixed and dramatic metaphors like "gird up the loins of the mind"!

> [1:13] *Therefore, gird up the loins of your mind, be self-controlled (sober), fully fix (your) hope upon the grace being brought to you at (by) the revelation of Jesus Christ.* [14] *As children of obedience, do not conform yourself to the desires you formerly had in your ignorance,* [15] *but like the Holy One who called you,*[78] *so also be holy in all (your) behavior;* [16] *for it is written, "Be holy, because I myself (am) holy."*

---

[78]Michaels, *1 Peter,* p. 51, is absolutely right that *kata* here is a preposition and is not equivalent to *kathōs*. The call is to imitate God's behavior.

One of the points often debated about 1 Peter is whether it actually uses participles as imperatives, as here in the outset of the proposition, where we have participial forms of the verbs for "gird up" and for "be sober."[79] In my view I do think we find this usage from time to time in this discourse, and here we have two examples of it: thus I have translated these verbs as imperatives here. I am unconvinced by the arguments of Leonhard Goppelt and Scot McKnight that these are just subordinate participles that explicate the verb "set your hope." No, getting ready for action and thinking clearly are prerequisites for being able to focus and set one's hopes on something in the future.[80] McKnight is right, however, that these verses show an extraordinary weaving of the theological and ethical together; on that particular score, he even suggests that there is no biblical passage comparable to this one.[81] As Goppelt notes, *all* the main verbs in 1 Peter 1:13—2:8 are imperatives except in the Scripture quotation. Indeed, they are aorist imperatives, indicating things that one must repeatedly do or initiate.[82] Hope is the fundamental posture of the Christian life and serves as a motivation to obey the imperatives.

The first thing Peter tells his audience to do in **1 Peter 1:13** involves a mixed metaphor: they are to gird up the loins—of their mind! The phrase "gird up your loins" refers to the practice of picking up and tucking one's full-length robe into one's belt so that one can run or do some sort of energetic activity (cf. 1 Kings 18:46; Jer 1:17; Lk 17:8; Acts 12:8; metaphorically at Lk 12:35 and Eph 6:14). It is the ancient equivalent of rolling up one's sleeves in order to get to work. There may be an allusion here to Exodus 12:11, and indeed to Jesus' use of that text in a parable found in Luke 12:35-36, where the same metaphor occurs.[83] However, Peter adds, "of your mind." Thus he likely means that they should prepare themselves for some heavy and serious thinking about what they will do in view of the suffering they are facing. He calls them to be fully self-controlled or sober.[84] Don't do anything irrational or panicky, but keep your act together, and fix your hope completely on the grace being brought to you. It is no surprise that this call to self-control is repeated in various places in the discourse (see 1 Pet 4:7; 5:8), since it is the function of the

[79]See the "Excursus" in Achtemeier, *1 Peter,* p. 117.

[80]But see McKnight, *1 Peter,* p. 85; Goppelt, *1 Peter,* pp. 107-9.

[81]McKnight, *1 Peter,* p. 88.

[82]Goppelt, *1 Peter,* p. 101.

[83]See Marshall, *1 Peter,* p. 51; Jobes, *1 Peter,* p. 111.

[84]The adverb *teleiōs* most likely goes with "self-controlled" here. See Michaels, *1 Peter,* p. 55; Marshall, *1 Peter,* p. 51, takes the exhortation to remain sober literally, seeing abstinence from drink as part of Peter's holiness message here. This is unlikely in this verse since we have just had the reference to actions of the mind. Cf. 2 Tim 4:5.

proposition to state the essential theses of the discourse. Note the present tense in the phrase "the grace being brought to you." It appears to imply they already have grace in part (or is it seen as on the way?). In favor of the idea that it is coming is that Peter adds "in the revelation of Jesus Christ" (cf. 1 Pet 1:8, where it refers to Christ's second coming). Peter likely expresses himself as he does because of the tension between the present and future aspects of salvation and because he believes that Christ *can* come at any time (cf. 1 Pet 4:7; 5:10). C. E. B. Cranfield is right to say:

> We shall be on the wrong track, if we understand this verse to mean that the grace that is being brought to us is something quite separate from the person of Jesus Christ who is going to be revealed. Grace cannot be separated from Jesus Christ. Grace in the New Testament means the redemptive action of God in Christ, whether we are thinking of it in the phase of the Incarnation or the Cross, or the Resurrection, or as here, in the final phase of the Consummation. So here what is meant is that we are to set our hope without reserve on Him, who "shall come again with glory" as our Judge and Redeemer.[85]

First Peter 1:14 provides us with the phrase "children of obedience," which is Semitic, like "sons of disobedience" (Eph 2:2). Here it means that their character is revealed by and springs from obedience. The source of their life is obedience. From the human side of things, it is what will help them persevere through suffering and is the aim of the Spirit's work in them (1 Pet 1:2). First Peter 1:14a calls these Christians not to conform themselves to their previous desires, though the form of the verb here could lead to the rendering "Don't let the world squeeze you into its mold," or "Do not allow yourself to be conformed," as at Romans 12:2 (the only other occurrence of this verb in the NT).[86]

While *epithymia* could refer to "desire" in a positive sense, in most New Testament contexts it refers to sinful cravings, as it certainly does here. We must bear in mind that it is the audience, far more than the author, who seems to have been affected by Hellenization when it comes to ethical concepts. Thus "desire" here is not seen as a "neutral" thing or a "positive" thing, or even as an "inevitable" part of the warring of body versus soul in a Greek dualistic sense. Rather, it is seen in the ethical sense as a root cause related to sin, as we find in the LXX and in other early Jewish literature. At this juncture we may compare James 1:14, where it has exactly this same negative sense.

The word *agnoia* (ignorance), coupled with the phrase "your futile behavior inherited from your fathers" (1 Pet 1:18) has suggested to many commentators that

[85]Cranfield, *First Peter,* p. 33.
[86]See Elliott, *1 Peter,* p. 357.

Peter's audience, or the vast majority of it, is Gentile. They argue that those who have converted from Judaism did not inherit such ways or ignorance from their fathers. Selwyn is representative of this view: "The picture given is of a society where men are without knowledge of God, . . . without objective moral standards . . . and without any plan or purpose which they expect to be able to fulfill. . . . Out of a life so characterized Christians have now been called."[87]

The problem with this view is that Peter is addressing Christians in highly Hellenized settings, in the various provinces of what we now call Turkey. Diaspora Jews, as we have pointed out in the introduction, would often be viewed as ignorant and engaging in futile pagan behavior by their more conservative counterparts in Judea or Galilee, especially if they had intentionally tried to fit into their pagan environment. In such an environment it was difficult to maintain not only ritual purity but also moral holiness: there were a vast array of temptations, many of them subtle. It is thus perfectly possible that Peter would speak of an audience that is largely made up of Hellenized Jews that he has evangelized and some Gentiles, perhaps God-fearers, in this way (but cf. Acts 17:30; Eph 4:18; 1 Thess 4:5 on the ignorance of pagans in regard to the true God). Yet the ignorance that Peter is referring to is linked to sin and evil desires, *not* to a general knowledge of God.[88] Sinful desires lead to a blinding of one's mind about what is right. Notice how our author calls all non-Christians ignorant at 1 Peter 2:15.[89]

In **1 Peter 1:15-16** Christians are called to be like God's Old Testament people, who were called to be holy in all their behavior because God himself (*egō* in emphatic position) is holy (cf. Ex 3:5; 15:11; Lev 20:26; Hos 11:9). Indeed, they are called to be like God himself. Here Peter quotes Leviticus 19:2 (cf. Lev 11:44, 45; 20:7). Notice that part of Peter's rhetorical strategy is to use Old Testament quotes in this discourse "to ratify its exhortations (see 1:18, 24; 2:3, 4-10, 22-25; 3:10-12, 14, 15; 4:8, 18; 5:5, 7, 8)."[90] Now this strategy is singularly inept and not apt if the audience is not Jewish, perhaps with some God-fearers. The audience (1) must respect the authority of the Old Testament; (2) must be familiar with at least some portions of it to catch the drift of the quotes and allusions, which are often just partial, and in some cases assume the context from which they have been taken; (3) and it would help if they also knew something about Jewish hermeneutics in regard to things

[87]Selwyn, *First Peter,* pp. 41-42.
[88]See the lengthy discussion in pp. 23-25 above.
[89]See Senior, *1 Peter,* p. 41.
[90]Ibid., p. 41.

like midrash pesher and the use of catchword connections in the use of the "stone" material.[91] In short, a purely or mostly Gentile audience converted from paganism does not fit the strategy of persuasion and the sort of proofs offered by our author.[92]

What is this holiness? In this context it obviously involves one's conduct, but more is entailed. Holiness is obviously not optional for the Christian, nor merely something that is added as an extra after their conversion. It is the essence of Christian living, involving both what the Spirit is doing in the believer (sanctifying, cleansing, 1 Pet 1:2), and what they are doing by the power of the Spirit in all their ways and behavior. It is thus a comprehensive term for good Christian living and conduct. Notice that the term *anastrophē* occurs six times in 1 Peter and twice more in 2 Peter, but only five times in the rest of the New Testament. Here Peter refers to "all conduct" being conformed to God's standards. Lest one think that God would demand less under the grace of Christ than he did under the law of Moses, Peter disabuses us of such thoughts; he definitely affirms that God's character has not changed from the time of the old covenant to the time of the new, nor has God's ethical standards for his people. Indeed, as we shall see, Christians in some ways are called to an even higher standard of rectitude than Israel was. In this intensification, Peter is simply following Jesus' lead (see Mt 5—7).[93] Notice as well that the use of Leviticus here in a text directed toward priests and their behavior prepares us for the assertion that the audience is to be part of a new royal priesthood of the new covenant. There is a further consideration as well: If a holy God is going to dwell in the midst of his people, they also need to be holy to come into his presence (e.g., cf. Is 6; 1 Jn 1:6-7).[94]

Christian ethics can be summed up in the notion that we are to become what God already is: holy, loving, and so forth. This certainly is impossible without God's grace enabling believers to approximate the character and deeds of God. I. Howard Marshall reminds us that the word "conduct" here and elsewhere in this discourse refers to public conduct.[95] Notice the reference to "all" conduct being conformed to God. Peter is not interested in constructing an isolationist sect:

---

[91]On the use of the OT in 1 Peter, see Bauckham, "James, 1 and 2 Peter, Jude," pp. 309-13.

[92]Yet I think it is right to assume that, even with mostly Gentile audiences, such as Paul's congregations, leaders had begun to initiate the believers into the rudiments of the OT Scriptures. But if one is dealing with pagans who have recently converted to Christianity, one could not assume any knowledge of the OT. The level of sophistication of knowledge and interpretation expected of Peter's audience most likely points to a largely Jewish audience that has been grounded in the OT since they were young.

[93]See the discussion in Goppelt, *1 Peter*, pp. 110-11.

[94]See Davids, *First Peter*, p. 69.

[95]Marshall, *1 Peter*, p. 53.

he is interested in their public witness for the gospel's sake. In the debate between whether Peter is constructing an ethic that seeks to make Christians stand out from the pagan crowd or blend in, the answer is that this ethic is mostly of the former nature; yet at the same time Peter wants them, for the sake of the witness, to do what they can to "seek the welfare of the city" (Jer 29:7 NRSV) and be good citizens and neighbors. If indeed Peter's audience is mostly Jews, then the use of Leviticus here will come as no surprise. What is a surprise is that Peter no longer thinks that the rest of Leviticus is also incumbent on the audience, because there is now a new covenant, which does not mean a mere renewal of the old one.[96] Only some of the moral stipulations of the old covenant are carried over into the new, as Peter himself learned through a vision, as Acts 10 tells the tale.[97]

The root meaning of holy *hagios* is to be separated out for something or someone, so be set apart. The term "saints" (holy ones) comes from this root, indicating that we are set apart by God and perhaps also set apart by our behavior from sin. Ernest Best says: "The idea of 'separation,' in so far as it continues to flavour the word, is separation to God rather than separation from the world: naturally separation to God means separation from sin because God and sin have no common meeting point."[98] The New Testament writers, however, picked up the ethical rather than ritual cast of "be holy" primarily from the Old Testament prophets, though Peter quotes Leviticus and the Holiness Code here, Cranfield is right to caution:

> The application of "holy" to Israel did not mean a blurring of the contrast between God and Israel, but rather that He had laid hold upon them to be His special people, set apart for His service. The contrast was still there; in fact, the holiness of the Holy One of Israel constituted a continual threat to their very existence, for it implied His judgment of their sins. The holiness of Israel derived from God's choice, but it involved the obligation on their part to be and to do what was in accordance with the character of the Lord their God.[99]

This also applies to the church. The proper way, indeed the only correct way, to relate to a holy God is by being holy like God: in this world, believers are to reflect his character, his will, his glory. Parenthetically, we may notice that Peter

[96]The lack of reference to ritual law is striking in 1 Peter and James compared to many other early Jewish discussions. I take this to reflect what Luke says Peter learned through the Cornelius episode (Acts 10-11) and perhaps also through his tête-à-tête with Paul (Gal 2). In addition, if Mark is reflecting Peter's conclusions at Mk 7:19, we have further proof of his view about such matters.

[97]See Jobes, *1 Peter,* pp. 114-15.

[98]Best, *1 Peter,* p. 86.

[99]Cranfield, *First Peter,* p. 36.

is certainly not talking about some postconversion experience. He sees holiness as a lifetime process and endeavor, not a spiritual booster shot. He would not have recognized or agreed with the idea of two or three stages in a Christian life: saved, sanctified or saved, sanctified and glorified. The saving begins the sanctifying; indeed, sanctifying may in one sense be said to precede salvation, when salvation is depicted as a future goal (cf. 1 Pet 1:7).

1 Peter 1:17—2:10—Argument 1: Live as Redeemed Resident Aliens

> If the price of our life is the blood of the Lord, see to it that it is not an ephemeral earthly field which has been purchased but rather the eternal salvation of the whole world. (Maximus of Turin [*Sermons* 59.2])

This first argument is remarkable in several respects. At the end of the argument in 1 Peter 2:10, we are informed that "this is the word announced as good news unto you." In other words, we are being told that in this first argument Peter is reviewing for the audience some of the initial proclamation of the good news to them. It involved both theology and ethics, with the latter grounded in the former. The saving work of Christ both for and in the believer is the ground of Christian ethics.

It was good rhetorical practice to lead from strength, or to put it another way, make sure that one's first argument has the best chance of receiving assent by the audience before going on to more difficult matters. This argument says nothing about the difficult matter of suffering. We continue to have the longer convoluted sentences characteristic of Asiatic rhetoric, with the ready use of dramatic metaphors. At the end of this argument's second segment, Peter clinches the argument with a quote from Scripture, using an inartificial and indisputable authority to do so just as he rounds off the proposition in the same fashion (see Quintilian *Inst.* 5.11.36-37; anon. *Rhet. Her.* 2.29.46). It is surely no accident that Peter chooses to quote from Isaiah 40:6-8 at this juncture: the word of comfort to those in exile, that God will lead them back to the Promised Land. The larger context of these words about the Word would not be lost on a largely Jewish Diaspora audience.[100]

Lauri Thurén is right that Peter is dealing with general Christian belief and behavior here, before he addresses the social crisis the audience is currently facing in the second argument, which begins at 1 Peter 2:11.[101] And yet in the be-

[100]Notice as well that the use of the same Scripture in Jas 1:11-12 is a bit less verbatim and more creative. See Campbell, *Honor, Shame,* p. 79.

[101]Thurén, *Rhetorical Strategy,* p. 135.

ginning verses, Peter reminds the audience of their social status, and also their standing with God, lest they think that their tendency to assimilate to the larger society makes no difference in their relationship to a God who is an impartial Judge (meaning that he impartially judges even Christians). The "author's basic goal is to deepen the addressees' Christian identity so that its central facts would not remain on the cognitive level but also reach the volitional level."[102] This remarks suits this first argument well, but he must deal with rhetorical necessity, the real bone of contention in the second argument; the later arguments are built on this first one and presuppose it. This first argument merely lays the groundwork and establishes the common ground between author and audience in preparation for what follows.

The proposition preceding this first argument established that God is holy, and God expects his people to be holy as well. But how exactly does this affect belief and behavior? In his rhetorical analysis of 1 Peter 1:17, Campbell calls it a *ratio* for the proposition. It would be better to see this as introducing the first argument on behalf of the thesis that believers need to be holy, even if they are strangers in a strange land. Here the first reason is given: God, not society, is their ultimate Judge and indeed also the one who ransomed them. Therefore it is God, not society, whose approval they should seek and whose wrath they should fear.

Notice the Asiatic use of invented multisyllabic word here, ***aprosōpolēmptōs,*** which literally means "not receiving the face of" = "impartial."[103] Likewise, the redundancy or repetition for emphasis in the phrase "perishable things" = "silver or gold" is so typical of Asiatic rhetoric. Furthermore, reading 1 Peter 1:18-21 out loud makes it clear that Peter is also striving here to use the device of end rhyme, "when in the same period two or more words appear in the same case, and with like terminations" (anon. *Rhet. Her.* 4.20.28). Thus we have a whole series of words ending with *-iō, -ou, -ous, -on,* and *-ta.* The author is striving for a certain elevated and even eloquent and poetic style here that is totally lost in translation. For example, consider that in 1 Peter 1:19 the phrase ***hōs amnou amōmou kai aspi lou Christou*** serves to build up the simile or analogy between Christ and a lamb. Some have seen in the asyndetic 1 Peter 1:20 a quotation from a hymn, which is not impossible, but in any case the participial construction coupled with asyndeton reveals the ornamental Asiatic style of the phrasing.[104]

The audience is not called "resident aliens" in relationship to God. To the

---

[102]Ibid., p. 139.

[103]See the discussion in Campbell, *Honor, Shame,* p. 68.

[104]See the discussion in ibid., pp. 74-75.

contrary, they are God's ransomed children. But in relationship to society, they continue to have this resident alien status. Peter is suggesting that the controlling paradigm for their life and conduct should be their relationship with God, not their relationship with society. In other words, mere assimilation is the last thing on his mind, yet since Peter is promoting an evangelistic faith, he does want the audience to be good neighbors in their cities and towns in ways that are compatible with their faith.

Peter draws on the standard deliberative rhetorical topic, love in 1 Peter 1:22-25 (cf. Aristotle *Rhet.* 1.4.1359a—1.8.1366.7; Cicero *Top.* 21.79—23.90). As it turns out, loving is the essence of holy behavior. In this case the exhortation is to love "one another" and thereby to strengthen the bonds of Christian community. Campbell identifies 1 Peter 2:1-10 as the *conplexio*, or conclusion and summation, of the first argument, and in this he is right. Peter repeats the key ideas of election (1 Pet 2:4, 6, 9) and what is precious or valuable (1 Pet 2:4, 6) as he busily seeks to redefine the honor and holiness code of his audience.[105] The first verse of this argument's final section is noted for its use of the rhetorical device called "polysyndeton," the use of an excessive number of conjunctions to pile up and intensify the effect of a phrase: "Rid yourself of all malice *and* all guile, *and* hypocrisy *and* envy *and* all slander" (1 Pet 2:1). This is another typical example of the verbosity and ornate nature of Asiatic rhetoric. In 1 Peter 2:1-3 we find, and Campbell has rightly noted, an enthymeme as follows:

> Major premise: Newborn infants long for milk.
> Minor premise: You are like newborn infants.
> Conclusion: Long for pure spiritual milk so that by it you may grow into salvation, putting off various vices like a garment.

This enthymeme is followed by a supporting maxim (1 Pet 2:3), a one-liner from Psalm 33:8 LXX (34:8 ET).[106] Note the use again of a mixed metaphor: infants cannot very well put garments on and off, or vices like garments, but this way of using colorful metaphorical language even to the point of oxymoron is typical of Asiatic rhetoric.

Peter has now established a pattern of punctuating or reinforcing his argument at regular junctures with Scripture quotes or allusions, a tactic especially apt to persuade and sway Jewish Christians in the audience. By one estimate, Peter makes reference to the Old Testament some 46 times in this discourse or about once every other verse! William L. Schutter demonstrates that one could

---

[105]Ibid., pp. 80-81.
[106]See ibid., pp. 82-83.

expand the list exponentially if one took account of all the echoes of Scripture as well.[107] Hence such use surely suggests that the author assumes a lot about the audience's knowledge of the LXX, and in addition that the author is not just using the Old Testament as a proof text or a way of validating an independent argument. His own argument and its vocabulary (in this case in 1 Pet 2:4-5) arise out of the biblical text quoted in 1 Peter 2:6-10. The quoting of the Scripture shows the source of the ideas. It is not brought in as merely an afterthought to clinch the argument.[108]

This brings us to the use of the extended or stone metaphor, applied both to Jesus and to believers. One can argue that the metaphor is used for the purpose of typology: Christ is the type; believers become "living stones" of the type and in imitation of the type.[109] But we actually have not just one metaphor but two, the stone and the house; the latter refers to the house of God, which is being composed of living stones and has Christ himself as its most important stone.

Some of this argument reflects a knowledge of Jesus' own use of some of this sort of language, and also of common early apostolic thinking about Christ and the church; at the same time it is an especially apt metaphor for someone whom Jesus himself nicknamed "Rocky" to develop! This in part is autobiography as theology. And the imagery is poignant and bound to stir up pathos in the audience as well. They are *paroikoi* (1 Pet 2:11), those who live outside the house of Hellenistic culture. Now they are told that they have a home right here on earth: their house is the community of Christ and his followers. This is the house they are a part of here and now, and not only that: since it is God's house, God is bequeathing them a special role in it as a royal priesthood.

Ezekiel 1 tells about a man of priestly lineage who is in exile and thus unable to fulfill his responsibilities as a priest, yet is granted a heavenly vision that enables him to be a prophet of God's people while being a stranger in a strange land; such a scene can help us begin to catch the drift and power of Peter's argument. Jews in the Diaspora had no hope of being priests in any full sense, since they lived nowhere near the cultic place, the temple in Jerusalem. Now they are being told that as Christians, and in the "house of God" that exists as a living community where they are, they can fulfill this role even in Anatolia. This argument can only be called masterful in several respects, in both form and substance, and it shows the rhetorical skill of our author. The honor and status denied Peter and the audience by the larger culture they find within their own

[107]Schutter, *Hermeneutic and Composition in 1 Peter*, pp. 35-37.
[108]See Campbell, *Honor, Shame*, pp. 84-85.
[109]See the discussion in ibid., pp. 87-92.

"house," the Christian community.[110] The honor denied them by their absence from Jerusalem they also find "in house" as they embrace their Christian faith and holiness code of conduct.

[1:17]And if (as you do) you call upon the one who impartially judges according to each one's work (deeds), live in fear during the time you are a resident alien, [18]knowing that you were ransomed from your useless/futile conduct of the forebears not by perishable silver or gold, [19]but by the precious blood as of a lamb without blemish or spot, [the blood] of Christ, [20]who on one hand was foreknown before the foundation of the world, but on the other revealed in this age for your sake. [21]Through him you have confidence (believe) in God, who raised him [Christ] from the dead and gave him glory so that your faith and hope might be in God.

[22]Having purified yourselves in the obedience of the truth (by obeying the truth) unto sincere brotherly love, love one another out of a pure heart, [23]having been born again, not from perishable seed but imperishable, through the living and abiding word of God—[24]for "all flesh is as grass, and all its glory as a (wild) flower of the grass. The grass withers and the flower falls off, [25]but the word of the Lord remains forever." But this is the word announced as good news unto you.

[2:1]Put off, then, every form of wickedness—all deceit and hypocrisy and envy and all evil speaking, [2]as newborn infants (do), long for the world's unadulterated milk so that in it (in him?) you may grow unto salvation, [3]if you have tasted (as you have) that the Lord is good. [4]Coming to him, the Living Stone, having been rejected by humanity but chosen and valuable to God, [5]you also as living stones were built as a spiritual house to be a holy priesthood, to offer spiritual sacrifices acceptable to God through Jesus Christ. [6]So it says in the Scripture, "Behold I lay a stone in Zion, a precious, elect (chosen) cornerstone, and the one who believes (trusts) in him will not be put to shame." [7]To you who believe, then, belongs honor, but to unbelievers a stone that the builders rejected; this one has become the head of the corner, [8]and a stone that causes stumbling and a rock (that is) a stumbling block. Those who stumble disobeying the word were also appointed unto that end. [9]But you (are) a chosen race, a royal priesthood [or, "a royal house, a body of priests"], a holy nation, a people in (his) possession, in order that you might proclaim the redemptive acts of the one who called you from darkness into his marvelous light: [10]those (of God) who at one time were not a people, but now are a people of God; who were not shown mercy, but now have received mercy.

The thoughts about holiness in 1 Peter 1:16 naturally lead to **1 Peter 1:17** and the mention of God as the Judge of each person's life, character and work (singular). God is not just the Judge of nonbelievers; he also judges the work and lives of believers. Christians have the privilege of calling upon God as "Fa-

[110]See ibid., pp. 93-94.

ther" but must also remember that God is an impartial Judge of believer's works (cf. Rom 2:6, 16; 2 Cor 5:10).[111] This seems to mean that God will not give them any special treatment on judgment day, any special lenience in regard to believer's *deeds.*[112] Indeed, if we who know and believe do not do right, we may be held more accountable than nonbelievers. This thought should be enough both to impel believers to holy living, and also to arouse a proper sort of fear or reverence of God. Respect and reverence for God means a constant awareness that God is God and we are but his creatures: we do not relate to God as equals but as children. We do not control our fate: God does. It has been said that reverence is the religious virtue par excellence.[113] It is or involves our attitude of worship toward God, recognizing him as both holy and just, both loving and merciful. This attitude is especially appropriate for those who are sojourning in a foreign land (earth) and have no one else they can totally trust or rely on. But the word *chronos* here suggests that when Jesus returns, they will be resident aliens and sojourners no more, even in relationship to society.[114] It is intriguing that we have a nearly identical phrase in 3 Maccabees 7:19, referring to the time when Ptolemy IV uprooted Alexandrian Jews and moved them to Ptolemais. Their stay there is called *ton tēs paroikias autōn chronon*, "the time of their being resident aliens." This language was especially apt when applied to transplanted Jews.

Read together, **1 Peter 1:18-19** reveals what Christians know or ought to know about their redemption. The key term we must examine first is the verb *elytrōthēte,* which here means either "redeem" or "ransom." The idea of ransoming implies a form of redeeming, but the converse is not necessarily true.[115] So we must examine how to translate this term. In favor of the translation "ransom" is that

- the "not . . . but" structure we have here contrasts two means by which one can be ransomed.
- money, mentioned here, is so often used to ransom various sort of captives or slaves.

[111]As Michaels, *1 Peter,* p. 61, points out, both *1 Clem.* 1.3 and *Barn.* 4.12 may well reflect a knowledge of this discussion, which again means that this discourse cannot be dated as late as the 90s. Peter believes that judgment does indeed begin with the household of God, and that divine election and calling do not in any way exempt one from such judgment. Indeed, the house of God is more accountable, having been given more by God.

[112]On God's impartiality as Judge, see Acts 10:34; Rom 2:11; Eph 6:9; Col 3:25. See Marshall, *1 Peter,* p. 54.

[113]Selwyn, *First Peter,* p. 143.

[114]See Michaels, *1 Peter,* pp. 62-63.

[115]In 1 Pet 1:18 the verb is passive, but it still has its same strong "ransom" sense as in the inscriptions. See *NewDocs* 3:72.

- “ransom” must be the meaning of the cognate noun in Mark 10:45, and it is quite possible and likely that Mark depended on Peter for his Gospel, which would thus suggest a similar translation here (cf. Tit 2:14).
- the use of the term in pagan and Gentile contexts would normally conjure up the idea of being bought out of slavery or buying oneself out of slavery (cf. Rom 6:14-23; 1 Cor 7:21-24; Gal 5:1).

If we ask to whom this ransom was paid, the text does not say; however, it surely cannot be Satan since neither Christ nor God owed Satan anything. Later patristic theology went in the wrong direction here. Most assuredly it is the price paid to God himself and the Judge who will indeed condemn us and cast us out if our sin is not dealt with, covered, paid for. A just God requires a just payment for sin—no more, but definitely no less. This implies that forgiveness for God is very costly indeed: nothing but Christ’s death was a sufficient price for ransoming believers from sure destruction and slavery to sin. God’s love thus is a holy love: holy in that sin must be dealt with and paid for before forgiveness can be offered or a declaration of no condemnation pronounced; loving in that Christ paid that price with his blood in our stead. Not all the money in the world could have paid for our multitude of sins and bought us salvation. Such things, though valuable, are perishable and cannot purchase something of eternal worth.

Peter’s emphasis is on being ransomed from previous useless (or futile) and sinful behavior. There is probably a play on words here: the word *timiō* refers to the price, in this case the price of manumission paid in the temple to the deity; in turn the deity then pays the slave owner back, less a commission. But it is not a *timiō* of silver or gold that ransomed the believer, but rather the *timiō*, the “precious” or “valuable,” blood of Jesus that did the ransoming and paid the price.[116] Notice as well the aural and rhetorical dimension to *amnou amōmou kai aspilou,* with both assonance and alliteration (cf. 1 Pet 1:4 and many other examples of alliteration such as 1 Pet 2:12, 15, 18-20, 21; 3:17; 4:4).[117] In this verse we may hear an echo of Isaiah 53:7 in preparation for the fuller christological statement in 1 Pet 2:22-25, where Christ is more extensively portrayed as the Suffering Servant of Isaiah; but already here Peter begins to paint that portrait.[118] Jesus is seen as the flawless and faultless lamb.[119]

In this reference to the futile or useless behavior passed down from the forefathers, many have seen a clear reference to the audience being Gentiles. This

---

[116]See Jobes, *1 Peter,* pp. 116-17.
[117]Achtemeier, *1 Peter,* p. 129.
[118]See Elliott, *1 Peter,* p. 374.
[119]See Michaels, *1 Peter,* p. 375.

depends on whether Peter agreed with some of the sentiments of Paul about how the law was not able to save even Jews, and how all those outside of Christ are lost and in a futile condition until they are ransomed by Christ. Notice for example Galatians 4:5, where Paul says that Christ came to redeem those under the law out from under the law, and he goes on to speak of their condition as bondage, even slavery. The language here comports with such ideas, and so the audience need not be Gentiles.[120] The Peter who in Acts 15:10 calls the law a yoke that neither current Jews nor their ancestors could bear is certainly a person who could have seen the traditions of the elders and ancestral customs as exercises in futility when it comes to the all-important matter of being saved.[121] Karen H. Jobes puts the matter well: "He argues that all knowledge without Christ is profitless and therefore is ignorance. One need only think further of Paul's testimony in Philippians 3:4-9 to hear a Jew describe his heritage passed down to him as 'garbage' (useless) compared with 'the surpassing worth of knowing Christ Jesus my Lord.' . . . Since the ignorance in 1 Pet. 1:14 is specifically in the context of the redemption achieved by Christ and because the adjective 'useless' in verse 18 generally describes all cultural systems that are not based on the reality of Christ, these verses do not decisively indicate that only Gentiles are in Peter's view."[122] Indeed not. And it should be stressed that the "futility" lies not in the law itself, which was seen as good by Peter equally with Paul; the "futility" lies in the behavior of those trying and failing to be able to keep it due to their bondage in sin and lack of the Holy Spirit.

We need to recognize that Christianity began in a culture where older was considered better, especially when it came to religion, and honoring the religious traditions of the ancestors was considered the height of piety. We get a feel for this from the saying of Fronto: "That which is preferable is commonly called *antiquius*" (Fronto *Ep.* 162.9). In this culture it was not assumed that the new was true or the latest was the greatest, especially when it came to religion; thus most ancients looked askance at the idea of conversion to a new religion, and many were even skeptical about the concept of "new birth" or "conversion." In this light many would consider Peter's discourse as controversial, subversive, even seditious.[123]

In fact, the language of ransoming here could be especially poignant for Diaspora Jews who were taken captive and transported as workers to these very

[120]But see the discussion in van Unnik, "Critique of Paganism in 1 Peter 1.18," pp. 129-42.
[121]Contrast the discussion in Michaels who thinks Gentiles are in view here, *1 Peter,* p. 64.
[122]Jobes, *1 Peter,* p. 119.
[123]Elliott, *1 Peter,* pp. 370-71.

regions some 150 years or more before this document was written. They knew what it was to be slaves, as well as to be resident aliens, and some of them, or at least their ancestors, knew what it was to be bought or ransomed out of slavery by someone.[124] To this we may add: Donald P. Senior may be right in holding that Peter is drawing on "biblical tradition that portrayed God as one who ransomed and liberated Israel from slavery and sin."[125] If so, no group of people would resonate more with these images than Jews, in this case Jewish Christians who are experiencing their own exile and are now being told that Christ has ransomed them from that bondage right where they are. Finally, Goppelt rightly points out that our author is reflecting on the general human condition, not on paganism in particular. All those outside Christ are subject to the futility of human striving, which never quite connects with God by human efforts, even with the aid of good religious traditions.[126]

Christ also did not die so that believers might sin all the more, now having a sure means of forgiveness. As Paul says in Romans 6:1-2, "Shall we go on sinning, so grace may increase? God forbid!" Rather, Christ spilled his precious blood so that believers might be purified and holy. Christ's death, if we are to receive its benefits, implies our death to our previous sinful ways.

The reference to Christ's blood as like that of a pure and spotless lamb[127] conjures up the idea of a sacrificial lamb. In Old Testament times the Passover lamb was apparently not seen as an animal that if sacrificed made atonement (see Ex 12:5). However, as Best says, it had begun to have this significance in Jesus' day in contemporary Judaism (cf. Jn 1:29, 36; 1 Cor 5:7).[128] Since Isaiah 53:7 seems to be in the background here, the atoning significance is surely implied. A lamb, if it was to be offered, had to be perfect (Ex 12:5; 29:1). Blood served as a means of redemption or as a price (see Eph 1:7; Heb 9:12, 22; Rev 1:5; 5:9; *1 Clem.* 12.7).

In **1 Peter 1:20** the concept of the preexistence of Christ is implied not by the term "foreknown" (God foreknows believers as well, but it does not make them preexistent) but in the phrase "but revealed . . . ," implying that he existed before his incarnation (which is surely referred to here). The question is, Does "foreknown" refer to Christ as a person or to his death and ransoming activity? In Peter's speech in Acts 2:23, it refers to God's foreknowledge of Christ's being

---

[124]See Perkins, *First Peter*, p. 38; Senior, *1 Peter*, p. 44.

[125]Senior, *1 Peter*, p. 45.

[126]Goppelt, *1 Peter*, p. 117.

[127]On Christ's sinlessness, see 2 Cor 5:21; Heb 4:15; 7:26; 1 Pet 2:22; 1 Jn 3:5; Goppelt, *1 Peter*, p. 116.

[128]Best, *1 Peter*, p. 90.

handed over (to death). Here, however, the scope seems wider, referring to Christ himself and God's plan for him to come as Redeemer, a plan made even before the world was formed. "Foreknown" parallels "revealed" and refers to an activity of God the Father, who does both. Notice the *men . . . de* construction here. The point is not simply the idea that God knew Christ or even that he knew Christ before creation, but that God knew Christ as Redeemer and planned on that shedding of blood even before creation. This means that God with certainty knew beforehand that humans would fall, though God did not make Adam fall. Nonetheless, God had already worked out plan B in advance because God loved his creatures so much.[129] All of this foreknowing and revealing was done "for your sake," for those who believe in Jesus and receive the benefit. It is wrong, however, to suggest that the foreknowing is not of the Son personally, but only of some events involving him or some role he would assume. Being "revealed" is no more a role than being "foreknown."[130]

First Peter 1:21 tells us how gracious God really is: he would do all this just for believers. This could not help but bolster the courage and strength of those in Peter's audience facing persecution. Through Christ's work they have come to have confidence in God and what he can do for them. The God who raised Jesus from the dead and gave him glory[131] can and will also do great things and similar things for believers (cf. 1 Pet 1:7b). The general New Testament witness is that it was God who raised Jesus: Jesus did not do it on his own strength or power but was acted upon by his Father (cf. Acts 3:15). All through this section are numerous parallels to Peter's speeches in Acts. Against those who might be

---

[129]For those who think God's foreknowledge is a kind of predetermination, this text should give one pause. If the preexistent Christ is the subject of God's foreknowledge, do we really want to argue that God (the Father) predetermined the destiny of God (the Son)? If so, this certainly means that God himself, in at least one of the divine persons, is not free or the master of his own fate. There is the further problem that foreknowledge in Rom 9—11 involves foreknowledge of Israel's sin and even apostasy. Do we really want to argue that because God foreknew this, he predetermined Israel to sin and indeed sin so severely that some committed apostasy when they had been part of God's chosen people? This seems to go counter to everything we know about how a holy, loving and sovereign God would act.

[130]Against Elliott, *1 Peter*, p. 377, and others who seek to minimize the witness for the personal preexistence of Christ or God's personal relationship with Christ before creation.

[131]First Pet 1:21 provides an interesting example of saying that God the Father gave glory to someone other than himself—in this case to Jesus, whom he raised from the dead and vindicated, honored, glorified. The close connection of the resurrection with the glorification reminds us that we are talking about the Son of God in his human nature, not in his divine nature, which in any case did not need to be glorified since it was inherently glorious. This is one more piece of evidence that God is not merely one who should receive glory and honor; he is also one who bestows it, even on humans who are said to be honored in this same context.

tempted to see Christianity as polytheistic or at least tritheistic, Peter stresses that what happened to Christ, happened so that believers can put their confidence in God and believe and hope in God, who is one (1 Pet 1:21).

First Peter 1:22 refers to the fact that believers can purify themselves by or in their obedience to the truth.[132] This sanctifying process, however, is not an end in itself: it is so that believers will be enabled to love one another earnestly and wholeheartedly, in sincere brotherly love (*philadelphia*; cf. Rom 12:10; 1 Thess 4:9; Heb 13:1; 2 Pet 1:7)[133] coming from a pure heart.[134] Here again we have an echo of Jesus' teaching, in this case John 13:35. It is notable that only 1 Peter has the characterization of believers as *adelphotēs* (1 Pet 2:17; 5:9), and only in 1 Peter do we have the adjective "brotherly" applied to believers.[135] Part of Peter's rhetorical and social strategy is to convince his audience that they have a home in God's house, they have a family in their spiritual family, they are a royal priesthood; hence, whatever social alienation they experience from the world's rejection or slander should not concern them. They are not orphans in the world. They have a place, and they are a chosen people, a spiritual family, with a special mission to be a light to the world.

Notice the Asiatic redundancy once more: they are to love one another deeply from the heart! If it is from the heart, it is bound to be deeply. At this juncture Pheme Perkins rightly observes that "the command which governs their [Christians'] relations does not echo the reverent obedience of the patriarchal household but the egalitarian love between brothers."[136] We must keep this steadily in view when we examine the household codes in the next argument in this discourse. Rather different from Perkin's conclusion is that of Elliott, who argues: "Here more than in any other writing of the New Testament, the themes of God's fatherhood, the rebirth of the believers, their identity as children of God, and the ethic of the household, its proper order, and behavior contributing to its cohesion and reputation, are unified in one concerted message concerning the dignity and honor of the household of God."[137] What is missing from this statement is

---

[132]The word "purified" is in the perfect tense here, which Goppelt, *1 Peter,* pp. 125-26, suggests means "permanently." I suggest that it simply means a past action that has enduring effects and validity into the present. Nothing here suggests that this is a reference to baptism. The purification comes from the internalization of God's word.

[133]And as Achtemeier, *1 Peter,* p. 137, says, "brother" here means fellow Christian, not fellow human being. The focus is on the behavior toward and within the community in these exhortations.

[134]See McKnight, *1 Peter,* p. 90.

[135]See Goppelt, *1 Peter,* p. 124.

[136]Perkins, *First Peter,* p. 39.

[137]Elliott, *1 Peter,* p. 385.

something Elliott elsewhere admits: The basis of Christian community and brother/sisterhood is conversion, not patriarchy nor ethnicity. What Elliott misses altogether is that the fatherhood of God as here enunciated has nothing to do with propping up patriarchy in the physical family's household or in the empire. It has to do with the intimate relationship of God with Christ in the first place, and with those who are in Christ in the second place.[138] It is not the father in the household, even where the church meets, who is said to be the "father" of the Christian family that meets there. As Jesus was to put it, his leaders were not to accept the title "father" for they had one Father, God (Mt 23:9).

Here we see the connection between love and holiness: love, if it is to be real and sincere and wholehearted, must be pure and coming from a pure heart. Conversion leads to holiness, which produces love in the believer, though the converse is also true—loving sanctifies the lover.[139] Thus, Wesley stressed that holiness was a loving of God with whole heart and neighbor as self. The word "unhypocritical" *(anypokritos),* or as we would say "pure and genuine," is also elsewhere connected to loving in the New Testament (Rom 12:9; 2 Cor 6:6).

In **1 Peter 1:23** the word of God is a living and abiding thing (cf. Ps 33:6, 9; Is 55:10-11), living because it produces life in the believer, and abiding because it produces eternal life and is eternally true and relevant. We do not, however, have the idea here of the word planted in the believer. Rather, the word is the means through which the seed of new birth and eternal life or salvation is planted in believers, and this is something imperishable planted in one's perishable nature (cf. 2 Cor 4-5). Peter thus states here what we also have from Paul in Romans 10:14-21, preaching as the indispensable means to new birth and eternal life. The good news announced to this audience is that God's word never fades or perishes: it remains forever, and so will we who believe in it. Because this new birth or "rebegetting" comes about through the word, it is clear enough that we have no reference here to baptism at all.[140]

First Peter 1:24-25 is from Isaiah 40:6-8 and stresses the transitory nature of human life or "flesh" (a synonym stressing our contingent nature, which withers and eventually dies), in contrast to the eternal word of God, never changing, failing, dying, never losing its life; and in contrast to hope-giving power. This indeed is good news for those who can rejoice only in that proclamation and in their reception of it when they suffer and lose much, perhaps even physical life

[138]See Ben Witherington III and Laura M. Ice, *The Shadow of the Almighty: Father, Son, and Spirit in Biblical Perspective* (Grand Rapids: Eerdmans, 2006).

[139]See the discussion in Marshall, *1 Peter,* pp. 60-61.

[140]See Achtemeier, *1 Peter,* pp. 138-39.

itself. Suffering cannot touch or snuff out their ultimate source of new birth, life, salvation, nor even qualify it. In this quotation the word *theos* is changed to *kyrios,* perhaps because Peter is referring to the gospel about Jesus.[141] William L. Schutter points out:

> It [the quoted text of Isaiah] no longer concerns merely a vivid picture of the vital, enduring nature of God's word. Rather, in his hands it has been made to apply particularly to the Christian experience, because "the message from the Lord (God)" of Isaiah's prophecy is none other than "the message about the Lord (Jesus)" which imparted to the addressees a new experience. Thus the relationship of the Isaianic quotation to 1 Peter 1:22-23 is more than simply a proof-text which ascribes the enduring nature of Christian existence to properties inherent in God's word, because it specially identifies that word with the message about the Lord Jesus. What seems to be involved is an eschatological disclosure of an oracle's hidden meaning on the order of 1 Pet. 1:10-12.[142]

Just so. Peter's hermeneutic is both eschatological and christological in character, and one could also say ecclesiological, when he talks about believers as living stones. Not only is Isaiah seen as something like the Fifth Gospel, in which Jesus was prepreached, but so are the messianic psalms.

Chapter two begins with more ethical enjoinders, as does the argument beginning at 1 Peter 2:11, and in the latter case we may see a summary of the holiness code referred to in 1 Peter 1:13-25.[143] There is no question but that ethical matters are Peter's chief concern.

In **1 Peter 2:1** The term *apothemenoi,* "put off," is often used in contexts where baptismal language is in the forefront, but not necessarily baptismal practice. Thus, "put off" would conjure up the image of the convert putting off his clothes and walking naked into the river, and then after leaving the water putting on a new garment. The imagery of "putting off" quickly came to be used of a spiritual matter, divesting oneself of sinful attitudes, habits, ways, as here. What we must always bear in mind is that New Testament writers could use baptismal language to refer to the Spirit's work in the believer without intending to say anything about the rite of water baptism itself. Thus, it is not necessary to declare that because Peter uses this language, he is speaking to new converts and alluding to their recent water baptism. Rather, he is taking about spiritual transformation after conversion, since salvation is an ongoing matter.[144] *Pasan*

[141]See Senior, *1 Peter,* p. 48.

[142]Schutter, *Hermeneutic and Composition,* pp. 126-27.

[143]See Selwyn, *First Peter,* pp. 153-54.

[144]See Ben Witherington, *Troubled Waters: Rethinking Our Theology of Baptism* (Waco: Baylor University Press, 2007).

kakian in 1 Peter 2:1 may refer to all sorts of wickedness or to malice in particular. If it is the former, then it is a general and omnibus heading referring to all the sins that follow and are listed. Most of these sins involve speaking: deceit, hypocrisy, evil speaking, perhaps even envy. The plurals here suggest a reference to any and all acts of malice, hypocrisy, slander.[145] Peter is thus referring not just to attitudes, but attitudes that give birth to actions. The verb "put off" is an aorist and suggests he is saying, "start putting off." Scot McKnight is right that Peter is dealing with social networks and the corporate body of believers growing in the right direction and shunning the things that make for division and bad public witness.[146]

First Peter 2:2 is an analogy to newborn infants who strongly desire their mother's breast milk. This verse could imply he is talking to new converts, however as Ernest Best points out: "In 1 Pet. 2:2 there is no contrast between the present state of the newborn and a later state and milk is sufficient food to nourish the believer to full salvation; as we shall see in verse 3 'milk' means Christ himself; there can be no food beyond Christ. The whole image need not necessarily mean more than 'long for spiritual nourishment as eagerly as newly born babies do for physical nourishment.' . . . The phrase does not then imply the recent baptism of those addressed."[147]

In other words, we should not assume the same context as we find in 1 Corinthians 3:1-2 or Hebrews 5:12-13. The phrase *to logikon adolon gala* probably should be translated "of the word" ("milk of the word," not "spiritual milk," though that is a secondary possibility).[148] *Adolon* means that nothing harmful or impure is mixed in: unadulterated milk. It can also mean milk that is not watered down.[149] Desiring and feeding upon such milk of the word (and its subject Christ) is necessary in order that one may start growing in (by) it unto salvation. Salvation is again seen as a goal to be received at the end of the process of growth, when Christ returns. One may compare Paul's exhortation to let the word dwell richly in the person in Colossians 3:16. Scot McKnight is correct to stress that Peter is not suggesting that the hearers are a group of immature or

---

[145]Marshall, *1 Peter*, pp. 62-63.

[146]McKnight, *1 Peter*, p. 103.

[147]Best, *1 Peter*, p. 90. See Moule, "Nature and Purpose of 1 Peter," p. 6; Achtemeier, *1 Peter*, pp. 145-46.

[148]This possibly means "your logical/reasonable milk," and thus the reference would perhaps be to Christ himself, the true source of nurture and nourishment for the believer. This comports well with the quote from the psalm where the Lord himself is tasted and found good. See the discussion in Jobes, *1 Peter*, pp. 139-40. One can also argue that imbibing the written Word also involves imbibing the living Word as well.

[149]Marshall, *1 Peter*, pp. 63-64.

new Christians. He is drawing an analogy, and the way that sort of rhetoric works is that he is saying that their craving for the Lord and God's word should be like the craving of newborn infants for their mother's milk.[150]

First Peter 2:3 begins with "if," but what follows states a real condition: they are actually tasting (continuing the milk metaphor) that the Lord is good (or delicious; the idea is feeding upon Christ and/or his word). Peter assumes that their conversions have been real, that they have already experienced Christ and his word. Hence *ei* should be translated "since" here. "1 Peter conceives of Christian life not as an instantaneous and easily attainable experience but as a lifelong process of growth toward the full beauty of one's humanity before God."[151]

Quite clearly Peter here alludes to Psalm 34, and one may say that he has this psalm in mind throughout 1 Peter (in LXX, cf. Ps 33:5 [34:4 ET] to 1 Pet 1:18; Ps 33:11 [34:10] to 1 Pet 1:15-17; Ps 33:13-17 [34:12-16] as quoted in 1 Pet 3:10-12; Ps 33:23 [34:22] with 1 Pet 1:13, 18).[152] There is also a play on words here for the word for "good" or "delicious" is *chrēstos,* which is like *Christos*. The "Lord" here is Jesus, another example of transferring Old Testament terminology to Jesus, terms earlier applied to God the Father. Jesus, the Living Stone (1 Peter 2:4), has and is coming to believers. This play on words qualifies as the rhetorical device known as paronomasia: the One that one is tasting and finding good is the Lord Jesus. In various inscriptions a king is called the "living image" *(eikōn zōsa)* of some deity.[153] Here in 1 Peter 2:4, however, "living" seems to allude to the fact that Christ was raised from the dead. This Psalm 34 text seems to be one of Peter's favorites, and he will use it again at 1 Peter 3:10-12. Here Peter does not quote the words "and see," for his audience has not "seen" the Lord, though they have experienced him.[154]

In **1 Peter 2:4** Peter makes the transition to talking about the community of God by way of talking about its founder, Christ.[155] What is a "Living Stone"? First of all, we are talking about a stone that has been tooled by a craftsman, whether a building stone or a precious stone. It is not simply a rough uncut stone lying out in the field.[156] It is a "Living Stone" because Christ is living, and

---

[150]McKnight, *1 Peter,* pp. 104-5.

[151]Senior, *1 Peter,* p. 51.

[152]See Selwyn, *First Peter,* pp. 156-57.

[153]See *NewDocs* 9:36-37.

[154]See Jobes, "Got Milk?" pp. 1-14; Snodgrass, "1 Peter ii.1-10," pp. 97-106.

[155]It does not appear that the messianic interpretation of the stone first occurred with Jesus or his followers. *Tg. Ps.-J.* on Is 28:16, for example, sees the stone as referring to a mighty king yet to come; and 1QS 8.8 may be based on this speculation. See Jobes, *1 Peter,* p. 147.

[156]Just the opposite of what Martin, *Metaphor and Composition,* pp. 175-76, suggests when he refers the phrase to "uncut" or rough stones. See Perkins, *First Peter,* p. 42.

the church of which he is founder is a living organism; the rejection in view seems to be "living" as well, being current and part of the audience's experience. Thus, we are not referring here to the original rejection of Christ in Judea since the audience is not there, and the author is writing to them some thirty-plus years later. Peter does not develop the body imagery but rather the temple imagery, adding a dynamic to it by saying "living." Peter contrasts human (perhaps he is particularly thinking of Jewish) response to God. What people rejected, God elected. What was a cast-off stone for humanity was valuable to God. The verb "rejected" here is in the perfect, which suggests that the rejection is ongoing, perhaps including the rejection the "living stones" are currently experiencing in Anatolia.[157]

Peter says that Christ is the Living Stone, and in **1 Peter 2:5** that believers are as or like living stones. Believers are the copy of the original, the metaphor of which Christ is the reality.[158] "You" is emphatic and placed first here: "You also" are like Christ. The verb *oikodomeisthe* is imperfect passive: "were/are being built." Should we take it as indicative or as imperative? Probably it is an indicative, with the emphasis being on what God is doing: he selected Christ; he is building believers up into a spiritual house, which does not mean a house made of spirit or immaterial substance, but rather an edifice or structure characterized by and filled by God's Spirit.[159] It nevertheless is possible, with Leonhard Goppelt, to take *oikodomeisthe* as middle rather than passive voice, in which case it means "Let yourself be built," which suggests synergism in the process. God is doing the building, but we must cooperate.[160] On the whole, since the emphasis in the verses that follow is on divine action, God's action is likely meant here as well.[161] It seems quite clear that our author views the Christian community as the new temple of God, where God dwells. *Oikos* is clearly enough used of the temple in 2 Chronicles 36:23; Psalm 68:10 LXX [69:9 ET]; and Isaiah 56:7, and there is no reason to doubt that our author is building on such texts, as 1 Peter 4:17 also suggests.[162] The image of house as temple certainly does not exclude

---

[157]See Senior, *1 Peter,* p. 53.

[158]I am not buying the argument of Jobes, *1 Peter,* p. 151, that the "on this rock" saying in Mt 16:18 does not refer to Peter the person; it certainly does refer to him as a confessing person with a living faith, not merely his confession. And similarly here the "living stones" that are like the Living Stone are persons, confessing persons with a living faith but nonetheless persons. Here Peter doesn't distinguish himself from the other living stones.

[159]See Perkins, *First Peter,* p. 43, takes it as a passive imperative: "Let yourselves be built." This is not impossible, but in any case it is God doing the building.

[160]Goppelt, *1 Peter,* pp. 139-40.

[161]See Elliott, *1 Peter,* p. 412.

[162]See Senior, *1 Peter,* p. 54, against Elliott, *Elect and Holy,* p. 159.

the image of house as household or family. Peter plays with both these images, but here temple is alluded to, as the reference to the priesthood makes clear.

As part of a holy priesthood, all believers are also to have a function in that house or community. Here we see a definite contrast to Old Testament religion. Believers are collectively and together God's temple, his spiritual house (he is not talking here about individual Christians being God's temple or of the individual body of the believer being a temple; cf. 1 Cor 3:16-17; 6:19). All believers are his priests, not just a particular segment, as in the Old Testament. The New Testament knows no priesthood except Christ's high priesthood and the priesthood of all believers. The job of all believers is to offer up the world to God in praise, or more particularly, to offer up themselves to God, and therefore to offer spiritual sacrifices. The Old Testament does speak of spiritual sacrifices of various sorts (cf. Ps 19:14; 51:9; Is 1; Hos 9—whether it is songs of praise or righteousness, or a pure heart offered to God). It is possible that Peter had Romans 12:1-2 in mind here, in which case he is referring to believers as spiritual sacrifices offered to God. Best's qualification is important here: "There is no idea that the priesthood acts on behalf of the world as the Levitical priesthood acted on behalf of Israel; nowhere in the references of the New Testament to the sacrifices which Christians offer is there any suggestion that these are provided by others or presented on their behalf. The New Testament priesthood presents its own sacrifices."[163]

In the New Testament there is no basis for the idea that Christian clergy offer vicarious sacrifices, for others or for the world, nor is there any re-offering of Christ to God. First, this passage is about *all* believers, not about clergy. Second, one has to import all sorts of Old Testament ideas into the New Testament practice to come up with what we have in some high-church practice. This is a questionable hermeneutical leap at best. Nor is the Lord's Supper seen as a sacrifice; instead, like Passover, it is a celebration of redemption once for all accomplished by God in the past, the benefit of which is appropriated in the present.[164] The main sacrifice believers offer to God in worship or in particular in the Lord's Supper is what Paul suggests in Romans 12:1—themselves. However, we must remember that even this offering in itself is not acceptable, but as 1 Peter 2:5b suggests, only through Christ, who offered the one perfect and sufficient sacrifice. Cranfield stresses, "The living Stone implies the living stones, the Foundation implies the edifice that is built upon it, the Elect One implies the elect ones (1:1) not in isolation but as an elect race (2:9)."[165] We may add that his sacrifice

[163]Best, *1 Peter*, p. 104.
[164]Achtemeier, *1 Peter*, pp. 156-57.
[165]Cranfield, *First Peter*, p. 46.

requires the believers' spiritual sacrifices in response, in offering themselves. Finally, I. Howard Marshall is quite right to point out that in the Old Testament, and in Leviticus in particular, different sorts of sacrifices served different purposes, and many of them were not for atonement for sin. The grain and fellowship offerings described in Leviticus 1—2 were expressions of thanksgiving and even communion with God.[166] In sum then, Peter can be discussing here the offering of self for communion with God, the offer of praise, the offering of thanksgiving—none of which has to do with atoning for one's own sin. The Lamb took care of that.

As we turn to **1 Peter 2:6-8**, we must notice how Peter uses the Old Testament. In quoting the Old Testament here, he in part confirms what he has said in 1 Peter 2:4-5, and then he goes on to advance his argument (not just prooftexting his point), using Old Testament phrases after that. Sometimes Peter, like other New Testament writers, uses the Old Testament to mean things that probably were not the main point that the Old Testament writer had in mind. First Peter 2:6 is a quote from Isaiah 28:16 (LXX; cf. Rom 9:33). The phrase "in him" is not found in the MT, but only in some LXX versions. Our author cites the version that makes the christological point clearest. During the whole course of this argument, Peter seems to have Jesus' own words about "the stone the builders rejected" in mind (cf. Mk 12:10-11; 13:1-2; 14:58). Notably Mark, Peter's interpreter, highlights Jesus' use of these terms near the end of his Gospel. I am inclined to agree with the argument of Thomas Lea that Peter learned how to handle texts in these christological and ecclesiological manners from observing the praxis of Jesus himself.[167]

The quote in **1 Peter 2:6** is strikingly introduced by a unique phrase that literally reads, "for it says in writing," but Peter certainly is not talking about just any kind of writing: he means the Old Testament. The question about the phrase is this: Is Peter implying that because it is in writing, it has more authority? This would depend on his theology of sacred texts, but I think the answer to this question is yes. In an oral culture, texts, especially religious texts, take on an even more sacral aura than they do in our culture of endless texts.[168]

The quote refers to God laying a stone in Zion, which is a synonym for Jerusalem in general, and more often indicates the city of God, the place of his indwelling, or his sanctuary, the temple hill being called Mt. Zion (cf. Ps 20; 48;

---

[166]Marshall, *1 Peter*, p. 69. Contrast Elliott, *1 Peter*, p. 420.

[167]Lea, "How Peter Learned the Old Testament," pp. 96-102, esp. 96-98. He makes this suggestion on the basis of observing how Jesus used Ps 118:22 in Mt 21:42 and par. And then Peter uses it in Acts 4:11. I suggest that he also learned a thing or two from James and Paul as well.

[168]See Michaels, *1 Peter*, pp. 102-3.

74). Here the usage makes sense because Christians look forward to a new Jerusalem. They *are* the new temple, but they also expect a new Zion (cf. Rev 14:1).

By etymology the Greek word in question means "extreme" *(akro)* "[at the] corner" *(gōniaion),* and so certainly cornerstone is a possible meaning here. But is it a bottom corner, like a modern cornerstone (for which there is little ancient evidence) or a top corner? I suggest that *akrogōniaion* probably means a stone designed for the top corner of a wall, not a capstone of an arch, but it could be the latter. This interpretation has the advantage of matching up with the Scripture citation in 1 Peter 2:7 and means that there is not a different sort of stone in view when one compares Psalm 117:22 LXX (118:22 ET) and Isaiah 28:16. This interpretation also has the advantage of matching up with *Testament of Solomon* 22:7-9; 23:1-4, which speaks of Solomon's erection of a temple in which "there was a great cornerstone *[lithos akrogōniaios]* that I wished to put at the head of the corner *[kephalēn gōnias]*." The stone is then set on the pinnacle of the temple, at the top and juncture of the two walls.

It would be impossible to stumble on a capstone or a head of the cornerstone unless it is (envisioned as being) on the ground and not yet in place in the building, which is why various commentators think a cornerstone is meant. Also, a foundation stone, which is below ground, is not likely in view.[169] We are not talking about the foundation here, but a special stone around which the rest of the edifice is built, which could be either a cornerstone, a keystone, or a head of the cornerstone, which is clearly referred to in the second part of the quotation. So Christians are viewed as being built into the community that is vitally linked to and designed around Christ. Christ is the elect and precious one, or one held in honor, who makes it possible for believers who are "in Christ" to be elect and precious to God.[170] Indeed, 1 Peter 2:6 even refers to honor that comes to the one who believes in Jesus.[171] It is interesting to contrast the discussion here with that at Qumran, where the Qumran community itself is characterized as the "precious cornerstone," using this very same text from Isaiah 28 (1QS 8.7; cf. 1QH 14.26 [Sukenik: 6.26]).[172]

The quote itself also says that those who believe in him will not be put to

[169]But see the discussion in McKelvey, "Christ the Cornerstone," pp. 352-59, makes a strong case against Joachim Jeremias that this means a foundation stone, not a keystone, even in the citation of Is 28:16 in Eph 2:20. On the latter text see Ben Witherington III, *Philemon, Colossians, and Ephesians: A Socio-Rhetorical Commentary* (Grand Rapids: Eerdmans, 2007), ad loc.

[170]See Selwyn, *First Peter,* pp. 162-65.

[171]Marshall, *1 Peter,* p. 72.

[172]See the discussion in Goppelt, *1 Peter,* p. 138.

shame. This is an Old Testament idiomatic expression referring to being condemned by God at the last judgment, the ultimate disgrace one can undergo, which results in shame rather than honor for the person involved. Believers share in the honor that belongs to Christ. But to unbelievers, those who build the edifice of their life rejecting the keystone, Christ, it becomes a stone over which they stumble, sin (just as walking implies obeying in OT). Christ is said to be a rock that is a stumbling block. The Greek term here is *skandalon,* from which we get "scandalous." Here it means that which occasions sin or stumbling, generally an obstacle in the way of the sinner. The irony is that these builders rejected the very one whom God selected and made into the head of the corner. Far from continuing as a cast-off stone, he was the one of chief importance, the head of it all, particularly in the matter of salvation.

In **1 Peter 2:7** and the next verse, Peter develops his argument by drawing on two other stone passages: Isaiah 8:14-15 and Psalm 118:22. Both Romans 9:33 and our text here are closer to the MT than to the LXX, perhaps because, as William L. Schutter suggests, the LXX leaves out the notion of offense or scandal. There was another reason to follow the MT for several of these texts as well: Isaiah 28:16 LXX refers to the stone in question being sunk in the foundations, and therefore something one could not likely trip over.[173] This has led some to suggest that Peter is following here a catena of "stone" texts that he and Paul shared in common. This is possible, but it is also possible that Peter, in Rome, had read Romans or knew of its argument, especially since Romans had been available to that community for some years, since about A.D. 57 or 58. In favor of the *testimonia* view is J. Ramsey Michaels's point: "If Peter were using Paul [here], it is unlikely he would separate out two quotations that Paul had so carefully integrated into one. Moreover his middle quotation, Ps. 117:22 LXX [118:22 ET], is not found in Paul's epistles . . . but (within the NT) only in 1 Peter and the Gospels (cf. Mark 12:10//Matt 21:42//Luke 20:17; cf. the paraphrase attributed to Peter in Acts 4:11)."[174]

First Peter 2:8 is certainly very difficult. The stumblers do so because they do not believe; and because they do not believe, they refuse to obey the word. *Apeithountes* is a strong word, implying refusal to obey (not simply disobedience), though the phrase in question could also mean "unpersuaded by the word." Stumbling is caused by their disobeying, which derives from their disbelieving: this much is clear. But what about what follows in the text? Peter adds, "Unto which end they were also appointed." ***Etethēsan*** is the same word that we translated "lay" in 1 Peter 2:6. It is one used specifically of God's predestining

[173]Schutter, *Hermeneutic and Composition,* pp. 131, 133.
[174]Michaels, *1 Peter,* p. 94.

(cf. Is 49:6; 1 Thess 5:9). Some are elect unto salvation, some are appointed to other ends. Or so it seems to say.[175]

However, we are not told that those who have stumbled cannot be made to rise up again. Indeed, in the context of the discussion, Peter goes on to talk of those who were not a people of God, who were not chosen, yet under God's new plan are chosen and saved (1 Pet 2:9-10). Note as well that human violation is involved in this stumbling: they refused to obey and so stumbled. God did not force them to do so against their will. Some commentators have suggested that what is meant is that disobeyers are inevitably destined for stumbling. They are heading for a fall, which suggests that God has appointed disobeyers to that end. If this is what is meant, then there is no reference to the idea that God chose these people to stumble, much less that he chose them to be damned.[176] There is a possible parallel here to Romans 8, which talks about a Christian's destiny, conformity to the image of Christ, and not about predestining people to become Christians. In Romans 9 as in 1 Peter 2, God's predestination is on the basis of what God knows or foreknows: God foreknows people completely, which includes his foreknowledge of whether they will respond to his call or not. Hence I conclude that what Peter is suggesting is that there is a moral mechanism programmed into a moral universe, such that disobedience inevitably leads to stumbling and falling. Put another way, it means that there are moral consequences to one's actions, good or bad.

In **1 Peter 2:9** Christians are seen as a chosen race, a holy people for God's possession: Exhibit A, revealing the mighty acts of God. Indeed, they are chosen for the specific purpose of proclaiming God's mighty acts. What has happened to believers has happened so that these acts might be proclaimed, and thus God be glorified. Redemption is for believers' succor, and it is also for God's glory. God is the one who called persons from the darkness of sin and spiritual blindness into his marvelous and everlasting light. As Michaels stresses, there is nothing here about an old Israel being replaced by a new one. To the contrary, Peter's view is that the one people of God has kept going all along, only now the true expression of them is found in Jew and Gentile united in Christ. This is more of an eschatological completionist schema than a replacement schema.[177] There is certainly no anti-Jewish sentiment in this discourse, nor even any po-

---

[175]See Achtemeier, *1 Peter,* pp. 162-63.

[176]See Jobes, *1 Peter,* p. 155.

[177]Michaels, *1 Peter,* p. 107. It is true that on my reading 1 Peter is not mostly addressing Gentiles. As I have said, however, it is very likely that some God-fearers came into Peter's churches through evangelism of Jews, as was true with other apostolic work. Thus, Peter is thinking of true Israel as Jew and Gentile united in Christ the living stone.

lemic against the synagogue. But Exodus 19:6 is being appropriated and applied to the community of Christ here.

One phrase calls for close scrutiny in 1 Peter 2:9. Is *basileion hierateuma* an adjective and a noun, or two nouns? Does it mean (1) royal priesthood? or (2) house of the King, body of priests? or (3) a priesthood in service of the king? or (4) a kingdom of priests? or (5) a group of kings, a body of priests? In favor of view 4 is the Old Testament background, Exodus 19:6 as translated in the LXX. The Hebrew reads "a kingdom of priests," but the LXX translates it as two substantives, two nouns in apposition to one another—kings and priests. It may seem odd to place two nouns side by side, but if the LXX could do it, so could Peter. If view 4 is the right rendering, it does not imply that believers are kings, only that they are priests in service of the King. Against view 5[178] we may argue that there is no precedent for the word *basileion* meaning a "group of kings." Against views 1 and 3 we must argue: (a) If *basileion* was an adjective, it would normally follow its noun, as *eklekton* follows *genos*, and *hagion* follows *ethnos*. (b) In the only other use of *basileios* in the New Testament (Lk 7:25), it means palace or king's house and is not an adjective; in parallel Hellenistic literature it is normally a noun (cf. 2 Macc 2:17; Philo *Sobr.* 661; Philo *Abr.* 56). (c) What precedes this in 1 Peter 2:5, a reference to a spiritual house, may suggest a parallel here: king's house.[179] Thus, perhaps we should see this as two nouns in apposition, and if so, view 2, "house of the king, body of priests" will be the best translation. If the LXX and Hebrew background is in view, as the other terms in the list may suggest, perhaps we should translate "a kingdom of priests" or even "a royal priesthood," because the other four honorific phrases here involve a noun and a modifier.[180] If the latter, it is simply affirming that all believers are priests; if the former, it stresses that believers collectively are both God's house and his priests.[181] Whichever translation we opt for, I. Howard Marshall is clearly right in stressing: "There is no justification here or elsewhere in the New Testament for labeling certain people in the church 'priests.' If some Christians are set apart to perform the functions of ministers in the church, they are not to be regarded as priests different in kind from that of all Christians. . . . The term 'priest' should be dropped as a way of designating ministers of the Gospel."[182]

First 1 Peter 2:10 presents a contrast: "You who were once not a people are now a people." Here Selwyn urges: "What Peter's words conveyed to people so

[178]See Best, *1 Peter*, pp. 107-9.
[179]See Selwyn, *First Peter*, pp. 168-69.
[180]Michaels, *1 Peter*, p. 108.
[181]See the discussion by Schweizer, "Priesthood of all Believers," pp. 285-93.
[182]Marshall, *1 Peter*, p. 75.

placed was that they now once again belonged to a community which claimed their loyalty; and it was something which could give all their instincts of patriotism full satisfaction. In short, the term connotes in Greek, community. In the mixed society of the Roman Empire, where freedom of association was suspect and subject to restrictive laws, as in modern despotic states, this sense of community must have worn very thin, and produced a widespread feeling of homelessness."[183] As we have noted in the introduction, these words from Hosea originally referred to Jews, and there is no reason why they cannot refer primarily to Jewish Christians here either.[184]

Notice as well the "now" in this text. Peter emphasizes both what God has now done and what he will yet do. To be a people, a community, means believers have experienced the mercy of God. Many commentators think that 1 Peter 2:10 could not have been spoken of Jews: here Peter can only be talking about Gentiles, who now are included in God's new chosen race. But this is forgetting Peter's view that when Jews have rejected Christ, they at least temporarily cease to be part of the people of God (cf. Rom 11). As we have emphasized in the introduction,[185] Peter is here quoting Hosea 1:6-7 and probably the second part of Hosea 2:25 LXX/MT (2:23 ET) as well; Hosea was certainly applying these texts to Jews, as Peter likely is here as well. What we have seen in this section of the discourse is the very sort of tour de force use of the Old Testament as a basis for argumentation, loaded with allusions and partial quotes tailored to fit the context here, and as such it rivals what we find in Romans 9—11 and the use of the Scripture there. For Peter, it was essential to ground his argument in such a way that he could say, as he does in 1 Peter 2:6, "For it is contained in Scripture that . . . " For him, this is the final and irrefutable authority that clinches the arguments and makes the case. No audience would be more likely to pronounce the Amen to that theology of the Word than Jewish Christians, who also knew and resonated with these very texts. But how poignant must these texts have been for Peter himself, who was called Cephas, but also a "stumbling block/*skandalon*" on the same occasion when he confessed Jesus as the Christ (Mt 16:23)! One can understand his wrestling with these very texts to understand not only Jesus' identity but also his own. This argument is brought to a close by a reminder to the audience that they have a high calling, they are a temple and indeed they are a royal priesthood; as such, they are God's option in their own pagan environment, and so they must live in a fashion that makes them good witnesses, good neighbors, good people.

---

[183]Selwyn, *First Peter,* p. 101, col. 2.
[184]On which see pp. 23-25 above.
[185]See section in introduction about Peter the man.

A CLOSER LOOK

Recycled Ideas—Peter's Sermons in Acts and 1 Peter

Almost from the very beginning of 1 Peter, it becomes apparent to any close reader of Acts and 1 Peter that there is some connection between the speeches of Peter in Acts and 1 Peter. In 1 Peter 1:2 we heard about the elect who had been chosen according to the foreknowledge of God, and Acts 2:23 contains the only other reference to *prognōsis* in the New Testament, where we hear about "this [Jesus], delivered up according to the foreknowledge and plan of God." If this were the only correspondence, one might pass it off as a coincidence.[186] But there actually are many other parallels that one discovers as one works through 1 Peter, and it is always with the speeches of *Peter* in Acts, not with Acts in general or speeches in Acts in general.

I have dealt at length with the speeches in Acts, including Peter's speeches in another commentary.[187] These speeches present the largest challenge to the student trying to evaluate the historical substance of the book of Acts, since in many cases Luke could not have been present to hear these speeches, and in all, or nearly all, cases what we have are summaries of speeches, not a transcript of whole speeches. These speeches make up some 365 verses of Acts, about a third of the whole book. The goal of a good Hellenistic historian was to present the major points of a speech, not just the singular main point, and to do so in a style and form that comported with Peter and his own ethos. Luke has made his source material his own, but precisely because there are correspondences between the Petrine speeches in Acts and the diction in 1 Peter, it becomes clear that he must have been rather faithful to those sources and their style and substance. I have made the case elsewhere that Luke was a careful Hellenistic historian, following the conventions of his predecessors like Thucydides and Polybius.[188] This result will be assumed here, not argued for. One of the important conclusions of that study was that since Luke believed that the early Christian movement was in one sense created and carried along by evangelism, the spreading of the word (as in Acts 6:7), he spent disproportionately more time on speeches in his work than his Hellenistic predecessors did. There actually are some longer speeches in Polybius and Thucydides than in Acts, but far less in number or percentage of the entire verbiage of the work.

We have some eight speeches by Peter, all of them in the first half of Acts (Acts 1:16-22; 2:14-40; 3:12-26; 4:8-12, 19-20; 5:29-32; 10:34-48; 11:4-17; and a

---

[186]See Elliott, *1 Peter,* p. 376.

[187]Ben Witherington III, *The Acts of the Apostles: A Socio-Rhetorical Commentary* (Grand Rapids: Eerdmans, 1998), pp. 116-23.

[188]Ibid., pp. 1-65.

bit in 15:7-11), and a further nine speeches by Paul (Acts 13; 14; 17; 20; 22; 23; 24; 26; 28); thus we see that Paul is depicted as picking up where the trail of Peter goes cold. These two are given by far the most space for speeches in Acts, the next closest being the one long speech by Stephen in Acts 7 and two speeches by James in Act 15 and 21. What is especially interesting about the place where Peter's speeches stop is that this is the juncture where Peter apparently goes to the very places listed in 1 Peter 1:1-2. The correspondences between 1 Peter and these speeches, as we are now about to see, suggest that Peter continued to preach in the same fashion and using the same subject matter as he had earlier.

Three important impressions stand out from reading through Peter's speeches in Acts: (1) In these speeches, Peter is always addressing Jews or in one case God-fearers like Cornelius. He gives no representative speeches to pagan Gentiles. (2) In the paradigmatic speech at Pentecost in Acts 2, which sets the tone for all that follows in Acts, Peter uses the Old Testament in much the same Jewish and messianic ways that we find him using it in 1 Peter. (3) As has often been noticed, the rough Semitic style and primitive doctrine in these speeches (e.g., esp. Acts 10:34-43) comport with what we know of Peter elsewhere in the Gospels, in Paul's letters, and in 1 Peter.

Over fifty years ago Edward Gordon Selwyn pointed out in detail the correspondences between the speeches of Peter in Acts and 1 Peter.[189] It will be good for us to review that data here.

Acts 2:14-40. The following parallels are worth noting. The reference to the Spirit that Christ sends, falling on the church as the signal of the eschatological age being in process, should be compared to what is said about prophets in 1 Peter 1:10-12. In this speech, Christ's death is said to take place according to God's counsel and foreknowledge (cf. 1 Pet 1:20 and 1:2). The statement that Christ was not left in Hades and his flesh saw no corruption but rather he was raised from the dead (Acts 2:27, 31) should be compared to 1 Peter 3:18 and also 4:6. Christ's resurrection and ascension are closely linked in Acts 2:32-36, and we can compare 1 Peter 1:21; 3:22. According to Acts 2:38 the purpose of baptism is said to be remission of sins—which should be compared to 1 Peter 3:21. The universality of grace promised in Acts 2:39 becomes a theme that runs through 1 Peter (see esp. 1 Pet 1:10-12; 2:9-10).

Acts 3:11-26. Here we have the references to Jesus as God's servant (Acts 3:13, 26 and Acts 4:27-30), which seems clearly enough to echo Isaiah 40—55, a christologically used source text that certainly crops up in 1 Peter with some regularity. Particularly, the language Peter uses about the death and vindica-

[189]Selwyn, *First Peter,* pp. 33-36.

tion of Jesus seems to echo Isaiah 53. Equally interesting and instructive is the theme of *agnoia* found in Acts 3:17 (cf. 1 Pet 1:14), especially since the ignorance in the Acts passage is predicated of Jews, as is probably the case in 1 Peter 1:14, as we have seen.[190] The various general parallels between these speeches and 1 Peter provide support for seeing a close parallel on the ignorance issue. Notice as well the parallel references to Christ's second coming in Acts 3:20 and 1 Peter 1:7, 13, and 4:13; to the rejection and slander of believers (cf. Acts 3:23 and 1 Pet 2:7-8); and also to the inevitable nature of Christ's suffering (cf. Acts 3:18 and 1 Pet 1:11, 20).

Acts 4:9-12. This is only a brief speech, but notice the use of the Old Testament stone material here and in 1 Peter 2:7, in both cases drawing on Psalm 117:22 LXX [118:22 ET].

Acts 5:29-32. Here and in Acts 10:39 the cross is called *xylon,* "a tree" (cf. 1 Pet 2:24; Acts 13:29). This undoubtedly echoes Deuteronomy 21:23. In Acts 5:32 the disciples are called witness of *tōn rhēmatōn,* "these things," where things refers to actions or events or even words (cf. 1 Pet 1:25).

Acts 10:9-16, 34-43. Notice the use of *prosōpolēmptēs* in Acts 10:34, and in 1 Peter 1:17 see the use of *aprosōpolēmptōs*. One can also compare the phrase "the judge of the living and the dead," referred to Christ in Acts 10:42, and what is said in 1 Peter 4:5.

Acts 15:7-11. Compare the emphasis on God's choice in Acts 15:7 and in 1 Peter 1:1 and 1 Peter 2:9, and on the cleansing power of faith in Acts 15:9 and 1 Peter 1:22.

In addition to the above, it is striking that we have the reference to the name *christianos* (Acts 11:26; 26:28) and in 1 Peter 4:14-16. The "name" arises when Christians live in a predominantly Gentile environment.

After reviewing this evidence, Selwyn concludes:

> Few would suggest that the parallels of thought and phrase between the speeches and 1 Peter are based upon St. Luke's reading of the Epistles: for in both documents they clearly belong to their contexts, and the doctrinal issues in the speeches, notably the idea of Christ as *pais Theou,* are obviously original and not deductions from the Epistle. On the other hand, they are what might be expected if both alike are utterances of the same mind, given on different occasions. The connexion, that is to say, is not literary but historical: the common ground lies in the mind of St. Peter who gave, and was known to have given, teaching along these lines and to a great extent in these terms.[191]

[190]See discussion of 1 Pet 1:15-16 above.
[191]Selwyn, *First Peter,* p. 36.

Though being in strong agreement with Selwyn, I would phrase things a bit differently. The evidence that we have considered here is sufficient to say that the implied author of 1 Peter certainly reflects various speech traits and thematic interests of the Peter who speaks in the sermons in Acts. The question is, How do we explain this? One possible explanation we have already seen in our introduction. Carl R. Holladay suggests that the author of 1 Peter wrote so late in the New Testament era that he knew various other New Testament works.[192] This is not impossible, but it could even be true at a time well before the ninth decade of the first century: *it depends on the dating of the other New Testament books.* But what neither Holladay or others have been able to show is a "literary relationship" between 1 Peter and Acts, or with various of Paul's letters or the Synoptics. It seems rather to be more on the level of oral tradition or familiarity of the author with some of this material directly: the author of 1 Peter knew some of the people who wrote these books, such as Paul and Mark, and perhaps the author of Hebrews.

Here is where the issue of social location comes into play. The author of 1 Peter is in Babylon (a code name for Rome in 1 Pet 5:13). Whether he is Peter or some later figure writing in Peter's name, he is a Christian who could have had access to Christian documents written in or sent to Rome—such as Romans, Hebrews, Mark, and perhaps even Acts—to judge from Acts 28, where the narrative breaks off. In my view, the correspondences between 1 Peter and the Petrine speeches in Acts are too subtle and convincing to be the work of a mere copier or imitator who decided to mimic the Petrine style of the speeches when he wrote 1 Peter.

It is a far better and more economical thesis, and one that avoids the serious problems of seeing 1 Peter as a pseudepigraphon, and therefore a deceptive work,[193] to suggest that the Peter who was a disciple of Jesus and knew his teaching—and was an associate of James and knew some of his teaching; and was an associate of Paul and knew some of his teaching; and had Mark, the author of the earliest Gospel, as a collaborator in Rome—is responsible for 1 Peter. Furthermore, we must consider the possibility that Luke also finished his career in Rome, and perhaps had access to Peter while he was there during the period of Paul's house arrest in Rome in A.D. 60-62. If so, then Peter is the source of the summaries of his own sermons in Acts, and it is accordingly no surprise at all that 1 Peter then sounds like some of that sermonic material. This is not because Luke is a good imitator and editor. It is because, while Luke is a good editor, in the case of Peter's sermons

[192]See note 2 above.

[193]See Witherington, "General Introduction to the Commentaries," in *Letters and Homilies for Hellenized Christians*, 1:23-38.

at least, he had a good eyewitness and original preacher source (just as he claims in Lk 1:1-4): the man called Cephas. While all roads may not lead to Rome, all these rabbit trails and echoes of other Christian sources in 1 Peter eventually lead back to the historical figure of Peter himself. He is the best candidate, perhaps with the help of Silvanus, for the authorship of 1 Peter, just as he is the one who spoke of these things on many occasions to Jews in Jerusalem and elsewhere during the first decade of the life of the church, and beyond.

1 PETER 2:11—3:12—ARGUMENT 2: SUBMISSION TO AUTHORITY FIGURES

What is humility? It is to bear the insults, to accept sins against oneself, to bear punishments. Indeed, this not just humility, but prudence as well. (Andreas Capellanus)[194]

The next major rhetorical unit of this discourse is found in 1 Peter 2:11—3:12, as Lauri Thurén argues.[195] It has surprised some that, in the face of suffering abuse, a fair degree of optimism undergirds this material about what good behavior and a good witness can accomplish; nevertheless, it is an optimism about God's grace, not in the main an optimism about human nature. Suffering leads to glory and perhaps also to winning some for Christ, but this paradigm is thought to work because Christ exhibited and enables it to do so.[196] We have arrived now at the heart of the discourse and argumentation, with all the more general and preparatory discussion left behind. It becomes clear that Peter is especially concerned about two sticky subjects—submission to authority and suffering, and how one can endure both of these conditions in a manner that is in accord with Christian holiness. Submission is the easier of the two subjects to address in Peter's world, and so he tackles it first under the broader rubric of ways one can live an honorable life, being a good witness, and doing good to others. He leaves the more difficult subject of suffering for his third argument, which begins at 1 Peter 3:13. But as is typical of rhetorical arguments, there is some overlap: already in 1 Peter 3:9 we hear the message of no retaliation to persecution and pressure and slander.[197]

Peter is concerned that they not merely avoid bad behavior, but that they ac-

[194]ACCS 11:102.

[195]Thurén, *Rhetorical Strategy,* pp. 146-47.

[196]See e.g. Achtemeier, *1 Peter,* p. 172.

[197]On the deliberate use of chainlink, or overlapping, rhetorical construction, see Longenecker, *Rhetoric at the Boundaries,* pp. 11-83.

tually, to the extent they are able, seek the good of their city or town by doing good deeds and even blessing those who misuse them. Peter sees this as a response modeled on the way Jesus handled such situations. "It does not suffice that they are not evil-doers but ordinary citizens, they should do even more and be extraordinarily good ones. This serves, according to the author, God's strategy: by doing good the addressees can convert the Gentiles to praise God."[198] Hence, we should likely see the so-called household code material in this section of the discourse as pragmatic advice that is part of a missionary or evangelistic strategy. In other words, it is *not* Peter's attempt to reinforce the patriarchal structure of society as a matter of principle. As 1 Peter 3:1 suggests, active resistance to and the despising of the structures of society makes it more difficult to win over pagans (1 Pet 3:1), which is the prime mandate. Peter recognizes that they *have* the freedom to behave otherwise (see 1 Pet 2:16), but it is a bad witness in the heated and hostile situation in which they seem to live where pressure, abuse, and persecution are not unusual. The "addressees, who are assumed not to have reacted in the crisis by resisting their oppressors, are encouraged to be more active and so good. They should not assimilate in the sense that they lose their Christian identity, but be ready to defend and even proclaim their faith."[199]

Thus Peter is not trying to create either an isolationist sect or an accommodationist one. There is a delicate balance, a tightrope he wants the audience to walk: they are to be in the world, do good to the world, convert the pagan world, but without being of the world and being assimilated to various of the dominant values and moral lifestyle of that world. The line is drawn on the basis of theology and ethics, and also on the basis of good evangelistic strategy.

Notice what marks off this rhetorical unit. It begins with the address "Beloved" (the author is not at odds with his audience but in fellowship with them; the term is also clearly transitional at 1 Pet 4:12)[200] and ends with a clinching and confirming quotation from Scripture, an inartificial proof, as we have seen Peter do previously in this discourse. This is not a grab bag of loosely connected paraenesis and theological remarks. There is a carefully thought-out structure to it. At the very heart of it stands the example of Christ's nonretaliation and doing good to others (1 Pet 2:21-25), which the audience is urged to emulate. But they do this *imitatio Christi* with the recognition that not only is the Lord's eye on them watching out for them, but the Lord also is the Judge of those who do them wrong, and so there is neither a need nor a warrant for them to respond

[198] Thurén, *Rhetorical Strategy,* p. 147.
[199] Ibid., p. 148.
[200] Campbell, *Honor, Shame,* p. 99.

to abuse, slander, persecution in kind. The Lord is sovereign over the situation: vengeance and vindication are tasks he alone can and should undertake. But there is in addition the not-so-subtle message that God will hold the audience responsible if they lapse into wrongdoing, and they will be judged as well. Thurén calls this a rhetorical strategy of entrapment: Peter first gets the audience to agree in principle that certain behaviors are wrong, even if one has endured such things; and then he implies that if they engage in such behavior, they are not following the example of Christ and are themselves in danger of losing their salvation and being judged. He may also be right that this sort of discourse presupposes that the letter will be read out on more than one occasion, so the audience can be allowed to gradually absorb the thrust and cut of the discourse and figure out its implications for belief and behavior.[201] It seems clear to me that, since Peter is here calling for a change of behavior to some extent, this must be seen as deliberative rhetoric.[202] Peter is not simply celebrating their present behavior: he wants them to change in certain respects.

This argument in the discourse begins with a strong warning against sin, "fleshly desires," which sets the rhetorical tone of this argument off from what precedes in the form of personification of "desire" (Quintilian *Inst.* 8.6.11). Campbell detects an enthymeme here:

> Major premise: One must abstain from things that make war on the soul.
>
> Minor premise: Fleshly desires do this.
>
> Conclusion: Keep away from fleshly desires.[203]

As we saw in our study of the Pastoral Epistles, many of these enthymemes are compressed due to space, leaving the audience to supply missing elements.[204] Appearing in 1 Peter 2:24-25 is another good example of an enthymeme:

> Major premise: Wandering sheep who return to their shepherd are healed by Christ's wounds.
>
> Minor premise: You were wandering sheep who have returned to your shepherd.[205]
>
> Conclusion: By Christ's wounds you are healed.[206]

---

[201]Thurén, *Rhetorical Strategy,* pp. 151-52.

[202]See rightly Campbell, *Honor, Shame,* p. 99.

[203]Ibid., p. 102.

[204]See Witherington, *Letters and Homilies for Hellenized Christians,* 1:69-72.

[205]This argument is rhetorically far more persuasive if the audience is largely Jewish Christians, who could "return."

[206]Campbell, *Honor, Shame,* p. 142.

One of the telltale signs that we are dealing with deliberative rhetoric that is seeking to affect change in the near future is the use of honor and advantage language, as we find here at the outset of this particular argument (cf. Cicero *Inv.* 2.51.156—58.175). Lest we miss it, Peter is not simply reaffirming the existing honor code of the society or its "family values": he is actually "rewriting the social code of honor, taking his cue from Jesus himself (2:23)."[207] For example, our author wants the audience to establish their honor in public not by engaging in what would be called agonistic honor challenges, but rather by doing the "good" for one's neighbors and avoiding getting in what I would call spitting contests. They are not to revile if they are reviled, not to retaliate if they are abused. This is a quite different ethic than the dominant one of that society. Bruce W. Winter is probably right that Peter is thinking through not only the implications of Jesus' ethic of nonretaliation but also of prophetic teaching like what Jeremiah gave to the Babylonian exiles, exhorting them to settle in Babylon, marry, and seek the welfare of the city (Jer 29:4-14). One was not to try to plot against the powers that be or to undermine the fabric of their society, but rather to seek to be a blessing to them. "They are not to retaliate, but are to bless (3:9). The twin concepts 'to do good' . . . and 'to seek peace' . . . are picked up later in the letter (3:11) in a citation from Psalm 34:12-16, but the language is also reminiscent of the theme of Jeremiah to seek the welfare of the city and pray for its peace (29:7). The parallels between Jeremiah 29 and 1 Peter . . . are compelling."[208]

As Winter goes on to stress, the argument we are considering now stresses that the audience is to continue to do observable good works as a good witness to their faith, and to abstain from the usual pagan immorality to also add to their honor rating among their neighbors. Doing benefactions or good works implies they have the time and/or resources to do them, which in turn implies something about how Peter views the audience's social level.[209] What we find in 1 Peter that is missing in Jeremiah is the evangelistic motive for the behavior. Christians are not just called to be good and honorable neighbors: they are also called to be good witnesses, which in turn makes clear that Peter's rhetoric is not attempting to inculcate an isolationist sect. Indeed, Winter goes so far as to argue that seeking the praise of rulers and doing good in their eyes (1 Pet 2:14-15) implies the doing of major civic benefactions, which again implies having the wherewithal to do them, at least in the case of some of the audience. The

---

[207]Ibid., p. 104.
[208]Winter, *Seek the Welfare of the City*, p. 17.
[209]Ibid., pp. 16-21.

evidence Winter provides from inscriptions of the period suggests that he is right: Peter is using certain buzzwords for public benefactions.[210] This in itself should change how the rhetoric of Peter's second argument is so often read. It carves out its own honor niche in society, not compromising on the distinctive Christian ethic, while at the same time seeking ways to be a recognized blessing to those who live in the same city. The desideratum is that those who observe Christian good works will then glorify the one true God.

One of the ways rhetoric works is that sound reinforces sense, with key ideas being punctuated by the repetition of sounds that aurally hammer home the message. For instance, as Campbell notes, in 1 Peter 2:12 the alliterative effect of *kalēn . . . katalalousin . . . kakopoiōn . . . kalōn,* using a rhetorical device called "homoiophonpheron" *(homoiophōnpheron),* hammers home the need to do the good and avoid the evil.[211] We may compare *aphronōn anthrōpōn agnōsian* in 1 Peter 2:15. Clearly some of the persuasive effect of this material is lost if one does not hear it in the original language.

But it is not just the use of such individual rhetorical devices that characterizes what is going on here. Campbell also points out the rhetorical progression of the argument: in the material leading up to the summary in 1 Peter 2:17, we have an introduction and then the rationale given for the imperative "Keep away from fleshly desires." We can describe the form as imperative, followed by rationale for the imperative, followed by confirmation and examples meant to reinforce the imperative (in this case the example of Christ), followed by a summary imperative working out the implications. Seen in this light, 1 Peter 2:17 becomes the trigger and introduction for the submission code teaching that follows, and that code presupposes the rationale and argument already made for the ethic being inculcated. It does not stand alone and should not be excerpted from the larger argument of which it is a part.[212]

I stress this here because what we are going to notice about the so-called household code in this argument is that it is *unlike* the ones we find in Colossians and Ephesians in crucial respects. Two differences can be mentioned here because it affects the way we hear Peter's rhetoric. First, as Michaels has stressed, Peter is concerned with the social *interface* between Christians and non-Christians as it transpires both in society and in the household. He is dealing with a mixed society and religiously mixed households. This is why the symmetry or mutuality so striking in the household codes in Colossians and Ephe-

---

[210]Ibid., pp. 26-40.

[211]Campbell, *Honor, Shame,* p. 106.

[212]Ibid., pp. 108-9.

sians is absent here. There is only one pair addressed, husband and wife, and the husband gets exactly one verse worth of attention (1 Pet 3:7). Otherwise, Christian slaves are addressed but not masters, the discussion of parents and children is omitted altogether, and the duty of all Christians but not that of rulers is discussed. And the discussion of one's duties to rulers and all those in authority is actually discussed first and sets the tone for what follows. This is because Peter is focusing on Christian duties to *those outside the Christian community*, even if they live in the same household as the Christian. Thus we do not, I repeat, *do not* at all have a discussion in 1 Peter of the "Christian household," unlike what we find in Colossians and Ephesians. And the discussion of duty to rulers can hardly be called part of a household or duty code. The rhetorical rubric being used to bind all this together is the Christian's duties to non-Christians, and "1 Peter alone makes his readers' civic obligations the framework in which to present more specific duties within the household."[213]

But that is not all. As Michaels stresses, in this document God is the only being to whom Christians are called to offer absolute and unconditional obedience. Bear in mind again 1 Peter 2:16, where Peter assumes and stresses that his audience is free to respond properly or not to respond properly to these exhortations. He is not referring to political or social freedom here but rather spiritual freedom that comes through new birth in Christ, and frees one from bondage to sin, darkness, ignorance, paganism (1 Pet 1:14; 2:9).[214] They can cooperate with their rulers, masters, spouses, or not. Peter is urging cooperation "for the sake of the Lord," because of the witness to the non-Christians one is relating to.

Michaels then notes that unconditional and unquestioned "obedience," *hypakoē*, is a term reserved for the Christian's relationship to God in Christ (see 1 Pet 1:2, 14, 22). He thus suggests that, since Peter under no circumstances would advise Christians to compromise their faith or obedience to God in order to comply with some lesser authority figure, we should see the verb *hypotassō* here as applied to one's relationship to a non-Christian ruler, master or husband (cf. 1 Pet 2:13, 18; 3:1, 5; 5:5) as meaning something closer to "defer" or "respect" rather than "submit" or "subject" in English.[215] I agree. This leads to the further necessary point that *ktisis* in 1 Peter 2:13 should be allowed to have the same meaning it has everywhere else in the New Testament (cf. Rom 8; Col 1:15, 23; Mk 16:15): creature or creation. Peter is not calling for Christian submission

---

[213]Michaels, *1 Peter*, p. 122.
[214]Ibid., p. 128.
[215]Ibid., p. 124.

to every creature on the planet, and the examples that follow of the emperor or governor are people, not institutions. No, Peter is inculcating the need to show respect and deference to all other human beings starting from the top of that hierarchical society and on down. Campbell aptly notes that Peter has modified the instructions found in Proverbs 24:21 LXX on this subject. "Fear" is reserved now for God alone, but the ruler is to be honored (1 Pet 2:17).[216]

Thus as Michaels concludes, "'Defer to every creature' simply prepares us for vs. 17 where we hear 'Show respect for everyone.'"[217] The rhetorical effect of this reading of the argument is that it turns out to be far more profoundly Christian and far less conventional than is often imagined: it is not counseling believers to baptize the existing social structures and call them good. It is calling Christians to act as Christians on the basis of first Christian principles in all their relationships, for the sake of the Lord and the witness, whether in the household or in society, *especially* when they are relating to pagans.

In some ways the most impressive and surprising rhetorical move of this particular argument is the use of Christ as a paradigm for the behavior of household servants (and others). Christ as exemplar is common enough, but only here is the "servant" Christ seen as specifically the model of behavior for Christian household servants. There were detailed rules for how a paradigm should be used in a deliberative speech (Aristotle *Rhet.* 1.2.1357b.25-37; anon. *Rhet. Her.* 1.8.13; 4.49.62; Quintilian *Inst.* 5.11.1-37).

Of importance here is that the example is used for paraenetic purposes, and that the example chosen is an historical one, indeed, the most important historical one for this audience, which considerably strengthens the force of the example to its maximum potential, especially because of the authority of the example over the audience (see Quintilian *Inst.* 3.8.26: appeal to authority is a deliberative move). In the midst of this surprising example is a dramatic play on the verb *pherō*. In 1 Peter 2:19 the household servant is exhorted, "*Bear up* under the pain," and 1 Peter 2:24 says, "Christ *bore* our sins in his body." "The pun unites the experiences of both the believer and Christ"[218] while deftly distinguishing them. Only Christ suffered for other's sins and made atonement, and Peter indicates the distinction by using the prefix *hypo-* with the former verse and *ana-* with the latter. The ultimate irony of this argument, which makes a tour de force, is that the household servants become examples for the whole community, showing how they should respond to society! The last shall indeed be

[216]Campbell, *Honor, Shame*, p. 120.
[217]Michaels, *1 Peter*, p. 124.
[218]Campbell, *Honor, Shame*, p. 136.

first.[219] Here David Balch helpfully reminds us that slaves were expected to take the religion of their masters; hence, when a slave became a Christian, there was a problem on this front, and Peter is suggesting that household servants should give no other offense than the offense of their faith.[220] The same applies to wives as well, as a glance at Plutarch's *Moralia* 140D and 144D-E shows. The wife was supposed to worship her husband's gods. What was she then to do if she became a Christian? Peter's advice is that in other respects she is to defer to her husband and so be a good witness to him. "Peter's advice is, unlike Plutarch's, . . . not for wives to abandon the worship of Christ, but for them to continue Christian living so as to win their husbands over to the Christian faith. The summons is not to acculturation to Greco-Roman society, but to [creative] adaptation to its domestic realities and norms. Thus will the Christian mission advance in a home despite a mixture there of religious beliefs."[221] As Peter H. Davids stresses, if Peter were simply an accommodationist to Greco-Roman norms, he would never have encouraged women and slaves to live out and be loyal to their Christian faith in clear violation of the normal patriarchal expectations of the day. The insistence on no religious accommodation to the master or husband is quite revolutionary.[222]

Near the end of this remarkable piece of argumentation, we have a second paradigm appealed to, this one as an example for women: the example of Sarah. Sarah is presented as a model of deference to one's husband, but with a bit of tongue in cheek, if one recognizes what is happening with the use of the Old Testament here. In Genesis 18:12 LXX Sarah calls Abraham "my lord," but she is being somewhat facetious. The context is not deference but rather "incredulous amusement at the announcement of her future child bearing."[223] Here Peter says the wife must hope only in God (honoring only God as God), but she must respect her husband as Sarah did. Though Peter refers to Sarah obeying and calling Abraham master, what he asks of Christian women is "doing good and not fearing intimidation"! What has happened here? Sarah becomes a general example of respecting one's spouse, but the Christian wife is not called to follow her example exactly. Rather, she is to do good and not be cowed or act on the basis of intimidation. In other words, her behavior should be guided by positive Christian principles of honor and respect, not be grounded in fear-based or cra-

[219]See ibid., p. 143.
[220]See Balch, *Let Wives Be Submissive,* pp. 68-75.
[221]Campbell, *Honor, Shame,* p. 148.
[222]Davids, *First Peter,* pp. 15-16.
[223]Campbell, *Honor, Shame,* p. 159.

ven behavior![224] This goes well beyond what Sarah modeled in that Old Testament story. Doing the good here suggests that there are women capable of benefactions, and Peter would rather have them do that, than spend their money on jewelry and luxurious apparel. They are to dress modestly. Perhaps the reference to fear has to do with concerns about verbal or physical abuse based on the wife's newfound religion, but Peter does not say so.[225]

Peter ends this argument with the longest Old Testament quotation in this entire discourse, and it is clear from the word "finally" in 1 Peter 3:8, which introduces the conclusion of the argument, that he is summing up. This conclusion shows that he is most concerned with inculcating nonretaliation (a counterintuitive virtue that distinguishes Christians), kindness in behavior toward non-Christians and brotherly/sisterly love and concord within the fellowship of Christ. Thus it turns out that Peter is concerned with both internal behavior in the community and also the interface between Christians and society in this entire argument.

2:11 *Beloved, I urge you as aliens and sojourners/settlers, keep away from fleshly desires, which war against the spirit/life.* 12 *Let your life among the pagans be honorable in order that those who speak ill of you as being evildoers, being spectators of your good works will glorify God in his visitation.* 13 *Defer/be subordinate to every human creature for the sake of the Lord. Whether emperors as supreme* 14 *or governors as sent through (by) him for the punishment on evildoers but praise of do-gooders,* 15 *because that is the will of God—in doing what is right to silence the ignorance of silly people.* 16 *(Do this) as free persons, and not having freedom as a pretext for evil, but as servants (slaves) of God.* 17 *Show respect (honor) to all, love the brotherhood, fear God, respect (honor) the emperor.*

18 *Let household slaves defer/be subordinate in all fear (with all respect) to their masters, not only to the good and considerate ones but also to the perverse (crooked) ones.* 19 *For this is a credit (commendable), if because of consciousness (knowledge) of God,*[226] *someone bears grief, suffering unjustly.* 20 *For what sort of fame is it if you do wrong and when beaten endure it? But if you endure while doing good and suffering, this is a credit (commendable) before God.* 21 *For unto this you have been called because Christ suffered*[227] *for you, leaving behind for you an example in or-*

---

[224]Here I part company with Campbell's reading (ibid.) of this text and Balch's as well *(Let Wives Be Submissive).*

[225]See Campbell, *Honor, Shame,* p. 161.

[226]Various scribes had problems with the phrase "through the conscience/consciousness of God," which is found only here in the NT, but it is strongly supported by Codexes ℵ, A, B, K, L, P and other manuscripts. Some witnesses, following Acts 23:1 and 1 Tim 1:5, 19 (C, 94, 206 and others) replace God with *agathē*, and in other witnesses the two readings are conflated. See Metzger, *TC,* p. 690.

[227]The reading *apethanen* is found in ℵ and a few other witnesses, but *epathen* is well supported by $\mathfrak{P}^{72}$, A, B, and a host of other witnesses. The variant is probably caused by 3:18.

der that you might follow closely in his footsteps, [22] *"who committed no sin, nor was deceit found in his mouth,"* [23] *who being abused did not return abuse, suffering did not threaten but handed it (himself?) over to him who judges justly,* [24] *who took up our sins in his body upon the tree so that dying (departing) to sin we might live to righteousness, by whose wounds we are healed.* [25] *For you were as sheep being lead astray, but now turned back to the Shepherd and guardian of your beings (souls).*

[3:1] *Similarly wives should defer/subordinate themselves to their own husbands, so that if some disbelieve (or disobey?) the word, he is won over through the behavior of the wife without a word,* [2] *watching over the reverence and purity of your behavior.* [3] *Your (behavior) must not be (marked) by the outward adornment of plaiting of hair and wearing gold or putting on (fine) clothes,* [4] *but the hidden person of the heart in the imperishability of a gentle and quiet spirit, which is precious before God.* [5] *For that (was) once the way also holy women, women hoping in God, adorned themselves, deferring to their own husbands,* [6] *as Sarah obeyed Abraham, calling him master, whose children you become (by) doing good and not fearing any intimidation (fear).* [7] *Similarly, husbands live with your wives according to knowledge (of her) as a weaker vessel, showing honor (respect) to the woman in her as also to fellow heirs*[228] *of the grace of life, lest you hinder your prayers.*

[8] *Finally, be all of one mind, be sympathetic, showing brotherly love, being compassionate, being humble minded,* [9] *not repaying evil for evil or insult for insult, but on the contrary, blessing, because for this you were called in order that you might inherit a blessing,* [10] *for "the one wishing to love life and see good days must stop the tongue from evil and the lips so they do not speak deceit,* [11] *but turn away from evil and do good, seek peace and pursue it* [12] *because the eyes of the Lord are on the righteous and his ears [inclined] unto their prayer, but the face of the Lord is against those who do evil."*

If we ask for the connecting thread in this crucial second argument, it is that Christians are called to live exceptional lives, even amid various sorts of suffering, for the glory of God and so as to be a good witness to outsiders.[229] Peter takes neither the tact of suggesting an ethic that is completely at odds with larger society, nor one that completely conforms to its dominant values. Karen H. Jobes puts things aptly:

> Peter expects that his readers can live in a way that will be recognized as good even by the standards of unbelieving pagans, which "presupposes overlap between Christian and non-Christian constellations of values." . . . The implication of this overlap

---

[228] There is a textual issue here of some note. The dative of "coheirs" is well supported by $\mathfrak{P}^{72}$, ℵ^{c}, B^{c} and various other witnesses, while the nominative reading is supported by A, C, K, P and others. If the former reading is original, the reference is to the women being coheirs; if the nominative is original, the husbands are coheirs. The structure of the sentence favors the dative and the reference to the wives. See Metzger, *TC*, pp. 690-91.

[229] See McKnight, *1 Peter*, p. 124.

> is that Peter does not seem to be thinking in binary categories that characterize society as evil and the Christian community as good. The apostle does not condemn all of the values and customs of first-century culture and society or advise complete withdrawal from it. . . . Peter recognizes that non-Christian values of his culture overlap in some ways with those of the Christian faith. . . . Peter challenges his readers to live by Christian values and, when they conflict with those of society, to be willing to endure graciously the grief and alienation that will inevitably result.[230]

Christians in **1 Peter 2:11** are said to be beloved (by God and Peter), but socially they are aliens and sojourners.[231] Let us consider the spiritual term "beloved" first. *Agapētos* is a term hardly found outside of early Christian literature in the writings of the New Testament period. It seldom appears at the outset of a letter or discourse, but rather usually shows up as a transition marker somewhere in the middle of a discourse (cf. Rom 12:19; 1 Cor 10:14; 2 Cor 7:1; 1 Thess 2:8; Heb 6:9; Jas 1:16, 19; 2:5 [in James, always with "brothers"]; 2 Pet 3:1; 1 Jn 2:7; Jude 3; etc.). Rhetorically speaking, its function is twofold: (1) It serves as a term of endearment to bind the author emotionally with the audience, letting them know that they are loved by the author, by God, by the body of Christ. In short, they are not abandoned or alone though they may feel that way as "resident aliens and sojourners." (2) As a term of endearment, it makes what follows it have more pathos and be emphatic. It is like when my parents or grandparents used to say to me, "Now listen, honey." I knew something crucial was going to follow those words.[232] Here Peter "appeals" to his audience and then at 1 Peter 5:12 characterizes the entire discourse as an "appeal." This tells us two things: (1) This discourse should be seen as deliberative in character. (2) Peter understands both the need for persuasion and its power. He could command, but he would rather appeal. This is the approach of a good rhetorician who has the authority to do more, but would much rather work with the free consent of the audience.[233] As Elliott notes, the force of *parakalō* is more than "request" but less than "command." "Urge" is closer to its sense.[234]

---

[230]Jobes, *1 Peter,* pp. 170-71, quoting Volf's "Soft Difference," pp. 15-30, esp. 25.

[231]Here is one of those places where some translations are far too overinterpretive. For example, in 1 Pet 2:11 there is no warrant to add the phrase "in the world," as the NIV does. That assumes that these social terms are used in a spiritual way here, referring to the pilgrimage from this life to the next, which as we have seen is probably incorrect.

[232]See Goppelt, *1 Peter,* p. 155.

[233]Michaels, *1 Peter,* p. 115. As Michaels says, what is interesting is that Peter appeals not on the basis of his own authority, but on the basis of their social situation as resident aliens. "Their identity as 'aliens and strangers' in Roman society is what necessitates the moral demands that will follow."

[234]See Elliott, *1 Peter,* p. 457.

The social term *paroikos* emphasizes that these believers are not citizens, but rather resident aliens, and it is no accident that as his examples our author would appeal to patriarchal figures who also were resident aliens, like Sarah and Abraham (see below). The next term, *parepidēmos,* implies believers' transitory stay in this locale. These social descriptions are crucial to understanding what follows here, which is advice to those who are *not* citizens of their towns and are therefore in a precarious social position if they should be found on the wrong side of the law.[235] Although their conversion had not created their social condition as resident aliens and sojourners, it had made that condition more precarious and problematic. Accordingly, especially those at the low end of the social spectrum must live lives that never provoke any authority figure. Peter's advice thus is not a call to martyrdom but actually an attempt to lessen the suffering in various ways.

Let us assess the situation: (1) Christians could not worship the emperor or any other pagan god or participate in other religious ceremonies for such gods. (2) This in turn meant that Christian women, particularly wives, could not be the "keepers of the flame" of the religion of hearth and home, the Greco-Roman religion that focused on the spirits of the ancestor. (3) Christian slaves also could not participate in the religion of their pagan masters. (4) Christians could not engage in the honor challenges of their society because of the ethic of Jesus, nor could they involve themselves in various of the familiar pagan vices. (5) Peter is already seeing persecution and suffering of Christians where he is and expects it to be exported to the provinces. Hence, the advice Peter gives here, especially to the most marginalized of noncitizen Christians, slaves and wives, is not only *not* surprising; it is actually rather bold and in some ways unconventional, as we shall see, especially for Jews whose ancestors may have originally come to live in these regions as slaves deported to the area. "As long as 1 Peter's readers are aliens, they must be careful not to provoke jealousy among local citizens. The warnings to be subordinate to all governing authorities and to honor all people are directed toward the situation of aliens. As long as nothing in their conduct causes offense, Christians can expect assistance from Roman officials."[236] Clearly this is written before the first major martyrdoms in Rome and Anatolia, but not before Christians have already suffered various forms of lesser abuse. Here we have advice on how to live in existing fallen and compromising situations that are not of the believers' making, and to do so in a Christlike manner.

But what sort of suffering does Peter actually think the audience has already undergone and is currently enduring? First of all, **1 Peter 2:12** suggests that they

[235]See the discussion above (pp. 23-35) on the meaning of these key social terms.
[236]Perkins, *First Peter*, pp. 49-50.

have been accused of doing wrong. First Peter 2:15 suggests that ignorant things have been said about these Christians: slander, accusations not based on facts. In 1 Peter 2:18-21 we will learn about slaves being mistreated, and in 1 Peter 3:1-7 there seems to be some complaint about more high-status women dressing in ways that the husband saw as provocative. If we go further into this discourse, we again hear about Christians being insulted and also persecuted (1 Pet 3:9, 13, 17; 4:12-16). Nothing is said about any martyrdom in these locales yet, but Peter's ethic and theological remarks as well are preparing them to follow the example of Christ to the bitter end, if need be. In other words, the social situation seems volatile and seems to involve minor violence, but as of yet there are no Christian casualties nor any direct official governmental action against these Christians. This best suits the period after the Neronian crackdown in Rome, which began after the fire in A.D. 64, a crackdown that had a ripple effect elsewhere, because what Nero did gave others in the empire a license to persecute, prosecute and even execute.

Peter begins this argument in 1 Peter 2:11 with a general exhortation about keeping away from the sort of desires of the flesh that war against one's *psychē*. Here if anywhere in 1 Peter one might be able to translate *psychē* as "soul." What is meant, however, is the believers' life, perhaps particularly their spiritual life within them, given them by the Holy Spirit, not some immaterial part of them that supposedly they were born with and would always exist, such that we could talk about the immortality of the soul. Perhaps better, with Cranfield, we should just see a reference here to the Christian as a person seen from the prospect of the believer's eternal or born-again nature. God will save new creatures, and indeed, new creatures are what salvation is about at its inception. It may be that "flesh" here is used as Paul uses it, to refer not simply to physical desires, but rather to evil or carnal desires, in which case Peter does not see physical desires as necessarily evil. Cranfield argues:

> The fleshly lusts are forces, which war against the soul. "Soul" (Greek *psychē*) is sometimes used in the New Testament to denote the natural life, and the adjective *psychikos* always denotes "natural" as opposed to *pneumatikos* (spiritual, i.e., indwelt by the Holy Spirit); but at other times "soul" has the sense of "person" (e.g. Rom 13:1). Quite often *psychē* is used as equivalent to a reflexive pronoun (e.g. Mk 8:35ff.). Here and in the other places in 1 Peter where it occurs (1 Pet 1:9, 22; 2:25; 3:20; 4:19) it has a similar meaning. It denotes a man's self, his individuality. While "flesh" describes him in his alienation from God, "soul" describes him simply as a self or person. It is this "soul" that is the object of redemption according to 1 Peter 1:9; 2:25. In the picture of the warfare of the Christian life in Galatians 6:16ff. the two protagonists are the Holy Spirit and the flesh, but there is a third party men-

tioned—the individual Galatian Christian, who is not just identical with his flesh, but is distinguished from it in St. Paul's use of the second person plural ("walk," "ye shall not fulfil," "that ye may not do the things that ye would," "if ye are led, . . . ye are not under the law."). The "soul" here in 1 Peter is equivalent to the "ye" in the Galatians passage.[237]

I disagree with Cranfield that *psychē* here means the self, or "you." Rather, the author is referring to the inner person or the inner life of the person in question. Christians are called to live an honorable life in public as well as in private: if they do so, those who watch them on an ongoing basis—having suggested that Christians were wrongdoers, and thus speaking ill of them—will be impressed and perhaps even glorify God. The principle here is one enunciated already by Jesus: his disciples are to let their light shine in such fashion that people will see their good works and glorify God (Mt 5:16; cf. 1 Cor 10:32; Col 4:5; 1 Thess 4:12; 1 Tim 3:7; 5:14; 6:1; Tit 2:5-10). The subject of glory or glorifying comes up more in 1 Peter than in any other New Testament book in proportion to length of document, and the language of honor is frequent as well.[238] This tells us something about Peter's perception of what would concern his audience in a honor-and-shame culture. First Peter 2:12 refers to "the day of his visitation," which probably refers to the Christ's second coming and the judgment that ensues (cf. Ex 32:34; Is 10:3; Jer 6:15; 10:15; 11:23; Wis 3:7-8; Lk 1:68; 19:44; *1 Clem.* 2.3), in which case Peter is saying, You may win God's eternal praise by the witness of your life at the day of his return.[239] We should likely see 1 Peter 3:16 as a parallel here, in which case the point is that believers are not shamed when Christ comes back, but those who vilify Christians will be put to shame.[240] It is thus vital to obey and have a good witness not just for one's own sake, but also for the sake of those who are watching the Christians. Peter at a minimum is hoping for tolerance and less abuse, but occasionally there are also hints that he thinks good Christian conduct can transform a pagan so that they embrace Christ. Achtemeier is right to stress that Peter assumes the possibility of conduct that both Christians and non-Christians would recognize as good. This makes clear that Peter does not take a purely binary approach to Greco-Roman society.[241]

---

[237]Cranfield, *First Peter,* pp. 54-55.

[238]See Elliott, *1 Peter,* p. 470.

[239]Though the phrase could refer to the immediate impact of the witness on these pagans and would mean something like "on the day that he was visited by the illumination and transformation of the Spirit and became a Christian."

[240]There are more than enough references to the day of judgment in 1 Peter to make this interpretation of the "visitation" to be likely (cf. 1:5, 7, 13; 4:7, 13, 17; 5:1). See Jobes, *1 Peter,* p. 172.

[241]Achtemeier, *1 Peter,* p. 177.

First Peter 2:12 speaks quite specifically about conduct "before non-Jews" *(ethnesin)*. Donald P. Senior says this merely means all those outside the community, all non-Christians.[242] This is unlikely, since clearly enough there were Jews outside these communities as well whom we could not say to be "of the nations." It is far more likely that we have here a clue not only that the author is Jewish, but also that the audience is viewed as overwhelmingly Jewish Christian as well.[243] It is not adequate to talk about "Peter's consistent way of referring to his Gentile Christian readers *as though they were Jews*."[244]

Now in **1 Peter 2:13**, after 1 Peter 2:11-12 has enunciated the principle about good Christian behavior, we begin what may be called the duty or social code section of the epistle, urging deference or possibly submission to rulers, masters, and husbands.[245] This is seen as one manifestation of good and godly Christian conduct. Leonhard Goppelt is exactly right that we must recognize the differences between what is going on here and what we find in the so-called household codes in Colossians and Ephesians. Here the focus is not primarily on Christians' relationships to each other, within the household structure. Rather, "1 Peter has in mind individual Christians in the institutions of a non-Christian society that discriminates against them."[246] Thus Peter starts with the largest institution: government; then he moves down to the largest economic unit: slave labor; finally he speaks to the smallest unit of society: marriage and family. Compared to Ephesians and Colossians, "in 1 Peter the sequence is reversed, moving from the civil order surrounding all society to the smallest unit, marriage."[247]

In other words, Peter is dealing with the interface between individual Christian lives and pagan society. Why does he concentrate on the subordinate member in certain relationships? Because "for them the tie to non-Christians is especially problematic. The relationship of children to parents is left out since Christian children of non-Christian parents would be hardly thinkable in the situation at hand."[248] The atmosphere or ethos out of which this teaching comes is one of threat, slander, persecution, danger to the Christian community, not from within, but at its interface with larger society. What is given thus is advice about conduct under such circumstances, with the desire to keep the commu-

[242] Senior, *1 Peter,* p. 65.
[243] But see Senior, "Conduct of Christians in the World," pp. 427-38.
[244] Michaels, *1 Peter,* p. 117, emphasis added.
[245] For the recent German discussion on the household codes, see Feldmeier, *Der erste Brief des Petrus,* pp. 102-28.
[246] Goppelt, *1 Peter,* p. 164.
[247] Ibid.
[248] Ibid., p. 165.

nity intact and continuing in its witness to the world, all the while minimizing the causes for abuse of Christians. Equally, we may notice the difference between what is going on here, and what we find in Romans 13, written at an earlier time in Nero's reign. Here there is no hint of suggesting that God has set up the Roman system or given it the divine imprimatur. The emperor is treated as a subset of the class called "every human creature," a not-so-subtle critique of the growing importance of the emperor cult in the regions addressed. As Achtemeier says, while there is some similarity of vocabulary between what we find here and Romans 13, the arguments and emphases go in different directions and do not suggest literary dependence one way or the other.[249] Elliott adds that the differences between the two texts are significant, particularly in 1 Peter: (1) there is no mention of taxes, (2) no reference to divine wrath, (3) no reference to governing officials being God's servants, and (4) the discussion of "fear" is in relationship to God, not governors.[250]

The first segment of this paragraph deals with rulers directly, but probably we should see 1 Peter 2:13 as a general introduction to this section, paralleling 1 Peter 2:17a, "Show honor/respect to all." First Peter 2:13a is sometimes translated, "Submit to all human institutions," but this will hardly do because *ktisis* in the Bible refers to creation or its human element as creatures. The notion that this refers to "human institutions" has no basis in all of Greek literature, and the examples that follow are all human individuals: emperors, proconsuls, masters.[251] Thus we must translate, "Defer/be subordinate to every human being" for the Lord's sake. It is possible that Peter says, "every creature" here to emphasize that even the emperor is just a creature, just another human being, and in principle one shows him no more respect or deference than one would show to other human beings.[252] It may be significant that Peter uses the word "king" *(basileus)* here rather than "emperor" *(kaisar)*. This was the preferred term in the Greek-speaking east, particularly in Anatolia. One other corollary is worth mentioning: If Peter says, "Subject yourself/show deference and respect to every human creature," as I think he does, this exhortation is hardly gender specific either in its object or in its performer. All Christians are to do this, and the object of this behavior is all other human beings. Thus, this does indeed parallel closely what is said in 1 Peter 2:17a.

What does this deference or submission amount to? Obviously it does not

---

[249]Achtemeier, *1 Peter,* pp. 180-82.

[250]Elliott, *1 Peter,* p. 493.

[251]See ibid., pp. 486-87; Achtemeier, *1 Peter,* p. 182.

[252]See Marshall, *1 Peter,* pp. 82-83, and the notes.

amount to doing anything that contravenes God's will because the believer is called to do it for his sake (cf. Rom 13:1-7; 1 Tim 2:1-3; Tit 3:1-3). *Kyrios* (Lord) here probably refers to God the Father, not Jesus, as the one who created human beings. If "Lord" means Jesus, the implication would be, Do this as a witness for Christ. More likely it means, "Do this because these are creatures God made, and you are to serve and witness to them." The verb *hypotagēte* is in the aorist, meaning "start deferring/subordinating," and is an action taken up voluntarily by people whom the Lord has set free. The verb *hypotassō* has the literal sense of ordering oneself under another or under a group of others, in this case governing officials. It is found nowhere in classical Greek, and only 1 Chronicles 29:23-24 LXX is of relevance when the subject is deference or submission to governing authorities. Notice that the term "obedience" *(hypakoē)* or "obey" *(hypakouō)* is not used for this relationship but rather is reserved for one's relationship with God (1 Pet 1:2, 14, 22).[253] The Christian is always to do God's will (1 Pet 2:15) because God would never ask of his creatures something immoral or inappropriate. But here it appears that "God's will" refers to the doing of good, not the divine ordering of government. All of these exhortations are grounded on the premise that Christians are "free" (1 Pet 2:16) in themselves to either be a good Christian witness or not, to either defer to governing authorities or not. Wolfgang Schrage aptly sums up Peter's view: "They are free with respect to the authorities, and *normally* this freedom manifests itself in respect and loyalty, submission and honor."[254] With this background we can now examine things in a bit more detail.

First Peter 2:14 is somewhat ambiguous. Are the *hēgemones* sent by God, or does this actually refer to their being sent by the emperor as governors and proconsuls to the various provinces? Donald P. Senior argues convincingly that since 1 Peter 2:13-14 is part of one sentence, it is likely the latter: the emperor has sent these governors to the provinces to administer justice.[255] A good example of this very language is found in Josephus (*Ant.* 17.314), where the Judean Jews asked to be freed from the rule of Herod Archelaus and "be made subject *[hypotassesthai]* to the governors sent there."

What about the phrase "the will of God," which follows in **1 Peter 2:15**? Does it refer to the divine authority of the governors and king? It would appear

---

[253]For a survey of usage, see Elliott, *1 Peter,* pp. 486-88.

[254]Wolfgang Schrage, *The Ethics of the New Testament,* trans. David E. Green (Philadelphia: Fortress, 1988), p. 278.

[255]See Senior, *1 Peter,* p. 69.

not since it seems to go with what follows (see below). This being the case, Peter, possibly unlike what we find in Romans 13, does not speak of the divine authority of these rulers.[256] They are simply creatures who should be honored and respected and deferred to, but not feared and revered, and not obeyed unconditionally, as God is to be obeyed. This posture is interesting and stands somewhere between what Paul wrote about government in Romans 13 and what the author of Revelation thinks about the emperor and his minions after considerable persecution.

If, as we think, Peter wrote this letter, what follows is notable because Nero was indeed a perverse emperor; at least he did some perverse things to some Christians in the period following the fire in A.D. 64.[257] Peter may be writing at the very inception of all this, before Nero's true character came fully to light. Emperors (literally, "kings") were supreme; but even governors are probably seen by Peter as sent by God for administering a basic reward-and-punishment system (noting the passive voice of "are sent" in 1 Pet 2:14).[258] This is, of course, the basic function of any government: to maintain law and order and to judge justly. With regard to the functions of a Roman proconsul, Edward Gordon Selwyn notes:

> [According to] *Digest* i.16.9, a Roman proconsul was concerned not only with the suppression of crime but [also] with the promotion of deference on the part of subordinates, e.g., children and freedmen, to their elders and betters, much as a colonial governor in British territories is concerned with social behaviour today. St. Peter and St. Paul are one in their teaching here, and what they teach is of great importance for Christian political philosophy; for they insist that the State is concerned not only with living, . . . or as we say with men as economic units, but [also] with the good life, . . . i.e., with men as political and moral beings. In so doing, they give us the standard Christian interpretation of the *verbum Christi*, "Render

[256]See Michaels, *1 Peter*, p. 126.

[257]For a good and fair assessment of the reign of Nero, see Miriam T. Griffin, *Nero: The End of a Dynasty* (New Haven: Yale University Press, 1985), pp. 125-33, on the fire and its aftermath. The important point is that it was not immediately after the fire that Christians were blamed. This only happened somewhat later, when there were suggestions that Nero himself had had the fire set. To deflect the criticism, Nero found his scapegoat and took a further step down the ladder into tyranny. This in turn means that we should place the martyrdoms of Peter and Paul in the period A.D. 65-67, before Nero's death in 68. In assessing Peter's advice here, one must remember that the first five years of Nero's reign had been good, steered as they were by Seneca the philosopher. Peter is writing in the wake of that, but may see trouble on the horizon. Since there is no mention of Paul in this document, we must assume he has been set free from house arrest and gone back east, an event that seems to have transpired in A.D. 62. On the timing of Paul's release and the writing of the Pastorals, see Witherington, *Letters and Homilies for Hellenized Christians*, 1:49-79.

[258]See McKnight, *1 Peter*, pp. 144-45, and the notes.

unto Caesar" etc. Emil Brunner's statement *(The Divine Imperative)* that "in its reality the State is always organized selfishness" is true; but since the alternative is anarchy in greater or less degree, its functions are necessary to the diffusion of the good life.[259]

First Peter 2:15 begins with ***houtōs,*** which could look back to what has just been said. A government offering of rewards and punishments for good and bad conduct is God's will. But Ernest Best suggests that it may also refer to what follows: God's will is that Christians silence the calumnies of foolish and ignorant people by doing what is good and right.[260] There is a good possibility that Peter is referring here to some Christians' ability to "do the good." Bruce Winter has shown that this phrase normally refers to benefactions, the doing of civic good. What would they entail? "Benefactions included supplying grains in times of necessity by diverting the grain-carrying ships to the city, forcing down the price by selling it in the market below the asking rate, erecting public buildings or adorning old buildings with marble revetments such as in Corinth, refurbishing the theatre, widening roads, helping in the construction of public utilities, going on embassies to gain privileges for the city, and helping in the city in times of civil upheaval."[261] One must bear in mind that this whole region was often subject to earthquakes and the devastation they caused, both then and now. Christians would frequently have opportunity to help towns and cities overcome adversity in this region.

If Winter is right, and I am inclined to think he is, this tells us, as does the discussion of women's clothing, that there are some rather high-status Christians among the audience of this circular document. W. C. van Unnik is in agreement with Winter. He says that the reference to the "do-gooders" in 1 Peter 2:14-15 must signify more than just those who obey the law and act as expected. "It is well known that *euergetai* (= *agathopoiountes*) of Greek communities were often honored by tablets in the marketplace extolling the great services they rendered to the State. Therefore, something more than doing one's duty is implied here; it means people who do something deserving a special distinction."[262] Thus we are dealing with persons of some social status capable of doing public "liturgies" (acts of civic benefaction), for which they would perhaps receive an honorary

---

[259]Selwyn, *First Peter,* pp. 172-73. Here he is following Charles Briggs, *A Critical and Exegetical Commentary on the Epistles of St. Peter and St. Jude,* 2nd ed., ICC (Edinburgh: T & T Clark, 1902).

[260]Best, *1 Peter,* p. 115.

[261]Winter, *Seek the Welfare of the City,* p. 37. See the additional comment by Rosalinde A. Kearsley in *NewDocs* 7:240.

[262]Van Unnik, "The Teaching of Good Works in 1 Peter," *NTS* 1 (1954-1955): 92-110.

plaque or column.[263] Campbell notes: "Giving public distinction *(epainos)* to benefactors is a role of the Roman ruler. If the Christians of Asia Minor work for the public good, the official commendations that they receive will silence the ignorant criticisms of their foolish accusers."[264]

Peter in **1 Peter 2:16** recognizes a Christian's ultimate freedom from the world, for they are sons and daughters of the kingdom (Mt 17:26). But he says, "Do not use that as a pretext or 'cloak' or 'guise' to do evil; rather, act as God's servants and be his witness to the world and serve the government and people he placed in your world," which is quite similar to what we find in Galatians 5:13. Various moralists of the age spoke of inner freedom and stated that it was something even a slave could have. Epictetus, both a Stoic and a former slave, says, "He is free who lives as he wills, who is subject neither to compulsion, nor hindrance, nor force, whose choices are unhampered, whose desires attain their end, whose aversions do not fall into what they would avoid" (Epictetus *Disc.* 4.1.1-2). On this basis he goes on to discuss how a slave can be more free (of the impulse of the passions) than his master.

Christian service and citizenship are done not because believers are earthly citizens but because they must serve God, and God ordained the state and governors. Christians serve them in obedience to God, and where there is a conflict, they must serve God alone. Martin Luther put it well: "A Christian is a perfectly free lord of all, subject to none. A Christian is a perfectly dutiful servant of all, subject to all."[265] Jobes puts it equally aptly: "The 'certain star' to which all our acts and words as Christians must have reference is not the Supreme Good of Greek philosophy but the Supreme God revealed in Jesus Christ."[266] We should not see this material as lightly Christianized Greco-Roman ethics.

First Peter 2:17 is a general summary statement before going on to the next section. Believers are called to honor or respect everyone, which includes slaves, who had little or no honor and no rights in society; but believers must go beyond that in special brotherly affection for fellow Christians. The term *adelphotēs,* "brotherhood," is rare, and we will find it again at 1 Peter 5:9 (cf. 1 Pet 5:13) but not elsewhere in the New Testament, nor is it normally used of

---

[263] I am not arguing that the term "doing good" in itself is a technical term for benefaction. Its use in 2:20; 3:6, 17, applying it to wives and even slaves, suggests a broader meaning, as Jobes, *1 Peter,* p. 175, points out. However, good deeds observed by rulers is surely a reference to a quite public act, a benefaction to society. As such, this must be included in what Peter means by doing good in this discourse.

[264] Campbell, *Honor, Shame,* p. 112.

[265] John Dillenberger, ed., *Martin Luther: Selections from His Writings* (Garden City, N.Y.: Doubleday, 1961), p. 53.

[266] Jobes, *1 Peter,* p. 182.

"spiritual" kinship outside Christian literature. We do find this unusual term in *1 Clement* (2.4) and in the Shepherd of Hermas (Herm. *Mand.* 8.10), suggesting that it was a term used in the Roman church to describe the relationship between Christians.[267] Peter may have inaugurated this usage, based on what he learned from Jesus about the concept of the family of faith. Brotherly affection must be done in the context of reverence for God. Peter concludes with "Show honor to the emperor." He does not insist that believers love him in the same way they love fellow Christians, but they are called to honor or respect him. Peter does not insist that Christians agree with everything the ruler says, but just submit to his rule. Here we may echo Cranfield's remarks:

> At this point we must notice a significant difference between the situation envisaged by the New Testament writers and our own. They were thinking in terms of an authoritarian State, which was the only form of State they had to deal with, and therefore regard the citizen solely as a subject, whose duty to the State was mainly passive, a matter of obedience and paying taxes. We live under a different form of State—a democracy, which needs from its citizens not merely respect for authority and submission to taxation, but [also] an active and responsible cooperation. The citizen is not merely a subject; he actually shares in the responsibility of government. We have no reason to think that a democracy is any less acceptable to God as a form of human State than an authoritarian State. On the contrary, there are reasons for thinking that democracy agrees better with the Christian understanding of man.[268]

We must also note that God is alone said to be the object of "fear" or reverence. Not even slaves are called to "reverence" their earthly masters, just to serve them. As Achtemeier puts it, "The concluding verse of this section thus establishes a hierarchy of values and allegiances: all people, including the emperor, are to be shown due honor and respect; fellow Christians are to be regarded as members of one's own family and shown appropriate love; God alone is to be shown reverence."[269] The structure here is that of a chiasm, with external relationships referred to in the "honor" clauses at the beginning and end, and internal relations ("Love the brotherhood" and "Revere God") in the middle.[270]

Various people at various times have been deeply disturbed by the apparent selling out of the gospel in an attempt to live peacefully in a fallen world. Nowhere has this issue been more seriously and severely debated than in the context of the New Testament passages on slavery. How, it is argued, could one

---

[267]See Elliott, *1 Peter,* pp. 499-500.
[268]Cranfield, *First Peter,* p. 60.
[269]Achtemeier, *1 Peter,* p. 188.
[270]See Elliott, *1 Peter,* p. 497.

like Paul or Peter, who affirm that God has set people free from the effects of sin, have acquiesced to the reprehensible institution of slavery? These are serious questions, and they deserve a serious answer, though any answer will be partial at best. We need to see the discussion about slaves in the larger context of the discussion about social relations and duties in those relationships. There is a tension in this material admirably described by Elliott:

> Where respect for authority and order is possible without compromise of one's loyalty to God, this respect ("honor" and "subordination") is appropriate. Where, however, adaptation to societal values and norms endangers exclusive commitment to God, Christ, and the brotherhood and obliterates the distinctive identity and boundaries of the Christian community, Christians are to stand fast and resist the encroachments of society, behind which stands the Devil (1 Pet 5:8-9). Keeping open the channels of communication between believers and nonbelievers is not to be confused with advocacy of social assimilation (against Balch). Contacts between believers and nonbelievers are to be utilized as an opportunity for demonstrating the honorable character of the Christians and their God and are essential for recruitment to the Christian faith."[271]

Even a slave can model Christlikeness, indeed in some respects especially a slave can do so.[272]

We must begin by observing that here we are dealing with the *oiketai,* the household or domestic slaves, and in relationship to non-Christian masters (cf. 1 Tim 6:1-2; Ign. *Pol.* 4.3). The focus here is quite narrow and specific. Furthermore, it is noteworthy that slaves are addressed at all in these Christian codes, because in the Greco-Roman codes they were not addressed. Here they are treated as persons capable of moral discernment, which is the opposite end of the spectrum from classical theory, which treated them simply as property lacking the essential qualifications of humanity.[273]

One of the best sources for the study of this issue is S. Scott Bartchy's work.[274] It now needs to be supplemented by the work of J. Albert Harrill.[275] We can only summarize briefly some of their remarks, but it will be well if we start by a caution

---

[271]Ibid., p. 510.

[272]The suggestion that the advice to slaves here betrays a later, postapostolic period is simply nonsense. In the earliest Christian period, there were Christian slaves whose masters were not yet converted, as a close reading of the Pauline corpus shows (see, e.g., 1 Cor 7; Philem 11 and 16; Col 3—4) shows. But see *NewDocs.* 7:195.

[273]Judge, *Social Pattern of the Christian Groups,* p. 28.

[274]S. Scott Bartchy, *[Mallon chrēsai]: First-Century Slavery and 1 Corinthians 7:21,* SBLDS 11 (Missoula, Mont.: Society of Biblical Literature for the Seminar on Paul, 1973).

[275]J. Albert Harrill, *Slaves in the New Testament: Literary, Moral and Social Dimensions* (Minneapolis: Fortress, 2006).

from Pheme Perkins: "First Peter never says that it is right for a master to beat his slaves irrationally, but that it is a common fact of life. Rebellious behavior would not gain anything. Therefore, 1 Peter counsels taking Christ as one's model and submitting to such treatment. This exhortation is a way of gaining what dignity and honor the oppressed slave can from the situation. It does not claim that the situation itself is ideal."[276] Peter is a sensible enough pastor to help his charges make the best of a bad situation, trying to alleviate the problem while figuring out what would be the best witness to the non-Christian involved in the situation.

A CLOSER LOOK

Domestic Slavery and First Peter

In the first place, first-century slavery is not to be identified with the agricultural slavery of the southern United States in the eighteenth and nineteenth centuries. In the latter institution, there was no real hope of manumission for the vast majority of slaves, because it was illegal in most states; this was not the case in first-century slavery, where it was a frequent and viable alternative. Indeed, many ancients deliberately chose to become slaves because they knew it was often not a permanent condition in life, and indeed could lead not only to their manumission but also to their becoming Roman citizens. One could see it as a temporary expedient on the way to a better life.[277] Second, in 1 Peter and also in Paul we are not talking about agricultural slavery but, as I have already stressed, household slaves, whose situation was usually much better than that of those who were slaves in agricultural or industrial settings. Indeed, as S. Scott Bartchy makes clear, it was often the case that if one had a good master, a person would be much better off financially, economically, and otherwise than they would be if they were a poor freedman or woman. Slavery was the very foundation of ancient society and economy, including as slaves up to a third of the population in some parts of the empire, particularly in urban regions. Practically speaking, to counsel a total rejection of slavery would have been suicidal for Christianity, and the alternative—a world full of poor, often very poor, freed persons—was likely worse. Cranfield stresses:

> Many of them were well-educated; the doctors, schoolmasters, secretaries, clerks would normally be slaves. Those employed in the labour-gangs lived under appalling conditions and were literally worked to death with the utmost heartlessness. But the lot of *domestic* slaves was usually very much better, and the abominable cruelties we sometimes

[276]Perkins, *First Peter,* p. 46.
[277]See McKnight, *1 Peter,* p. 165.

> hear of were exceptional. Quite often there was real affection between master and slave. But the slave had no rights. He was a mere chattel. He could be tortured or put to death by his master for any offence or for no offence. The normal method of execution for a slave was crucifixion. In court his evidence was only valid if given under torture. His marriage had no legal force; his children belonged to his master. When old or sick, and so no longer useful, he might be left to die of exposure. Slavery was taken for granted as something natural. . . . But it must be remembered that they were for the most part addressing slaves, and to denounce the system to them would have been either useless or else much worse; for the slaves had no peaceful constitutional way of protesting and if they attempted to free themselves, that could only mean a bitter and futile servile war. Such servile wars there had been, as for instance that generally called the Second Servile War, in which a force of 40,000 slaves had been defeated by Lucullus; but the result was always the same, the slaves were defeated, and then the roads far and wide were lined with crosses bearing the rotting bodies of the slaves, and afterwards masters were all the more oppressive and vindictive, fearing a fresh outbreak. To incite Christian slaves—or pagan slaves, for that matter—to revolt would have been to condemn them to certain death, and to increase the hardships and sufferings of those who did not revolt.[278]

In addition to this S. Scott Bartchy points out that none of the great slave revolts of 140-170 B.C. were attempts to *abolish* slavery because even slaves saw it as an indispensable way of life. Bartchy adds:

> To the contrary, those who had been owners were forced into slavery, and the homes and workshops remained private property in the hands, then, of the former slaves. In addition, it is significant that none of the authors who had been in slavery, whose works are known to us, attacked the institution in which they had once lived. They did write about the behavior (bad or good) of individual owners and slaves, but they never counseled the slaves to rebel. Indeed, no freedman-author comes near championing either slaves or freedmen as groups in themselves.[279] . . . By no means was the slave's position always a "subordinate" one, for in the household he served not only as cook, cleaner or personal attendant but also as tutor of persons of all ages, doctor, nurse, or close companion. In business he was not only delivery-boy and jan-

[278]Cranfield, *First Peter,* pp. 62-64, excerpts.
[279]Bartchy, *First-Century Slavery,* pp. 63-64.

> itor, he was also secretary or manager of estates and shops and ships, contracting as an agent for his owner. Often he joined in partnership with his owner or others on the basis of his *peculium*. In the handcraft factories he was not only fuel-carrier and artisan, he was also foreman and salesman. In the civil service he was not only a part of the street-paving gang or the sewer-cleaning department, he was also an administrator of funds and personnel and an executive with decision-making power. Indeed, during the first century, slaves and freedmen became the most important part of the Roman administrative force.[280]

In his handling of the "household codes" in the New Testament, J. Albert Harrill takes a very different tact than one finds in most commentaries. He argues that there is actually nothing very unique or special about the forms of these domestic codes as we find them in the New Testament. He sees them as adaptations of the ancient agricultural handbooks that address slaves directly and remind the local farm master of his obligation to the owner of the farm, the paterfamilias.[281] There are two methodological problems with this: (1) In no place in the New Testament are agricultural slaves discussed or addressed. It is always domestic slaves. This is especially clear in 1 Peter where the term *oiketai* is used. (2) From the historical evidence, particularly the Roman evidence, we know perfectly well that domestic slaves not only tended to be treated better and differently than agricultural slaves or those who worked in the mines; we also know that most domestic slaves had a reasonable prospect of manumission, and even becoming a freedman member of the wider family, and a Roman citizen, which was certainly beyond the purview of most agricultural slaves. Aristotle himself distinguished between two sorts of slaves: brute laborers and those in position of trust (Aristotle *Oec.* 1.5.1-2; cf. Seneca *Ep.* 47). The fact that many domestic slaves turned down the possibility of manumission shows that they knew perfectly well which choice would be more economically advantageous in their particular situation. In short, Harrill has read the agricultural situation and rules into the urban situation; while there is some overlap and he presents helpful insights, on the whole he has misread the historical evidence, it seems to me. It is striking and unfortunate that Harrill in his extensive study does not at all deal with the household material in 1 Peter. If he had done so, he would have discovered that advice for a religiously mixed household such as we find in 1 Peter takes a form somewhat different than advice for a Christian home, where there can be mutuality and a more egalitarian context, and all members of the family can be addressed as Christians. In 1 Peter

[280]Ibid., p. 73.

[281]Harrill, *Slaves in the New Testament*, p. 86, plus all the discussion on pp. 85-117.

the call to be a witness within the household to non-Christians plays large in what is said. Or as it says in 1 Peter 3:1-2, the reason for the behavior is so that the wives can win their husbands over to the faith. This is, quite frankly, never a motivating factor and indeed never a factor at all in pagan household materials. Just the opposite is true: the subordinate members of the household are expected to conform to the religion of the master.

We must add to this that Paul and Peter and various secular authors were arguing that "inner" freedom or real freedom was the freedom to submit one's own will to God's will, to allow God to direct one's path. In early Christianity, however, there was what can only be called an inner dynamic that gradually undermined such institutions as slavery. It was this: "in Christ there is no slave or freedman, but all are one" (Gal 3:28).[282] This leveling in the Christian community eventually led to leveling in the larger society, in a quiet revolution in some quarters. Early Christians believed that to change institutions, they must first change individuals who run them: this is what Christianity set out to do. Couple this with the belief in the equality of all created and re-created persons in God's image, the belief that Christians could be free in salvation whatever their station or situation in life, and a commitment to nonviolence and no retaliation strongly inculcated by Jesus: all this gives us a basic explanation for the New Testament view of slavery.

In conclusion, slavery was seen as a mere human institution, not one ordained of God, which Christians may have to endure while passing through this life. Its force was seen as mitigated if one was in Christ and in his community. It was at times seen as a lesser of two evils—if poverty was the other option. Nevertheless, it was well known that slaves could be and were abused physically and sexually by brutal masters (Seneca *Ep.* 47), and slaves were basically viewed as property without rights. This was far from ideal; indeed, it was the parade example of a fallen, all-too-human institution. The Christian response to slavery was to concentrate on changing people and to let other changes flow out of that salvation change. This is hardly what we would call Marxist liberation theology, which ignores Jesus' maxim "Those who live by the sword shall perish by it." It is a rather more subtle means of leavening the lump of society with Christians and the gospel, which nonetheless could lead someone to say, "These are the men who have turned the world upside down" (Acts 17:6). Indeed, by the time of Constantine, Christianity had begun to take over the empire in many regards. Let us look at what Peter says in light of all the above.

[282]See the discussion of Philemon in Witherington, *Philemon, Colossians, and Ephesians*.

First Peter 2:18 begins with a general exhortation, as did 1 Peter 2:13. All household slaves are to submit themselves to the master of the house, whether he is good and considerate or "crooked," which is the literal meaning of *skoliois*. This submission is to be offered in all respect, regardless of the treatment one receives in response. It is thus a matter of principle and of being proactive rather than reactive, and it is also a witnessing tactic, as we shall see. Peter recognizes that there is such a thing as unjust treatment of slaves; in contrast, Aristotle thought no true injustice could be done to slaves since they were property.[283] Peter views slaves as persons and wants them treated as such, persons capable of a relationship with God and moral decision making.

There is debate about the referent of the phrase "in all fear." Leonhard Goppelt thinks it refers to fear of God (on *phobos* in LXX, cf. Gen 31:42, 53; Ex 20:20; Neh 5:9; Prov 1:7, 29), which is possible, but the natural reference is the *despotais* in the clause that follows.[284] Still, 1 Peter 2:17 may suggest otherwise.

First Peter 2:19 begins with the phrase "for this is *charis*," which probably means "a credit to you" or "commendable"; it does not likely mean grace here, as it does elsewhere in the New Testament.[285] Peter then speaks in terms of a real condition: "If you bear grief, suffering unjustly, this is to your credit" (*ei* plus the present tense verb indicates a real condition, not a hypothetical one). The phrase *dia syneidēsin theou* is difficult. Does it mean (1) "through the conscience of God" (a literal rendering)? (2) "through consciousness or awareness of God"?[286] (3) "through common knowledge of God"? In favor of the first translation is the fact that elsewhere in the New Testament and in 1 Peter 3:16, 21 the word *syneidēsis* usually means "conscience." But the problem here is that we cannot be talking about God's conscience, and that is normally how one would have to construe the genitive, as here. Edward Gordon Selwyn has suggested the translation "for conscience sake before God," but this seems to make the phrase "of God" an unnecessary added extra (cf. the textual variants where it is left out).[287] At this point the argument can go either way, but perhaps it is best to see view 2 or view 3—which amounts to saying, "being conscious of God" ("being aware he is taking note of your behavior")—as the most likely rendering. Yet view 1, though awkward, is not impossible.[288] Notice the use of the

[283]See Jobes, *1 Peter,* p. 188.
[284]Goppelt, *1 Peter,* p. 194.
[285]Selwyn, *First Peter,* p. 178; Elliott, *1 Peter,* p. 518.
[286]See Senior, *1 Peter,* p. 75; Achtemeier, *1 Peter,* p. 196.
[287]Selwyn, *First Peter,* p. 179.
[288]See Kelly, *Epistles of Peter,* p. 117; Best, *1 Peter,* p. 118.

word *tis* here. The advice to slaves is actually advice to all Christians: all should be prepared to suffer unjustly.

In **1 Peter 2:20** Peter goes on to say that there is certainly no glory in suffering quietly when one deserves a beating from having done wrong. Creditable or grace-filled *(charis)* behavior in God's eyes is when one suffers for or with the doing of what is right. The focus is on doing right here, not on developing a martyr complex or seeking out suffering. Here is advice on how to bear it, if it does come, even if it is unjust punishment. Peter assumes this to be really happening (*ei* plus the verb). Such patience and suffering, even if one is wronged, is what Christians (not just slaves) are called to.[289] The context may suggest that he is simply talking about suffering "in house," at the hands of one's master. Here, really for the first time, Peter begins to broach the subject of suffering, which is to be a major theme throughout the rest of the discourse (*paschein,* as in 2:20-21, 23; 3:14, 17, 18; 4:1, 15, 19; 5:10). Twelve of the forty-one occurrences of this verb for suffering occur here in 1 Peter, as do four of the sixteen occurrences of the cognate noun, *pathēma* (1:11; 4:13; 5:1, 9). It is obvious that how Christians will respond to suffering is a major concern of Peter.

Not accidentally or incidentally, grace is also a major concern of 1 Peter. In fact Leonhard Goppelt says, "No other New Testament document appropriates this technical term as densely and in a similarly broad variety of usage as does 1 Peter."[290] It begins at the very outset of the letter in 1 Peter 1:2, where we have the wish or request for grace. The God of this discourse is called the God of all grace (1 Pet 5:10), even to the extent of bringing the believer to the eschatological finish line where grace is once more encountered (1 Pet 1:13). This grace bestows new life in the first place (1 Pet 3:7), is given to the humble (1 Pet 5:5), and becomes the essence of what is proclaimed in the gospel message (1 Pet 1:10). It is interesting that outside of the Pauline corpus, only in 1 Peter do we have the mention and discussion of *charismata* (1 Pet 4:10). In sum, Peter has a full-orbed theology of grace comparable to that of Paul.

Peter does not mention slaves by name after 1 Peter 2:18. This is advice for all such Christian household members, including slaves. They must remember that Christ "suffered" (not "died" here)[291] for you, leaving behind an example, so believers might follow in his footsteps. Here Peter sees Christ's suffering as vicarious. It is *"for us."* This may mean just for believers' benefit, but as we shall see, it is also

---

[289]The later discussions (as in Ign. *Pol.* 4.3; *Did.* 4.10; *Barn.* 19.7) reinforce the need for Christian masters to treat their slaves equitably, but they do not really advance the principles of Christian freedom as espoused in Philemon.

[290]Goppelt, *1 Peter,* p. 200.

[291]See Metzger, *TC,* p. 690.

Peter's view that Christ's suffering was in place of "us," as a substitute. This call for slaves to imitate Christ becomes a general call for all Christians in 1 Peter 3:9.

Beginning with **1 Peter 2:21** we have something of a meditation on Isaiah 53:4-12 LXX. Scholars have debated whether Peter here is taking over some source, but probably Elliott is right that the poetic diction of Isaiah 53 has inspired the more exalted prose of this little paragraph.[292] In any case it was customary in Asiatic rhetoric to increase the eloquence when one reached a crucial passage in a discourse, and this is such a passage. This meditation is framed by references to the believer's conversion (1 Peter 2:21, 25). First Peter 2:22 directly quotes Isaiah 53:9b LXX, and there are quite clear allusions to Isaiah 53:4 and 12b in 1 Peter 2:24 (e.g., "He bore our sins"). We thus can see 1 Peter 2:23 as a reformulation of Isaiah 53:7 about the silence of the sheep before their slaughterers, making it applicable to the experience of persecuted Christians. We can also point directly to 1 Peter 2:24, where we have the quote "by whose wounds you have been healed" (Is 53:5b), but note the shift from Isaiah's first person plural to the second person plural. Peter does not follow the order of the narrative in Isaiah 53, and here the result of Christ's passion is healing of sinners.[293] The reference to the shepherd and sheep probably echoes Isaiah 53:5-6, but there is also another intertextual echo here that rounds out the brief passage, drawing on Ezekiel 34:5-16, the promise about God the shepherd looking after his sheep. In this case Christ is the shepherd in 1 Peter 2:25.[294] The passage thus strikingly ends with an allusion to a word of comfort to resident alien Jews in Babylon, now applied to Peter's resident alien Jewish Christians in Anatolia.[295]

We are now prepared to look at these crucial verses in some detail, bearing in mind what I. Howard Marshall says about its importance: "Here then is the fundamental theological statement of the basis of the Christian life in terms of the death of Jesus. It becomes obvious that Christ cannot be an example of suffering for us to follow unless he is first of all the Savior whose sufferings were endured on our behalf."[296] Finally, it is worth noting that Clement of Rome offers an exact quotation of Isaiah 53:1-12 LXX in *1 Clement* 16.3-14, which suggests that the church from which Peter is writing did some rather serious reflection on this Old Testament passage in the last third of the first century A.D., and clearly Clement's citation shows that the LXX form of the text was known in Rome.[297]

---

[292]See Elliott, *1 Peter,* pp. 543-50.
[293]See the discussion of Achtemeier, "Suffering Servant and Suffering Christ," pp. 176-88.
[294]See Jobes, *1 Peter,* pp. 198-99.
[295]See the discussion in Perkins, *First Peter,* pp. 54-55.
[296]Marshall, *1 Peter,* p. 91.
[297]See Michaels, *1 Peter,* p. 136.

There is something quite interesting about this meditation that we should note at the outset. This is the only place in the New Testament where Isaiah 53 is so explicitly referred to the death of Jesus as a way of explaining that death. Jobes even suggests that we may owe to Peter himself the insight that Christ's passion is specifically referred to in Isaiah 53. She may well be right. Of the six direct quotes of Isaiah 52:13–53:12 in the New Testament (Mt 8:17; Lk 22:37; Jn 12:38; Acts 8:32-33; Rom 10:16; 15:21), only two of them are used by others in reference to Jesus in particular (the Acts 8 quote and here). In Acts 8:32-33 there is no actual meditation as here (in 1 Pet 2) on Jesus and the relating of this passage to Jesus and his sacrifice. "We are thus indebted to the apostle Peter alone for his distinctive Christological use of the Suffering Servant passage to interpret the significance of the suffering and death of Jesus. The Suffering Servant Christology may even have originated with Peter, possibly based on Jesus' teaching."[298]

First Peter 2:21 uses some interesting language to describe the example of Christ. First of all, we have the term *hypogrammos,* which refers to the exact pattern of alphabetic letters, impressed on a wax tablet, which children copied or traced so as to learn their letters. The patterns of the letters was impressed into the wax so that the children could copy them, learning how to form their ABC's (cf. 2 Macc 2:28; Clement of Alexandria *Strom.* 5.8.49; cf. *1 Clem.* 5.7; 16.17; 33.8).[299] Second, the word "steps" appears in this verse. The image is of walking behind someone and literally following in their footsteps (cf. Philo *Virt.* 64).[300] The verb here is in an intensified form, *epakolouthēsēte,* producing the meaning "follow closely," as a disciple (cf. Rev 14:4).[301] The essence of ancient education was following good models, imitating or copying them, and repetition to the point of memorization. The most basic idea here is the patient endurance of unjust suffering, of which Christ is the model. Nothing is said here about seeking martyrdom or suffering, nor even about suffering being the will of God for the audience's life. Peter is saying, "If it comes, let it be for a just cause, and therefore be an unjust form of suffering, not the sort that amounts to punishment for wrongs done." Finally, we should also note that the verb *paschein* sometimes has specific reference to the death of Christ, not merely his preliminary suffering (cf. Lk 22:15; 24:26, 46; Acts 1:3; 3:18; 17:3; Heb 9:26; 13:12), though it can also

---

[298]Jobes, *1 Peter,* p. 193. See Bellinger and Farmer, *Jesus and the Suffering Servant.* There is surprisingly little discussion of this passage in 1 Peter in this volume, though the focus of the volume is supposed to be on Jesus.

[299]See Michaels, *1 Peter,* p. 144.

[300]Goppelt, *1 Peter,* pp. 204-5.

[301]See Senior, *1 Peter,* p. 75.

refer to the sufferings leading up to the death (Mk 8:31; but cf. Heb 2:18 and 5:8, referring to Christ's suffering of temptation or in the Garden of Gethsemane). Christians in 1 Peter not only have sufferings for which the same term is used (1 Pet 5:9-10); they also participate in Christ's sufferings in some sense (1 Pet 4:13). The paralleling of Christ's story and the story of the audience can be seen in this light: just as Christ suffered in the past, so now believers suffer in the present; just as Christ was glorified thereafter, so also believers will one day be glorified. In the meantime believers are to follow the pattern of Christ: (1) Avoid committing sin. (2) Do not retaliate. (3) Bear abuse and injustice. (4) Recognize in Christ's death a healing.[302]

First Peter 2:22 refers to the sinlessness of Christ, a common New Testament teaching.[303] Here indeed was unjust suffering. Jesus had never done wrong, and yet he was experiencing the punishment reserved for the worst slaves and individuals. Peter here and in 1 Peter 2:23-25 is quoting and alluding to Isaiah 53. Christ is seen in light of the Suffering Servant. Some, like Ernest Best, argue that because of the use of Isaiah 53 to describe Christ's passion, this is not likely the testimony of an eyewitness. Several things may be said in response: (1) It is possible that Peter, here and elsewhere in this epistle, makes reference to his own behavior and even his name "Rock" (*petra;* cf. 1 Pet 2:8b). (2) The Gospels do not claim that Peter saw the crucifixion. He is not said to be among those standing at the cross, though he did witness the preliminary events until his denial and disgrace, at which point he broke down and wept. We are not told of his whereabouts until resurrection morning. Possibly he was too distraught or depressed to witness the gruesome spectacle.

Yet (3) **1 Peter 2:23** could be a remembrance of what Peter did see of Jesus' response at or before his trial. There is no reason why he could not have used Scripture to describe what he saw, since he saw Jesus as fulfilling the Scripture, and Scripture said it so much better than this ordinary fisherman. There is nothing here, contra Ernest Best, that argues against Peter as author of this letter.[304] Jesus' response was not just "no retaliation" but also to rest his case in the hands of the one truly fair Judge: God. The implication is that Christians should do likewise. Peter is saying, "Act as Christ did, on Christian principles, not in response to unchristian persecution. Do not react in a way that vitiates your Christian life and witness." This teaching and use of Isaiah 53 implies that Jesus' teaching about not resisting the one who is evil (Mt 5:39) was perhaps derived

[302]See Jobes, *1 Peter,* p. 196.
[303]See the discussion of Christology in 1 Peter above.
[304]See Best, *1 Peter,* pp. 120-21.

from his own reflections on Isaiah 53; yet here it notably is also used as the basis for the disciple's code of conduct as well (cf. 1 Pet 3:9).

First Peter 2:24 gives Peter's view of the atonement in some depth. Christ took up the cross or bore our sins on the cross in his own body: he bore the punishment for our sins.[305] That it is "in his body" stresses Christ's humanity. He was truly human, and redemption came through a real historical person. He suffered too, he suffered unjustly, he suffered for those who deserved to suffer as sinners. Here we may understand sins as a burden that Christ lifts from human beings. Since Isaiah 53 is likely in the background, the implied idea likely is that Christ bore the punishment for human sins *in their stead.* Thus, here we have substitutionary atonement by the Suffering Servant. It is also implied that Jesus takes away human sins, that he heals us. To what end? Not just so humans may experience redemption, but so they may die to sin[306] and live to righteousness, as Christ himself died for sin and lived to righteousness.[307] Christ's death, if one accepts it, requires of us a willingness to go and sin no more, lest one crucify Christ afresh by one's further sins (Heb 6:6). Thus, theology leads to ethics necessarily in 1 Peter. To accept Christ means to agree to follow in his righteous footsteps, and not to crucify him afresh by sinning again.

"By his wounds (welts, weals) we are healed of our sin sickness." Here *mōlōpi* means "weal" and refers to the welts on the body of one who has been whipped, such as a slave (cf. Is 53:5). Philippians 2:7 calls Jesus a suffering slave, and he received a slave's final punishment: crucifixion. What better way to encourage Christian slaves than to say that Jesus voluntarily became a slave for their sake? "He knows what you go through. He's been there too." Sin is also seen here as a disease that affects the whole person, not just one's behavior, but also desires, thought patterns, and so forth. It is a deadly cancer of which a person must be healed—or be lost.

First Peter 2:25 adds that believers are like wandering sheep, who have now turned back to the Shepherd. Perhaps Peter is thinking of his own encounter in John 21, where Jesus said to him, "Feed my sheep." Jesus as the Good Shepherd is an image found also elsewhere (cf. 1 Pet 5:4; John 10:11, 14; Heb 13:20). Christ is the believer's Shepherd and guardian. *Episkopos* refers to an "overseer" and later meant "bishop," but here in application to Christ, not humans, it surely means "overseer, guardian," guardian of ourselves (or possibly our spiritual well-

---

[305]Goppelt, *1 Peter,* p. 213.

[306]The verb *apoginomai* is found only here in the NT. It means to be away from or have no part in something. This seems to be Peter's way of talking about dying to sin. Cf. Rom 6:11.

[307]See Marshall, *1 Peter,* p. 94.

being or life). Interestingly, in 1 Peter 5:2 he will use the verb "shepherd" to refer to Christian leaders. Jesus, however, is the "chief shepherd" and overseer of God's people (1 Pet 5:4). As John H. Elliott notes, the idea of the sheep returning to the Shepherd is not derived from Isaiah 53, but it may come from Ezekiel 34.[308] It is especially appropriate if the "sheep" of Peter's flock here were Jewish.

In **1 Peter 3:1-7** we come to the conclusion of Peter's social code, or the household ethics section of it. We have not really discussed the underlying motivations behind this material, nor its interrelationships with the same sort of material not only in the New Testament but also elsewhere in the first century. Both these issues are vitally important. In general there have been two major sorts of approaches to 1 Peter. Some have seen it as a baptismal homily, a catechetically oriented document, but this trend has waned in the last few decades. Others see it as fundamentally a response to persecution and suffering, with its injunctions conditioned by that context of suffering and persecution. The latter explanation better accords with the content of the letter, though Peter does use various traditional materials in his argument: hymn fragments, Old Testament, Christian teaching, words of Jesus, and so forth. In 1 Peter 2:13—3:7 we are definitely dealing with material that was common to the early Christian Church, not Peter's invention, as shown by glances at 1 Corinthians 14; 1 Timothy 2; Ephesians 5—6; Colossians 3—4; Titus 2; and 1 Peter.[309]

There is an especially close correspondence between 1 Peter 3:3-5 and 1 Timothy 2:9-15 in terms of both vocabulary and substance. We should compare 1 Peter 3:3 to 1 Timothy 2:9 on clothing and hairdressing, 1 Peter 3:4 to 1 Timothy 2:11-12 on the call for quietness, and *ekosmoun* in 1 Peter 3:5 to *kosmiō* and *kosmein* in 1 Timothy 2:9. How do we account for this? It is possible to argue that there is some literary dependency here, but far more likely is the suggestion that both authors are drawing on some standard early Christian teaching.[310]

Peter adopts and adapts this basic Christian teaching to his situation of Christians being persecuted; he urges them to continue to bear witness to their non-Christian family members and neighbors. This raises the question of how much this material is to be seen as prudential or tactical and situational, and how much a matter of principle it is for Peter.

In his helpful monograph, David Balch states:

> Close attention to the text of the household duty code in 1 Peter in its Greco-Roman context enables further specification of the socio-religious situation in which the

---

[308]Elliott, *1 Peter,* p. 537.
[309]See the chart in Selwyn, *First Peter,* p. 432.
[310]See Goppelt, *1 Peter,* pp. 217-18, and the notes.

code functioned. The general situation was similar to the tensions described in chap. V: Greco-Roman society suspected and criticized foreign religions. Many of the Christians addressed by the author had rejected traditional religion (1:18b), and the author exhorted Christians to the kind of behavior that would silence the negative reactions which such conversions generated (2:11-12, 15). The stress on "harmony" in the conclusion of the code (3:8) reveals that the author was especially concerned about divided households: many masters and husbands were still pagans while some slaves and wives had converted to Christianity. In these divided houses, the harmony demanded by the Hellenistic moralists had been disturbed, which was judged to be a negative reflection on the new religion. The author exhorts his readers to make a "defense" (3:15) by reassuring the masters and husbands, perhaps even the governor, that they are obedient slaves and wives, just as the culture expected them to be. Christians are not to exacerbate the situation by meddling in others' domestic affairs (4:15). The readers are warned that governors punish insubordinate persons but are reassured that the authorities praise those who accept their role in the socio-political system (2:14).

The household duty code addressed by the author to this situation is adapted from the Aristotelian topos "concerning household management." He modified the form by addressing the persons in those roles where tension was focused: slaves and wives. As was traditional in certain strands of Platonic and Neopythagorean literature, the author exhorted wives to be submissive. He silently passed over the Greco-Roman expectation that such submission would include worship of the gods of the husband and master. Some of the husbands had not converted, and given the cultural assumptions of that society, they were probably among those persons slandering the converts. The author exhorted the women to submissive, gentle, quiet, chaste behavior, which might gain the husbands for Christ. They were to take Sarah for their model, who was submissive to Abraham, in whose house God had made "peace," and who led Abraham to a higher vision of God. Whatever domestic, social, or political developments might occur, the wives were not to be terrified (3:6).

As Dibelius suggested, the code is paraenetic; it is addressed to Christians, not outsiders. But it was not adopted because eschatological hopes had faded and Christians felt more at home in society. Rather, the code has an apologetic function in the historical context; the paraenesis is given in light of outside criticism. Persons in Roman society were alienated and threatened by some of their slaves and wives who had converted to the new, despised religion, so they were accusing the converts of impiety, immorality, and insubordination. As a defense, the author of 1 Peter encouraged the slaves and wives to play the social roles which Aristotle had outlined; this, he hoped, would shame those who were reviling their good behavior (3:16; 2:12). The conduct of the slaves was not expected to convert masters. However, the author hoped that the wives would convert their husbands by laudable behavior.[311]

[311]Balch, *Let Wives Be Submissive*, pp. 108-9.

This assessment seems to me to largely account for the occasion of this section, but it does not entirely do justice to its function. What Peter advises here is indeed a matter of principle for him. Thus, for instance, submission to governors is simply positive Christian teaching. Submission is not merely because persecution looms; it is also because it is seen as good missionary practice. Further, part of the point of citing the example of Sarah in 1 Peter 3:6 is that this pattern of behavior has a biblical basis, not merely a basis in contemporary culture. Peter is urging these women to conform to the type, and the implication is that the basic behavioral model or conduct or mode of relationship has not and should not change.

Further, here Peter is dealing exclusively with mixed marriages, where tensions obviously exist. He says in 1 Peter 3:1 that "some" disbelieve (disobey), referring to some husbands, not all. Peter thus cannot simply be telling Christian women how to behave toward non-Christian mates, though that is certainly the central thrust of 1 Peter 3:1-2. A woman's actions are to be taken within the context of the "pure reverence of God," not merely because it will prevent abuse by non-Christians. Christian women are to stand on their principles and not be intimidated by hostile mates (cf. 1 Pet 3:6b). Thus we must conclude: (1) This material is a specific application of general Christian social teaching about submission or deference. (2) It is occasioned by Christians being persecuted and partially addresses the Christian–non-Christian tension, but its advice is of value and relevance to a wider context as well. (3) Not only is such behavior to be based on matters of Christian respect and holiness principles, but also the failure to behave in the way described can interfere with one's relationship to God through prayer (1 Pet 3:7b). (4) There is also a missionary motive for at least some of the behavior. It is not all a matter of apologetics, and it certainly is not primarily a matter of accommodation to society in general. Rather, it is a Christian adaptation of the social structures to make it possible for Christians to continue to practice their religion, which includes bearing witness and being a good citizen.

One more thing can be said: Achtemeier is likely right that here the text makes some distinction between a Christian husband-wife relationship and that in a mixed marriage. The Christian husband is expected to honor the women in his household, and to see them, or at least the wife, as coheirs of the grace of life. "So necessary is this second admonition that for the Christian man to ignore it is to have God ignore him: the prayers of a Christian husband and head of a household who acts otherwise will be ignored by God."[312] In other words, it is

[312]Achtemeier, *1 Peter*, p. 209.

incorrect to see here a fall from the high-water mark of equality in Galatians 3:28. We are now ready to look at the section in detail.

In **1 Peter 3:1** the term *homoiōs*, "similarly," indicates a new subsection of the household code. Peter is not saying that women are just like slaves and must defer/submit like them, but a general pattern of orderliness and deference has similarities with all these cases, whether we are talking about all believers respecting and deferring to rulers, or all household members respecting and deferring to the head of the household. We must stress here that this is in-house advice. Peter is not talking about women in general submitting to men in general, bur rather within the structure of the house or home, wives and husbands are the sole focus. This is especially clear from the use of the word *idios* here, which means "your own." Obviously family relationships were a vital part of early Christianity. Peter wishes them to see such relationships within the context of the wider Christian family, and allow Christian principles and behavior to structure the situation in the physical family, not vice versa. Hence, this is not merely acquiescence to cultural norms for prudential or other reasons; it is the Christianization of non-Christian institutions by changing the Christian individuals and their behavior in these institutions.[313]

We can say with some assurance that women in Anatolia (in all the provinces mentioned in 1 Pet 1:1-2), had opportunities to engage in private businesses, serve in some public offices, have prominent roles in religious cults, run their own households, have some property rights, and gain some education in a degree that was not true in Peter's native setting, in the Holy Land.[314] What "respect" and "defer" to your husband would normally be understood to mean in these provinces would be something less restrictive than what it would be in other settings, and since Peter has apparently been to these regions, he will know this fact. What amounts to respectable behavior in one social setting is different than what that entails in others. This is why Leonhard Goppelt rightly stresses that 1 Peter 3:1-2 suggests that wives are primarily to defer because of the Christian influence it will give them. In other words, this advice is to an important degree pragmatic and missional in conception.[315] The wives are to win over their husbands without a word. I. Howard Marshall nevertheless is right to stress that it is tremendously significant that there were wives in Peter's audiences who did not practice the religion of their mate, or perhaps of their parents. This tells us some-

---

[313]See the more extended discussion of women in the Greco-Roman world in Ben Witherington III, *Women in the Earliest Churches,* SMTSMS 59 (Cambridge: Cambridge University Press, 1988), pp. 1-23.

[314]See the discussion in ibid., chap. 1.

[315]See Goppelt, *1 Peter,* p. 218; McKnight, *1 Peter,* p. 183.

thing about the freedom at least some women had in these areas.[316]

Notice that Peter starts with wives here, as he started with slaves earlier, and before that with those being ruled. His subject is submission or deference, perhaps because here is where problems are arising, as Balch suggests, but also because here is where guidance is needed. Peter does not say, "Husbands, counsel your wives to submit," or vice versa. This must be an individual and willing action of the party involved, not enforced subordination. The very word ***hypotassō*** here is in participial form and used as an imperative, but perhaps not with the full force of an imperative, as Balch says: "The participle never attained the full strength of an imperative but rather had the character of describing what should be."[317] The form is mild and passive and may be seen as reflexive here: not "submit," but "you *should* defer/submit yourselves." But to whom is this voluntary serving to be rendered? The answer given is "your own husband" (cf. 1 Cor 14:34-35). Peter does not extrapolate this act to include all husbands or all men.

In the case of a mixed marriage, the motive for submission is at least in part "so that if some disbelieve the word," you can win them without a word. There is a play on the word for "word" *(logos)*. In the first instance it means the gospel; in the second it means a spoken word, or possibly verbal propaganda. There is a definite article, "the," before the first reference to distinguish it from the second. The verb *kerdainō,* "to win" or "to gain," has a clear missionary sense here and in Matthew 18:15 and 1 Corinthians 9:22.[318]

Thus, **1 Peter 3:2** continues the paradigm of silent, irreproachable and deferential conduct as a total witness to a possibly irritated husband, who perhaps had already grown tired of hearing about Jesus! The example of Monica, Augustine's mother, and her silent witness to his father is proof of the effectiveness of such a tactic (Augustine *Conf.* 9.19-22).[319] The wife acts in fear of God: with proper awe and morality and due respect for all authority that God has ordained, including the head of the household.

Here I stress that Peter's advice goes absolutely against the flow of normal household advice when it comes to the subject of religion. Consider, for example, what Plutarch says:

> A wife ought not to make friends on her own, but to enjoy her husband's friends in common with him. The gods are the first and most important friends. Therefore it

[316]Marshall, *1 Peter,* p. 98.
[317]Balch, *Let Wives Be Submissive,* p. 97.
[318]See Daube, "*Kerdainō* as a Missionary Term," pp. 109-20.
[319]Kelly, *Epistles of Peter,* p. 128.

> is becoming for a wife to worship and know only the gods that her husband believes in, and to shut the front door tight upon all peculiar rituals and outlandish superstitions [Eastern religions like Judaism and Christianity and the worship of Isis and Serapis]. For with no god do secret rites performed by a woman find any favor. . . . Since some [men] . . . cannot well endure the sight of scarlet and purple clothes, while others are annoyed by cymbals and drums, what terrible hardship is it for women to refrain from such [religious] things, and not disquiet or irritate their husbands, but live with them in constant gentleness. (Plutarch *Mor.* 140D, 144 D-E)

According to Plutarch, religion is the number one thing on which wives should follow the lead of their husbands, and they certainly should abstain from trying to influence their husbands to join some pernicious Eastern *superstitio*. Peter advises just the opposite of Plutarch. He wants wives to win their husbands to the Christian faith. As Jobes says, a wife's practice of a nontraditional religion would be seen as an act of rebellion by many a husband and a violation of the social order. Furthermore, if she persisted in attending Christian worship, this could shame the husband if his friends and neighbors found out. Furthermore, Peter himself could be accused of usurping the role of the husband by daring to give imperatives to slaves and wives in these religiously mixed homes.[320] Therefore, since there is to be no compromise on religion, they must find other forms of behavior that please their mates, such as in how they dress. But there is no escaping that the uncompromising stand on religion could be seen as unsettling at the least and subversive at the most.

What follows in **1 Peter 3:3** is a typical contrast between outward and inward beauty, a not infrequent subject in pagan writers. The point here is that character, not appearance, is what really matters to God, and what will also be likely to win people to Christ. A woman who simply dresses like other well-to-do women will appear no different than other people. But a person who chooses a simple appearance, demeanor and pure behavior will attract attention. That is getting attention in the right way and might lead some to ask, Why is she different? This section is similar to 1 Timothy 2 and implies some well-to-do women are already involved in Christianity and have money for such clothes and hairdos. It is possible, but uncertain, that Peter wishes Christian women to avoid ostentatious outward appearance because this is also how *hetaerae* (companions)[321] and prostitutes often dressed in Hellenistic style. For example, consider the Neopythagorean advice:

---

[320] See Jobes, *1 Peter*, pp. 203-4.

[321] "Companions," or "courtesans," were women who accompanied prominent men to social and public functions, particularly in sections of the empire when it was deemed immodest for the wife to go to the theatre or the gladiatorial contexts.

> The temperate, freeborn woman must live with her legal husband adorned with modesty, clad in a neat, simple, white dress. . . . She must avoid clothing that is either entirely purple or is streaked with purple and gold, for that kind of dress is worn by *hetaerae* when they stalk the masses of men. . . . You should have a blush on your cheeks as a sign of modesty instead of rouge, and should wear nobility, decorum, and temperance instead of gold and emeralds. (Pseudo-Melissa *Letter to Kleareta* 160-62)[322]

If Peter alludes to such a form of dress, it might be associated with immoral behavior and be a bad witness, suggesting that the Christian wife is either immoral or too worldly (cf. *1 En.* 8:1; Philo *Virt.* 39-40). It is clear that women in Asia Minor, Greece, Rome, and Egypt had more freedom and access to money than Jewish women in the Holy Land, and so Peter is not likely dealing with a hypothetical case. Some of the church fathers saw this as a prohibition of women wearing jewelry at all, but clearly that goes well beyond what the text says.[323] Braided hair, gold jewelry, and fine clothes refer to refined apparel and the coiffure of the elite, especially if they wove jewels into the hair.[324] Peter in no way counsels divorce in the case of a mixed marriage, but rather, as 1 Corinthians 7 urges, "You may win him to Christ by staying" (cf. 1 Cor 7:16).

First Peter 3:4 stresses the contrast: develop and be beautiful in "the hidden person of the heart" (*ho kryptos tēs kardias anthrōpos;* cf. Rom 2:8-9; 2 Cor 4:16; Eph 3:16). Lurking in the background here is the idea that God looks upon the heart, not the outward appearance, and that this is what generally matters. The phrase may mean "the inner person who dwells in the heart"; or "the unseen person, the heart" if the genitive phrase is in apposition; probably the former. The focus is on the whole person, as determined from the heart.[325] What is really of lasting and imperishable or even immortal (the literal meaning of *aphthartos*) value is a gentle and quiet spirit, which Jesus himself is said to have modeled (Mt 11:28; 21:5). This can surely only refer to the human spirit and is not a reference to a part of one's being: it refers to one's disposition, frame of mind, way of relating to and dealing with the outer world. It is a quality of character, not an anatomical part. Several things weigh against this being a reference to the Holy Spirit: (1) The context refers to human behavior. (2) Sarah, the model that

---

[322]See Perkins, *First Peter,* p. 56.

[323]See, e.g., Clement of Alexandria *Paed.* 3.66.3 (ironically he quotes 1 Tim 2:9 as if it were in 1 Peter!); Tertullian *Or.* 20; Tertullian *Cult. fem.* 1.6; 2.2, 7-13; Cyprian *Hab. virg.* 8. Note that all of these particular fathers were adopting the Christian asceticism that characterized their period.

[324]See Witherington, *Women in the Earliest Churches,* pp. 120-22.

[325]Goppelt, *1 Peter,* p. 221.

follows, did not receive the Holy Spirit. (3) In the New Testament the Spirit is hardly quiet, but rather dynamic, and the Spirit inspires words and does not hinder them. Interestingly, this positive character trait is described as imperishable. The point is that it cannot fade away as outward beauty does.[326] Peter stresses that this is what pleases God: it is precious to him.

In **1 Peter 3:5** Peter begins to speak of holy women of the Old Testament. "Holy" may mean morally upright here, or just chosen by God, or both, but in any case the phrase "holy women" is unique in all the canon. Peter cites but one example, and it is probable he has Isaiah 51:2 in mind, "Look to Abraham your father, and to Sarah who gave you birth," as well as Genesis 18:1-15 in the LXX (cf. Gen 12 and 20, where she is also prominent). Not just Old Testament texts but also intertestamental literature about Sarah may lie in the background here. Thus, for instance, in the *Testament of Abraham* (Recension A: 5:12-13; 6:2, 4, 5, 8; 15:4) Sarah appears as an example of good deeds and fearlessness, and is called the mother of the elect.[327]

According to **1 Peter 3:6**, Sarah in a whimsical mood calls Abraham "Master." This is conventional terminology of respect meaning "Sir," or refers to him as head of the household. It need not imply more here. Peter is simply trying to insist on respect even for non-Christian husbands.[328] It is perhaps fair to say that Peter is relying more on the portrait of Sarah as in the *Testament of Abraham*, where she appears as a rather conventional Hellenistic woman addressing her husband as "Master," rather than the less-submissive portrait we actually find in Genesis.

It is hard to say what Peter has in mind when he says, "She obeyed Abraham." It could mean that she followed Abraham's directions even when he told her to say he was her brother, or more likely that she obeyed him in preparing the meal on the spot when he requested it in the first part of Genesis 18. Although Sarah follows her husband's religion, Peter does not suggest that the Christian wife should obey her pagan husband in the matter of following his religion: after all, Hellenistic culture normally expected the family to believe as the head of the household did. This is why in 1 Peter 3:7 Peter addresses husbands and assumes that all Christian husbands have Christian wives in Anatolia. They are all fellow heirs of grace.[329] Various Byzantine texts with an anti-feminist bias try to take this

---

[326]See Marshall, *1 Peter*, p. 102.

[327]See the discussion in Martin, "The TestAbr and the Background of 1 Pet 3,6," pp. 139-46. Also worth a look is Kiley, "Like Sara," pp. 689-92.

[328]See Spencer, "Peter's Pedagogical Method," pp. 107-19.

[329]We have evidence from the papyri letters of the use of *synklēronomos* to refer to joint heirs of an estate. See *NewDocs* 1:135.

reference to heirs of grace and apply it to only the husbands.[330] The danger was that Christian wives in a mixed marriage would lose heart or become intimidated, perhaps due to persecution or verbal abuse. Peter insists that she stick to her guns and live as Sarah did, doing good, trusting God, and hoping in God (1 Pet 2:5a).

First Peter 3:7 may mean only that Christian husbands should respect their wives,[331] remembering that they are the weaker vessel. It has been suggested, however, that "live with/cohabit according to knowledge" is a euphemism for fulfill your conjugal duty in regard to sexual intercourse (cf. Gen 20:3 [of Abraham and Sarah]; Deut 22:13; 24:1; 25:5; Is 62:5; Sir 25:8),[332] in which case 1 Corinthians 7 supplies a commentary here.[333] Probably, however, it involves all of their interaction including their intercourse. Least likely is the view that "according to knowledge" means knowing God is watching. Showing the wife respect or honor is vital and is indeed a means of the husband serving and submitting to his wife and her needs, just as *timē* above in reference to the emperor refers to the form of submission (cf. 1 Pet 2:13, 17b). This advice was necessary because men were likely to take the social code about women being subordinate to mean more than it ought to mean in a Christian context.[334]

The use of the term *skeuos* has caused a lot of controversy. Does it mean (a) body? (b) vessel? or (c) person? It has been argued that "vessel" implies that the woman is an object, indeed a sex object, and this is degrading. However, since Peter says "weaker *skeuos*," he is implying that the husband is also a *skeuos*, so no such implication can be drawn here. The sentence literally reads, "as with a weaker vessel, a feminine one."[335] Probably the reference is to woman as physically weaker. It is certainly not a reference to woman as morally, spiritually, or intellectually inferior, since Peter goes on to say that she is coheir of the grace of life. Donald P. Senior stresses, "Here the author is speaking not of the husband-wife relationship as such, but of the deference a man owes to women as the weaker 'vessels.'"[336]

Too often in pagan remarks about women and the household, derogatory

---

[330]Metzger, *TC*, 690-91. See note 299 above on the textual variants.

[331]The word in 1 Pet 3:7 is *gynaikeiō*, the adjective used as a noun; it could even be translated "the female," which might refer to a class of persons rather than to one individual such as the wife. See Jobes, *1 Peter*, p. 207. Jobes also probes the possibility that the wife is not seen as a Christian here, but that is surely a less likely possibility in view of the end of the verse, where she is called a coheir of God's grace.

[332]Kelly, *Epistles of Peter*, pp. 132-34.

[333]In the inscriptions the word *synoikeō* simply means "cohabit." See *NewDocs* 3:85-86.

[334]See Achtemeier, *1 Peter*, pp. 218-19.

[335]Elliott, *1 Peter*, p. 576.

[336]Senior, *1 Peter*, p. 84.

comments are made about women and their inferiority to men. We may compare, for example, the *Letter to Aristeas* 250, which says, "The female sex is bold, positively active for something which it desires, easily liable to change its mind because of poor reasoning powers, and of naturally weak constitution." Peter's remarks are restrained by comparison. So *skeuos* here probably means "person" with a special emphasis on the frail mortal form. In 1 Thessalonians 4:4 *skeuos* likely also refers to wife, not to one's own physical body.[337] In addition, there is material of relevance where women call themselves "those of weaker nature" (cf. CPR 15 from Hermopolis; P.Oxy. 1 [1898]: no. 71, col. 2 [p. 303]). A few are worth quoting. In one (P.Oxy. 34 [1968]: no. 2713 [p. 297]) a woman named Aurelia Didyme, obviously of high status, has written a prefect named Aristius Optatus and says, "And you are well aware, my lord governor, that the female sex is by nature easily despised because of the weakness of nature on our part" (lines 8-9). Such phrases, seeking to incite pathos and engender a favorable treatment of a request, are typical of petition of this era made by women (cf. P.Flor. 1 [1906, repr. 1960]: no. 58). In his extended discussion of this material, A. R. Connolly points out the formulaic and rhetorical nature of such material.[338] What he does not note is that there is a difference between these entreaties and what we find in 1 Peter 3. Peter is simply talking about a physical weakness, as is especially clear from the use of the word "vessel," a term that never occurs in these inscriptions, which are talking about either a weak "nature" or a weak social position.

Peter is saying that women equally with men stand before God as fully heirs of God's kingdom and grace and salvation and eternal life.[339] There is no higher privilege. If that will govern our thinking—and we are called to have the attitude God has, as Peter insists—there can be no denigrating of the female or relegating them to an inferior place in life on the basis of this text. We see here the reformation, though not the outright abolition, of patriarchal culture, as also is the case with Paul. Finally, Peter points out that unless a husband acts with full respect for his wife, it will hinder his prayers. His relationship with God is intertwined with his love and respect for his fellow humans, especially his wife. One relationship affects the other. Here it is probably just the husband's prayers that are in view since 1 Peter 3:7 addresses *hoi andres*.[340]

---

[337]See Ben Witherington III, *1 and 2 Thessalonians: A Socio-Rhetorical Commentary* (Grand Rapids: Eerdmans, 2006).

[338]See A. R. Connolly's helpful discussion of such material in *New Docs* 4:131-33.

[339]On the textual variants here, see Goppelt, *1 Peter,* p. 228, n. 11. He is right that the nominative reading distorts the meaning here.

[340]There are now two detailed studies about early Christian families and household and also about the family of faith that should be consulted: Balch and Osiek, *Families in the New Testament World;* and Hellerman, *Ancient Church as Family.*

First Peter 3:8-12 begins with the phrase *To de telos* (finally) and concludes this argument with a return to the themes involving Christian character enunciated before (cf. esp. 1 Pet 2:23—to 3:9). There is considerable verbal similarity between what we find here and Romans 12:10-17, which implies that there was an early Christian ethical tradition shared rather widely, and close examination also suggests that it was in various respects grounded in the ethic of the Sermon on the Mount (cf. *Did.* 1.3; Pol. *Phil.* 2.2).[341] Notice as well that the function of citing Psalm 34 is to provide further backing from the sacred text for the ethic of Jesus. In other words, Peter does not derive the ethic from the Psalm, but rather bolsters and supports it from the Psalm.[342] And this is the same Psalm that Peter has previously used to urge the audience to taste and see that the Lord is good (1 Pet 2:3). Here Peter returns to a general exhortation to all his audience and concludes with a quote from a source he often has in mind: Psalm 34. Proverbs 3 and 4 also are often in the background here.

In **1 Peter 3:8** Peter calls Christians to harmony, to be all of one mind (*homophrōn* only here in the NT; cf. Phil 2:2-5) and have real feeling and compassion for one another (*sympathēs,* from which we get "sympathy," meaning "suffering with"; cf. Rom 12:15; 1 Cor 12:26; Heb 4:15; 10:34). Leonhard Goppelt aptly says that what results from harmony is "not uniformity but unanimity."[343] *Tapeinophrōn* is an interesting Greek word for it has a unique meaning in Christian contexts. In pagan contexts it means something like base minded, ignoble, low, mean—a derogatory term. Here it is seen as a virtue. It expresses a character directly modeled on Christ and "humbling oneself." Best adds "'a humble mind' (cf. 5:5f.; Eph 4:2; Phil 2:3ff.). This represents a new quality of life which was introduced by Christianity into the Hellenistic world. In classical Greek the underlying word possessed the sense 'base,' 'mean'; in the Christian faith it obtained a new meaning and signified a new virtue 'humility.'"[344] Elliott is right to add: "In the highly competitive and stratified world of Greco-Roman antiquity, only those of degraded social status were 'humble' and humility was regarded as a sign of weakness and shame, an inability to defend one's honor. Thus the high value placed on humility by Israelites and Christians is remarkable."[345]

This virtue is expected of all believers. They are all called to be servants. Humility comes not from a low opinion of self, but from a high opinion of God, realizing how much believers owe God and are dependent on God. This is real

[341]See Elliott, *1 Peter,* p. 602, for a chart of the similarities.
[342]See Goppelt, *1 Peter,* pp. 230-31.
[343]Goppelt, *1 Peter,* p. 233.
[344]Best, *1 Peter,* p. 129.
[345]Elliott, *1 Peter,* p. 605.

humility, not false modesty, that Christ calls believers to, and it involves deeds of service, not a craven attitude that denigrates self. This first verse of the summation seems to refer primarily if not exclusively to behavior among Christians themselves. Peter may be remembering what it was like early in the Jerusalem church (cf. Acts 2:42-47; 4:32-35).

First Peter 3:9 simply repeats the theme of nonretaliation found in 1 Peter 2:23.[346] Retaliation is a natural and normal response, but it is not a Christian response. Rather, we are to bless those who curse us, so that we ourselves might inherit a blessing (cf. 1 Cor 4:12; Lk 6:28a). The teaching here is closest to what we find in Luke 6:27-28.

Here we see the influence of early Christian teaching (cf. Mt 5:12; 25:31-46; Rom 15) and the teaching of Jesus, which was widely known and used in the early church. Notice in 1 Peter 3:9b how a believer's inheriting of a blessing is contingent on their giving one through certain forms of behavior. Again the connection between ethics and grace is clearly seen. The receiving cannot be isolated from the giving. It is not clear what "blessing" is to be inherited. It could be a reference to longer life on earth in view of the Psalm that follows this verse, but it could look forward to final salvation.[347] If the latter, it is important to note that an inheritance is not something one *earns* by good deeds.

It is telling that in **1 Peter 3:10-12** "the author does not alert the reader that he is quoting Scripture but simply incorporates it without comment into his argumentation, perhaps able to assume that his readers will recognize the Psalm."[348] This strongly suggests to me that the audience must involve mostly Jews. Otherwise, it is an inept rhetorical move to finish one's argument with a flourish by quoting a source of inartificial proof, a strong one, the force and authority of which would be missed by a largely pagan audience. Peter's quote of Psalm 34 here has modified it in several ways: (1) He omits Psalm 34:16, which discusses the destruction of the evildoers or their "remembrance" being "cut off." Probably quoting this would have upset Christians with pagan mates or friends, which would not help. (2) He has smoothed out the awkward LXX wording. (3) The original reference was to length of life on this earth, which Peter may have altered to a love of and longing for eternal life here—"wishing to love life" seems to imply something the author does not have (cf. 1 Peter 3:9, a coming blessing). (4) There is a change from questions to statements.[349] This

[346]Notice how the NIV clarifies the matter at 1 Pet 3:8 by adding the phrase "with one another."
[347]See Goppelt, *1 Peter,* pp. 234-35; Michaels, *1 Peter,* p. 179.
[348]Senior, *1 Peter,* p. 92.
[349]See Selwyn, *First Peter,* p. 190; and the chart in Jobes, *1 Peter,* pp. 221-23.

is but a part of a larger pattern of use of Psalm 34 LXX, as we can see if we compare as follows:

Psalm 33:2 [34:1 ET]	1 Peter 1:3
Psalm 33:5 [34:4 ET]	1 Peter 1:17
Psalm 33:6 [34:5 ET]	1 Peter 2:6
Psalm 33:8 [34:7 ET]	1 Peter 1:17
Psalm 33:10, 12 [34:9, 11 ET]	1 Peter 2:17
Psalm 33:18 [34:17 ET]	1 Peter 3:12
Psalm 33:20 [34:19 ET]	1 Peter 1:6
Psalm 33:23 [34:22 ET]	1 Peter 1:18; 2:16[350]

In this discourse Peter is not sequentially working through the psalm, nor is he really expositing it. Rather, he uses the text sometimes to reinforce what he is saying, sometimes to provide him with the biblical vocabulary to speak meaningfully to the audience, implicitly drawing an analogy between the sufferings they are going through and that of the righteous sufferer spoken of in the Psalm. Many of these echoes and allusions would have been lost on a formerly pagan audience, though some God-fearers may have picked up an echo here and there. The use of the text is remarkably skillful and subtle at points, and one might add that it reflects sensitivity to the text's original sense and context as well.

In a nutshell, **1 Peter 3:10** urges believers to cease speaking evil and deceit, and **1 Peter 3:11** calls them to turn from evildoing, and on the positive side to do "the good," to actively work for and seek peace (both in the Christian community, but perhaps elsewhere as well, thus fulfilling Mt 5:9; cf. Rom 12:18). Then in **1 Peter 3:12** we are told why: God's eyes and ears are on believers and listening to their prayers; but his face is set against evildoers. Whoever wants one's prayers to be heard (cf. 1 Pet 3:7) must hear and do God's will. Whoever does not do God's will finds oneself opposing God, and God opposing the evildoer. Thus we have come back full circle to 1 Peter 2:12, and we can see how intentionally and carefully Peter's rhetoric has been crafted here to convey, reinforce, and make persuasive his message in a rhetoric-saturated environment.

1 PETER 3:13—4:11—ARGUMENT 3: SUFFERING AND SELF-CONTROL

No one can harm a person who does not do evil himself. Peter shows that trials which come from Gentiles cannot harm those who live according to virtue. On the

[350]Here I have basically followed Jobes, *1 Peter*, loc. cit.

contrary, they turn those who endure them into blessed ones. (Chrysostom)[351]

Christ descended into hell in order to acquaint the patriarchs and prophets with his redeeming mission. (Tertullian [*The Soul's Testimony* 55.2])[352]

Without question, 1 Peter 3:13—4:11 includes the most difficult material in this discourse in terms of (1) textual, (2) grammatical, and (3) interpretive possibilities. It is not too much to say that this section takes us back into a thought world very different from our own. The major problems arise with 1 Peter 3:19-22 and 1 Peter 4:6 and deal with (1) fallen angels, (2) baptism, (3) the dead in Christ. Furthermore, if the subjects themselves are not complex enough, one needs to know *1 Enoch* to understand what Peter is saying, in particular *1 Enoch* 6—16. Fortunately, the rhetorical design of the material is more straightforward than some of the interpretive issues. As I. Howard Marshall and others have stressed, within this section 1 Peter 3:18-22 is a passage for which it is as difficult to ferret out the original meaning as any text in the New Testament.[353]

Both Thurén and Campbell agree that the next rhetorical unit is 1 Peter 3:13—4:11; it begins with a rhetorical question and a beatitude, and ends with the rhetorical flourish of a benediction of sorts.[354] Also, as at the end of the previous argument, Peter uses the conclusion of his argument to sum up some of the pith or essence of what has been said earlier in this argument. Thus, in 1 Peter 4:1-11 we have suffering (cf. 1 Pet 4:1; 3:14, 17-18), the slander of pagans (cf. 1 Pet 4:4; 3:16) and the called-for good conduct (cf. 1 Pet 4:7-11; 3:13, 16).[355] One might think that in so short an argument, this much repetition would not be necessary, but that would be forgetting that this is Asiatic rhetoric, which has as its trademark repetition, reduplication, even redundancy and certainly dramatic hyperbole.

As Campbell says, the third major argument in this discourse builds on what has come before, especially the second argument. The subject of suffering could raise latent fears in the audience. It is also the wise rhetor who recognizes the emotional state of the audience and names it and responds to it. Here our author clearly articulates that the audience is afraid, and not without good reason. Aristotle says that the rhetor's knowledge of the emotional state of the audience is crucial to persuading them about something, for if the audience sees that the speaker knows and names what they are feeling, they are more

---

[351]*CEC* 64; see ACCS 11:104.

[352]See ACCS 11:107.

[353]Marshall, *1 Peter,* p. 118.

[354]See Thurén, *Rhetorical Strategy,* p. 153; cf. Campbell, *Honor, Shame,* p. 172.

[355]Campbell, *Honor, Shame,* p. 186.

liable to trust him (Aristotle *Rhet.* 2.1.1378a.5).

Forestalling objections the audience may have to an act of persuasion is something any good rhetorician is called upon to do. One could even argue that the rhetorical question beginning this argument gives us something of the diatribe style, where the author has an imaginary dialogue with a potential objector (cf. Cicero *De or.* 3.54.207; Quintilian *Inst.* 9.3.90), in this case a rather naive person, who assumes that no one will harm anyone who is zealous for the good. This assumes a positive correlation between behavior and one's fate or what happens to a person. Such was indeed a common assumption in antiquity, often in the form of the negative: "I am in danger because I have not reflected the proper ancestral piety." Here Peter is answering potential objections to what he has said in the second argument about suffering. He denies the correlation claiming that suffering necessarily indicates the lack of divine favor or even the wickedness of the person suffering.[356] He does this by echoing a beatitude of an unimpeachable source—Jesus (Mt 5:12). The ongoing discussion suggests an environment where Christians will be under close scrutiny and need to think in advance about how they will cope with and respond to challenging situations as a Christian witness, not merely as a Christian.

There is an element of "reduplication" in this argument, not surprisingly since a call to suffering is almost always a hard sell. Thus Lauri Thurén notes how 1 Peter 3:13-17 to some extent repeats and builds on 1 Peter 2:19-20; then the christological section in 1 Peter 3:18-22 corresponds to and builds on 1 Peter 2:21-24.[357] As this discussion progresses, Peter goes beyond the theme of witnessing, to that of apologetics, the actual giving of a reason for one's belief and behavior. Exemplars are brought into play once more, in this case Jesus, and perhaps one could argue for Enoch in the background, and perhaps Noah as well. Historical examples are always the rhetorically strongest sort.

There is more "reduplication" in 1 Peter 4:1-11 with a repeat of the theme about avoiding Gentile behavior (cf. 1 Pet 2:11), but the tone here is sharper. At the end of this argument, Peter applies an eschatological sanction. Since the end of all things may be near, there is all the more reason to renounce bad behavior and do a better job of emulating Christ, being willing to suffer and also to answer for one's faith.[358] But the reduplication and repetition, both forms of amplification so characteristic of Asiatic rhetoric, does not happen simply at the

[356] I find ibid., p. 172, a bit off the mark if he thinks the audience would be saying, "If we do good, we will still continue to suffer." This is an unlikely hypothetical response, particularly if the audience is mainly Jewish.

[357] See Thurén, *Rhetorical Strategy*, p. 154.

[358] See ibid., pp. 155-57.

level of content but also at the level of verbiage and the very sound of the words, thus reinforcing the repetition of the themes. For example, in 1 Peter 3:14 we have "But the fear of them do not fear," perhaps a partial allusion to Isaiah 8:12. In the vice list (1 Pet 4:3) Peter lines up Greek words so that the sound-alike ones are bunched together in threes: *aselgeiais, epithymiais, oinophlygiais,* followed by *kōmois, potois kai athemitois*. Again, I must stress that this material was meant to be heard: a fair bit of its persuasive power depends on the way it sounds.

But this is not for a minute to deny that the argument itself is supposed to carry weight with the audience. As he has done before, Peter will use maxims, echoes of Jesus' teaching or the Old Testament, and enthymemes to get his point across. Their persuasive character depends to an extent on how much of a universe of discourse the author shares with the audience. If they are Jews like himself and know the Old Testament and at least some of the Jesus tradition and the sacred traditions of early Christians, then echoes and mere reminders can be enough to persuade. And make no mistake: Peter is using short-form argumentation here. The audience is expected to give an *apologia,* but Peter does not pause to elaborate in detail what exactly they should say when challenged, whether formally or informally. There is not enough space, nor does Peter really take time to elaborate and give full syllogisms. Rather like a good preacher with an audience who respects his authority and with whom his ethos is established, he assumes that if he can simply allude, hint, quote, repeat and emphasize, this will carry the day. This is far more likely to be the case with a knowledgeable audience, an audience perhaps he has mostly led to Christ, and in particular a Jewish Christian one.

The use of the rhetorical device that we call typology was common in antiquity, especially in deliberative rhetoric, where a comparison would be made to gain the assent of an audience to a change in behavior, or the avoidance of a change in behavior. Here we have the typological use of the Noah story to some effect, although the logic of the comparison with baptism is not entirely or immediately apparent to us at our great remove from early Jewish and Greco-Roman use of typology. Quintilian reminds us that the quickest method of securing assent to some course of action (or in this case refraining from a course of action, defecting) was to point the audience to historical parallels from which they would feel one could draw valid inferences (Quintilian *Inst.* 3.8.36). The rhetorical assumption is that the audience would know the story of Noah, and accept it as part of Scripture and therefore be persuaded by the narrative logic of the use of this analogy. Noah and his kin were saved through the water, just as "baptism saves" the believer. The irony of this analogy is that Noah and his kin were saved by staying *out of and above* the water, though the water helped them rise above the disastrous consequences the land-bound experienced. The sense in which Peter wants to suggest that baptism saves, on the basis of this analogy, is almost as clear as those murky waters of judgment themselves that flooded the earth.

From a rhetorical point of view, 1 Peter 4:7-11 can be seen as a *transitus*: a transition bringing the preceding material to a conclusion and foreshadowing what comes thereafter. J. Ramsey Michaels notes a thematic correspondence between 1 Peter 4:7-11 and 1 Peter 4:12—5:11 as follows: (1) There is an announcement of the end of the age (cf. 1 Pet 4:7; 4:12-19; 5:8-9). (2) Next come instructions on how Christian believers are to treat one another (cf. 1 Pet 4:8-10; 5:1-5). (3) This is followed by a reminder of God's sovereignty and the need to glorify God (cf. 1 Pet 4:11; 5:6-7, 10). (4) All this is concluded with a doxology (cf. 1 Pet 4:11b; 5:11).[359] What Michaels does not note or notice is the way this material functions rhetorically, as summary and preview, but also following the dictates of Asiatic rhetoric, which calls for repetition and amplification; so the lesson is backed up and learned, using what we might call "redundant systems." What Michaels also does not notice is that 1 Peter 5:6-9 followed by a closing doxology is the peroration of this discourse. The first two parallels (the first half of the comparisons of points 1 and 2 above) with the last two arguments that precede the peroration (1 Pet 4:12-19 and 1 Pet 5:1-5) are not all that convincing. Is 1 Peter 4:12-19 really about the End, or is it about self-control, an ever-present theme for those facing suffering? Moreover, 1 Peter 4:8-10 is about general Christian behavior, whereas 1 Peter 5:1-5 is about leaders and "the younger," who are given specific instructions suitable to their station in the community. The parallels with the peroration are much stronger. This is in no way surprising since a peroration is supposed to rehearse, amplify, sum up some or many of the previous arguments, and stir the deeper emotions.

Last, it is quite likely that Peter is drawing on some traditional materials here; yet he has skillfully woven it into his own discourse to serve his own rhetorical purposes. Discovering where this material comes from is far less important than recognizing how it is being used in this particular text. Reinhard Feldmeier observes the rhetorically skillful way our author weaves this traditional material into the context here, such that it helps him make his own points about the suffering of Christians.[360]

---

[359]Michaels, *1 Peter*, p. 244.

[360]Feldmeier, *Der erste Brief des Petrus*, p. 133: "Auf diese Weise autorisiert der 1Petr seine Aussagen zum Leiden der Christen mit Hilfe des urchristlichen Bekenntnisses, wobei der Wechsel in Stil und Diktion diese rhetorisch eindrucksvoll vom Kontext abhebt. Im Übrigen ist auch hier wieder zu sehen, mit welcher Souveränität der 1Petr diese vielfältigen Traditionen zu einer in sich geschlossen Textpassage verwebt."

[3:13] And who will harm you if you are an enthusiast of the good? [14] But even if you should suffer because of righteousness, (you are) blessed. Do not be terrified with fear of them, do not be disturbed, [15] but treat as holy the Lord Christ in your hearts, being always ready (to give) a rational explanation/defense to all asking you for the reason for the hope that is within you, [16] but (do it) with gentleness and respect, having a good conscience so that in the matter for which you are disparaged, the slanderers will be put to shame by your good behavior in Christ. [17] For it is better to suffer for doing good, if the will of God should wish/decree it, than to suffer for doing evil, [18] for even Christ suffered once (for all time) on account of sin [or "as a sin offering"], the righteous for the unrighteous, in order to bring you before God.

On the one hand he was put to death in the flesh, but on the other he was brought to life in the spirit, [19] in which also he went (and) spoke to the spirits in prison, [20] who disobeyed once when the patience of God waited in the days of Noah (while) the ark was being built, into which a few, that is, eight persons, were saved through water, [21] which also is the antitype of what saves you now—baptism, not by the putting off of the dirt of the flesh but through the appeal/pledge/request of a good conscience unto God, through the resurrection of Jesus Christ, [22] who is at the right hand of God, gone into heaven, angels and principalities and powers being subjected to him.

[4:1] Christ then suffered in the flesh, and you arm yourselves with the same thought that the one suffering in the flesh has ceased to sin, [2] thus no longer satisfying desires of human beings but the will of God (during) the remaining time in the flesh. [3] For enough time has passed doing the will of the Gentiles, leading one's life in debauchery, desires, drunkenness, orgies, carousing, and forbidden idolatry. [4] Being surprised at your not remaining together (with them) in a flood of dissipation, they blaspheme. [5] But they will render account to the One judging the living and the dead, because for this also he preached to the dead, [6] so that on the one hand they might be condemned according to human judgment in the flesh, but on the other hand according to God's judgment, be alive in the Spirit.

[7] But the end of all (this?/things?) is near/has arrived. Be reasonable, then, and self-controlled unto prayer. [8] Above all (be) eager in having love among yourselves because love covers a multitude of sins; [9] be hospitable to one another without grumbling, [10] just as each has received a free gift to be in service of one another as stewards of the variegated grace of God. [11] If someone speaks, (treat that one) as a spokesperson of the words of God. If someone serves, (treat that one) as the servant from the power which God supplies, so that in all things God through Jesus Christ may be glorified, to whom is the glory and might unto the eternity of eternity. Amen.

This is a place where it is not sufficient to deal with the textual problems in the notes. We need to discuss them here. First, in 1 Peter 3:18 we have a host of variants that fall into two larger categories: (1) "He suffered for *[hyper]* sins [with 'our' or 'your' added by various manuscripts]." Another reading is along this same line: "He suffered on account of *[peri]* sins," or one could translate "as a sin offering." (2) "He died for sins [with 'your' or 'our' added in various manuscripts]." The other reading is, "He died on account of sins" (and once again *peri* plus *hamartia* can mean "as a sin offering"). There are thus two major issues. What is the original verb? What is the original preposition? On the whole, it seems more likely that scribes would change "suffered" to "died" since that was the more common expression in early Christianity when speaking of Christ's death. Another thing is important in this decision: this is a discourse that has as its major theme suffering, with the verb *paschein* used some eleven times and the verb *apothnēskein* not found elsewhere in 1 Peter. To give his audience hope, Peter is drawing an analogy between a suffering audience and a suffering Christ, not a dead Christ and a dead audience. Thus option 1 above is the more likely reading in regard to the verb. Bruce M. Metzger suggests that if *peri hamartiōn* is original, then it is understandable why some scribes changed the verb to "died": he died on account of sin, or as a sin offering. This makes good sense.[361]

Second, in 1 Peter 3:21 we have an even larger textual problem with the first word of the verse. Do we read

ho . . .	which also . . . saves
hos . . .	who also . . . saves
omit the word	baptism saves
hō . . .	to/for which . . . also saves
hōs . . .	as an antitype . . . saves

Some basic text-critical principles come into play here. Normally one takes the reading that best explains the others and/or the reading that is most difficult and/or the best supported reading, or some combination of these three principles. On all three grounds "which [*ho*] . . ." is the best reading, even though it is difficult to understand. Thus, we have translated it "which."

First Peter 3:13 picks up where the previous verse left off. First Peter 3:12 spoke of evildoers, and verse 13 now speaks of those who can do evil or harm to the audience. Obviously, 1 Peter 3:13a cannot mean "You will never suffer if you are a sincere Christian" because he is busily preparing sincere Christians for that precise eventuality. It could mean something like "No one can harm you in any serious or spiritual way." The word *zēlōtai* seems strange to some commentators. Ernest Best, for example, says of "zealous":

> this word has an interesting background. . . . One Jewish party which opposed the Romans by force in the first century A.D. was known as the Zealots. The word is

[361]See Metzger, *TC*, p. 692.

> an odd choice here since excessive zeal is associated with a tendency to annoy and irritate others rather than with the gentleness and reverence desired in 1 Peter 3:16. We must take it to stress the active nature of right behavior, and we find the noun or its cognate verb associated with goodness elsewhere in the New Testament (Acts 21:20; 1 Cor 12:31; 14:1, 12; Gal 1:14; Tit 2:14). Bo Reicke, who dates our letter before the fall of Jerusalem, when the Zealots were very active, suggests that this explains the choice of word; Christians ought not to be carried away by revolutionary activity but be zealous for what is good.[362]

Christian zealots are still to submit to the emperor, yet contend for and defend the faith (1 Pet 3:15b). But does this really explain the connection between this verse and what precedes?[363] It is better to recognize the way a rhetorical question functions here.[364] This represents a voice other than that of the author, in diatribe style, which the author then answers in the next verse. The voice could be that of a naive questioner from the audience, perhaps a young Christian. Jobes suggests that here may be an echo of Isaiah 50:9 LXX: "Behold, the Lord helps me. Who can harm me?"[365] However our interlocutor does not say anything about God or divine protection. He is asking about the human response if one does good. It is best to stick with the rhetorical explanation of this rhetorical question. In any case this verse has a close parallel at 1 Peter 4:14, which also may involve the adapting of a beatitude or saying of Jesus.[366]

First Peter 3:14 speaks of suffering with an optative verb form, which is very rare. *Ei* plus the optative suggests that suffering may or may not happen in a particular case, or possibly as Achtemeier suggests, that it is sporadic.[367] But the grammar is such that Peter may mention suffering in this tentative way because (1) some of his audience is certainly not suffering, at least not yet; (2) some are seeking to avoid it even now and do not need a painful reminder of its reality. However, the second half of the verse, "You are blessed/fortunate," may suggest that some are suffering, and receiving the "blessing" of suffering not just for any reason, but because of their Christian faith; certainly by 1 Peter 4:12 we seem to be hearing that suffering is either happening or inevitable, using quite similar language but without the optative. Donald Senior puts things this way: "So the sense here is probably not purely hypothetical (i.e.,'if' suffering should come),

---

[362]Best, *1 Peter,* p. 132, following Bo Riecke, *The Disobedient Spirits and Christian Baptism* (København: E. Munksgaard, 1946; repr., New York: AMS Press, 1984).

[363]Notice the head-scratching in Goppelt, *1 Peter,* p. 240.

[364]See Elliott, *1 Peter,* pp. 619-20.

[365]Jobes, *1 Peter,* p. 226.

[366]See Michaels, *1 Peter,* p. 186; Elliott, *1 Peter,* pp. 622-24.

[367]Achtemeier, *1 Peter,* p. 230.

but conditional (i.e., in those instances when suffering does come)."[368] It is a high privilege to suffer in this way and for such a great cause and faith, and it appears likely that Peter is drawing on Matthew 5:10 here: "Blessed are those who are persecuted for righteousness' sake."[369] J. N. D. Kelly aptly sums things up: "In neither section is the picture one of Christians continuously undergoing concrete ill-treatment; in both it is an environment charged with suspicion and hostility which has erupted, and is liable at any moment and in any place to erupt again, in painful incidents. This risk, always imminent but for the most of the time a threat rather than an actuality, is itself sufficient to explain the optative."[370]

First Peter 3:14b refers to Christians not being afraid of their persecutors and is like 1 Peter 3:6. Christians are not to be overly disturbed by persecution: in a hostile environment it comes with the territory. According to **1 Peter 3:15**, the way to handle such persecution is twofold: (1) Christians must hallow Christ in their heart but (2) also be prepared to defend their faith when someone asks concerning the hope within them. Under persecution the temptation might well be to do action 1 but neglect action 2, or quite possibly to neglect both. Instead of fear in the heart, there is to be faith and treating Christ as holy. To acknowledge Christ as holy involves recognizing that he is Lord over the situation and also the Lord who is coming as Judge. Thus, Christians should not take matters into their own hands, nor curse their persecutors or their fate. In 1 Peter 2:8 Peter drew on Isaiah 8; he seems to return again to this text in 1 Peter 3:14-15. Isaiah 8:12-13 reads: "Do not fear what they fear, and do not dread it. The LORD Almighty is the one whom you are to regard as holy; he is the one you are to fear, he is the one you are to dread." Once again we are dealing with simply an echo, not a straight quotation here, and it is closest to the LXX.[371] What Peter is doing is substituting Christ for Yahweh in the second verse of this allusion. It is now Christ who is hallowed, and in the heart.

First Peter 3:15b may suggest defense of the faith before a judge or a court, but probably we have a more general use of the language here. Believers are to be prepared, not just in special circumstances or when authorities ask, but if *anyone* should ask.[372] The term "hope" in 1 Peter is almost synonymous with

---

[368]Senior, *1 Peter,* p. 94.
[369]As was the case with James, Peter follows the Matthean form of the Q material in the Sermon on the Mount. This once again suggests to me that the Matthean form is likely to be older, for the most part. See as well 1 Pet 2:12, which also follows the Matthean form of the text.
[370]Kelly, *Epistles of Peter,* p. 141.
[371]See Marshall, *1 Peter,* p. 114, and the note on 1 Pet 3:14.
[372]See Kelly, *Epistles of Peter,* pp. 142-43.

faith. Peter is talking about a defense of one's basic life orientation and philosophy: one's faith (cf. 1:13, 21; 3:15).[373] Notice that the phrase "requiring an accounting from someone about something" *(aitein tina logon peri tinos)* is a classical phrase, perhaps almost a technical phrase (Plato *Pol.* 285E).[374] Yet it is clear from the broad language ("*always* be ready . . . to give to *anyone*") that a courtroom situation is not the narrow focus here, but it would be included in this exhortation.[375] In light of Philippians 1:7, 16, the sense of giving a defense may be at the forefront of what Peter is urging here. It is an answer given in response to criticism or attack, not just a neutral inquiry.[376]

Nevertheless, people who are being persecuted live in hope, in a special sense of the phrase, and look forward to a better life. *Apologia* here refers to a rational explanation, or possibly a defense. In a rhetorical context, for instance in a law court, it most certainly had the sense of "defense" in the face of opposition (cf. Lk 12:11-12; Acts 22:1; 25:16). It is used here in a somewhat more generalized way, in view of the animus in the environment already experienced by these Christians, who have not yet been taken to trial, so hence the translation "testimony" by Achtemeier, Senior and others.[377] As Perkins points out, Peter is not merely talking about lifestyle evangelism here: he means actually verbally explaining or defending his faith.[378] Christians need to prepare intellectually to explain and give reasons or proofs for their faith. We may remember the admonition in 1 Peter 1:13 to gird up the loins of one's mind. The phrase "the hope within you" may mean the hope within the individual Christian (see 1 Pet 3:16), or perhaps more likely the hope shared within the community. In any case, the "atmosphere of this passage and of the letter as a whole suggests that the encounter between the nonbeliever and the Christian envisioned here is not a dispassionate discussion but a more aggressive challenge to the Christian way of life mounted by the dominant majority that has little sympathy for these spiritual 'aliens.'"[379]

First Peter 3:16 urges Christians to act out of a good conscience and not let

---

[373]Best, *1 Peter,* p. 134.

[374]See Goppelt, *1 Peter,* p. 243.

[375]Ibid., p. 244; cf. Achtemeier, *1 Peter,* p. 233.

[376]See Michaels, *1 Peter,* p. 188; cf. Elliott, *1 Peter,* pp. 627-28. He is right that the reference to "the hope within you" surely points away from a legal situation where they are normally asking about past or present behavior. There are exceptions to this: for instance, the Areopagus in Athens was set up to deal with matters of religious belief, including teaching about the future—a very touchy subject in a superstitious and omen-consulting age.

[377]Achtemeier, *1 Peter,* pp. 234-35; Senior, *1 Peter,* p. 95.

[378]Perkins, *First Peter,* p. 62.

[379]Senior, *1 Peter,* p. 98.

suffering become an occasion for giving in to or seeking out sin. Gentleness under fire, not aggressiveness, is called for here. The purpose of such good behavior is "in order that" (*hina*) the slanderers may be put to shame (cf. 1 Pet 2:6b on "put to shame"; 1 Pet 2:15; 3:13). Peter uses the *en Christō* formula here (see also 1 Pet 5:10, 14), which we find so often in Paul's discourses (some 134 times); Peter may have derived it from Paul or from one or more of his writings. The formula is found in no other canonical document than here and in Paul. In many cases the phrase is not merely a cipher for the word "Christian." It alludes to the real spiritual link between Christ and his people. Here the reference is to Christlike behavior.

First Peter 3:17 may simply allude back to what was said about suffering for wrongdoing in 1 Peter 2:20, but perhaps it more likely considers suffering for doing good now as better than suffering for doing evil later, at the judgment day. This suits the eschatological content of this discourse.[380] First Peter 3:17b reminds hearers that it can be God's will for Christians to suffer in some contexts and ways—if it will produce some good result, or if the alternative is worse (such as apostasy). But the verb *theloi* here is in the optative mood and could well be translated "if he may will [it to be so]." Clearly, from Peter's viewpoint, it was God's will that Christ suffer; so why should his followers be exempt forever? "Avoid suffering at all costs" is not a Christian motto, for there are worse things, such as eternal punishment for sin or apostasy. We may observe here that Peter seems well aware of the early Jewish pattern of describing the righteous sufferer as one who suffers and then goes on to glory (see, e.g., Wis 2—5). That seems to affect the portrait of Christ here and elsewhere in 1 Peter. Last, Elliott has just the right balance of understanding of this verse: "The qualification, *if this should be God's will*, refers to suffering *for doing what is right* and not simply suffering per se. The point is not that God wills suffering but that God wills *doing what is right* rather than doing what is wrong . . . , even if this results in suffering."[381] God wills that Christians always and everywhere remain faithful and true, even if that entails suffering.

We may count **1 Peter 3:18** as beginning the third major christological reflection in this discourse (cf. 1 Pet 1:18-21; 2:21-25),[382] possibly drawing on traditional materials.[383] It brings out a further insight into Peter's view of the atone-

[380]See Best, *1 Peter*, pp. 134-35.

[381]Elliott, *1 Peter*, p. 635.

[382]Achtemeier, *1 Peter*, p. 240 characterizes 1 Pet 3:18-22 as rambling in style, not recognizing that lengthy and often convoluted sentences are a hallmark of Asiatic rhetoric.

[383]Achtemeier, *1 Peter*, pp. 241-43. Though on pp. 244-46 his discussion of the basic possible ways to interpret this passage provides a helpful summary, see the more-thorough discussion in Elliott, *1 Peter*, pp. 693-705, on the traditional materials used here.

ment. Isaiah 53:11 LXX is likely in the background here: "The righteous one my servant, shall make many righteous, and he shall bear their iniquities." First Peter 3:18a reminds the listener that even Christ suffered on account of sins, and yet Peter certainly is not just drawing an analogy to his audience's suffering. The use of *hapax* here likely means "only once" (cf. Rom 6:10; Heb 7:27; 9:12, 26-28; 10:10), and thus the stress is on the uniqueness of Christ's suffering and death.[384] Here *epathen* likely includes death, as in the phrase "suffered under Pontius Pilate." The use of "sins" as plural may well suggest that Peter is not using *peri* plus the object to indicate that Christ is a sin offering, but just to stress that sin was what made it necessary, and indeed made it God's will, for Jesus to suffer. The next phrase, "the righteous for the unrighteous," again conjures up Isaiah 53 and clearly refers to a vicarious death by one who did not deserve to die at all, much less to die on a cross. The purpose of the death is clear: to bring people before God, to reconcile them to God, to make it possible for people to come into God's presence even though we are unrighteous. Thus, Christ's death is viewed as an act of pure grace. The verb *prosagō* means "to procure access." Christ's death provided access into the very presence of God (cf. the cognate noun: Rom 5:2; Eph 2:18; 3:12). It is perhaps not an accident that this is the same term used to refer to the leading of the animals to sacrifice (LXX: Ex 29:10; Lev 1:2). Access comes through sacrifice, in this case the sacrifice Jesus offered in person.[385]

The last clause of 1 Peter 3:18 is difficult to interpret, but clearly it refers to Christ. *Thantōtheis* implies that Jesus was forcibly put to death, and *sarx* indicates that he was a person of real flesh and blood, fully human. The form *sarki* cannot be instrumental here (and thus does not mean "by his flesh"); this rules out the idea that the parallel phrase means brought to life "by his (the) Spirit." In other words, *pneumati* cannot be a reference to Christ's divine nature since it never died nor could be said to be brought to life. His human spirit is another matter. Michaels is right to emphasize the parallel construction here and the *men . . . de* contrast. On the one hand, he was put to death in the sphere of the flesh. On the other hand, he was made alive in the sphere of the spirit/Spirit.[386]

---

[384]Marshall, *1 Peter,* p. 119, points out *hapax* could also mean "at one point in time" (once back then as opposed to now—somewhat like the meaning of *pote* in 1 Pet 2:10; 3:5; or 3:20) but that would be innocuous, and besides, the use of *hapax* in the book of Hebrews also points in the direction of seeing the uniqueness and finality of Christ's sacrifice in this term. Cf. Michaels, *1 Peter,* pp. 201-2; Achtemeier, *1 Peter,* p. 251. Elliott, *1 Peter,* p. 641, is prepared to translate it "once for all time." In any case the word sets Christ's suffering apart from that of his followers in a crucial way. His alone was for atonement of sins.

[385]See Goppelt, *1 Peter,* p. 252.

[386]See Elliott, *1 Peter,* pp. 646-47.

But what does *pneumati* means here? Does it mean (1) in his spirit, (2) in the Spirit, (3) spiritually, or (4) in the realm of the spirit, or with reference to the spirit? Here is an intended contrast—"on the one hand, . . . on the other"—but in both halves of the contrast we are talking about something that *happened* to Jesus, not something he did. Possibly 1 Peter 4:6b should be seen as a parallel here: dead Christians have been judged in the eyes of humans and are dead in regard to the flesh, but in God's eyes they are alive in regard to the Spirit. But if 1 Peter 3:18 is talking about the human spirit of Jesus, did it die on the cross, or did it merely pass on into God's hands? Sometimes "spirit" means the animating life breath of a physical body (the *psychē,* e.g.), but Peter does not seem to mean that here. He is probably not talking about a body-soul dualism here. Normally "made alive" in the New Testament means resuscitated (cf. Jn 5:21; 6:63; Rom 4:17; 8:11); if that is meant here, then clearly Peter is not talking about some spiritual existence that Jesus had between death and resurrection. Thus, either *pneumati* refers to the Holy Spirit here, or there is a reference to the realm or sphere of the spirit, the spiritual realm. If it is the latter, then presumably *sarx* here refers to the physical or material realm. Now if Christ's being "made alive" points to his resurrection, then *pneumati* does not describe Christ's anatomical condition (that he was nonmaterial at that point), but rather says that the controlling sphere or factor in his life was the spiritual sphere, not the earthly, fleshly one. This might mean that he had a resurrection body but was living in a heavenly or spiritual sphere (in a realm or condition dominated by God's Spirit). Best puts it this way:

> The contrast is not between two parts of man's nature, his flesh and his spirit (a contrast which is on the whole foreign to the New Testament) nor between two parts in Christ (his divine nature could not be said to be made alive in his death), nor is it possible to take "spirit" to mean that Christ went in a bodiless fashion to preach to the "spirits" (verse 19). When spirit is opposed to flesh in the New Testament, the opposition of divine Spirit to human existence is intended; cf. Gal 5.16ff.; Rom 8.1ff. . . . Both "flesh" and "spirit," datives without a preposition, are best taken as datives of reference. . . . The phrase then means that Christ died in the human sphere but was made alive and continues alive in the sphere of the Spirit.[387]

Unless one wants to argue that the second phrase refers to Jesus' human spirit being revived, it is hard to escape the conclusion that the second phrase refers to the resurrection. And the further implication of the grammar here is that Jesus' visit to the spirits in prison took place *after* he was quickened "in the

[387]Best, *1 Peter,* p. 139.

spirit/Spirit."[388] What can be added to this is that the verb *zōopoiētheis,* "made alive," is clearly used to refer to the resurrection of Jesus elsewhere in the New Testament (cf. Jn 5:21; Rom 4:17; 8:11; 1 Cor 15:22; Col 2:13). The passive voice here and elsewhere makes clear that Jesus did not raise himself, but rather was raised by God.[389]

Furthermore, even texts like Romans 10:7 or Ephesians 4:8-10 do not actually refer to Jesus going down and preaching to dead human beings. The Ephesians text surely refers to the preexistent Christ's descent *to earth,* not to Sheol/Hades; the Romans text, though it may refer to Christ's spirit being in the land of the dead at some juncture, says nothing about preaching to anyone, and in any case it is part of a rhetorical question. Furthermore, Paul is speaking to his own Roman audience in the present tense and believes very clearly that Jesus is not currently among the dead: instead, he is in heaven. Therefore the rhetorical function of the remark is not to comment on the location of Jesus but rather on the fact that human beings could not go and retrieve Christ from *anywhere* in the spiritual realm.

There is no doubt that **1 Peter 3:19** follows on from the previous verse and should not be separated from it. However, there are at least six hard questions this text does raise:[390] (1) What is the antecedent of "in which"? (2) When did Christ preach to the spirits?[391] (3) Who are these spirits? (4) Where is their prison? (5) What did Christ preach to them? (6) Do 1 Peter 3:16 and 1 Peter 4:6 refer to the same event? In addition to our other problems with this text, it is not clear what Peter's view of baptism is. Elliott claims that there are some 180 options for interpreting these complex verses, but still certain issues can be sorted out reasonably clearly.[392] Grammar should have guided the discussion, but in many cases it has not. As Michaels says, "The words *en hō kai* serves to link *zōopoiētheis* closely to the *poreutheis ekēryxen* that follows, making Christ's proclamation to the spirits a direct outcome of his resurrection from the dead."[393] In other words, the preaching, whatever its nature, is surely *not* an activity that

---

[388]Michaels, *1 Peter,* pp. 204-5; Achtemeier, *1 Peter,* p. 258.

[389]See Senior, *1 Peter,* p. 101.

[390]So many questions arise that even so fine a scholar as Scot McKnight (in *1 Peter,* pp. 215-17) throws up his hands and simply presents the three major options for interpreting this text.

[391]The substitution of Enoch for Christ here by Moffatt and Goodspeed has no textual warrant at all. But see Moffatt, *General Epistles,* p. 141. See the critique in Achtemeier, *1 Peter,* pp. 253-54. This brilliant conjecture for 1 Pet 3:19, turning "in which," *en hōe,* into Enoch, *enōch* (only one letter different in the Greek), can be traced back to the Greek NT of William Bowyer in (London) 1763, after which this conjecture took on a life of its own. See Elliott, *1 Peter,* p. 652.

[392]See the laying out of the basic options in Elliott, *1 Peter,* pp. 648-50.

[393]Michaels, *1 Peter,* pp. 205-6.

took place between his death and his resurrection.

Of necessity we must deal with the central thrust of these complex verses, which clearly enough are not primarily focusing on baptism. Attending to question 1, which is dealing with the beginning of 1 Peter 3:19, as commentators have rightly pointed out, when Peter uses the phrase *en hō,* its antecedent is always a whole phrase that precedes, not a single word. It is thus unlikely that "in which" means "in the Spirit." Rather, it is more likely to mean "in which condition" (the condition of being made alive by the Spirit or spiritually, meaning resurrected). Second, we need to answer the question about who these "spirits" (plural) are, which are in some sort of prison.

We may note first that they cannot simply be the dead, to whom 1 Peter 4:6 indeed refers, because here these spirits are not said to be all spirits, but only those who are *en phylakē,* and furthermore, they are the same spirits who disobeyed in the days of Noah. In the New Testament this language about prison is *never* used to refer to Sheol/Hades, the land of the dead, much less to hell. It always refers to an incarcerating place for fallen angels or demons (cf. Rev 18:2; 20:7; *1 En.* 10:4; 14:5; 15:8, 10; 18:12-14; cf. 2 Pet 2:4). Now if Peter was talking about human beings here, he surely would not have chosen the phrase "in prison" or the phrase "spirits who disobeyed," because human beings were neither spirits nor in the Spirit in the days of Noah. He would rather have said "the spirits *of those* who once disobeyed," not "the spirits who disobeyed." Furthermore, the phrase *ta pneumata,* which does not mean "the spiritual ones," is never used elsewhere to refer to human beings who have died, with the possible exception of Hebrews 12:23. By contrast, we have plenty of evidence of supernatural beings called spirits in the New Testament (e.g., cf. the unclean spirits in Mk 1:23, 26, 27; 3:11; etc.). More important, in Jude and in 2 Peter the phrase is used of disobedient angels (cf. Jude 6; 2 Pet 2:4; *T. Reu.* 5.2). In view of this fact, that 1 Peter comes out of the same apocalyptic Jewish Christian milieu as these two books; that these sources seem clearly to be drawing on *1 Enoch* 6—16; and finally since 2 Peter 2:4 represents the first canonical interpretation of our passage (and the one in Jude)—then most assuredly what we are dealing with here is angels.[394] In *1 Enoch* 15:8-10 we hear about the giants being born of the union of "spirits and the flesh" (of angels and human women).

Obviously nowhere in Judaism and also nowhere in early Christianity in the first century, unless it is here in 1 Peter, do we find the idea of a descent into hell (as distinct from "prison" in 1 Pet 3:19). The first noncanonical mention of

[394]See what happens when exegesis goes awry and the angelic interpretation is rejected in Goppelt, *1 Peter,* pp. 258-62.

the idea of a descent into hell seems to be found in Justin's *Dialogue with Trypho* 72, but it is not associated with the interpretation of this text. That does not come until Clement of Alexandria interprets 1 Peter 3:19 this way, and this then became the dominant interpretation, at least by the time of Irenaeus at the end of second century A.D.[395] Nevertheless, the first time that the phrase "He descended into hell" appears in any creedal discussion or creed is in about A.D. 400, in Rufinus's exposition of a Roman creed. It is also worth remarking at this juncture that the Apostles' Creed does not originally seem to have had this clause, but even if it did, no council ever endorsed this particular early creed, unlike the Nicene Creed.[396]

The notion that the preaching was to the disobedient sinners of Noah's generation, giving them a second chance at redemption, so to speak, raises a perplexing question. How exactly rhetorically would that effectively steel the audience to face persecution and possible death? Would it not rather have the opposite effect? Achtemeier puts it this way: "If God relented on such evil entities, why not rely on the same treatment and deny Christ now to avoid suffering?"[397]

With I. Howard Marshall, we may also stress that there are insuperable problems with the idea that Christ preached to the lost during the time of Noah in the person of Noah. As we have stressed, the Greek grammar here favors the view that this proclamation by Christ took place after Christ had been "made alive," which is to say, "was raised," not before he even took on flesh. Second, the spirit of Christ inspiring Old Testament prophets is one thing; his inhabiting Noah and speaking through him is quite another. If that were the case, the text should have read, "He preached when the spirits disobeyed," but it does not. Third, the spirits in prison would be a very odd way to speak about ordinary human life during the time of Noah.[398] For these difficult verses, we surely need better exegesis than this. In these verses nothing is said about Christ going *down* anywhere, much less that he went *down to Hades*. The verb *poreutheis* in 1 Peter 3:19 and in 1 Peter 3:22 describes Jesus' travels, and it simply means "he went" or "he has gone," with no direction

---

[395]See Senior, *1 Peter,* p. 101.

[396]On the history of the *ad infernos* interpretation, see esp. Elliott, *1 Peter,* pp. 706-9; cf. Jobes, *1 Peter,* p. 236.

[397]Achtemeier, *1 Peter,* p. 261. The same problem follows if Jesus is preaching good news to the wicked angels of Gen 6:1-4. The word "preach" in itself is not a technical term for "preach the good news." The noun form *kērygma* in Mt 12:41//Lk 11:32 is used for the content of Jonah's message, which was closer to the Baptist's message than to Jesus' preaching. In 1 Pet 3:19 the use of *kēryssō*, just meaning "announce," differs from 1 Pet 4:6, which indeed does have *euangelizō*.

[398]See Marshall, *1 Peter,* p. 124.

implied in the verb at all. Only the context indicates that, if anything does. If 1 Peter 3:22 provides the guiding clue, then this proclamation took place not *between* death and resurrection but *after* Jesus experienced resurrection, as 1 Peter 3:18 implies. In other words, it refers to what happened as or while Jesus ascended to heaven. We have to read the idea of "between death and resurrection" into this story. But there is a much better option than suffering these sorts of exegetical gymnastics: it involves recognizing the influence of *1 Enoch* in our text.

A CLOSER LOOK

Ascending Enoch; Jesus and Falling Spirits

Commentators have long known that there is some connection between *1 Enoch* and what is said in 1 Peter 3:18-22, but the exact connections have been vigorously debated. Indeed, so vigorous has the debate been that some have dubbed this passage in 1 Peter the most difficult one in the whole New Testament to understand. We certainly cannot obtain clarity if we fail to read this material in the light of its Jewish and apocalyptic contexts. This passage especially presumes a lot of the audience. Indeed, it presumes too much if the audience is largely composed of converted pagans not privy to the vagaries of early Jewish apocalyptic speculations. It will be useful at this juncture to consider the relevant material from *1 Enoch* in a closer way, to see if we cannot unravel some of the mysteries of our text.

First a little background. *First Enoch* is a book composed and edited over several centuries before the turn of the era: it is a composite document. The important point for our consideration here is that it was all extant long before the time when 1 Peter was written. George W. E. Nickelsburg, one of the few real experts on *1 Enoch*, tells us that *1 Enoch* was "composed and edited over the three and half centuries before the turn of the era, the earliest [parts] of them were composed within a century after the time of Ezra. Running through these texts is the belief in an imminent great judgment that will terminate the present age dominated by the evil spirits generated by the rebel angels, and that will usher in a new creation and new age marked by God's final and universal sovereignty."[399] It should be immediately apparent why Peter would find this text of use and interest for what he wants to claim in 1 Peter. Nickelsburg rightly characterizes what we find in *1 Enoch* as apocalyptic eschatology. The same could be said about the eschatology in 1 Peter, especially 1 Peter 3:18-22.

[399]George W. E. Nickelsburg, *Ancient Judaism and Christian Origins: Diversity, Continuity, and Transformation* (Minneapolis: Fortress, 2003), p. 123.

Notably, however, Peter seems to be familiar with and possibly indebted to not just one verse here or there; he seems to have a wider range of familiarity with the *1 Enoch* literature. But let us start with the most obvious echo.

First Enoch tells the tale of the fallen angels of Genesis 6:1-4 and their fate. Enoch, who ascended into heaven without first dying on earth (cf. Gen 5:24), is sent on a mission to speak a word of judgment to these fallen angels. He is commissioned by the "watchers of the Great Holy One" (the unfallen angels still serving God in heaven):

> Enoch, righteous scribe, go and say to the watchers of heaven, who forsook the highest heaven, the sanctuary of their eternal station, and defiled themselves with women. As the sons of the earth do, so they did and took wives for themselves. And they wrought great desolation on the earth. [Say to them,] "You will have no peace or forgiveness," and concerning their sons in whom they rejoice, "The slaughter of their beloved ones they will seek; and over the destruction of their sons they will lament and make petition forever, and they will have no mercy or peace." And Enoch, go and say to Asael, "You will have no peace. A great sentence has gone forth against you, to bind you. You will have no relief or petition, because of the unrighteous deeds that you revealed." (*1 En.* 12:4—13:2)

On this passage we must stress that the content of the message to the fallen spirits is clearly negative and condemnatory. If, as seems likely, the story of Jesus in 1 Peter 3 is being patterned after this, then we are meant to assume that his message to these spirits was one of judgment, or perhaps even announcing triumph over the spirits. Notice as well that in *1 Enoch* 10:4-6 (cf. *1 En.* 67) these fallen spirits are said to be imprisoned in the burning valley of Gehenna or Dudael. Both *1 Enoch* (21:10) and *2 Enoch* (7:1-3; 18:3) tell us quite specifically that we should call the dwelling place of these fallen spirits a "prison." *First Enoch* 18:14 speaks of "the prison house for the stars and the powers of heaven."

Nickelsburg has been able to show considerable parallels between *1 Enoch* 108, the very end of the Enoch corpus, and 1 Peter in general, including 1 Peter 3:18-22 in particular. For example, *1 Enoch* 108 speaks of the spirits punished (*1 En.* 108:3-6), and this follows hard on the announcement in *1 Enoch* 106:16-18 that Noah and his sons were saved.[400] He notes the reference to "perishable seed" in both 1 Peter 1:23 and *1 Enoch* 108:3b. The reference to disdain for silver and gold in 1 Peter 1:7, 18 is like that found in *1 Enoch* 108:8.

[400] Van Unnik, "Role de Noé," pp. 207-39.

The discussion of blessing and reproach in 1 Peter 3:9, 16; 4:4, 16 is like that in *1 Enoch* 108:7-10. The discussion of exaltation in 1 Peter 5:4, 6 is similar to *1 Enoch* 108:12. And the similarities in the discussion of righteous judgment in 1 Peter 1:17; 2:23 should be compared to *1 Enoch* 108:13. In addition there is the common use of Psalm 34 (see *1 En.* 108:7-10; cf. 1 Pet 3:10-12).[401] None of this is a surprise when we recognize that *1 Enoch* is influential in various of these Jewish Christian eschatological works: for instance, Jude not merely refers to the text of *1 Enoch* in Jude 4, 6, 13; he even cites *1 Enoch* 1:9 in Jude 14-15 of his discourse. Second Peter as well also is directly dependent on *1 Enoch* at 2 Peter 2:4 and 3:13. For our purposes here we note that it is the Book of Noah part of *1 Enoch,* which includes *1 Enoch* 6—11; 64—69; 106—108 that is almost exclusively being drawn on in 1 Peter.[402]

The story of the "sons of God" coming down and mating with the daughters of humanity immediately precedes the story of Noah and the flood (see Gen 6:1-4). Especially important are *1 Enoch* 106:13 and *2 Enoch* 7:3, which connect the story of Noah with the punishing of the fallen angels. As Jude 6 says, these fallen angels are "bound in chains in everlasting darkness," or as 1 Peter puts it, they are "in prison."[403] Just as Enoch went and spoke to them according to the tradition in *1 Enoch,* so too does Jesus; 1 Peter depicts Jesus as the new and true Enoch. Again, Sheol, or the land of the dead, is never called a prison in the Bible. In 1 Peter 3:19 we are talking about the confinement of some (rebel) angels: that is all. We are told that Jesus proclaimed something to them—but what? If we see Peter as continuing to draw on the Enoch material, then we must remember that Enoch proclaimed their punishment to these fallen angels (cf. *1 En.* 12:4—13:2; 1 Pet 3:19). Further, 1 Peter 3:22 tells us of the angels being put in subjection to Christ. The context mentions nothing about how they respond to the preaching. This is understandable if Christ simply went to proclaim their punishment, not to try to convert them. We certainly do not find here any sort of second-chance, beyond-death theology, not least because the text is about angels and not humans; and Peter does not tell us that the resurrected Jesus went and preached any good news to anyone. And lest we find it hard to imagine that Jesus preached to these fallen angels in heaven somewhere on his way to the throne, consider *2 Enoch*

[401]See George W. E. Nickelsburg, *1 Enoch: A Commentary on the Book of 1 Enoch,* Hermeneia (Minneapolis: Fortress, 2001), p. 560.

[402]The definitive and detailed study of Dalton, *Christ's Proclamation to the Spirits,* esp. pp. 164-71, makes so very clear the connections between 1 Pet 3:18-22 and various materials in *1 Enoch* that it is hard to understand why some scholars are so insistent on denying these parallels.

[403]See the detailed discussion in Ben Witherington III, *Jesus the Seer: The Progress of Prophecy* (Peabody, Mass.: Hendrickson, 1999), introduction, pp. 1-15.

7:1-3, where Enoch is taken to the second heaven and shown "a darkness greater than earthly darkness" and "prisoners under guard, hanging up, waiting for the measureless judgment."

After the extensive work of George W. E. Nickelsburg and William Joseph Dalton and others, it is very difficult for me to doubt that we are talking about a considerable influence of the Enochian material in 1 Peter, and especially in 1 Peter 3:18-22. The import of this is hard to underestimate. It means, among other things, that this text has nothing to do with proclaiming the gospel to the human dead. It certainly also has nothing to do with the coming of the preexistent Christ to earth either during the time of Noah or in the incarnation. Here we have a story about the proclamation of judgment on the principalities and powers, and the triumph beyond death of Christ in glory. Its relevance to the Jewish Christian audience is quite apparent. Peter is telling them that they are following the same trajectory as Christ, and indeed of Noah even earlier. Though others may be reviling, slandering and abusing them during their earthly life, nevertheless despite their current suffering, they will one day triumph over their foes whose "doom is sure." Peter does not specifically connect the "spirits" with the powers behind the pagan government, but rather he makes the association more broadly with the fallen world in general, which is abusing the audience. Truly 1 Peter 3:18-22 is one text about which it is most accurate to claim that, without knowledge of the context of this material, in particular the Jewish apocalyptic context, all sorts of misinterpretations are likely to follow, including even the generation of doctrines of purgatory, second-chance theology and the like.[404]

If we ask the rhetorical function of this elaborate argument, it would be a further way that Peter is trying to encourage suffering Christians. "Do not worry," says Peter, "about the powers of evil that motivate such persecutors. They have already been told that their doom is sure." Here is where we observe the close parallel in 1 Timothy 3:16—"appeared in flesh, vindicated by the Spirit, seen by angels"[405]—though that could refer to being seen by nonfallen angels. Presumably we should see this prison as a holding place until the final judgment (cf. Rev 20:1-2), and thus not hell or Sheol. This all comports nicely with the idea that angels and such spirit beings are above, in the air or the heavenlies (cf. Eph 2:2, "the prince of the power of the air"; Eph 3:10; Eph 6:12).[406]

---

[404]See the helpful summary in Bauckham, "Spirits in Prison," pp. 177-78.

[405]On this see Witherington, *Letters and Homilies for Hellenized Christians,* 1:245-46.

[406]See the discussion in Witherington, *Philemon, Colossians, and Ephesians.*

The point of the analogy in **1 Peter 3:20** is that just as God saved his people, though only a few, while the wicked pagans were many in the days of Noah, so will he do with Peter's audience, who are only a few Jews in comparison with a large pagan majority. Peter is rehearsing Jesus' triumphant story to reassure the persecuted Christians that though they are also going the route of suffering, their triumph afterward will be like Christ's. They need not fear or worry.

First Peter 3:21 is one of the more difficult verses to decipher in this section. First of all, we hear about the "antitype," a term elsewhere (in the NT) found only in Hebrews 9:24 (cf. *2 Clem.* 14.3; Polybius *Hist.* 6.31.8 for the use with the dative), to refer to the temple.[407] Here it must mean something like the waters of Noah's day prefigure the greater judgment and salvation event in Christ, which is symbolized in baptism.[408] *Only here* in 1 Peter do we have a brief discussion of baptism, and only here in the whole New Testament do we have a statement that baptism in some sense "saves." It is a mistake to build a whole theology of baptism on the basis of one text, which all sides of the discussion admit is obscure, perhaps the most obscure and difficult text in the whole New Testament canon.

At some point after Jews arrived in the region of Asia Minor to which 1 Peter is addressed, after about 200 B.C., a remarkable thing happened. There were already at least four flood stories in Asia Minor even before the proliferation of Jews in the region, but when the Jews arrived, they became fascinated by a town named Apamea Kibotos (modern Dinar). This is because the second word in the name of this town means "ark," and Jews drew the conclusion that the town likely preserved the location where Noah's ark came to rest, or at least on the nearby mountain. Over the course of the next two and half centuries, the one Old Testament figure that became a household name in this region was Noah. Even Gentiles knew about Noah and his possible connection with Asia Minor. It thus is in no way surprising that Peter would choose Noah to draw an analogy while addressing persons in these regions, and all the more so if they were Jews familiar with their Old Testament history. Even more remarkable, the legend of Noah continued to grow in this region well into the Christian era. For example, five Roman emperors from Septimus Severus (A.D. 193-211) to Trebonianus Gallus (251-253) issued coins depicting Noah and his wife on one side and the emperor's image on the other! In short, Peter was a wise rhetorician, who drew on the story of a very popular "local hero" to make his points about

[407]We now have inscriptional evidence for the word *antitypos* (1 Pet 3:21). In *IGUR* 1167.3-4 it means something like "corresponding." To this we should compare *IGUR* 1327.5, which refers to an "exact" copy. See the discussion in *New Docs* 4:41-42.

[408]See Senior, *1 Peter*, pp. 104-5.

Christ and baptism and salvation and the fallen angels.[409] The story, and Peter's rhetorical move in using it, is all the more telling if the audience is Jewish Christians. Finally, we should remember that Noah was seen as a preacher of righteousness to a wicked world that rejected his message (2 Pet 2:5; Heb 11:7). He indeed provides another example of how Peter's audience should respond to their situation, whatever the reception, when they give a reason for the hope that is within them.[410]

This verse seems to be saying that what saves a person is either the plea/entreaty for or the pledge/plea of a good conscience to God, not the rite itself, which simply involves the putting off of the filth of the flesh. William Joseph Dalton has made the interesting and plausible suggestion that the phrase "filth of the flesh" alludes to circumcision since early Jews thought of the foreskin as unclean. The point thus would be that baptism, unlike circumcision, the sign of the old covenant, does not accomplish its work by an outward physical act. Rather, there must be an inward and spiritual transformation that amounts to real "immersion," and it is not somehow directly accomplished by the water ritual (noting the contrast here).[411] In any case, this is the only direct reference to the rite of baptism in this whole discourse, and one should not therefore turn the whole discourse into some sort of baptismal liturgy or catechism. If baptism is just an appeal or request for a good conscience, then it neither presupposes one, nor creates one.[412]

Here are some factors that help us to figure out this conundrum:

1. The word *eperōtēma* is a crucial one in the whole discussion. This word has a legal or contractual sense of a clause in a contract containing a formal question/request and its answer. It can then certainly mean "question" or even "formal request." The evidence that the term means pledge seems to be lacking before the second century A.D. (but see P.Cair.Preis. 1.16 on

[409]On all of this, see Trebilco, *Jewish Communities in Asia Minor,* pp. 86-91.

[410]Columbia University geologists William Ryan and Walter Pitman, *Noah's Flood* (New York: Simon & Schuster, 1998), and Ian Wilson, *Before the Flood* (London: Orion, 2001; repr., New York: St. Martin's Griffin, 2004), show archaeological evidence that around 5600 B.C. waves from the Mediterranean, caused by melting glaciers of the last ice age and rising sea levels, broke over the land linking Turkey to Europe, creating the Bosporus Strait and raising the (formerly inland freshwater) Black Sea level ca. 300 feet (human settlements found 300 feet below surface) in a matter of months (6 inches a day!), flooding farming settlements around the Black Sea, creating worldwide diaspora: some survivors went south into Egypt, Mesopotamia and other parts of Middle East and, they argue, carried stories that might be a basis for the Genesis tale of Noah, stories likely remembered in some fashion in Peter's Asia Minor communities!

[411]See Dalton, *Christ's Proclamation to the Spirits*, pp. 199-206; cf. Achtemeier, *1 Peter,* p. 269.

[412]Against Goppelt, *1 Peter,* pp. 268-69; Heb 10:22 does not suggest otherwise: it simply parallels the internal cleansing of the conscience with baptism, the external sign of cleansing.

a legal sense of a formal question). Going back to Herodotus, this term refers to the inquiry made of the gods through an oracle (Herodotus *Hist*. 1.53.1). In other words, it refers to a ritual act that is making a request, petition or entreaty of a deity (cf. this verb in Mt 16:1). We may compare Shepherd of Hermas's *Mandate* 11.2, where in the plural it has the sense of requests. Baptism is clearly enough a ritual act. If we take the word to mean request, which is certainly possible, then baptism is seen as a prayer or plea to have one's conscience, one's inner self cleansed.

2. The text does indeed say "baptism saves," but Peter then proceeds to qualify the remark in several ways, including denying that the outward washing accomplishes the inward transformation. I. Howard Marshall is quite emphatic about this: "[Peter] clearly does not mean this [baptism saves] in any material sense, as if an outward rite could convey spiritual salvation; or in any magical sense, as if the water possessed some spiritual power; or in any automatic way, so that anyone who is baptized is saved. We should not make the mistake of limiting baptism to the precise moment and action of being immersed or sprinkled with water. Rather, for Peter, the word "baptism" symbolically represents the whole process by which the Gospel comes to people and they accept it."[413] This makes some sense if Peter had actually heard Jesus use the term "baptism" in a broader sense, for example to refer to his death or even to refer to the coming and powering of the Spirit.

3. What precisely is the antitype here? Is it baptism itself? The NIV, for example, takes the relative pronoun "which" to refer to the water itself, as if the text reads, "which water also saves you." Should we think that Peter means "and as an antitype to the whole Noachic event baptism now saves you"? Or is he saying that believers are the antitype of the family of Noah? Elsewhere in the New Testament, for example in Hebrews, the antitype kind of comparison is made between persons, Moses and Jesus, or even better Melchizedek and Jesus (but Heb 9:24 uses the temple/tabernacle in a typology). This is why the idea of saved believers being the antitype of Noah's family makes some sense.

4. Notice how 1 Peter 3:21 reads literally, "Which also you [object] antitype now saves (you) baptism [subject], not the flesh removal of dirt but a good conscience request unto God." If we expand that just a little it can read, "Which also is (true of) you, the antitype in the present—baptism saves

[413]Marshall, *1 Peter,* p. 130.

you, not through the removal of dirt from the flesh, but through the request for a good conscience." And further, we must ask what it means to call baptism the antitype of the flood. This seems to view baptism as a water ordeal that involves redemptive judgment: judgment on sin, but redemption of some who repent or are righteous or are in the ark, so to speak. Is the ark here seen as an emblem of the church? Some church fathers thought so.

Yet here we need to deal with a further point of grammar. The phrase contrasting something with the outward washing of water reads literally, "but of a good conscience a plea/request unto God." The phrase "good conscience" is in the genitive, and the question is whether this genitive is objective (noun in genitive receives the action) or subjective (noun in genitive produces the action): is baptism a symbol of a plea *of* or *by* a good conscience unto God (subjective genitive), or is it a plea unto God *for* a good conscience (objective genitive)? One's theology of baptism is dramatically affected by how one reads this genitive, and scholars are about equally divided. In my view the objective genitive makes better sense. Baptism symbolizes cleansing, in this case the cleansing of the conscience, which takes place by means of conversion (see 1 Pet 1:2). Only God can produce such inner cleansing by the saving work of Christ; hence comes the following phrase "through the resurrection." If we are dealing with a subjective genitive, then we have no answer to the question Plea or request for what? But if we are dealing with an objective genitive, then baptism is seen as a plea for internal cleansing, a plea for a clean conscience.[414]

This makes better sense not only in terms of Peter's soteriology, but also in terms of his theology of baptism. Baptism, the outward washing, does not produce what it depicts, and what it depicts is entrance into the community of faith. It is a rite of passage, not a rite of confirming a preexisting faith. This is why whole households of persons were baptized, surely including children, even infants (see, e.g., 1 Cor 1:16), for the term "household" is never used exclusively of adults. It is always an all-encompassing phrase, even including the slaves.[415] Baptism does not symbolize a human response, much less a human self-help program. It symbolizes the grace of God, which regenerates and has washed

[414]See the detailed discussion in Achtemeier, *1 Peter*, p. 272, which shows why the objective genitive reading is far more probable, not least because the parallel phrase about the filth of the flesh involves an objective genitive as well. If baptism really is a plea or request for a good and clean conscience, then it presupposes that the person does not yet have one and so is pre-Christian or at the point of conversion.

[415]On all of this, see Ben Witherington III, *Troubled Waters: Rethinking the Theology of Baptism* (Waco: Baylor University Press, 2007).

away our sins, even the grace that worked in us before we ever responded to God. It is a passive sacrament, not an active sacrament, by which I mean that the participant simply "receives" an act of baptism performed by another on their behalf. It is to be contrasted with the Lord's Supper, which is an active sacrament.

First Peter 3:22 presents us with an interesting conclusion to this whole paragraph. It speaks of the supernatural beings as "angels, authorities, and powers," a style found elsewhere only in Paul. This supports our view that our author knew Paul, and perhaps some of his writings, or at least his characteristic speech and discourse (cf. Rom 8:38; 1 Cor 15:24; Eph 1:21-22; 3:10; cf. Col 2:10).[416] Another interesting feature of this verse is we have reference to the ascension, which is not an idea found only in Luke-Acts in the New Testament, but here ascension and exaltation are joined together, so to speak. Peter reassures the audience that the angelic powers are already in submission to Christ.[417] We may compare what is said here to Acts 1:9-11 (cf. Lk 24:51); Hebrews 4:14; 6:20; and Mark 16:19, from the later long ending of that Gospel.

First Peter 4:1-6 then draws out certain implications of all this and links back with 1 Peter 3:18a, on the suffering of Christ. But in **1 Peter 4:1**, are Christians meant to arm themselves with the thought that Christ suffered in the flesh? This may be so. The "then" seems clearly resumptive here of 1 Peter 3:18, and suffering was the subject in that verse.[418] The word *ennoia* is an interesting word and can have the sense of "insight" or "wisdom." Note its use in the LXX of Proverbs 2:11; 3:21; 16:22; 23:19, where it almost seems to have the sense of "resolve," or "settled disposition."[419] This thus would be a plea to arm themselves with the wisdom or resolve that Christ had when he suffered.[420] We are reminded of Philippians 2:5, "Have this mind in yourself which was also in Christ Jesus." I quite agree with Karen H. Jobes in commenting on Jesus' resolve: "It would not do justice to the full human nature of Jesus Christ to assume that he fulfilled God's redemptive plan for his life without thought, deliberation, or decision. Jesus' agony in Gethsemane indicates otherwise. In fact, throughout his human development Jesus had consciously to embrace his calling and commitment to his relationship to the Father (Luke 2:52; Heb. 5:8)."[421]

[416]All these three documents could have been available in the community of Christians in Rome when Peter wrote 1 Peter: Romans was written to Rome in A.D. 57; Colossians and Ephesians were likely written from Rome in 60-62.

[417]See Goppelt, *1 Peter,* pp. 273-74.

[418]See Cranfield, *First Peter,* p. 88.

[419]See Jobes, *1 Peter,* p. 262.

[420]Perkins, *First Peter,* p. 67.

[421]Jobes, *1 Peter,* p. 265.

The question then becomes, What does 1 Peter 4:1b mean? Let us consider several options: (1) Suffering on the believers' part atones for their own sins. (2) Suffering causes the believer to cease from sinning, and thus suffering is so much better than other alternatives such as sinning (see 1 Pet 4:2-3).[422] (3) 1 Peter 4:1b refers to being dead to sin and alive to Christ (cf. Rom 6:7). (4) 1 Peter 4:1b, like 1 Peter 4:1a, means suffering unto death, at which point one has obviously ceased sinning. (5) Suffering purifies the believer from sin. (6) "He who suffers" in this verse actually refers to Christ, not to Christians.[423]

In weighing these views, we can rather easily dismiss option 1 since elsewhere Peter affirms that only Christ's death atones for sin (see, e.g., 1 Peter 3:18), and we must remember that the term "sin" in 1 Peter normally means sinful behavior, not a sin nature (see 1 Pet 4:2-3). Option 3 is unlikely not only because we ought not to read Paul into Peter, but also because "suffering in the flesh" is not the same as "dying to sin." Option 4 is too obvious to need saying: death certainly stops sinful behavior. But here the issue is sin itself and its relationship to suffering. If Peter wanted to tell us that suffering purifies us from sin, *pepautai* is not the most obvious or likely verb to use. What about option 6? The problem with this is severalfold: The natural and closest antecedent for the phrase "whoever suffers . . ." is the "yourselves" who are arming themselves.[424] We need to realize that here we are dealing with an enthymeme, a compressed argument, and we need to identify the suppressed premise:

> Major premise: Christ suffered in his body and yet was vindicated beyond death.
>
> Minor suppressed premise: You will also have such an outcome if you will arm yourself with the same attitude as Christ had about suffering (and death).
>
> Conclusion: The one busily suffering for a just cause has ceased from sinning. It is better to suffer as a righteous person than to sin and face the ultimate suffering—final judgment and punishment.

Thus, on the whole, view 2 seems the most likely option here. Suffering is preferable to sinning, and suffering for Christ means one has ceased to sin against him.[425] And it certainly is a comforting thought that Christ himself had to suffer in the flesh.

First Peter 4:2 follows quite naturally from the above conclusion. Peter now introduces a stock list of things pagans do which no Christians, during their re-

---

[422]See Achtemeier, *1 Peter,* p. 280.
[423]See Michaels, *1 Peter,* pp. 225-29.
[424]McKnight, *1 Peter,* p. 225.
[425]But see the discussion in McKnight, *1 Peter,* pp. 224-26.

maining time in the flesh, should be involved in.[426] Pheme Perkins rightly warns: "The descriptions of a past life of drunken licentiousness should not be taken as evidence for the particular vices that the audience had abandoned. They are part of the stock language of conversion stories."[427] In this particular case, Hellenized Jews may well have done some of these things, especially if they went to dinner parties at temples. I. Howard Marshall puts it this way: "The reference to pagan pursuits need not imply that the readers were all former pagans. Jews too were quite capable of falling into such sins. The point is rather that these were the kind of practices one might expect from people without any knowledge of God, whereas the Jews should know better."[428]

"Desires" here must mean "sinful desires"; 1 Peter 4:2 functions as something of a heading for **1 Peter 4:3** and says, "For the rest of your life avoid indulging sinful desires." Notice that all of these vices listed are things that went on at pagan festivals or dinner parties, including in temples. Drunkenness and orgies are forbidden, but notice also the prohibition against idolatry, here called "disgusting" or "lawless *[athemitois]* idolatry."[429] Pagan idol feasts is a subject that Paul addresses as well at length in 1 Corinthians 8—10, as does Acts 15's decree articulated by James, and we may see this as one subject for taboo in Revelation 2—3 as well. Second Corinthians 6:14—7:1 is the Pauline form of the same advice: "Do not become entangled in pagan idol feasts and so be unequally yoked spiritually with unbelievers." The association of idolatry and immorality is quite natural in Jewish polemic, because it all happens in the same venue: the pagan temple.[430]

As **1 Peter 4:4** describes, it is natural for pagan friends to feel shamed when their friends who have become Christians start to refuse dinner invitations to the idol feast. This could lead them to retaliate by blaspheming (whether Jesus' name or that of the believer is not specified). If we seek other evidence written by Jews that criticizes Jews for idolatry and immorality, we can point to the *Testament of Judah;* though written in the second century B.C., it was translated into Greek in the first century A.D. *Testament of Judah* 14:2-3 tells us that Israel practices "debauchery" *(aselgeia),* the first word in our vice list, and *Testament of*

[426] This last phrase is certainly not a reference to the nearness of the parousia. Peter has already quoted the OT to the effect that "all flesh is as grass," which quickly withers and fades (cf. 1 Pet 1: 24). See rightly Michaels, *1 Peter,* p. 229.

[427] Perkins, *First Peter,* p. 68.

[428] Marshall, *1 Peter,* p. 135, note on 1 Pet 4:3.

[429] This may allude to the chaos of an orgy. See Michaels, *1 Peter,* p. 232, on the meaning of "lawless" and Acts 10:28.

[430] See at length Ben Witherington III, "Not so Idle Thoughts about *eidōlothyton,*" *TynBul* 44, no. 2 (1993): 237-54.

Judah 23:1 accuses the Jews of idolatry and even witchcraft. As Karen H. Jobes says, it is quite impossible to conclude that this section of the discourse proves that the audience must have been overwhelmingly Gentile.[431]

Sometimes it is hard for us to understand why polytheistic people would be so upset if their neighbors are worshiping a different god than they do. Why would they slander Jews or Christians or their God? There are several important reasons enumerated by John Barclay: (1) There was a belief in communal effect if proper piety was not exhibited by some member of the city. The wrath of one god or another was feared if even one segment of society did not propitiate or appease them. Earthquakes, famine, disease, flood, war—these were all attributed to the gods' displeasure if there were people who did not exhibit ***eusebeia*** in the place where these things happened. (2) "Family members who broke with ancestral traditions on the basis of their new-found faith showed an appalling lack of concern for their familial responsibilities." They were home wreckers and family dividers. (3) Christians, like Jews, practiced an exclusive worship of one God, which meant that they would not honor others nor even participate in the emperor cult. Pagan neighbors saw this as both arrogant and unpatriotic.[432] And we know that exhortations to Christians such as this very one in 1 Peter had an effect on Anatolia. Pliny the Younger, writing in about 111 A.D. to the Emperor Trajan, says that what he calls "depraved, excessive superstition" has not merely infected the cities of Asia Minor (he is holding court in Pontus), but has also spread to the countryside, with the result that people are abandoning "their normal way of life," "deserting the temples," no longer frequenting the meat markets (which got their meat mostly from the temples), and abandoning the festivals (Pliny *Ep.* 10.96.9-10). These complaints are all interrelated. What Christians are abandoning is temple feasts, idol meat sold in the markets, and the whole liturgical calendar around which celebrations in an ancient town revolved. As an evangelistic religion, Christianity was aggressively changing the religious climate in the region, such that some Christians had been executed and others were forced to renounce their faith; yet this was not stopping them, leading Pliny to seek further instructions from the emperor.[433] Peter is writing well before those days, but his words in 1 Peter must have been recognized as prophetic for many generations of Christians in Anatolia after he wrote, at least until the time of Constantine.

In any case, Peter in **1 Peter 4:5** wants his audience not to worry about such

---

[431]Jobes, *1 Peter,* p. 268.
[432]See Barclay, "Conflict in Thessalonica," pp. 512-30, esp. 515.
[433]See Achtemeier, *1 Peter,* p. 234-35.

abuse. Slanderers will have to account to the just Judge when he comes to judge the living and the dead. The phrase "the living and the dead" refers to everyone, whether they are alive at the parousia or not.

If Peter had stopped here, all would be relatively clear, but he does not stop. Instead, he gives us **1 Peter 4:6**, which is almost as difficult as 1 Peter 3:19, though clearly it refers to something different than 3:19. In 1 Peter 4:6a we have *eis touto gar* . . . , which makes it quite clear that 1 Peter 4:6 is linked back to 1 Peter 4:5. It is most unlikely that Peter means for us to find the antecedent all the way back at 1 Peter 3:15. Here "preached" is in the aorist tense and is in the passive voice as well. There are few if any examples in the New Testament of an impersonal subject with a passive verb such as this one.[434] It is talking about a past onetime activity that was done and is no longer done. It appears that its object is "the dead," and clearly in 1 Peter 4:5 the dead are human beings, not fallen angels. We need to bear in mind that Christians who died before Christ returned presented something of a pastoral problem, as we can clearly see in 1 Thessalonians 4:13-18.[435]

Have we finally found evidence that Christ preached to the dead in 1 Peter 4:6? John 5:25-30 might on the surface seem to support such a view, but in fact there the subject is Christ calling people out of their graves to face the music at the last judgment. Christ is not depicted as evangelizing them, but if he were, John 5:25 might well refer to the spiritually dead. Here in 1 Peter 4:6 it clearly is the physically dead who are in view. As Selwyn points out, the normal subject for "was preached" should be Christ.[436] This follows naturally from 1 Peter 4:5, where Christ is the (acting) subject as Judge. This means that if Christ is the one preached in 1 Peter 4:6, he is not also the preacher. So who is? It is possible that Peter has in view past missionaries who preached to living people who now are dead, a preaching that obviously transpired on earth, not in the nether regions. *Nekrois* might mean all the believers and nonbelievers, but the point of 1 Peter 4:5 is that nonbelievers who have slandered Christians will be judged. It is thus likely that 1 Peter 4:6 has a specific reference as well, in this case to the dead in Christ (who had accepted the gospel proclaimed to them while they were living). Here we recognize that this is a possible reference to one or more martyrdoms in the regions Peter is addressing. Since 1 Peter 4:5 is clearly connected with 1 Peter 4:6, the drift of the argument could be that while those who have tormented Christians will face final judgment, those who

[434]See rightly Kelly, *Epistles of Peter,* pp. 172-76.
[435]Achtemeier, *1 Peter,* pp. 288-91; Elliott, *1 Peter,* pp. 733-34.
[436]See Selwyn, *First Peter,* pp. 214-15.

have been faithful even unto death will have everlasting life.[437]

It is also believable that unbelievers are ridiculing the belief in resurrection, when even believers keep on dying (perhaps partly due to persecution?). Peter's point would thus be like Paul's in 1 Corinthians 15 and 1 Thessalonians 4:13-18: "Do not worry about those who die before the last day of judgment. Even if from a human viewpoint they have experienced punishment in the flesh (the human punishment for sin is death), from God's viewpoint they are alive in the spiritual realm by his power." Possibly, however, 1 Peter 4:6b means "condemned according to human estimation," by which is meant that pagans were saying: "Those Christians die like everyone else and experience the ultimate curse of sin, which is death. Where is their God and this resurrection?" By contrast, according to God and God's view, they are not condemned but rather are saved and living in the spiritual realm.[438]

In conclusion, it seems clear enough that Peter was indebted to the same Jewish Wisdom tradition as Jesus was in various ways. What has been said in this passage is certainly reminiscent of what we hear in Wisdom of Solomon 3:1-6 RSV: "But the souls of the righteous are in the hand of God, and no torment will ever touch them. In the eyes of the foolish they seem to have died, and their departure was thought to be an affliction, and their going from us to be their destruction; but they are at peace. For though in the view of [human beings] they were punished, their hope is full of immortality. Having been disciplined a little, they will receive great good, because God tested them and found them worthy of himself; like gold in the furnace he tried them, and like a sacrificial burnt offering he accepted them."

One of the distinguishing features of Peter's discourse is the focus on the inward disposition to be able to endure and prevail over outward opposition, trials, persecution, suffering, and the like. Donald Senior sums this point up well: "The author had urged his readers to 'gird up the loins of your minds' and 'be self-controlled' with their hopes set entirely on God's grace (1:13); they were to 'purify' their lives through 'obedience to the truth' (1:22); the slaves were urged to maintain 'consciousness' . . . of God, even when enduring unjust suffering (2:19); wives married to non-Christian husbands were to adorn themselves with 'the hidden person of the heart' (3:4); husbands should live with their wives 'with awareness' of God (3:7); and the entire community was urged not to give way to fear but to sanctify Christ 'in your hearts' and to have a 'good conscious-

---

[437]See Omanson, "Suffering for Righteousness' Sake," pp. 439-50; Achtemeier, *1 Peter,* pp. 290-91.

[438]The most helpful discussion on all of this remains Dalton, *Christ's Proclamation to the Spirits.*

ness' [conscience] (3:15)."[439] Peter does not emphasize these things because he is a mystic or a visionary. He emphasizes interiority because he is dealing with the wellspring of behavior. He knows that to a real extent, as persons think, so they are and will behave. He focuses on things that Christians actually have some control over, which is certainly not the case all the time in regard to one's circumstances. In effect, he says, "You cannot control what will happen to you, but you can control what will happen in you if you are proactive rather than reactive to life's circumstances." This sort of advice was especially necessary in a hostile environment, where bad things were increasingly likely to transpire. The goal here was conforming one's own thoughts to the pattern of Christ's thoughts and life, and acting accordingly.

First Peter 4:7 begins a section with what may be called an eschatological sanction for behavior. Christians should behave as follows because ***pantōn de to telos ēngiken*** (literally, "but the end of all things is near"). The *oun* (then) in 1 Peter 4:7b indicates that this behavior is related to the eschatological timetable. On first blush it appears that the letter comes to a close at 1 Peter 4:11 with an "amen." Because various scholars have seen in 1 Peter 4:8—5:14 a section about a certain and present suffering, not just a possible suffering, some have posited that two letters are combined here. It perhaps is just as possible that 1 Peter 4:8—5:14 was written later, perhaps when fresh news arrived, yet before 1 Peter 1:1—4:7 was ever sent, and both were incorporated into one letter. This makes better sense to me. Letter writing was an expensive proposition. If the material through 1 Peter 4:7 had already been drafted, there would be more than enough room for the rest of what we find in the document to be added. Rhetorically, however, 1 Peter 4:11 need be no more than an indication that this particular argument is over, not the discourse as a whole.

First Peter 4:7 raises for us the same question that James 5:7-9 raises.[440] Does Peter believe that the End is necessarily just around the corner, a few days or weeks away? This is how many scholars interpret this verse, and we cannot dismiss such a view without evidence to the contrary. We look back and admit, If this was Peter's view, then he was wrong. The end of all did not come in A.D. 64-66. The verb *engizō* here and elsewhere in the New Testament (in perfect or aorist tense) means "has drawn near" (cf. Mt 3:2; 4:17; 10:7; 21:1, 34; Lk 7:12; 15:1; Rom 13:12; Heb 10:25; Jas 5:8; and cognate adverb: Phil 4:5; Rev 1:3; 22:10). It is used in the Gospels of the dominion of God breaking into human history (see Mk 1:15) and can mean "has arrived." It is possible, especially if Pe-

[439]Senior, *1 Peter,* pp. 110-11.
[440]On which see Witherington, *Letters and Homilies for Jewish Christians,* pp. 536-38.

ter is addressing Jewish Christians, that "the end of all" would naturally mean to them the destruction of Jerusalem and the temple: the end of the heart of their Jewish world. I am suggesting that this discourse was written while the Zealots were busily fighting the Romans, which was already the case in the mid-60s. James the Just had already been martyred in A.D. 62. Peter could be talking about the end of "their world" as they knew it, and he was right. Things changed irrevocably for Jews after A.D. 70.[441]

It is also quite possible that "the end of all things has arrived" means that this end Peter is referring to has already begun. In other words, when Jesus was raised from the dead, the end times began. That event took place in the past and has enduring effects into the present (the meaning of a perfect tense verb). On this scenario "end" refers not to a point in time in the future, but rather in the past.[442] This comports with 1 Peter 5:10, where we hear that believers have already been called into God's eternal glory. The problem with this particular interpretation is the phrase "of all things." We can say that the resurrection of Jesus began the eschatological age, but not that it was "the end of all things." Nevertheless, it is possible to translate *telos* here as completion or even perfection. If we translate the phrase "the completion/perfection of all things has arrived," we could take it to be a description of a series of events already in progress, again honoring the thrust of the perfect tense verb. At the least Peter is talking about the possible imminence of these things that are yet to come as an eschatological sanction promoting ethical seriousness.[443] For some Romans the fire of A.D. 64 in Rome signaled or was seen as an omen of something catastrophic, perhaps even the end of an era. Could Peter be taking cognizance of this fear here?[444] As it turned out, Romans were right to be alarmed. The end of the Julio-Claudian dynasty in the person of Nero was soon at hand, and this led to the descent into "the year of three emperors" and absolute chaos in A.D. 69.

What other views may represent Peter's perspective? It is possible that 1 Peter 4:7 indicates that the end of all "this" means that the end of all the audience's suffering is near. Against this view is the fact that what Peter was talking about in 1 Peter 4:5-6 is what will happen at judgment day, when the scoffers are judged and dead believers are made alive. The presumption thus is natural that "the end of all" means "all of these last and eschatological events." Indeed, one

---

[441]See McKnight, *1 Peter,* pp. 236-37; and Ben Witherington III, *Jesus, Paul, and the End of the World: A Comparative Study in New Testament Eschatology* (Downers Grove, Ill.: InterVarsity Press, 1992).

[442]See the discussion in Jobes, *1 Peter,* p. 276.

[443]See Achtemeier, *1 Peter,* p. 294.

[444]See Elliott, *1 Peter,* p. 746.

could argue that the "but" *(de)* introducing 1 Peter 4:7 is intended to indicate that, lest someone see these events as remote, Peter intends to assert that they are near or at hand. But we can ask, Near in what sense? Since we are talking about events, not people, it is unlikely that Peter means spatial nearness. This leaves two other options: (1) By these dramatic words Peter means, "The end could come at any time without its actual timing being known or certain to be near." On this view Peter is agreeing with other New Testament writers that the eschatological age has broken in with the incarnation of Christ (cf. 1 Pet 1:20), and since Christ's death and resurrection, there are no other major eschatological events left to happen before the End. Thus, one can say in earnest, the End is at hand, seen from the perspective of significant events that must precede the End. (2) C. E. B. Cranfield enunciates a second possibility:

> The supreme event of history has already taken place, that event in which the meaning of history (which is outside and beyond history) did actually become for a while a part of history. That was the climax, the final chapter; all subsequent history is but epilogue, a period, in which men have opportunity to come to terms with the meaning of history and of their lives, as it has been revealed in history. So in this letter Peter has already spoken of the time of Christ's Incarnation as "the end of the times" (1:20). We may compare Acts 2.16ff., where Peter in his Pentecost Day Sermon says that Joel's prophecy of the last days has been fulfilled (cf. also Heb. 1:2; 9:26). The epilogue may soon end or it may go on for a very long time; but the end is all the time near, because this world is a conquered world. Christ has already won the decisive battle, and what remains of the war is merely the last skirmishing of a beaten foe. The end is near, because it is the meaning of the present, and every historical crisis is a kind of dress rehearsal of the end.[445]
>
> It will be the end—both in the sense of termination and in the sense of consummation. It will be the end, inasmuch as history will then be over and done with, its course brought to a stop. But the end is also the goal, the meaning of history, the thing which gives significance to its whole course. It is the last day, which gives meaningfulness to all our days. . . .The new order is not a part of the historical process, it does not evolve from the present order; on the contrary, it is the breaking in of that which is outside and beyond history, the replacing, not the self-fulfillment, of this order.[446]

Now it seems to me that either of these two options is closer to the truth than the views of many scholars. As even Ernest Best says, we have no speculation here in 1 Peter on the precise nearness of the End or its designs.[447] Best is also

---

[445]Cranfield, *First Peter,* p. 93.
[446]Ibid., p. 92.
[447]Best, *1 Peter,* p. 159.

right to say: "The New Testament writers frequently use eschatological expectation as a motive for Christian behaviour, . . . but not, as 4:7b-11 shows, to suggest an other-worldliness; what could be more mundane than hospitality! The readers may be aliens and exiles, . . . but they are not to abandon the ordinary duties of life. The awareness of the proximity of the end is not then used to devaluate life but to give it new depth of meaning (cf. 1 Th. 5:1-11)."[448] It is instructive to compare what is said here with 2 Peter 3:3-10, where some of the same language occurs, but which offers a quite different perspective. Among other things, what this suggests is that 1 Peter is an early document, written before the great martyrdoms in Rome; and that 2 Peter is a much later document, written at the end of the first century, when at least for some the language of imminence was not so readily on a Christian's lips.[449]

We thus conclude that this verse does not *necessitate* the view that Peter was wrong in his eschatology, and there is no indication that God had given him the knowledge of how long the historical pilgrimage would last.[450] In view of the coming vindication of their cause, Peter urges his audience to be reasonable and self-controlled. They are not to abandon the normal course of human activities, nor to stand around on street corners proclaiming, "the sky is falling." Peter wants neither fanaticism, which goes for the eschatological jackpot and predicts the exact time of the End, nor coolness, which denies or ignores in practice if not in principle the End and its potential nearness. He tells Christians to hold on firmly to the tension of the already and the not yet, living in this age, but being aware of the shadow of the age to come. They are to live in hope, with expectation, but without calculation. Christians are to be disciplined about prayer, or perhaps he means to be clear-minded, having been informed of the true state of affairs through prayer—seeing things from God's perspective. At this point Scot McKnight is right to point out how eschatology and ethics are closely linked throughout this discourse (cf. 1 Pet 1:3-5, 7, 9, 13; 2:12; 3:15; 4:5-6, 13, 17-19; 5:1, 4, 6).[451] Finally, notice the way 1 Peter 4:7 ends. Because "the end or goal has arrived/is near," they are to prepare themselves mentally and devote themselves to prayer. Mental toughness and alertness and a close connection with God are required in view of what is coming now that the eschatological age has been set in motion (cf. 1 Pet 1:13).[452]

First Peter 4:8 indicates that the most important thing is having love for each

[448]Ibid., p. 158.
[449]On the eschatology in 2 Peter, see below on 2 Pet 3.
[450]See Hiebert, "Living in the Light of Christ's Return," pp. 243-54.
[451]McKnight, *1 Peter,* p. 235.
[452]See Michaels, *1 Peter,* pp. 245-46.

other as believers.[453] *Ektenē* comes from a word that means stretching. It suggests the sustained and constant and strenuous effort of an athlete. This calls for a love that endures and is flexible. Tough love or love fully stretched to its limits is especially called for in tough times when suffering is going on.[454] The reason that Peter exhorts believers to love above all else is because "love covers a multitude of sins." This may be an allusion to the Hebrew form of Proverbs 10:12, which says, "Hate stirs up dissension, love covers over all wrongs." It does not appear in this form in the LXX, which tells us something about our author and the Jewish traditions he had access to. We wonder, What does "cover" mean in 1 Peter? And whose sins are being covered—the one loving or the one loved? This was obviously a popular proverb in early Christianity, to judge from this text's use: 1 Corinthians 13:7, James 5:20, *1 Clement* 49.5 and *2 Clement* 16.4. The idea here is clearly not the covering up or veiling of sins, and the one who sees these sins clearly is God. Then is this atonement by good works? One controlling factor must be that, as here, ***hoti*** (because) in 1 Peter always indicates the reason or ground for the prior ethical injunction to love, not its consequence: love, and this will result in covering sins.[455] Thus, Peter must be giving the reason for loving in the second clause.

Here Psalm 32:1 may be relevant, with covering as God's activity in forgiving. Hence, Peter urges believers to continue to love their brothers and sisters who may be hard to love and may even wrong them, because Christian love forgives and indeed overlooks a multitude of sins. Support from this can be garnered from Romans 4:7-8, which also draws on Psalm 32 and speaks of the covering of sins. Christians are to have a tough love that keeps on loving despite reasons to quit, remembering that the love coming from God forgives and keeps loving. Probably, then, Peter is not suggesting that our love atones for or makes up for our many sins (a thought that goes against Peter's teaching about Christ's death) or anyone else's. Rather, he is talking about love overcoming, overwhelming, overriding a multitude of sins and winning the day. This comports with what we also hear in Matthew 18:21-22 and 1 Corinthians 13:4-7.

First Peter 4:9 continues this interpretation. Christians are to go on being hospitable even when nerves are on edge and some may be wearing out their welcome. The onomatopoeic word ***gongysmos*** literally means saying something in a low voice, muttering, talking under one's breath, perhaps grumbling (cf.

[453]Rhetorically speaking, there is a possible play on words here as Achtemeier, *1 Peter,* p. 294, notes: since the end of "all" things (*pantōn*) is near, one must above "all" else (*pantōn*) love one's fellow believers.

[454]See Marshall, *1 Peter,* p. 143.

[455]Cf. Selwyn, *First Peter,* p. 217

Did. 4.7; Ex 16:7-9; Acts 6:1; Phil 2:14). Peter does not want hospitality done in a grudging fashion.[456] As we know, the early church met in homes and shared in meals, which went along with sharing in worship. Probably what prompts the doxology in 1 Peter 4:11b, at least in part, is Peter's remembering Christian worship in the homes and thinking of what happens there: hospitality, the word proclaimed or taught, practical ministry, the glorifying of God. Thus we can see 1 Peter 4:9-11 as a quick overview of a worship service in the house context and what flowed out of it.

In **1 Peter 4:10** the word *oikonomos* has as its normal meaning "steward," one who takes care of the house, and in various cases it can be a slave. In 1 Peter 2:5; 4:17, Peter compares the church to a house, which certainly fits the scene: the early churches were almost always house churches. The function of a steward in the church probably grew out of the "house steward," one who administered the household, saw that hospitality was provided, and so forth. Thus, the practical work of the steward in the church grew out of such a context (on stewardship, cf. Lk 12:42; 1 Cor 4:1). As Cranfield reminds us: "There were no church buildings for the first two hundred years or so, and each local church would have to meet in the house of one of its members (cf. Rom 16:5; Philem 2)."[457] As Marshall suggests, in the ANE only Jesus and Christians seem to have viewed work as a service to others (cf. Mk 10:45; Lk 22:24-27). Indeed, more elite Greco-Roman persons saw some kinds of work, particularly manual labor, as beneath their dignity. There thus was something different about the Christian approach to work.[458]

The meeting is naturally in the house of one of those who is better off, with a bigger house. Thus, well-to-do Christians are expected to take on the responsibility of using their wealth to support and house the church, as well as various traveling missionaries, evangelists, prophets, and so forth. In 1 Peter 4:10 Peter indicates (as Paul also does in 1 Cor 12) that God has given each believer a gift and that there are many such gifts (*poikilēs* means "diversified").

Nevertheless, in **1 Peter 4:11** he focuses on the two major sorts: gifts of speaking and gifts of doing. We are to treat the speaking and preaching as God's word, not just human conjecture, and the service as God-empowered. It is not completely clear whether Peter is talking about divine oracles here from Christian prophets, or if he simply means that believers should hear and regard any genuine Christian preaching or teaching as the word of God, God's very *logia*.

---

[456]Senior, *1 Peter,* p. 120.
[457]Cranfield, *First Peter,* p. 96.
[458]Marshall, *1 Peter,* pp. 146-47.

The word is used in oracular contexts elsewhere (Num 24:4, 16; Ps 106:11 LXX [107:11 ET]; Acts 7:38; Rom 3:2; perhaps Heb 5:12).[459] As Michaels says, it appears that "Peter is broadening traditional understandings of prophecy so as to include all the teaching and exhortation that goes on in connection with Christian worship."[460] Peter is saying this about "whoever speaks" and not just the prophets (cf. *Did.* 15.1). The use of the word *hōs* should not be taken to indicate approximation here ("as if it were God's very words"). Peter means "as" not "as if." The sentence is elliptical and conditional, literally says, "If speaking, as the words of God," and is dependent on the previous clause about serving "as good administrators of God's diverse grace," and the *hōs* there also in 1 Peter 4:10 simply means "as." Their speech must bear the character of God's word.[461]

All the believers do and say is empowered and prompted by God if they act in accord with his will. Senior suggests, "[The] sense is that whenever such teachers or preachers use their gift, they are to do so in a manner worthy of God's own utterance."[462] Remarkably, Peter uses the same word, *charisma,* "grace gift," as does Paul to talk about these grace-empowered functions (cf. 1 Cor 12:4, 9, 30-31), yet one more piece of evidence that our author is indebted to Paul, or at least some of his letters. The doxology in 1 Peter 4:11c may be to Christ or to God, probably the latter, and we should compare it to 1 Peter 5:11. Of the sixteen doxologies in the New Testament, only three come at the end of a letter; here it does not indicate the end of this letter, just the end of the train of thought in this particular argument (cf. Rom 11:36; Gal 1:5; Eph 3:20-21). "Amen" is the congregation's Hebrew response to words preached or worship given. It means "So be it." Peter rounds off this argument much like what we find in 3:8-10, once again counseling mutual love and respect within the community of faith.

1 PETER 4:12-19—ARGUMENT 4: SUFFERING AND GLORY

> Peter said "according to God's will" either because our afflictions are part of God's providence and are sent to us as a form of testing, or because although we are afflicted by God's will, we depend on God for the outcome. For he is faithful and sure and does not lie when he promises us that we shall never be tempted beyond what we are able to endure. (Oecumenius [*Commentary on 1 Peter 4*])[463]

Here is a place to say something more about the ideas of a combined docu-

[459]Achtemeier, *1 Peter,* p. 298.
[460]Michaels, *1 Peter,* p. 250.
[461]Achtemeier, *1 Peter,* p. 299. See *New Docs* 6:68.
[462]Senior, *1 Peter,* p. 121.
[463]PG 119:569; see ACCS 11:120.

ment here: 1 Peter 1:1—4:11 and 1 Peter 4:12—5:14. First, we may note that the style is such in both segments to make it unlikely that we have two documents written by two different people. Second, the subject matter is also definitely related (e.g., cf. 1 Pet 2:25; 5:2), though of course the later segment could be based on the earlier. Many have thought that there is a shift at 1 Peter 4:12 and the following verses to a situation where persecution is not just a possibility but even an actuality. If one goes this route, then there seem to be three possibilities:

1. Peter had the second segment written (by Silas perhaps) after he received further information about the changing situation, but before he sent the second letter.
2. First Peter 4:12—5:14 was originally sent as an addendum to one particular church in Asia Minor that was already undergoing persecution. The two documents were sent together and quite naturally later combined.
3. First Peter 4:12—5:14 was a fragment of an entirely separate letter sent on a different occasion.

Both options 1 and 2 are possible, but there is no textual evidence for either of these views. Against option 3 we must argue: (a) 1 Peter 4:12—5:14 is not a whole letter, and we have no textual evidence to show that it was later added to 1 Peter 1:1—4:11. (b) The final greetings in 1 Peter 5:12-14 would be lacking for 1 Peter 1:1—4:11 if both were not part of the same document. It would seem more natural to have closing greetings with a longer, more formal letter, though since this is a circular document like Ephesians, it may not have been expected or required. (c) Peter uses verb tenses somewhat loosely anyway. We thus conclude that option 2 is the best view, but perhaps with this modification: the copy sent to the churches who were being persecuted probably already had the section 1 Peter 4:12—5:14 combined with 1 Peter 1:1—4:11. This, then, is the copy that survived. Obviously, those who were being persecuted would recognize themselves in this segment, and they did not need to be formally addressed at 1 Peter 4:12. They too would receive the circular letter 1 Peter 1:1—4:11. But having pursued the logic of this form of reasoning, it turns out to be quite unnecessary when one recognizes the rhetorical signals and structure of this document. As Leonhard Goppelt says: "This explanation of 4.12-19 [that it is the beginning of a separate letter] is . . . exegetically indefensible. The difference in relation to what precedes reflects not a new situation but new aspects of the interpretation of suffering."[464] Just so, and John H. Elliott, provides an extensive demonstration of the thematic unity of the whole document.[465] He is right to add

[464]Goppelt, *1 Peter*, p. 311.
[465]Elliott, *1 Peter*, pp. 768-70.

that since this discourse is written to various areas and churches, it is not surprising that Peter speaks both of the possibility and the reality of suffering, for it was unlikely that the experience of the entire audience was uniform in this matter. Persecution in this era was more sporadic and local. In my judgment it is time to pronounce the case closed on the partition theory.

First Peter 4:12 begins with "beloved," which indicates the beginning of a new section of the discourse (cf. 1 Peter 2:11). The rhetorical unit ends in a by-now familiar pattern (e.g., cf. 1 Pet 1:24-25; 3:10-12), with a Scripture quote that comes at or near the end of the particular argument, this time from Proverbs 11:31 and a final conclusion drawn from it in 1 Peter 4:18-19. As Michaels points out, we have a *parakalō* clause in 1 Peter 5:1, coupled with the indication of a new and smaller group being addressed (the elders),[466] which sets off this unit from the one that follows in 1 Peter 5:1-5.[467] Rhetorical study of a discourse's structure has a distinct advantage over epistolary study: one is able to recognize and distinguish individual arguments without lumping too many things together under a heading like "body middle" or "body closing," which tells us nothing about the content of those sections, nor does it really explain the argumentative structure of the discourse at all. For the record, 1 Peter 4:12—5:11 does not fit any known epistolary patterns of letter closings. First Peter 5:12-14 is another matter, with its closing greetings and final farewell.

The material in 1 Peter 4:12—5:11 needs to be recognized for what it is: two small arguments in 1 Peter 4:12-19 and 1 Peter 5:1-5, followed by a final peroration in 1 Peter 5:6-11. This explanation makes far better sense of the conclusion of the argumentative portion of this discourse than an epistolary one does because it is actually based on the literary form *and the content* of this material. We have arrived then, in 1 Peter 4:12, at the closing arguments that sum up certain themes already introduced and make some concluding crucial remarks about leadership and discipleship in 1 Peter 5:1-5. J. Ramsey Michaels is right to note: "The difference in tone between, 1:6-8 and 4:12-19, on the one hand, and most of 2:11—4:6, on the other, is the difference between a rhetorical summary [in the former two sets of texts] of the Christian community's position in a hostile world and a series of directives on how to respond to specific aggravations and challenges."[468] The final emotional appeal and summation follows in 1 Peter 5:6-11, in succinct and stirring fashion.[469] Michaels has also rightly noted that in

---

[466]See Achtemeier, *1 Peter,* p. 304.
[467]Michaels, *1 Peter,* p. 257.
[468]Ibid., p. 258.
[469]Achtemeier, *1 Peter,* p. 188.

1 Peter 4:12-19 we have two lesser-to-greater sorts of arguments (of the how-much-more variety: 1 Pet 4:12-13; 4:17-18). Goppelt is quite right that we have not finished with the arguments when we arrive at 1 Peter 4:12 and thus have not arrived at a peroration. He puts it this way: "This is not to be the concluding part of the letter. It not only adds new perspectives to what has already been said, but also alters the descriptive mode. Until now the author has laid out principles, but now the thought developments are connected to circumstances in a more concrete and direct way."[470] There is a rhetorical reason for this development. Peter is dealing with a delicate subject: suffering. He has chosen to follow the procedure called *insinuatio*, and thus he does not broach the main subject, the real bone of contention at the outset of the discourse or in the first argument. No, this must wait until some groundwork had been laid. Then, in arguments 2 through 4 he is able to discuss suffering with increasing degrees of specificity and detail. We see this latter here in 1 Peter 4:12-19.

In the rhetorical analysis of this material, Lauri Thurén is only partially helpful. Though he recognizes that a rhetorical unit begins at 1 Peter 4:12, he wants it to continue until 1 Peter 5:7. But this fails to see that a new subject, the church elders, is introduced at 1 Peter 5:1, and the transition to the peroration is made fluid by the final Scripture quotation in 1 Peter 5:5, which leads naturally to the final peroration of exhortations in 1 Peter 5:6. Furthermore, Thurén fails to recognize that 1 Peter 5:12-14 is not part of the final harangue. It is rather the normal epistolary closing of a letter.[471]

More helpful is Campbell, who wants to see 1 Peter 4:12-19 as a rhetorical unit, as an *exposito* on suffering, but unfortunately he sees this as the beginning of the peroration that extends all the way to 1 Peter 5:14 rather than another argument, which it is.[472] This confuses several rhetorical units and rhetorical and epistolary categories, for 1 Peter 5:12-14 is a purely epistolary ending. One of the reasons for this confusion on the part of both Thurén and Campbell is plain enough to see. They do not realize that we are dealing with Asiatic rhetoric, and so there is lots of repetition and amplification all along through the discourse. The fact that we find some in 1 Peter 4:12-19 is not necessarily a sign that we have reached the peroration at all, which is the final summing up, amplification and emotional appeal. He is certainly right, however, that 1 Peter 4:12 does not signal a separate correspondence tacked on here at the end. If that were the case, we would expect another epistolary opening, or at least a new exordium/

---

[470]Goppelt, *1 Peter,* p. 311.
[471]But see Thurén, *Rhetorical Strategy,* pp. 157-59.
[472]See Campbell, *Honor, Shame,* pp. 199-228.

thanksgiving section, but in fact we have neither here. And as Elliott reminds us, it is not correct to see a difference in perspective in these last sections of 1 Peter from that in 1 Peter 1:1—4:11.[473]

Campbell, however, is absolutely right that we do have an *exposito* here (anon. *Rhet. Her.* 4.42.54—4.44.57): the development of a particular theme (in this case suffering) according to a rhetorical pattern of looking at the subject from various angles. The unit is not composed of a bunch of loosely connected maxims. To the contrary, we have the announcement of the theme of "fiery trials" and a ***hina*** clause explaining a reason, followed by an antithesis in 1 Peter 4:15-16, a brief example in 1 Peter 4:17, a Scriptural quote in 1 Peter 4:18 and a final conclusive statement in 1 Peter 4:19, introduced by ***hōste***. This unit is something of a rhetorical tour de force: it packs a great deal into a short span of verses, drawing on both artificial and inartificial proofs (such as Scripture), with Scripture once more serving as a way to strengthen and indeed clinch the argument. We also have a brief example, an enthymeme and a rhetorical question, all tightly packed together.

As Quintilian reminds us, deliberative rhetoric is a form of rhetoric used whenever there is an issue about which there is some doubt in the audience (Quintilian *Inst.* 3.8.25). One can imagine that Peter's audience had considerable doubt about suffering for the faith, for putting up with verbal and then physical abuse was not the way most ancients operated. They believed in honor challenges and in responding to provocations. And yet as Quintilian (*Inst.* 3.8.30-33) says, when one can make the issue of suffering or martyrdom a matter of honor, honor is supposed to trump expediency and even common sense in that culture. Indeed, Quintilian adds that nothing that is not honorable is expedient. He says that if deliberative rhetoric is to be effective, it must reflect a real knowledge of what will and will not persuade a particular audience. For example, he declares that most persons' minds are more easily swayed by fear of evil than by hope of good, and that is because they find it easier to understand evil than good, harm than blessing (Quintilian *Inst.* 3.8.40). In this argument, Peter uses both the carrot and the stick: as the discourse draws to a close, he holds before the audience's mind the prospect of glory, but also the specter of judgment beginning with God's house.

> [4:12]*Beloved, do not be surprised at the fiery trial among you that comes to test you, as if something strange (alien) were happening to you.* [13]*But insofar as you share in the suffering of Christ, rejoice, so that also in the revelation of his glory you may rejoice, being jubilant.* [14]*If you are reviled on account of the name of Christ, blessed*

[473]Cf. ibid., p. 199; Elliott, *1 Peter*, pp. 768-70.

are you because the (presence) of glory and the Spirit of God rests upon you.[474] [15]*Let not any of you suffer as murderers or thieves (or evildoers or as a meddler in others' affairs).* [16]*But if you suffer as a partisan of Christ, do not be ashamed, but glorify God on the account of his name* [17]*because the time for judgment to begin with the house of God [has come], but if first upon us what (will be) the end of the disobedient to the gospel of God?* [18]*"And if the righteous scarcely are saved, where shall the godless and sinners appear?"* [19]*Thus also those suffering according to the will of God commend themselves unto a faithful Creator in (by) well doing.*

First Peter 4:12 indicates that the believers are surprised at their fiery trials. The verb here is present tense for continuous action and could be rendered, "Stop being regularly or habitually surprised when . . ."[475] Again we have the word *peirasmos*, which can refer to a "testing/trial" or a "temptation" (cf. 1 Pet 1:6-7). Here it is clearly a trial. But that the trials are "fiery" probably means Peter is once again drawing on the image of refining of metals (cf. 1 Pet 1:7; Prov 27:21; Wis 3:5-6; *Did.* 16.5).[476] The word *pyrōsis* is rare and means "burning" or even "destruction by fire" (see Rev 18:9, 18). An allusion to the fire in Rome would not be surprising or out of the question here.

Surprise would be a normal response of Gentiles who are not used to suffering for their faith, but it no doubt would *also* be the response of Diaspora Jews who have Hellenized and are doing their best to fit in with their cultural environment. Peter sees this trial as a testing, which will reveal the genuineness or lack of faith that each one has. God allows it to happen to believers for that purpose, perhaps in conjunction with others. Peter may or may not be reflecting on the fire of A.D. 64 in Rome and what it augured for Christians, but in any case the metaphor is biblical.[477] Since 1 Peter 4:12-13 shares so much common diction with 1 Peter 1:6-7, it is hardly likely that these passages are from different hands.[478] Rhetorically speaking, we need to note the threefold repetition of the word *hymin* in this verse, a clear example of Asiatic reduplication for the sake of emphasis. Thus we should read: "*You* should not be habitually surprised at

[474]In 1 Pet 4:14 the Textus Receptus adds a full clause: "On one hand he is blasphemed on their part, but on the other he is glorified on your part." It has the support of K, L, P, most minuscules and some versions. Michaels, *1 Peter,* pp. 265-66, actually takes it to be original to the text, as does Rodgers, "Longer Reading of 1 Peter 4.14," pp. 93-95. But as Metzger, *TC,* p. 695, says, these manuscripts are not our earliest and best witnesses for 1 Peter, and furthermore, this is the kind of explanatory gloss that scribes would add to clarify what the text meant by referring to "glory" here. See the critique of Rodgers's view in Jobes, *1 Peter,* p. 296.

[475]See Campbell, *Honor, Shame,* p. 200.

[476]Marshall, *1 Peter,* p. 150.

[477]See Senior, *1 Peter,* p. 128.

[478]See Dalton, *Christ's Proclamation to the Spirits,* p. 96.

the fiery trial among *you* that comes to test *you*." The ball is being placed in the audience's court, and they are being urged to respond.[479]

First Peter 4:13 indicates that in some way a suffering for the faith can be seen as "a sharing in the sufferings of Christ" (cf. 2 Cor 1:5; 4:10-11; Phil 3:10; Col 1:24). This is probably not an example of some sort of Christ mysticism; instead, it involves Christians having a similar set of circumstances happen to them as happened to Jesus and for the same reason: bearing Christ's name (cf. 1 Pet 2:20-21).[480] The language is so clearly Pauline that we must assume some sort of relationship or influence on Peter's diction here. The adverb *katho* has the literal meaning "to the extent that" or "to the degree that." The upshot of the adverb is that only suffering like Christ is suffering that Christians should rejoice about, and to the degree that they so suffer, to that degree they should rejoice. Ernest Best is probably going too far to read the messianic woes into this text, though in this last age we can certainly count all suffering by Christians for the faith as a foretaste of that final judgment of God that begins with the house of God (cf. 1 Pet 4:17-18).[481] Peter's rhetorical strategy is to try to convince the audience that it is an honor to share in Christlike sufferings, and therefore there is some cause for rejoicing.[482] The theme of suffering as a divine test and often as a cause for rejoicing is not a completely new idea in the New Testament. It is found elsewhere in early Judaism (cf. 2 Macc 6:28; 4 Macc 7:22; 9:29; 11:12; Tob 13:13-14; Jdt 8:25-27; Wis 3:4-6; 1QH 17.24 [Sukenik: 9.24]; et al.). What is distinctive is linking this theme to suffering with the Messiah.[483]

If one suffers as a Christian, like Christ, one should rejoice and be very glad to have had the honor to bear his name and be enough of a witness that one undergoes persecution. The reason for rejoicing in the midst of such suffering now is in order that when Christ appears in his glory, a believer may be able to rejoice completely, as one recognized and honored by Christ, as one who persevered despite heavy opposition and trials. This is not quite what Paul refers to in Colossians 1:24 in speaking of filling up the sufferings of Christ himself, but it is close. The verb here *koinōneite* means a sharing in common with someone in something (cf. 1 Pet 5:1). This probably means sharing the same sort of sufferings for the same cause. First Peter 4:13, with its emphasis on present and future joy, is a positive restatement of what Peter already warned about in a

[479]Campbell, *Honor, Shame*, p. 203.
[480]See rightly Marshall, *1 Peter*, p. 151.
[481]Best, *1 Peter*, p. 162.
[482]McKnight, *1 Peter*, p. 248.
[483]Elliott, *1 Peter*, p. 776 and the notes.

sterner voice in 1 Peter 4:12.[484] They suffer now "in order that" they may share in the big rejoicing at the revelation of Christ's glory at the second coming (see 1 Pet 1:7; 5:4). This verse depicts the second coming as Jesus' coming-out party, when he is revealed in his divine nature and glory to one and all.

First Peter 4:14 indicates a simple condition, which (assumedly) is already happening: "If/since you *are* [now] being reviled on account of Christ's name . . . " The *ei* plus the present indicative verb (as here) can even be translated "When you are reviled . . . "[485] There is no need to see any more in this than what Jesus himself foresaw would happen to his disciples (cf. Mt 10:22 and par.).[486] We need not take this as an indication of a formal persecution by Rome that is because "the name Christ" is now proscribed. But on the other hand, this certainly could reflect the starting up of the troubles in Rome and elsewhere in the wake of the fire in A.D. 64 and Nero's scapegoating of Christians (to deflect accusations against himself, he blamed Christians setting the fire). As Campbell notes, we have an enthymeme here as follows:

> Major premise: Blessed are you on whom God's Spirit rests (on you who are reviled for bearing the name of Christ, on you rests the Spirit).
>
> Minor premise: You are reviled for the name of Christ.
>
> Conclusion: The Spirit is resting on you and you are blessed.[487]

First Peter 4:14a indicates that such reviling is a blessing, not least because it indicates that you really are persevering to be a bearer of Christ's name (possibly an echo of Mt 5:11-12; cf. Lk 6:22). First Peter 4:14b probably refers to the presence of God and his Spirit resting upon believers, perhaps in a special sense upon persecuted believers, to strengthen and protect them (cf. Is 11:2a; Mt 10:20; Mk 13:11; Lk 12:11-12; Jn 14:26; 16:7-15).[488] The sense of the sentence is that when a Christian is abused, they paradoxically are also blessed, for then the Spirit comes upon them and gives them a share of God's glory in advance.[489]

The redundancy of the phrase "the Spirit of glory and of God" is typical of Asiatic rhetoric and the attempt to amplify the majesty of what is being described. Nevertheless, Paul Achtemeier sees the prolixity as inspired by the string of genitives in Isaiah 11:2 ("the spirit of wisdom and of understanding,

---

[484]Campbell, *Honor, Shame,* pp. 204-5.

[485]See Achtemeier, *1 Peter,* p. 307.

[486]See Selwyn, *First Peter,* p. 222.

[487]Campbell, *Honor, Shame,* p. 207. I see it structured a little differently than does Campbell, but we are in basic agreement.

[488]Ibid.

[489]See Goppelt, *1 Peter,* p. 325.

. . . of counsel and might"), which cannot be completely ruled out.[490] Since Isaiah 11:1-2 is a messianic prophecy, Peter with this allusion would suggest that just as the same sufferings of Christ fall on his followers, so the same Spirit that sustained Christ through suffering will also sustain them: the Spirit of the Lord.[491]

First Peter 4:15 simply reiterates that Christians should not suffer for doing evil (1 Pet 2:20), and perhaps the thought here is of doing evil as a response to persecution; Peter sees even this as unacceptable. We have a miniature vice list here, probably in descending order in terms of gravity of offense, with the last one being annoying but not criminal behavior. The last term, *allotriepiskopos,* indicates a meddling that is reprehensible, though perhaps not criminal (cf. 2 Thess 3:11; 1 Tim 5:13, though Paul uses a different term). It literally has the sense of overseeing the affairs of another,[492] but as Jobes rightly stresses, all words that have the *allotrio-* root denote an activity that is not the proper concern of the doer.[493] We should compare it to Greek words with the *allotrio-* prefix for which we do know the meaning: (1) *allotriophagos,* eating someone else's bread; (2) *allotriopragia,* meddling in another's affairs; (3) *allotriopragmosynē,* meddlesomeness. In all these cases the word refers to involving oneself in matters that are not one's proper business or concern.[494]

Peter has apparently coined this word since it is not known to have existed in Greek literature before the writing of 1 Peter. Epictetus (*Disc.* 3.22.97) uses a partial parallel from a slightly later time, but not this exact term: its two components are in adjoining phrases.[495] But in later Christian literature, it does not show up again until Epiphanius in the fourth century A.D.[496] The word seems to be a combination of *allotria,* or possibly *allotrio,* and *episkopē*. In his more detailed discussion of the term, Achtemeier concludes that it most likely refers to defrauding—which is possible, but that would be a crime and would not distinguish this item from the previous ones in this list, and the above list of words with the same root suggests meddling or interfering in another's affairs is at issue.[497] Here the word seems more likely to do with meddling in the business of outsiders, non-Christians, which would be especially offensive if the Christians are indeed resident aliens and sojourners in their area. Asiatic rhetoric was redolent with convoluted sentences and made-up words. For the Christian, med-

[490]Achtemeier, *1 Peter,* p. 308; see D. Johnson, "Fire in God's House," pp. 285-94.
[491]See Jobes, *1 Peter,* p. 288.
[492]See Senior, *1 Peter,* p. 130.
[493]Jobes, *1 Peter,* p. 297.
[494]See Elliott, *1 Peter,* p. 786.
[495]See Feldmeier, *Der erste Brief des Petrus,* p. 151.
[496]Campbell, *Honor, Shame,* p. 211.
[497]Achtemeier, *1 Peter,* pp. 311-13. See now J. Brown, "Just a Busybody?" pp. 549-68.

dling is wrong and falls into the category of "judging outsiders," which Paul bans in 1 Corinthians 5:12.[498] As Perkins suggests, one may see this as a way of avoiding suspicion as a practitioner of an unsanctioned religion.[499] Here we see a list of sins likely in decreasing order of severity, all of which believers are to avoid, even if under persecution. Goppelt may be right that at the end of the list we find items for which Peter is concerned that the audience is actually doing or contemplating.[500]

First Peter 4:16 presents us with the word *Christianos*, mentioned only three times in the New Testament: once here and twice in Acts (Acts 11:26; 26:28; cf. *Did.* 12.4; Ign. *Eph.* 11.2; Ign. *Pol.* 7.3). There is an interesting variant in Aleph (א): *chrēstianos,* "good fellow," but this is clearly a mistake or later emendation. The name "Christian" was apparently a nickname that outsiders at first applied to Christians, meaning something like "partisans of Christ" or "belonging to Christ." The term follows a regular practice of describing the followers or partisans of someone by using their leader's name (e.g., *Herodianoi;* Mk 3:6; 12:13).[501] It was applied to Christians in Antioch near the middle of the first century and probably was coined by Gentile outsiders, since non-Christian Jews would hardly call Jesus "Christ."[502] As such, it may well have the pejorative sense of a "Christ sychophant," lackey or even "Christ's slave."[503] This is the term from which the English word "Christian" comes. There is absolutely nothing here to suggest that governmental officials in some official policy are already causing Christians to suffer punishment for the name "Christian" itself.[504] But what Peter has just seen happen in Rome is that for the first time a Roman official took action, focusing on finding people who bore this "name." This is sufficient to explain the warning here. Not until much later, in A.D. 249, did Decius declare Christianity to be formally illegal in the empire. It is not before Ignatius of Antioch in the early second century (e.g., Ign. *Eph.* 11.2; Ign. *Magn.* 4) that the term *Christianos* seems to have become a self-designation Christians themselves were comfortable in using. Even in his day people were not consistently persecuted just for bearing "the name" of Christ.

Again, the *ei* with a present tense verb suggests a real condition. Christians who are Jews or Gentiles might feel ashamed of facing charges or punishment

---

[498]Elliott, *1 Peter,* p. 788.

[499]Perkins, *First Peter,* p. 72.

[500]Goppelt, *1 Peter,* p. 326.

[501]See Achtemeier, *1 Peter,* p. 313.

[502]See Selwyn, *First Peter,* p. 225.

[503]See Elliott, *1 Peter,* pp. 791-92.

[504]Against Knox, "Pliny and 1 Peter: A Note on 1 Pet. 4.14-16 and 3.15," pp. 187-89. See the critique in Elliott, *1 Peter,* pp. 792-93.

if they have been good citizens or of some social status in Anatolia, but Peter calls them to praise God for the name and the honor of bearing Christ's reproach and fate.[505]

First Peter 4:17 says that believers who suffer such should remember that the time is coming (or "has come," but probably "is coming" since one must supply the verb) for judgment. The concept of judgment beginning with the house of God is Old Testamental (cf. Ezek 9:6; Amos 3:2; Mal 3:1-5; *2 Bar.* 13:9-10; 1QS 4.18-22).[506] Notice again that Peter uses the term "house" to refer to the Christian believers. He has in mind the idea that God will hold more responsible and judge first and foremost those to whom he has revealed more. Knowledge implies responsibility. Peter may be saying that this judgment has come, in which case he sees his audience's present suffering from persecution as part of that judgment. One could compare 1 Corinthians 11:32 here: "When we are judged by the Lord, we are being disciplined so that we will not be condemned with the world."[507] In other words, they are disciplined now so they will not have to face the final judgment later. But as Jobes points out, the word *to krima* (only here in 1 Peter, but the concept of judgment is found esp. in 1 Pet 1:17; 2:23; 4:5) does not need to refer to penalty or punishment; it can simply refer to the action of the judge, which is likely in this case. Christians are not being punished by the fiery ordeal: they are being tested and purified. Peter assumes that the audience is not committing apostasy but needs to be strong to undergo further trials and persecution. Peter here contrasts the audience with those who reject the gospel. Therefore the suffering of Christians is not to be seen as a punishment here.[508]

First Peter 4:17b makes this view seem likely since Peter says judgment is first upon us, including his present contemporaries and himself.[509] The judgment has in effect proleptically begun even though the Judge has yet to appear (cf. Jer 25:17-26; Ezek 9:6). The next verse helps to reinforce the point of the rhetorical question: if believers undergo close scrutiny and are barely (*molis,* "scarcely") saved, what will happen to those disobeying "God's gospel"? It is not "our" gospel: it belongs to God. The phrase "gospel of God" also appears elsewhere (Mk 1:14; Rom 15:16; 2 Cor 11:7; 1 Thess 2:2, 9). What our reference probably has

---

[505]Here we probably have another small clue that there were some more socially elite Christians in the audience.

[506]I quite agree with Jobes, *1 Peter,* pp. 291-92, that Peter is not alluding here to texts like Mal 3:1-3 and Zech 13:9 because Peter is not saying that the suffering of the audience is for sin or breaking the covenant.

[507]See Goppelt, *1 Peter,* pp. 330-32; McKnight, *1 Peter,* p. 251.

[508]Jobes, *1 Peter,* pp. 293-94.

[509]On which concept see above on 1 Pet 2:4-9.

in common with the first two of these is a Roman provenance.

The point of **1 Peter 4:18** and the quote from Proverbs 11:31 LXX (another quote from Proverbs!) are not to frighten believers into thinking that their chances to be saved are slim, but to remind them that the alternative to a faithful persevering under the test and apostatizing is worse: suffering eternal judgment as a sinner and disobeyer (cf. 1 Pet 2:8). The message of this verse is that however many bad things may befall Christians now, things will be worse for those who are non-Christians later. Possibly we see here a crescendo of judgment like in Luke 23:31. Cranfield remarks, "What is said is a warning that it is no use seeking an escape from the present sufferings of persecution by apostasy, because that would be simply a case of 'out of the frying pan, into the fire.'"[510] As Pheme Perkins suggests, Peter is trying to give the audience some perspective so they will see what is happening to them in an eschatological perspective and as part of the larger history of final salvation and final judgment.[511]

In **1 Peter 4:19** we possibly have an allusion to Jesus, who commended himself to God when he suffered according to God's will. God is faithful: the one who has made you will not abandon you anymore than he did Jesus (cf. Lk 23:46, *paratithemai;* 1 Pet 4:19, *paratithesthōsan*). The "doing well" in 1 Peter 4:19b may refer to outlasting the suffering and passing the test, or simply not giving in to the temptation to renounce Christ under fire. Peter regards such suffering for Christ as a suffering according to God's will. There is no suggestion here that all suffering done by believers is God's will in any active sense. Some of it may indeed be the devil's work. But as I. Howard Marshall says: "Part of the mystery of evil is that it cannot be wiped out but only overcome by the suffering love of God incarnate in Christ. It would be wrong, then, to say that God's will for us is suffering for its own sake or because he delights in suffering; on the other hand, it is right to say that God's will for us is suffering because there is no other way that evil can be overcome. When we suffer it is not a sign of God's lack of love or concern for us."[512]

This brief argument ends with a truly beautiful and unique phrase: Christians who suffer like Christ should place themselves into the hands of a faithful Creator. This is reminiscent of the word of Jesus from the cross: "Into your hands I place my spirit" (Lk 23:46), which in turn is a citing of Psalm 30:6 LXX (31:5 ET). Remarkably enough, this is the only time in the whole New Testament that God the Father is called *ktistēs* (cf. Rom 1:25, *ktisis;* Col 3:10, *ho ktisas;* LXX: 2 Sam

---

[510]Cranfield, *First Peter,* p. 105.
[511]Perkins, *First Peter,* p. 73.
[512]Marshall, *1 Peter,* p. 157.

22:32; Sir 24:8; 2 Macc 1:24-25; 7:23; 4 Macc 5:25; and *1 Clem.* 19.2), here expanded to "faithful Creator." As we might say, one should continue to do good even if one suffers for it, leaving the results in God's hands. The verb ***paratithemai*** literally refers to placing one's life in the hands of another, in this case God's.[513]

It will be useful to sum up the points made about Christian suffering, particularly in this argument, drawing on Elliott's conclusions: (1) Christians should in no wise be surprised at their suffering, since they are in communion with a Christ who suffered at the hands of the world. (2) Reproaches like being labeled a Christ partisan and innocent suffering that results therefrom should be seen as a test from God, a test of one's trusting in God. (3) Since innocent suffering "for the name" effects solidarity with Christ and involves bearing witness to Christ, it is a cause for rejoicing not lament. (4) Such experiences of suffering involve the special blessing of the rich presence of the Spirit, which produces joy and is the special sign of the divine presence. (5) If believers are maligned and suffer as Christians, this should not be a cause for shame, but rather a cause for glorifying God. (6) This suffering is a sign that the eschatological judgment of God has begun with the household of God, *before* the End, and in order that final judgment not fall on God's people. (7) All who suffer innocently can with confidence place themselves in God's hands, because we have a faithful Creator.[514]

1 PETER 5:1-5—ARGUMENT 5: APPEAL TO THE ELDERS AND YOUNGER ONES

In the Greek the meaning is still plainer, for the word used is *episkopeuontes*, that is to say, "overseeing" and this is the origin of the "bishop." (Jerome [*Epistulae* 146])

Here Peter is telling the leaders of the church exactly what the Lord told him: "Feed my sheep." (Hilary of Arles [*Introductory Commentary on 1 Peter 5*])[515]

We have now reached the end of the argumentative section of the discourse, with the exception of the concluding peroration, which follows directly and flows naturally out of this last argument, beginning at 1 Peter 5:6. One may expect that Peter might turn to addressing or speaking about church leaders here near the end of the discourse, for this seems to have been a regular pattern in early Christian discourses (as in Rom 16:1-16; 1 Cor 16:15-18; Phil 4:2-3; 1 Thess 5:12-15; Heb 13:7-8).[516]

---

[513]See Senior, *1 Peter,* p. 133.

[514]Cf. Elliott, *1 Peter,* pp. 807-8. I have modified his list a bit where my exegesis differs from his, but we are in basic agreement on almost all these points.

[515]PL Sup. 3:104; see ACCS 11:121-22.

[516]See rightly Elliott, *1 Peter,* p. 812.

Rhetorically this last argument stands out not only because of the selective group of persons being addressed, but also because here Peter speaks in the first person singular—elder to elder.[517] This is a succinct exhortation for the leaders to lead, and for the younger members of the congregations to submit themselves to this leadership, but only in the wider context of the mutual submission and service of every believer to every other believer. Peter is here dealing with delicate "internal affairs," which is probably why he has reserved this for his last argument. The last argument in a discourse has a climactic and especially prominent and important place in a discourse, and in this case Peter intends to sort out some practical matters about the social structures and interrelationships of leaders and followers.[518] The remarks are generic enough that they could apply to a wide range of congregations. Nothing here suggests later ecclesial structures, including monarchial bishops. Peter is an elder and an apostle (eyewitness of Christ), but he relates to his leaders in the provinces as fellow elders, setting an example of humility, to which he urges the audience as well at the close of this argument.

Campbell has suggested that 1 Peter 5:1-5 be grouped together with 1 Peter 5:6-11 and counted as part of a farewell speech. But in fact 1 Peter 5:1-5 is not about Peter, nor is it about his saying farewell. Nor does the peroration serve such a function.[519] Though brief, this argument also shows the rhetorical skill of Peter (or his scribe). For example, we have the neologism "co-elders" or "fellow elders," showing skill in "invention." Then Peter sets up a nice antithetical structure involving both *epanaphora,* the use of identical words at the beginning of each colon, and we also have rhyming with the concluding *-ōs* and *-oi* and *-ou* sounds on a series of words We can see this from 1 Peter 5:2-3:

mēde	*alla*
anankastōs	*hekousiōs kata Theon*
aischrokerdōs	*prothymōs*
hōs katakyrieuontes tōn klērōn	*typoi ginomenoi tou poimniu*

But this is not all. At the close of this petite argument, we once more have the use of a sacred text, in this case Proverbs 3:34 LXX, to punctuate and conclude the argument by means of inartificial proof (cf. Cicero *Part. or.* 2.6; but cf. Quintilian *Inst.* 5.11.43-44, calling such a creative use of a text as this an artificial proof). The proof for Peter's point on humility comes from a text he has cited various times in this discourse: Proverbs, associated with the ultimate Jewish

[517]See Thurén, *Rhetorical Strategy,* p. 157.
[518]Ibid., p. 159.
[519]See Campbell, *Honor, Shame,* pp. 216-17.

sage, Solomon, who himself was a leader of God's people. This doubly reinforces the authority of the exhortation; but what is so remarkable about it is that this saying from Solomon is used to undergird the nontraditional exhortation about mutual submission and deference of all Christians to all other Christians. As Jesus advised, the real sage should be able to bring out something old and something new from his sapiential storehouse and blend them together (Mt 13:52), and Peter models that here. Finally we observe the ongoing penchant for using new and longer Greek words, which especially pleases audiences raised on Asiatic rhetoric.

> [5:1]*To any elders among you, then, I appeal (as a) fellow elder and witness of the sufferings of Christ, who also is a sharer of the coming glory to be revealed.* [2]*Tend the flock of God among you as overseers, not under compulsion but spontaneously according to God('s way), not for shameful gain but wholeheartedly,* [3]*not as one lording it over the portion (inheritance), but being a pattern of the flock.* [4]*And at the appearing of the chief shepherd, you will receive the unfading crown of glory.* [5]*Likewise, younger ones, submit to the elders, and all of you (submit) to one another; bind humility around yourselves because God resists the arrogant, but gives grace to the humble.*

We need to deal with certain textual problems in 1 Peter 5. At 1 Peter 5:2 Peter uses the word *episkopos* in its verbal form *episkopountes,* literally meaning "overseeing." Its meaning is not significantly different from *poimanate,* "tend," earlier in the same verse. Various important manuscripts omit *episkopountes.*[520] Perhaps we should see it as a later addition to this epistle, intended to associate the functions of the "overseers" with Peter and elders. But there is actually a good reason for retaining it. As I. Howard Marshall points out, it has good early attestation ($\mathfrak{P}^{72}$, $\aleph^2$, A and most other witnesses), and later scribes, once the office of bishop had developed, would have had a problem with assigning the task of overseeing to mere elders.[521]

The manuscript evidence suggests that either reading 1 or 3 is the original text, with 1 perhaps having the best support, but in either case the meaning is essentially the same.

In 1 Peter 5:1-5 we come to a section about leadership functions. It should be clear from this that whatever one makes of the earlier teaching about the priesthood of all believers, it does not in any way rule out particular persons being singled out for leadership positions like that of elders. In light of the description of what these "elders" do, it is entirely unlikely that Peter simply means

[520]Metzger, *TC,* pp. 695-96. See the discussion in Elliott, *1 Peter,* p. 824, n. 665.
[521]See Marshall, *1 Peter,* p. 161, note on 1 Pet 5:2.

"old men" in some generic sense.[522] The term "co-elder" here makes no sense if "elder" is simply referring to age. Peter is not trying to empathize with the old men in his audience![523]

A CLOSER LOOK

Leadership Structures in the Early Church

In the early church there were basically four sorts of labels applied to church workers and leaders: apostle, overseer/bishop, elder, deacon. To this one could perhaps add prophet, teacher, evangelist. It appears likely that in most cases function preceded office (but cf. Acts 6). Probably leadership developed at different rates and in different ways in different places. Fortunately for us, the New Testament does not strictly mandate a polity, though it does tend to favor certain kinds of polity: hierarchical types. The term *presbyteros,* which we translate as "presbyter," literally means "elder," as for an older person. This apparently came to be applied to the leaders of the church (as previously done in the synagogue: cf. 1 Macc 11:23; 12:35; 1QS 6.8-9; Mk 7:3; 8:31; 11:27; 14:53; 15:1; Lk 7:3) because they were of the older age bracket, chosen for their experience and especially their Christian experience, and they led a local congregation, perhaps in their own home. We hear about Christian elders as leaders in local churches in Acts 14:23 and 20:17-38 and in the Pastoral Epistles (1 Tim 5:1-2, 17, 19; Tit 1:5). In our study of the material in the Pastorals, we pointed out that these elders had local authority, but some of them apparently were also "overseers" and some had authority over a circuit of churches.[524] It is simply wrong to hold that the term "elder" implies a stage of church leadership development that could not have existed in Peter's own day. A glance at texts like Philippians 1:1 shows that considerable leadership structures existed already in the 60s in various places. There actually was a long history of the use of the term "elder" in Jewish circles. For example, in Exodus 24:1 LXX (a translation of the third century B.C.) the leaders Moses addresses are called "elders." We may also compare 1 Maccabees 14:20. Holding such a post does not seem to have been based purely on age or prestige of one's family or household, though these may have been partial factors in determining this matter.

The "apostles" seem to have been limited to three sorts of groups: (1) the Twelve; (2) those who have seen the risen Lord and were commissioned for

[522]Michaels, *1 Peter,* pp. 277-79, contrasts with Achtemeier, *1 Peter,* pp. 812-16.

[523]See Senior, *1 Peter,* p. 137.

[524]On this see Witherington, *Letters and Homilies for Hellenized Christians,* 1:105-07.

mission by him (cf. 1 Cor 15); and (3) church members sent on a specific mission for a particular church (cf. 2 Cor 8—9; Acts 13; 14, esp. 14:4) but sent to a region or group of churches.[525] "Apostle" in the first two senses died out in the first century A.D., and the term was apparently only occasionally used of the third group. It seems to have been a term used primarily of certain sorts of missionaries, sent ones, not of local church officials. Nonetheless, obviously *apostles* had apparent authority over such local officials. Elders on the other hand were indeed local church officials (in 1 Pet 5:2 charged "to tend the flock among you"), and it appears that the office of bishop developed out of the overseeing function or office of elder by the time of Ignatius in the second century. Clearly a bishop was a regional and overarching authority, perhaps seeing himself as one that supplied the place of the apostolic office. As Karen H. Jobes says, elders performed the tasks in various cases of pastoral oversight, and so of the terms used here, "elder" is closer to a title, while "overseeing" is closer to a job description. In such remarks we are a long way from bishops. Even in the time of Clement of Rome, the terms ***episkopos*** and ***presbyteros*** were used basically interchangeably (*1 Clem.* 42.4; 44.4-5).[526]

Nothing in this material suggests that Peter is now dead, and 1 Peter 5:1-5 is a sort of homage and passing of the baton to the postapostolic leaders in this area, perhaps due to some power vacuum. Rhetorically speaking, this material is deliberative rhetoric and does not take on the form of an encomium or farewell speech at all.[527] Nevertheless Peter truly is concerned about the leadership of his churches as the apostolic age, at least for him and other leaders in Rome, comes to a close. There is nothing here about setting up monarchial bishops, and deacons are not even mentioned in passing.[528] As fleshed out, the polity here is local and simple. One can call it primitive, and it seems little different than the way elders seem to have functioned in the synagogues, which is precisely what we would expect in largely Jewish Christian communities. The polity of the two major sects of Judaism was similar at this juncture.

We may be frustrated by the brevity of these remarks, since we would like to know much more about the leadership structures of early Christianity. Marshall rightly notes: "Peter assumes there will be leaders in the church. He does not discuss how they are appointed or what their duties are. He is concerned, as so often in the biblical discussions of leadership, with how they do their appointed duties. It is the style of leadership that matters. Reading between the lines, we can form some idea of what these leaders' duties were,

[525] I would argue that Rom 16:7 fits in category two of the three slots.
[526] See Jobes, *1 Peter,* p. 303.
[527] Against Goppelt, *1 Peter,* pp. 337-39.
[528] Against Feldmeier, *Der erste Brief des Petrus,* pp. 154-56.

but the main point is the way the leadership is exercised."[529] It is worthwhile to compare this little address to elders and the more substantial one that Paul gives in Acts 20:18-35. In both cases tending, guarding, guiding, overseeing the flock is paramount, and in both cases the character description of what it takes to be a leader is quintessentially Christian, following the example of Christ. We may learn one more thing here though. The elders may be paid, and so Peter warns them not to be greedy. Acts 5:1-5, 2 Corinthians 8:20 and Polycarp's *Letter to the Philippians* 11.1-4 all suggest that there was a group in the church, apparently elders, who managed donations from the congregation and indeed from benefactors.[530] In particular notice the sad case of the Christian elder Valens, whom Polycarp accused of graft and avarice in the text just mentioned.

Finally, it is probable that more general references in the New Testament to "those who lead/preside" are references to those who are assuming the tasks of elders. This responsibility in the synagogue was given to the synagogue ruler or to another elder. Thus note the 1 Thessalonians 5:12 reference to those who preside over the congregation, or the same description in Romans 12:8. We may compare Hebrews 13:7, 17, where we have a participle used to describe leaders who seem to be fulfilling these sorts of functions.

It does not appear that there was any sort of uniformity to the leadership structures in earliest Christianity, and a variety of factors determined such things: gifts and graces, age and availability, length of time in the faith, who had a house big enough for the congregation to meet there, and so on. What does seem likely to me is that in congregations mainly composed of Jewish Christians, there would more likely be a carryover of the leadership structures of the synagogue, including elders, and there would more likely be an appointive system (see below on "not from compulsion"). In the more Gentile congregations there seem to be more loose and charismatic forms of organization at the local level. For example, in Corinth whoever had the gifts and graces seems to have vied for opportunity to use them in the church. Thus Paul in 1 Corinthians 16:15, for example, quite revealingly speaks of how the first converts of Achaia "devoted themselves to the service of the saints," and then he exhorts, "Submit to such as these." We see nothing about them being appointed; instead, they devoted themselves to be servant leaders.

The lesson to be learned from all of this is that there was a variety of leadership structures in varying degrees of complexity, differing from place to place and congregation to congregation. But one thing that does seem likely

[529]Marshall, *1 Peter*, p. 159.
[530]See Goppelt, *1 Peter*, p. 346.

is this. Beginning with the Jerusalem church, there were elders in Jewish Christian congregations (see Acts 15:6). It thus is not a surprise to hear about elders in the Jewish Christian congregations to whom James wrote (Jas 5:14), nor in the congregations to whom Peter wrote (1 Pet 5). *Charismata* (grace gifts) were found in such congregations, as 1 Peter bears witness, influencing who spoke, who served, who presided, who managed the money, and who shepherded; yet there seems to be a carryover from the synagogue structures in these congregations when it comes to shepherds/elders/overseers.

Finally, we should observe that apostles and elders are grouped together in Acts 15 (cf. Acts 16:4), and also here in 1 Peter. There is apparently some overlap between these two leadership roles: notice how Papias calls the original disciples of the Lord "elders," and Eusebius in quoting Papias calls the same persons "apostles" (Eusebius *Hist. eccl.* 3.39.7). Apostles could also be called elders then, but local church elders were not necessarily apostles.

The cautionary word of Raymond Brown about 1 Peter 5:1-2 is worth repeating here when we think of Peter as an elder: "We should not be deceived by this modest stance as if the author were presenting himself as their equal. He has already identified his authority as apostolic (1:1); and so the use of 'fellow presbyter' is a polite stratagem of benevolence, somewhat as when a modern bishop of a diocese addresses his 'fellow priests.'"[531] Peter is a skillful rhetorician. He is using some tact as he addresses Christian leaders in the provinces and trying to establish rapport with them so they will do what he is urging them to do and persevere through persecution. In this last argument in 1 Peter, his words of wisdom should be viewed with these things in mind. Elliott is right to say that what we discover in 1 Peter reflects "a stage in the development of a ministry and order tradition, rather than dependency upon an already-fixed tradition. [First Peter 5] vv. 2-3 reflected part of an early, flexible ministry and Church order tradition that was shaped by teaching concerning leadership, status, humility and Jesus as model, teaching associated by Luke and John with the Lord's supper (Luke 22:24-27; John 13:1-20) and with the Apostle Peter (John 13:1-20; 21:15-21)."[532] Indeed, and there was no one in the early church more likely and able to make such connections and adjustment on the basis of the Jesus tradition than Peter himself.

[531]R. Brown et al., *Peter in the New Testament*, p. 152.
[532]Elliott, *1 Peter*, p. 811.

Peter here connects **1 Peter 5:1** to what has preceded *(oun)* as if to say, "So then in light of the persecutions and trials you face, and in light of judgment beginning with the house of God, church leaders need to do a good job in tending the sheep, making sure that they do not stray, or get scared, or scattered." Some scholars have observed that 1 Peter 4:17 has some affinities with Ezekiel 9:5-6 LXX, where judgment begins with the elders who are in front of the temple. The point of this connection here would be to suggest that the Christian elders especially must not shrink back or fail in their leadership responsibilities in this time of trial, even though the leaders may be most subject to persecution.[533] Perhaps the warning about "not out of compulsion" reflects the fact that elders are chosen and appointed. They do not choose themselves, and so when times become rough, they may well need this sort of exhortation.[534]

Here Peter in 1 Peter 5:1 calls himself an elder because he addresses a special group of leaders in the churches as fellow elders. Michaels is probably right that the lack of definite article at the beginning of this sentence suggests a situation where some congregations in the regions Peter is addressing had elders and some did not.[535] But why are such leaders called "elders"? R. Alastair Campbell has tried to argue that Peter in using the term "elder" is referring to the heads of households and their senior status in the house churches, and that they had an entirely informal authority based on their prestige and age.[536] My problem with this suggestion is that it ignores the connection between the synagogue elder role and those who were leaders in early Christianity. Not all older and well-to-do men were elders in the synagogue or for that matter in the early church. There is evidence that in some cases they were appointed, as is especially clear in the Pastoral Epistles, *which do not represent a later and post-Pauline development.*[537] This in no way disputes the suggestion that age and prestige may well have been factors in deciding who were elders, especially for Christians who needed a house to meet in. My point is simply that these were not the only determining factors. Synagogue elders had the functions of organizing congregational events, watching over synagogue life, and accepting donations in order to fund the synagogue activities.[538] Broadly speaking, this comports with the description of what Christian elders seem to be doing as well (note the shepherding language and the warnings about greed). But in the church, as 1 Peter itself

---

[533]See Jobes, *1 Peter,* p. 300.

[534]See Goppelt, *1 Peter,* pp. 345-46.

[535]Michaels, *1 Peter,* p. 279.

[536]Campbell, *The Elders.*

[537]See Witherington, *Letters and Homilies for Hellenized Christians,* 1:49-90.

[538]See Goppelt, *1 Peter,* p. 345.

bears witness, *charismata* helped determine who took leadership roles of speaking and serving.[539]

These Christian elders are envisioned as having authority over local congregations: *klēroi* in 1 Peter 5:3 likely refers to these individual house churches, literally called "portions" (cf. LXX: Num 33:54; Josh 14:2; 18:6; NT: Acts 1:17; 8:21; 26:18; Col 1:12). Nothing suggests that the general structure of the household itself is the basis of Peter's thinking about elders. Indeed, it is significant that Peter sees himself as a fellow elder and yet is not confined to or only exercising authority as the head of some particular household (was he even connected with a particular one on an ongoing basis? cf. 1 Pet 5:1). In this discourse Peter has already spoken of Christians who live in houses not headed by Christians, and he has also manifested a theology of *charismata,* which suggests that speaking and serving roles in the church are determined by gifts and graces, not by household structure. Last, where is the evidence that the head of an ancient household was or would be called "elder"? Father, yes; Master, yes; Husband, yes; but "elder," no. This in no way denies Alastair Campbell's other point that in a seniority-oriented society, it is likely that older Christians, older in age, would often be naturally expected to take various of the leadership roles in a congregation. Finally, Marshall is right to add: "Peter exhorts a style of leadership for the elders in terms of a metaphor drawn not from the household but from the field."[540]

This word *sympresbyteros* is found only here in the New Testament; as Peter calls himself "fellow elder" with the other elders, it is obvious that he is trying to inculcate a collegial relationship with them even though he has already said he is also an apostle (1 Pet 1:1). We should think of the leveling language of Jesus coming into play here, as when Jesus talks about disciples all being brothers, but there being but one Teacher (Mt 23:8-12).[541] Jobes is surely right that the use of this unique, perhaps even new word here surely must count against the theory of pseudonymity here, in view of the fact that the author has already self-identified at 1 Peter 1:1 as an apostle. The pseudonymous author seeking to am-

[539]The discussions of Campbell, *The Elders,* and Elliott, *1 Peter,* pp. 814-17, both fail to come to grips with the possibility that from the start Jewish Christian congregations may have been organized differently than largely Gentile ones, with the former being more influenced by synagogue structures than the latter. They also fail to seriously conjure with the possibility that 1 Peter is a document written to Jewish Christians, just as James is.

[540]Marshall, *1 Peter,* p. 162.

[541]The order of deacons is not dealt with here, but it appears in various other places in the NT and seems to have been a group from the first dedicated to practical service in the church; the word *diakonos* itself means "servant" or "helper" (cf. 1 Tim 3:8-13), yet in some cases (e.g., Rom 15:8; 16:1-2; 2 Cor 6:4) the term seems to refer to more than just practical service.

plify his authority would more likely have used the term "apostle" here again in this exhortation to leaders.[542]

Peter also says he is a witness of the sufferings of Christ. This might suggest that Peter saw Christ's death, but it can equally well mean a witness *about* Christ's sufferings.[543] It is unlikely that we should read the phrase to mean a witness to Christ's sufferings, unless the torture of Jesus at Caiaphas's house rather than his death is in view, for the Gospels do not tell us that Peter was present at the Roman scourging or at the crucifixion. The term *martys*, from which comes the English word "martyr," refers to one who "witnesses with a life." It does not necessarily imply eyewitness, but one who witnesses about something. Certainly in this letter Peter has been witnessing about Christ's sufferings. In favor of this interpretation of what is said here is the fact that the Greek has one definite article *(ho)* before the two nouns "co-elder and witness." This may suggest that the second word should read "co-witness," in which case Peter would not be distinguishing himself from his fellow elders who are also witnesses about the sufferings of Christ.[544]

Peter also describes himself as a sharer *koinōnos* (same root as *koinōnia*) of the coming glory to be revealed on the last day. This sounds a familiar note, as a quick comparison with Romans 8:18 will show. Peter, or his scribe Silas, may well have read Paul's letter to the Romans while in Rome. It is most unlikely that this is an allusion to Peter's having seen the transfiguration.[545] As we shall see, that reminiscence shows up in 2 Peter 1:16-18. The glory Peter is referring to here is in the future, not the past.[546] He implies he has a share in it now, but the glory is yet to be unveiled. This is another example of the present-future tension of salvation. Believers now have an earnest or down payment, a foretaste of glory, but in the main it is yet to come. Believers hold stock in it now; they receive the dividends of that stock later.

Peter's advice to the elders in **1 Peter 5:2** is to tend the flock of God among you. This has rich application. It implies that (1) the church and all parts of it belong to God: it is God's flock, not ours. (2) Elders are called to tend the flock assigned to them and in their midst, not someone else's. (3) This tending in-

---

[542]Jobes, *1 Peter,* pp. 300-301.

[543]It could also refer to Peter seeing Jesus being abused by the temple police in the garden or at Caiaphas's house.

[544]See McKnight, *1 Peter,* p. 259 and note 5. McKnight is right that it makes little sense to establish rapport with the elders with one of these terms and distance oneself from them with the other if Peter's appeal is based on commonalities, which it is.

[545]Senior, *1 Peter,* p. 139, contrasts with Selwyn, *First Peter,* pp. 228-29, who thinks he refers to seeing the Transfiguration here.

[546]See Marshall, *1 Peter,* p. 161.

volves all that being a good shepherd involves: not just feeding them, but also protecting them, disciplining them, and so forth. As Donald Senior says, it involves "attentive compassionate care."[547] And it is an ongoing task, not a one-shot deal. Elders are to do this eagerly or spontaneously, not under compulsion. The language here is distinctive. For examples, *hekousiōs* (freely) is rare in the New Testament (cf. Heb 10:26), and unique to 1 Peter are the adverbs *anankastōs* (under compulsion) and *aischrokerdōs* (greedily). Failure or fear or rejection or fear of unpopularity or a host of other possibilities could affect the way an elder acts. The image of the shepherd as applied to leaders of God's people is traditional, and what makes it most interesting is that it is applied to God and God's leadership style as well as to human leaders in the biblical tradition (cf. Ps 23:1; Is 40:11; Ezek 34, of God and his undershepherds; of Jesus: Mt 15:24; Lk 12:32; Heb 13:20 and 1 Pet 5:4, Christ as chief shepherd; of Christian leaders: Jn 21:16; Acts 20:28-29; Eph 4:11; Jude 12). The term *episkopos* is a term naturally associated with shepherds (cf. Acts 20:28; 1 Pet 2:25; CD 13.7-12) since oversight is an essential part of their job. It is telling that the Latin word "pastor" is a translation of the Greek word for shepherd.

Why would elders ever have to be compelled? Perhaps because of fear of persecution, failure, rejection, unpopularity or a host of other possibilities. They are to do the job according to God's ways and will, not human ways. Certainly they are not to be in it for shameful gain. This statement is not against a paid elder (cf. Mt 10:10; 1 Cor 9:7-12), but against becoming an elder or acting as an elder so as to feed yourself and have personal gain instead of seeking the feeding and gain of the sheep. *Didache* 12.5 warns against "making business on Christ" *(christemporos)*. There is nothing wrong with a paid clergy: a worker is worthy of his hire, said Jesus (Mt 10:10). But there is something wrong with those who minister in certain ways for the purpose of making money. They are to serve God and their fellow believers wholeheartedly, not halfheartedly.

In **1 Peter 5:3** Peter also tells elders not to lord it over their charges. Believers already have one Lord; they do not need another. In addition, Peter knows that Jesus took on the form of a servant and ministered to the people as their slave, even washing their feet. Mark 10:42 (and par.) clearly gives Jesus' view of a leader's role. It should be a servant ministry and should not involve *katakyrieuontes,* "lording it over" others. This is what characterizes pagan leadership; but Peter, following Jesus, thinks it should never characterize Christian leadership style. *Klēros* means "portion" or "inheritance," probably here a reference to the portion of the flock entrusted to the elder; from it we derive the word "clergy."

---

[547]Senior, *1 Peter,* p. 139.

"If you want your flock to follow Christ, you must be their pattern," says Peter. "If you want them to serve Christ, you must be their example." One picture is worth a thousand words. The minister and his life is a picture or pattern, here called *typos* or "type" of Christ's life. Similarly, Paul and his fellow workers are examples (as in Phil 3:17; 2 Thess 3:9), and so are Timothy (1 Tim 4:12) and Titus (Tit 2:7). The leader is to model humility and service for the followers. The qualities that make a good leader also make a good follower.

In **1 Peter 5:4** Jesus is called the chief shepherd (*archipoimenos*, another word found only here in the New Testament; cf. 2 Kings 3:4 Sym.).[548] This implies that ministers (pastors) are undershepherds. The term originally referred to a supervising shepherd (chief herdsman), who oversees the work of various shepherds caring for a flock too large for one to handle (cf. *T. Jud.* 8:1; cf. Is 63:11 LXX, on God as the great shepherd of the sheep). They have the high honor of having the same task as Christ, tending the flock, though they do so as hired hands bought with a price and sent on into the pasture. Jesus, as chief shepherd, will host the awards banquet, and those who have been good shepherds will receive a crown, which consists of eternal glory when he returns. Here the image is of a crown of unfading flowers (amaranths are in view, considered especially durable, and their red color did not quickly fade) such as was presented to those who won an event in the Greek games (see Philostratus *Her.* 19.14). Selwyn argues:

> But St. Peter's Gentile readers, who were acquainted with the Greek gymnasia and the Greek games and festivals, would have found his phrase equally significant, and for them too it would have religious, or at least sacral, associations. For the four Panhellenic festivals, famed in Greek tradition and celebrated by Pindar and Bacchylidas, "were distinctively the sacred meetings . . . and the games of the crown," . . . in contrast with the numerous games where prizes of value were given.[549]

These remarks are equally apt if the audience is largely Hellenized Jews who participate in the games and their observances. We may compare here the reference to the crown/reward given to all believers in Revelation 2:10 and 3:11, but perhaps we should also compare Paul's words about the imperishable crown that is given for his apostolic labors (1 Cor 9:25; 2 Tim 4:8).[550] In Philip-

---

[548]Achtemeier, *1 Peter,* p. 329 and note 114, noting a mummy label with an inscription in Greek including this term.

[549]Selwyn, *First Peter,* p. 232; at the end he is quoting Edwin Norman Gardiner, *Greek Athletic Sports and Festivals,* Handbooks of Archaeology and Antiquities (London: Macmillan, 1910), p. 67.

[550]See Achtemeier, *1 Peter,* p. 330, on the various sorts of crowns and their purposes.

pians 4:1 and 1 Thessalonians 2:19-20 Paul also calls his converts his crown, his reward. On this we may compare Daniel 12:3, where teachers especially are exalted to heavenly glory. Peter thus may have in mind the specific reward of church leaders.[551]

The prize will not be money, the crown will not be gold: it will be the glory of having shared in Christ's mission to humanity, and hearing him say, "Well done, good and faithful servant" (Mt 25:23 KJV). God does not promise leaders their own street of gold in the new Jerusalem: he offers something far more precious, a chance to share in the glory of Christ's mission to save the world and the rewards that come from that.

In **1 Peter 5:5** Peter inculcates deferential conduct among the younger members of the audience. The verse begins with *homoiōs,* which suggests a comparison, as if the younger were to behave in a fashion similar to the older or elders. Some have puzzled over this, but there is no mystery if one recognizes that the second clause here calls *all* to mutual submission to each other. The Greek literally reads, "In the same manner, younger folks should defer/submit to the elders, *and all to one another.* Clothe yourselves with humility, because . . . " This way of reading the text assumes that the "and all to one another" phrase is elliptical and is to be filled out by inserting the immediately preceding verb, which is the normal way to read such a phrase. To take this phrase with what follows is very awkward. It would then read, "But all to one another clothe/bind humility (to yourselves)."

There are two problems with such a reading: (1) The verb "bind to yourselves" is in the second person plural, and we quite naturally take it as an imperative directed to the whole audience, for *each one of them* to bind humility to themselves (individual actions). But "all" here is so clearly associated with "one another," and it is hard to imagine that the imagery is of all binding humility to one another. Thus Leonhard Goppelt has to insert the phrase "in relation to" to make sense of this phrase when read prospectively: "All put on humility in relation to one another." But the Greek does not suggest this; indeed, the *de* in "and all to one another" appears to continue the previous thought.[552] Surely this is a task meant for each individual in regard to themselves. (2) This in turn means that the elliptical second phrase here is retrospective, not prospective, and we must insert/repeat the verb "submit." This reading comports nicely with texts like Ephesians 5:21, and it also fits with previous "all" statements in this discourse, particularly 1 Peter 2:13 ("submit/defer to all creatures"), and 1 Peter

[551]See Perkins, *First Peter,* p. 77.
[552]See Goppelt, *1 Peter,* p. 352.

3:8. This reading is also precisely what produced the scribal emendation we find in Codex P and in the Majority text including the Byzantine Koine text, where *hypotassomenoi* is inserted after the pronoun, yielding the phrase "and submitting to one another"; and in minuscule manuscripts 614 and 1505 we have the insertion of *hypotagōmen* (let us submit) at this point. Though these emendations are not original, they do rightly interpret the drift and structure of this text. Once more we have here the call to mutual deference of all to all as the context in which these ordered relationships should be played out.

Though it is not impossible that Peter means just younger men here, the fact that there are clearly women in these churches cuts against such a suggestion, nor is it likely that by younger he means "younger elders in training" since this Greek term for "younger" was never used for some church function or office.[553] Ancient understanding of what constituted younger and what constituted older differs from our own. Persons forty or a bit older could still be called young men *(neōteroi),* and if one had only two categories, some ancients suggested that old age did not begin until one was sixty. As Senior says, "The term 'younger men' may simply be a way of referring to those in the community who are not in leadership positions, thus it is equivalent to the 'rest of the congregation' who must respect the elder's authority."[554] But if the focus was just on them being young men, we would have expected the term *neanias* or perhaps *neaniskos* for "young man." Nevertheless, we still cannot rule out the idea of chronologically younger persons. But there is absolutely nothing here to suggest that the discussion is about neophytes, or brand-new converts, for which we would expect a different term to be used.[555]

There is one further possibility. We are dealing with churches under duress and distress. There is some abuse and persecution being doled out. Impressionable young men seeking to make their way in the Greco-Roman world and to establish their honor and honor claims in public as they become men would be especially vulnerable to the gravity-like pull of the culture to defect from the Christian circle, and they might wilt under the heat. Perhaps, then, Peter really is exhorting them to stick close to and submit to their leaders, some of the older members in their congregation. In support of this conclusion, one could point to Titus 2:2-10 and perhaps 1 Timothy 5:1-2, where young men are but one stratum of a congregation; this sort of usage continues in *1 Clement* 1.3, 21.6 and

---

[553]See McKnight, *1 Peter,* p. 263; Jobes, *1 Peter,* p. 307.

[554]Senior, *1 Peter,* p. 141.

[555]Against, Elliott, *1 Peter,* pp. 836-40. There is no reason why the term "neophyte" could not have been used here if that were the subject of this address.

Polycarp's *Letter to the Philippians* 4.1—6.3, where young men are a specific target group within the congregation. If 1 Peter is an ad hoc document in any sense, it could also deal with a particular recurrent problem involving the reaction of young men to social pressure to abandon their Christian faith.

Some have seen this as a fragment from the household code, yet Peter is not talking about behavior in the physical family, but rather behavior in the family of faith. We can compare this advice to what is said in 1 John 2:12-15.[556] It is not clear whether these are the younger members of the church in age, in years of Christian experience or both. Perhaps the latter. What is clearer is that all members of the congregation are expected to recognize the authority of their sole leaders—in this case elders who are also overseers. They are to submit/defer to their elders, but only in the context in which all bind humility around themselves when they interact with one another. Here Peter may be remembering the foot-washing episode, when Jesus bound a cloth around himself and washed the disciples' feet (Jn 13). All leadership and all following is to be done in the context of a mutual respect, mutual deference and submission, mutual serving of one another. As Pheme Perkins stresses, the call for elders and the younger to mutual submission surely is a call to the whole community to submit and defer to one another in all humility. This changes altogether the character of the hierarchical relationships, though it does not obliterate the hierarchy altogether.[557] When we see leadership as a form of service, with humility and mutual submission involved, we do indeed have a uniquely biblical view of how leadership should work and should be seen. The flock is Christ's, and he is the overseer and Great Shepherd of it, so this places the elders not at the top of the hierarchy, but as persons under authority, even in a local house church.[558]

"Humility" is the translation of the Greek word *tapeinophrosynē,* yet the translation does not adequately portray either the origins or negative connotation this word normally had in the Greco-Roman world. As its basic sense the word means "to be base minded, have the mind of a slave or servant," though we may translated it "humble minded."[559] It is normally associated with the overly deferential and obsequious behavior of slaves, bowing and scraping, which the elite ridiculed and parodied in their comedies. Nevertheless, there is a biblical tradition that sees "humility," the stooping down to serve others, as both gracious and good. When humility became synonymous with the name Jesus, who came

[556]On which see Witherington, *Letters and Homilies for Hellenized Christians,* 1:474-80.
[557]See Feldmeier, *Der erste Brief des Petrus,* p. 158.
[558]About all of this unit, see Elliott, "Ministry and Church Order," pp. 367-91; Spicq, "La place ou le role des jeunes," pp. 508-27.
[559]See Senior, *1 Peter,* pp. 141-42.

not to be served but to serve and then die a slave's death (Mk 10:43-45; Phil 2:5-8), this marginal virtue became central to the Christian ethic and part of the real essence of what it means to be like Christ. It surely is no accident that Peter uses the metaphor about footwashing in this text, thinking of Jesus, and then tells his leaders that they are to model this virtue, following the lead of their head Shepherd. This discussion remarkably ends with a call to mutual deference and submission between elders and younger persons, and presumably this means between all Christians.

Humility involves an action here: suffering for or serving one another. Peter presents the same Scripture, Proverbs 3:34 LXX, quoted in James 4:6 for a slightly different purpose, and Peter, like James, substitutes *theos* for *kyrios* in the quote to make evident that he means God the Father.[560] Here it is simply a reminder that God resists the arrogant and struggles against them, but he gives grace to the humble, not so they may exalt themselves, but so they may go on serving and thus humbling themselves. And so, having announced the theme of humility, our author has launched us into his peroration, his parting remarks and conclusions in this discourse, smoothly binding the final argument to the rhetorical conclusion of the discourse.[561]

1 Peter 5:6-11—Peroratio: Between the Mighty Hand of God and the Roaring Satanic Lion

> There is a world of difference between God and the devil. If you resist God, he will destroy you, but if you resist the devil, you will destroy him. (Hilary of Arles *[Commentary on 1 Peter 5]*)[562]

> Who could avoid encountering the teeth of this lion, if the Lion of the tribe of Judah had not conquered? (Augustine *[Sermons* 263*]*)

> The word *humiliation* can be understood in many different ways. It may be self-induced, as when someone who is starting out on the way of virtue humbles himself in repentance for the sins which he has committed. It may be what one sees in those who are closer to perfection when they voluntarily agree not to pursue their rights but to live in peace with their neighbors. And of course, it may be what we see when a person is caught up in the whirlwind of persecution and his spirit is unbowed, thanks to the power of patience. (Bede *[Commentary on 1 Peter 5]*)[563]

A peroration in a deliberative discourse can serve one or more of three pos-

---

[560]Perhaps one more little hint that the author of 1 Peter knew the homily of James.
[561]See Feldmeier, *Der erste Brief des Petrus,* p. 162.
[562]PL Sup. 3:105; see ACCS 11:125.
[563]PL 93:66; on these last two quotes, see ACCS 11:124.

sible purposes: summation, amplification, rouse the deeper emotions. As Quintilian says, whatever the style of the earlier rhetoric in the discourse, the peroration should be brief, succinct, to the point, stirring (Quintilian *Inst.* 6.1.1). Certainly 1 Peter 5:6-11 meets all these requirements and more. The sound and fury and pathos in this peroration are amplified by painting a picture of the humble Christian leaning on the mighty hand of God, but all the time scanning the horizon, watching out for the ravening lion known as Satan. In other words, Peter leaves us with a picture of the spiritual battlefield that his converts live on, and the discourse ends with a roar rather than a bang.

In the peroration it is especially necessary to arouse the deeper emotions of love or hate, fear or faith, anger or pity and the like. In deliberative oratory, the appeal to these emotions, especially in the peroration, is especially needed (Quintilian *Inst.* 3.8.12). In Greek rhetoric the peroration is called the "epilogue," where things are summed up, and certainly in this peroration we have a summing up of the themes of humility, watchfulness in view of the fiery ordeals and eschatological realities, self-control and firmness of faith in the face of suffering; it concludes with a stirring promise that some have seen as a doxology. All of this has been heard earlier in this discourse, with the exception to the direct reference to the devil and his present role in history, which raises the spiritual temperature of the peroration. As such, this peroration as summation meets the requirements for deliberative discourses (cf. Demosthenes *Or.* 2.31; 3.36; Isocrates *Or.* 5.154; Aristides *Or.* 23.80).

The peroration is the conclusion of the discourse, and so here we find out what it is that Peter most wanted his audience to remember, what he wanted to leave ringing in their ears on this occasion. What becomes crystal clear here are the paraenetic aims of the whole discourse. The call to humble oneself, to cast one's cares on God, to watch out, to be self-controlled, to be prepared to suffer—this call characterizes most of the entire discourse. Peter indeed is trying to get the audience to embrace the kind of Christian behavior truly needed in crisis, especially in a crisis that involves persecution and real suffering. As Lauri Thurén says, once the peroration is reached, ambiguous expressions are left behind: we are confronted with direct exhortations in regard to behavior.[564]

In a fluid discourse it was desirable for the peroration to flow quite naturally out of the last argument, and so it is no surprise that here the quotation from Proverbs about grace and humility and their opposite, which clinches the final argument, leads directly and smoothly into the peroration. Indeed, the peroration is based on the truth of the quotation that God gives grace to the humble

[564]Thurén, *Rhetorical Strategy,* p. 169.

while opposing the proud. The *oun* (then) in 1 Peter 5:6 signals a conclusion: since Scripture says this is the way God operates, then this peroration sums up how believers should respond and behave as a result, humbling themselves and so on. By now none of this should catch the audience by surprise: the peroration is the place for reaffirmation of things—for example, the call to be alert echoes 1 Peter 1:13 and 4:7 reminding the audience of the place where they stand in the eschatological scheme of things.[565]

There is room to introduce one final dramatic rhetorical figure here, so that there will still be some "invention," even in the peroration. I am referring to the *descriptio* of the devil in 1 Peter 5:8-9, where Peter is drawing on a familiar dramatic image used in earlier perorations, using emotive rhetoric to grab the audience's attention one last time and galvanize them into action. Consider this example from the peroration of another skilled rhetorician:

> But, men of the jury, if by your votes you free this defendant, immediately, like a lion released from his cage, or some foul beast loosed from his chains, he will slink and prowl about in the forum, sharpening his teeth to attack everyone's property, assaulting everyone, friend and enemy, known to him or unknown, now despoiling a good name, now attacking a life, now bringing ruin upon a house and its entire household, shaking the republic from its foundations. Therefore, men of the jury, cast him out from the state, free everyone from fear, and finally, think of yourselves. For if you release this creature without punishment, believe me, gentlemen, it is against yourselves that you will have let loose a wild and savage beast. (anon. *Rhet. Her.* 4.39.51)

In both cases of the final *descriptio* in this ancient speech and in 1 Peter, the figure is meant to reveal the dangerous and predatory nature of the person in question. Peter pulls out all the stops and uses the onomatopoeic word *ōpyomenos*, "which blends an audible vibrancy with the visual detail about stalking prey. The image captures for the audience the ferocity of its adversary and fosters self-pity for the hearer's plight. Their misery is to be matched by the graciousness of God in vs. 10."[566] But the goal of using this figure, which may well be based on the audience's own witnessing of what lions in arenas can do, is not to frighten the audience either into cowering or into going on the attack; this is shown by the word "resist" and the call to self-control and humility. Rather, the point is to reassure the audience that the slanders they undergo ultimately come from a diabolical source, and so these slanders are not legitimate criticism or punishment. Peter reminds them that though Satan is fierce, their

---

[565]See ibid., p. 160.

[566]See the entire helpful discussion of this parallel in Campbell, *Honor, Shame,* pp. 223-24.

God is mightier still, and he will restore, strengthen, establish and indeed lead them into eternal glory. They are not victims but rather victors in Christ, even in and through their sufferings.

> 5:6 *Be humbled, then, under the mighty hand of God, so that you may be exalted in due time (in his time),* 7 *throwing all your anxieties upon him, because he cares about you.* 8 *Be self-controlled. Watch out! Your adversary, the devil, is walking about like a roaring lion, seeking someone to devour,* 9 *whom you must resist, being firm of faith, knowing that the same sort of sufferings are being perpetuated on your brothers and sisters in the world.* 10 *But the God of all grace, the one who called you into his eternal glory in Christ Jesus (after) your suffering a little while, he himself will restore, stabilize, strengthen and establish you.* 11 *To him be the might unto eternity. Amen.*

A significant textual problem arises at 1 Peter 5:8, with some alternate readings:

seeking someone to desire	*tina katapiein*
seeking whom he may devour	*tina katapiē*
seeking to devour	*katapiein*

First Peter 5:6 simply picks up where 1 Peter 5:5 left off, except that here it is a matter of humbling one's self before the mighty hand of God, in view of the fact that God exalts the humble and resists the proud. The note about humbling oneself and the promise of exaltation probably draws on a saying of Jesus (Mt 23:12//Lk 14:11//Lk 18:14). The verb here actually is an aorist passive imperative (be humbled or accept being humbled; cf. LXX: Gen 16:9; Jer 13:18), rather than a reflexive middle verb (humble yourself).[567] The reference is not to a state of mind but to a condition that is the result of an action. Peter says, "Be humbled (or accept being humbled) *so that* you may be exalted." Human action affects the human outcome. The reference to God's mighty hand probably presupposes the Old Testament idea of God being strong to deliver, or more likely to God's hand of judgment (cf. LXX: Ex 13:9; Deut 3:24; 4:34; 5:15; 7:19; 9:26; 11:2).[568] Believers are to act in relationship to God while bearing in mind that their present conduct matters and will affect their standing later. Thus Peter adds, "so that you may be exalted in due time." Peter does not say how long. It is certainly not the timing that he stresses. "All in God's good time" is what he is promising. As Perkins says, "Humility is not humilia-

[567]Senior, *1 Peter,* p. 145; Achtemeier, *1 Peter,* p. 338. The word "yourselves" is not in the Greek text of 1 Pet 5:6.

[568]So Selwyn, *First Peter,* pp. 235-36.

tion in human terms. Rather, humility describes the position of every human being before God. The eventual goal of this humility is the final exhortation experienced by the faithful."[569] Humility at its core has to do with being steadily aware that we are creatures and not the lords of our own lives. We are those who live under the authority and reality of God and therefore "do not think more highly of ourselves than we ought to think" (Rom 12:3). "Christians are to acknowledge that such status conforms to God's will and to accept it for that reason, since it is the path God wishes Christians to take, a path that will lead finally to God's exaltation of them."[570]

In **1 Peter 5:7** Christians are exhorted to cast all their anxieties on God (an allusion to Ps 55:22), not just the major ones, because he does indeed care about even the smallest difficulties (cf. Mt 6:25-34; Herm. *Vis.* 3.11.3; 4.2.4). Here we find the same verb used as in Marcus Aurelius (*To Himself* 2.11), who says that the gods are interested *(melei)* in human affairs. If we do not trust God in small things, how will we do so in large things? As Donald P. Senior points out, the theme of God's protective care for his suffering people is continuous throughout this letter (1:5, 21; 2:9-10; 3:12; 4:14, 19).[571] "This casting off of fear is just as necessary as submission: If a person does not succeed at separating himself or herself from fear, fear separates him or her from God. Affliction either drives one into the arms of God or severs one from God."[572]

Christians are called in the Sermon on the Mount not to worry, but rather to trust God (Mt 6:25-27 and par.; cf. Lk 12:11, 22-32): worry is something that reflects a lack of faith and trust in God, or at least if we have anxieties, we need to put them onto God's strong shoulders and not dwell upon them. Faith is the opposite of fear; the former casts out the latter. Peter stresses that God is in control (cf. this stress in Wis 12:13; Philo *Flacc.* 102; Josephus *Ant.* 7.54), but this never leads Peter to add that Christians may take off their armor or let their guard down. Instead, God's sovereignty should be the solid foundation for a believer's watchfulness and self-control.

Not surprisingly, this discourse, which began on an eschatological note, also ends on one as well here in **1 Peter 5:8-9**. The Asiatic style has near repetition in the two aorist verbs: "Be self-controlled" and Watch out!"[573] or as Michaels translates them, "Pay attention! Wake up!"[574] Marshall reminds us that

[569]Perkins, *First Peter,* p. 79.
[570]Jobes, *1 Peter,* p. 312.
[571]Senior, *1 Peter,* p. 146.
[572]Goppelt, *1 Peter,* p. 359.
[573]Feldemeier, *Der erste Brief des Petrus,* p. 163.
[574]Michaels, *1 Peter,* p. 292.

the first verb literally refers to avoiding the effects of intoxication; the second refers to shaking off the effects of sleep (cf. Mk 13:35; 1 Thess 5:6).[575] These two verbs end exactly alike: the repeated *-sate* produces a memorable rhetorical or rhyming effect, meant to leave these two imperatives ringing in the audience's ears.

The reason for the wake-up call and warning is that the dangerous Adversary is on the prowl. It is clear enough here that Peter is connecting the assault of Satan with physical suffering of some Christians throughout the empire.[576] Again, we should probably see this as pointing to a date in the mid-60s for this document. Persecution had begun in Rome, but it would by no means end there, for Christians were now singled out, even by name. Yet I agree with Achtemeier: "The incompatibility of Roman society and Christian community is enough to account for the universality of Christian suffering."[577] True enough, but Nero's action gave official permission for it to be open season on Christians and so exacerbated the problem throughout the empire.

Aside from the passing reference to the spirits in prison in 1 Peter 3, this is the only reference to the powers of darkness in this entire discourse.[578] The demonic is not a major theme of this discourse; it operates on a far more mundane and practical plane. There are other more elaborate treatments of the theme "Resist the devil" (cf. Eph 6:10-17; 1 Thess 5:6-8; Jas 4:7). Here resistance is linked to being "strong in faith" (*stereoi* denotes something strong or firmly established; cf. 2 Tim 2:19). "The call to resistance against the devil . . . shows that calls to subordination within certain social institutions have the final limitation in the need to resist any subordination to evil. . . . Subordination of any kind therefore has as its limit faithfulness to God."[579] The term used for Satan here is *diabolos*,[580] which has the root meaning of the slanderer or accuser (LXX: Zech 3:1; Job 1—2; cf. Rev 12:10) or even tempter (1 Chron 21:1). Here alone he is called *antidikos* (cf. Lk 18:3), which has the root sense of legal adversary (cf. Rev 12:10). The image of a hungry lion, as we have already seen, is especially appropriate where one wants a peroration in one sense to close by putting the fear of God (rather than the fear of the devil) into the audience. The imagery of the ravenous lion is commonly used to describe some kind of abuse or affliction (Ps 22:13; Amos

---

[575]Marshall, *1 Peter,* p. 170.
[576]See McKnight, *1 Peter,* p. 278.
[577]Achetemeier, *1 Peter,* p. 344.
[578]Jobes, *1 Peter,* p. 313.
[579]Achtemeier, *1 Peter,* p. 338.
[580]In 1 Pet 5:8, $\mathfrak{P}^{72}$ adds *ho* before "devil," to make clear that the noun is a substantive, which it surely is, with or without that definite article. See Elliott, *1 Peter,* p. 853.

3:8). We may compare Sirach 21:2, "The teeth of sin are the teeth of a lion, slaying the souls of men"; and also texts at Qumran (1QH 13.7-10 [Sukenik: 5.7-10]; 4QpNah frgs. 3 + 4 col. 1.5-6; 4QpHos frg. 2 line 2) about God's people being persecuted, likening the persecutors to lions (cf. 2 Tim 4:17; Rev 13:2). Job 1:7 provides us an image of the Adversary stalking human prey. Even the righteous could not survive eschatological traumas without the strong arm of God's protection and support. In funerary art the ravenous lion is the symbol of the ravening power of death.[581]

The goal of going through such trials is not destruction but indeed its opposite: purification and glorification. The language here would strengthen future generations of Christians who faced martyrdom. The account of the martyrdom of Polycarp, in about A.D. 155 at Smyrna, says that he was martyred "when Statius was proconsul but when Jesus Christ was reigning forever" (*Martyrdom of Polycarp* 21). Finally, Donald Senior is right to note that the verb (in 1 Pet 5:9) *epiteleisthai* has the sense of being completed, finished and the like, and in the passive it means causing something to happen, thus he suggests the translation "Sufferings are being placed upon your brothers [and sisters]," with the implication that God is the ultimate source, and perhaps meaning that suffering is being brought to its completion or goal.[582] Notice the dawning consciousness of a worldwide body of Christ or "brotherhood" (on *adelphotēs* see 2:17) that is interconnected and suffering together. Peter does not use the language of "assembly" *(ekklēsia)* as does Paul. The terms *adelphotēs* (brotherhood) and *oikos* (house) serve in its stead.

A CLOSER LOOK

Christians Having the Devil of a Time

First Peter 5:8 is the most cited of all verses in this wonderful discourse insofar as the use of 1 Peter in later literature is concerned, and it became the main scriptural reading for the close of the day, as part of the liturgy for the order of Compline.[583] Here alone in the New Testament is the devil called the believers' adversary (but the thought seems present in Rev 12:10), though of course there was a long tradition of viewing the devil this way, indeed calling him *ha-satan*, "the adversary."

One of the striking features of the New Testament when one contrasts it with the Old Testament is the amount of attention given to demons and the

[581]See *New Docs* 3:50.
[582]Senior, *1 Peter*, p. 148.
[583]Elliott, *1 Peter*, p. 860.

devil. It is hard to find passages in the Old Testament about demons per se, though there is frequent comment about angels and also departed human spirits; it is only a little less difficult to find discussions of Satan himself in the Old Testament. This is not a surprise since it was only after the exile and during the period we call early Judaism that a robust demonology came into full play in Jewish literature. The New Testament is actually restrained in its reference to angels and demons and the devil compared to some of that literature, but our focus here must be on what New Testament authors have to say about the devil in particular.

The correct beginning point for this discussion should actually be texts like Job 1:6-12, 2:1-7 and Zech 3:1-2 (cf. Num 22:22, 32). In such texts the image of "the Satan," or "the Adversary," is of a sort of prosecuting attorney in the form of an angel. He was under the control of God, initially, and his function was to test the character and virtue of God's people, as well as others. Yet already in the later parts of the Old Testament (1 Chron 21:1; Zech 3:1-2), he has turned into a rather independent rogue, a personal injury lawyer, seeking to damage people rather than merely to test them.

In early Jewish literature Satan has many names in addition to the ones already mentioned: Belial/Beliar, Beelzebul (a pun on Baal-zebub), Sataniel, Sammael, Semayaz, Azazel, Mastema, Abaddon, Apollyon, Lucifer.[584] The understanding of Genesis 6:1-4 went through dramatic development: it refers to fallen angels mating with human women, and their fate thereafter is described in Jude and 2 Peter, among many other early Jewish sources.[585] Satan and his minions are seen as causing illness, injury, division, war, death and a host of other ills (see *1 En.* 6—16). Satan is then identified as the prince of demons or the head of the fallen angels (cf. *1 En.* 6:3; *Jub.* 10:8; *T. Dan* 5:6; *T. Naph.* 8:4, 6; *T. Ash.* 3:2); sometimes fallen angels and demons are seen as one and the same, and sometimes they are seen as different ranks in the powers and principalities. At some point in the exilic or postexilic period, further thought was given to Satan's possible role in original sin, and so he is portrayed in more vivid and more than biblical hues as the original tempter in the Garden of Eden, who even envied Adam and Eve (see Wis 2:24; *Life of Adam and Eve; 2 En.* 31:4-7; *Apoc. Mos.* 15:1—19:3).

The full story of the fall of Satan is not told in the Old Testament, but we do find it in literature that predates our book of Revelation, where we hear about a threefold fall of Satan from heaven to earth (Rev 12), from earth to the Pit (Rev 20) and from the Pit to the lake of fire (Rev 21). This story is told in

[584]In what follows here I am indebted to Elliott and his fine work. See, e.g., his summary in *1 Peter,* pp. 853-58.

[585]See the discussion in Witherington, *Letters and Homilies for Jewish Christians,* pp. 606-14.

more graphic detail in *2 Enoch* (29:4-5; 31:3-4; cf. *Jub.* 10:7-11). What distinguishes the New Testament presentation is its christological referent: Satan's fall is correlated with the death and resurrection and exaltation of the Son (see Col 2:14-15; Eph 4:8-9). Christ triumphs over the principalities and powers through his death and resurrection. This theme makes better sense in light of Wisdom of Solomon 2:24, which says that through Satan death entered the world; in a later echo of this, Hebrews 2:14 identifies Satan as having the power of death. Satan is said to be able to disguise himself as a human being (cf. *T. Job* 6:4; 17:2; 23:1; cf. 2 Cor 11:14, where Satan is said to masquerade as an angel in light, though the allusion is to false apostles). The Enochian literature suggests that Satan was cast from heaven into the air or atmosphere, and so it is not a surprise that we hear Satan called "the prince of the power of the air" and like phrases (Eph 2:2 KJV).

Already in pre-Christian literature it was anticipated that evil and the Evil One would one day be conquered (cf. Is 14:12-15; *T. Levi* 3:3; 18:12; *T. Dan* 5:10-11; *T. Zeb.* 9:8; *T. Benj.* 3:8). In the meantime, however, the Gospels report the devil claiming to have all kingdoms of the world in his hand (Mt 4:9//Lk 4:6). Even Jesus calls him "the ruler of this world," but Jesus adds that he has been judged (Jn 16:11; cf. the description of the devil as the ruler of this age: Eph 2:2; 6:11-12; 2 Thess 2:9-10; Rev 12—18). Jesus during his earthly ministry already claims that he saw Satan fall like lightning from the sky (Lk 10:18). The devil's doom is sure, predicted by Jesus in Matthew 25:41 and depicted in Revelation 20:10. In the meantime the devil is described as deceiving persons and nations, even causing massive delusions (cf. 2 Thess 2:9-12; Rev 20:3, 8), and he is the one who puts betrayal into the heart of Judas (Jn 13:2). The devil is the one who tempts and seduces believers (1 Cor 7:5; 2 Cor 2:11; 11:14; Eph 6:11; 1 Tim 3:7; 5:15; 2 Tim 2:26) and tempts Jesus (Mt 4; Lk 4). Satan is the one who sows tares amid the wheat, even in the Lord's field (Mt 13:39; Lk 8:12). He blinds the minds of unbelievers (2 Cor 4:4), hinders missionary work (2 Cor 2:11; 1 Thess 2:18). With all of this, it is no surprise that the devil, Satan, is also described as the great dragon of ancient mythology (Rev 12:9).

Even with all of this, there are remarkable statements about the Christian's ability to resist the wiles of the devil and even promises that with such resistance, Satan will flee (cf. Jas 4:7; 1 Pet 5:9). An even stronger statement is made in Romans 16:20 about God crushing Satan under the feet of believers. The picture of Christ proclaiming victory over the fallen angels in 1 Peter 3:19, 22 is part of this Christus Victor motif. Again, some other early Jews such as the Qumran community thought they were living in the eschatological age, filled with angels and demons and battles and spiritual warfare, as thought various

Christians; yet, due to the work of Christ past and present, early Christian literature sounds a remarkably triumphalist note not only about the future but even about the present. Outside of the Gospels, and on this side of Pentecost, we do not hear much about demons at all in Acts or in the epistolary literature of the New Testament. Peter, like other New Testament writers, does not ascribe bad human conduct solely or wholly to demonic influence; like other such writers, he holds Christians themselves responsible for their own behavior. They are able to resist even Satan, they are able to put on sufficient Christian armor to withstand the onslaught of evil powers (Eph 6), they are told that no temptation has overcome them that is not common to humanity and that cannot be dealt with at least by fleeing and escaping it (1 Cor 10). Nothing in this literature speaks about demon-filled Christians, not least because Christ and the Spirit are said to dwell in the believer, and "greater is he who is in you, than he who is in the world" (cf. 1 Jn 4:4 KJV). Thus, in sum the devil is able to bewitch, bother, and bewilder Christians. He is able to confuse, deceive, mislead, and attempt to seduce Christians. But there is nothing inevitable about this: indeed, there are reassurances that he can always be resisted and will even flee the resister. When the New Testament literature speaks of Satan, it presents a tension between warning of his wiles and power on the one hand, and reassuring Christians on the other hand that "his doom is sure" and he can be resisted and overcome even now. First Peter reflects this healthy tension as well. Though from another era, one can well imagine Peter affirming the sentiments of the great Reformer (Luther) in the great Reformation hymn "A Mighty Fortress Is Our God":

> And though this world, with devils filled, should threaten to undo us,
> We will not fear, for God hath willed his truth to triumph through us:
> The Prince of Darkness grim, we tremble not for him;
> His rage we can endure, for lo, his doom is sure;
> One little word shall fell him.

This thought leads Peter to a doxological conclusion in **1 Peter 5:10-11** celebrating God's eternal might, which enables God to restore, stabilize, strengthen, even establish them. Notice the rhetorically effective accumulation of four future tense verbs here at the end of the peroration, offered in a certain sequence. Establishing can only be accomplished once the restoring, stabilizing and strengthening have all happened.[586] The suffering they endure is temporal

[586]See Campbell, *Honor, Shame,* p. 227.

and temporary, and in any case it is a fellowship of suffering with other believers throughout the world. They are not alone in their suffering, and God has not left them alone to endure it on their own.[587] As Marshall notes, this doxology stands out in that it includes a promise, not just a praise.[588] The four verbs here thus provide reassurance that God will be with the suffering believers, helping them through the trial.

Clearly, while Peter knows and uses some Pauline diction (see 1 Pet 5:10b, "in Christ" once again), he is his own person with his own ideas and style. This letter was not written by a slavish imitator of the style of Paul, James or anyone else for that matter. In other words, the case for this letter being pseudonymous on stylistic grounds is weak. We have here a creative use of Greek and of Christian ideas, and there is no striving whatsoever to gild the halo of a now dead saint by one of his later admirers. Sometimes those who simply assume this document is by a later hand forget that an audience other than the one specified would likely be required as well for the pseudonymity to work.[589] There is no reference here at all to internal struggles in these communities or to false teachers. Rather, the problems are due to persecution, not later power vacuums caused by the martyrdom of apostles like Peter. In this letter the appeals to the author's authority seem genuine and are not all that prevalent, unlike what we might expect in a document written by a later admirer or imitator. Finally, the personalia at the end of the letter all seem genuine, not contrived, and as such are marks of a genuine correspondence between the author and audience. Since this is an oral document, and Silvanus's name is not mentioned until the end, no one would know or think that Silvanus (= Silas) might be the author of this discourse before it was over, a rather ineffective rhetorical strategy, and doubly so if Silvanus composed this discourse after Peter's death. There is no reason he could not have spoken in his own voice in this letter, since he was a respected and recognized leader in early Christianity.

Finally, the peroration in 1 Peter 5:6-11 is quite similar to what we find in the latter half of the homily of James. One should compare the use of the same Scripture in James 4:6-10 followed by exhortations to submit to God's hand, resist the devil, and humble oneself before the Lord.[590] It is true that various ele-

[587] As Feldmeier says, the ball is left in the court of the audience and God and their interrelationship, as Peter in effect turns the audience back over to God here at the end of the peroration; see Feldmeier, *Der erste Brief des Petrus,* p. 164.

[588] Marshall, *1 Peter,* pp. 171-72.

[589] On this point see Witherington, *Letters and Homilies for Hellenized Christians,* 1:23-38.

[590] These parallels are discussed in some detail in Goppelt, *1 Peter,* p. 355; Michaels, *1 Peter,* pp. 293-95; McKnight, *1 Peter,* pp. 276-77.

ments of the tradition are in a different order in 1 Peter than in James, and different wording is sometimes used, so each writer has used this material in his own way.[591] Should we merely put this down to common or shared Christian tradition, or should we entertain the notion that Peter knows the letter of James written to Diaspora Jews and is echoing it here to some degree? The difference in the two documents at this point is that Peter is addressing a situation of some serious suffering, while James is mainly dealing with internal struggles and divisions.[592] Nevertheless, the use of the same Scripture followed by three similar exhortations is telling. It provides more evidence for the thesis that Jewish Christianity as led by James, Peter, and the Beloved Disciple was a more tight-knit phenomenon than we have previously thought, with considerable shared communication.

1 PETER 5:12-14—EPISTOLARY POSTSCRIPT: A "BRIEF" CONCLUSION

Epistolary postscripts are traditionally brief, sometimes exceedingly so, even as brief as the word *errōsthe* (farewell/be well; 2 Macc 11:21, 33; Acts 15:29) or in more elite correspondence ***eutyxe*** (good luck; Plato *Ep.* 4.321c), and this one is brief. To say that this letter is "brief" is a rhetorical conceit that we also find in Hebrews 13:22, where it is even less warranted if one takes it literally (cf. Ign. *Rom.* 8.2; Pol. *Phil.* 7.13-14; Isocrates *Ep.* 2.13; 8.10; Pliny the Younger *Ep.* 3.9.27). First Peter is some 105 verses long, which puts it in the top 10 percent or so for length of all known letters in antiquity. The rhetorical conceit was necessary because the letters were *supposed* to be short, and so in a sense here it serves as something of an indirect apology (cf. Demetrius *Eloc.* 228, 231, 234; Jerome *Epist.* 57.8; 68.2). New Testament letters were indeed long compared to most ancient letters, and that judgment includes 1 Peter, which is much longer than the average papyrus letter. This speaks volumes to us about the nature of early Christianity. It was an intellectually serious enterprise, which involved a good deal of appeals and exhortations and education and the building up of considerable social networks between Jerusalem and Rome and in all sorts of places in between.

If we took time to look at the conclusion of various ancient letters, they tend to be even briefer than this one, with an oath, a health wish, a word of farewell, and occasionally a reference to the letter carrier. As will be seen, various of these features are missing from the ending of 1 Peter, and various other specifically

[591]Achtemeier, *1 Peter,* p. 337.

[592]See the discussions of James 4 in Witherington, *Letters and Homilies for Jewish Christians,* pp. 504-25.

Christian features have been added. In no sense should this conclusion of the letter be seen as merely pro forma.

Christians seem to have used their own couriers, and apparently Silas was one that various Jewish Christian leaders entrusted with the task, such as James, Peter and Paul (cf. Acts 15:22-32; 1 Thess 1:1; 2 Thess 1:1).[593] The interesting phrase *hōs logizomai* means "in my judgment," or "as I consider/reckon him" (on the verb's use in the sense of a personal testimonial, cf. Rom 3:28; 8:18; 2 Cor 11:5).[594] This little phrase, which serves as something of a recommendation, strongly suggests that Silas is the bearer of this letter, now with the apostolic imprimatur stating that he is a faithful brother. The word *dia* (through) here perhaps also suggests that he had a hand in writing this letter as well, and not merely as one who took dictation.[595] In a rather close parallel, Cicero (*Att.* 1.19) commends Cossinius, perhaps because he was not well known by the letter's recipients.[596]

The epistolary opening and closing of this document are quite close in content, showing the care in the composition of the whole, as shown here:

1 Peter 1:1-2	*1 Peter 5:12-14*
to the chosen	she . . . chosen with you
Diaspora	Babylon
peace to you	peace to you[597]

We can also point out that it is hard to doubt that Peter had read one or more of Paul's letters because this closing sounds more Pauline than it does like a generic epistolary ending.[598]

[5:12] *Through Silas, a faithful brother, as I consider him, I wrote to you briefly, appealing and testifying this to be the true grace of God. Stand fast in it.* [13] *Those likewise elect in Babylon, greet you, and Mark, my son.* [14] *Greet one another with a kiss of love. Peace to you all that (are) in Christ.*

---

[593]It is a mistake to make too much of the Latin equivalent of Silas's name, "Silvanus." "Silas" is perhaps the Aramaic form of the name Saul, and the Latin cognomen would be adopted, as was Paul's at the juncture where the person had contact with Latin speakers who preferred to deal with Latin equivalents or at least Greek names. Nothing in his name nor in his felicity with Greek needs to suggest at all a non-Palestinian origin for this man. Indeed, Acts 15 suggests otherwise, as does the name by which he is introduced in Acts: "Silas." One cannot conclude that 1 Peter's audience is largely Gentile on the basis of the name of this letter writer and carrier!

[594]Senior, *1 Peter,* p. 152.

[595]See introduction above.

[596]See Moffatt, *General Epistles,* p. 169.

[597]Jobes, *1 Peter,* p. 319.

[598]See the discussion in Achtemeier, *1 Peter,* p. 349.

There is debate as to whether the phrase "through Silas" in **1 Peter 5:12** means that he is the scribe of this document or the deliverer of the document, or perhaps both.[599] If he is just the deliveryman, it is not the first time he is charged with delivering a letter to Jewish Christians (see Acts 15:23). The phrase "as I consider him" suggests a recommendation of him as letter bearer to the audience. There is no doubt that the phrasal pattern *graphein dia tinos,* "write by way of someone," can refer to a letter carrier (e.g., cf. Acts 15:23; BGU 1079; P.Mich. 15:751 lines 4-7; Ign. *Rom.* 10.1; *Phld.* 11.2). However, this is not the end of the matter. In the first place, some of the examples cited by Elliott from the papyri do not prove his point. To say "I sent *[epempsa]* through someone" is one thing. To say "I wrote through someone" is something else.[600] We have the example where the same "through" language is used by Dionysius of Corinth to refer to Clement of Rome writing on behalf of the church in Rome (see Eusebius *Hist. eccl.* 4.23.11). Though in that case the "through" language refers to the author rather than the scribe, it does mean someone writing on behalf of others. More germane is 2 Thessalonians 2:2, where it is quite clear that *dia* refers to the person through whom the letter was written, not the person through whose help it was delivered or sent.[601]

More important, here in 1 Peter 5:12 the reference to writing or sending "briefly" through Silas here surely does not mean sent or delivered briefly through Silas! The phrase *di' oligōn* must count against the theory that Silas is referred to here as nothing but the deliveryman.[602] The rhetorical conceit of referring to "writing briefly" must be recognized and given due weight (cf. Acts 24:4).[603] It is not a conceit about "sending briefly" or quick delivery! There could be no "quick" delivery of a letter in antiquity anyway, and certainly not to all these regions mentioned in the superscript. Thus the main thrust of this phrase alludes to Silas writing, while the commendation suggests he also delivered the missive.

We must remember that Peter was not a lettered man (see Acts 4:13). This does not mean that he was illiterate, but it does mean he was not learned, and this comports with the later tradition from Papias that Peter had and needed the services of Mark in order to convey the Gospel tradition to another generation. Finally, we

[599]On which see Introduction above.

[600]See Elliott, *1 Peter,* pp. 872-74. We can now compare *New Docs* 3:9, presenting the inscription fragment that says, "I write you through the household of the boatman of the monastery," and uses *dia*. It is not clear whether this really refers to sending or writing.

[601]See McKnight, *1 Peter,* p. 279 and n. 10.

[602]See Marshall, *1 Peter,* p. 174.

[603]See rightly Goppelt, *1 Peter,* p. 369, who stresses that the word "briefly" must be given its due. Goppelt adds that, considering the great distances between the churches in all these locales, a single carrier of the letter is difficult to imagine.

must also take into account that the scribe of Romans, Tertius, is only mentioned at the end of the letter as well (Rom 16:22). There thus is precedent for mentioning the scribe here at the end of document.[604] In my judgment, Silas should probably not be seen as a mere secretary here. He has helped in the composition of this document, putting Peter's oral communication into a more effective, rhetorically adept Asiatic form. As Jobes points out, however, the Greek of 1 Peter does reflect Semitic interference (suggesting a Jewish composer whose native language is not Greek), and it also suggests less facility and rhetorical skill with Greek than shown by the author of Hebrews, but then Hebrews is the gold standard of such Greek in the New Testament. All of this comports well with what we can know of Silas's background from Acts (where he is connected with the Jerusalem church: see Acts 15) and from Paul's letters (cf. 1—2 Thessalonians).[605]

Here is not only the return to the language of "appeal" (1 Pet 2:11; 5:1), but even more strikingly the verb *epimartyrōn* (only here in the NT) has the sense of "testify" or "declare," and in this case he is declaring the nature of the true grace of God. Peter sees himself as a witness of the true grace of God, not only in the sense that he has seen Jesus personally, but also that he has experienced pure grace after his threefold denial of Christ. But here the word "this" seems to refer to a grace already mentioned in this discourse (see 1 Pet 1:13; 5:5, 10), and perhaps we have a reference to the whole discourse, which is indeed about God's grace in times of trouble and suffering.[606]

In **1 Peter 5:13** the reference to "Mark, my son" could refer to John Mark being converted through Peter's efforts in Jerusalem in the A.D. 30s.[607] The early church there had as one of their meeting places the house of John Mark's mother (Acts 12:12).[608] Two emissaries who formerly served as part of the Pauline mission are here in close contact with Peter, and at least Silas is working in the service of Peter. One needs to compare the different spiritual and social language used: Silas is the "faithful brother," while Mark is "my son," the one who would go on to be Peter's translator or interpreter in the writing of a Gospel in and for Roman Christians (see Eusebius *Hist. eccl.* 3.39.15).[609]

---

[604]Here I must agree with Davids, *First Peter,* p. 198 and n. 2, against Michaels, *1 Peter,* pp. 306-7.

[605]See the excursus in Jobes, *1 Peter,* pp. 325-38, esp. the conclusions on the last two pages.

[606]See ibid., p. 324.

[607]I do indeed think this Mark is the same as the youth who ran away in the Garden of Gethsemane, according to the Gospel of Mark. That does not make him already a disciple of Jesus; he may have simply been an interested observer who would report to his mother. See Witherington, *Gospel of Mark.*

[608]See Marshall, *1 Peter,* p. 175.

[609]On this see Witherington, *Gospel of Mark.*

They are all currently residing in "Babylon," which is to say they share in the "exilic" or resident alien state and status of their audience. Perkins is right to note that ordinarily a letter to the "Diaspora" (1 Pet 1:1) would come from the Holy Land, in particular from Jerusalem (see Jas 1:1). But this one comes from Rome. "Babylon" was the Jewish code name for Rome, as is perfectly clear from many references (*2 Bar.* 11:1-2; 67:7; 2 Esd 3:1-28; *Sib. Or.* 5:143, 157-160; cf. Rev 14:8; 16:19; 17:18; 18:2-24). It is a term Peter could expect a Jewish Christian audience to understand without further explanation. Otherwise they might think he was dwelling on the Euphrates or in Egypt, which is where the two Babylons of that era were.[610] "Here the political center of the empire, which controls the provinces of Asia Minor, is also the epitome of a place of exile."[611] In other words, Peter shares the condition of the audience, and so they should be able to trust him in his exhortations. That Mark and Silas are now with Peter is perhaps a sign that Paul by this time is dead.[612]

The language in 1 Peter 5:13 is applied to the church in Rome collectively: "she who is likewise chosen."[613] The use of the feminine for a church is to be compared to the reference to the elect lady in 2 John 1 and 13. The imagery of the church as the bride of Christ appears in Ephesians 5:22-23 and in Revelation 19:7-8, 21:2-3, and 22:17. Peter's concept of election here at the end and also at 1 Peter 1:1-2 certainly involves an elect group. It is corporate election of a group of persons he has in mind, and one is only elect insofar as one remains a part of the group. There is nothing here that encourages the notion of pretemporal choosing of individuals to be the elect.

The closing greetings from the church in Rome, and in **1 Peter 5:14** the appeal to greet one another with the "kiss of love" (here only, but on the holy kiss, cf. Rom 16:16; 1 Cor 16:20; 2 Cor 13:12; 1 Thess 5:26).[614] The ascetical move-

---

[610]See Best, *1 Peter*, p. 178. On the Babylon that was a garrison town in Egypt, see Josephus *Ant.* 2.15.1; Strabo *Geogr.* 17.1, 30. It is extremely unlikely that the text means the famous Babylon in Mesopotamia, not least because most of the Jewish community there left that city for Seleucia a long time before this discourse was composed (see Josephus *Ant.* 18.9.8-9).

[611]Perkins, *First Peter*, p. 82.

[612]See Davids, *First Peter*, p. 203.

[613]The suggestion that this is a reference to Peter's wife (see 1 Cor 9:5) is unlikely in the extreme, and most commentators have abandoned it. This would be an oddly formal and detached way to refer to one's own wife, without even providing her name. Moreover, personal greetings usually included personal names, including women's names. For the revival of this old theory, see Applegate, "Co-Elect Woman of 1 Peter," pp. 587-604.

[614]By the mid-second century this kiss of love or holy kiss was a regular part of the Lord's Supper liturgy. See Justin Martyr *1 Apol.* 65.2. See Klassen, "Sacred Kiss in the New Testament," pp. 122-35. For an outsider's comment on this custom, see Minucius Felix *Oct.* 9.2. See the discussion in Feldmeier, *Der erste Brief des Petrus*, p. 171 and n. 647.

ment, which would run through the whole church beginning in the second century A.D., was to effect the way this family custom was applied. Clement of Alexandria complains about the churches being noisy with the loud smacking of kisses, and the *Apostolic Constitutions* (2.57; 8.11) expressly orders that men kiss only men, and women kiss only women.[615] *Shalom* (*eirēnē*, peace) as Peter's last word of blessing in 1 Peter 5:14 thus reminds us once more of the family nature and family meeting and family setting of this document. In that regard it is in-house advice for the household of God, which has taken over the customs of the household and applied them to all those with whom they have a faith kinship. This is not something superficial or ephemeral. Though it is technical sociological language, the phrase "fictive kinship" is not entirely apt here for the good reason that early Christians really were, and really believed they were, united in Christ and by the Spirit.

Bridging the Horizons

First Peter is a rich and diverse book, which provides lots of material for good preaching and teaching. Sadly, when it is not being entirely neglected, it seems mostly to be used as cannon fodder for the assumption that the author was an unreconstructed oppressor of women and slaves, hidebound to the fallen conventional cultural values of his age. Fortunately, as we have sought to show in this commentary, this is by no means true, but few seem prepared to listen. Once buzzwords or phrases like "the weaker sex" or "slaves obey even abusive masters" begin to be bandied about, it is hard to convince those who are not already convinced that on such subjects 1 Peter stands with, rather than against, the more enlightened views of Jesus, Paul and other early Christians. Completely ignored in such discussions is Peter's emphatic exhortation to "live as free people" but to use their freedom responsibly, acting as servants of God (1 Pet 2:16). Equally underappreciated are Peter's statements about mutual submission in the body of Christ, indeed submission, by which is meant deference and respect and service to "every human creature" (2:13). And when one sees the strong stress on women being coheirs of grace immediately after the reference to physical weakness (1 Pet 3:7), and the exhortations to husbands to behave accordingly, it becomes quite impossible to paint Peter into the male chauvinist corner.

Equally unhelpful are some of the usual treatments of what 1 Peter says about kings and governors, as if Peter's call to suffering were some tacit endorsement of governments behaving badly, or worse, even a call to masochism. But Peter

[615]See Moffatt, *General Epistles*, p. 170.

says nothing about seeking out suffering. He sounds nothing like later overly eager Christians yearning for martyrdom (e.g., Ignatius of Antioch). Rather, 1 Peter seeks to prepare the audience for the worst the world can do, all the while helping the audience to live in the light of God's grace, knowing that the resurrection makes clear that God's yes to life is louder than the persecutors or even death's no. And Christ, who is coming back, will indeed have the last word.

In my own evangelical context, I suspect that one of the reasons why interpreters have avoided 1 Peter is because it has been one of the pet texts that Reformed exegetes have used to prove the Calvinistic approach to the doctrine of election and predestination. Yet 1 Peter surprisingly says nothing about individuals being selected to be saved quite apart from their own will or wishes. The entire discussion of election in this book has to do with a corporate concept of election. Christ is the elect one, whom God has chosen in advance, as 1 Peter 1:20-21 makes very apparent, and if one is "in Christ," one is in the group of the Chosen One. Furthermore, as 1 Peter 1:2 stresses, God's choosing is done on the basis of what he knows, or more precisely what he foreknows about those in question. His choice is not arbitrary, and it indeed has to do with something he knows about those who respond in faith.

In evangelical circles of late, it has been fashionable to trash the doctrine of penal substitutionary atonement; this is unfortunate, since Peter is certainly an advocate of such a theology. Jesus' blood atones for our sins by means of his death, which he endured in our stead, or place. Indeed, it is even said graphically that he bore our sins in his own body (1 Pet 2:24). Jesus is portrayed not merely as the Suffering Servant, but also as the dying one who atones for sin thereby. And if a suffering Savior is placarded before the eyes of the audience, this is in part because they too are expected to participate in similar sufferings, which can even be called participation in the sufferings of Christ. While Peter does not see the suffering of the saints as atoning for sin or purchasing forgiveness of sin, he does see suffering as an event that puts an end to the sinning of the person in question at that point. Perhaps after all, 1 Peter is not much preached in the U.S. because suffering for Christ is the experience of so few, and indeed it flows against the drift of middle-class culture, which would much rather hear about a health-and-wealth gospel, however false that gospel might be.

There is no cheap grace in this discourse either: it tells us that Christians will be held accountable for their behavior by a Father who judges everyone's works impartially (1 Pet 1:17). Those who want "the crown without the cross, the palm without the pain, the glory without the gall," to use William Penn's words,[616]

[616]William Penn, *No Cross, No Crown* (London: Andrew Sowle, 1669).

need to look elsewhere for something to preach or teach than 1 Peter. Peter also makes it as clear as can be that the new birth or conversion is only the beginning of salvation, and that after conversion our behavior most certainly can negatively affect the ultimate outcome. Most often in 1 Peter the term "salvation" refers to the end of the salvation process that comes with the parousia and the day of reckoning and redemption and resurrection.

The day when 1 Peter could be seen as some baptismal liturgy has come and gone, not least because apart from 1 Peter 3:21 the author does not really mention or much discuss water baptism. And when he does wish to talk about the means of grace, he says things like "for you have been born again, . . . through the living and enduring word of God." So much for baptismal regeneration. Even in 1 Peter 3:21, when Peter says in shorthand that "baptism saves you," he quickly adds that this is not actually by the washing with water, but by the resurrection of Jesus, which is not repeated or enacted in the baptismal ritual. Like so many preachers, Peter speaks in compact and pithy phrases, which require the broader context for readers to properly unpack them. And if one does not take account of the fact that preachers often say things for rhetorical effect and for their emotional impact, one is bound to misunderstand a good rhetorician like Peter.

Sometimes lost in the shuffle of the due attention to all the rich Christology of 1 Peter is the theocentric orientation of the document. It is God the Father who creates, judges, raises Jesus from the dead, and under whose mighty hand one is to humble oneself, according to Peter. There is no succor here for those who like to be christomonistic preachers. And if there is any historical substance to the charge that Jesus is said to have given Peter in Matthew 16, we should not be surprised that there is considerable focus on ecclesiology in this discourse. One could make the case that his theology of the Living Stone and the living stones is a reflex of that charge and his own reflection on his Jesus-bequeathed nickname. And in light of all the profound reflection on suffering in this discourse, one wonders whether it does not reflect Peter's knowledge that the handwriting was on the wall for him personally: after all, Jesus (in Jn 21) forewarned him that he would follow his master in a like death. In that light, this letter becomes the actual last will and testimony of Peter to the church, and a poignant one at that.

Peter's ethical warnings about the hostile world, the nagging flesh, and the roaring devil punctuate the discourse throughout and are well grounded in the theological reflections about suffering and salvation, but they never give way to the pessimism of a Qoheleth (in Ecclesiastes). To the contrary, they are seen as temporal and temporary problems: believers stand between the first and second advents of their Redeemer. The eschatological fervor and underpinning of this discourse is no less noticeable or substantial than we find in any of Paul's letters, including 1 or 2 Thessalonians. And it is precisely this fact that so distinguishes this document from a few of the remarks we find in 2 Peter. First Peter reflects the expectations of the earliest Christians, who stand on tiptoe with eyes wide open, awaiting the revelation of their Lord.

On balance we thus need not see 1 Peter as a late first-century document. We do not need to apologize for its content, or explain it by explaining it away. We can hardly fathom what it must have been like to live as resident aliens, and Jewish Christian aliens in Asia Minor; we are in no position to accuse Peter of serving up bourgeois ethics, or the ethics of knuckling under to the iron fist of tyrants and oppressive cultural mandates. This letter is meant as a means of comfort for those in distress, in despair, in dilemmas, in hostile environments, in the midst of persecution and various degrees and kinds of suffering. Peter the pastor is steeling them for what they face, strengthening them to endure and prevail, and trying to gird up the leadership structure of elders that existed in these regions so they can aid in this task. As such, this discourse is powerful and poignant, not offering pabulum or "chicken soup for the soul." We would do well to ponder it again and again.

The use of the Old Testament in the New Testament is always a controversial subject, and 1 Peter presents some special challenges in handling the matter. Peter, like various other New Testament authors, reads the Old Testament with christological and eschatological and ecclesiological glasses, if we can put it that way. His overarching conviction is that all previous revelation points to Christ and can be used as commentary on Christ and his people. He sees a clear continuity between God's Old Testament people and his New Testament people, not least because they are to a large degree in his day the same people, Jews, and they share the same sacred text. We can say that for the most part Peter uses the Old Testament in a homiletical rather than exegetical way; yet what he says about Old Testament prophets in 1 Peter 1:10-12 is quite interesting. He claims that when they offered predictive prophecy about messianic things and the Messiah, they realized that they were basically not serving their own immediate audience but a considerably later one, the audience of Peter's generation, or to put another way, the eschatological generation. Peter is in no way surprised that these prophets predicted the sufferings of Christ, because it was the Holy Spirit, called the Spirit of Christ, who inspired the prophets to prophesy as they did.

Peter clearly enough believes in predictive messianic prophecy, and he demonstrates this in detail from his use of both Isaiah 52:13—53:12 and Psalm 118:22, among other texts. Yet he is also quite content to use other Old Testament texts in a more straightforward ethical manner, verses such as Proverbs 3:34 or 11:31. He definitely agrees with the statement in 2 Timothy 3:16 that all Scripture, by which is meant all the Old Testament, was suitable for use with Christians, but some of it requires a figurative use, some a literal use, some a messianic use.[61] In some ways modern exegetes and preachers can follow Peter in this practice, and in some ways that they cannot follow without the danger of distorting the meaning of the Old Testament text. It is always dangerous to start trying to find Christ under every rock in the Old Testament. If 1 Peter is any guide, one would need to stick to the more obvious typologies, future prophecies and messianic psalms, and leave the Old Testament narratives and wisdom books alone. Abraham and Sarah, as we now understand, did not sit down to dinner with the Trinity, despite the way medieval exegetes and later iconographers interpreted the scene.

But what should it look like today to read the world situation as an eschatological one, as Peter does? We are all too painfully familiar with the prognosticators in whose hands the language of imminence in the New Testament, the language of expectation, is turned into calculation, and with disastrous results for people's faith. All such calculations have one thing in common: throughout the course of two millennia of Christian history, they have all been wrong! There has been an 100 percent failure rate in such predictions. This should have taught us all a lesson about calculations, but sometimes pious curiosity knows no limits.

I have a theory on how God intended and intends future prophecy to function: God reveals enough about the future to give us hope, but not so much that we do not have to keep on trusting God and exhibiting faith. This means, among other things, that God is not intending in any way to set up a specific timetable showing how long it will be until the End. That would be rather like telling us how long we have to live, and most of us would rather not know that sort of information since it would irrevocably change the way we would then live our lives, for the worse. The language of "imminence" in the New Testament, including in 1 Peter, serves the function of preparing the saints for the possible nearness of the return of Christ. It is an unpredictable event, but believers do not count it as uncertain.

By this I mean that since all of Christian history has been a part of the end times, meaning the eschatological age since Jesus' resurrection (as is perfectly

---

[61]It would appear that by the 60s A.D. the sections of the Old Testament including the Law and Prophets were pretty much fixed, with some debate about the "Writings" and what it included. What we do not seem to find is a suggestion from Josephus or elsewhere that documents like *1 Enoch* should be included in the Scriptures.

clear from reading the New Testament, for all the writers think that they are living in the eschatological age),[618] it follows that Christ could come at any time. We might think that certain things must happen before that event, but according to Mark 13, all or almost all of those things have already happened in the events that led up to the destruction of the temple in A.D. 70. The earliest Christians, including Peter, did not look for the reestablishment of Israel in the Holy Land before Christ's return. They did not expect a battle of Armageddon before Christ's return. They did not look for a pretribulation rapture before Christ's second coming. No, they simply expected to suffer as Christ did, and when Christ returns, to be gloriously transformed as he was. First Peter is a call to expect and respond in a Christian manner to suffering and even death for the cause of Christ. There would be no exemption from tribulation and suffering for Christians at all. Indeed, Peter calls such suffering a sharing in the sufferings of Christ, which only Christians could share with him.

This to be sure is an uncomfortable truth. All of us would rather hear about a promise that we are exempt from the final sufferings that happen before the Lord returns. But to preach that is to preach a gospel that would be unrecognizable to Peter. All he sees in front of him until Christ returns is a hostile world that will cause Christian suffering, which must be endured, absorbed, and transformed into Christlikeness in the person of the believer. This gospel does not play well in our day and culture, unlike the rapture gospel or the health-and-wealth gospel, but this is the true gospel. As Dietrich Bonhoeffer once said, When Christ calls you to take up your cross and follow him, he bids you to come and die.[619] But we do so with the prospect of resurrection hovering just beyond the horizon, because we do so with the prospect of the Risen One hovering just beyond the horizon. First Peter must be preached in our age of wars and rumors of wars and much suffering. For in it is contained the secret of turning such suffering into a witness for Jesus, into an "end to sin," (Dan 9:24; 1 Pet 2:24) into a way to stop the cycle of violence with forgiveness.

My colleague Joel Green has been one of the pioneers in hermeneutical and narratological studies of the New Testament, including now 1 Peter. As I write, his Two Horizons commentary on 1 Peter is with the press. Yet he has an article already in print in the July 2006 issue of *Interpretation*, one of the better journals for pastors and teachers, in which he discusses "Narrating the Gospel in 1 and

---

[618]See Witherington, *Jesus, Paul, and the End of the World.*

[619]Dietrich Bonhoeffer, *The Cost of Discipleship*, trans. Reginald Horace Fuller (New York: Macmillan, 1949): "When Christ calls a man, he bids him come and die."

2 Peter."[620] I want to briefly interact with some statements in this piece as we draw these reflections to a close.

When we catch up with his discussion, Green is talking about the usual approach to handling New Testament texts, in which we first study the text in its original and various historical contexts, and then we take materials from that study and recontextualize them for our own quite different age, time and culture. He then adds:

> In spite of its hoary pedigree, this approach too often stops short, its frames abandoned on the cutting room floor. This is not surprising. First, it has an effect that is the exact opposite of what it intended. Rather than bringing the message of the New Testament more fully to bear on the life and mission of the church, it tends instead to segregate that message from the contemporary church. To a large degree, this is because it perpetuates the erroneous claim that these New Testament materials are written to folks back then and not to the church now. The task of theological interpretation cannot bypass the theological claim that the church is one—one across time and space. The church out of which 1 Peter was written, the church to which 1 Peter was addressed, the church that received 1 Peter as canon, the church that has engaged in the interpretation of 1 Peter, and the church that today turns to it as Scripture—these are all the same church. Second, it places the need for transformation in the wrong place. This is because it assumes that what is needed is our moving into the world of the New Testament, tracking and capturing its message, then carrying it back into our worlds for transformation, into contemporary idiom. But it is we who need transformation, not the Word of God. The essential division between the biblical world and our own is not *historical* but *theological*, having to do with our capacity to read ourselves into Scripture's theological vision and so to enter into its world that we are transformed for faithful life in our world. What I am urging is a narrative-theological approach to our craft.[621]

Green then goes on to talk about the fact that this new narrative theological approach involves an antipathy to theological approaches that involve the systematic organization of a bunch of propositions gleaned from the text and usually arranged topically (e.g., the doctrine of creation followed by the doctrine of the fall followed by the doctrine of redemption, and so on). As an alternative to such schematizing ways of doing theology, he suggests a narrative approach, even for the materials in an epistle like 1 Peter. He does so because he is convinced that narrative is central to identity formation: narrative helps people make sense of what they experience day by day. "From this perspective, narrative is not the absence of referentiality, but rather the admission that persons

[620] Joel B. Green, "Narrating the Gospel in 1 and 2 Peter," in *Int* 60, no. 3 (2006): 262-77.
[621] Ibid., p. 265.

and events in the world receive their significance by means of their being located in particular narratives. From this perspective, 'ideas' are not ruled out of court, but gather meaning within a particular narrative by which imaginative structures are (trans)formed. In this context, narrative representation is identity formation through theological intervention."[622]

This approach is both problematic and promising at the same time. First, let me enumerate some problems. The first task of any reader of Scripture is to respect the historical givenness of the text. By this I mean that it was not in the first instance written for twenty-first-century Christians. It was written for first-century ones, in their language, in their historical circumstances, in their cultural forms of expression, and so on. Too often narratological approaches to theology jump the hermeneutical gun by not first dealing with the historical givenness of the text. We must study the text in its original historical contexts to even be able to understand what it *means*. Simply studying the Bible in the literary context of the Bible itself is not by any means sufficient to figure out the meaning the first-century authors encoded into these texts. If it were just a matter of reading the Bible in its canonical contexts, we would never need historical commentaries of any sort on the text. Before we can say what uses and significance we can make of these texts today, to help us understand our stories and lives, we must respect the original authors, audiences and contexts in which the material is given. Only thus can we discover the meaning in these texts.

Second, it is both true and false to say that the church has been the same forever, and that provides us with an instant continuity and point of contact with the original audiences. If one means no more by this than that these texts are written to Christians, and we also are Christians and part of the body of Christ today, that is true; but it also is innocuous and does not help us get at the meaning of the text. More to the point, it does not give us permission to omit the hard work of studying the text in its original historical givenness. Christians, just because they are Christians, *especially* need to take seriously the cautionary tasks of historical work because they are liable to read all sorts of things into the text from modernity that are not there. And thus exegesis becomes eisegesis (reading one's own ideas into the text), and the original meaning of the text is not applied to the modern believer's life. Distorted interpretations lead to distorted applications today. In fact, the Christians to whom Peter was writing were quite different from most readers of this particular commentary series. They were Jews, which most of us are not; they lived in Asia Minor, which most of us do not; they spoke Greek, which most of us do not; they knew rhetoric, which most

[622]Ibid., pp. 266-67.

of us do not; and they were suffering, which most of us are not. What divides us from that original audience is just as profound as what unites us, and it does no good to gloss over these facts because *these very factors have shaped how Peter has addressed this audience, the words he chose, the ideas he used, the Scriptures he handled,* and so on.

I agree with Joel that systematicians are often guilty of ahistorical methods of abstracting McNuggets from the text and then arranging them in some logical order. Nevertheless, some narratological-theological-canonical approaches unfortunately are just as guilty of taking an ahistorical approach to the text. And this simply will not do. It is just another form of modern docetism, which is an especially deadly thing when one is dealing with a historical religion based on a certain irreducible number of historical events and persons and processes.

It would be nearer to the mark to say that we are in the same eschatological situation as the original readers, than that we are in the same ecclesiological situation. By this I mean that we also stand between the two advents of Christ and live in the eschatological age and should view history in that light. The story of Christ's coming and his coming again is such that we are inherently and inevitably in medias res, in the middle of things, whether we realize it or not. And eschatology in the first instance is not all about texts and ideas, though it involves them. It is about historical events—then and in our present and future. For example, if we are suffering for some Christian cause or purpose right now, as when Jim Elliott and his fellow missionaries gave their lives for the Waodani Indians in South America (see the movie *The End of the Spear*), then we are actually living the sort of messianic sufferings that Peter was clearly talking about: suffering for the faith, suffering inflicted by a hostile outside world. In the first instance this was not all about texts and interpretations and how one reads oneself into the Christian story: this was about dramatic real-time life experiences. Precisely because so few Christians are really engaged in frontline witnessing for Christ to a hostile world and so many are isolated and insulated from such experiences, there is often an air of unreality in the way they study the text, read the text, and read themselves into the stories in the text.

Joel Green however is quite right that it is not the Word of God that needs to be transformed. It is us. Just so, but the Bible does need to be helpfully interpreted in our very different world and context so that transformation can transpire. I would not see contextual exegetical study of the Bible, if properly done, as a transforming of the text. To the contrary, I would see it as a process of being illuminated about what the text actually says, and allowing it to have its own say, not trying to tell it what it must say. Only then can I apply the real meaning of the text to my own life, or allow myself to be exegeted by the text and allow the text to make a claim on me. As Johann Albrecht Bengel said long ago, we must apply the whole of ourselves (including our historical study skills) to the text, all the while allowing the whole of the text to exegete us, interpret us, be applied to us.[623]

The essential differences between our world and the world of Peter are both historical and theological and also to some extent ecclesiological. Although I agree that a narratological theological approach can be quite helpful in our understanding of the text, I do not see it as a replacement for traditional historical study of the text, but rather as a supplement thereto, a necessary supplement, to be sure. In particular, I quite agree that isolated ideas are not what we are looking for when we do theology. Ideas do indeed take on their meaning from how they are embedded in texts, sometimes in stories, sometimes in discourse, sometimes in law tables, sometimes in hymns and other sorts of poetry, sometimes in wisdom sayings and so on. Story is not the only fish in the biblical sea, but it is a very important and large one that promises to help us understand ourselves better as Christians.

After all, precisely because we care about history, we also care about the stories that are and have been told about historical events. Stories about suffering, death and resurrection are not inherently helpful in themselves unless suffering, death, and resurrection have happened at least once in real life in space and time. Then the story has not merely an air of reality; it also has the possibility of historical actualization again, as Jesus' story ceases to be only history and also becomes our story. In short, Christ's history becomes our destiny, if and only if his story actually happened, was a historically "true" story. Thus we must care at least as much about the history that generated the tale as about the telling of the tale in 1 Peter and other New Testament texts, and about our retelling the accounts and so inscribing ourselves into that tale once more.

In this way we recognize that history and story both matter, and we do not collapse the two horizons into one, as if we were the original audiences who heard these stories. We are not, and we must not engage in identity theft. First Peter is not written in the first instance to late Western Christians like me. It cuts me no slack when it comes to my modern encumbrances and understandings, and it is only through hard work and the conversion of my understanding as well as my imagination that I can enter into their historically given world.

Even so, I still will not become an early Jewish Christian in the process, but at least I can come to understand them, understand what Peter said to them, and then be prepared to ask the question of how I can stand with them, learn with

[623] Preface from his 1734 edition of the Greek New Testament.

them, and affirm Christian truths and praxis with them. Only then can I say that what unites us is substantial: the living Christ, the Holy Spirit, being a part of the people of God reading God's Word. But this unity, while a given, does not in any way obliterate difference, important historical differences between myself and the average believer in Pontus in the first century, for example. A good missionary must engage in indigenizing the gospel into a native culture; likewise, I must indigenize my imagination into that original biblical culture if I am to understand the meaning of its texts and their significance for my life. Otherwise, I am truly guilty of glossing over profound differences and will inevitably read my own modern predilections into the text.

We must especially bear these things in mind when interpreting a theologically rich text like 1 Peter. The danger is that we will try to abstract the theological gems from the Petrine mine and forget the "rock from which we were hewn" (cf. Is 51:1). But who knows? That might be the historical stone that the modern theologians and narratologists have rejected, but that God has chosen to be the Living Stone, the head of the corner, the most important building block in the ecclesial structure.

Introduction to 2 Peter

Second Peter is a mystery wrapped in an enigma cloaked in a conundrum, to coin a redundant phrase that gives one a feel for the florid nature of Asiatic Greek. The vocabulary facts show just how different this book is: out of a total of 401 different words (total word count, 1,103), some 57 words are found nowhere else in the New Testament, half of these do not occur in the LXX, half of the rest are unknown in early Jewish literature, and at least three words *(akatapaustos, empaigmonē, paraphronia)* occur nowhere else in all of Greek literature before or during this period. Although 2 Peter repeats only 38 percent of its vocabulary—less than do some 21 books of the New Testament—there are more than enough examples, at least 25, of paronomasia and transplacement to make parts of this discourse sound quite repetitive.[1] Add to this that there are no, or almost no, Semitisms in this work.[2] If style makes, or at least expresses, the individual, the author of this document is not much like the other New Testament authors. But not just the language issues make 2 Peter difficult. Without question, 2 Peter is the most difficult New Testament book to deal with in terms of the basic authorship, date and composition issues. This may to some extent explain why Fred Craddock bemoans that "this epistle is seldom read and studied even less."[3] And in a remarkable statement James Dunn opines, "I would want to insist that not a few compositions of Martin Luther and John Wesley, for example, were as, if not more, inspired than the author of 2 Peter."[4]

Furthermore, there is a strong consensus among most scholars, even many evangelicals (such as Richard J. Bauckham), that 2 Peter *cannot* have been writ-

---

[1]See Callan, "The Style of the Second Letter of Peter," pp. 202-24, esp. p. 209 and nn. 37-38.

[2]There do appear to be a couple of Latinisms, however.

[3]Craddock, *First and Second Peter*, p. 85.

[4]J. D. G. Dunn, *Unity and Diversity in the New Testament* (Philadelphia: Westminster, 1977), pp. 285-86.

ten by Peter and certainly not by the Peter who was responsible for 1 Peter. In terms of perspective, Greek style, theological content, language, dependency on Jude and a host of other factors, 2 Peter is said to be a clear example of a New Testament pseudepigraphon. Thus, we get such dogmatic statements as that of Werner G. Kümmel: "But this letter cannot have been written by Peter."[5] That is a quite definite and dramatic conclusion. In a famous lecture in 1952, Ernst Käsemann insisted that 2 Peter not infrequently presents us with irreconcilable theological contradictions and then concluded that 2 Peter is "from beginning to end a document expressing an early Catholic viewpoint and is perhaps the most dubious writing in the canon."[6] Yes, it is true: 2 Peter has been something of the stepchild or even the whipping boy of New Testament studies, especially in Germany.[7]

This has led to the conclusion that the letter must have been written in the postapostolic era, reflecting later concerns, and some have been willing to say that it comes from as late as the mid-second century if not later. We are also not much encouraged to think of this letter as authentically Petrine when we examine how the church viewed this document. Origen is our first clear evidence that the church fathers knew and used it (A.D. 185-254), and along with Jude, 2 Peter was regarded as of doubtful value if not spurious altogether. It is listed by Eusebius as one of the "disputed" books (of uncertain apostolic authorship and canonical value). Origen even held, says Eusebius, that Peter had written one letter and perhaps a second, "for it is disputed" (Eusebius *Hist. eccl.* 6.25.8). Indeed, in giving his own evaluation, Eusebius says, "But the so-called second epistle we have not received as canonical, but nevertheless it has appeared useful to many, and has been studied with the other writings [or Scriptures? *graphai*]" (Eusebius *Hist. eccl.* 3.3.1). At most, this suggests a deuterocanonical status for 2 Peter in Eusebius's view (A.D. 260-340). Jerome resorts to the view that Peter uses a different amanuensis in 2 Peter, and perhaps his authority led to its eventual acceptance. He does so because he recognizes that for the most part the style and vocabulary of 2 Peter betrays "another hand." At one point Jerome actually seems to reject Petrine authorship (Jerome *Epist.* 120.11).

Even the Reformers had serious doubts. Erasmus saw 2 Peter as spurious or

---

[5]Werner G. Kümmel, *Introduction to the New Testament* (London: SCM Press, 1975), p. 427.

[6]Ernst Käsemann, "An Apologia for Primitive Christian Eschatology," in *Essays on New Testament Themes,* SBT 41 (London: SCM Press, 1964), pp. 135-57, esp. pp. 156-57.

[7]E. G. Günter Klein says our author does a miserable job of presenting his case, botching his presentation of early Christian eschatology. See his "Der zweite Petrusbrief und der neutestamentliche Kanon," in *Ärgernisse: Konfrontationen mit dem Neuen Testament* (Munich: Kaiser, 1970), pp. 109-14, esp. pp. 111-12.

written by Silvanus. Luther only thought it *might* be written by Peter. Even Calvin resorted to the view that it was written by a disciple at Peter's direction. None of this inspires confidence in the apostolic and Petrine nature of 2 Peter. Nevertheless, the external evidence is not decisive, and some of it may help us date our epistle earlier than has been done in some quarters. First, there can be little doubt that two apocryphal second-century works knew 2 Peter and drew on it: the *Apocalypse of Peter* (ca. 110-140 A.D.), and the *Acts of Peter* (180). This means that 2 Peter must have been written before A.D. 140. Thus, we cannot date it a whole century after the apostle Peter's death.

Second, with the newly discovered *Letter to Theodorus*, we have more sure grounds for stating that Clement of Alexandria knew of 2 Peter.[8] This also would suggest that this document was known and used in the second half of the second century and thus was probably written before A.D. 150. Perhaps it is even more helpful for us to note the obvious affinities between our letter and certain other letters and documents that came from Rome between A.D. 80-100, such as *1 Clement, 2 Clement*, and the Shepherd of Hermas. As Bauckham shows in his commentary, these letters and their content bear the closest resemblance to 2 Peter among noncanonical works, while Jude and 1 Peter are its nearest canonical relatives. The noncanonical material might suggest a date in the period A.D. 80-100.

With regard to sources, there are several views: (1) Jude used 2 Peter.[9] (2) Both Jude and the author of 2 Peter used a common source. (3) 2 Peter definitely used Jude. In regard to the last view, Ralph P. Martin reports that 19 out of 25 of Jude's verses seem to exist in some form in 2 Peter, as suggested in his chart:

Jude	*2 Peter*	*Jude 2*	*Peter*
4	2:1-3	11-12a	2:15, 13
5	2:5	12b-13	2:17
6, 7	2:4, 6	16	2:18
8, 9	2:10, 11	17	3:2
10	2:12	18	3:3[10]

In short, almost all the significant material in Jude is taken over, used, and expanded upon or adapted in 2 Peter 2. Just as impressively, the material is found *in exactly the same order* in both documents, covering the same themes and topics. This is not a case of just borrowing an idea or two, or a term or

---

[8]See Bauckham, *Jude, 2 Peter,* p. 163.

[9]See Moo, *2 Peter, Jude*, pp. 16-18.

[10]Ralph P. Martin, *New Testament Foundations,* vol. 2 (Grand Rapids: Eerdmans, 1978), p. 385. For a more extensive list, see pp. 337-38 below.

phrase or two. The argument here for literary dependence is indeed strong. Why not conclude that they used a common source? For one thing, since both of these authors seem to arrange their material according to their own purposes, we would not necessarily expect to find all of this material in the same order in the two documents. And why would they have borrowed exactly the same material from the third source, and not other material?

The suggestion of direct literary dependency is far more plausible and convincing, not to mention a far simpler explanation. There are very good reasons for not concluding that it is Jude borrowing from 2 Peter: (1) The noncanonical books referred to in Jude are deleted from the common material in 2 Peter. This indeed suggests that 2 Peter was written later, and for a broader audience than the Jewish sectarian one Jude is addressing. (2) Jude appears to be composed freely and without any such copying of sources; 2 Peter is rather clearly a composite document. One can argue that the false teaching combated in 2 Peter is of a somewhat different and perhaps later variety than what we find in Jude. We must give due weight to Duane F. Watson's detailed demonstration of the dependence of 2 Peter on Jude (and not vice versa).[11] In my view his arguments are compelling, and there has been no successful refutation of it since it was put forth in 1988. It is confirmed by the detailed comparisons in the landmark commentary by Bauckham as well.[12] We should also cite the detailed monograph of Michael J. Gilmour, who concludes after a lengthy evaluation of the parallels: "Scholarship is on solid ground in postulating a literary relationship between 2 Peter and Jude; the evidence is best explained by the hypothesis that 2 Peter was dependent on Jude."[13]

This means that 2 Peter can certainly not be earlier than Jude and thus not earlier than A.D. 50-60. More helpful, however, is the likelihood that 2 Peter was written after 1 Peter and is possibly in part dependent on it, or its writer at least knows of 1 Peter's content. The reference in 2 Peter 3:1 is most naturally taken as an allusion to 1 Peter since this letter (2 Peter) also purports to be by Peter, and we know of no other Petrine letters in the first century.[14] On the surface of things, 2 Peter appears to be Peter's last words and personal testimony to the church, and as such it could not have come earlier than 64-66, since this is when 1 Peter was likely written and when Peter died.

We have thus narrowed the time gap to A.D. 64-100. Roughly, this makes it a

---

[11]Watson, *Invention,* pp. 163-87.

[12]Bauckham, *Jude, 2 Peter,* pp. 141-43. Strictly speaking, Bauckham's evaluation predates Watson's, though the conclusion is the same.

[13]Gilmour, *Significance of Parallels,* p. 120.

[14]This allusion provides a strong hint that 1 Peter is seen as authentic by our author. It is unlikely that he would appeal to a pseudepigraphon as by Peter.

first-century document, but it does not thereby make it by Peter in its final form. A key factor suggests that at least part of 2 Peter depends upon something Peter wrote or said. The section 1 Peter 1:12-21 reads like Peter's personal and final testimony; linguistically, we may note two phrases in particular in common with 1 Peter. Joseph B. Mayor notes two phrases in particular: (1) 2 Peter 1:16 and 1 Peter 2:12; (2) 2 Peter 1:21 and 1 Peter 2:15.[15]

In addition, in the small section of 1:12—2:3 we have the following words shared with 1 Peter: *agapētos, aei, apothesis, aselgeia, blasphēmeō, graphē, despotēs* (though used of different objects), *dio, thelēma, idios, laleō, lambanō, oida, pote, prōton, stēridzō, phainō, pherō*. In so short a segment of text, having eighteen common words cannot be ignored: they are not accidental. Some of the words are common, yet various of the terms are not. *Apothesis,* for instance, is found only in 1 and 2 Peter and nowhere else in the New Testament. In addition, H. E. W. Turner identifies a similar use of *kathōs* in 2 Peter 1:14 and in 1 Peter.[16] Also, Turner gives evidence that an earlier "Jewish Greek" original has been revised and redacted,[17] and that we find certain Hebraisms in our section, such as *ou pote* at 2 Peter 1:21, to which we may compare the use of 1 Peter 2:10; 3:5, 20. Another Hebraism is perhaps the use of *pas . . . ou* for *oudeis* at 2 Peter 1:20, as well as the avoidance of the divine name at 2 Peter 1:17. Nor can we say that the section 2 Peter 1:12-21 exhibits especially grandiose Asiatic Greek or any significant number of Hellenisms. Perhaps also we should note the fine rhythm at 2 Peter 1:16-17 and the alliteration at 2 Peter 1:19-21. Second Peter 1:12-21 generally does not have the heavy, cumbersome sentences we find at 2 Peter 1:3-4, 2:4-10 and 3:5-6. This is significant because the rest of 2 Peter does definitely reflect Asiatic Greek. As we have said, there are some 57 words in this discourse not found in any other New Testament document, and 32 of which are also not found in the LXX. So 2 Peter is hardly an example of Septuagintal Greek. This number of unique words is considerable in view of the brevity of 2 Peter. Taken altogether, this information may suggest three things:

1. The person who wrote or dictated 1 Peter could also have written 2 Peter 1:12-21, or at least have spoken it.
2. The Greek in this short segment, 2 Peter 1:12-21, is not overly Asiatic but is more like the Greek of 1 Peter.[18]

---

[15]Cf. Boobyer, "Indebtedness of 2 Peter to 1 Peter," pp. 44-51.
[16]MHT 4:181.
[17]MHT 4:143.
[18]Here is where I stress that, yes, 1 Peter does reflect Asiatic Greek to some extent, but outside the passage in question, 2 Peter is far more obviously Asiatic in style; 2 Peter's style outside the section 2 Pet 1:12-21 could be said to reflect Asiatic Greek on steroids.

3. Nevertheless, there are some evidences of an editor who may have touched up this section or even put a bit of it into some of his own words later. The importance of this will be seen later.

On the other hand, it is fair to say that what we have elsewhere in 2 Peter is rather pompous, bookish Greek that is different from 1 Peter in many ways and words. Thus, Bauckham says:

> As [Bo Ivar] Reicke points out (146-7), 2 Peter must be related to the "Asiatic" style of Greek rhetoric which was coming into fashion in 2 Peter's time, and which, with its love of high-sounding expressions, florid and verbose language, and elaborate literary effects, was an artificial style which Reicke aptly compares with European baroque. If 2 Peter's language can seem bombastic and pompous to us, it must be judged by the taste of its age and circle, and we should not too quickly decide that the writer overreached himself in his literary ambition.[19]

The matter needs to be characterized a bit differently. First Peter actually reflects to some degree the Asiatic style, but not in nearly the pronounced fashion that we find in 2 Peter. The difference is immediately apparent to anyone who is familiar with New Testament and Asiatic Greek. Wilbert Francis Howard states:

> It is a book which stands apart in many ways, by general consent decidedly the latest in the Canon, and the solitary New Testament example of pseudepigraphic writing. *2 Peter* is written in Greek which seems to have been learnt mainly from books, Greek proverbs, Greek inscriptions, and Greek books which we can no longer handle, contributed to the writer's vocabulary, and moulded the fine sense of rhythm to which Mayor bears effective testimony. It is to literature rather than to vernacular inscriptions and papyri that we go when we seek to illustrate rare words in this little book; and the general style is far removed from the language of daily life, as any tiro can see.[20]

It is unlikely that Peter the fisherman had picked up such bookish Greek, and nowhere does 2 Peter tell us that an amaneuensis is being used.

Lauri Thurén, in his fine study of the style of 2 Peter, has some important observations that bear repeating. It is well to keep in mind that judgments on style are often a matter of personal taste, and so when we hear scholars today, completely removed from the ethos in which the author of 2 Peter lived, say such things as "We have bombastic, pompous, or bookish style in 2 Peter," these are modern value judgments, and value judgments that the author of 2 Peter and

[19]Bauckham, *Jude, 2 Peter,* p. 137.
[20]MHT 2:5-6.

doubtless many in his audience would not have agreed with (though if there were some Atticists in the audience, they might well have agreed). But as Thurén rightly says, the "main idea of rhetorical criticism is that in human communication it is at least as important to ask *how* something is said as what is said."[21] This is especially a crucial point in a largely oral culture, where discourses are meant to be heard, not silently read. Asiatic rhetoric especially is rhetoric that is meant to be heard: in large measure it depends on its aural effect if it is to persuade someone of something. In such a style, words are often chosen on the basis of how they *sound* because the author, if he has a good Greek vocabulary, knows that many words have synonyms, and so one has a choice about the matter.

We are contending that 2 Peter is a document that can truly be said to be one of the first Christian attempts at "mass communication." It is written to all Christians in the empire, unlike 1 Peter, for example. And Asiatic Greek was, especially in the middle of empire where Christianity was beginning to flourish, the vox populi. If we put together the old adage "vox populi, vox Dei" with the understanding that 2 Peter is a mass communication of a religious sort, then we may pick up one clue as to why this document looks and sounds like it does. This is persuasion for the masses, and only more traditionalist patricians, upper-crust Romans and other well-educated members of society were likely to turn up their noses at it. Like modern musical snobs who love classical music but look down their noses at pop or country or rap music, style in the empire was often a reflector of class, education and ambitions. But in our case, it tells us most about the audience 2 Peter addresses. And this audience is Christians, both Jews and Gentiles, throughout the empire, who need to be galvanized to continue to embrace the apostolic values and virtues, beliefs and behaviors of the previous generation of believers. Both the style and the content of the document suggest that we are addressing Christians considerably after the end of Peter's and Paul's lives.

Certain other factors also make it likely that the letter in its present form comes from a time after the death of Peter:

1. The reference to Paul's letters in 2 Peter 3:14-18. Here Paul's letters are spoken of as "all his letters" and as Scripture. This strongly suggests a time after the death of Paul when his letters or at least several of them had been collected, or the writer of 2 Peter at least knew of them, and Christians had come to regard them as Scripture. This likely happened in the period A.D. 70-100. We must also note, however, that the author of 2 Peter appears to have been little influenced

[21]Thurén, "Style Never Goes Out of Fashion," p. 337.

by Paul's thought (although cf. on 2 Peter 3:10-11), unlike the person behind 1 Peter. Further, the person behind the *present* form of 2 Peter shows little dependence on the thought and theology of 1 Peter. He writes in his own way and uses different terms for common concepts (e.g., 1 Peter calls the second coming "the revealing of Jesus Christ," while 2 Peter speaks of the "parousia"). Whoever wrote 2 Peter knew *about* Paul and his letters but had formulated his thoughts independently, and this is true also with regard to the thought of Peter for the most part (although 2 Peter 3:6-9 suggests that he had read 1 Peter).

2. Perhaps as important is the reference to "*your* apostles" in 2 Peter 3:2, which suggests that the writer is not one of them and certainly not his audience's apostle. The words of "your apostles" are being called to memory, perhaps suggesting that they are of a previous era. It is uncertain as to whether "the fathers" in 2 Peter 3:4 is a reference to early Christian fathers, meaning the apostles, or to the Old Testament saints. If it is the former, then here is more evidence that we are in the subapostolic era. The problem of perceived "delay" of Christ's coming may also be a sign of the lateness of 2 Peter.

3. We may distinguish the author from Jude in that he mostly edits out Jude's use of extracanonical material, though he does share some Jewish apocalyptic thought with him. More clearly, he also, like those of the apostolic age, maintains and speaks of the second coming and its vital importance for and effect on Christians and their behavior. He does not write like one who lived when their hope had faded, as some authors of the second century do. Indeed, it is his purpose to stress it in this letter.

4. Against Ernst Käsemann, there are no signs of highly advanced church organization or insistence on creedal orthodoxy that would cause us to date this material late.

5. Note the change in the discourse from 2 Peter 2:1-3 prophesying about future false teachers to 2 Peter 2:10, 12-16, 20, 22 describing them as a present reality or even a reality going on for a while (cf. 2 Pet 2:15, 22). Scholars sometimes explain this as carelessness on the author's part. Bauckham argues that the author has included material in the form of a testament of Peter prophesying to an age after his death, though it is a literary fiction, but elsewhere he includes apocalyptic material addressing the present problem. Now if we are right that 2 Peter 1:12-21 (and perhaps also 2 Pet 3:1-4 with certain editorial changes, as for example "your apostles") is indeed a real testimony of Peter that has been incorporated by our author and used to address a later situation, then the change in verb tenses to describe the false teachings is quite natural, not part of a literary fiction.

Several aspects of Bauckham's argument for a pure and indeed transparent pseudepigraphon here are unsatisfactory. He tries to distinguish between a pseudepigraphon and a testament (the latter being a fictitious literary genre).[22] Then he suggests that testaments and farewell discourses were all well known to be fictional. Now, whatever may be true of Jewish pseudepigraphic literature such as the *Testament of Moses*, it is doubtful that either the Fourth Evangelist in John, much less Luke in Acts 20, intended for his audience to see such material as a fictional or at least a *purely* fictional farewell message. For one thing, Acts 20 is in the midst of a "we" section in Acts, and Luke likely heard this farewell address. John 13—17 in the Fourth Gospel appears to be based on the testimony of the beloved disciple, though edited by a later tradent of his, and thus also could go back to an eyewitness. Thus there were genuine testaments and fictitious ones, and we must evaluate them on a case-by-case basis. The *Testaments of the Twelve Patriarchs* are neither letters nor rhetorical speeches, and in terms of genre this is what we are dealing with in 2 Peter. Other factors also argue against a pure pseudepigraphon or a purely fictional testament in 2 Peter. Donald Guthrie points out:

> It must at once be recognized that there are no close parallels to 2 Peter, if this Epistle is pseudepigraphic. The normal procedure was to adopt a fairly consistent first person style, particularly in narrative sections. This style was not specially adapted for Epistles, and this is probably the reason for the paucity of examples of pseudepigrapha in this form. . . .
>
> It must at once seem strange that the author uses the double name Simon Peter, when the name Simon does not appear in 1 Peter, which was presumably used as a model, if 2 Peter is pseudepigraphic. The difficulty is even greater if the form "Symeon" is the correct reading, for neither in the Apostolic Fathers nor in the Christian pseudepigraphic literature is it used. Indeed, it occurs elsewhere only in Acts xv.14 and is obviously a primitive form.[23]

Further, there is little or no precedent in earlier Jewish apocalyptic literature for a fictional letter testament addressed to a real audience with real problems. As Guthrie argues:

> Yet there is a great difference between this Epistle and Jewish apocalyptic books in testamentary form, which all share the pattern of a discourse addressed to the immediate descendants, but which are really destined for future generations. This latter type of literature proceeded from a review of the past to a prophecy of the future. While both these elements may be found in 2 Peter, the Epistle can be clearly understood without recourse to the testamentary hypothesis, which could

[22]Bauckham, *Jude, 2 Peter,* pp. 134-40; cf. 158-62.

[23]Donald Guthrie, *New Testament Introduction* (Downers Grove, Ill.: InterVarsity Press, 1990), p. 828.

certainly not be said of the farewell discourses of Jewish apocalyptic.[24]

It must also appear strange, on Bauckham's view, that a pseudepigraphon ascribed to Peter is found to be obviously so heavily dependent on Jude. This does not suggest an author who was concerned to make most of this document really appear to be by Peter. Guthrie argues:

> If Jude is prior to 2 Peter, therefore, it must be regarded as unexpected that such use is made of it and this would weigh the evidence rather against than for authenticity. At the same time it is equally, if not more, unexpected for a pseudepigraphist to adopt such a borrowing procedure. Indeed, it is quite unparalleled among the Jewish and early Christian pseudepigrapha. The question arises why so much of Jude needed to be incorporated. About the only reasonable suggestion on the late-date theory is to suppose that Jude's tract had failed because of its lack of an impressive name and so the same truths with considerable additions were attributed to Peter.[25]

Beyond all this, we must once again insist that there *was* a critical concern, and not only in the second century and afterward, that a document with Christian teaching be by, or include material from, its reputed author. Paul in 2 Thessalonians 2:2 and 2 Thessalonians 3:17 already shows concern about and against pseudepigrapha, and we may also note Luke's concern in Luke 1:1-4 for authentic testimony, not just verisimilitude. We must remember that in the second century the author of the fictitious *Acts of Paul and Thecla* was defrocked for writing such fictitious books about or in the name of an apostle. Around A.D. 180 Serapion, the bishop of Antioch, became very upset because some Christians were treating the *Gospel of Peter* as authentic and valuable; he said, "For our part, brethren, we revere both Peter and the other apostles as Christ, but the writings which falsely bear their names we reject."[26] When one studies such material, it is rather amazing that many contemporary scholars just assume that pseudepigrapha was an accepted literary genre and practice that raised no ethical concerns for ancient Christians. This is not so.

But it is equally surprising that many scholars today do not seem to realize that there are other options besides declaring this document to be a pseudepigraphon or a letter composed by Peter himself. I attribute this to the fact that most New Testament scholars do not know sapiential literature as well as they should, and they especially seem unaware of the scribal practices found in early Judaism and early Christianity, where scribes would not merely copy but also edit together collections of valuable sacred traditions, just as we see happening

[24] Ibid., p. 830.
[25] Ibid., p. 838.
[26] Cf. M. Green, *2 Peter Reconsidered*, pp. 32ff.

in 2 Peter. These are not exercises in pure creativity or in pseudonymity. They are ways of preserving sources and traditions from the past and applying them in later situations, with the editors neither claiming authorship nor trying to deceive anyone about the sort or identity of their sources.[27]

The very reason 2 Peter had so much trouble getting into the canon was because the church even as early as Paul was indeed suspicious of and closely scrutinized documents that claimed apostolic authority. No doubt this process was only exacerbated by the rise of so much apocryphal material used to support particular heresies. As I see matters, it does not appear that 2 Peter had any special ax to grind or new or unique doctrine to promulgate that would provide a motive for composing a pseudepigraphon. Bauckham comes closer than others to giving such a rationale, but even he falls short. I thus conclude:

- At least 2 Peter 1:12-21, perhaps also 2 Peter 3:1-3, must be seen as the testimony of Peter, perhaps orally passed on to the church at Rome shortly before his martyrdom. This testimony draws on some of Jesus' own teaching about false prophets (cf. Mk 13) as well as Peter's own experiences (at the transfiguration).
- This section has been somewhat edited and written up to fit into a larger document that draws heavily on Jude, but its style is not as bombastic or Hellenistic as what we find elsewhere in the epistle and suggests use of a source, possibly even a written source, with more Hebraisms and Semitic Greek.
- We should see 2 Peter 1:3-11 as a summary of apostolic teaching or, better said, of Peter's apostolic preaching, which comported with general apostolic teaching. It is written in Asiatic Greek and suggests that the author relied on memory or an oral source, composing it himself for the first time.
- We should see 2 Peter 2:3b-22 as a recasting of Jude into Asiatic Greek to address a different situation. Here again is a reliance on authentic tradition from a church leader of the first generation. The writer of 2 Peter is not intending to promulgate his own doctrine but to combat certain opponents by adopting and adapting authoritative Christian material. Even his reference to Paul must be seen as an appeal to previous apostolic authority, which his audience to called upon to heed.
- First Peter 3:1-18 may be a mixture of Petrine testimony (2 Pet 3:1-3) and Petrine and Pauline ideas about the parousia. There is nothing particularly original here

---

[27]Take, for example, the book of Proverbs, attributed to Solomon, which contains only some material that likely goes back to Solomon and various other sources of wise sayings as well, some of which Solomon may have collected and some of which was collected later. Similarly in Ecclesiastes we have the sayings of Qoheleth, but this book is put together by a later scribe or tradent, as its last chapter manifests. The same seems to be the case with 2 Peter, which is edited by a scribe, perhaps Linus(?), assembling and editing earlier apostolic material here of various sorts: Petrine testimony, eschatological teaching, comparative polemic amplifying on Jude, proverbs and sayings of various sages (including Jesus).

except for the idea of the world's final conflagration, which has some precedent in Hellenistic sources.

- Agreeing with Bauckham, it is likely that this document was drawn up after Peter's (and Paul's?) death, by someone in the Petrine circle, likely a colleague, probably *not* an understudy. Bauckham's guess of Linus, the second great leader and bishop of Rome (cf. 2 Tim 4:21; Eusebius *Hist. eccl.* 3.13, 21; 5.6.1), is plausible. Bauckham's conjecture may stand with the above modifications. Linus, if he is the compiler and writer of 2 Peter, did not intend for anyone to see this document either as a forgery or as his own composition. Rather, it is in part Peter's last testament and as such bears Peter's name, though he may never have written it. The affinities with *1* and *2 Clement*, 1 Peter and Shepherd of Hermas suggest that it was sent from Rome to at least some of the same audience as that which had been evangelized by Paul and received his letters; and may have read 1 Peter.

Most definitely the sort of problems and opponents here do not warrant seeing this document as arising when Gnosticism was a full-fledged system. There is no reference here to the Demiurge or other characteristic features of mature Gnosticism. But it does appear that we may be dealing here with libertine tendencies such as we also find in 1 Corinthians and elsewhere in the New Testament. Perhaps, then, this epistle comes to us from end of the first century. In conclusion we may quote J. Ramsey Michaels:

> Posthumous publication in Peter's name does not necessarily imply any intent to deceive. If the tradition behind Second Peter is genuinely Petrine [at least in part], then the only kind of compiler of this material who might be guilty of deception would be one who presumptuously signed his own name to the apostle's teaching. This testament, however, frankly calls itself a "second" or "secondary" epistle (3:1), a designation that perhaps glances back not at First Peter or at a lost epistle but precisely at the traditional Petrine teachings out of which Second Peter is built.[28]

Second Peter is a composite document that draws on material from both Peter and Jude, two earlier apostles, and reflects some knowledge of Paul as well. It bears neither the form nor the character of a pseudepigraphon, and since it includes some genuine Petrine material, it is understandably attributed to its first and most famous contributor.[29] Because of the ever-increasing importance of

---

[28]Glenn W. Barker, William L. Lane and J. Ramsay Michaels, *The New Testament Speaks* (San Francisco: HarperCollins, 1969), p. 352.

[29]On the problems with the genre "pseudepigrapha," see Ben Witherington III, *Letters and Homilies for Hellenized Christians,* vol. 1, *A Socio-Rhetorical Commentary on Titus, 1-2 Timothy and 1-3 John* (Downers Grove, Ill.: InterVarsity Press, 2006), pp. 23-38. Note Lewis R. Donelson's remarks in *Pseudepigraphy and Ethical Argument in the Pastoral Epistles* (Tübingen: Mohr, 1986), p. 11: "No one ever seems to have accepted a document as religiously and philosophically prescriptive which was known to be forged. I do not know of a single example."

Peter in the Western church, the church fathers assumed that Jude borrowed from Peter, but literary study of the material shows that Jude is surely the earlier of the two documents. Nevertheless, 2 Peter may well be the latest New Testament document, with the possible exception of Revelation. Possibly reflective of the late date of the document is the elimination of the extracanonical material found in Jude, but not in the directly parallel portion of 2 Peter. Since the Roman church seems to be the repository or point of origin for many New Testament documents, including various of the letters of Paul, 1 Peter, Hebrews, and presumably the encyclical homily of James made it to Rome as well, there is no location more likely for the composition of 2 Peter than the growing church in Rome, drawing on its apostolic resources.[30]

THE RHETORIC OF 2 PETER

The rhetorical discussion of 2 Peter is not nearly as advanced as it ought to be: little has been accomplished since the discussions of Watson and Jerome H. Neyrey in the period 1988-1993. Thomas J. Kraus's work on the style of 2 Peter is helpful in distinguishing this discourse from most of the rest of the New Testament and showing that it has a more cosmopolitan style, but alas, he fails to compare 2 Peter to other Asiatic rhetorical discourses. Even less helpful is the study of Anders Gerdmar, who wants not only to protest against 2 Peter being Asiatic Greek, but also tries to stand on its head the usual conclusions that Jude is the more Jewish and 2 Peter the more Hellenistic form of their common material. This can only be called special pleading, going against the vast majority of scholars who have examined the matter closely. Gerdmar is right, however that the line between Judaism and Hellenism was not rigid; indeed, it was especially fluid in Asia Minor, it would appear, and so we have to conjure with numerous very Hellenized Jews in that region especially.[31]

Kraus suggests that to some degree 2 Peter is reacting to the circulation of the Pauline corpus. One could have wished for a careful comparison with Ephesians—that other epideictic rhetorical piece that is in the form of Asiatic rhetoric.[32] Furthermore, Ephesians, like 2 Peter is an encyclical, and so there is a general character to it as well. The difference is that 2 Peter is heavily indebted to source material, being composite, whereas Ephesians is a fresh composition, though it too has at least one partial source or parallel text: Colos-

[30]On the use of Petrine material in 2 Peter, see Witherington, "Petrine Source in 2 Peter," pp. 187-92.

[31]Gerdmar, *Rethinking the Judaism-Hellenism Dichotomy*.

[32]Kraus, *Sprache, Stil und historischer Ort des zweiten Petrusbriefes*.

sians.[33] More helpful is the study of Thurén. He shows that "change of style" is a central redactional and rhetorical feature of this discourse.[34] Too often we forget that for those adept at Greek, style could be a matter of choice of form of expression, not merely a reflection of personality. Also quite helpful is the detailed essay by Terrance D. Callan, who lays out the basic case that here we have Greek in the grand or more ornate style, specifically in the Asiatic style and with a cogent understanding of rhetoric.[35] He finds this style in inscriptions of the period, particularly the Nimrud-Dagh inscription found in Turkey.[36] The inscriptions demonstrate that this style was quite popular with the public and used especially in honorific inscriptions that people wanted at least to sound grand, if not grandiose.

To moderns like ourselves, on first glance the style of 2 Peter will mostly seem to be an example of a person overcome with the exuberance of his own verbosity, loving rare words, the coining of terms, solemn and sonorous and grandiloquent language and phrasing. Cicero tells us that in terms of ornament, one should use rare words only occasionally, new words more frequently, and metaphors and tropes the most frequently of all (Cicero *De or.* 3.153-155). We certainly find all of this and more in 2 Peter. There are some twenty-six metaphors in play in 2 Peter, as identified by Watson; in addition we have a barrage of tropes: hyperbole, metonymy, synecdoche, onomatopoeia and others.[37] All of them remind us that this document was meant chiefly to be heard, not silently read. It is an oral document. Several long periods characterize Greek in the grand style: 1 Peter 1:3-7, 2:4-10a, 2:12-14. Sometimes 2 Peter 1:19-20 and 3:1-4a are pointed to as well, but these latter two are not nearly as lengthy or convoluted as the first three mentioned.[38] In fact, 2 Peter 1:12-21 and 3:1-3 read much like the Greek of 1 Peter, which is simpler in style, though still Asiatic in tone.

Lack of a knowledge of Asiatic Greek and its great popularity in the first century and anachronistic applying of modern tastes to 2 Peter has led to the conclusion that the style is too elaborate, grandiose, baroque or even artificial. And to some extent the ancient rhetorical experts preferred a more sedate and less florid and emotional style and would agree. Quintilian calls Asiatic style too in-

[33]On which see Ben Witherington III, *Philemon, Colossians, and Ephesians* (Grand Rapids: Eerdmans, 2007), the introduction.
[34]Thurén, "Style Never Goes out of Fashion," pp. 329-47.
[35]Callan, "Style of the Second Letter of Peter," pp. 202-24.
[36]See ibid., pp. 217-18.
[37]Watson, *Invention,* pp. 123-25.
[38]See Callan, "Style of the Second Letter of Peter," pp. 212-13.

flated and empty (Quintilian *Inst.* 12.10.16), but then he was a patrician training patricians to be orators. Cicero, early trained in Asiatic style and an aficiando of it, seems to have changed his mind, and there was a pragmatic reason. As he raised the *cursus honorum* and toadied to patricians, Cicero gradually toned down his use of the Eastern style (see Cicero *Brut.* 13.51). As Thurén says, Cicero was swimming against the tide of the cultural mainstream of popular rhetoric in making this stylistic adjustment in his rhetoric.[39] But Callan is clearly right: "We can see that many negative assessments of style of 2 Peter are not evaluations of it according to the canons of style recognized by its author and readers. Instead, they are implicitly expressions of preference for a different style, like the criticism of Asianism in its own time."[40] Turning the matter around, Callan asks, What does the choice of the grand style tell us about our author's rhetorical purposes? Callan highlights several good points: (1) the use of the grand style indicates that the author sees himself as expressing powerful and important thoughts. The style suits the lofty subject matter. (2) Writing in the grand style implies that the author is primarily seeking to appeal to the emotions, not to inform them of things they do not already know. This comports well with the epideictic nature of this discourse. (3) The author wishes to arouse the audience to continue to develop their Christian virtues in light of the return of Christ.[41]

As Neyrey and Watson both intimate, we are dealing with a polemical rhetorical document in 2 Peter, at least in 2 Peter 2—3. Neyrey sees it as epideictic, focusing mostly on praise and blame, while Watson sees it as mostly deliberative in character, with brief forays into the other two species of rhetoric. They both recognize that the rhetoric begins immediately after the briefest possible of epistolary introductions in 2 Peter 1:1-2. There is no epistolary conclusion at all: no personalia, no travel plans, no concluding farewell, only a final doxology that is not really an epistolary feature, but rather a feature of early Jewish and Christian worship, since this discourse will have been delivered in worship. In other words, epistolary conventions explain next to nothing about this discourse, but rhetorical conventions explain the vast majority of it. Here is the rhetorical analysis offered by both Watson and Neyrey:

1. Second Peter 1:3-15 is the exordium, which provides the preview of coming attractions in the following discourse.
2. The *probatio* is seen as encompassing 2 Peter 1:16—3:13. Here is the meat of the discourse.

[39]Thurén, "Style Never Goes Out of Fashion," p. 340 n. 65.
[40]Callan, "Style of the Second Letter of Peter," p. 223.
[41]Ibid., pp. 223-24.

3. The *peroratio,* or conclusion, is found in 2 Peter 3:14-18a, with a concluding doxology rounding out the final verse.

This analysis is generally helpful but could use a little amplification and modification. First, it needs to be stressed that not all polemical rhetoric is judicial in character. Galatians is a good example of polemical deliberative rhetoric. Watson argues for a mixed species of rhetoric in 2 Peter, but is it really so? He finds 2 Peter 2:10b-22 to be a digression. In fact, what we seem to have in 2 Peter 2:3b-22 is a long narration of pertinent facts associating the present false teachers with the previous fallen angels in Noah's day. We have the beginning of a new segment of the argument at 2 Peter 3:1, set off by both the use of "beloved" and the reference to a previous letter indicating that these false teachers are in fact the scoffers predicted to show up in the last days; in this case they are scoffers about the Christian eschatological message, a subject that is dealt with up to 2 Peter 3:13. They are quite right in seeing 2 Peter 3:14-18a as the peroration.

While our discourse as a whole is *not* really a testament, it clearly contains a testimony in the second half of 2 Peter 1, which carries on to the beginning of the second chapter. Following the testimony is a narrative comparison of past and present beguilers, coupled with value judgments about the perpetrators. Next comes the warnings about eschatological judgment in a final argument that concludes with the peroration. At 2 Peter 3:1 we are told that what is being said is a "reminder." Deliberative rhetoric is not really about reminders: it did not require a narration of past facts, and we would have expected some examples in a deliberative discourse. As it is, in 2 Peter 2 we have only one extended *synkrisis,* or rhetorical comparison, between fallen angels and false teachers in the past (e.g., Balaam) and current false teachers.[42]

The eschatology in this discourse is, then, not new information, even though it does involve discussing the future. The future can certainly come into epideictic rhetoric if it is pertinent to the praising and blaming that is going on in the present. In epideictic rhetoric the primary temporal focus will be on action in the present, and so we find it in 2 Peter where the real focus is on the present false teachers and the present proper response of the audience to them. Blame is being laid on those scoffers, and this discourse shames them by displaying all the

[42]Commentators have puzzled over the fact that on the one hand in 2 Pet 2:1-2 the author speaks of false teachers in the future, whereas further into the discourse he speaks of them as present. Some have suggested solving this problem by source criticism since this discourse is a patchwork quilt of sources. While that is possible, it seems more likely that we should take seriously the encyclical character and broad audience of this discourse. The author knows that some locales are already experiencing false teachers, and he is rather certain that others will do so, since this is the character of the "last days," the denouement of the eschatological period.

florid Asiatic vocabulary and lengthy sentences one could want. We may ask what sort of discourse was likely to have (1) a testimony or testament from a now deceased hero being cited; (2) a lengthy narration of pertinent information so that blame could be laid at the right doorstep; (3) a discussion of eschatology that is called a "reminder," is primarily hortatory in character, is not really focused on the nature of the future and is rapidly followed by an emotional peroration. I submit that this looks a lot like epideictic rhetoric from start to finish.

Listen to the judgment of Thurén: "The addressees . . . are presented throughout as good Christians, who only need some encouragement in their life. . . . Here we do not deal with logical arguments, but above all a modification of values at the emotional level."[43] On the whole this discourse does not urge the audience to change opinions and behavior; rather, it says they are "established" in the truth (2 Pet 1:12) and are being asked to recall these matters (2 Peter 1:15). Peter has left a brief testimony that is now being read aloud to help them do so; in this period, funeral oratory often contained testaments from the deceased. The past and the future are brought into the narration by way of reminder of things the audience already knows, to ground the blaming of the false teachers in a properly arced narrative of salvation history, which has an eschatological punch line forthcoming. Finally, it was not necessary to have a proposition in epideictic rhetoric for the good reason that one is not offering formal proofs in trying to win over the audience to a new point of view. You are not trying to demonstrate a particular thesis statement in such rhetoric. You are affirming standing values and condemning existing vices. This is the essence of the discourse in 2 Peter.

We can outline 2 Peter as follows:

Epistolary Prescript (2 Pet 1:1-2)
Exordium (with a 2 Pet 1:5-7 being an interlocked catalog of virtues) (2 Pet 1:3-11)
Quoted Testimony (2 Pet 1:12-21)
Beguilers Past and Present: A Rhetorical Roundup of the Blameworthy (with a treatment of vices) (2 Pet 2:1-22)
Eschatological Reminders (2 Pet 3:1-13)
Peroratio (2 Pet 3:14-18a)
Concluding Doxology (2 Pet 3:18b)[44]

[43]Thurén, "Style Never Goes Out of Fashion," p. 34. This is a textbook description of epideictic rhetoric.

[44]After doing the rhetorical analysis, I discovered that David Edward Aune basically sees the same structure as I am proposing. See his article in his dictionary: "Peter, Second Letter of," in *The Westminister Dictionary of New Testament and Early Christian Literature and Rhetoric* (Louisville: Westminister John Knox, 2003), pp. 353-54. For a similar breakdown of the structure, see also Thurén, "Style Never Goes Out of Fashion," p. 344.

There certainly is a great deal of microrhetoric and subordinate acts of persuasion and rhetorical devices along the way, some of which we will consider in due course. We must keep steadily in view that "the aim of the text is not to meet ancient academic standards [or modern ones], but to affect the values, emotions, and life of the addressees, [and so] an Asian style may be appropriate."[45]

The Social Location of 2 Peter

The social location of 2 Peter has been remarkably difficult to judge for the good reason that if any of the so-called General Epistles deserves the label, it is this one. It indeed is a more generic discourse written apparently to all extant Christians, recycling earlier material and applying it to a later generation. The author assumes that at least a great deal of the audience not only knows some of Paul's letters and a letter of Peter (and Jude?), but has also come to see them as something of a sacred corpus. We are in a social location in which the apostolic presence either is no more, or is so sparse that its texts can be drawn on or alluded to as the valuable resources of the past. This surely points to the end of the first century. And furthermore, the warnings here about itinerant false teachers sound much like some of the warnings in the *Didache* (11—13) about itinerant false prophets in the postapostolic era.

Michael J. Gilmour has dealt with this matter of 2 Peter's social location at some length, through comparing 2 Peter to other early Christian literature, and it will be well if we dialogue with his arguments briefly.[46] Basically, after a detailed comparison of 2 Peter to a variety of other early Christian documents, Gilmour reports that such comparisons only reinforce the conclusion that 2 Peter is more of a generic broad-brush document, not like an ad hoc discourse addressing one particular area or situation or problem. He puts it this way: "This thesis has argued that the final word about certain background matters related to 2 Peter cannot be given. . . . The value of parallels with other texts is limited; they do not provide a reliable basis to determine a specific context. . . . [But] Second Peter can properly be located in a broad context, namely early Greek-speaking Christianity of the first and second centuries."[47] While more can be said, what this conclusion rightly points to is that this encyclical was intended to be suitable for a broad audience. It is not locale-specific.

One of the great problems with arguing that 2 Peter is simply a pseudepigraphon is that it has no specific or particular target audience. Indeed, it appears

---

[45]Thurén, "Style Never Goes Out of Fashion," p. 341 n. 65.
[46]Gilmour, *Significance of Parallels*.
[47]Ibid., p. 123.

to be written to all Christians. Did the author really think he could deceive the lot of them? I doubt it, and as Richard Bauckham has pointed out, in any normal case one needs a pseudonymous audience (not the one said to be addressed in the document) to go along with the pseudonymous author if the deception is going to work.[48] If our author, then, was not trying to fool anyone, what is he doing, and where could he have written from?[49]

Perhaps we need first to ask, What is he opposing? What is the nature and object of his polemics? The standard answer used to be some form of Gnosticism, but this theory has been thoroughly discredited by Neyrey and others. Neyrey shows that the polemic our author is *opposing* here is closer to what we find in Plutarch's *De sera numinis vindicta*—where we hear about the Epicurean polemic against divine providence, divine judgment, unfulfilled prophecy, injustice and the like—than it is to Gnosticism. The four main themes of the Plutarchian response to Epicureanism involving cosmology, freedom, unfulfilled prophecy and injustice sound quite like what we find in 2 Peter at certain points, though our author couches his discussion in much more Jewish and biblical language. And one thing we know about the discussion in Plutarch: it reflects a first-century A.D. debate, not the later second-century Gnostic ones.[50]

The opponents of our author are (1) moral relativists; (2) those who reject early Christian eschatology, and especially the notion of the second coming; (3) those who seem to assume a steady-state universe, one that will certainly not end in final judgment or conflagration. Bad eschatology leads to bad ethics, and so our author must critique both (cf. the way Paul approaches the issue of the relationship of eschatology and ethics, more specifically resurrection and ethics, in 1 Cor 15). The primary thrust of the response in 2 Peter is to focus on ethics, not doctrine. If we ask how our author chooses to address a growing church, David Horrell's suggestion makes the best sense: "The nature of the opposition, and the character of the letter itself, suggest a context in which the Hellenistic environment exerts an increasing influence upon the debates current within the

[48] See the discussion in *Letters and Homilies for Hellenized Christians,* 1:23-38.

[49] It could be argued that if the compiler of this document is neither Peter nor a pseudepigrapher, then why would he open it with the name of Simon/Simeon Peter and then speak in the first person? This is a good question, but not without an answer. The editor is weaving together various sources of material, and since he is sending this as a letter, it requires a first person voice, and so he attributes it to its most famous contributor: Peter. He neither wants to pass the letter off as by himself—after all, he is just collecting and editing earlier material by earlier and apostolic figures—nor does he want to neglect to explain what stimulated or was the catalyst for this composition: the personal testimony of Peter.

[50] See Jerome H. Neyrey, "The Form and Background of the Polemic in 2 Peter," *JBL* 99, no. 3 (1980): 407-31.

church. Just as Jewish writers of the first century had expressed their faith in terminology and language drawn from Hellenistic culture, so II Peter is engaged in the task of translating the Christian message into 'Hellenistic cultural terms.'"[51]

With regard to the "who?" question, I suggest that we are dealing with someone from the Petrine circle who wishes to preserve the apostolic and especially the Petrine legacy for the next generation of the entire church. He is a Jewish Christian who knows, for example, that the Jerusalem Church and probably other Jewish Christians called Peter "Simeon" (Acts 15:14) rather than Simon, and so that is how he is labeled in 2 Peter 1:1. But he is also called "Peter" in the prescript because this discourse is for both Jewish and Gentile Christians in the empire. And at this juncture we need to say something about 2 Peter 3:1. Neyrey is not alone in his conclusions. Bauckham and Tord Fornberg are equally clear that *what* our author is problematizing here is not later Gnosticism. But there are other dimensions of the "what?" question, to which we must attend.

On any showing, Peter was the leader of the original disciples of Jesus. In addition, so far as we know, he was the foremost missionary to Jewish Christians throughout the empire.[52] To understand what is going on, then, in this composite discourse, we must always remember that the author is editing preexisting material. He is especially keen to put the testimony of Peter up front, and its diction is like that of 1 Peter, setting it somewhat apart from the rest of the discourse, which has the full exotic quality of Asiatic Greek. Although he is happy to turn Jude's material into more Asiatic sounding rhetoric and not even mention that it comes from Jude, he treats the Petrine material in a more reserved manner, basically quoting it verbatim. Why? Because of the great respect he and his circle have for Peter and his legacy.

And this brings us to 2 Peter 3:1. Since it can be argued that 2 Peter 3:1-3 seems to revert back to the more sedate Greek style of a testament in 2 Peter 1, my theory is that originally the author intended to simply have 2 Peter 1 and 2 Peter 3 in this discourse. It was going to be just a testimony-plus-eschatology discourse. But he knew that false teachers were a chronic problem in various places in the empire, and he knew that Peter would have addressed the problem if he had still been alive. How should he handle the matter? Not daring to simply speak in his own voice, since he wanted the document to carry apostolic weight and the voice of earliest Christianity, he refocuses the sectarian Jewish material from Jude for his audience, deleting the more obscure apocryphal ma-

[51]Horrell, *Peter and Jude*, p. 139.

[52]See my discussion in *What Have They Done with Jesus?* (San Francisco: HarperCollins, 2006).

terial that Gentiles would not know, and hence we have 2 Peter 2. Our author, or better said, final editor is himself a Hellenized Jewish Christian, like those addressed in 1 Peter. He is at home with Asiatic Greek and Asiatic rhetoric. And so he puts together this composite document.

One more thing: 2 Peter 3:1 suggests that Peter himself had intended to send out his last will and testament to his converts, but did not manage to do so before his martyrdom. For that very reason our author definitely wants his discourse to be accepted as the sequel to 1 Peter. He is following the wishes of the great apostle, making sure that Peter's testimony and other material reach as broad an audience as possible. He is speaking *for* Peter, knowing Peter's intent, not *as* Peter in this discourse, and he would have been horrified if he had been accused of forgery. The voice is the apostolic voice, but the hands (apart from the testimony) and the style are that of this Hellenized Jewish Christian. Because of the epistolary format of the document and the citing of a first-person testimony, the document had to be in the first person.

From where was this author writing? The best and most likely answer to this question is Rome, where he might well have had access not only to earlier documents meant for Jewish Christians like Jude and 1 Peter, but also to some of the Pauline corpus as well. This comports with Bo Ivar Reicke's argument that notes similarities between 2 Peter and *1 Clement*, similarities that lead Reicke to date 2 Peter to about A.D. 90, before the persecution of Domitian.[53] It also comports with Bauckham's point that 2 Peter seems to be written just after the first generation has entirely or almost entirely died out, thus in the period 80-90 or thereabouts. There is another reason to see this document as coming from Rome. Once Jerusalem was destroyed in A.D. 70, the center of Christianity in general became Rome. It is certainly true that there were centers of Jewish Christianity in Galilee and Syria, such as Capernaum, Pella, Damascus, Antioch. However, the missionary work of Peter had been in the West and had ended in Rome. The Petrine legacy was in Rome. Hence our author is likely to be in the place where there was the great deposit of the Petrine legacy and, equally important, where the Petrine circle was still a living entity.

What was Rome like for Jewish Christians in the last couple of decades of the first century, and after the persecutions of Nero? In his detailed and magisterial study of the origins of Christianity in Rome, Peter Lampe makes these telling remarks:

> The Jewish Christians and *sebomenoi* who brought with them cultivated traditions

[53]Reicke, *Epistles of James, Peter, and Jude,* p. 145.

> from Jewish teaching and set into motion a process of passing on the Jewish cultural riches within the Christian circles of Rome, remain in large measure anonymous for us. *How* these traditions were handed on among Christians often remains opaque in the sources: through individual teachers, to whom Hermas in *Similitude* 9.16.5; 9.25.2 looks back as phenomena of the past or in any way analogous to Jewish schools? . . . What is important here is *the fact that* such a process of passing on Jewish-Christian knowledge existed in Christian circles in Rome. It shows (a) that at least some Christians were able to spare time for such activities (socially from a higher class?) and (b) that, independently of the pagan educational systems, there was among Christians their own educational and tradition-passing process.[54]

I submit that our author/editor was one such teacher among these Jewish Christians in Rome. He may have come with Peter to Rome many years before, from one of those churches in Asia Minor. Like a Cicero, he may have simply been a Roman who had a love for Asiatic Greek and Asiatic rhetoric. Whichever is the case, he is a literate person whose Greek is not of the rudimentary Koiné sort. We need to give some thought as to where the great library and scribal resources were in the empire, places where even Jewish documents could be safely kept, copied and even disseminated rather rapidly throughout the empire. Rome was certainly one such place.

Our author not only wants to transfer the legacy of the previous generation to the next; he also needs to be in a place where he can access that legacy. And make no mistake, it is primarily the Jewish Christian legacy our author wants to pass on, and he offers a cautionary remark about the Pauline corpus. This also suggests that he is a Jewish Christian writing at a time where he sees the Pauline influence spreading wider and wider, and the Pauline letters becoming increasingly treated as sacred texts.[55] He may have thought, Should not the final legacy of Peter be respected and disseminated in such fashion as well?

Scholars have sometimes pointed out that there are some similarities between 2 Peter and the Pastoral Epistles.[56] This is a good observation, especially when one is comparing 2 Timothy with 2 Peter. In both cases the legacy and a sort of last will and testament of a great apostle is being passed on. In both cases a disciple of the great man is responsible for writing up the document in its present form. I suggest that 2 Peter is meant to function rather like 2 Timothy in this respect: it passes on the final legacy and exhortations of the great Christian leader, calling those who follow him to pursue the Christian virtues and avoid the tempt-

---

[54]Peter Lampe, *From Paul to Valentinus: Christians at Rome in the First Two Centuries* (Minneapolis: Fortress, 2003), p. 78.

[55]See the discussion on social location in Neyrey, *2 Peter, Jude,* pp. 128-32.

[56]See Gilmour, *2 Peter and Other Early Christian Literature*, pp. 125-28.

ing vices and false teaching that have plagued the postapostolic church. If I were to be asked to guess who composed 2 Peter, my guess would be Linus (2 Tim 4:21), who is a member of the community in Rome and knows Paul and some of Paul's letters and presumably even the letter 2 Timothy. He lived well into the latter part of the first century in Rome, and according to various church traditions was in a sense the successor to Peter in the community in Rome. Consider, for example, the following entry from a popular encyclopedia:

> **Pope Saint Linus** (d. ca.79) was the second pope of the Roman Catholic Church. According to Irenaeus, Jerome, Eusebius, John Chrysostom, the *Liberian Catalogue* and the *Liber Pontificalis*, Linus was the second Bishop of Rome, succeeding Saint Peter and succeeded by Anacletus. Irenaeus identifies him with the Linus mentioned in 2 Timothy, although this identification is not certain. The *Liberian Catalogue* and the *Liber Pontificalis* both date his Episcopate to AD 56–67 during the reign of Nero, but Jerome dates it to 67–78, and Eusebius dates the end of his Episcopate to the second year of the reign of Titus (80).
>
> Other sources disagree on Linus's place in the succession of Popes. Tertullian says that Peter was succeeded by Clement I. The *Apostolic Constitutions* says that Linus was the first Bishop of Rome, ordained by Paul, and was succeeded by Clement, who was ordained by Peter.
>
> Saint Peter's view is preserved in the *Apostolic Constitutions*' comment on the appointment of Saint Linus as Rome's first bishop. Saint Peter writes: "Now concerning those bishops which have been ordained in our lifetime, we let you know that they are these: . . . Of the church of Rome, Linus the son of Claudia was the first, ordained by Paul; and Clemens, after Linus' death, the second, ordained by me Peter." Peter's words are credible since Paul arrived in Rome prior to Peter, and therefore Paul was in a more likely position to appoint a bishop.
>
> The apostolic church elder Irenaeus (born ca. AD 130), a disciple of Polycarp and later Bishop of Smyrna, also confirms Linus's appointment. He wrote: "After the holy apostles founded and set the church in order (in Rome), they gave over the exercise of the episcopal office to Linus. The same Linus is mentioned by Saint Paul in his Epistle to Timothy [2 Tim 4:21]. His successor was Anacletus" ([Irenaeus] *Haer.* 3.3.3).[57]

Obviously this material has to be critically evaluated since it involves later legendary material, but when one sifts it the following likely historical points still remain: (1) Linus is likely a socially elite, literate Christian in Rome, with strong connections to both Paul and then Peter. He likely knew the legacy of both. (2) He is indeed a leader and teacher in the church in Rome after the

[57]This comes from the online *Wikipedia* entry <http://en.wikipedia.org/wiki/Pope_Linus> (with minor stylistic adjustments). Nevertheless, the information is correct and the best short summary of the data, whatever *Wikipedia*'s shortcomings elsewhere.

deaths of Paul and Peter and uniquely positioned to pass on the Petrine legacy, with authority to do so. We must not think of the author of 2 Peter as some archaeologist on a scavenger hunt in Rome, who just happened to find some Petrine material and material from Jude. The Christian source documents in Rome were not likely available to the general public after the odium cast upon Christians due to the fire of A.D. 64, the martyrdoms that followed and the aftermath. Rather, these documents were more likely carefully preserved within the tight-knit Christian circles in Rome. (3) Notice that Linus takes over after the death of Peter in Rome, whether one dates that to 69, or more likely to 66-67. The tradition about Linus's date of death seems to be less well grounded. He surely was not called a pope in those days; he may not even have called himself an apostle. Yet he could have carried on as a leader until the time of Domitian (81-96), though we cannot be sure. But in any case he was the ideal bridge figure in Rome between Peter and other early apostolic figures like Jude and Paul on the one hand, and his own audience on the other. He was uniquely positioned to pass on their legacy.[58] (4) The connections with both Paul and Peter are important for another reason. In another volume in this series, we have seen that Jewish Christianity continued to grow alongside Gentile Christianity well into the latter part of the first century, with some cross-fertilization between the two branches of the movement.[59] But at some point someone had to realize that the movement needed to be more closely bound together. Something had to be done to appreciate the contributions of all the great apostles and remind all Christians to appropriate their entire heritage. Particularly as the church became increasingly Gentile, there would be concern that the Jewish part of the legacy not be lost, especially at a time when the Pauline legacy was already widely known and being treated as Scripture.

Here, then, I think we find part of the rhetorical exigence, the bone of contention, that prompted the assembling of 2 Peter and its dissemination. More than just the issue of false teachers who were scoffing at early Christian eschatology, our author is worried about losing the Petrine and early Jewish legacy, in the wake of the Pauline one sweeping across the church. He thus writes this encyclical to the whole church. I would suggest that *this may well be the very first document and the very first encyclical ever written to the entire extant church*. This makes it a very important document indeed in terms of the history

[58]Apparently Linus is not in Rome in A.D. 57, when Paul sends his letter to the Romans, for he is not mentioned in Rom 16. But he is present in the mid-60s, when Paul writes his last will and testament in 2 Timothy (2 Tim 4:21).

[59]Witherington, *Letters and Homilies for Jewish Christians,* pp. 401-5.

of the development of the Christian movement. And unlike the way it has sometimes been treated in New Testament studies, I will treat it as a precious relic of an era we know too little about: the beginnings of the postapostolic era. Something had to have happened before an Ignatius of Antioch comes along early in the second century and addresses Jewish and Gentile Christians alike in his letters and assumes authority over them. In 2 Peter we gain a little glimpse of what led to that development. Finally, it is possible that Linus was one of Peter's converts in Asia Minor who came to Rome, possibly with Peter, in the 60s. This would explain why he was not present in the Roman churches when Paul wrote Romans 16 in about 57 and so is not greeted then.

Finally, it is time to lay to rest the whole theory of "early Catholicism" as supposedly represented in a document like 2 Peter (or for that matter the Pastoral Epistles). That theory of early Christian development argued that beginning with the second generation of Christians, there was a movement toward the institutionalization of offices in the church and toward treating the "faith" as a body of orthodox doctrine and praxis to be believed and received, with less emphasis on the centrality of Christian experience. In other words, this was seen as a movement toward formalization and more formality, as orthodoxy began to take a more definite and even rigid form. It was supposed that this movement was nurtured by the waning of early Christian eschatological belief in the possible imminence of Christ's return, and the rise of heresy in various forms; these necessitated both centralization of authority and clear articulation of doctrine.[60]

The not-so-implicit message was that we should see such texts as 2 Peter not as preserving the earlier legacy, but as a fall from the original grace of the early apostolic gospel and movement. But do we actually find anything like "early Catholicism" in 2 Peter? Is there any discussion of church office at all in 2 Peter? The answer is no, unless you count the false teachers, which you should not do. Is there anything in 2 Peter that suggests that "the faith" means some prescribed body of doctrine and practices in 2 Peter? No, there is not. What about the eschatology we find in 2 Peter? Listen to the conclusion of Watson in his recent 2 Peter commentary:

> Yet 2 Peter should not be classified as early catholic. Although the delay of the parousia underlies the echatological skepticism of the false teachers (2:3b; 3:4, 9), the author expects both the churches and the false teachers to be alive when the parousia does arrive (1:19; 2:12; 3:1-4). The judgment of the false teachers at the pa-

---

[60]See, e.g., Käsemann, "An Apologia," pp. 169-95; but he is simply doing a new take on Ferdinand Christian Baur's nineteenth-century hypothesis about orthodoxy. See the discussion in Gilmour, *Significance of Parallels*, pp. 24-27.

> rousia will not forever be delayed, and when it comes it will be swift (2:1-3a). The author does not address any church officers (unless the false teachers of 2:1 hold an office), but assumes that the churches will understand the situation and respond as desired. Also, faith is not understood as a set body of orthodox doctrine. The author is defending apostolic tradition, against perversion of its eschatological and ethical teachings, but there is no indication that these are encapsulated in creedal formulae and governed by church authorities.[61]

Bauckham rightly had earlier come to the same conclusions.[62] And scholars cannot have it both ways. If the audience is still worked up about a "delay" in the parousia, then the eschatological expectation is still quite intense. Yet these same scholars generally correlate such intensity with earlier dating of a document that manifests it. The actual eschatological discussion in this document suggests it was *not* written well into the second century.

The only qualification I would make about Watson's remarks is that our author, like other earliest Christians, was not involved in setting a date for the parousia. He only speaks about the possible imminence of the event, not its necessary imminence, and he does so as a hortatory device, much as other early Christians did. It is the false teachers, not our author, who got involved in date setting and therefore can talk about delay or even no second coming at all. Nevertheless, the fact that our author must combat such notions does provide us one more clue that this document was written late in the first century A.D., when such problems were likely to arise, especially well after the fall of Jerusalem. We thus must turn to the commentary itself and let it speak without the pejorative grid of either seeing the letter as warmed-over second-rate second-generation Christian thinking, or as some dreaded "early catholicism" that turned a dynamic Spirit-filled movement into some left-behind, cold, formal, rigid orthodoxy and orthopraxy. Second Peter reflects no such fall from grace, and it is time we respected its contribution to the canon a bit more, for as I have said, it appears to be *the very first encyclical addressed to the whole church in the postapostolic era.*

BIBLIOGRAPHY FOR 2 PETER

Not surprisingly, considering the low opinion of 2 Peter in many scholarly circles in the twentieth and early twenty-first century, we do not have nearly as much helpful scholarly treatment of 2 Peter as we did on 1 Peter. Philip B. Harner's eleven pages of introduction on 2 Peter in his *What Are They Saying*

[61]Watson, "2 Peter," pp. 326-27.
[62]Bauckham, *Jude, 2 Peter,* pp. 151-54.

About the Catholic Epistles? (New York: Paulist Press, 2004)[63] gets the ball rolling, but it is too cursory a treatment of too complex a subject to help us very much. There are no other introductory guides to 2 Peter that serve us better, and the general introductions to 2 Peter in the standard New Testament introductions tend to be only a little more substantial. David A. deSilva's treatment in *An Introduction to the New Testament: Context, Methods and Ministry Formation* (Downers Grove, Ill.: InterVarsity Press, 2004) is perhaps the most helpful since he discusses pseudepigraphic writings in that context, without just assuming that 2 Peter is such a document.[64] We must mainly rely on the monographs and the detailed commentaries and some articles to sort out the mysteries of 2 Peter. Still, a quite helpful article by Michael J. Gilmour, "2 Peter in Recent Research: A Bibliography," *JETS* 42 (1999): 673-78, provides a useful bibliographic starting point.

Commentaries on 2 Peter

Commentaries appear on various levels. Of the more technical ones that are older, we give pride of place to Joseph B. Mayor's *Epistles of Jude and Second Peter* (London: Macmillan, 1907; repr., Minneapolis: Klock & Klock, 1978). Mayor's grasp of the Greek text and the differences in Greek style between the testimony and the rest of the discourse are important. J. N. D. Kelly's *A Commentary on the Epistles of Peter and of Jude,* BNTC (London: Black, 1969), is still quite useful and is more readable than Mayor's work. The gold standard of all commentaries in English is clearly Richard J. Bauckham's *Jude, 2 Peter,* WBC 50 (Waco: Word, 1983), and it can now be supplemented by Peter H. Davids's *The Letters of 2 Peter and Jude* (Grand Rapids: Eerdmans, 2006).[65] All further study (in any language) should have taken account of Bauckham's magisterial volume, but sadly it seems not to have the influence on the Continent it should have. The Anchor Bible series has published two commentaries on 2 Peter: the first is by Bo Ivar Reicke, *The Epistles of James, Peter, and Jude,* AB 37 (Garden City, N.Y.: Doubleday, 1964), where the discussion of 2 Peter is too brief; the more recent volume, by Jerome H. Neyrey, *2 Peter, Jude,* AB 37C (New York: Doubleday, 1993), is a niche commentary, approaching the text from a social-scientific and more particularly a cultural-anthropological point of view (in the style of Bruce Malina and the Context group). Neyrey also treats the rhetoric of 2 Peter, though in a cursory fashion: with less than 150 pages of actual discus-

---

[63]See Harner, *What Are They Saying?* pp. 47-58.

[64]See deSilva, *Introduction,* pp. 685-89, 875-84.

[65]This substantial commentary (xxxii + 348 pp.) unfortunately arrived on my doorstep too late in 2006 to be taken account of.

sion, we could have wished for more in this interesting study. Daniel J. Harrington is the contributor of the study of Jude and 2 Peter in the Sacra pagina series, *1 Peter, Jude, and 2 Peter,* SP (Collegeville, Minn.: Liturgical Press, 2003), with Donald Senior writing the part on 1 Peter. Here as well, 2 Peter gets short shrift (72 pp.), but there are some helpful comments.

Of the really brief more popular commentaries, several can be commended. Especially helpful with the rhetoric is Duane F. Watson's "2 Peter" in the *New Interpreters Bible,* vol. 12, ed. Leander Keck (Nashville: Abingdon, 1998), pp. 323-61, which distills the material from his important monograph for a broader audience. Also to be commended is Norman Hillyer's *1 and 2 Peter, Jude* (Peabody, Mass.: Hendrickson, 1992), pp. 157-227; Pheme Perkins's *First and Second Peter, James, and Jude* (Louisville: John Knox Press, 1995), pp. 159-94; and Fred B. Craddock's *First and Second Peter, and Jude* (Louisville: Westminster John Knox, 1995), pp. 85-124. Especially helpful on the social side of issues is David Horrell's *The Epistles of Peter and Jude* (Peterborough, U.K.: Epworth, 1998). We owe much to the work of Michael Green over a long period of time on 2 Peter. Besides his monograph (listed below), he also published a commentary on the epistle (London: Tyndale Press, 1968); its second edition, regularly cited here as *2 Peter,* has the title *The Second Epistle General of Peter, and the General Epistle of Jude: An Introduction and Commentary,* TNTC (Downers Grove, Ill.: InterVarsity Press, 1987), has the merit of responding to Bauckham's magnum opus to some extent.

Of older popular, quite readable but less substantive volumes is James Moffatt's *The General Epistles: James, Peter and Judas* (London: Hodder & Stoughton, 1928), pp. 173-213. I have listed the page numbers to give a feel for how brief the treatments of 2 Peter are in some of these studies. Douglas Moo's *2 Peter, Jude* (Grand Rapids: Zondervan, 1996), pp. 31-220, is the most substantial of all the popular commentaries, but over half the discussion has to do with how to use this material in the church today. This is the best volume for pastors looking for ways to teach and preach this material. Also helpful is Thomas R. Schreiner's *1, 2 Peter, Jude,* NAC 37 (Nashville: Broadman, 2003), based on the NIV; it has helpful discussions of recent Continental literature on 2 Peter, though it breaks no new ground, and Moo has more direct application material.

Of the commentaries in German and French, only a few can be really commended here. Horst Balz and Wolgang Schrage's quite popular *Die "Katholischen" Briefe: Die Briefe des Jakobus, Petrus, Johannes und Judas,* NTD 10 (Göttingen: Vandenhoeck & Ruprecht, 1973), has gone through many editions, but this is more of a midlevel commentary, with limited technical discussion. More recent and helpful is Henning Paulsen's *Die zweite Petrusbrief und der Judas-*

brief, KEK 12/2 (Göttingen: Vandenhoeck & Ruprecht, 1992). Ceslas Spicq's French commentary *Les Épîtres de Saint Pierre,* SB (Paris: Gabalda, 1966), is the work of a master exegete, though this commentary is not as well known as some of his Pauline ones. Important for its wealth of linguistic analysis is the study by Eric Fuchs (along with Pierre Reymond, who tackles Jude) in *La deuxième épître de Saint Pierre; L'épître de Saint Jude,* CNT 2/13B (Lausanne: Neuchatel & Niestle?, 1980).

Monographs on 2 Peter

It would be nice to say that we have a plethora of monographs on 2 Peter that make up for the lack of good commentaries, but alas, there are only a handful that can really be called seminal or very helpful. In terms of the rhetorical discussion, Watson's landmark work has stood the test of time and is still extremely helpful: *Invention, Arrangement, and Style,* SBLDS 104 (Atlanta: Scholars Press, 1988). Watson paved the way for the rhetorical discussion of Jude and 2 Peter, and we are all greatly in his debt. Another interesting more-literary study is E. M. B. (= Michael) Green's older volume *2 Peter Reconsidered* (London: Tyndale Press, 1961). Like Moo and Hillyer, Green defends the Petrine authorship of 2 Peter. One thing that characterizes such studies is that they do not seem really to reckon with the fact that there are options that lie in the middle of the spectrum between calling a document a pseudepigraphon and suggesting that Peter himself authored this document. The most interesting of the recent monographs on 2 Peter is that by J. Daryl Charles, *Virtue Amidst Vice* (Sheffield: Sheffield Academic Press, 1997), which analyzes material in 2 Peter 1 in terms of ancient virtue catalogs. What Charles does not emphasize, but I will, is that such catalogs are characteristic of epideictic rhetoric. More helpful is his chapter refuting the notion that 2 Peter should be seen as an example of early Catholicism.

We have two studies to compare with each other since they are seeking to socially locate 2 Peter by studying the text in light of apparently parallel or similar noncanonical texts. Gilmour's *The Significance of Parallels Between 2 Peter and Other Early Christian Literature* (Leiden: Brill, 2002) is more reticent in drawing strong conclusions about such parallels; indeed, he thinks 2 Peter is a rather generic and at the same time somewhat unique document when it comes to canonical literature; I agree. Thomas J. Kraus's *Sprache, Stil und historischer Ort des zweiten Petrusbriefes,* WUNT 2/136 (Tübingen: Mohr Siebeck, 2001) is able to show that the ethos of the Greek and indeed some of the discussion in 2 Peter is much more cosmopolitan than other New Testament documents and more nearly sounds like some late classical literature, including pagan religious literature. This is not surprising since we are dealing with Asiatic Greek in the first place, and we are also dealing with a writer trying to speak in a way that reaches as wide an audience of Christians as is possible.

An older monograph that has been too often neglected is Tord Fornberg's *An Early Church in a Pluralistic Society: A Study of 2 Peter,* ConBNT 9 (Lund: Gleerup, 1977), which challenged the consensus about the social locale of 2 Peter, and instead found internal clues in 2 Peter suggesting that the author is writing to those in a pagan (not Gnostic) environment striving to live a Christian life of virtue and avoid pagan vices. This was a step in the right direction in the analysis of 2 Peter. The theological discussion of 2 Peter by Ralph P. Martin in *The Theology of the Letters of James, Peter, and Jude* (Cambridge: Cambridge University Press, 1994), pp 134-63, actually spends more time on prolegomena than on actual theology, but still it has some useful insights, including the fact that this discourse is intended as a reminder and a call to stand firm in the face of false teaching—a clearly epideictic strategy. Though never published, Neyrey's Yale dissertation, "The Form and Background of the Polemic in 2 Peter" (Ph.D. diss., Yale University, 1977), is an important study as it lays to rest the theory that 2 Peter is a response to Gnosticism. In summary form his thesis can be found in an article as listed below. There are specialty monographs that analyze some of the special theological language in this discourse, such as James M. Starr's *Sharers in Divine Nature: 2 Pet. 1.4 in Its Hellenistic Context,* ConBNT 33 (Stockholm: Almquist & Wiksell, 2000). In the same series is Anders Gerdmar's *Rethinking the Judaism-Hellenism Dichotomy: A Historiographical Study of Second Peter and Jude,* ConBNT 36 (Stockholm: Almquist & Wiksell, 2001), which argues the hard case that 2 Peter is more Jewish in flavor than Jude; I am unconvinced.

Articles of Note on 2 Peter

Alexander, T. Desmond. "Lot's Hospitality: A Clue to His Righteousness." *JBL* 104 (1985): 289-91.

Barrett, C. K. "Myth and the New Testament: The Greek Word *Mythos*." *ExpTim* 68 (1957): 345-48.

———. "*Pseudapostoloi* (2 Cor. 11.13)." Pages 377-96 in *Mélanges bibliques en homage au R. P. Béda Rigaux*. Edited by Albert Descamps and André de Halleux. Gembloux: Ducolot, 1970.

Boobyer, G. H. "The Indebtedness of 2 Peter to 1 Peter." Pages 44-51 in *New Testament Essays: Studies in Memory of Thomas Water Manson*. Edited by A. J. B. Higgins. Manchester: Manchester University Press, 1959.

Callan, Terrance D. "The Christology of 2 Peter." *Bib* 82 (2001): 253-63.

———. "The Soteriology of 2 Peter." *Bib* 82 (2001): 549-59.

Cavallin, Hans Clemens Caesarius. "The False Teachers of 2 Pt. as Pseudo-Prophets." *NovT* 21 (1979): 263-70.

Chang, Andrew D. "Second Peter 2.1 and the Extent of the Atonement." *BSac* 142 (1985): 52-63.

Charles, J. Daryl. "On Angels and Asses: The Moral Paradigm of 2 Peter 2." *Proceedings: Eastern Great Lakes and Midwest Biblical Societies* 21 (2001): 1-12.

Dalton, William Joseph. "The Interpretation of 1 Peter 3.19 and 4.6: Light from 2 Peter." *Bib* 60 (1979): 547-55.

Danker, Frederick W. "II Peter 3.10 and *Psalms of Solomon* 17.10." *ZNW* 53 (1962): 82-86.

———. "2 Peter 1: A Solemn Decree." *CBQ* 40 (1978): 64-82.

Duke, Thomas H. "An Exegetical Analysis of 2 Peter 3.9." *Faith and Mission* 16, no. 3 (1999): 6-13.

Dupont-Roc, Roselyne. "Le motif de la creation selon 2 Pierre 3." *RB* 101 (1994): 95-114.

Farkasfalvy, Denis. "The Ecclesial Setting of Pseudepigraphy in Second Peter and Its Role in the Formation of the Canon." *SecCent* 5 (1985-1986): 3-29.

Feuillet, André. "Le péché évoqué aux chapitres 3 et 6, 1-4 de la Genèse: La péché des Anges de l'Épître de Jude et de la Seconde Épître de Pierre." *Divinitas* 35 (1991): 207-29.

Finegan, Jack. "The Original Form of the Pauline Collection." *HTR* 49 (1956): 85-86.

Fischel, Henry A. "The Uses of *Sōritēs* (Climax, *Gradatio*) in the Tannaitic Period." *HUCA* 44 (1973): 119-51.

Fitzmyer, Joseph A. "The Name Simon." *HTR* 54 (1961): 91-97.

Gamble, Harry. "The Redaction of the Pauline Letters and the Formation of the Pauline Corpus." *JBL* 94 (1975): 403-18.

Gilmour, Michael J. "Reflections on the Authorship of 2 Peter." *EvQ* 73, no. 4 (2001): 291-309.

Green, Gene L. "'As for Prophecies, They Will Come to an End': 2 Peter, Paul, and Plutarch on the Obsolescence of Oracles." *JSNT* 82 (2001): 107-22.

Heide, G. Z. "What Is New About the New Heaven and the New Earth? A Theology of Creation from Revelation 21 and 2 Peter 3." *JETS* 40 (1997): 37-56.

Kraus, Thomas J. "*Para kyriou* oder *para kyrio* oder omit in 2 Petr 2,11." *ZNW* 91 (2000): 265-73.

Kuske, Daniel P. "Conveyed from Heaven—2 Peter 1:17, 18, 21." *Wisconsin Lutheran Quarterly* 99 (2002): 55-57.

Lee, Edwin Kenneth. "Words Denoting 'Pattern' in the New Testament." *NTS* 8 (1961): 166-73.

Lövestam, Evald. "Eschatologie und Tradition im 2 Petrusbrief." Pages 287-300 in *The New Testament Age: Essays in Honor of Bo Reicke*. Vol. 2. Edited by William C. Weinrich. Macon, Ga.: Mercer University Press, 1984.

Lunn, Nick. "Punishment in 2 Peter 2.9." *Notes* 12 (1998): 15-18.

Makujina, John. "The 'Trouble' with Lot in 2 Peter: Locating Peter's Source for Lot's Torment." *WTJ* 60 (1998): 255-69.

Meier, John P. "2 Peter 3.8-18: Forming the Canon on the Edge of the Canon." *Mid-Stream* 38 (1999): 65-70.

Miller, Robert J. "Is There Independent Attestation for the Transfiguration in 2 Peter?" *NTS* 42 (1996): 620-25.

Neyrey, Jerome H. "The Apologetic Use of the Transfiguration in 2 Peter 1:16-21." *CBQ* 42 (1980): 509-14.

———. "The Form and Background of the Polemic in 2 Peter." *JBL* 99, no. 3 (1980): 407-31.

Overstreet, R. Larry. "A Study of 2 Peter 3.10-13." *BSac* 137 (1980): 354-71.

Pearson, Birger A. "A Reminiscence of Classical Myth at II Peter 2.4." *Greek, Roman and Byzantine Studies* 10 (1969): 71-80.

Picirelli, Robert E. "The Meaning of '*Epignōsis*.'" *EvQ* 47 (1975): 85-93.

Snyder, Graydon F. "The *Tobspruch* in the New Testament." *NTS* 23 (1977): 117-20.

Thiede, Carsten P. "A Pagan Reader of 2 Peter: Cosmic Conflagration in 2 Peter 3 and the *Octavius* of Minucius Felix." *JSNT* 26 (1986): 79-96.

Wenham, David. "'Being Found on the Last Day': New Light on 2 Peter." *NTS* 33 (1987): 477-79.

Witherington, Ben, III. "A Petrine Source in 2 Peter." Pages 187-92 in *Society of Biblical Literature 1985 Seminar Papers*. Edited by K. H. Richards. Atlanta: Scholars Press, 1985.

Wolters, Al. "Worldview and Textual Criticism in 2 Peter 3:10." *WTJ* 49 (1987): 405-13.

Zmijewski, Joseph. "Apostolische Paradosis und Pseudepigraphie im Neuen Testament: 'Durch Erinnerung wachhalten' (2 Petr 1,13; 3,1)." *BZ* 23 (1979): 161-71.

Bibliography for Rhetoric in 2 Peter

Aune, David Edward. "Peter, Second Letter of." In *The Westminister Dictionary of New Testament and Early Christian Literature and Rhetoric* (Louisville: Westminister John Knox, 2003), pp. 353-54.

Callan, Terrance D. "The Style of the Second Letter of Peter." *Bib* 84 (2003): 202-24.

Forbes, Christopher. "Paul and Rhetorical Comparison." Pages 134-71 in *Paul in the Greco-Roman World: A Handbook*. Edited by J. Paul Sampley. Harrisburg, Penn.: Trinity Press, 2003.

Moore, Bruce R. "Rhetorical Questions in Second Corinthians and in Ephesians through Revelation." *Notes* 97 (1983): 3-33.

Neyrey, Jerome H. *2 Peter, Jude*. AB 37C. New York: Doubleday, 1993 (esp. pp. 23-29, 113-20).

Thurén, Lauri. "Style Never Goes out of Fashion: 2 Peter Re-Evaluated." Pages 329-47 in *Rhetoric, Scripture and Theology: Essays from the 1994 Pretoria Conference*. Edited by S. E. Porter and T. H. Olbricht. JSNTSup 131. Sheffield: Sheffield Academic Press, 1996.

Watson, Duane F. *Invention, Arrangement, and Style: Rhetorical Criticism of Jude and 2 Peter*. SBLDS 104. Atlanta: Scholars Press, 1988.

2 Peter

2 PETER 1:1-2—EPISTOLARY PRESCRIPT: INCLUSIVE LANGUAGE

> [1:1] *Simeon Peter, servant and apostle of Jesus Christ, to those who have received a faith of equal worth with ours through the justice of our God and Savior, Jesus Christ.* [2] *Grace to you and peace in abundance in the knowledge of God and of Jesus our Lord.*

This introductory prescript in **2 Peter 1:1** reflects continuity with 1 Peter and tries to stress the continuity with the original apostle to the Jews. *Symeōn* here is in all likelihood the more original reading since it is rarer (only one other time for this apostle in the New Testament: Acts 15:14; cf. Lk 2:25, 34; 3:30; Acts 13:1; 15:14; Rev 7:7) and more Jewish.[1] It is a transliteration of the Hebrew (cf. 1 Macc 2:65). The weight of the external evidence is almost equal: the reading *Symeōn* has ℵ, A, K, P and a host of minuscules; *Simōn* (cf. 1 Macc 15:24; Sir 50:1) has $\mathfrak{P}^{72}$, B, Psi (Ψ) and a different group of minuscules. As Bruce M. Metzger says, the former term is rarer, occurring only one other time in the New Testament, and was more likely to be changed to the more familiar term "Simon" found everywhere else in the New Testament.[2] *Symeōn* is a term more likely to be used by fellow Jewish Christians of Peter, such as his colleagues in the inner circle at Rome. The term also indicates that the author of 2 Peter is not *deliberately* trying to imitate 1 Peter (as does the use of *doulos* here, unlike 1 Pet 1:1), which implies that our author does not see himself as creating a pseudepigraphon.

Rather, he is writing *on behalf of* Simon Peter, as one who has known him and his teaching, not intending to speak for himself, but on behalf of Peter

---

[1]See the discussion in *NewDocs* 1:94-95.

[2]Metzger, *TC*, p. 699.

to a situation after his death, using Petrine material, at least in part. It is just possible that our author (Linus?) was also an apostle, though not in the churches he is presently addressing. This may perhaps explain the *hēmin* in 2 Peter 1:1: "with ours" is more literally "with us." The point is not that in Christianity Gentiles have a faith as equally valid as do Jews (this is not at issue in this letter); instead, the point is that even ordinary believers have a faith of equal worth and standing, and that gives them equal privilege and standing in the kingdom with that of the apostles, for all are one in Christ. There must be no partiality or ranking of Christians, because all are equal in God's eyes and grace. *Hisotimon* here, then, could mean "equally precious" or of "equal worth," but it could also mean "of equal honor" (cf. Philo *Conf.* 170).[3] The problem with the latter translation is that clearly enough the writer has just finished calling Peter a servant (in the OT sense in which it is a honorific applied to prophets and others, as in Ex 32:13; Deut 9:27; 34:5; 1 Sam 3:9-10; 17:32) and an apostle. Clearly Peter has higher honor claims than members of the audience, who are not apostles but rather have "had" apostles come to them (2 Pet 3:2). Thus the translation "of equal worth with us" is to be preferred here if it refers to one's person. But since it appears to refer to one's faith, the point, then, is that Peter and the audience have been equally blessed with Christian faith. The author is seeking to gain the good will of the audience by suggesting what they share in common with the great apostle. The faith of the second-generation Christians is no less valid or precious or worthy or honorable than that of the original apostles, and it is equally a gift from God, which they must make use of to benefit from. At the same time the author must establish the ethos of Peter at the outset so that the words of the discourse will carry his weight and authority as apostle and servant of God.[4]

Our author does *not* specify an audience, though we may presume it includes the audience of 1 Peter (cf. 2 Pet 3:1). But this discourse actually seems to be addressed to a much broader audience, and since it is written well after Peter's own day, 2 Peter 3:1 simply reflects the fact that 1 Peter has been circulated much more widely than to its original intended audience in Asia Minor. We have both the Hebrew and Greek forms of Peter's name, the Hebrew and Greek forms of greeting and the designations "servant" and "apostle," which would presumably make better sense to Jews and Gentiles respectively as indicators of Peter's leadership roles. In other words, this prescript is deliberately being inclusive in its

[3]See Perkins, *First and Second Peter,* p. 167.

[4]See Watson, "2 Peter," p. 333.

wording to address all the church, Jews and Gentiles alike.[5]

The faith that these believers have is a gift of God's grace: it has been "received" (*lachousin,* aorist) or more literally, "obtained by (sacred) lot."[6] ***Pistis*** here probably does not mean a body of doctrines, but the basic trust in God through Christ for salvation. It is not unprecedented for faith and even repentance to be said to be a gift received from God (cf. Acts 11:18; Rom 12:3; 1 Cor 12:9). ***Dikaiosynē*** here is perhaps not used of God's righteousness or divine saving activity, as we find it in Paul. Here it seems to mean God's justice, as it does in 2 Peter 2:5, 21 and 3:13 (as in 1 Pet 2:24; 3:14 perhaps). God has justly bestowed this faith equally on apostle and ordinary believer, showing no partiality. In this sense, faith has come through the justice of God, not because God owed it to anyone.

Before examining the phrase "our God and Savior Jesus Christ," we must look briefly at 2 Peter 1:2a, "grace and peace in abundance." Here, despite Bauckham, we have a definite parallel to 1 Peter 1:2. This suggests our author knows 1 Peter, but it is obvious that he is not modeling this epistle entirely on 1 Peter. A pseudepigraphist would surely have wanted to model the epistle more closely on 1 Peter, through conscious imitation. This we do not have in 2 Peter.

The phrase "our God and Savior Jesus Christ" in 2 Peter 1:1 may be taken to mean that Jesus is both our God and our Savior. In favor of this conclusion is the phrase "our Lord and Savior, Jesus" at 2 Peter 1:11 and 3:18 (cf. 2 Pet 2:20; 3:2). Furthermore, as J. N. D. Kelly points out, if we distinguish two persons here, then the word "our" only refers to God, and we are left with the awkward phrase "Savior Jesus Christ" applied to Jesus.[7] Against this, however, is said to be the immediate context in 2 Peter 1:2, where the phrase "of God and our Lord Jesus" is definitely a reference to two persons, not just one. It is hard to say which view should be adopted; however, the absence of the definite article and the presence of "our" tips the evidence in favor of Jesus being called "God" in 2 Peter 1:1.[8] If so, this text is like John 1:1, 20:28, Romans 9:5 and Hebrews 1:8-9 in calling Jesus "God." The term *sōtēr* "Savior," was used of God the Father in the Old Testament. Here it is applied to Jesus as the one who brings salvation. It was, however, a popular Hellenistic word, widely used of pagan deities and even the emperor, and this may explain its use here. It is a term only sometimes

[5]See rightly Craddock, *First and Second Peter,* p. 95.
[6]See Kelly, *Epistles of Peter,* p. 296.
[7]Ibid., p. 298.
[8]Bauckham, *Jude, 2 Peter,* p. 168.

used in the New Testament as a christological title (16 times, of which 5 are in 2 Peter and 4 in the Pastorals).[9]

In **2 Peter 1:2** we read that "grace and peace" come to the believer through knowledge of God and Jesus. It does not happen by accident or without cognitive content. The point here is that peace is multiplied by the fuller *knowledge* of God.[10] *Epignōsis,* an amplified or intensified form of the noun for "knowledge," is a favorite term in 2 Peter (1:2-8; 2:20; cf. 3:18), and some have suggested that this is because the false teachers were claiming some esoteric knowledge. This may or may not be the case, and certainly the term does not have that sort of meaning in Hebrews 10:26 or for that matter in its numerous occurrences in the later Paulines (cf. the Pastoral Epistles: 1 Tim 2:4; 2 Tim 2:25; 3:7; Tit 1:1).[11] Our author implies that intimate knowledge of God is to be found only in what has already been taught them from Jesus through "your apostles" (2 Pet 1:1; 3:2), not through false prophets or teachers, not through any esoteric or secret teachings. As Pheme Perkins puts it, the author is speaking about the recognition and understanding of God that comes through conversion.[12] The author's use of the intensified form is in keeping with his Asiatic style, and we should not make too much of its difference in meaning from *gnōsis,* though sometimes it has the sense of "full knowledge."[13] Robert E. Picirelli suggests that the intensified form of the word refers to knowledge received in and at conversion, while the term *gnōsis* refers to what can be learned after conversion (2 Pet 1:5-6; 3:18).[14] It is also important that our author begins and ends this document with this reference to "knowledge of God" (cf. 2 Pet 3:18).[15]

The phrase "your apostles" in 2 Peter 3:2 is important for understanding the entire discourse. It reflects the editorial work of the one who assembled these apostolic traditions from Peter and Jude. Our editor is not claiming to be an

[9]There are various parallels between 2 Peter and the Pastorals, which may reflect our author's knowledge of those documents.

[10]Mayor, *Jude, 2 Peter,* p. 82.

[11]*Epignōsis* occurs 15 times in Paul, 4 times in 2 Peter, once in Hebrews, nowhere else in the NT. Here we have another small correspondence between the Pastorals and 2 Peter. On the use in the Pastorals, see Witherington, *Letters and Homilies for Hellenized Christians,* 1:254-55.

[12]Perkins, *First and Second Peter,* p. 167.

[13]See Hillyer, *1 and 2 Peter,* p. 158.

[14]Picirelli, "Meaning of '*Epignōsis*,'" pp. 85-93.

[15]See Moo, *2 Peter, Jude,* p. 36. Neyrey, *2 Peter, Jude,* p. 149, reading this through an honor-and-shame grid, prefers the translation "acknowledgement." The problem with this is that the "knowledge" is said to come from God in the grace and peace. Here the "in the knowledge" phrase modifies "grace and peace." This greeting is talking about the blessings of God, not our response to the blessings.

apostle, much less the chief Jewish apostle, Peter. He distinguishes himself from the audience's apostles. If Peter were writing this to even some or any of his own converts, one can hardly imagine him phrasing 2 Peter 3:2 the way we have it. One could perhaps argue that 2 Peter 3:2 indicates that Peter is addressing audiences not his own, such as Pauline audiences, but absolutely nothing in this document suggests that a particular audience is being targeted, much less that a purely Pauline one is being addressed.

This document is meant for all Christians and is intended to allow the apostolic witness of Peter and Jude and even Paul to address them all. In stressing that they are "your apostles," our author is trying to link the audience to the apostolic founders of the previous generation. This remark functions much like what we find in Hebrews 2:3-4, where the author indicates that he is in touch with the original ear- and eyewitnesses of Jesus but is not one of them. In this case, the point is to remind the audience that some of the original apostles have converted them, and so they should maintain continuity with the apostolic teaching.

2 Peter 1:3-11—Exordium: Manifesting Virtues, Making Firm One's Calling, Sharing in the Divine Nature

> Realize your dignity, O Christian! Once you have been made a partaker of the divine nature, do not return to your former baseness by a life unworthy of that dignity. Remember whose head it is and whose body of which you constitute a member. (Leo the Great [*Sermons* 21.3])

> When we hear these things, we must fortify ourselves and obey what is said, and cleanse ourselves from earthly things. If we do that, we shall share in his blessings, and we shall not need anything else. But if we do not obey, we shall be destroyed. What difference does it make whether we are destroyed through wealth or through laziness? Or if not through laziness, through cowardice? For when a farmer destroys his crop, it hardly matters how he does it. . . . Therefore it is necessary that once someone has been cleansed and has partaken of holiness, that he hold on to it through thick and thin, for without it he will not see the Lord. (Chrysostom)[16]

An exordium can serve different kinds of functions in the differing species of rhetoric, but in all of them some of the major themes of the coming discourse will be announced in advance. In an epideictic discourse the focus will necessarily be on praiseworthy or blameworthy behavior, and on the virtues and vices that correspond to them. In such a discourse the issue is honorable or dishon-

[16] *CEC* 86.

orable character and behavior in the present, and so it tends to be hortatory and focus on ethics rather than ideas.

In this exordium our author will focus on the nature of Christian character as produced by God's work in the life of the believer, and on how that character should manifest itself in honorable behavior. It thus is no accident that we have a virtue list in the very heart of this exordium, and at its end the author characterizes what he has just said as a reminder, not a change of policy or direction; he is not preparing the audience for a deliberative discourse on how change of behavior in the near future is necessary and beneficial.

Our author's rhetorical strategy thus is to make clear up front the nature of praiseworthy character and behavior; then he will present Peter's testimony, which presents to the audience the ultimate example of honorable and glorious character and behavior in the person of Jesus. There is an implicit comparison: just as the believers have received faith and can be partakers in the divine nature, so Jesus at the transfiguration received glory and honor from God and was certainly a partaker of the divine nature. Peter was a witness of his splendor. Such glory is the destiny of believers if they continue to stand firm in their faith and develop their character.

This opening exordium and testimony perfectly sets up the following contrast by way of rhetorical *synkrisis,* with a series of examples of blameworthy and dishonorable conduct as exhibited by the fallen angels and ancient and modern false teachers. At 2 Peter 3:1 this in turn leads to a final lengthy argument about eschatology grounded in both the exordium and the previous two major expositions on praiseworthy and blameworthy character and behavior. Finally, at 2 Peter 3:14 our author will come to the peroration, where he reiterates the call for the audience to continue to live praiseworthy lives and avoid the blandishments of the false teachers. The audience has secure footing and is standing firm, but the author does not want them to be shaken, distracted, misled or beguiled by the false teachers who may be approaching them. The audience must continue to grow in the knowledge and favor of the Lord Jesus Christ. Hence, I submit that from start to finish this is an epideictic argument about honorable and dishonorable character and behavior, and its essential ethical and hortatory character is notable throughout.

Asiatic Greek was especially compatible with epideictic rhetoric, which in any case tended to be hyperbolic and lavish in character. When the two were combined, one could expect lengthy and sometimes convoluted sentences, grandiloquent phrases and vocabulary, amplification and redundancy—all to make the honorable look more glorious and the dishonorable look more despicable. What one does not have in such rhetoric is formal arguments. Rather, it presents polemics, emotive characterizations, appeals to the deeper emotions, casting of odium or offering of lavish and exorbitant praise and the like. Second Peter does not disappoint on any of these scores. The classic discussions about epideictic rhetoric all emphasize these things (cf. Aristotle *Rhet.* 1.9.1368a.38-40; Anaximenes *Rhet. Alex.* 3.1426b.19ff.; 6.2428a.1ff; Cicero *Part. or.* 21.71), and I have little doubt these rhetoricians would have recognized in 2 Peter a first-rate presentation of epideictic oratory, with all the emotional stops pulled out so that the apostolic tradition will continue to be embraced and manifested, and the teachings and behaviors of the false teachers be rejected.

In this discourse our author does not begin with polemics, but rather with praise and piety before he turns on the pyrotechnics and polemics in 2 Peter 2. This is not a surprise since epideictic rhetoric was often all about religion and what amounted to real piety, and its opposite: impiety. Nothing could be more dishonorable than impious behavior, nor more glorious than true *eusebeia*, "piety," often considered the queen of all the virtues, the height of *aretē*. For example, consider the Greek inscription found in Sardis, dating from the reign of Claudius:

> Tiberius Caesar god Augustus, the imperator, uncle of Tiberius Claudius Germanicus Caesar Augustus, the imperator, the founder of the city and benefactor of the world, out of piety *[eusebeia]* and thanksgiving *[eucharistia]* did the people hallow. . . .[17]

Clearly enough our author knows the language of religious praise, only he is directing it to quite different objects, a very different sort of God, who walked upon the earth in the first century: not Caesar, but Christ.

One of the real problems in overconcentrating on the source criticism of this discourse is that one fails to see how skillfully our author has blended this diverse source material into a powerful discourse, which reflects skill especially in the manipulation of style. Nowhere is this more evident than in the use of the material from Jude, where our author is by no means simply quoting his source. Rather, he is rephrasing it in Asiatic style, and here it is especially evident what skill he had in transforming a source. This makes it all the more remarkable that in the Petrine testimony in 2 Peter 1 the text does not really reflect such a transformation. Instead, it reads more like something one would find in 1 Peter. It was especially appropriate in epideictic oratory, which had chiefly become funeral oratory in the second half of the first century, that one trot out the testimony and testament of an honorable and now-deceased man, and this we have in 2 Peter 1.

[17] *NewDocs* 9:22.

In 2 Peter this testimony honors Peter's legacy by using his eyewitness story, and yet it is not an encomium of Peter or about him. No indeed. Peter's testimony is not primarily about himself but about the most noble hero and example of piety of all—Christ himself, whom even God glorified and honored at the transfiguration! Thus what we have here is a testimony to Christ, not so much a testament, like the *Testaments of the Twelve Patriarchs*. Peter here is nowhere said to be passing on the baton to the next generation or dispensing his personal largesse, but rather is pointing away from himself to the glorified and ultrahonorable Jesus. Peter is only the servant and messenger of that Savior. We do not hear a recounting of Peter's ministry, but rather a reminder of the apostolic tradition regarding what amounts to good character and behavior and what does not. There is a brief allusion to the promised outcome of Peter's life in 2 Peter 1 in the style of John 21, but it is only brief and helps to set up the Christophany. This is the rhetoric of commendation and condemnation with the volume turned up; it is not the rhetoric of advice and consent.

One interesting feature in the *synkrisis* in 2 Peter 2 is its narrative form, following the source material from Jude in the same order, but shaping it for a more generic audience. The old bad guys and the new ones are compared, and both are found wanting, despicable, dishonest, and likely to bewitch, bewilder and beguile. The portrait could hardly be more negative. Rhetorically speaking, one could not lead with this sort of odious subject in an epideictic discourse. One needed first to establish rapport in a positive way with the audience (see Cicero *De or.* 2.80.325; Quintilian *Inst.* 4.1.23-27). Therefore the author is all sweetness and light in the prescript, the exordium, and in the first exposition, which is Peter's testimony. Once the audience is on board with the author and receptive to the discourse, then the author can tackle the bone of contention, which he does at great length in 2 Peter 2.

But again, since this is epideictic material, he cannot not simply lead them somewhere and leave them there in the darkness. He has to return to the positive teaching, in this case about eschatology and ethics in 2 Peter 3, which will naturally lead up to the final appeal in the peroration. This is not a lengthy speech by ancient standards, but it is full of emotive language of both a positive and negative sort about the Beloved and the despised. The author gets the most out of his verbiage, and he does not mince words. Like a Rembrandt painting, the contrast between the light and the dark is stark, such that the choice between the two ought to be obvious.

Finally, the topic of honor is one that is at the forefront of epideictic rhetoric. Duane F. Watson says of our text: "2 Peter's exordium is prompted by the honorable cause which wins the approval of the audience by its very nature [see

Cicero *Inv.* 1.15.20; Quintilian *Inst.* 4.1.41]. . . . 2 Peter's cause is honorable because it is defending the teaching of Peter (3:1) and Paul (3:15-16) against attack. The audience [already] holds this teaching in great respect (1:1, 12; 3:17) and its defense is sure to win their approval."[18] Our author has chosen his material wisely, starting with the common Christian ground he shares with the audience, and he does not need to argue for or about that ground. His strategy is to make the audience attentive, receptive and well-disposed to what follows—the three main functions of an exordium. In other words, at the outset our author takes the high road, going out of his way to establish rapport so that he can later deal with the issue of the false teachers. Remarkably, he is able to pull it off in a relatively brief exordium, which still provides the first flashes of his Asiatic skill. Nothing less than the spiritual welfare, faith, relationship with God and true worship of the audience is at stake. They must continue to stand firm in their already-embraced values and virtues. With this rhetorical summary, we are ready to delve into the rhetoric of the last, or nearly the last, canonical document to be written in the New Testament era.[19]

> [1:3] *Seeing that the divine power has bestowed on us all that contributed (everything necessary) to life and piety through the knowledge of him who called us (by) his own glory and excellence,*[20] [4] *through these (things) he has given us the precious and sublime promises so that through them we may be sharers in the divine nature, having escaped the corruption because of sinful desire in the world.* [5] *And for this very (reason) having brought to bear all zeal, add to your faith virtue, but to virtue knowledge,* [6] *and to knowledge (add) self-control, to self-control (add) endurance, to endurance (add) piety,* [7] *to piety (add) brotherly affection, to brotherly affection add love.* [8] *For these are belonging to you and are increasing; they make you neither idle nor fruitless in the knowledge of our Lord Jesus Christ.* [9] *For anyone who does not have these is blind, he is (deliberately) closing his eyes, being oblivious to the cleansing from his sins long ago (in the past).* [10] *Therefore, all the more, brothers, be zealous to make firm your calling and election, for doing this you will not ever stumble.* [11] *For in this way (thus) the entrance into the eternal kingdom of our Lord and Savior Jesus Christ will be richly afforded.*

---

[18] Watson, *Invention,* p. 88.

[19] Only Revelation may be later, and perhaps the final assembling of the Beloved Disciple's Gospel materials.

[20] We have a rather severe textual problem at this juncture. Although the Textus Receptus (see 𝔓[72], B, K, L and most minuscules) has *dia* here; ℵ, A, C, P, various minuscules and all the ancient versions have *idia* here. Metzger, *TC,* p. 699, prefers the latter reading in part because *idios* is a favorite word of our author, occurring six times in three chapters. The former reading "called through glory and virtue (or might)" makes less sense as well. The emphasis here is on God's qualities or character traits.

Our author deliberately casts his message into Hellenistic and more specifically Asiatic Greek. For example, observe the use of *theias, epignōseōs, aretē* in this section and the mention of being sharers in the divine nature. The author is trying to relate to his audience in a language they are familiar with; however, he modifies the Hellenistic ideas to suit a Judeo-Christian and eschatological perspective. Daniel J. Harrington calls this an attempt at enculturation. I disagree: it is rather an attempt at indigenization of the gospel and at the same time taking captive certain cultural notions and giving them a Christian ethos and content.[21] But before one can talk about Christians manifesting virtues, our author quite rightly must focus on the work of God in the lives of the audience. "These verses make the God who is known by Christians the source of the highest good that ancient moral philosophy could imagine, actual participation in the divine nature itself."[22] In these verses is absolutely nothing that deserves to be called a thanksgiving period or a blessing period or a eulogy, for that matter. Epistolary conventions are nowhere in evidence here. They have been left behind at 2 Peter 1:2. What we find here is the beginning of the exordium, and only rhetorical conventions are in play.

It nevertheless is possible to see 2 Peter 1:3-11 as being like an honorific decree. Frederick W. Danker has analyzed this segment in detail in relationship to decrees in which a patron's benefaction is first praised (2 Pet 1:3-4 here), followed by a list of statements of how the clients ought to and will respond (2 Pet 1:5-11 here). He also observes that the more formal and grandiose language here matches up with that of the decrees, even in the way this section begins with "whereas" or "as" (*hōs* here).[23] The problem with this analysis is that the style to which he refers is not found just in this segment of the discourse; instead, it reflects the style of Asiatic rhetoric found throughout most of this discourse. Furthermore, the language of patron and client is not used here, and in any case our author's theology does not simply view God's grace and the human response as another example of reciprocity: You scratch my back and I'll scratch yours. The relationship between God and believers is rather characterized as a parent-child relationship, which is quite different from a patron-client relationship.[24] Nevertheless, it is possible that the audience would hear some

---

[21]See Harrington, *Jude and 2 Peter,* pp. 247-48.

[22]Perkins, *First and Second Peter,* p. 168.

[23]See the discussion in Danker, "2 Peter 1," pp. 64-82.

[24]In my opinion the Context Group overreads a large portion of the NT in regard to this matter. But see Neyrey, *2 Peter, Jude,* pp. 150-62. Modern cultural anthropology is not the place to start in analyzing ancient cultural scripts, although it is certainly true that there are some parallels between Greco-Roman culture then and Mediterranean culture now. Normally it is not the patron who makes promises, but rather the client—promising to pay back the patron or honor the patron in some way. The patron gives gifts or benefactions, which sets the cycle in motion.

similarities between what is said here and such decrees.

Second Peter 1:3-4 are not merely transitional verses but rather foundational for the ethical summary of the preaching that begins at 2 Peter 1:5 and continues until 2 Peter 1:11. **Second Peter 1:3** stresses that God's power has already bestowed on believers everything necessary for godly living (an example of hendiadys: more literally, "life and piety"). The implication is that no additional information from false teachers is wanted or needed. This power to do God's will and live a godly life has come to believers through knowledge of the One who has called them. This presumably refers to Christ and possibly, if we ask what has lured them to Christ, it may be answered that they were called and attracted to him by his uniquely excellent glory (another hendiadys: literally, "glory and excellence"). This paves the way for the reference to the transfiguration in 2 Peter 1:12-21. In any case, it refers to Christ in his incarnation.[25] In the transfiguration we see in Christ the presence and qualities of God. "Called" is aorist and probably refers back to the believers' first hearing of the proclaiming or first receiving of Christ.

Second Peter 1:4 is somewhat difficult to decipher grammatically. In beginning the verse, to what does *di' hōn* refer? The most natural and nearest antecedent is "his own glory and excellence." The point could be that through Christ's manifestation and witness, God has given believers these great and precious promises.[26] Elsewhere in 2 Peter these promises are clearly seen to be fulfilled at the eschaton (cf. 3:4, 9, 13), and this may be the case here as well.[27] The last portion of 2 Peter 1:4 is one of the most discussed segments of the epistle. In the beginning of the verse we are told the result (or purpose) of receiving the great and precious promises:[28] (1) Believers are able to escape the ways of the world. (2) Positively, they become sharers in the divine nature. In some ways the first of these is easier to deal with, so we will tackle it first. Bauckham suggests that "having escaped the corruption in the world on account of desire" refers to escaping from human mortality.[29] This, however, may be doubted precisely because of the phrase *en epithymia,* "because of sinful desire."[30] This could be a ref-

[25]See Bauckham, *Jude, 2 Peter,* pp. 177-79.

[26]As Moffatt, *General Epistles,* p. 178, points out, this verse was crucial to the faith development of John Wesley, and on May 24, 1738, it helped get him beyond a spiritual crisis, by reminding him that the gospel was all about God's promises, which provide the means of becoming partakers of the divine nature through the knowledge of God in Christ.

[27]See Watson, "2 Peter," p. 336.

[28]*Epangelmata,* referring to promises, is found only in 2 Peter in the NT: cf. 2 Pet 1:4; 3:13.

[29]Bauckham, *Jude, 2 Peter,* pp. 179-80.

[30]On *epithymia* having the sense of sinful or fleshly desire in early Jewish sources, see pp. 138-39 above.

erence to the Genesis story, which may imply that mortality entered the world as a result of the original sin. However, it could just as easily be a reference to how moral corruption entered the world through the original sin, and this much better fits our context, which discusses moral corruption. Further, *apophygontes* is a participle in the aorist. "Escaped" is the most likely translation, and this means that our author is talking about an event in the Christians' past, *not* their future. This is a verb found only in 2 Peter in the New Testament (cf. also 2:18-20; Sir 22:22). Craddock puts it this way: "In other words, the conversion from this life to the next is not achieved simply by dying and therefore passing from mortality to immortality. Rather the change is moral and ethical. This point must be insisted on because the 'corruption' *(phthora)* is not the world itself but rather moral corruption which the believer is to flee. To be sure sinful desire leads to corruption which in turn leads to destruction, but the corruption and the destruction of the world (or of the individual physical existence) are not identical here.[31] It is the knowledge of God as revealed in Jesus Christ and not simply a funeral which provides 'entry into the eternal kingdom.'"[32] Further, the common Hellenistic expectation was that there was a way to become a participant in the "divine nature," at least in part here and now. Thus, Michael Green points out how it was commonly expected that one could enter into such a nature:

> Rival pagan schoolmen asserted that you escaped from the toils of *corruption (phthora)* by becoming *partakers of the divine nature* either by *nomos* ("lawkeeping") or by *physis* ("nature"). Peter takes up their language and replies that it is by sheer grace. Did the false teachers . . . suggest that their adherents became more godlike as they escaped the trammel of the material world? Far from it, says Peter. Participation in the divine nature is the starting point, not the goal, of Christian living. He writes to those who have escaped from the seductive allegiance to society at odds with God.[33]

Plutarch by contrast complains that humans feel the passion for immortality (a quality of God they cannot really share) far more than the passion for God's moral excellence, which is within their reach (Plutarch *Arist.* 6). All of this buildup is part of the author's attempt to combat the false teachers, only he is taking the rhetorical approach known as *insinuatio.* He is working up to his broadside against those teachers indirectly. His tactic will be to take up common terms and even buzzwords and give them a proper Christian content. Michael Green suggests:

---

[31]Against Neyrey, *2 Peter, Jude*, p. 157.
[32]Craddock, *First and Second Peter,* p. 98.
[33]Green, *2 Peter,* p. 65.

> The false teachers laid emphasis on knowledge; so Peter stresses that the object of knowledge in the Christian life is the Lord who calls men. They thought that knowledge dispenses with the need for morality, so Peter emphasizes two words common in pagan circles for ethical endeavor, *eusebeia* (godliness) and *aretē* (virtue). They appear to have thought that holiness of living was impossible (see ii.19, 20), so Peter speaks to them of the *divine power,* a Hebrew periphrasis for God.[34]

Thus, we must reject Bauckham's view of what is escaped from and when participation in the divine nature begins. He is, however, right as to what participating in the divine nature means: (1) It involves union with God, not divination of the human. (2) It involves a work of grace in the believer so that one can become godlike. It thus means participation in eternal life and eternal goodness and eventually involves everlasting life and an incorruptible body; but we must remember that, strictly speaking, participation in the divine nature can have nothing to do with a resurrection body.[35] Even Christ's divine nature never took on human flesh. Rather, as the God-man, Christ had two natures: divine and human. To be like God or Christ in divine nature can have nothing to do with escaping physical mortality. We may, for example, compare Wisdom of Solomon 2:23: "God created the human for incorruption and made him in the image of his own eternity." In the Christian way of viewing this, immortality or everlasting life is not an inherent property of the soul: it is rather a gift obtained when one is saved, and it is fully realized at the eschaton. Our author says this divine nature is something believers share: "We are sharers" *(koinōnoi)* in it. It is not a believer's private possession, but it is something that they share together with other believers. The concept of the spiritual union of believers in Christ may be behind this terminology. General confirmation of our view is found in 2 Peter 1:9, which refers to the "cleansing from sins *long ago.*" It is this sort of corruption that our author has in view. Craddock is right to stress that while in Greco-Roman thought participating in the divine nature meant things ranging from immortality even to apotheosis and entering the Elysian fields, here it has an ethical dimension: participating in the holiness of God and thereby being enable to act ethically.[36]

Kosmos here as in James and the Fourth Gospel refers to the world as organized by human beings against God, stressing its influences and fallenness. Our writer, then, is talking not about the good material (natural) existence God has created, but about the bad human society that humans have perpetuated in the

---

[34]Ibid.

[35]Against Bauckham, *Jude, 2 Peter,* pp. 190-91.

[36]See Starr's *Sharers in Divine Nature;* and Craddock, *First and Second Peter,* p. 98.

world. This is what Christians escape at conversion. Human sinful desires have led to this state, beginning with the original sin. But believers are no longer slaves to, nor should they be active partakers in, the world in its sinfulness. This will be the author's point as he continues to write. Notice the already-and-not-yet perspective. "We *have been* given great promises. We are however now only partial sharers in what we may receive through those promises": thus we need ethical exhortation here. Moffatt reminds us that though some see Christianity as essentially about a conversion experience that guarantees one eternal life regardless of one's subsequent behavior, and thus "an initial spasm is followed by chronic inertia," our author will have none of it.[37] Real faith works: it produces not only godly character but also behavior that glorifies God.

Second Peter 1:3 has begun a segment of the letter which at **2 Peter 1:5** goes even further into Hellenistic language and Asiatic Greek. It is rather grandiose, like a Rubens work of art. Green has shown how this was a popular way to write, especially for those with a certain literary bent. He cites an inscription from Asia Minor showing the popularity of such a style in the very locality from which this sort of Greek emerged. Green points out:

> Two examples of this style come from the Decree of Stratonicea in Caria, Asia Minor, and the grandiose inscription of Antiochus the First of Commagene in central Asia Minor. Bo Reicke, who has acutely seen the significance of this inscription for the whole question of the language of 2 Peter, gives the following extract: "It was as being of all things good not only a most reliable acquisition, but also—for human beings—a most pleasant enjoyment that I considered piety; and the same conviction I held to be the reason for a most successful authority as well as for a most blessed employment thereof; furthermore, during my entire lifetime I appeared to all in my monarchy as one who regarded holiness as both a most trustworthy safeguard and an inimitable satisfaction."[38]

Precisely because Christians have escaped corruption, they must go on avoiding it, and it is precisely because they are in part partaking in the divine nature that they must be very zealous and make every effort to add every positive Christian virtue to their arsenal. Before dealing with individual points, we need to say several things about the *sōritēs,* the developing and interlocked catalog of virtues here. First, Bauckham has correctly shown that our list is an amalgam of Christian and pagan Hellenistic terms.[39] There may indeed be an intentional development from the foundation and starting point of faith to the

[37]Moffatt, *General Epistles*, p. 181.
[38]Green, *2 Peter,* p. 18.
[39]Bauckham, *Jude, 2 Peter,* pp. 174-75.

ultimate goal and end of all Christian behavior: love. Strikingly, the verb "supply" or "add" in its noun form is the Greek word for "chorus," or as a verb "to make provision for the chorus." It is as if the author is saying: "Orchestrate your life as follows."[40] At this juncture it would be well to set this rhetorical device in its larger context, for virtue catalogs were characteristic of this ancient world, since it was an honor-and-shame culture.

A CLOSER LOOK

The Christian Face of Virtue

The rhetorical device being used in this virtue catalog is called *sōritēs,* or *gradatio,* providing us with an ascending chain of virtues that leads to a climax, or in this case to the supreme virtue: Christian love. It is a device that involves repetition, something near to the heart of Asiatic rhetoricians, and it takes the form A . . . B, B . . . C, C . . . D and so on. In this era chains of virtues were not uncommon in Hellenistic and Stoic philosophy (cf. Seneca *Ep.* 85.2; Maximus of Tyre 16.3b), as were vice lists. The other example of this sort of rhetorical construction using virtues is found in Romans 5:3-5, which is similar enough to this *gradatio* that one may wonder if the author of 2 Peter knew of the one in Romans. In later Christian literature, the *Acts of Peter* (Vercelli: 2) is very similar and is probably based on this one in 2 Peter 1, and we may also compare the *Epistle of Barnabas* 2.2-3 and *1 Clement* 62.2. We should also especially compare this list in 2 Peter 1 to Philippians 4:8, with which it shares the characteristic of having a mixture of Hellenistic and more-Christian virtues. The 2 Peter 1 list is like the one in 2 Corinthians 8:7 in beginning with faith and ending with Christian love (cf. 1 Cor 13:13).

In some cases in this list the author has taken terms prominent in Hellenistic lists, such as "knowledge," which was sometimes listed either first or last on the list, indicating its preeminence, but here it is in the middle of the pack. Faith and love are more important. Notice as well that some words like *pistis* do occur in the pagan lists, but with the very different meaning of loyalty or even faithfulness.[41] The list in 2 Peter, then, has something old, something new, and something borrowed but transformed into another concept. Craddock rightly adds that it would have been striking to the ancients to have a list with *both* mutual affection between brothers and sisters and some other kind of love listed. "But that is just the point: mutual affection, reciprocal love, pertains to life in the church, to the fellowship. Beyond that, however, is love

---

[40]Craddock, *First and Second Peter,* p. 100.
[41]See ibid., p. 101.

agapē. Love does not require reciprocity; it includes the stranger, and even the enemy."[42]

There are early Jewish chainlink lists of virtues as well, the most similar in form of which is from Rabbi Phineas ben Jair (ca. A.D. 90): "Zeal leads to cleanliness, and cleanliness leads to purity, and purity leads to self-restraint, and self-restraint leads to sanctity, and sanctity leads to humility, and humility leads to the fear of sin, and the fear of sin leads to piety, and piety leads to the Holy Spirit, and the Holy Spirit leads to the resurrection of the dead" (*m. Soṭ.* 9.15).[43] To this one may wish to compare Wisdom of Solomon 6:17-20, which moves from "wisdom" to a "kingdom."

In some ways this is just the opposite of our list, which presupposes that the audience already has the Holy Spirit, who is helping produce these virtues in the believer. Ritual purity is not an issue in our list in 2 Peter. The near-contemporary Shepherd of Hermas (*Mand.* 5.2.4) lists vices that have a snowballing effect, with one engendering the next (e.g., "from foolishness is engendered bitterness"). This, however, is not the nature of 2 Peter 1, which lists virtues. Bauckham points to another passage in Hermas (*Vis.* 3.8.7) that does use the *sōritēs* (chainlink, *gradatio*) form, beginning with "faith" and ending with "love." Hermas lists seven virtues, 2 Peter lists eight. But also in that list one virtue produces the next, which despite Bauckham's argument does not seem to be the case here in 2 Peter.[44]

What is not at all clear is whether Bauckham is right in translating the key verb *epichorēgēsate* as "produce," indicating that each virtue is the means of producing the next. There are various problems with this view, as Joseph B. Mayor demonstrates at length.[45] The basic idea of this verb is one who supplies, furnishes, provides, or makes possible something originally; it was used, for example, of a financial backer of a Greek chorus and drama.[46] He was a provider, not a producer. Furthermore, in 1 Peter 4:11 the basic form of this verb means "supply," "provide": God provides strength. Again, in 2 Corinthians 9:10, the idea is the same: God supplies. Here in this text we have both forms of the verb, with and without the prefixed *epi*. In 2 Corinthians 9:10 Paul supplements "supplies" with "and will increase." The idea here is providing and adding to, but not *producing*. Mayor cites an example where the force of *epi* in *epichorēgēsate* is accumulative.[47] Theophilus of Antioch (*Autol.* 73B) uses the

[42]Ibid.
[43]See the detailed discussion in Fischel, "The Uses of *Sōritēs*," pp. 119-51.
[44]Bauckham, *Jude, 2 Peter,* pp. 175-76.
[45]Mayor, *Jude, 2 Peter,* pp. 90-91; and also M. Green, *2 Peter,* pp. 66-67.
[46]See Hillyer, *1 and 2 Peter,* p. 164.
[47]Mayor, *Jude, 2 Peter,* p. 91.

word as meaning "to add further supplies," or "to provide more than was expected." Here in 2 Peter, to "supply" further means to "add more." In addition, as Mayor notes, it is not at all clear how some of these virtues could be said to be produced by the preceding virtue, but it is not difficult to see how they could be added to them. Thus, as Mayor suggests, we may here have a poetic or rhetorical use of *en de* to express addition, not production.[48] On Bauckham's view *en* has a rather strained force of "by." What the author is saying is not "by virtue produce knowledge," but rather, "to virtue add knowledge." We must not confuse the interlocking rhetorical structure with a chain of dependent causes or ideas. On all this Kelly should be compared.[49] All of these qualities are things Christians should add to their arsenal. There is a general progression here from faith through knowledge to affection to love, but this is not because one virtue produces the next, but because the author has the foundational virtue first, and the greatest or climactic virtues last. As Norman Hillyer stresses: "Believers . . . must be lavish in the time and effort they put into developing their Christian lives—not being satisfied with getting by on the minimum, but striving like the *chorēgos* [the drama's patron, financial backer] of old to achieve the finest and most attractive production."[50]

What especially makes 2 Peter 1:5-7 stand out is that even more than in either the Roman or Philippian list, our author chooses to use terms that are more directly accessible to those who know the buzzwords of Hellenistic moral philosophy: *aretē,*[51] *enkrateia,*[52] *eusebeia, philadelphia.*[53] The terms more characteristic of Christian moral discourse are *pistis* in the sense of faith/trust, *hypomonē* in the sense of endurance/hope and certainly *agapē*.

J. Daryl Charles makes the point that what the author is doing is linking the theological virtues to the natural ones, the ones admired and manifested in the wider culture.[54] He sums up as follows:

> Whereas the acquisition of virtue in pagan ethics is an absolute good and the highest human goal, for the Christian it is evidence of deeper theological realities. . . . [Just] because God through Christ has made provision for the ethical life—and this *abundantly*—does not mean that there is no cooperation in the ethical enterprise. To the contrary, the readers have a necessary part to play: "For this reason make every effort

[48]Ibid.
[49]Kelly, *Epistles of Peter,* pp. 305-6.
[50]Hillyer, *1 and 2 Peter,* p. 164.
[51]Cf. 1 Pet 2:9; Phil 4:8.
[52]Said by Xenophon (*Mem.* 1.5.4) to be the foundation of all virtues.
[53]See Harrington, *Jude and 2 Peter,* p. 248.
[54]Charles, *Virtue Amidst Vice,* pp. 126-52.

to supply . . . " Arranged in pairs and then distinguished for rhetorically stylized effect, the virtues build upon faith . . . and culminate in love. . . . The purpose of the catalog is its demarcation of exemplary—and by implication, unacceptable—behavior. . . . At bottom, Christians are to live a life *worthy* of their calling.[55]

In a piece of epideictic rhetoric, we are often dealing with an effort at character building or character formation. It is not an accident that such an exercise happens right in the exordium of this discourse. So formed, the audience will be better able to judge the behavior (and pedagogy) of the false teachers (who are a part of some Christian communities) for what it is. Indeed, the very next verse helps the audience to see the contrast: in 2 Peter 1:8-9 we have a contrast between the audience and blind guides, or at least nearsighted ones. One of the evidences of our author's considerable rhetorical skill is that he is able to integrate, adopt and adapt other people's material into his discourse without interrupting the flow of the discourse. He knows how to make the material his own, and he also knows when to treat a sacred tradition carefully without doing an extreme makeover of it, as in his use of Peter's testimony. What emerges from this entire first chapter is that the character of Christians is to be like the character of Christ, and being praiseworthy will result in honor and glory, as they become sharers in the divine nature. Perhaps we should end this discussion with the apt commentary of Ignatius: "The beginning is faith and the end is love, and when the two are joined in unity, it is God" (Ign. *Eph.* 14.1).

A *sōritēs,* as we have beginning in **2 Peter 1:5**, tends to climax in the supreme virtue or vice—which here is *agapē,* and it may be implied that this virtue encompasses and crowns all the rest, being the context out of which the rest are manifested and the manner of their manifestation. "Faith" appears to be the basic trust in God through Christ or belief in the gospel, which results in such trust, not a reference to some body of doctrines. *Aretē* is indeed a term often used in Hellenistic lists, meaning "virtue," or perhaps "excellence," the proper fulfillment of anything (cf. Phil 4:8). In Hellenistic thought, it involves the achievement of human excellence, not obedience to God. "Knowledge" is mentioned next and possibly should be distinguished from *epignōsis* (cf. 2 Pet 1:2-3), which could mean for the author "that fundamental knowledge of God in Christ which makes a person a Christian."[56] The reason for hesitating on this

[55]Ibid., p. 157.
[56]Bauckham, *Jude, 2 Peter,* p. 186.

point is that in Asiatic rhetoric one often, for the sake of "invention," varies the word one uses, saying the same thing in slightly different terms.[57] Possibly, though, *gnōsis* here means "practical wisdom" necessary for Christian living and progressively acquired.

In **2 Peter 1:6** *enkrateia* means "self-control" and is another characteristic Hellenistic virtue (cf. Aristotle *Eth. Nic.* 7.1.11); it is usually taken to mean "reason winning out over passion." Here the term is particularly appropriate in view of the apparent antinomianism or libertinism of the false teachers. *Hypomonē* means a "steadfastness" and may refer to endurance under pressure or persecution, but here may be allied to endurance in a Christian way despite temptation. *Eusebeia* is yet another characteristic Hellenistic virtue; literally it means "good worship," but it normally has the broader sense of "piety" or "godliness," and in a pagan context it means giving the gods their due in respect and in sacrifice and perhaps also to some extent in living a life of virtue.[58] In a Christian context it refers to the godliness that necessarily entails both honoring God in worship, and also in one's behavior.

As in **2 Peter 1:7**, *philadelphia* means "brotherly or sisterly affection" and occurs elsewhere in ethical lists only in 1 Peter 3:8. Perhaps our author was led to include it here as a result of his knowledge of Petrine teaching. It is not to be confused with *agapē,* a more distinctively Christian virtue. Green notes:

> The crown of Christian "advance" (to return to the martial metaphor of the Stoic *prokopē* [progress/advance], on which this list of qualities seems to be modeled) is love. "The greatest of these is love" (1 Cor. xiii.13). This word *agapē* is one which Christians to all intents and purposes coined, to denote the attitude which God has shown Himself to have to us, and requires from us towards Himself. In friendship (*philia*) the partners seek mutual solace; in sexual love (*erōs*) mutual satisfaction. In both cases these feelings are aroused because of what the loved one is. With *agapē* it is the reverse. God's *agapē* is evoked not by what we are, but by what He is. It has its origin in the agent, not in the object. It is not that we are lovable, but that He is love. This *agapē* might be defined as a deliberate desire for the highest good of the one loved, which shows itself in sacrificial action for that person's good. That is what God did for us (Jn. iii.16). That is what He wants us to do (I Jn. iii.16). That is what He is prepared to achieve in us (Rom. v.5).[59]

[57]See the discussion of this phenomenon in 1 John in Witherington, *Letters and Homilies for Hellenized Christians,* 1:431-36.

[58]See the detailed discussion in ibid., pp. 254-60. One of the notable ways 2 Peter is like the Pastorals is in its use of Hellenistic virtue language. Our author is clearly writing at a time in which he believes it is still possible for Christians to be good citizens and model some of the widely accepted virtues of the Greco-Roman culture, while also modeling the distinctively Christlike traits.

[59]Green, *2 Peter,* p. 71.

This conclusion must be tempered somewhat since *agapē* is used in the LXX even for sexual love, as in Song of Songs (e.g., Song 1:7). There is, then, more overlap in these terms, particularly between *agapē* and brotherly love, than one might expect. The borrowing from pagan virtue lists bespeaks a desire to use the language of the common culture of the audience, but also makes clear that "Christian ethics cannot be totally discontinuous with the moral ideals of non-Christian society."[60] Nevertheless, here they are invested with Christian context and content.

Second Peter 1:8 makes clear that Christians are not only to have these virtues; they are also to increase in them. They must not regard these virtues as static qualities or permanent possessions once given. The Christian life of witness, insists our author, leads neither to idleness nor fruitlessness (perhaps a litotes, a way of affirming something by negating its opposite, here using two terms for emphasis). This verse's point is that the believer's initial knowledge *(epignōsis)* of Christ leads not to indolence but to activity, not to spiritual bareness but to a fruitful life of Christian virtue (as exhibited in the qualities/activities listed in 2 Pet 1:5-7).

It is not sufficient to simply have an initial knowledge (or experience) of Christ. Without Christian virtue and behavior, **2 Peter 1:9** stresses, a person is *typhlos, myōpazōn*.[61] It is not clear whether these are two ways to say the same thing or not. The former word normally means "blind" and the latter "nearsighted"; but in Asiatic rhetoric it is typical to be redundant, saying the same thing in two slightly different ways. On the surface of it, these terms might seem to contradict one another. As Green says, "If a man is blind, how can he be short-sighted?" Presumably what is meant is that a man is blind to spiritual or heavenly things, because he is so shortsighted as to focus on earthly things. "This makes excellent sense in view of the immorality and earthiness of the false teachers."[62]

Mayor also points out that *myōpazōn* does not in itself imply willful blindness.[63] It has the basic sense of squinting to block out the bright light. To deny the need for a virtuous life and progressive sanctification is to be oblivious to the cleansing that took place at the point of one's conversion—cleansing of the effects of one's preconversion sins. This is probably not a reference here to the

---

[60]Bauckham, *Jude, 2 Peter,* p. 187.

[61]Here is another one of the those telltale passages that reveals the oral and rhetorical character of the document: here we have a Greek phrase in trochaic tetrameter, which may suggest that it was borrowed from some popular poem or quote.

[62]Green, *2 Peter,* p. 72.

[63]Mayor, *Jude, 2 Peter,* p. 96.

effect of water baptism, but rather to the effect of regeneration spoken of in "baptismal" language, as is so frequent in the New Testament.[64] The false teachers (of 2 Pet 2) possibly assume that the freedom they have in God's grace is freedom to do as they please.[65] This is to ignore the fact that God's converting grace is intended to save and cleanse the believer from sin, not to save them so they can sin all the more without fear of judgment or with impunity.

Second Peter 1:10 makes quite clear how our author views the matter of election and human responsibility. A person cannot sit around after conversion, resting on God's laurels, and assume "once saved, always saved," regardless of one's postconversion conduct. Rather, the author says, believers must strive to make their calling and election firm or steadfast, in other words, to make it stand up. *Spoudasate* carries the sense of making every effort, being exceedingly zealous and the like, picking up the same idea from 2 Peter 1:5. As Galatians 5:21 stresses, the ethical fruits of election (Gal 5:22-23) are necessary not only to prove or demonstrate one's election and calling, but also to obtain final salvation. Green says rightly:

> So here, election comes from God alone—but man's behaviour is the proof or disproof of it. Though "good works" (gratuitously read here by some mss.) are possible only through the appropriation of God's gracious aid, they are absolutely necessary, and fairly and squarely our responsibility. Hence the use of the middle voice, *poieisthai*, "make sure for yourself." Christian calling and Christian living go together. It seems that the false teachers boasted of their divine calling and election, while making an "excuse for every kind of license, as though they had permission to sin with impunity because they are predestined to righteousness" (Calvin).[66]

Only by such working out of our salvation do believers make their election steadfast, certain, sure. **Second Peter 1:10b** simply stresses that a person who is working out his salvation will not ever stumble so as to fall, that is, to fail to see the goal of final salvation. Here the author is probably not referring to some immunity to sinning even for those who are zealously striving to be immune, but he is talking about an assurance that they will not ultimately lose out on eschatological salvation *if* they are making their calling and election firm. Even with all such efforts, according to **2 Peter 1:11**, the eternal kingdom (here as something we enter at the last day) is still to be understood as something God gives

[64]See Ben Witherington III, *Troubled Waters: Rethinking the Theology of Baptism* (Waco: Baylor University Press, 2007).

[65]See Moo, *2 Peter, Jude,* p.48.

[66]Green, *2 Peter,* p. 74.

believers in the end out of his grace (richly afforded).[67] Christian behavior is a necessary but not sufficient condition to enter that kingdom, to obtain final salvation. It is necessary because in a negative sense, without Christian living we shall not obtain it, but insufficient because we will still fall short of the goal without God's grace and mercy being added to even our best efforts. The word *eisodos* (entrance) is the opposite of "exodus" and refers to a triumphal entry into the kingdom of Jesus, at the eschaton. It is even translated "welcome" in the NIV. This seems to be a reference to the messianic kingdom that precedes the final kingdom of God on earth (cf., e.g., 1 Cor 15; Rev 20; Mt 13:41; 16:28; Lk 1:33; 22:29-30; 23:42; Jn 18:36; Col 1:13; 2 Tim 4:1, 18; Heb 1:8; Rev 11:15).[68] It is clear enough that our author reflects the same sort of eschatology that eagerly looks forward to the parousia, just what we find in the earliest New Testament material in Paul's letters. It is the false teachers, not our author, who feel as though the clock has run out on such hopes in the latter part of the first century A.D. The Asiatic and redundant nature of the phrasing here is made clear in the translation by Hillyer: "The entry for you will be richly abundantly supplied."[69]

Bauckham adds:

> In this passage the author provides a kind of miniature "farewell sermon" of Peter's, summarizing Peter's definite teaching as he would wish it to be remembered after his death. Although the substance of the passage is no doubt faithful to the historical Peter's message, its form and terminology must be attributed to the author, whose distinctive way of expressing the Christian faith is very evident in these verses. Following the path already pioneered by Hellenistic Judaism, he employs Hellenistic religious ideas and language to interpret the gospel in terms appropriate to his Hellenistic environment. At the same time he gives these borrowings a definitely Christian context which determines their meaning.[70]

We must now turn to the actual testimony section of the letter, which not merely summarizes Peter's eternal exhortations to Christians, but also offers us his eyewitness reflections as spoken or written by Peter and adopted and adapted here by our author, with very little touching up.

2 Peter 1:12-21—Lively Testimony from a Dead Apostle

> There used to be many people who thought that this letter was not written by Peter. But it is enough to read this verse [2 Pet 1:17], and you will soon see that it was

[67]Noting here the passive form of the verb "be provided." See Harrington, *Jude and 2 Peter,* p. 246.
[68]Ibid.
[69]Hillyer, *1 and 2 Peter,* p. 169. Cf. Heb 10:19 on the entrance.
[70]Bauckham, *Jude, 2 Peter,* p. 192.

Peter who stood with Jesus on the mount of transfiguration. It is therefore the same Peter who heard the voice testifying to the Lord who wrote this letter. (Gregory the Great [*Sermons on Ezekiel* 2.6.11])

The prophets heard God speaking to them in the secret recesses of their own hearts. They simply conveyed that message by their preaching and writing to God's people. They were not like pagan oracles, which distorted the divine message in their own interest, for they did not write their own words but the words of God. For this reason the reader cannot interpret them by himself, because he is liable to depart from the true meaning, but rather he must wait to hear how the One who wrote the words wants them to be understood. . . . Some interpret Peter's words to mean that the Spirit inspired the prophets in much the same way as the flutist blows into his flute, so that the latter were no more than mechanical instruments in God's hands, saying what the Spirit told them to say without necessarily understanding or believing it themselves. This is ridiculous. For how could prophets have given such good counsel to people if they did not know what they were saying? Are prophets not also called seers? How could a prophet possibly have communicated what he saw in secret heavenly visions to a wider audience if he did not fully grasp what it was that he had seen? (Bede [*On 2 Peter*])[71]

If we ask why our author has chosen this bit of Petrine material found in 2 Peter 1:12-21 for his discourse, the answer is not far to seek. The false teachers are denying the parousia, and so our author trots out a tradition that not only has the great apostle speaking of the coming parousia, but also actually presents him as an eyewitness to the great parousia preview that transpired during Jesus' ministry: the transfiguration of Jesus. Peter thus is an eyewitness to this preview and can prophetically speak about its sequel, which he begins to do at the end of this testimony, and we will find further eschatological reflections in detail in 2 Peter 3.

Why not recount the appearance of the risen Jesus to Peter (see Lk 24:34)? The answer is quite simple: our author wants to foreshadow the return of Christ for judgment, in particular for judgment on the false teachers, and resurrection is about the beginning of Jesus' leaving, not a foreshadowing of his return for judgment. Thus we have here only a brief allusion to the appearance of Jesus to Peter in John 21, followed by the recounting of Peter's reflections on the transfiguration. But there is another point as well. At the transfiguration we have the figures of Moses and Elijah, and many in early Judaism believed that both of them were taken up into heaven miraculously. Thus we have a chain of prophetic witness to Jesus from both Old Testament history and New Testament his-

[71]PL 93:73-74.

tory. Peter is presented as a prophetic figure pointing to Christ, just as the Old Testament prophets were viewed as doing. There are true prophets and false prophets, true teachers and false teachers, and Peter is being ranked with the true leaders just as the false teachers will be compared with the false ones. This is said to be a reminder, and so the audience is being nudged in the direction of praising the good prophets and teachers who point to Christ and blaming the false ones who do not.

Yet there is the additional reason for choosing this fragment: it appears to be Peter's last words to other Christians. "Final words are very important, carefully chosen, not to be forgotten."[72] This is all the more the case when we are dealing with genuine last words, not just a fictive testament masked as someone's last words. But why were these words so important to our author at his time of writing in the 90s A.D.? The answer is not hard to find: "Tradition has replaced the living voice, and the legacy of the past must be preserved. This urgent need put pressure on the church to choose its leadership carefully, to teach its membership thoroughly, and to define 'the true faith' precisely."[73] Just so, and if we can judge by the length of the treatment of false teachers in 2 Peter 2, our author believes that the church is facing a leadership crisis in his day, and there is a danger of losing the essence and character of the apostolic teaching due to the influence of false teaching.

Our author responds to this crisis by dusting off a piece of Petrine tradition, a piece of material from Jude, the Lord's brother, and also alludes to the Pauline tradition, which needs to be properly interpreted as well, weaving these things together, like a student using excellent sources and putting together a good term paper. "Obviously, the author is not an advocate of the church's continual reassessment and reinterpretation of the positions held by a previous generation. The apostolic tradition is for him a package of truth to be handed on."[74]

And make no mistake about it: to good rhetorical effect our author will make a truth-versus-myth contrast, with the myths being said to be the character of the false teaching, and the truth being the character of the apostolic tradition. Nothing less is at stake. And he will trot out a threefold cord of testimony: Peter's, the Old Testament's, and the Holy Spirit's; all three bear witness to the truth of the apostolic tradition. Our author clearly thinks, as did Peter, that he lives in dark days, and that the apostolic tradition is a lamp to guide the church in transition along the way as it walks carefully into the postapostolic era. It is

[72]Craddock, *First and Second Peter,* p. 103.
[73]Ibid., p. 102.
[74]Ibid., p. 104.

certainly hard for us, in an age where innovation and change is so highly valued, to enter into the mindset of a culture where tradition was much more highly valued than it is today, and innovation and change, especially in religion was viewed with great suspicion. If a religion was not ancient, with a hoary pedigree, it qualified as a *superstitio*, something to be looked at with great skepticism.[75] In his rhetoric our author is able to play off of this cultural dynamic by setting forth the apostolic tradition and contrasting it with the innovations of the false teachers.

But we must ask once more: Here in the second half of 2 Peter 1, are we actually dealing with a Petrine fragment? Elsewhere I have argued this case at some length, but here it is necessary to review the data. First of all, one should review the data presented in the introduction.[76] In addition to that evidence, we note the following points: (1) Notice the similarities between 1 Peter 1:10-12 and 2 Peter 1:21. (2) Mayor rightly compares the discussion of the will of God found in 2 Peter 1:21 and 1 Peter 2:15; 3:17; 4:2, 19. (3) Mayor also compares 2 Peter 1:16 to 1 Peter 1:12.[77] What is important about the comparisons previously listed and those mentioned here is that six times as many differences in vocabulary appear as do similarities between 1 and 2 Peter,[78] and many of these similarities in wording are clustered in the segment 2 Peter 1:12-21. There are approximately 85 nouns, verbs, adjectives and adverbs in our segment (not counting the verb "to be" in its various forms or pronouns). If we eliminate mundane ones (words that occur more than 250 times in the New Testament), we are down to about 60 words. If we eliminate the familiar phrase "our Lord Jesus Christ," which occurs twice in this section, then we are down to about 50 words. Of these 50 words, 18 from this small section receive significant use in 1 Peter. But there is more. Of the some 57 hapax legomena in 2 Peter, only five are found in our segment, and they all occur in 2 Peter 1:19-20 with one exception (***hekastote*** in 2 Pet 1:15, though it is a variant of the common word ***tote***). The specific subject matter accounts for some of this in 2 Peter 1:19-20. What is absent from this segment is just as noteworthy. Here we do not find the long convoluted sentences that characterize Asiatic style at its most florid. Rather, the style here is more like what we find in 1 Peter, which involves what I would call restrained Asianism. Since we have already made the case that 1 Peter comes from the mind and heart of Peter,[79] the similarities we have noted be-

[75]Neyrey, *2 Peter, Jude,* p. 166.
[76]See pp. 264-65 above.
[77]Mayor, *Jude, 2 Peter,* p. lxix.
[78]Ibid., p. lxxiv.
[79]See pp. 270-74 above.

tween this section and 1 Peter are sufficient to warrant the conclusion that the person largely responsible for 1 Peter could certainly have penned 2 Peter 1:12-21 as well.[80]

Nevertheless, we are still not yet out of the woods. Could 2 Peter in general and 2 Peter 1:12-21 in particular really be a fictitious testament cleverly disguised and presented here? The first question to be asked is this: Does 2 Peter really read like the fictitious *Testaments of the Twelve Patriarchs,* where the baton is passed to the next generation, leaving them with the final wisdom of the dying man? The answer to this question is that while 2 Peter has some similarities with such stories, the differences from them outweigh the similarities. In those *Testaments* there is always a specific group of people, sons and/or future leaders of God's people, to whom the legacy is being passed. The classic biblical example of the testament genre is Jacob's in Genesis 49:1-28. In the fictive and much later *Testaments*, the great patriarch, be it Jacob or someone else, is directly bequeathing a testimony to the next generation of leaders. But in 2 Peter we have no mention at all of leaders or future leaders, unless one counts the false teachers, and they are hardly candidates to whom Peter would hand over his legacy. Nor is there any mention of Peter's offspring in 2 Peter. Further, unlike in 1 Peter, the author of 2 Peter knows that he is not simply writing to Peter's converts here. Rather, this document is written to "all of you," so that what gives the discourse clout and authority is not the personal relationship of Peter with this particular audience of the apostle's converts, but rather the generally apostolic character of the teaching and the apostolic credentials of Peter himself.

Lets take two other features that Richard J. Bauckham and others say characterize the testament genre: ethical exhortations and revelations or prophecies about the future.[81] Though it is certainly true that these features do often show up in such fictional testaments, neither of these items are testament-specific and send a genre signal in and of themselves. Only a moment's reflection on an obviously authentic letter of Paul, such as Philippians, will make our point: (1) We have ethical exhortations aplenty in this letter. (2) We find the usual eschatological discussion and future orientation as well. And (3) we actually also have reflections on Paul's coming demise, or possible demise. Does this make Philippians a fictional last will and testament? No, it does not, not least because Paul is still alive, and even more to the point, these features regularly occur in nontestamentary literature.[82]

[80]See especially, Boobyer, "Indebtedness of 2 Peter to 1 Peter," pp. 44-51.
[81]Bauckham, *Jude, 2 Peter,* pp. 133-35.
[82]A few scholars think Philippians is not by Paul, but they are in a distinct minority.

And furthermore, what does characterize the prophetic material in those fictional *Testaments of the Twelve Patriarchs* is that revelations are received through dreams or visions. There is no recounting of dreams in 2 Peter, and unless one says that 2 Peter 1:16-18 recounts a vision, we have none of them in 2 Peter either. Bauckham finds the features of the testament in 2 Peter 1:3-15, 2:1-3a and 3:1-4, but when we come to the actual eyewitness testimony in 2 Peter 1:16-18, he does not single out this segment as reflecting that genre.[83] Yet it is the one segment that involves an actual recounting of an eyewitness experience. Even more telling is the fact that Bauckham admits that other large parts of 2 Peter do not reflect the testamentary genre's features: the bulk of 2 Peter 2–3 (he cites the apologetic material in 2 Pet 2:3b-22; 3:5-10, 16b). He admits this because there the epistle speaks of the false teachers in the present tense, not as future foes. "In other words the convention of prediction, necessary in a testament, is not maintained but alternates with passages in which it is abandoned."[84] Bauckham rightly rejects the suggestion that our author is just being sloppy or careless and concludes that he is intentionally breaking with the conventions. In other words, 2 Peter as a whole *cannot* be seen as a testament, and it is not seen that way even by its strongest advocates. And I add that precisely the juxtaposition of present and future language about the same subject in 2 Peter suggests that our author is actually using a Petrine testimony, just as he is using older material from Jude to make his case.

Furthermore, as Charles says, how can Bauckham and others be so sure that the pseudepigraphic quality of this document would have been so apparent to the audience *by its very nature or character?*[85] Why did the later assessment of 2 Peter by the church fathers not include a discussion of the option that it might be a fictive testament? There are no answers forthcoming to these questions, and since 2 Peter has no specific fictive audience for this testament, other signs of pseudonymity here are also lacking.

Just how convoluted the logic can become can be seen by reading the article by Joseph Zmijewski in which he argues that because our author was "making present" the apostolic tradition, he could legitimately claim apostolic authority, presumably for himself, or at least for his document.[86] There are two problems with this: (1) If he was claiming such authority for himself, then why is he hiding behind Peter's name in 2 Peter 1:1? He could have written in his own name but

[83]Bauckham, *Jude, 2 Peter,* pp. 132-34.
[84]Ibid., p. 134.
[85]See Charles, *Virtue Amidst Vice,* pp. 50-51.
[86]Zmijewski, "Apostolische Paradosis und Pseudepigraphie," pp. 161-71.

quoted earlier sources, as Clement does with Pauline material. (2) We do not need the literary fiction of either a fictive testament or a pseudepigraphon to make present the apostolic tradition. This was done all the time by the church fathers, who simply quoted the apostolic sources. The further one probes the notion of a fictive testament in a pseudepigraphon, the less probative value the argument seems to have. Finally, Neyrey is forced to admit: "Formal analysis of the regular elements of a testament or farewell address has proved difficult to establish because of the variety of examples available to us."[87] That is, there is no set pattern. But when Neyrey tries to boil things down to four or five characterizing features, one of them is the giving of a commission or charge to one's successors or children or future leaders. But there is absolutely nothing like this either stated or implied in 2 Peter. Our author is not commissioning anyone: he is simply praising and passing on the apostolic tradition, including the testimony of Peter, and contrasting all of that with the false teachers and their message.[88]

One more factor worth mentioning is brought up by Douglas Moo. As Moo points out, the *Testaments of the Twelve Patriarchs* are documents written between 200 B.C. and 200 or so A.D. In other words, they were written long after these patriarchs had been dead, indeed millennia later! Second Peter on any dating is not written that many decades later than the lifetime of Peter. There was indeed a danger that this document, if pseudonymous, would deceive various early Christians, and indeed would be seen as attempting to do so because of the short time span between when Peter died and when this was likely written (at most perhaps 30 years after Peter's death).[89] This being the case, it seems far more plausible to argue that this is a composite document that includes a Petrine fragment near the outset of the discourse, which led to it being named after its most famous contributor.

We need to consider another point as well. There does not appear to be a single other good candidate within the corpus of the New Testament that meets all the criteria for being a pseudonymous document, as we have pointed out in this series at length in our studying of all the New Testament books most often thought to be pseudonymous (the Pastorals and some of the General Epistles).[90] Is 2 Peter the odd book out? This is possible, but it would have to be demon-

---

[87]Neyrey, *2 Peter, Jude*, pp. 163-64.

[88]Equally unhelpful is Neyrey's (ibid., p. 164) honor-and-shame analysis of our passage, where he suggests that the revelation to Peter of his imminent death (2 Pet 1:14) is a benefaction from Christ! How exactly is news of one's coming demise a benefaction?

[89]Moo, *2 Peter, Jude*, pp. 64-65.

[90]See the discussion on pseudonymity in the introduction to Witherington, *Letters and Homilies for Hellenized Christians*, 1:23-38; and the prolegomena material to each document studied in ibid. and in Witherington, *Letters and Homilies for Jewish Christians*.

strated with a more viable thesis than the fictive testament idea. We must conclude from this discussion: Though 2 Peter has some features similar to those we find in fictive testaments, so much of 2 Peter does not match up with such testaments that the hypothesis does not work as an explanation of either the genre or character of 2 Peter as a whole. Furthermore, as Moo points out, no one has shown any substantive evidence for epistolary testaments either (testaments presented in the context of an epistle).[91] But there is plenty of evidence for eyewitness testimonies cited within an epideictic oration, as even a glance at some of Demosthenes' or Cicero's funeral oratory will show. I submit that what we have here is a testimony of the deceased incorporated into the larger whole of this epideictic discourse.

At this point I need to say a few things about such orations. Epideictic oratory, as its very name implies (the word *epideiktikē* means "display"), is rhetoric meant to impress the audience with its verbal pyrotechnics. Long words, new words, impressive phrases, alliterative phrases, strong rhythms and even rhymes characterize this rhetoric, and this was especially the case with Asiatic rhetoric. But in Roman oratory there needed to be a practical function for such rhetoric, beyond trying to impress someone with mere verbal eloquence or entertain someone with the same. This is why the Romans adopted this style of rhetoric for funeral oratory, as Quintilian (*Inst.* 3.7.1-4) tells us plainly. It continued to be the rhetoric of praise and blame, and often it was the rhetoric of praise when it came to the deceased, and blame when it was dealing with the living. This is precisely what we see in 2 Peter. The great apostle, other deceased apostles and indeed the apostolic tradition in general are being praised and commended, while living false teachers are coming in for some heavy weather. "The proper function of panegyric . . . is to amplify and embellish its themes" (Quintilian *Inst.* 3.7.6).

Proofs were not required in such rhetoric, but one of the major themes of such rhetoric was to praise those who were born immortal or "others because they won immortality by their valour, a theme which the piety of our sovereign has made the glory even of these present times" (Quintilian *Inst.* 3.8.9). There are two quite striking things about what Quintilian says here: (1) He is writing in the 90s and talking about how Domitian has deified his father, Vespasian, and his brother Titus. In other words, he is talking about the emperor cult. But (2) our author, writing in the selfsame period, has just brought up the praise of becoming partakers in the divine nature, and now he is recounting an eyewitness testimony about the honor and glory given to Jesus by God himself at the transfiguration, and by implication the honoring of Peter and the disciples who

[91]Moo, *2 Peter, Jude*, pp. 24-25.

were allowed to partake in that experience, which has authorized them to speak about receiving such glory and even partaking in the divine nature. In other words, our author is telling his audience that for information on how mortals may become sharers in the divine nature, they should look to Jesus and their Christian faith, not to the emperor cult. The subject of glorification coming from God downward is used to replace the notion of divination or apotheosis, as humans overreach and anoint themselves as divine. In other words, there are some implicit polemics even here in the 2 Peter 1 testimony section.

One of the things on which Quintilian insists in an epideictic speech involving a testimony from the deceased that presents him in a praiseworthy light is that "in the case of the dead, *we must distinguish the period following their death*" (Quintilian *Inst.* 3.7.10, emphasis added). I submit that this may explain why, when we hear the voice of Peter, one thing is happening; but when we hear the voice of our author, another thing is happening as we talk about time frame of the false ones. Our author is preserving the integrity of his source by quoting it in its original time frame, making clear that the current era is to be distinguished from the age in which Peter lived. Quintilian goes on to say that when an orator is praising the deceased, even if indirectly, one needs to pick some deed he did or experience he had that "our hero was the first or only man or at any rate one of the very few to perform" (Quintilian *Inst.* 3.7.16). Here is a striking parallel: more than being a witness to the resurrection, witnessing the transfiguration qualifies here because only three disciples saw it, but many saw the risen Lord. The transfiguration not only makes clear the special character of Jesus; it also makes clear the praiseworthy character of Peter, though not focusing directly on Peter. This is a quite skillful example of what Plutarch was to call "inoffensive self-praise."[92] Thus, Peter's witness to the Son of God, like God's own testimony to his Son, is to be listened to, and this is in stark contrast to the testimony of the current false leaders, who are like other false ones in the past. The comparison by contrast between the apostolic testimony and the false teacher's testimony is being set up quite nicely here. And yes, Quintilian says that contrasting a praise with a blame should be done in stark terms, such that the ones denounced should be presented as cowards or debauchees or a curse to those whose lives they influence (Quintilian *Inst.* 3.7.19-21). Darkness makes the light seem brighter. Thus, by this testimony our author sets up the subsequent polemics in 2 Peter 2. Finally, eyewitness testimony and personal experience were the first among the proofs when one was making a rhetorical argu-

[92]On which see Ben Witherington III, *Conflict and Community in Corinth* (Grand Rapids: Eerdmans, 1996), pp. 432-37.

ment (Anaximenes *Rhet. Alex.* 36.1442b.37). Our author knows how to lead from strength as he sets before his audience's eyes the things that are first praiseworthy, and then the things that are blameworthy in the present.

> [1:12]*Therefore I mean to always remind you about these things, although you know*
> *(them) and have been confirmed (established) in the truth that is present with you*
> *(or has come to you).* [13]*But I think it right as long as I am in this tent, to wake you*
> *up by a reminder,* [14]*knowing that it will soon be time to divest myself of my tent, just*
> *as also (even) our Lord, Jesus Christ, showed me.* [15]*But I will make every effort that*
> *after my exodus (departure) you may bear in mind these things on each occasion*
> *(necessary).*
>
> [16]*For we have not followed cleverly concocted myths (when) we made known to*
> *you the power and parousia of our Lord, Jesus Christ, but we have been made eye-*
> *witnesses of his majesty.* [17]*For he received from God the Father honor and glory*
> *when a voice came to him such as that from the Majestic Glory (God); "This is my*
> *Son, my Beloved, in whom I am well pleased."* [18]*And we ourselves were hearing this*
> *voice, which came from heaven, being with him on the holy mountain.* [19]*And we*
> *with very great certainty (reliance) have the prophetic word, which you do well to*
> *heed as a light shining in a dark place, until the day dawns and the daystar rises*
> *in your hearts.* [20]*Understand this first (or above all), that all prophecy of Scripture is*
> *not a matter of one's own interpretation,* [21]*for it was not ever brought about by the*
> *will of a human being, but by being carried by the Holy Spirit, human beings spoke*
> *from God.*

We have suggested that beginning at **2 Peter 1:12** Linus (?) has drawn on Peter's actual testimony given shortly before he died. It is probable he has only used part of it due to the necessities of confining himself to the size of a papyrus letter. Nonetheless, he has made certain effort to make the transition smooth. Thus, verse 12 begins with *dio,* "therefore." In its present context it refers to the summary made by our author of the typical Petrine ethical exhortation found in 2 Peter 1:3-11. In its original context it may have referred to a similar message or a different one; we do not know which. In fact, the *dio* may well be part of the original testimony (cf. 1 Pet 1:13 for an example of Peter's use of it). We may picture Peter as facing his demise and being concerned over how false teachers in the church are disturbing it. He wishes to remind them of what they have already heard, a message on what the Christian life ought to be like, and so wake them up to the dangers they face from a teaching that undermines their faith once received. Our author has made this possible by including the condensed and transformed message in 2 Peter 1:3-11 of the apostle's typical message. As we shall see, this will account for certain peculiarities in our passage.

Mellēsō is a future verb (I will be . . .). But how can Peter be "always" reminding them if he is about to die? The answer to this perplexing question is that he may well have provided a means in writing to serve as that ongoing reminder: his own testimony. The audience, knowing that Peter has died, will recognize the testimony form and treat it as such. Does this mean that they will deduce it to be a literary fiction, as Bauckham argues? This is by no means certain or necessary. People did leave real testaments and testimonies in New Testament times (cf. Acts 20, etc.) and it is doubtful that the author or audience would have seen this as a mere literary device to make it possible to speak with apostolic authority to a later age.

For one thing, the language of 2 Peter 1:12-21 is sufficiently different from 2 Peter 1:3-11 that for those who know Asiatic Greek, the style change is apparent. Here we have another hand and style. In all likelihood the audience will recognize this as a real testimony or testament from their beloved departed, Peter. Second Peter 1:15 indeed indicates that Peter, as is likely, would make after-his-death provision for the ongoing needs of the churches he addresses in 1 Peter. By having someone write to them to remind them once he is gone, Peter has made sure to provide for these churches after his death, so that they will remember his teaching. The discourse that they have now received here will serve that very purpose, on any and every necessary occasion. The word "remind" is important, because in its Christian context it means more than bear in mind: it also implies a required heeding of apostolic teaching given at an earlier occasion (perhaps at conversion). Further, it may imply that Peter is reminding them of what he said in 1 Peter (hence the 18 words shared with 1 Peter might ring a bell in this way). Neyrey rightly stresses that in a culture honoring the past and tradition and talking a lot about the "good old days" or the golden eras of the past, what is older is valued much more than what is new. So Peter once more is presenting the old story of the transfiguration as a sacred tale from the past, and not incidentally, a tale with which Peter was involved as an eyewitness.[93]

Verse 12 suggests that they have already been established in the truth that has come to them, and this is probably not just politeness on Peter's part. They have indeed received all the know-how that is necessary for godliness (2 Pet 1:3). However, they must act on that knowledge lest their foundation become shaky (2 Pet 2:14). Bauckham says: "Here it means that the readers are well grounded in the Christian faith, instructed in it, firmly committed to it, and therefore not likely to be easily misled by false teaching. Of course, the communities included those who were coming under the influence of the false teachers and

[93]Neyrey, *2 Peter, Jude*, pp. 166-67.

who could therefore be described as 'unstable' (2:14), while the whole letter shows the writer's concern that his readers should not 'lose their stability.' So there is probably an element of hopefulness in the description of them in this verse."[94]

Second Peter 1:13 essentially indicates that Peter feels it to be his apostolic responsibility to remind them of that proper foundation for Christian living, as long as he is living and indeed beyond (2 Pet 1:15). The last part of this verse literally says, "as long as I am in this tent." Though this may be an allusion to the "sojourners" language of 1 Peter 2:11, more likely Peter is drawing on a common image of the body as a somewhat flimsy and mobile outer shell of the human personality, or perhaps he is even thinking of what Paul said about his own departure in 2 Corinthians 5:1-4 (cf. *4 Bar.* 6:6-7). In 1 Peter we did see evidence that Peter knew and was definitely influenced by some of Paul's letters and thoughts, unlike the author of 2 Peter, who shows little influence from Paul. Not only the reference to the body as a tent, but also in 2 Peter 1:14 the "putting off" (language used for taking off clothes) of it seems to recall 2 Corinthians 5:1-10.[95] Peter like Paul says nothing about a body/soul dualism, but there is no doubt that some sort of body/personality or body/life dualism is here as in 2 Corinthians 5. The point in our text, however, is not to teach about such matters. Nonetheless, the words of a hymn convey the image well: "Here in the body pent, absent from Him I roam, yet nightly pitch my moving tent a day's march nearer home" (James Montgomery, "At Home in Heaven"). If this idea is in Peter's mind, then indeed 2 Corinthians 5:1-10 may be in the back of Peter's mind.

In **2 Peter 1:14** Peter says he knows that it will soon be time for him to divest himself of this tent. Here Bauckham seems right on target. *Taxinē* in all likelihood means "soon," not "suddenly." Perhaps there has been a recent prophecy of Peter's death. This is perhaps not an allusion to John 21:18-19a, though we cannot rule that out. However, as Bauckham rightly notes, the second half of 2 Peter 1:14 adds an additional reference to a prophecy by Jesus of Peter's death ("just as also Jesus showed me"), and there John 21:18 is likely in view, which implies that when Peter is old he will die by crucifixion. As Bauckham notes: "But (a) John 21:18 does indicate that Peter's martyrdom will occur when he is old, . . . and this may be sufficient indication of time to satisfy the requirements of 2 Pet 1:14. If our exegesis, according to which Peter knows that his death is imminent independently of Christ's prophecy, is correct, then the prophecy itself need not contain too precise an indication of

[94]Bauckham, *Jude, 2 Peter,* p. 197.
[95]Cf. Mayor, *Jude, 2 Peter,* p. 101; Kelly, *Epistles of Peter,* p. 313.

time. (b) John 21:18 is too obscure and ambiguous as a reference to Peter's martyrdom for it to be a *post eventum* prophecy, . . . and therefore it cannot be the creation of the author of John 21."[96]

Some have taken **2 Peter 1:15** as an allusion to Peter's missionary work and his being a source for Mark's Gospel; however, one can only hold such a view if either Peter wrote this whole letter personally (which he likely did not), or the whole letter is a pseudepigraphon (which it likely is not).[97] In any case the Gospel of Mark is hardly apposite here, but Peter's ethical exhortations are.[98] The most likely view is that 2 Peter 1:15 refers to Peter making every effort to ensure that his testimony is written down and conveyed to the same audience that received 1 Peter, and in addition to a much wider audience, as things turned out. In this he succeeded, and no doubt this discourse had a special poignancy for those who did receive it after Peter's death, and heard his words speak to them after he had met a violent end.[99] Here Peter's talking about his own "exodus" or departure connects with at least one tradition of the transfiguration story. Luke 9:31 uses the exact same word *exodos* to describe what Moses and Elijah are talking to Jesus about during the transfiguration experience (cf. Wis 3:2 and 7:6, also using it of death; and especially Josephus *Ant.* 4.189, where Moses in his farewell message uses this term).

There is a remarkable tradition found in the much later apocryphal document called the *Acts of Peter*, in which Peter has a *quo vadis* experience. The legend relates that as Peter is leaving Rome to escape arrest by Nero's men, he is met and confronted on the road by Jesus himself. Peter asks Jesus, "Where are you going?" (Latin, "*Quo vadis*"). Jesus replies that he is going into Rome to be crucified again. Peter thus turns back and submits to crucifixion. We can date this story no earlier than about A.D. 180, and so we really cannot see this as the backdrop to these verses in 2 Peter, but it shows the trajectory of one way the Petrine tradition could go when not constrained by historical evidence.[100]

Second Peter 1:16, as Bauckham indicates, begins Peter's defense of the gospel he has preached to his hearers. He does not accuse the opponents of following myths, but he does rebut the charge that he has done so. The "we" no doubt refers to the apostle(s), presumably those who have preached in or

---

[96]Bauckham, *Jude, 2 Peter,* p. 200.

[97]See Mayor, *Jude, 2 Peter,* pp. cxlii-cxliv.

[98]At 2 Pet 1:15, P^{72} has "I am making every effort," and Hillyer, *1 and 2 Peter,* p. 173, sees this as a point in favor of it referring to Mark being able to remember these things. The first church father known to think that this verse alluded to Mark was Irenaeus (*Haer.* 3.1.1).

[99]Harrington, *Jude and 2 Peter,* p. 15.

[100]See Moo, *2 Peter, Jude,* pp. 62-63.

written to the churches in Asia Minor.

What was a myth in New Testament times? What did the term mean? The old Greek myths, the stories about the gods, could be seen as stories that were not literally true but expressed religious, moral or philosophical truth in pictorial form. They could be subjected to allegorical interpretation, as by the Stoics. In many respects the Hellenistic age showed a "growing preference for . . . [myth] over . . . [rational argument] as a means of expressing truth. . . . On the other hand, there was a strong tradition of criticism and repudiation of myths, as morally unedifying, or as childish, nonsensical or fabulous. Here *mythos* can come, like 'myth' in much modern English usage, to mean a story which is *not true*, a fable or fairy story (again in the derogatory senses)."[101]

In short, a "myth" was something not grounded in history, though it may have some philosophical or moral truth content (cf. 1 Tim 1:4; 2 Tim 4:4; Josephus *Ant.* 1.22).[102] Diodorus Siculus (1.2.2) puts it this way: "For it is true that the myths which are related about Hades, in spite of the fact that their subject matter is fictitious, contribute greatly to fostering piety and justice among human beings."

Peter sets about the task to refute the idea that there would be no future parousia and judgment in space and time. These false teachers, perhaps not unlike the problem in Corinth (cf. 1 Cor 15: "How can some of you say there is no resurrection from the dead?"), apparently see Christianity as a matter of totally realized eschatology: the resurrection or new life is seen as either what has happened at baptism or perhaps present spiritual life is constituted by ecstatic experiences leading to (false) prophecy. Peter uses the word *sesophismenos,* which indicates that the opponents think such stories about the parousia are clever but really fabrications of an overheated Christian mindset. In his *Republic* (2.364-66) Plato complains that tales about future divine judgment are being used by both nannies and rulers to enforce morality. This complaint is still being made much later by Epicureans like Lucretius (*Nat.* 3.966-1023). Something like this seems to be the complaint of the false teachers regarding the apostolic tradition on the parousia. As Perkins says, the word *sesophismenos* refers to something used to deceive people,[103] and it was actually used of quack doctors in antiquity.[104] On more than one occasion Philo makes the same sort of contrast we have here between a "myth" and a sacred oracle or testimony (*Fug.* 121, 152), using the formula "not a myth invented . . . but a sacred oracle."

[101]Bauckham, *Jude, 2 Peter,* p. 213.

[102]For the pejorative use of the term "myth" in Greek inscriptions, see Barrett, "Myth and the New Testament," pp. 345-48.

[103]Perkins, *First and Second Peter,* p. 173.

[104]See Hillyer, *1 and 2 Peter,* p. 177.

One of the small indicators of the character of the rhetoric here is that while Peter uses the term "revelation" to refer to the second coming in 1 Peter, here he uses the term "parousia," or "royal arrival/visit" (see 1 Thess 2:19).[105] The emphasis here is on the appearing of the glorious king in the future as he appeared in the past on the mount of transfiguration.[106] Thus the future, like the past, is related to the present of the speaker and present issues, as is usual in epideictic rhetoric.[107]

Beginning in **1 Peter 1:16b,** Peter rebuts this charge. Not only has he not followed myths; he has also made known to his audience the power and parousia of the Lord. Probably here, as elsewhere in this discourse, we have a hendiadys meaning "powerful coming" or "coming in power" instead of two separate matters. Far from concocting myths, Peter and other apostles have been eyewitnesses of and about the transfiguration. The word *epoptai* is a crucial one, meaning literally "observers" or "spectators." It is not found elsewhere in the New Testament, but we do have its verbal cognate at 1 Peter 2:12 and 3:2, another little piece of positive evidence that we should see 2 Peter 1:12-21 as a Petrine fragment.[108] On occasion it can refer to one who has been initiated into the greatest secrets of the Eleusinian mysteries (having seen the vision of the mysteries; cf. Plutarch *Demetr.* 26.1-2). If 1 Peter 2:16c is not written by Peter, this last usage might be appropriate here since he is going to talk about the transfiguration and their seeing a preview of Christ's parousia glory. However, as Michael Green points out, we have the verbal form of this word at 1 Peter 2:12 and 3:2, and this should likely be seen as another indication of a common source behind both pieces of material.[109] Notably in 1 Peter 2:12 it refers to being witnesses/spectators of believers' good deeds, but this is connected to glorifying God at Christ's parousia, a clear connection to our present text. Further, this ter-

---

[105]On 1 Thess 2:19, see Ben Witherington III, *1 and 2 Thessalonians: A Socio-Rhetorical Commentary* (Grand Rapids: Eerdmans, 2006), pp. 91-92.

[106]See Moffatt, *General Epistles*, p. 186.

[107]The term "parousia" could also be taken as a small sign that our author has touched up the vocabulary of Peter's testimony so that it fits more smoothly into his overall presentation, since he will use the term "parousia" later to refer to Christ's second coming (see 2 Pet 3:4, 12).

[108]Not surprisingly the Jesus Seminar member Robert J. Miller, "Is There Independent Attestation for the Transfiguration in 2 Peter?" pp. 620-25, wants to answer no to his own rhetorical question, possibly seeing what we have here as based on the account in Mt 17:1-8. This hardly explains the distinctive features in our account (e.g., the phrase "Majestic Glory"), and it especially does not explain why, if the author of this is not Peter, that he did not much more exactly quote at least the divine words from heaven, which here do not match any of the Synoptic witnesses. See rightly Hillyer, *1 and 2 Peter,* p. 178. On the Matthean account, see Ben Witherington III, *The Gospel of Matthew* (Macon, Ga.: Smyth & Helwys, 2006), ad loc.

[109]See the discussion in Bauckham, *Jude, 2 Peter,* pp. 215-16.

minology is used nowhere else in the whole New Testament in any form of the word, so the connection can hardly be accidental here. We must take this as strong evidence that 2 Peter 1:12-21 is from Peter himself.

What is it that Peter has seen at the transfiguration? He says in **2 Peter 1:17** that he has seen Christ's majesty, a majesty or "glory and honor" (as descriptors of God: cf. Heb 1:3; 8:1; *T. Levi* 3:4; of humans crowned with glory and honor: cf. Ps 8:5). The term majesty or glory is regularly a cipher for the divine presence. To see Christ's glory is to see the bright divine presence in and on him. Christ had received these things from God the Father on that occasion. We are unable here to go into detail, but it appears rather clear, as Bauckham has shown at length, that this description of the transfiguration is independent of the Gospel accounts. It can either be taken as the author (if it is not Peter) relying on an independent (oral?) tradition, or an eyewitness testimony of Peter. Now the later one dates 2 Peter, the more difficult it becomes to explain this independence from the four Gospel accounts. If 2 Peter was written around A.D. 90 or later, one must ask where 2 Peter's author could have been not to have known and used the richer, fuller accounts found in the Synoptics?

All of this difficulty disappears when we see that here Peter himself is likely giving his own remembrances, which would quite naturally not conform to any secondhand formulations of the event. It is probable that we should see Psalm 2 in the background here (esp. Ps 2:7b-12), an enthronement psalm that contains the line "You are my son; today I have become your father." Now the import of this allusion to Psalm 2 is this: Peter sees in the transfiguration a depiction of Jesus being installed as eschatological King and Judge over all the earth, an office he does not assume until the parousia. It is quite probable that the Synoptic Evangelists (especially Mark) also saw the transfiguration as a foreshadowing not of resurrection or ascension, but of parousia. In Matthew 16:28 there even is a direct reference to the coming of the Son in/into his kingdom just before the transfiguration story. And interestingly, later Christian tradition also wanted to connect the transfiguration with the parousia.[110] Neyrey is even prepared to suggest that the transfiguration is viewed as a prophecy of the parousia, when Christ comes in glory and honor as the king, the Beloved Son of God. He relates this to the later *Apocalypse of Peter* tradition, where Jesus discourses on the parousia in connection with his transfiguration.[111]

Presumably, in the Gospel accounts the reason Peter wants to set up booths is because he presumes that the great and final day of eschatological celebration

---

[110]See Neyrey, "Apologetic Use of the Transfiguration," pp. 504-19.
[111]Ibid., p. 519; and see Neyrey, *2 Peter, Jude*, pp. 173-74.

is at hand (see Mk 9:5-6). If this is a correct interpretation of our text, it explains why Peter refers to the transfiguration to refute the notion that there would be no parousia. Peter is saying, "At the transfiguration, which we saw personally, Christ was given an office in token that he will not fulfill until his parousia. Therefore, there must be a parousia, or else the transfiguration was pointless." Hillyer rightly notes that the terms "honor" and "glory" do not come up in the resurrection narratives, but certainly they are apropos for both the transfiguration and the parousia.[112] Now we are prepared to examine the rest of the particulars of vss.17-18.

Second Peter 1:17b is a reverential way of avoiding two things: (1) saying that God spoke directly and (2) saying God's name. The "Majestic Glory" is simply another Semitic way of saying "God" (cf. *1 Clem.* 9.2).[113] The word *toiasde* serves the function of saying the voice was "to the following effect" (perhaps out of reverence, Peter avoids quoting the voice directly). This reverential approach to the matter makes quite clear that the author of this section was a Jewish Christian who would be likely to use such circumlocutions, which may have the use in the Psalms as a background (Ps 144:5, 12 LXX [145:5, 12 ET]).[114] Peter intends to focus only on the investiture (2 Pet 1:17a) and what the voice said (1 Pet 1:17b). The literal rendering here would be "a voice was conveyed from the Majestic Glory."[115] Unfortunately, we have a textual problem with the key phrase of the voice from heaven. Basically there are two options: (1) the text as in the latest UBS and Nestle-Aland Greek editions: "my Son, my Beloved, this is"; or (2) as in ℵ, A, C, K and a host of other manuscripts: "This is my Son, the Beloved." The problem with the second reading is that although it has good support, it appears to be an attempt to conform the text to Matthew 3:17 and 17:5.[116] Thus, reading 1 is to be preferred: "This is my Son, my Beloved." Some scholars have thought that we should combine the two phrases here and make it read, "My Beloved Son," by which was meant "my chosen Son," or "my only (unique) Son." However, there is probably sufficient evidence to suggest that "my Beloved" was actually a separate messianic title for Christ (see Eph 1:6), meaning "my Elect One." This may suggest that Peter's doctrine of election was as follows: Christ alone was and is

---

[112]Hillyer, *1 and 2 Peter,* p. 175.

[113]See *NewDocs* 2:109. Only in this Petrine testimony do we find a Semitism like "Majestic Glory." The rest of the discourse is basically free of them, another clue that a source is being used here.

[114]We have already observed how frequently 1 Peter draws on the psalms. See pp. 169-70 above.

[115]See Kuske, "Conveyed from Heaven," pp. 55-57, who argues that the translation "conveyed" best conveys the meaning here and in all four occurrences of the verb.

[116]Metzger, *TC,* pp. 700-701.

the Elect One, chosen by God according to his eternal plan. Believers are elect only insofar as they are "in him." This would mean that the language of election as applied to believers has a transferred sense and does not suggest that God arbitrarily chose some to be saved and some to be lost, quite apart from and prior to their own choice or response (cf. 1 Pet 1:1-2). They become elect when they become a part of Christ's body and partake of the divine nature. This view, however, does not fully do justice to such texts as 1 Peter 1:2, where God's choosing of believers is based on his foreknowledge. Yet we may ask, Is it foreknowledge of those who will respond and be in Christ? In my view this is likely.

The last phrase in **2 Peter 1:17c** is "with whom/in whom I am well pleased." The phrase likely means "on whom I have set my favor" (glory/honor), and Isaiah 42:1 may be its source. Richard J. Bauckham states: "The very rare construction *eis hon* . . . probably carries the sense of God's favor selecting Jesus by coming to rest on him, while the aorist indicates an act of election. Presumably the election is considered as having already occurred, in God's eternity; it is now declared at the moment of Jesus' official appointment to the task for which God has elected him."[117]

The point of this is clearly that the transfiguration and that which it foreshadows (parousia) is part of God's eternal plan involving the election of Jesus as king and judge over the world. It is thus hardly a humanly contrived myth. In **2 Peter 1:18** Peter stresses that he was with Jesus then and heard all this so that he can vouch for it personally. It happened on the holy mountain. Here we may again see an allusion to Psalm 2:6—"on Zion, my holy hill." Peter thus has cast his own experience in scriptural terms, investing it with such language to indicate that this event was a fulfillment of messianic prophecy in the Psalms. This prepares us for what follows in 2 Peter 1:19-21.

Possibly we should see **2 Peter 1:19** as an allusion to the prophetic word in Psalm 2. Peter is probably not suggesting here that Psalm 2 has greater certainty than his own personal experience, but that it has very great certainty and is something on which one can firmly rely. The prophetic word, then, is seen here as a second witness to the truth of the parousia's historicity. The debate has been as to whether Peter is saying that Scripture confirms his experience, or that the apostolic witness fulfills and thus authenticates Scripture. But the meaning "made more sure" for *bebaioteron with echomen* is doubtful. Probably we should translate the term as a superlative: "made very firm."[118]

---

[117]Bauckham, *Jude, 2 Peter*, p. 220.
[118]Watson, "2 Peter," p. 342.

Nor is there likely a comparison between the value of prophecy vis-à-vis the value of personal experience. The point rather seems to be that Peter is introducing a second and objective witness here that they can check out for themselves. The drift of the argument seems to be this: If you do not believe me, check out the Old Testament messianic prophecies, here especially Psalm 2:6. The prophetic word has unquestionable clarity and certainty: you can rely on it. Second Peter 1:19b indicates that the audience must heed this word, for it is their only light in an otherwise dark and murky world; it can guide them through the darkness as nothing else can. We must see 2 Peter 1:19c as a reference to the parousia, which causes no problems if the author says only "when the day dawns." He says that these prophetic words guide us *until then*. There is a time-conditioned element even in Scripture. To be sure, it is eternal truth, but it is only applicable in and to situations in time, and when time expires, we will no longer need a guidebook to walk through the dark: believers will have the daystar in their very hearts to illumine them (cf. 1 Cor 13:8-13: prophecy and knowledge ceases, and the general thought of Jer 31:31-34 about God's word written on the heart).

Phōsphoros means literally "light bearer" (Latin, *lucifer*) and may be a reference to the planet Venus, the daystar, which accompanies dawn. Cicero says, "Lowest of the five planets and nearest to the earth is the star of Venus, called in Greek *Phōsphoros* and in Latin *Lucifer* when it precedes the sun" (*Nat. d.* 2.20.53). However, we should not puzzle for long about it because Numbers 24:17 LXX seems to be in the background here, referring to the messiah: "A star shall rise out of Jacob." The point is that Christ on the day of parousia will illumine the believer not just from the outside in, but also from the inside out, because his day of revelation will be their day of transformation. Hence the phrase "in your hearts" is natural and understandable. It is not a reference to believers being currently and slowly illuminated by God's presence or word. Craddock puts it this way: "'In your hearts' reminds us that the day of the Lord will not only be cosmic in its immensity but also personally transforming in its effect."[119] We may wish to compare the references to Christ as morning star in Revelation 2:28 and 22:16.

Second Peter 1:20-21 expresses why we may so firmly rely on Old Testament prophecy, or why it has such great certainty. Peter says that above all his audience ought to know (is this an example of imperatival participle as in 1 Peter?). Verse 21 gives the reason for verse 20, and we will tackle it first. In **1 Peter 1:21** we actually have a short-form syllogism, otherwise known as an en-

---

[119]Craddock, *First and Second Peter*, p. 107.

thymeme, as Watson has pointed out.[120] We can outline it as follows:

> Major premise: No real prophecy simply comes from the prophet's imagination and interpretation.[121]
>
> Minor premise: Rather, all genuine prophecy like that found in the Old Testament is inspired by the Spirit.
>
> Conclusion: Those prophecies in the Old Testament about the parousia are inspired and true.

Biblical prophecy was never brought about by the will of a human being, but rather humans were borne (carried) along by the Holy Spirit and thus spoke from God. In these words we find a definition of inspiration and how the prophetic Scriptures came to be; thus we need to observe several things: First, the author insists that true prophecy never is a purely human product, resulting from mere human will. The *ou* (not) in 2 Peter 1:21a contrasts with 2 Peter 1:21b's *alla* (but). Instead, these persons were borne along, carried, compelled by the Holy Spirit so that they spoke not merely human words but "from God." The key verb here, *pherō,* can be used of the wind moving something along or driving it in a certain direction, or it can be used figuratively of God's Spirit moving or motivating human beings (cf. Job 17:1 LXX). The phrases here suggest that God is the primary author of prophetic Scripture. These prophets, though they spoke in their own words, spoke from God. What does "carried along," "borne along," "impelled," "moved" by the Holy Spirit mean? We should probably not count this as any mechanical, dictation theory. The author intends to indicate that the Holy Spirit guided and directed and motivated human authors so that what they said was not their own creation or imaginings, but the very word of God himself: the truth. Thus, the Spirit is the motivator or originator, the guide or guard of the words of the human author so that what he says can be declared to be spoken from God. Green adds:

> It is interesting that in this, perhaps the fullest and most explicit biblical reference to the inspiration of its authors, no interest should be displayed in the psychology of inspiration. The author is not concerned with what they felt like, or how much

[120]Watson, *Invention,* p. 105. An interesting side note is that we have exactly the same phrase "knowing this first" repeated at 2 Pet 3:3. It is hard to know whether this makes our author a good imitator of Petrine style, or whether we should see 2 Pet 3:1-3 as from Peter's hand as well. I favor the latter suggestion.

[121]In 𝔓[72] we have the interesting variant "every prophecy and Scripture," while a few other manuscripts have "every Scripture of prophecy" (cf. 2 Tim 3:16). On any reading of this verse, Scripture surely must mean the Old Testament here. See Harrington, *Jude and 2 Peter,* p. 257.

they understood, but simply with the fact that they were the bearers of God's message. The relative parts played by the human and the divine authors are not mentioned, but only the fact of their cooperation. He uses a fascinating maritime metaphor in verse 21. . . . The prophets raised their sails, so to speak (they were obedient and receptive), and the Holy Spirit filled them and carried their craft along in the direction He wished. Men spoke: God spoke. Any proper doctrine of Scripture will not neglect either part of this truth. Certainly those who are convinced of God's ultimate authorship of Scripture will take every pain to discover the background, life situation, limitations, education and so forth of the human agent who cooperated with God in its production. For revelation was not a matter of passive reception: it meant active cooperation. The fact of God's inspiration did not mean a supersession of the normal mental functionings of the human author. The Holy Spirit did not use instruments; He used men. God's way is ever one of truth through personality, as was perfectly demonstrated at the incarnation. Moreover, He did not use any men, but holy men, those who were dedicated and pledged to His service. And even with such men, He did no violence to their personalities, but co-operated with them while revealing Himself through them. "He says they were *moved*, not because they were out of their minds (as the heathen imagine *enthousiasmos* in their prophets), but because they dared nothing by themselves but only in obedience to the guidance of the Spirit, who held sway over their lips as in his own temple" (Calvin).[122]

So then, we should not see here an overwhelming of human nature: it is too obvious that God used human beings and their own character and characteristics to produce Scripture. Thus, biblical inspiration is to be distinguished from pagan ecstatic utterance, in which the human being is a purely passive vessel through which "the god" speaks. What Peter says comports with what the Old Testament prophets themselves say (cf. Jer 14:13; 23:16, 18, 21-22, 26; Ezek 13:3). A prophet speaks on God's initiative, not his own (Jer 20:9; Amos 3:8), and it is God's word he proclaims in his own words. "Individual ingenuity cannot solve the problems of prophecy because individual ingenuity was not the origin of prophecy; 'prophecy never came by human impulse,' by any conscious cleverness on the part of the individual."[123] Justin Martyr (*1 Apol.* 33) interprets this notion further and says that the Old Testament prophets were carried away by God "by nothing but the divine word."

If we compare what is said here with 1 Peter, however, we cannot agree that our author is simply affirming the popular notion of ecstasy = inspiration, such that the prophet is literally *ek-stasis* (standing out of) his normal state of being

[122]Green, *2 Peter*, pp. 90-91.
[123]Moffatt, *General Epistles*, p. 189.

or consciousness and wholly taken over by God's Spirit. Philo advances this theory, drawing an analogy between biblical and pagan inspiration, when he says that in inspiration the human faculty of reason is replaced by the divine Spirit, which Spirit then uses the unconscious faculties of the prophet to predict and reveal the future. The prophet thus is uttering what lies beyond his own grasp, "for the prophet utters nothing that belongs to himself; another is prompting him to utter what is beyond his own range. And it is wrong for any worthless person to be an interpreter of God, so no rascal can be divinely inspired, in the strict sense of the term; the wise alone is the echoing instrument of God, sounding forth as he is invisibly struck by God" (*Her.* 51-52; cf. Philo *Mos.* 1.283; Philo *Spec.* 1.65; Philo *Mos.* 1.281 uses Balaam to prove that God overrides the prophet's own faculties). Philo, it seems, has been too influenced by Greco-Roman notions of inspiration, and what he says stands in contrast to the Petrine tradition about such matters. Peter even depicts the prophet as having a dialogue with God about the referents of their prophecies in 1 Peter 1:10-11.

In my view what is likely going on here reflects the Greek tradition of prophecy as it is found at Delphi and other shrines. In that tradition, there is a *Pythia* (female ecstatic) who receives the divine revelation; but then it is not the Pythia but a separate person, the *prophētēs* (male prophet), who goes outside the shrine and interprets the utterance to the inquirer. Peter is saying that the role of the biblical prophet is not like that. The prophet is not in essence a mere interpreter of some other person's inspired words or even his own. He or she is the mouthpiece of God, without needing another to perform the interpreting function.[124] The later radical Jewish Christian sect called the Ebionites took the opposite view. They claimed that prophets spoke "of their own intelligence and not the truth" (see Epiphanius *Pan.* 30.1.5). This is not a totally surprising view for them, since they were so tradition-oriented that anything looking pneumatic or like a fresh revelation from God was immediately under suspicion, as is the case today with many of the less charismatic Christian traditions.

Now we must ask, What does **2 Peter 1:20** mean? *Idias* can mean either one's own or the prophet's own. *Epilyseōs*—which literally has the sense of unraveling something (Josephus *Ant.* 8.157),[125] finding a solution or explanation for

[124]See at length my discussion of Greco-Roman prophecy in *Conflict and Community in Corinth,* pp. 276-81; also Neyrey, *2 Peter, Jude,* pp. 180-81; and the helpful discussion in Moo, *2 Peter, Jude,* pp. 77-79. As Moo says, "his own" most likely refers to the prophet's own interpretation, not just anyone's (though our author would agree that those prophecies are not just "a matter of interpretation" for us either).

[125]Hillyer, *1 and 2 Peter,* p. 181, rightly notes that we find the verb cognate to this noun in Mk 4:34, referring to the unraveling and so the explaining and understanding of parables.

something—in a context like this usually means explanation or interpretation.[126] Thus the question is, Do we read "No prophecy is a matter of one's own interpretation," or "No prophecy arises from the prophet's own interpretation"? Either of these is possible. Bauckham argues for the second view:

> This conforms to a widely accepted view of the nature of prophecy, according to which the prophet is given a sign (e.g., Amos 7:1; Jer. 1:11, 13), a dream (e.g., Zech. 1:8; Dan. 7:2) or a vision (e.g., Dan. 8:1), and then its interpretation. In true prophecy this interpretation is not the prophet's own explanation of his vision, but an inspired, God-given interpretation. Thus, it is possible that 2 Pet. 1:20 counters a view which held that the prophets may have received visions, but that their prophecies, found in the Old Testament, are only their own interpretation of the visions, mere human guesswork. This was one way of denying the divine origin of scriptural prophecy.[127]

Against this, however, must be the fact that 2 Peter 1:20-21 thus comes to mean the same thing said in two ways: it is not prophetic interpretation because it is God's Spirit that caused it. This seems somewhat tautological, which is certainly possible in Asiatic rhetoric, but we would expect verse 21 to give us a real reason why it is not this sort of interpretation. More likely then, it is saying, "It is not a matter of one's own interpretation, because it derives from God and is objective truth, not subjective opinion." Neyrey rightly reminds us that we are dealing with a collectivist culture, where the group is primary, the individual secondary, and "the right of private interpretation" is not even remotely on the horizon.[128]

Mayor says:

> When St. Peter says that "it was revealed to them that not unto themselves but unto us they did minister the things now reported unto us," he does not surely mean to deny that they ministered to their own generation also, although not exclusively nor in the highest degree. The prophets never cast themselves as it were into the midst of the ocean of futurity; their view reaches over the ocean, their hearts it may be are set on the shore beyond it, but their feet are on their own land, their eyes look upon the objects of their own land; there is the first occasion of their hopes, and there lie their duties. They are prophets in both senses of the term, preachers of righteousness to their own generation, as well as foretellers of blessing for generations yet to come.[129]

---

[126] Bauckham, *Jude, 2 Peter,* pp. 230-31.
[127] Ibid., p. 230.
[128] Neyrey, *2 Peter, Jude* p. 182.
[129] Mayor, *Jude, 2 Peter,* p. 197.

Perhaps, then, Peter is refuting an argument of his opponents: "So he says there is going to be a parousia and that the Old Testament says so. Well, that's just his interpretation of the matter." Kelly says:

> Much the most natural meaning, and the one which suits the context best as well as agreeing with the lexical evidence for ***epilysis,*** is the one implied by the printed translation (so too RV; RSV; NEB; etc.), vis., that no individual is entitled to interpret prophecy, or scripture generally, according to his personal whim. It is precisely this, as we shall later see (iii.16), that the troublemakers are guilty of, and it leads in the writer's view to disaster. But if one's own interpretation is excluded, what is the approved alternative with which "Peter" contrasts it? The next verse makes this clear: it is the interpretation intended by the Holy Spirit, whose inspiration lies behind prophecy.[130]

At the end of his testimony, Peter has thus left us on the high ground: with the witness of Scripture. In this discourse both Scripture and apostolic experience and testimony are on the side of the teaching. Paul, in texts like Galatians 3 and 1 Corinthians 11, also appeals to experience first, and then to Scripture to support his argument. And Paul has stressed that when it comes to interpreting Scripture, it is not just a matter of my opinion versus your opinion. The Holy Spirit is viewed as the "hermeneut" who interprets the words in and for the prophet. Teachings at variance with apostolic teaching and interpretation of Scripture are to be rejected.

1 Peter 2:1-22—False Teachers Past and Present

> Not everyone who speaks in the Spirit is a prophet, but only if he follows behaviorally the path of the Lord. Accordingly, from their conduct the false prophet and the true prophet will be known. (*Didache* [11.8])

> If the grace of God could work through an animal without affecting the animal—for the donkey was not saved—but only as a means of helping the Israelites, it is perfectly clear that he is prepared to work in us, which is why this story is so poignant. (Chrysostom)[131]

> A person is the slave of whatever vice that controls him. (Hilary of Arles [*Introductory Commentary on 2 Peter*])[132]

It is not really possible to discuss this chapter's worth of material without laying out plainly the parallels between Jude and 2 Peter at this juncture, which

---

[130]Kelly, *Epistles of Peter,* p. 324.
[131]*CEC* 96.
[132]PL Sup. 3:113.

surely indicate a literary relationship between the two. Here I am following the helpful chart of Perkins (the words in italics indicate the direct parallels between the two sources):[133]

2 Peter	**Jude**
False prophets also arose among the people, . . . *denying* the *Master* who bought them, . . . (2:1) and many will follow their *licentiousness.* (2:2)	Certain people sneaked in; . . . impious, they put aside the grace of our God for *licentiousness* and *deny* our only *Master* and Lord Jesus Christ. (4)
God did not spare *the angels* who sinned, but cast them into Tartarus *in chains of darkness,* keeping them until *judgment.* (2:4)	*Angels* who did not keep their own rank, . . . *he keeps* for the *judgment of the great Day,* with eternal *chains of darkness.* (6)
God condemned and reduced to ashes the *cities* of *Sodom and Gomorrah,* setting an *example* for those who would be impious. (2:6)	*Sodom and Gomorrah* and the *cities* around them, which committed fornication, . . . are set forth as an *example,* suffering a punishment of eternal fire. (7)
. . . especially for those who follow the *flesh* in passion for *corruption* and *despise authority.* Bold and arrogant, they are not afraid to *blaspheme the glorious ones.* (2:10)	Yet these dreamers *corrupt the flesh* and *set aside authority* and *blaspheme the glorious ones.* (8)
. . . strength and power, *do not* bring a *blasphemous judgment* against them from the Lord. (2:11)	. . . argued with the Devil, . . . *did not* dare *bring a judgment of blasphemy* but said, "The *Lord* will rebuke you." (9)
These people, like *irrational creatures,* born *physical beings* for capture and *destruction, blaspheme what they do not know,* and in their destruction *they will be destroyed.* (2:12)	*These* people, *what they do not know,* they *blaspheme;* what they understand *physically,* like *irrational creatures,* in those things *they are destroyed.* (10)
They are *stains* and blemishes, reveling in their deceitful . . .	These people are *stains* on your fellowship meals; *feasting.*
Leaving the straight path, *they*	Woe to those who *follow the*

[133]Perkins, *First and Second Peter,* pp. 179-80.

are deceived, following the way of Balaam son of Bosor, who loved the *wages* of wickedness. (2:15)	*way* of Cain and abandon themselves to the *deceit of Balaam for wages*. (11)
These people are *waterless springs* and mists driven by storms, for whom the *gloom of darkness is kept*. (2:17)	These are . . . *waterless* clouds carried about by wind, fruitless trees, . . . wild waves of the sea, . . . for whom the *gloom of darkness is kept forever.* (12-13)
Uttering foolish *boasts,* they deceive with the licentious *passions* of the flesh those who recently fled from people who live in error.	They are murmuring grumblers who follow their *passions,* and their mouths speak *boasts*. (16)
Beloved, I am now writing . . . (3:1)	But you, *beloved,* (17)
that you should *remember* the *words spoken before* by the holy prophets and the command of your *Lord* and Savior through the *apostles*. (3:2)	*remember the words spoken before by the apostles* of our *Lord* Jesus Christ. (17)
In the last days scoffers will come scoffing, *following* their own *passions.* (3:3)	They told you that *in the last* time there will be *scoffers following the passions* of their impiety. (18)

Even on a cursory examination of these two columns, and even examining them in English, three things are apparent: (1) They are covering the same ground in the same order. (2) Though there is considerable verbal overlap between the two accounts, 2 Peter cannot be said to be simply copying Jude's account. Rather, the author is adopting and adapting this source for his own purposes and audiences. (3) Our author is deeply indebted to the little sermon of Jude, using the vast majority of Jude's material in one way or another, but leaving out the very sectarian material in order to make the source more user-friendly for his own broader audience.

We can learn a variety of other things from carefully examining the omissions and reformulations. For one thing, it is understandable how Jude's "rocks" might become "blots and blemishes" in 2 Peter's hands, and Jude's "love feast" be transformed into "deceit," but the converse is hard to imagine. It is especially hard to understand why, if 2 Peter is the source and Jude the copier, the positive examples in 2 Peter 2:7-9 are omitted by Jude. The more one studies the parallels, the more convincing becomes the chronological order of Jude first and then

2 Peter.[134] A further thing that comes to light when one closely considers and compares 2 Peter with 1 Peter is that while there are various similarities, suggesting that our author may have known 1 Peter, clearly enough he did not derive either his Petrine testimony in 2 Peter 1 from a reading of 1 Peter, nor did he obtain the vast majority of the substance or diction we find in 2 Peter from 1 Peter. In other words, 1 Peter is hardly the main source of the material we have in 2 Peter, which is rather strange if our author is trying to create a plausible pseudepigraphon. We would have expected him to imitate the Petrine style, diction, phraseology more frequently than just in 2 Peter 1:12-21.

Bauckham has helped us see how skillfully our author has woven together his material taken from Jude with what precedes it. He notes the structure: (a) apostles (1:16-18); (b) Old Testament prophets (1:19-21); (b′) Old Testament false prophets (2:1a); (a′) false teachers (2:1b-3).[135] But even more important is the rhetorical structure that our author will draw on in 2 Peter 2, which is signaled so clearly in the very first verse of the chapter: "But there were even false prophets, . . . just as there will be false teachers." In other words, our author is setting up an analogy or rhetorical comparison right from the beginning of this part of his discourse, highlighting the blameworthy conduct of the past and present. How, then, does a rhetorical *synkrisis* work?

There are a variety of kinds of comparisons, including comparison by contrast. In this particular case, though, our author has chosen the easiest form of comparison: comparing two like things, one of which (ancient false ones) is found in a text that both the audience and the author accept as sacred. This is what would be called a strong form of comparison, likely to persuade, and all the more so if the audience knows that in addition to citing Old Testament examples, our author is actually following an authoritative apostolic use of that same material: Jude's. Aristotle declares that comparisons are especially apt, and apt to convince in epideictic rhetoric (Aristotle *Rhet.* 9.38.1368a). According to Cicero and Quintilian, who follows him, it was perfectly acceptable for comparisons to be polemical, ironic and critical in nature (Quintilian *Inst.* 9.3.32). One of the best ways to make a comparison is to use illustrious, or well-known, examples, famous or infamous, depending on whether one is praising a particular person or group of persons or is blaming. Thus, if one picks the bad boys of the Bible to compare to some contemporary false teachers, you are painting them black indeed.

---

[134]See Witherington, "Petrine Source in Second Peter," pp. 187-88; and Bauckham, *Jude, 2 Peter,* pp. 141-43.

[135]Bauckham, *Jude, 2 Peter,* pp. 236-37.

As Aristotle says, the point of such comparison is to amplify someone's virtues or faults: "You must compare him with illustrious persons, for this [is what] affords ground for amplification" (Aristotle *Rhet.* 1.9.38.1368a). Comparison in a sense is a form of shouting or turning the volume (and the heat) up to amplify someone's faults and flaws so as to create odium and avoidance of such persons. Arguments from an historical example were called ***paradeigma*** by the Greeks and ***exemplum*** by the Romans (Quintilian *Inst.* 5.11.7-9), and clearly our author thinks this is a strong form of argumentation. Quintilian (*Inst.* 4.2.99) recommends as effective rhetoric that "arguments be drawn from a comparison of the characters of the two parties." Just as in the schoolboy exercises comparisons were worked up for each of the virtues when one was doing an encomium, so also comparisons could be worked up for each of the vices. In his detailed study of rhetorical comparisons, Christopher Forbes makes clear how many rules and discussions there were about the use of comparisons in epideictic rhetoric.[136] It was used equally for praise and blame, encomia and invective. It is certainly used in the latter manner here, so the audience will not waver or give way to the siren songs of false teachers.

For our purposes I want to stress three points: (1) one did not need to be a master rhetorician to use rhetorical comparisons. This was taught as some of the initial training of schoolboys taking the beginnings of rhetorical instruction. (2) The conventions for this form of rhetoric were both widely known and widely practiced, as Forbes stresses, so it would be surprising if our author did not know about such a rhetorical device.[137] (3) In a discourse that uses Asiatic Greek and rhetoric, this device would be seen as de rigueur if one was going to persuade an audience of what was praiseworthy and blameworthy. Our author's rhetorical skill is shown in how he uses the material in Jude in a rather different way, to paint a portrait of rather different villains, as we shall see. As Craddock so rightly reminds us, here we have a classic example of the rhetoric of praise and blame, mostly the latter. "Most likely the original readers were more able than subsequent ones to hear this section with understanding and without offense. In fact, they may have found in it a measure of sober entertainment—assuming they were not the ones renounced."[138]

As Neyrey says, the glue that holds together the portion of this argument that modern scholars have found most difficult (2 Pet 2:10b-16) is actually an oral and rhetorical device: assonance, repeatedly used. This is true right throughout

[136]Forbes, "Paul and Rhetorical Comparison," pp. 134-71, esp. pp. 148-49.
[137]Ibid., p. 150.
[138]Craddock, *First and Second Peter*, p. 114.

these verses, and it was going to carry weight and make sense and be persuasive on the basis of its sound. Consider the following: (1) In 2 Peter 2:10b-12 we have *blasphēmountes . . . blasphēmon . . . blasphēmountes*. (2) In 2 Peter 2:12 we have *phthoran . . . en phthora . . . phtharēsontai*. (3) In 2 Peter 2:13 we have *adikoumenoi . . . adikias* and (4) *hēdonēn hēgoumenoi . . . en hēmera*. (5) In 2 Peter 2:14 we have *mestous moichalidos* and (6) *akatapaustous hamartias . . . astēriktous*. (7) In 2 Peter 2:16 we have *aphōnon . . . phōnē phthegxamenon*.[139] Very little of this does our author owe to Jude. He is a skillful rhetorical redactor of his sources.

One more thing becomes evident upon close inspection of 2 Peter 2. Our author is some sort of scribe, and he seems to be trained not only in Asiatic rhetoric, but also in the Jewish wisdom tradition and in Jewish stories that amplified and clarified the Old Testament stories. We cannot say that he is simply getting this from Jude, for the good reason that he adds positive examples of his own, and those very examples show that he knows more than just the Old Testament itself. I suggest that we should see our author as a Jewish Christian scribe, skilled at weaving together earlier traditions and making them into a compelling whole. In this respect, he seems much like the First Evangelist.[140] Scribes were editors of earlier source material. They were not authors, at least when they were doing their scribal work. I suspect that we need to revise our entire way of looking at 2 Peter as if there were only two categories: genuine author or pseudonymous author. No, there is a third possibility, that we are dealing with a genuine editor preserving and presenting, adopting and adapting earlier sacred material, and rightly ascribing it to one of its sources, the most famous one: Peter.

2:1 But there were even false prophets among the people (of Israel), just as there will be false teachers among you, who will struggle in destructive heresies, disowning the Master who bought them, bringing upon themselves swift (sudden?) destruction. 2 And many will follow their debaucheries; because of them the way of truth will be blasphemed. 3 And prompted by greed they will exploit you with (using) fabricated arguments.

The judgment on these (false teachers) waiting for a long time is not idle, and their destruction is not sleeping. 4 For if God did not spare the angels who sinned, but consigned them to the gloomy pits of Tartarus, being kept unto judgment (condemnation), 5 and he did not spare the ancient world, but protected Noah a preacher of righteousness along with seven others when he brought a deluge on the world of ungodly people, 6 and the cities of Sodom and Gomorrah being covered by ashes, they

---

[139] Neyrey, *2 Peter, Jude*, p. 206.

[140] On Jewish Christian scribes, see Witherington, *Gospel of Matthew*, pp. 6-9.

were condemned to ruin, making them a "proof" of what is going to happen to the ungodly, [7] *and righteous Lot being oppressed by the unprincipled one's sexual behavior was rescued,* [8] *for righteous in look and in hearing he tortured himself day after day at their lawless deeds, while he lived among them* [9] *(the Lord knows how to rescue the decent from a trial, but the unrighteous are to be kept under the prospect of punishment on judgment day),* [10] *but above all those who follow the sensual polluting desires of the flesh and despise the (final) authority (dominion) of the Lord.*

Daring arrogant men, they are not afraid to blaspheme the glorious ones, [11] *when angels greater in might and power do not blaspheme when they pronounce judgment against them on the part of the Lord.* [12] *But these men are as (like) irrational animals born of nature for capture and destruction, blaspheming in matters they do not understand; in this decadence they will also decay (or in their destruction they will also be destroyed),* [13] *being hurt as the wages (reward) for hurting (or being defrauded of the wages of fraud), thinking it pleasure to revel during the day, blots and blemishes, reveling in their deceptions while feasting with you;* [14] *they have eyes full of adultery, and not ceasing from sin, enticing unstable persons, having hearts trained in greed, they are children of a curse;* [15] *forsaking the straight way, they have gone astray, following the way of Balaam of Bosor, who loved the wages of unrighteousness.* [16] *But he received reproof (for) his wrongdoing (when) a dumb beast of burden spoke in a human voice (and) prevented the aberration of the prophet (or madness of the prophet).*

[17] *But these men are waterless springs and mists driven by a windstorm, for whom the gloom of darkness has been kept (reserved).* [18] *For speaking (with) inflated bombast, they entice, by appealing to sensual passions and debauchery, people who are just escaping from those who live in error,* [19] *promising freedom to them, whereas they themselves are slaves of destruction (corruption), for whatever a person is defeated by, to that he is enslaved;* [20] *for having escaped the corruption of the world in the knowledge of the Lord and Savior Jesus Christ, they are again entangled and are defeated, so that the last state is worse than the first.* [21] *It would have been better for them if they had not known the way of righteousness rather than known it and turned back from the holy commandment passed down to them.* [22] *The true proverb has happened to them, "The dog returned to his vomit" and "The pig having washed (returns) unto wallowing in mud."*

A CLOSER LOOK

How Was 2 Peter Composed? Elementary, My Dear Watson

Without question the first really important and formative discussion of the rhetoric of 2 Peter in the modern era is Watson's modification of his doctoral dissertation, entitled *Invention, Arrangement, and Style: Rhetorical Criticism of Jude and 2 Peter.* Compared to some more recent ones, this study has numerous virtues: Watson is rigorous in applying only ancient Greco-Roman rhetorical principles and ideas to the analysis of the text. In my view this is the right way to proceed, if one is focusing on the question What was the original author up to in his own era? Modern discussions that follow the methods of Vernon K. Robbins and others of the school of "New Rhetoric" are quite capable of producing many wonderful new insights into our biblical texts, but at the end of the day these methods fall more into the category of exercises in hermeneutics, not exegesis. They usually do not answer the question as to what the biblical writer himself was trying to accomplish rhetorically speaking, since the biblical writer obviously was innocent of modern communications theory, language theory, presuppositions about the epistemic principles of the mind, recent technical distinctions like "inner-texture" and "intratexture" and the like. There is nothing wrong with such distinctions, and they indeed can often be quite helpful in analyzing an ancient text, but they do not tell us much about how the original author structured or likely viewed the structuring of his own material. This study, like all of my socio-rhetorical commentaries, has stuck with the methodology exhibited in Watson's original study so far as the issue of rhetoric is concerned. This does not mean that I agree with all of Watson's conclusions, as will in a moment become evident. But I do agree with his restricting of his study and analysis to ancient rhetorical methods, forms and devices. This is where the discussion with a text like 2 Peter should begin, but it need not end there.

In spelling out how rhetorical criticism aids the study of 2 Peter, we can initially recognize its ability to help us to see the discourse as a whole and to avoid some of the problems caused by an overly stratifying approach to source criticism. Watson nonetheless glosses over some obvious problems when it comes to what he says about source criticism. I quite agree with him that theories of "later" (after the original composition of 2 Peter) additions or interpolations into this discourse do not merely fall down on the hard rocks of textual criticism, which suggests no such large-scale later additions; they also fall to the ground because there is an overall rhetorical structure to this discourse, which actually binds its disparate source material together. There is an epistolary opening, an exordium, several arguments or proofs, and a final peroration and closing doxology. We do not need to bring in any theories of interpolation or later addition to explain any of this material. But what is needed is not merely a frank recognition that this discourse uses Jude as a source, but also that there is good evidence of other source material as well.

Then too, the structure of 2 Peter is less elaborate than Watson suggests, in part because this is the rhetoric of praise and blame, not the rhetoric of advice and consent (deliberative rhetoric), with its elaborate proposition statement and detailed arguments working out the thesis statement. Watson knows that his deliberative rhetoric theory is not entirely satisfactory, so he resorts to finding epideictic and forensic bits, occasionally by way of digression, in this short discourse. But we have *no digressions* at all in this discourse and certainly not in 2 Peter 2. This discourse only has three main arguments or discussions: (1) the testimony of Peter; (2) the discussion of the false teachers, comparing them with the ancients; (3) the discussion of eschatology as a sanction for ethics. That's all.

Since my earlier study on Petrine sources in 2 Peter, however, I have come to the conclusion that Watson is right that 2 Peter 2:1-3 is indebted to Jude, as is the rest of 2 Peter 2; but I remain unconvinced that 2 Peter 3:1-3 is adapted from Jude. What Watson does not really adequately cope with is how our author himself deals with his sources apart from his handling of Jude. He clearly uses them, and just as clearly he uses them well to form a new whole, a coherent rhetorical discourse. But this in no way preempts us from identifying and recognizing that 2 Peter 1:12-21 and 1 Peter 3:1-3, for example, reflect a Petrine source just as 2 Peter 2 reflects a use of Jude. Watson intimates that the style of this discourse is so seamlessly uniform that we could never have guessed that sources were used to compose it; but this is simply false. The material in 2 Peter 2:12-21 and also 2 Peter 3:1-3 do not reflect the more grandiose Asiatic style that we find in the rest of this discourse. This material does not involve long convoluted sentences or lugubrious and lengthy terms and clauses. Has our author made the material from Jude his own and transformed it into Asiatic style? Yes, he has. Has he done this in the same way or to the same degree with 2 Peter 1:12-21 and 2 Peter 3:1-3? No, he has not, though I do not deny that he has touched up that material in small ways to make it fit better with the rest of 2 Peter. The change in style reflects not a change in rhetorical species from deliberative to judicial to epideictic, or a shift from the exordium to the arguments.[141] There is no difference in style between the exordium and the discussion of eschatology in 2 Peter 3:4-13. It is not a matter of which rhetorical part of the discourse we are in. In the case of 2 Peter 1:12-21 and 2 Peter 3:1-3, the different and more Petrine style reflects a change in source material, which needed only light editing to make it fit into our discourse.

There is a further problem with Watson's argumentation. One would have thought that a careful comparison of the parallels between Jude and 2 Peter would have led to the conclusion that 2 Peter is more generic rhetoric, not situation specific like Jude is. One would also have thought that more generic quality and a broader audience, coupled with the lack of a real proposition statement or a *narratio* and the lack of a discussion of what changes were "beneficial" and "necessary," would have led to a conclusion that 2 Peter is not

[141]Against Watson, *Invention,* p. 153.

a sample of deliberative rhetoric. I would have especially expected this when we do have praise-and-blame activities and language going on throughout the discourse, coupled with the language of reminder and standing firm.

Watson however is absolutely right on the mark when he says that the arguments for Jude drawing on 2 Peter are quite weak indeed. What is the point of having written Jude at all when 90 percent of it in one form or another is already in 2 Peter? In the other direction, Watson is quite right that Jude 4-18 is a rather tightly structured argument, whereas parts of 2 Peter, particularly 2 Peter 2:10b-18, are by no means as carefully structured. There is a reason why there are so many textual problems with 2 Peter 2:10b-18: scribes kept trying to fix its language and sentence structure.[142] In other words, it is hard to imagine Jude constructing his svelte argument out of what we find in 2 Peter 2, and furthermore, the specific verbal changes point to Jude being earlier (e.g., love feasts, rocks).

Finally, the positive examples in 2 Peter 2 (comparing old and new righteous ones) and the opening remark about comparing old and more recent false ones point to a later and more complex use of the material in the service of *synkrisis,* which leads us up to the closing proverbial invective and leaves us in no doubt what sort of person and behavior was being praised and what sort was being blamed. This same material is put to a very different and more deliberative and situation-specific use in Jude. "Borrowing" and using historical examples was especially prevalent in epideictic rhetoric, which is not surprising since this is the rhetoric of eulogies and encomia, where one normally cites the deceased's own "greatest hits" or significant sayings or traditions. In 2 Peter this is one of the key indicators of what sort of rhetoric we are dealing with in this discourse.

In conclusion, we may be deeply grateful for Watson's detailed and powerful analysis of both Jude and 2 Peter as rhetorically structured documents, even if at times he pushes the structural and species arguments too far. My response to his analysis of 2 Peter is to say thank you, but the epideictic rhetoric here is more elementary, my dear Watson. But seriously, Watson made as clear as it could be that one cannot just settle for accepting the fact that these authors used microrhetoric or the occasional rhetorical device. He showed that the very structure of the material *as a whole* is indebted to rhetorical convention, indeed far more indebted to those conventions between the epistolary prescripts and postscripts than to letter conventions of the era. For this we may be truly thankful. It has helped changed the face of New Testament studies, and especially the analysis of what used to be assumed to be just ancient letters.

[142]Ibid., p. 163.

Our author in **2 Peter 2:1** sets up his rhetorical comparison by pointing to historical precedent. Having false prophets or teachers is nothing new.[143] It happened also in Old Testament times, and so Christians should not be surprised about it happening in the New Testament era.[144] The author here draws on his audience's knowledge of the Old Testament characteristic actions of false prophets, summed up for us by Green: "Their teaching was flattery; their ambitions were financial; their lives were dissolute; their conscience was dulled; and their aim was deception" (cf. Is 28:7; Jer 23:14; Ezek 13:2-4).[145] It is possible that the social backdrop of this entire discussion is that our author is relying on the general skepticism in Greco-Roman culture about self-proclaimed prophets during this era.[146] There were three things especially that false prophets were criticized for in the Old Testament: (1) They did not speak with divine authority. (2) They preached peace and security when judgment was actually coming. (3) In both their beliefs and behaviors, they were shown to be worthy of condemnation. All three of these critiques will be applied to these false teachers/prophets of the New Testament era.[147] Yet our author does not want to grace these persons with the title of "prophet"; he simply wants to call them "false teachers," a more inclusive term in some respects (cf. 1 Tim 4:12; 2 Tim 4:3).

It appears that we are talking not about itinerant false teachers here but about indigenous ones who partake of the local fellowship, and in that household context introduce their destructive views.[148] Our author, then, will ring changes on the word "destruction" *(apōleia)* throughout this argument to show where following such false teaching leads a person.[149] Their "opinions are destructive; their activity is self-destructive; and God's destruction awaits them."[150] It is possible that our author sees himself as a true prophet for he foresees that false teachers will come to the church; however, he offers no oracles here, and it would not take a prophet to know this would likely happen since it was already happening in the 90s in some churches in areas where both Paul and Peter had evangelized (cf., e.g., Rev 2—3). I need to make clear that in terms of genre of

[143]Some scholars debate as to whether our author sees these false ones as prophets or teachers, but the attempt to nail this down is unnecessary. This is a more generic polemic and would include either or both, since both plagued the church. But see Cavallin, "False Teachers of 2 Pt. as Pseudo-Prophets," pp. 263-70, esp. pp. 269-70.

[144]There may be an echo of this verse in Justin Martyr *Dial.* 82.1.

[145]Green, *2 Peter,* p. 93; cf. Mayor, *Jude, 2 Peter,* pp. 115-16.

[146]Green, "'As for Prophecies,'" pp. 107-22.

[147]See Moo, *2 Peter, Jude,* p. 91.

[148]Horrell, *Peter and Jude,* p. 161.

[149]Perkins, *First and Second Peter,* p. 180.

[150]Craddock, *First and Second Peter,* p. 111.

material, we do not have prophetic material in 2 Peter, and it is time to stop calling it that. We have neither Old Testament style oracles, nor do we have apocalyptic visions here. What we have is inspired teaching and the passing along of the apostolic tradition.[151]

It may be significant that our author does not call these adversaries "prophets." They did not claim to be prophets; perhaps they even denied prophecy altogether. But certainly they denied the prophecies of the second coming and judgment. The irony here is that they are denying the coming of judgment, which is the very deed which will make them liable to judgment. There is nothing remarkable about the author, as a true scribe or teacher, warning of the coming of false teachers since Jesus himself (Mk 13:22) predicted false prophets and christs would appear. Here only in the New Testament do we have the word *pseudodidaskaloi*. Our author is simply following in the steps of Jesus at this point. False teachers are a sign of the eschatological age. Those false teachers, according to 2 Peter 2:16, are teaching heresies. This may go back to a saying of Jesus not recorded in our Gospels but mentioned in other early Christian sources (Justin *Dial.* 35.3; cf. 1 Cor 11:18): "There will be divisions and heresies." This suggests again that our author is just reiterating a prophecy of Jesus here, in which case he may not have seen himself as a prophet, but only a conveyor of Christ's prophecy.[152]

Hairesis is where we derive our word "heresy," and here it may refer to doctrinal error that leads to ethical error. Its original sense in classical Greek was simply "choice," and this is the meaning it had in early Judaism in some contexts. It came to have the sense of a chosen school of thought, and so a sect (see Acts 5:17; 26:5), but it is clear enough from texts like 1 Corinthians 11:18-19 and Galatians 5:20 that the term has come to have a pejorative sense: a chosen school of thought or view that is aberrant, "other," false.[153] The word *apōleias* could be an objective or subjective genitive: either heresies/views that are destructive in themselves, or heresies that lead to (final) destruction. Perhaps Bauckham is right to choose the second option in view of 2 Peter 2:1c, where our author talks about these false teachers bringing swift destruction upon

[151]On the discussion of what amounts to prophecy, see Ben Witherington III, *Jesus the Seer: The Progress of Prophecy* (Peabody, Mass.: Hendrickson, 1999).

[152]Bauckham, *Jude, 2 Peter,* p. 240.

[153]See Kelly, *Epistles of Peter,* p. 327; Harrington, *Jude and 2 Peter,* p. 261. Moo, *2 Peter, Jude,* p. 93, admits that the term *hairesis* does begin to have the sense of "heresy" in the late first century; yet because of how Moo wants to date this discourse, he goes for the translation "opinion" here. But clearly from 2 Pet 3 we discover that our false teachers held false theological views, and the pejorative nature of this whole section in 2 Pet 2-3 must count against such a translation.

themselves. *Taxinēn* can mean "imminent" and thus "soon," but it could also have a more adverbial sense of "speedy" or "quickly" here, rather than soon, and this is likely right.

These false teachers are smuggling foreign and wrong ideas into the church, ideas against the apostolic teaching, which they have already received (cf. 2 Peter 1:3-11, 12-15). By doing so, they were disowning the master who bought them. Here again we have the idea of Christ's death as the purchase price for buying believers out of bondage to sin (cf. 1 Cor 6:20; 7:23).[154] Christ has freed them from sin, but they are disowning their master by doing what Christ came to set them free from.

Our author here charitably assumes that these false teachers have once been true believers, bought with a price. Unfortunately, there will be many who will follow them in this error. In **2 Peter 2:2** *aselgeiais* here as elsewhere likely refers to sexual sins, or at least sins of a sensual nature. When Christians backslide to do such things, the way of the truth is said to be blasphemed, by which is probably meant the true Christian way of living a moral and upright life. According to **2 Peter 2:3a**, the motives of the false teachers are at least in part to exploit innocent believers and line their own pockets, accepting money from their supporters. The phrase *plastois logois* (molded words) is interesting. The first of these two words is the one from which we derive the term "plastic." In a rhetorical context such as this, the term is used to describe forgeries (Josephus *Life* 177, 377). Our author thus would be accusing the false teachers of counterfeiting the apostolic teaching, in a sense a reprise to what 2 Peter 1:16 may imply.[155] In view of the chiastic structure, Bauckham calls us to look back to its parallel in 2 Peter 1:16: cleverly concocted myths. Thus here the phrase means "humanly fabricated words," phony arguments or artificial proofs. It is the false teachers who are using bogus words to deceive the believers. *Plastois* can also mean "fictitious," in which case we might see an allusion back to 2 Peter 1:16b and the word "myth," though Mayor thinks otherwise.[156] The term "blaspheme" in 2 Peter 2:2 may have the broader sense of "slander" or "revile," but it could in fact have its more theologically loaded sense of misusing the divine name (see Lev 24:10-23).[157]

Second Peter 2:3b-10a begins a section of material more obviously adopted and adapted for a purpose different from Jude's. Necessarily we will only deal

[154]See Chang, "Second Peter 2.1," pp. 52-63.
[155]See Neyrey, *2 Peter, Jude,* p. 193.
[156]Mayor, *Jude, 2 Peter,* p. 119.
[157]See Harrington, *Jude and 2 Peter,* p. 262.

with the points where our author uses the material in a different way since we have dealt with Jude's use of the material at length in another volume of this series.[158] Moo helpfully shows how this one long sentence is structured, including all of 2 Peter 2:4-10a at least, if not also 2 Peter 2:3b. It works like this: "If God did not spare the angels, . . . and if he did not spare the ancient world, . . . and if he condemned the cities of Sodom and Gomorrah, . . . and if he rescued Lot—then [2 Peter 2:9a] the Lord knows how to rescue righteous people . . . and to hold the unrighteous for the day of judgment."[159]

Scholars are divided as to how situation specific this material could really be in 2 Peter, since it seems to be a broadside sent to the church as a whole. We do not need to think of this material as merely a literary exercise, to be sure, but on the other hand it is a mistake to see it as dealing with some specific situation in a specific city in the empire. No, our author is dealing with a more endemic problem: false teachers and false prophets who have both their eschatology and ethics wrong. And these two things certainly go together. When one loses the eschatological sanction, one assumes that one's behavior will not be called to account at the eschaton.[160] Our author will draw an especially adept comparison with Balaam and these false prophets or teachers. They are oblivious to the consequences of their own actions and are blind spiritual guides, heading for and leading others down the primrose path to destruction. Unlike 1 Peter, 2 Peter is entirely concerned about internal problems within Christian communities: external persecution, prosecution and execution (and the accompanying theology of suffering) are not to be found in this discourse.

Our author has just quoted Peter to the effect that apostolic experience and messianic prophecy predict a coming judgment/parousia. Now our author turns to further evidence of this kind, in this case Old Testament accounts of judgment that are historical examples and also types of the coming judgment. The message is clear: God destroyed the world once, has kept angels for future punishment and has leveled Sodom and Gomorrah. A wise person would conclude that God means it when he says that he will judge sin.

Quite clearly our author has tailored his Jude section to fit the Petrine material. *Hois* in **2 Peter 2:3b** makes the connection to the present situation, and the verbs are in the present tense. Possibly, as Bauckham suggests, the false teachers who do not believe in the future judgment have mocked the judgment, saying, "Where is it? Is it sleeping or waiting around to happen?" To this our author replies, "The

[158]See Witherington, *Letters and Homilies for Jewish Christians,* pp. 607-25.
[159]Moo, *2 Peter, Jude,* p. 101, with stylistic alteration.
[160]See J. Daryl Charles, "On Angels and Assess," pp. 1-12.

judgment has been prepared for these false teachers for a long time." Bauckham may be right to note the pagan parallels where deities were accused of being idle or sleeping (cf. 1 Kings 18:27; Ps 44:23; 78:65; 121:4), implying their impotence or lack of interest in the human scene. By contrast to this, our author suggests that judgment waits with unsleeping eyes, and indeed it is in a sense already active.[161]

Second Peter 2:4 begins another typically long, cumbersome Asiatic sentence like what we found in 2 Peter 1:3-11, and in contrast to what we found in 2 Peter 1:12-21. Further, this present section is full of colorful and un-Petrine vocabulary, all of which suggests that a different source is being used (Jude), but the modification of Jude in a way that works with Asiatic rhetoric is notable. Verse 4 begins by saying, "for if God did not spare . . . " This is not a hypothetical "if" *(ei)* but a real condition. Second Peter's treatment of the material differs from Jude's in several regards. (1) Our author mainly excises the apocryphal material from *1 Enoch* 10 and the *Testament of Moses*. (2) Most important, he adds some positive examples for his audience to follow, unlike Jude. (3) He puts his examples in biblical chronological order. He thus is a careful writer even if his style is rather grandiose and unwieldy. From an epideictic rhetorical point of view, this is important: it means here that our author is not engaging in unrelenting invective; he also sets forth some praiseworthy examples.

Verse 4 also indicates clearly that our author has interpreted Gen 6:1-4 to refer not to men but to angels, who sinned and were consigned to Tartarus (cf. *1 En.* 20:2, cf. *1 En.* 18:14-16; 21:1-10 Greek text).[162] This is also what we saw in 1 Peter and Jude. Tartarus was the nether regions of Hades, the very bottom of the pit reserved for disobedient gods and rebellious humans and other creatures presumably. One of the reasons not to translate this word as "hell" is because it is a preliminary holding tank, not a final destination.[163] The word *seirais* (chains) presents us with a textual problem, because the original reading may be *sirois* (pits), as attested by ℵ and other witnesses (alt. spelling *seirois* in A, B, C).[164] In favor

---

[161]Bauckham, *Jude, 2 Peter*, pp. 245-47.

[162]See Feuillet, "Le péché évoqué aux chapitres 3 et 6, 1-4 de la Genèse," pp. 207-29. Our author seems to have used the term "Tartarus" (Greek, *Tartaros*) to conjure up the mythological punishment of the Titans in such a gloomy place (cf. Hesiod *Theog.* 713-735). See Pearson, "Reminiscence of Classical Myth at II Peter 2.4," pp. 71-80. However, as Schreiner, *1, 2 Peter, Jude*, pp. 336-37, rightly notes, the term is used by various early Jews and is even found in the LXX (cf. Job 40:20; 41:24; Prov 30:16; cf. *Sib. Or.* 2.304; 4.186; Josephus *Ag. Ap.* 2.240; Philo *Praem.* 152). However, the parallels between the story about the Titans and the story about these angels may have prompted this usage here, bearing in mind that here our author is Hellenizing Jude for his broader audience.

[163]Moo, *2 Peter, Jude*, p. 103; Dalton, "Interpretation of 1 Peter 3.19 and 4.6," pp. 547-55.

[164]And as favored in the Nestle-Aland[25] (1963) text of the Greek NT but not in the text of Nestle-Aland[27] (1993).

of "pits" (literally, underground grain silos, from which we derive the word "silo") is the fact that in a text like Revelation 20:1-3, we hear of Satan being thrown into a pit. It is easy to see why scribes would change the original "pits" to "chains," since that is similar to Jude's text.[165] We thus conclude that "pits" is original here. After all, what would gloomy chains mean anyway? What the author is saying is that until the last day, these fallen angels are being kept in gloomy holding tanks. He identifies this place of confinement as "Tartarus." In Greek mythology Tartarus was a place of punishment for wicked departed spirits, or a place of confinement for the Titans. This was a dungeon or prison (cf. 1 Pet 3:19) and is in all likelihood not to be identified with the biblical hell. Once again we see our author's Hellenistic bent. In *1 Enoch* there was a special angel in charge of Tartarus: Uriel (Greek text of *1 En.* 20:2; cf. Rev 20:1-3).

Second Peter 2:5 is about God's not sparing the ancient world. Clearly the author of 2 Peter sees the flood as universal, the whole *kosmos* going under the deluge. This example we do not find in Jude. The two positive examples of Noah and Lot also appear in Philo (*Mos.* 253-265). One of the rhetorical functions of these examples is to provide some relief from the blaming, to cite praiseworthy examples. Even more important, it allows our author not only to link his audience to previous righteous ones being assailed by a sea of wickedness, but also to give them hope that they will prevail over it, and that the wicked will be judged.[166] But 2 Peter includes these little positive examples to remind the audience that "God did not establish commandments, send prophets, and ransom humanity through the death of Jesus in order to maximize the population of hell."[167] Rather, his redemptive judgments are all for the purpose of redeeming the world, just as the warnings of future judgment are to help keep the faithful on the straight and narrow. These particular two examples remind the audience that God could deliver them from even more drastic circumstances than they currently face (see Sir 33:1); not incidentally, Jesus also uses the examples of Noah and Lot back to back as well (Lk 17:26-29).

Notice how our author contrasts those whom God does "not spare" (a recurring verb: 2 Pet 2:4, 5) and those whom he "rescues" (also a recurring verb: 2 Pet 2:7, 9). He is building to a conclusion: (1) There is plenty of historical precedent for God acting in judgment, and also in redemption in history. (2) These examples are but types of the final judgment; therefore the false teachers and

[165] Cf. Mayor, *Jude, 2 Peter,* p. cxciv; Kelly, *Epistles of Peter,* p. 331; M. Green, *2 Peter,* p. 98.
[166] Perkins, *First and Second Peter,* p. 183.
[167] Ibid.

their followers had better beware. God protected Noah as one of eight he spared (Gen 8:18). Bauckham overexegetes the use of "eight" here, thinking there is an allusion to the "eighth day of creation," in this case the day God started over with the world (*2 En.* 33:1-2; *Barn.* 15.9).[168] The word translated "deluge" is where we get the word "cataclysm": an earth-shattering event. Noah is said to be a "preacher of righteousness," something also implied in Josephus (*Ant.* 1.3.1). Wisdom of Solomon 10:4 associates Noah with Wisdom, who saves the world. Genesis 6 does not say that Noah preached, but it does imply that God allowed a period of repentance. Perhaps our author is drawing on popular Jewish traditions about Noah, that he preached to the sinful world before he boarded the ark (see *Sib. Or.* 1:148-198).

In **2 Peter 2:6** we are told about Sodom and Gomorrah and that these events of judgment are *hypodeigma,* "examples" or "patterns," or if used in the rhetorical sense as here, "proofs"[169] of what will happen to the godless (cf. 3 Macc 2:4-5).[170] We may compare the above discussion of rhetorical *synkrisis*.[171] Our author sees God's saving and judging action as following a certain characteristic and even predictable pattern in human history. Rhetorically speaking, historical examples taken from commonly shared sacred traditions or texts were considered the strongest inartificial proofs of one's point, falling only behind direct eyewitness experience. Clearly the point is for the audience to take note and heed the warning, and thus to avoid such conduct. Here our author uses the verb *tephroō,* which literally means "reduce to ashes," the same verb Dio Cassius uses to describe what happened to Pompeii when Vesuvius erupted (A.D. 79); Philo likewise employs this same sort of language in discussing the destruction of Sodom and Gomorrah (Philo *Mos.* 2.56). Probably Mayor is right that the second phrase here involves an instrumental dative: a condemnation by destruction is what happened to Sodom and Gomorrah. Some quite good manuscripts have *katastrophē* (catastrophe), which is probably original here, for the good reason that it creates the proper repetitious Asiatic effect: *katastrophē . . . katekrinen.*[172] Mayor is probably right that the first half of the verse is an example of seeing a judgment that comes in two stages: covering by ashes and then destruction.

In **2 Peter 2:7** Lot is called "righteous," and here again certain popular Jewish traditions may be in mind, not in the Old Testament (cf. Wis 10:6; 19:17).[173] In

[168]Bauckham, *Jude, 2 Peter,* p. 250.
[169]See Neyrey, *2 Peter, Jude,* p. 203.
[170]See "Words Denoting 'Pattern' in the New Testament," pp. 166-73.
[171]See pp. 345-46 above.
[172]See Metzger, *TC,* p. 702; Harrington, *Jude and 2 Peter,* p. 267.
[173]See Bauckham, *Jude, 2 Peter,* pp. 251-52.

any event, he was righteous by comparison to his contemporaries in Sodom and Gomorrah. Lot is portrayed here as one who was oppressed by all the wicked and especially the sexual sinning around him. One suggestion is that Lot is called "righteous" here due to his being hospitable.[174] **Second Peter 2:8** is very difficult to translate, and we have rendered it rather literally in our translation above. It is probably right to see this description as aimed at our author's audience. They are like Lot, and he wishes them to reject or struggle against the trials and temptations to sin around them. The meaning seems to be that he vexed his righteous spirit or being by what he saw and heard. He was a morally sensitive person, and he went through internal turmoil due to the sin around him. The point is that the unprincipled actions and sins of the flesh of the false teachers should likewise trouble the audience. Our author is pleading: "Do not become anesthetized to sin just because it is so prevalent around you."

Obviously Gentile Christians may have often been tempted to fall back into the pattern of behavior they followed as pagans, but our author is probably not addressing just Gentile Christians. For Christians under such temptation and trial, our author in **2 Peter 2:9a** offers a hopeful word: "The Lord knows how to rescue the devout from that sort of trial or temptation" (here *peirasmos* does not mean physical suffering).

Second Peter 2:9b is somewhat difficult to interpret. It could imply either that (1) the unrighteous are being punished now as well as on judgment day, or (2) they are being held under (the prospect) of punishment on judgment day, or (3) they are being kept to be punished at judgment day. Kelly favors the first suggestion.[175] It nevertheless is possible that *kolazomenous* is proleptic: kept *now* for punishment *later*. Our author always has the false teachers in view, and they are not apparently being tormented now.[176] If the language suggests, and it does, an analogy to 2 Peter 2:4 (the angels being held awaiting judgment), perhaps this is intended here. So either option 2 or option 3 is more probable, and the second does best justice to the grammar. Hillyer makes the interesting point that the "Greek ethical writers on punishment (e.g., Aristotle *Rhetoric* 1.10) distinguished between *kolasis,* inflicted for the good of the sufferer, and *timōria* (Heb. 10:29), imposed for the satisfaction of justice. Since Peter's term is reflected in the former, he may be hinting at the notion of the penalty being corrective (cf. 1 Pet. 3:19; 4:6)."[177] For a grisly de-

[174]Alexander, "Lot's Hospitality," pp. 289-91; cf. Makujina, "The 'Trouble' with Lot," pp. 255-69.
[175]Kelly, *Epistles of Peter,* pp. 334-35.
[176]Bauckham, *2 Peter, Jude,* p. 254.
[177]Hillyer, *1 and 2 Peter,* p. 191.

scription of the punishments of the wicked after death but before final judgment, see 2 Esdras 7:78-87.[178] It is just possible that we have here a hint of a line from the Lord's Prayer: "Do not bring us to the time of trial, but deliver us from the evil one" (Mt 6:11).[179]

Second Peter 2:10a concludes this segment of the argument. In this verse it is not necessary to conclude that our author sees physical flesh as evil, for *sarkos* here may mean "sinful inclinations," not just "physical flesh." Judgment is especially reserved for those who commit grievous sexual sins (as at Sodom and Gomorrah) and despise dominion. Perhaps this is a reference to the Lord's dominion and rule as Judge on judgment day, as would suit the context. Dominion thus is a reference to God and not heavenly beings.[180] In short, our author wishes his audience to conclude that the polluted false teachers who deny final judgment are cruising for a bruising. It is not clear here who the *kyriotēs* is. It could be God or Christ, or even the church leaders or apostles like Peter, but in light of the use of blasphemy in this context, it likely refers to God.[181]

Beginning with **2 Peter 2:10b** and continuing down to the end of the chapter, we once again find our author relying heavily on Jude, though he adopts and adapts Jude's material to his own purposes. I am not convinced that our author is attacking a known and specific group of false teachers plaguing a particular part of the churches in Asia Minor, since this discourse involves more of a general polemic than Jude. Although I think the author may have in mind false teachers he already knows about, he is addressing a wider audience and warning them lest teachers of that sort come their way. Some in the audience will have run into such people, some will not have. Kelly is however right that here we have "the most violent and colourfully expressed tirade in the NT."[182] What we should not do is call this material a digression from the main argument of our discourse.[183] It is rather a further exposition of the false teachers' blameworthy conduct, concluding with powerful invective to make the audience know that they must disassociate from such people if they are to be praiseworthy themselves.

The Greek in 2 Peter 2:10b-22 is extremely difficult and convoluted, full of hapax legomena and imponderables, and this section especially shows how much our author is prepared to alter a source when he wants to do so. Our au-

---

[178]Lunn, "Punishment in 2 Peter 2.9," pp. 15-18.
[179]See Horrell, *Peter and Jude*, p. 166.
[180]Mayor, *Jude, 2 Peter,* p. 127; Bauckham, *Jude, 2 Peter,* p. 255.
[181]See Harrington, *Jude and 2 Peter,* p. 268.
[182]Kelly, *Epistles of Peter,* p. 337.
[183]Against Watson, "2 Peter," p. 350.

thor alters Jude in certain key ways. He omits Jude's reference to the story of Michael's dispute with the devil, perhaps because his audience does not know it.[184] He also omits the reference to Cain and Korah and expands the reference to Balaam. In verse 13 he gives words in Jude *(spilades, agapē)* a fresh turn or twist *(spiloi, apatais)*. But what is odd about this is that the changes involve words that look similar, which leads one to wonder if our author is copying a variant manuscript of Jude. We cannot be sure.

At 2 Peter 2:11, 13, 18 we have textual problems of varying degrees of severity. Clearly, scribes had a hard time making sense of the convoluted Greek here, and some of them seem not to know Asiatic Greek at all. In 2 Peter 2:17-22 we find a similar phenomenon to what we find in 2 Peter 2:10b-16. Second Peter omits the Jude 12-13 material from *1 Enoch,* and in 2 Peter 2:19-22 he begins to quote a series of popular sayings (of Jesus and others) and proverbs. Thus, for instance, we find in 2 Peter 2:19b a current proverb: "A man becomes . . . " In 2 Peter 2:20b we have a saying of Jesus: "Their final state is worse . . . " In 2 Peter 2:21 we have "It would have been better . . . ," possibly modeled on Mark 9:42-47, or Mark 14:21. Second Peter 2:22 informs us that a proverb is being quoted, indeed two: one from Proverbs 26:11 about the dog, and one from *Ahiqar* 8:15 (Arabic) about the pig. In short, our author continues to mine previous sources to make his point. He does not see himself as an original author, but as an adapter, synthesizer, applier of previous traditions and scriptures. Throughout this section he compares the false teachers to irrational animals (2 Pet 2:12, 16, 22: pigs, wild dogs, et al.) which certainly are unclean animals in a Jew's eyes. This invective works especially well with the Jewish part of the audience. It reminds the audience that sin, instead of elevating a person to ecstasy or to equality with God, in fact drags them down into becoming even lower than the most despicable animals a Jew could imagine.

The tone of the invective is heightened here, but we must bear in mind the reason for it: our author's grave concern over Christians being led astray to the pigsty of their old ways of life. These false teachers are both daring and insolent because they do not fear to insult the glorious ones. In view of the background in Jude, this likely means that they were deriding or dismissing the dangers of the devil or demons; "the glorious ones" thus is a reference to fallen angels. This is a quite vague allusion to Jude's citation of *1 Enoch,* but presumably the audience understands our author's drift.

Second Peter 2:11 then follows Jude 9, suggesting in a more general way

---

[184]Here 2 Pet 2:10-11 may reflect Jude's reference to Michael and the devil from *T. Mos.* 10. But if this is the case, our author has generalized the reference to make a broader point.

that even the good angels had a healthy respect for the powers of darkness, even though they had more power and might than these dark powers. Here is a comforting word: if the good angels are more powerful than the bad angels, how much more so Christ and the Father. These good angels do pronounce judgment on the bad, but do not use invective or insults in the process. It is easier to revile the defiled than to convert or judge them. This passage repeatedly uses forms of the word *blasphēmon* for the activity of false teachers (2 Pet 2:10, 12; unlike the good angels, 2 Pet 2:11). As Jude says, they blaspheme/insult what they do not understand (Jude 10; 2 Pet 2:12). The generalizing nature of our author's handling of Jude is especially clear here, and this points us in the direction of seeing this as part of a more general address to the church as a whole, dealing with its endemic and pan-local problems in the postapostolic era. There is a textual issue here: Are the false teachers blaspheming "judgment" *(kyriō)* or blaspheming "the Lord" *(kyriou)?* Probably the former, and the term for "blaspheming" may even modify the word "judgment": a demeaning judgment.[185]

Beginning in **2 Peter 2:12** our author starts comparing the false teachers to immoral animals and natural forces by way of analogy. In a striking analogy he says these people are like animals born to be captured and killed. Two qualities make them like this: (1) They act on animal passions and instinct and are *aloga* (irrational). (2) They are born to be slaughtered: a common idea about animals designed to be killed and used as food.[186] Verse 12c is difficult. It may mean either "in their decadence they will also decay," or "in their destruction they will also be destroyed" or even "suffering hurt for the hurt they inflicted." The obvious Greek wordplay here is hard to render into good English.[187] If the point is to continue the analogy with the beasts, the latter translation is more likely.

Yet a question remains: To whom does "they/their" refer? The "also" *(kai)* adds a further thought, so the last half of the phrase refers to the false teachers: they will also be destroyed or will also decay. It could mean they will share the same fate as the bad angels, or as others have suggested, the fate of irrational animals. We conclude that the translation "decaying" does not fit the context, which is about destruction. They will be destroyed in the same (eschatological) destruction as the evil angels. Our author is engaging in a series of redundancies (destroyed in destruction; hated with hatred, etc.), which is absolutely typical of Asiatic rhetoric, especially when it is trying to be emphatic.

The first part of **2 Peter 2:13** gives us another puzzle. It may refer to their

[185]Kraus, "*Para kyriou* oder *para kyriō* oder omit," pp. 265-73.
[186]Bauckham, *Jude, 2 Peter,* p. 263.
[187]See Horrell, *Peter and Jude*, pp. 166-67.

greed ("being defrauded of the wages of fraud"),[188] mentioned in 2 Peter 2:14b, or may be a presentation of the retribution-and-pain idea: they "are hurt as payback for hurting." Perhaps we should not follow the last translation here because the author has moved on to a new thought. At the day of reckoning those false teachers will be deprived of their ill-gotten gains. Green shows how the metaphor is essentially commercial here.[189] These men are so brazen that they engage in dissipation even during the day, always in hedonistic fashion looking for pleasure. Even by pagan standards this was considered inappropriate behavior and a sign of moral degeneration (cf. also Is 5:11; Eccles 10:16; cf. Acts 2:13, 15).

With a nice alteration of Jude's "rocks," our author calls them "blots and blemishes," which is the opposite to what he later says we ought to be in God's presence: "without blot or blemish" (cf. 3:14).[190] He may be continuing the image of them as animals, in this case animals not even fit for slaughter in a Jew's eyes. They revel in their deceits, and they delight in leading others astray in the way they have gone. Their behavior can be said to be both shameful and yet shameless.[191] *Apatais* is his alteration of *agapē*, "love feast," in Jude. He is saying that their love feasting involves deception, or perhaps that they feed (revel) on deceits. Verse 13b mentions the problem: they are eating with you, and the implication is that the audience should not be giving them such hospitable treatment.

Second Peter 2:14 charges the false teachers with lust. They always have an eye out for a likely sexual partner (literally, "eyes full of adultery"), and the implication is that they are looking for them at the love feasts or at least among God's people.[192] There may be a traditional pun in play here: the shameless man is said not to have "pupils" *(korai)* in his eyes but rather "harlots" (*pornai;* see Plutarch *Mor.* 528E).[193] Their practice is not just to drag Christians back into pagan ways, but also to drag the church itself down to the pagan level. They do not wish to leave the church or convert others to leave: they want to lead the church astray. They do not cease from sinning, and they are able to entice the unstable into it. They are quite capable of doing this, having been well schooled in how to bilk an unstable person of what they are worth.

Our author can only call them "children of a curse," a Hebrew metaphor (cf.

[188]See Metzger, *TC,* p. 703.
[189]Green, *2 Peter,* p. 109.
[190]See Moo, *2 Peter, Jude,* p. 125.
[191]Harrington, *Jude and 2 Peter,* p. 272.
[192]The words *akatapaustos hamartias,* meaning "unceasing lust" or "unceasing sin," here refer to "everlasting love" in the love charm inscription found on a lead tablet. See *NewDocs* 2:45-46.
[193]See the discussion in Watson, "2 Peter," p. 351.

Is 57:4; Hos 10:9; Sir 41:9-10). This means that they are accursed by God and are not his true representatives. In **2 Peter 2:15** to say that they have forsaken the "straight" or "righteous way" (cf. 2 Pet 2:2, 21; Acts 13:10) refers to their chosen way of life, pattern of behavior. They have done the opposite of "gone straight," as we would say. Our author says these teachers are like Balaam, probably not because they are prophets, but because they are mad and greedy. Again we see, as we did in Jude, the characterizing of Balaam as greedy (cf. Num 22:16-18; 24:10-14, presenting Balaam as resisting the temptation to be greedy). Here again our author relies on Jewish tradition, not the letter of the Old Testament. He is saying that they are like greedy Balaam in the popular story.

In the popular Jewish tale the donkey reproves Balaam; however, in Numbers an angel reproves him, and his donkey just complains (cf. Num 22:22-35). Here again in **2 Peter 2:16**, the discourse relies on popular expansion (*Tg. Ps.-J.* on Num 22:30). Our author calls Balaam "son of Bosor," but in the Old Testament Beor is his father (Num 22:5). This, however, is probably a play on words, on the Hebrew word *bāśār*, "flesh." Like Balaam, these false teachers are sons of the flesh.[194] The aural device here is particularly clever. Further, our author coins a word for madness, *paraphronia* (normally *paraphronēsis*), so that it will rhyme with the word for transgression: *paranomia*. Here is one more reminder that this is a discourse meant to be heard, not silently read. The implication of verse 16 is that even the dumb donkey (unable to speak in a human way) was smarter than Balaam, and by analogy even irrational animals are brighter than the false teachers, who did not heed or fear angels, but the donkey did in the Balaam story.

Second Peter 2:17-22 begins a new round of invective and apologies. Up through 2 Peter 2:16 our author was focusing on the false character of the false teachers; now he will turn to focus on their bad effects on others, and not surprisingly he turns up the volume on the invective here because it is one thing to destroy yourself, and another thing to destroy other unsuspecting Christians.[195] As in **2 Peter 2:17**, a "waterless well" was a cause for bitterness in Israel, "a dry and weary land" (Ps 63:1). Our author changes Jude's metaphors in Jude 12, which refers to waterless clouds. Here the image of an empty, dry well is apt. These men are empty of any life-giving sustenance and have quenched the Spirit in their own lives. The next metaphor, "They are like mists driven by a storm," may mean that they promise rain but do not produce it, or it may refer to the optical allusion of haze that appears to be rain. Calvin thinks of little

[194]On all this, see Green, *2 Peter*, p. 125; Bauckham, *Jude, 2 Peter*, pp. 267-68.
[195]See Moo, *2 Peter, Jude*, p. 140.

clouds that cast only a shadow but shed no rain. Green adds: "As for the darkness reserved for the heretics, Calvin writes, 'In place of the momentary darkness which they now cast, there is prepared for them a much thicker and eternal one.' Surely he has understood the link between the errorists' crime and punishment, which has escaped most commentators, who complain that darkness is a very inappropriate doom for mists or springs!"[196]

In any case the gloom of eternal darkness, as with the fallen angels, has been reserved for these false teachers. They are good at using empty and grandiose words to entice people to lead them into sexual sin, as well as to defraud them of their money. In **2 Peter 2:18** we have an interesting phrase, ***hyperonka mataiotētos,*** "empty bombast," a phrase sometimes used to describe Asiatic rhetoric by its cultured despisers![197] Clearly the false teachers might well see this as a case of the pot calling the kettle black, since our own author, and especially in this very chapter, is pulling out all the Asiatic rhetorical stops. Second Peter 2:18-20 presents a sad contrast between what 2 Peter 1:3-4 says that God offers and what the false teachers actually offer.[198]

The false teachers prey upon those barely escaping (*oligōs* here means "barely" or "just" or "scarcely," and it is the right reading). That is, they prey on new converts and convert back them into pagans. These converts are still in the process of breaking away from pagan ways. "Those living in error" are the pagans in general, not the false teachers. The teachers' empty words involve promising people freedom, presumably freedom from a coming judgment, which they deny, and certainly freedom from moral restraint. This so-called gospel may be a perversion of Paul's gospel of grace and justice, as 2 Peter 3:15-16 may suggest. Paul was surely one of the apostles who evangelized regions where part of this audience resided, and so his words would be carefully followed. It is likely that these false teachers are twisting Paul's words out of context to support their sin-free judgment-free gospel.

In **2 Peter 2:19**, however, the false teachers' promise of freedom is bogus and ironic because they themselves are slaves of corruption (or possibly destruction). Romans 8:21 may be in the background, which our author may know a bit of, being from and in Rome, though here may be the one and only place where he reflects his knowledge of Paul.[199] Perhaps he is avoiding Pauline terms so as to distinguish himself from the false teachers. Rather than being free, by

[196]Green, *2 Peter,* p. 115, following Calvin.
[197]See Hillyer, *1 and 2 Peter,* p. 205.
[198]See Horrell, *Peter and Jude,* p. 171.
[199]Bauckham, *Jude, 2 Peter,* p. 276.

choosing sin, they are bound to their sin: it has its grip on them, not vice versa. Here our author begins to apply well-known proverbs to the opponents, to suggest that these sort of deceivers and sinners are nothing new, and no one should be surprised or impressed by them. The proverb in **2 Peter 2:19b** suggests that if one does not have victory over something, one serves it as a slave serves a master (a bad habit, etc.) (Mt 6:24; Jn 8:34; Rom 6:6, 16).

Second Peter 2:20 makes a surprising statement, implying that these false teachers were once Christian converts. Some have suggested that the statement should probably be taken as hypothetical. Green, however, thinks that actual apostasy is described here of those who once were genuinely Christian, and he may well be right.[200] Our author is saying, "Even if they once came to know Jesus, having escaped pagan immorality, they have again been defeated/entangled by that sort of sin, so that as Jesus said (Mt 12:45//Lk 11:26), their last condition is worst than their first (pre-Christian) one."

Why? As **2 Peter 2:21** says, because it would have been better not to know Christ: then their judgment would ultimately have been less severe. They have turned back from obedience to the holy commandment (the sanctified way of life they were exhorted to follow), which was definitely passed down to them. It was not a case of their not knowing about the Christian call to moral behavior. Green, aptly says:

> No man can serve two masters; but all men must serve one. These men were not the last to set liberty against law. Yet their vaunted liberty turned into licence, and generated a new bondage. On the other hand glad bondage to the law of Christ, which was so disparaged by the false teachers, leads in fact to an emancipation more complete than the errorists could ever have imagined. Peter has already shown, in i.3, 4, that true liberty, true escape from the relentless grip of

---

[200]See Green, *2 Peter*, p. 131. On the basis of this text and Heb 6 and several texts, he stresses, "Apostasy would seem to be a real and awful possibility." He is right about this. For a good example of what trouble a faulty theological system brings someone, even leading to the denying of the straightforward meaning of a text and resorting to exegetical gymnastics, see the treatment of these verses about apostasy by Schreiner, *1, 2 Peter, Jude*, pp. 330-31, 355-59. He tries to argue that our author is using "phenomenological" language here. That is, the false teachers merely appear to be Christians, make a confession and appear to be converted and so on. But this is not what this text says. Our author claims that Christ died for these people, they had some benefit from this through conversion, and then they turned their backs on it. The whole point of the metaphors at the end of the argument is that they are turning back to a lifestyle that they had genuinely left behind for a period of time! Schreiner also wants to read 2 Pet 1:3 to mean that the audience was "effectually called" (irrevocably chosen by God). But this is not what the language of "calling" means here or elsewhere in the NT. One has to import the idea of "effectual" into it to make it mean "irrevocably chosen."

phthora,[201] comes through knowing Jesus Christ. So here he shows that precept and love, charity and chastity, law and gospel are not combatants but correlatives. It is ever the way of licence to champion gospel over law, and of dead orthodoxy to champion precept over love. Healthy Christian living comes when God's commands are seen as the kerbstones on His highway of love, the hedge encompassing His garden of grace.[202]

From a social point of view, one can say: "The danger of apostasy was clearly a reality in the early church; as has always been the case, people sometimes turned away from something to which they were once converted. A horror of apostasy and vivid declarations of the grievous state in which apostates find themselves are found both here and in Hebrews (6:4-6; 10:26). Gradually a system of penance for postbaptismal sin and even for apostasy evolved; but apostasy remained a particularly serious offense."[203]

In **2 Peter 2:22** we have the word *paroimia,* which here means something like a "proverb" or "maxim," but we can compare its use in John 10:6 and 16:25, 29, where it has the sense of a veiled or apocalyptic saying that conceals not merely secret but also profound truths.[204] Here the former sapiential sense prevails. It was traditional in Jewish religion to talk about the ethical life as a "way," in this case a "way of righteousness" (Prov 21:16, 21 LXX; Mt 21:32). Here we are talking about the teaching and tradition once delivered to the church by the apostles and now passed on to the next generation. Jerome H. Neyrey cites an interesting parallel in *Epistle of Barnabas* 5.4, where the author is reflecting on Proverbs 1:17 and takes it to mean that "a man deserves to perish who has knowledge of the way of righteousness, but turns aside into the way of darkness."[205] The "better than" form of the proverb here is quite familiar in the Wisdom literature (Prov 15:17; Eccles 7:2, 5; Mk 9:43-48; 1 Pet 3:17).[206]

Here in 2 Peter 2:22 our author suggests that these people are the most disgusting sorts of creatures imaginable: like a dog returning to sniff its own vomit. The analogy is that these false teachers have apparently rid themselves of such corruption at conversion only to turn back to it with a vengeance. The second proverb seems to come from a pagan source, perhaps chosen to suggest that even pagan writers condemn such behavior.[207] The rhetorical effect of this com-

[201]Kelly, *Epistles of Peter,* p. 346, points out that *phthora* does not allude just to moral corruption but also to spiritual death (cf. 2 Pet 1:4; 2:12).

[202]Green, *2 Peter,* pp. 117-18.

[203]Horrell, *Peter and Jude,* p. 172.

[204]See Harrington, *Jude and 2 Peter,* p. 278.

[205]See Neyrey, *2 Peter, Jude,* p. 224.

[206]See the discussion in Snyder, "*Tobspruch* in the New Testament," pp. 117-20.

[207]Green, *2 Peter,* pp. 121-22.

parison is meant to so cast odium on the false teachers that the audience will react viscerally, not merely by saying "yuck," but also by casting these teachers out of their fellowship meals and presence. Otherwise, they will be constantly cleaning up after them like one must do when a dog vomits in the house, leaving a stench for a long time to come. The first proverb comes from Proverbs 26:11, and the second from the book of *Ahiqar* 8:15: "My son, you have behaved like the pig that went to the baths with people of quality, and when he came out and saw a stinking ditch, he went and wallowed in it."[208] Notice that here the word *borboros*, "mud" or "filth," is not only rare (see Jer 45:6 LXX [38:6 ET], a miry pit; cf. "slimy pit," "mud and mire," in Ps 40:2 NIV); it is also onomatopoeic, one more small reminder this was meant to be heard, indeed to be delivered in an orally effective manner.

2 Peter 3:1-13—Last Argument About the Last Things

> All those who love our Lord's return must have a balanced approach to the whole question. We must not think that it is so near that it will come before time, but neither must we think that it will not come until much later. Rather we must be careful to make sure that, whether Christ comes sooner or later, he will find us ready and waiting for him when he appears. (Bede [*On 2 Peter*])[209]

> It must not be forgotten that this letter is counterfeit, and although it may be published, it does not form part of the earliest list of received writings. (Didymus [*Commentary on 2 Peter*])[210]

> A thousand years is the time that the temple worship lasted. For from the completion of the temple by Solomon, who built the Lord's house until it became redundant when Christ died on the cross, is a thousand years. This thousand years is compared to a day, or to a watch in the night, because everything appeared to be night before the coming of the Savior. For until the sun of righteousness arose, everyone dwelt in ignorance and confusion. (Athanasius)[211]

In a rhetorically effective Christian discourse, it was certainly not unusual to reserve the discussion of "the last things" until last, the final argument in the discourse. A good example of this from earlier Christian rhetoric would be either 1 Thessalonians or 1 Corinthians. Rhetorically speaking, a speaker wanted to have the last argument ringing in the audience's ears as he went into the final peroration and the close of the discourse. It thus is no surprise when the author

[208] There is a Syriac (*Ahiqar* 8:18) and an Arabic (*Ahiqar* 8:15) version, and they vary a little; the Arabic version is closer to 2 Peter and so is cited here. See Bauckham, *Jude, 2 Peter*, p. 279.
[209] PL 93:80.
[210] PG 39:1774.
[211] *CEC* 100.

declares that what he is about to say "last" is of "first importance." The first two or three verses in 2 Peter 3 are transitional in character, as our author is briefly returning to his Petrine source in order to set up the apostolic teaching about the parousia, which follows in this last argument. Watson rightly notices the similarity here in these introductory verses with 2 Peter 1:12-15. He simply does not see why: they are both part of the one Petrine source that our author is using in these places (see below). To support the teaching about the parousia and last judgment,[212] the discourse here appeals to the same two authorities as in 2 Peter 1:15-21: the Old Testament prophets and the apostles like Peter.

The transitional nature of these verses is important because the author is turning away from the invective and to the positive teaching about the parousia, by way of "reminder," a word signaling that we are dealing with values and views already affirmed by the audience, what our author wants them to continue to embrace. In a discourse of praise and blame, it is not surprising that our author would alternate back from what he is against (enunciated in 2 Pet 2) to what he is for. Interpreters have rightly noted that once again in this final argument, our author is drawing on traditional materials, in this case the Jesus tradition. Evald Lövestam has pointed out considerable parallels between 2 Peter 3 and Matthew 24:33-51.[213]

Transitioning here, then, back to the positive argument and drawing on more traditions, this amounts rhetorically to "a return to our point, [we must] repeat it and [then] draw our formal conclusions" (Quintilian *Inst.* 9.1.28). Originally this material may have begun Peter's last penned discourse, of which we have a fragment here and in 2 Peter 1:12-21, but our author is now using this material skillfully to transition to the climactic argument in his own discourse, 2 Peter 3:4-13. The fact that our author is able to perhaps incorporate, though with modification, an idea from Jude in these verses likewise shows just how skillful an editor he is.

For Bauckham and others who take the "testament" view as an explanation for the form of 2 Peter in general, it is a problem that 2 Peter for a large stretch shifts out of the genre of a testament. Chapter two does not really fit as a testament since it is dealing with present problems, not future ones, and there is no hint in 2 Peter 2:1-22 of any personal reflections, indications of death coming on, and so forth. Nor indeed is the transition as smooth between sections because we have no narrative framework as in Acts 20 or elsewhere to introduce the great man's testament. Here we simply shift between past and future sometimes

[212]See Watson, *Invention*, pp. 125-26.

[213]Lövestam, "Eschatologie und Tradition im 2 Petrusbrief," pp. 287-300.

abruptly (2 Pet 2:3a-3b). This suggests that our author is not trying to compose a testament, but rather include a testimony in his work, and sometimes the transition is a bit awkward. Not only so, the differences in grammatical style and word choice are quite apparent if one looks at 2 Peter 1:3-11 versus 2 Peter 1:12-21 and 2 Peter 3:1-3. Even Bauckham is forced to admit the following about 2 Peter 3:1-2: "Verses 1-2, which mention 1 Peter and echo 1:12-15, are doubtless intended to reestablish in the readers' minds the fact that it is Peter's testament they are reading, after a long section in which this has not been evident. In 2:10b-22 the author has been writing about the false teachers in the present tense, as his own contemporaries, but he now wishes to return to the conventions of the testament genre, in order to provide a second prophecy."[214]

When we look further at 2 Peter 3:1-3, we discover even further reason to think that we have a Petrine source here, and this is especially likely if it be allowed that at least 2 Peter 1:12-21 is Petrine. First, we note that Mayor, whose list is incomplete, shows that over half of the nouns, verbs, adjectives and adverbs (significant units) in 2 Peter 3:1-3 are found also in 1 Peter. Thus, for instance, the use of *agapētoi* can as easily be reminiscent of 1 Peter as of Jude 17. Much of the common vocabulary is simple words (unlike in 2 Peter 2 or 2 Peter 1:3-11), the words for write, day, thing, first, last, prophet apostle, holy. There is nothing very florid or special about these words. Bauckham has already admitted, as quoted above, that 2 Peter 3:1-2 are an echo of 2 Peter 1:12-15, and we may even say that even a key phrase is duplicated verbatim at 2 Peter 3:3 *(touto prōton ginōskontes)* from 2 Peter 1:20, so the parallels go farther than 2 Peter 1:12-15. If 2 Peter 1:20 is part of a Petrine source, 2 Peter 3:3 may be as well.

An obstacle in the way of this view, however, comes in the parallels Bauckham thinks he finds between 2 Peter 3:1-3 and Jude 17-18. Several things may be said about this suggestion. If 2 Peter 3:3 reflects 2 Peter 1:20, then 2 Peter 3:3 and Jude 18 need not show a literary relationship. This leaves 2 Peter 3:1 and 2. But we have already noted that the author of 2 Peter is fond of the word *agapētoi,* so it shows no necessary dependence of 2 Peter on Jude here. This leaves 2 Peter 3:2 and Jude 17b. Here again, the parallels at first appear striking but are not necessarily compelling. Christians are always being told to remember or heed the apostolic words or exhortations or commandments. The one word that is not common Christian parlance here is "said beforehand." However, it is precisely this word that we find in Mark 13:23//Matthew 24:25, in the very verse that adjoins Christ's prediction of misleaders who will come. Our au-

[214]Bauckham, *Jude, 2 Peter,* p. 282 n. 10.

thor may have simply passed on Christ's words and prediction of coming false ones in one form, Jude in another. The call to remember the things said beforehand corresponds to the Gospel message: "Behold, I have told you beforehand." The prophecy of the coming false ones is reiterated as a word of the apostles, who in turn have received it from Jesus. We thus conclude that the parallels between 2 Peter 3:1-3 and Jude 17-18, though certainly possible, do not require seeing Jude as the source for 2 Peter here. Both are likely relying on a common source ultimately going back to Jesus' saying in Mark 13:23. Thus we have nothing in 2 Peter 3:1-3 that could not have been part of an original Petrine source. What about 2 Peter 3:4? Bauckham has made a good case for this verse being the beginning of our author's use of a Jewish apocalyptic source. This is quite possible and plausible in view of the parallels with *1 Clement* 23.3 and *2 Clement* 11.2, which are using some such source. If this is so, then I think we likely should note the percentage of Petrine words in the section (2 Pet 3:1-3) is fifty percent, a significant crossover in vocabulary with 1 Peter, but we have no such crossover beginning with 2 Peter 3:4.

We should deal with two other points of note here. First, it is sometimes said that 2 Peter 3:1 cannot be a reference to 1 Peter since 1 Peter is so different from 2 Peter. Here we must agree with Kelly that Peter is thinking of the broad similarity of themes at certain points.

> What he has in mind, we may be sure, . . . are not so much slabs of identical material as, in more general terms, 1 Peter's pervasive concern with the avoidance of immorality and with living blameless, holy lives, and with the blessed inheritance for the righteous and the condemnation of the wicked which Christ's revelation in glory will bring (all themes close to his heart), as also the appeal the earlier letter makes to Christ as an example . . . to the Old Testament as inculcating the good life . . . and prophesying doom to evil-doers, and . . . to the combined authority of the Old Testament prophets, the Spirit of Christ, and apostolic teachers.[215]

Second, what about the troublesome reference to "your apostles" in 2 Peter 3:2? The issue here is who Peter in the Petrine sources is addressing if 2 Peter 3:1-3 goes back to him, not who the compiler of 2 Peter as a whole is addressing, which is all Christians. As Green points out, this is a perfectly possible phrase on Peter's lips if Peter did not evangelize the region he is addressing and if Paul and others did. But even if this refers to an audience that includes not merely areas that Peter evangelized but also areas he did not evangelize, this phrase would be natural. "Your apostles" simply means the ones who

[215]Kelly, *Epistles of Peter*, p. 353.

founded your church, and Peter is looking back on the recent past when the churches were formed, not the distant past, as if all the apostles were now deceased.[216] That he indeed calls them "your apostles" may imply that the audience was alive when they first came, and thus they know and need only to be reminded that those apostles have taught them in essence what Peter is now urging on them.

Finally, on a grammatical note, Max Zerwick and Mary Grosvenor suggest that we translate the phrase in question as "the apostolic command to you of our Lord," or possibly "the commandment of the Lord and Savior transmitted by the apostles to you."[217] If either of these translations is correct, the whole problem is solved. There is no reference to "your apostles" as distinguished from the author of this material. We may add that this phrase could thus actually indicate that 2 Peter 3:2 is referring to Mark 13:22-23, which records Jesus' words about such future troublemakers coupled with his command "Be on guard." We reaffirm the conclusion that 2 Peter 1:12-21 and 2 Peter 3:1-3 are likely from Peter, as was 1 Peter. Possibly it is right to think that 2 Peter 3:1-3 is the beginning of the letter to which we may append 2 Peter 1:12-21. Even so, 2 Peter 3:1-3 would, however, be a fragment of Peter's testimony, not the whole thing.[218]

Let us return for a moment to the rhetorical nature and effect of this argument we have in 2 Peter 3:1-13, taken as a whole. From a rhetorical point of view, speakers deemed it most effective to save the most important point and argument until last. Sometimes this was the matter that spawned the discourse in the first place, sometimes the bone of contention that one did not want to tackle until well and truly winning the audience. As Quintilian says, "The judge is always in a hurry to reach the most important point" (Quintilian *Inst.* 4.5.9), but the rhetor on the other hand must be patient and let his arguments build to a climax. Quintilian is right that a good orator will not merely instruct the mind but also appeal to the emotions throughout the discourse, to win both mind and heart. In epideictic rhetoric, the rhetoric of praise and blame, it is the orator's duty at the end to make clear the essential values and views that the audience needs to continue to embrace.

One way of looking at 2 Peter 3:4-13 from a rhetorical point of view is to say that here we have the elements of a diatribe, where the false teachers have asked a rhetorical question that implies a denial of orthodox eschatology, and

---

[216]See Horrell, *Peter and Jude*, p. 175.

[217]Max Zerwick and Mary Grosvenor, *Grammatical Analysis of the Greek New Testament,* vol. 2, *Epistles—Apocalypse,* English rev. ed. (Rome: Biblical Institute Press, 1979), p. 723; also MHT 3:218; BDF, sec. 168.1, p. 93.

[218]See Bauckham, *Jude, 2* Peter, p. 285.

our author answers and refutes their implied view in 2 Peter 3:5-13.[219] Note, however, how our author goes about this. He reminds the audience of what they already believe, which is to be contrasted with what has "escaped the notice" of these false teachers. By doing an exposition of what really is the case about the parousia, our author reminds the audience of what praiseworthy and blameworthy teaching on this subject looks like. Our author draws on Old Testament examples and early Jewish Christian teaching to make his point. He is actually amplifying what he has already said (cf. 2 Pet 2:4-9 and 2 Pet 3:5-7), as is typical in both Asiatic and especially epideictic rhetoric. Thus 2 Peter 3:4-13 does not bring up an entirely new argument or make an entirely new case. Watson has shown how we have several compressed syllogisms in this material, or enthymemes.[220] Notice how the argument ends with the exhortation to "wait" on the parousia since it will come in God's good time. Any such exhortation to wait, and to continue to hold on to values and views already embraced, is certainly forward looking but also focused on the present posture to be inculcated in the audience. The audience is not asked to change belief or behavior but to accept a reminder and to wait while standing firm: these all are characteristic epideictic appeals.

In terms of teaching, perhaps the one thing that concerns our author most about the false teachers is their denial of the parousia and ensuing final judgment. As a Christian teacher in his own right, he is indeed worried about what will happen during the postapostolic era in his audience's minds and hearts, as the clock ticks longer and Jesus has still not returned. While he knows that one cannot really talk about a delay of an event if there has never been a promise of a precise time frame in which it must happen, he knows that Christian expectation was such that it led some to move in their minds from eager expectation to calculation and thence to disappointment. He thus must set the balance back where it should be—with expectation and certainty about the fact of the coming parousia coupled with a denial of knowing the timing. But he goes further to suggest something the audience may never have considered: Christ has not come back yet due to God's great mercy, giving more time for amendment of life. This is an important theme, which would resonate through a good deal of the postapostolic era. And our author has provided a rubric for dealing with the problem of misguided calculations while affirming expectations. When we reach the close of 2 Peter, we will be able to reflect on the sort of theologizing and ethicizing into the new generation that our author is doing. We can say here

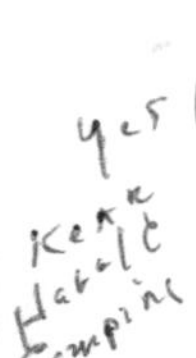

[219]See Watson, *Invention,* pp. 128-29.
[220]Ibid., pp. 129-30.

that there is a sense in which this discourse is one giant transitional argument, helping the audience to make the next step without leaving the essential apostolic teaching behind.[221]

3:1 Beloved, this is already the second letter I write to you, in which I arouse your pure
mind with a reminder. 2 Remember the things that were said beforehand by the holy
prophets and the commandment of the Lord and Savior transmitted by the apostles
to you, 3 knowing this first, that mockers will come at the ends (last) of the days in
mockery following according to their own lusts 4 and saying, "Where is the promise
of his parousia? For from the days in which the fathers fell asleep, all things remain
in the same way from the beginning of creation."
5 For, wishing this (to be so), they deliberately ignore that the heavens were from of
old and the earth had been put together out of water and by means of water by God's
word. 6 Through these, then, the world being deluged by water was destroyed. 7 But
the heavens and earth that now are by the same word have been preserved for fire,
having been kept unto the day of judgment and destruction of ungodly people.
8 But do not let yourself be ignorant in this, beloved, because one day with the Lord
is as a thousand years, and a thousand years as one day. 9 The Lord is not late (or
slow) in effecting the promise as some think of lateness, but shows patience unto
you, not wishing any to perish but all to be brought unto repentance. 10 But the Day
of the Lord will arrive, like a thief, on which (day) the heavens will pass away with
a loud noise, and the elements being burned will fall apart, and earth and all the
works in it will be found.
11 Since all these things are to be dissolved, what kind of (person) is it necessary for
you to be in holy life and godliness, 12 while waiting and hastening the parousia of
the day of God, because of which heavens being set on fire will dissolve and the
heavenly bodies burning will melt? 13 But we wait for a new heaven and a new earth,
according to his promise in which righteousness dwells.

Second Peter 3:1 likely refers back to Peter's first letter in a general way. Some scholars have assumed that this strongly suggests that both letters were originally intended to have the same audience. The most one can actually say is that our author assumes that his audience by now knows of 1 Peter, but then that would surely involve a much wider audience than the original one of 1 Peter, if 2 Peter is written at some point during the last decade of the century.[222] It is unlikely that the "first letter" refers to a now lost letter because, as seen above, there is some common material in the two letters.[223] Second Peter 1:12-21 and

[221]See Farkasfalvy, "Ecclesial Setting of Pseudepigraphy," pp. 3-29.

[222]See, e.g., Kelly, *Epistles of Peter*, p. 353: "All we need infer is that the author feels entitled to suppose that it is being read in the particular communities he has in mind in the first instance."

[223]Bauckham, *Jude, 2 Peter*, pp. 285-86; against M. Green, *2 Peter*, pp. 134-35.

2 Peter 3:1-3 indeed are where most of the similarities to 1 Peter appear.[224] Here the strong return to the first person singular again reflects the use of the source material, as well as the clear parallels: 2 Peter 3:1 and 2 Peter 1:13, also 2 Peter 3:3 and 2 Peter 1:20.[225] Since the earlier Petrine fragment refers to eschatology, these verses are the perfect introduction to our own author's further delineation of the apostolic teaching on that matter.

Peter calls them "beloved" and trusts that they are still mostly faithful. Here in verse 1 and at 2 Peter 3:8, 14 and 17 we have the use of *agapētoi* as our author seeks to cement his bond with the audience in a rhetorically effective way at the end of the discourse. Peter adds that they have a pure mind, probably meaning a sincere understanding or perhaps a wholesome mind. Plato uses this exact same phrase but to mean "pure reason" (*Phaedo* 66a). Nevertheless, perhaps here we have one more example of trying to relate to Hellenized Christians familiar with Greco-Roman culture. He is thus counting on them to remember and act on the truth as sincere Christians, though they are under temptation.

In **2 Peter 3:2** our author is waking them up by a reminder that both the Old Testament prophets and Jesus predicted such scoffers (cf. Is 5:18-20; Jer 5:12-24; Ezek 12:22; Amos 9:10; Zeph 1:12; Mal 2:17), and that Jesus himself by way of the apostles gave them a command as to what to do about it: be on guard, stay alert, watch out. The reference back to the prophets and apostles as the authority figures conveying the truth was to become standard in the postapostolic age (cf. *2 Clem.* 14.2; Ign. *Phld.* 5; 9; Pol. *Phil.* 6).

The reference to the holy prophets is not at all impossible on Peter's lips and is not at all a sign of lateness (cf. Lk 1:70). In fact, we find it in a speech by Peter in Acts 3:21. It is characteristic of the Peter of Acts and 1 Peter that he relies on Old Testament prophecy to refute his foes' slanders against the Gospel and to vindicate its truth. Second Peter 1:12-21 and 2 Peter 3:1-3 show the same sort of reliance. We may also compare the phrase "your apostles" to *1 Clement* 44.1, where "our apostles" refers to those who founded the Roman church.[226]

In **2 Peter 3:3** the phrase *eschatōn tōn hemerōn* literally means "the ends of the days" and could be translated, "when the days were drawing to a close" (cf. LXX: Gen 49:1; Deut 4:30; Dan 2:28).[227] The phrase clearly indicates that Peter

[224]If this material in 2 Pet 3:1-3 does go back to Peter, then Peter himself could be reminding the audience of his earlier letter now that he is writing down his testimony. Second Peter 3:1-3 need not just be a reference to Peter himself; indeed, the reference to writing previously must count against such a theory.

[225]See Moffatt, *General Epistles*, p. 201.

[226]See Green, *2 Peter*, p. 137.

[227]See Mayor, *Jude, 2 Peter*, pp. 146-47, who is following J. B. Lightfoot.

thought he and his audience were living in the last age of human history, the eschatological age. It is possible that he also thought the end was at hand, that the last days of the last age were nigh. However, we observe that these words are in a prophecy, and Peter may take it to mean no more than that the presence of scoffers (false teachers?) is a sign that the last times are upon us. Notice the rhetorical effect here: "Scoffers will come with scoffing." Thus, ironically, the presence of teachers who deny that the end of the world and judgment will come is a sure sign that we are in history's last period! These mockers follow their own desires, which are evil and not God's will, scoffing at his commandments and judgment and future coming. The "scoffer" or "mocker" is a stock figure in Wisdom literature and refers not just to the cynical but also to one who ridicules something he cannot understand. As such, he is close to the "fool," another stock figure in Wisdom literature (cf. Ps 1:1; Prov 1:22; 9:7-8; 13:1; cf. Amos 9:10 and Mal 2:17 for those who mock divine judgment).[228] Here the mocking is said to be "according to their passions." They ridicule the notion that their behavior will be judged at some future final occasion because such a belief interferes with their pursuit of their sensual lifestyle. The word here is *epithymia,* "passion," considered one of the cardinal vices.[229]

Second Peter 3:4 begins the use of Jewish apocalyptic material, which may be yet another source on which our author draws.[230] We may compare Ezekiel 12:22 and the cynical questions in Psalm 41:4, 11 LXX (42:3, 10 ET; cf. Jer 17:15; Mal 2:17). Here, however, we have a rhetorical question that is going to receive a full length rhetorical answer! The scoffers strike at a crucial issue in the early church: Why has the second coming not happened? There is no doubt that this was a problem even as early as when Paul wrote 1 Thessalonians, perhaps because of some of Jesus' teaching (cf. Mk 9:1; 13:30; Lk 21:32; Jn 21:22-23). It became an even more acute problem when the apostles or most of them died and the end had still not come.

The reference to the promise of his coming is likely to reflect Jesus' own words promising the parousia. The word *parousia* found here is not used in 1 Peter, perhaps a clue that 2 Peter 3:4 is not by Peter, as we have granted that it was not. Verse 4b is difficult because of its reference to the fathers: is it a reference to Old Testament patriarchs? This is its normal meaning. Indeed we have evidence in the New Testament to support the view that it does not refer to the

---

[228]See Moo, *2 Peter, Jude,* p. 166.

[229]Neyrey, *2 Peter, Jude,* p. 227.

[230]See Bauckham, *Jude, 2 Peter,* pp. 283-85. He compares material we find in *1 Clem.* 23.3 and *2 Clem.* 11.2, which seems to be citing such a Jewish source.

first Christian generation, or the apostles (cf. Jn 7:22; Acts 13:32; Rom 9:5; Heb 1:1). In favor of a reference to the Old Testament patriarchs here is that the author goes on to use the phrase "since the beginning of creation," and clearly the apostles were not around that long ago. Furthermore, this reference to the fathers is on the lips of the scoffers, not our author, and it is connected to the promise of his coming, which *may* suggest a reference to the first Christians, or early Christian leaders.[231]

Let us suppose that James, Peter and Paul are now all dead when 2 Peter is being written. It is possible that such skepticism would have particular force in that period, especially among those who understood that the end was promised to come before the first generation of believers or the apostles died (see Mt 16:28; Mk 9:1; Jn 21). They die, and now the scoffers can say, "See, nothing has happened!" The verb *ekoimēthesan*, "fell asleep," is a common metaphor for death. Here we may have its Christian usage, for in the Gospels and Paul it often means that death in God's hands is no more harmful than sleep, from which one awakes alert, alive, refreshed at the resurrection. Again, however, it is the scoffers who are using the term, and one wonders if they believed in any afterlife, so it probably just means death here. Possibly, then, "fathers" is indeed a reference, even if unprecedented, to the early Christian leaders who have died (perhaps cf. 1 John 2:13-14, referring to spiritual "fathers").[232] Obviously, the argument "Ever since the Old Testament fathers have died nothing has changed" could easily be rebutted. One could say, "But it did when *Jesus* came the first time," which the scoffers apparently believe did happen, or at least once believed it (cf. 2 Pet 2:20). As Bauckham notes, the point of 2 Peter 3:4b is not to argue the immutability of the universe, but that God will not or will not again intervene in human history. "It is not necessary to seek the background to the scoffers' ideas in the Aristotelian belief in the imperishability of the world, which was denied by Epicureans and Stoics. They are not influenced by cosmology as much as by a rationalistic skepticism about divine intervention in the world, to which the Epicurean denial of providence seems the closest pagan parallel."[233]

Basically they are denying divine intervention in history at all ("since creation all remains the same"), but it is also possible that they thought cause and effect would go on forever. In any case, our author responds: (1) the parousia is coming, and (2) so is the end of the world. There is going to be a big change, but for the scoffers it will be a change for the worse.

---

[231]See Horrell, *Peter and Jude*, p. 176.

[232]See Witherington, *Letters and Homilies for Hellenized Christians*, 1:474-77.

[233]Bauckham, *Jude, 2 Peter*, p. 294.

Beginning with **2 Peter 3:5**, our author begins to reply to the quoted scoffers. He gives a response both about the delay of the parousia and its reasons, and also about the falseness of supposing that nothing ever has and thus nothing ever will change in this world so far as divine intervention is concerned. It is possible that the false teachers' critique was not to say "no divine intervention" in human history, but to say "no divine judgment" in history. How could they deny intervention altogether without denying the incarnation of Christ? As in other New Testament texts, these verses posit a connection between the destiny and fate of humans and the destiny and fate of the physical earth (see Rom 8).[234] Redemption and judgment in a sense involves all creation, not just the creature, though clearly the focus is on the latter. In verse 5 our author accuses the opponents of wishful thinking and probably also of deliberately ignoring (not just overlooking) various Old Testament texts and events. This verse clearly refers to creation, and much here has been made of the use of Genesis 1:2-10: the creation of the world out of the primeval chaos waters (LXX *hydōr*; Heb *mayîm*) over which the Spirit hovered. Apparently these waters were then assumed to become the heavenly ocean, the waters above the firmament, out of which God pulled the plugs when he let down the rains that led to the flood.[235] The point of our passage is not to teach cosmology, except in general to make the following points, though the focus is clearly on God's judgment of humans (2 Pet 3:7b) and the attendant circumstances.[236]

1. God created the earth, bringing forth land by separating the waters (above) from the waters (below), and so forth. In this sense the earth could be said to be created by water. The reference to "out of waters" means probably out of the original chaos (Gen 1:2-10).
2. God caused the earth to experience an initial destruction at the flood (Gen 6:17: LXX *kataklysmos hydōr;* Heb *mabbûl mayîm*). Clearly our author sees it as a worldwide cataclysm, not a local flood.
3. All of creation was made and remade by God's word.

The final judgment will entail another worldwide cataclysm, but this time by fire.[237]

[234]It is possible that the scoffers held the eternal universe theory, that the universe has always been, to which the Christian rebuttal would be, "No, it was created at one juncture by God speaking." Nevertheless, it seems more likely that they are simply denying divine intervention in the recent past and into the future. But see Horrell, *Peter and Jude,* pp. 176-77.

[235]Bauckham, *Jude, 2 Peter,* p. 295.

[236]See Dupont-Roc, "Le motif de la creation selon 2 Pierre 3," pp. 95-114.

[237]Now, none of this can in fact be gainsaid by modern science, and in some ways Gen 1—2 comports with the big bang theory, on which see Paul Davies, *God and the New Physics* (New York: Simon & Schuster, 1984).

In 2 Peter 3:5-13 we have deliberate contrast among the old (then) world, the present world, the new heavens and new earth. The point of this all is to contradict the opponent's charge that nothing changes by saying: "God has started and changed things before, and he will do so again. It is the same God, and his same divine fiat that caused the first creation will cause, by the same word, the final conflagration."

Although **2 Peter 3:6** suggests a worldwide flood, it is not clear that it necessitates the view that our author thought that God made a whole new world after the flood.[238] At the beginning of this verse, it is not clear what the antecedents of *di hōn* are, but probably "through which things" refers to water and God's word, the proximate and ultimate cause of these things.[239] The notion of a whole new world would hardly comport with the Genesis story. Rather, it is a whole new *human* world, and all its organization and facets begin again after the flood. *Kosmos* is then used somewhat similarly to what we find in 2 Peter 2:5, where it specifies the world of godless people that is washed away. Bauckham stresses:

> We may therefore concede that in 3:6 his emphasis is on the Flood as a universal judgment on sinful men and women. But he evidently conceives this judgment as having been executed by means of a cosmic catastrophe which affected the heavens as well as the earth.
>
> The idea of the destruction of the antediluvian world need not be taken to mean total annihilation. Rather, just as it was created by being brought out of the primeval ocean, so it was destroyed when it was once again submerged in the primeval ocean. The ordered world . . . reverted to chaos.
>
> The author of 2 Peter (no doubt following his Jewish apocalyptic source) seems to envisage world history in three great periods, divided by two great cataclysms: the world before the flood, the present world which will end in the eschatological conflagration (v. 7), and the new world to come (v. 13).[240]

In **2 Peter 3:7** our author proceeds to argue that the world has been preserved, kept, stored up for fire, a fire that will come on judgment day, when ungodly people will be destroyed (cf. Is 30:30; Nahum 1:6; Zeph 1:18; 3:8). The participle of the verb *thēsaurizein* is found here, which means stored up, and is the source of our word "thesaurus," a storehouse of information.[241] At least at this point the text does not say that the known world will be annihilated, but

[238]See Horrell, *Peter and Jude*, pp. 177-78; Kelly, *Epistles of Peter*, pp. 356-57.
[239]Green, *2 Peter*, pp. 141-42.
[240]Bauckham, *Jude, 2 Peter*, p. 299.
[241]Hillyer, *1 and 2 Peter*, p. 215.

merely that it will be destroyed. In 2 Peter 3:10 we will see the world depicted as collapsing, falling apart, the melting of the stars, and the dissolving of the heavens—not unlike what would happen if the earth was absorbed back into our sun and our part of the universe collapsed. This still does not mean that the collapse leaves nothing out of which the new heavens and earth would and could be made. Obviously, there are numerous Old Testament texts that use fire to speak of the fate of the wicked (Deut 32:22; Ps 97:3, Is 66:15-16). Unlike our text, Stoics taught that such a conflagration was periodic and natural. Thus

> the essential element in most Jewish and Christian references to the eschatological conflagration is the destruction of the wicked by the fire of divine judgment; this idea, which differs from the Zoroastrian fire of purification and from the Stoic idea of a natural, deterministic cycle of destruction and renewal, is fundamentally Jewish and biblical. The author of 2 Peter, who is really interested in the conflagration as judgment on the wicked, . . . follows this Jewish tradition. If he was aware of the pagan parallels, he is unlikely to have been very concerned with them.[242]

The idea that the world has been kept until that judgment day may imply that the world will not end until then. Until then, the world will be preserved. The verb "are being kept" has been applied to the bad angels and perhaps to the unrighteous in 2:9 and to the false teachers, and now to the heaven and earth: it is reserved, set aside for, kept until judgment day, and will undergo judgment and destruction similar to the bad angels and humans. Josephus (*Ant.* 1.70) tells us that early Jews sometimes attributed to Adam himself the notion of a dual cataclysm by water and by fire. Later Zoroastrian or even Stoic speculations that involve the idea of a repeated restoration of the earth through fire need not enter into the discussion here.[243] Melito of Sardis, writing near the end of the second century, puts it this way: "There was a flood of water. . . . There will be a flood of fire, and the earth will be burned up together with its mountains, . . . and the just will be delivered from its fury as their fellow humans in the ark were saved from the waters of the deluge."[244] We may also quote the Jewish *Sibylline Oracles* 2:200-211: "For stars from heaven will fall into all the seas, and all the souls of human beings shall gnash their teeth. Burned both by sulphur stream and force of fire in ravenous soil, and ashes hide all things. And then the world shall be bereft of all the elements—air, earth, sea, light, sky, days, nights; and no longer in the air shall fly birds without number, nor shall living things which

[242]Bauckham, *Jude, 2 Peter*, p. 301.

[243]See the helpful analysis in M. Green, *2 Peter*, pp. 143-44; cf. Thiede, "Pagan Reader of 2 Peter," pp. 79-96.

[244]Green, *2 Peter*, p. 145.

swim in the sea, swim any longer, nor heavy cargo ship pass over the waves, nor straight-cutting plow carve the field" (cf. *1 En.* 83:3-5).

In **2 Peter 3:8** our author contrasts his readers with the false teachers, but it is particularly telling that our author thinks that at least some in his audience may share the doubts about the parousia expressed by the false teachers.[245] Though they may well fully ignore Old Testament prophecy and examples and the changes the universe has already undergone, his readers must not let it or several other factors escape their notice.[246] For instance, he refers to what Psalm 89:4 LXX (90:4 ET) says: "For a thousand years in your sight are like a day that has just gone by." Now 2 Peter 3:8 corresponds to this only in the second half of the sentence. The first half says, "One day is as a thousand years." In some ways it would be easier if we only had verse 8b and not also verse 8a to cope with. The general drift is clear enough: God's time is not the same as human time. If this is what is meant, then it is saying that in eternity a different time clock operates than in present time. This might lead to the conclusion that ever since Christ brought eternity and the eschatological things into present time, we are operating on a different clock: the last days in the eschatological age are days according to God's clock, not ours. "You must not use normal human reckoning to assess the Lord's time," our author would be suggesting. However, perhaps these words mean that God's view of human time is not the same as our view of it, in which case our author is simply saying, "You need to see things from God's perspective." Green, for example, points out that not only does God see time from a different perspective (a thousand years would seem but a day to an eternal being), but also God sees time with an intensity that we lack (one day can seem like a thousand years to God).[247] Bauckham reminds:

> In the first place, God, who determines the time of the Parousia, does so from a different perspective on time from that of men and women. He is not limited by a human life span, but surveys the whole course of human history, so that, as the psalmist observed (Ps. 90:4), periods which by human standards are of great length may be from his perspective very short. Those who complain of the delay of the Parousia, impatient to see it in their own lifetime, are limiting the divine strategy in

[245] See Horrell, *Peter and Jude*, p. 178, noting that the same verb "forget" crops up in both 2 Pet 3:5 and 2 Pet 3:8, only this time it is the audience who is forgetting.

[246] The contrast is made here between the false teachers, who ignore certain truths, and the audience, who is encouraged not to ignore one fact. See Watson, "2 Peter," p. 356. This speaks to the different spiritual conditions our author thinks the false teachers and the audience are in. The audience might overlook a truth, but they would not deliberately ignore or repudiate truth.

[247] Green, *2 Peter*, p. 146.

history to the short-term expectations to which transient human beings are accustomed. But God's purpose transcends such expectations. Thus the false teachers' accusation, that it is now too late for the Parousia to be expected, is based on their own evaluation of "lateness," not necessarily on God's.[248]

Yet the problem with this view is that it does not merely say, "A thousand years is as a day." It also adds the converse, suggesting that one day for God could be a thousand times longer than we reckon one day. Therefore in God's sight time is both contractible and expandable, depending on what God desires and intends. Here we may compare *2 Baruch* 48:13: "With you the hours are like the ages and the days like generations." This is not simply a remark about time's relativity. In its original context, the saying in Psalm 90:4 means that God is eternal and we are transient. Our whole life span is but a blink of an eye for God. If that were meant here, we would have expected only verse 8b, not verse 8a. Later Christians, taking their cue from this text's use of the psalm, came to the conclusion that each day of creation presaged a thousand years, so that the world would last six thousand years, and this would be followed by the return of Christ and a Sabbath of a thousand years for the saints (see *Barn.* 15.4-7; Justin *Dial.* 81.3-4; Irenaeus *Haer.* 5.28.3). Of this our author says nothing: he is not interested in speculations about the timing of the end. But there can be no doubt that most all the earliest Christian interpreters of Revelation 20 and of this text were premillennialists when it came to their theology about the return of Christ and his reign upon the earth.

Therefore, I conclude that our author is saying: "You must see things from God's broader perspective. For God, human time until the end is expandable or contractible, depending on various considerations. The time of the end is in God's hands, and he has chosen to expand the interval due to his long-suffering or patience, giving us time to amend our lives and repent so that we will not perish." Perkins is on the right track when she says that by coupling Psalm 90:4 "with an allusion to Hab. 2:3 LXX, that phrase from the psalm indicates that even the suspicion of delay is false."[249] The Qumranites also wrestled with what appeared to be a delay in the coming of the *Yom Yahweh* (1QpHab 7.6-14), and texts like *Jubilees* 4:30 and *2 Enoch* 33 likewise seem to have connected the number one thousand with the numbers of days of creation to figure out how long human history would last. Finally, it is good to keep steadily in mind that our author has simply drawn an analogy—for God, a day is *like* a thousand years and vice versa. Analogies compare two unlike things that in some partic-

[248]Bauckham, *Jude, 2 Peter*, p. 321.
[249]Perkins, *First and Second Peter*, p. 190.

ular way are the same or similar. The question to be asked is, In what way is a day like a thousand years for God, and the converse?[250]

Second Peter 3:9 has the verb *bradynō,* which means "is slow in effecting," "is delayed or late," or "is negligent about." The paronomasia in *bradynei . . . bradytēta* again shows how our author is concerned with the aural impact of his rhetoric.[251] Since the problem is lateness (the parousia is late and overdue), however, and not slowness, the translations stressing "late" better suit the context. But how can God be late for the messianic banquet, for which he is the host and time setter? In this verse, then, the author is denying that God is late or overdue (or slow). Lateness presupposes that you *definitely* know when the end should have happened, and our author is going on to point out that no human has such inside information. We have here, then, the rebuttal to 2 Peter 3:4 in the form of a "not . . . but" style of argumentation.[252]

The promise referred to in 2 Peter 3:9a is the promise of the parousia (cf. 2 Pet 3:4a). And those who think God is late are the false teachers. Verse 9b is important because it says that God's forbearance or lateness is deliberate. He is showing patience to you,[253] the believers. Verse 9c must not be separated from 9b. Obviously the Old Testament concept of God giving time for repentance and amending of life is in view here (cf. Exod 34:6-7; Num 14:18; Neh 9:17; Ps 86:15). But here God is giving these Christians being addressed time to straighten up, not just anyone. He shows patience unto *you,* says the text. Therefore verse 9c must mean that God does not desire for any Christians to perish, but that all should repent and be saved. This in turn presupposes that it is indeed possible for Christians to apostatize and then be judged by God. Elsewhere in the New Testament (cf. Acts 17:30-31; Rom 11:32; 1 Tim 2:4; cf. Ezek 18:23, 32; 33:11) we certainly find the thought that God wants all to come to know Christ, but that is not the point here. The focus here is more narrowly on Christians who stand in danger of perishing if they do not forsake the false teachers' ways and repent. Therefore verse 9 states, "God has expanded the time till the end to give you an opportunity to repent, for that is God's compassionate character" (see Joel 2:12-13; Jon 4:2; *1 En.* 60:5; *2 Bar.* 12:4; 21:20-21). The corollary of this is found in 2 Peter 3:12. Here it is suggested that we might hasten the parousia if we did live an upright life. This is not to suggest that be-

[250]See Moo, *2 Peter, Jude,* p. 186.

[251]See Watson, *Invention,* p. 131.

[252]See ibid., p. 130.

[253]There is a textual issue here, and the text could read "on your account" rather than "unto/upon you." This might refer to being patient with them until they come to faith or those they care about come to faith.

lievers can force God's hand, but rather that if they do amend their lives, this may shorten the time until the end. Yet that length of time is flexible in God's hands for a host of reasons; only God knows when it will finally come.[254]

For humans and from a human perspective, however, **2 Peter 3:10** expresses the fact that "that day will come suddenly," unexpectedly, so far as its timing is concerned. Notice the emphatic position of the verb "will come," which is at the very beginning of the sentence. It will break in like a burglar. Verse 10a is a common image in the New Testament, sometimes used to speak of the timing of Christ's coming, sometimes speaking of the timing of the day of Christ, both of which are simultaneous and come together. This teaching clearly goes back to Jesus and his parable in Matthew 24:44//Luke 12:40. We find it used in all sorts of strands of New Testament teaching both early and late (1 Thess 5:2; 2 Pet 3:10; Rev 3:3; 16:15). It may be said to be a governing metaphor for Pauline and other Christian theological reflections on the parousia chronology.[255] If the coming is as a thief, it cannot be calculated and therefore can happen soon (or later). One can thus argue that there is a consistent view of parousia chronology throughout the New Testament era. It is constantly used to correct overrealized or underrealized or nonrealized eschatologies. The second coming will burst in upon humankind suddenly, and it will not be a quiet affair.

At that time the heavens will pass away with a loud noise or with a rushing, crackling sound (perhaps the sound of burning). The word *rhoizēdōn* is onomatopoeic: it sounds like snoring, hissing, roaring or whizzing by. After the heavens are destroyed, then the *stoicheia* will fall apart, being burned up. These *stoicheia* are either the elements of the universe (earth, air, fire, water) or perhaps the heavenly bodies. Probably our author has Malachi 3:19 LXX (4:1 ET) in view, "for the Day of the Lord is coming, burning like an oven," possibly coupled with Isaiah 34:4 LXX, "All the powers of the heavens will melt"[256]—texts to which *2 Clement* 16.3 also alludes. One can also compare the Greco-Roman ideas about the world/universe going up in flames at the end of things (Cicero *Nat. d.* 2.46.118). Our author has thus expressed himself in ways to which both the Jewish and the Gentile Christians in the audience can relate.[257] This latter is likely right, and we quote Mayor: "A further reason for supplying the entire predicate to both clauses, is that the heavens and earth make up the *kosmos* (vv. 6, 7, 12, 13) and that the water by which *ho tote kosmos* [v. 6] was destroyed be-

[254]See Duke, "Exegetical Analysis of 2 Peter 3.9," pp. 6-13.

[255]See Ben Witherington III, *Jesus, Paul, and the End of the World* (Downers Grove, Ill.: InterVarsity Press, 1992).

[256]Using variant reading of LXX; see Green, *2 Peter*, p. 151.

[257]Neyrey, *2 Peter, Jude*, p. 241.

longed alike to earth and heaven (Gen. 7:11; 8:2)."[258] The stars will fall from the sky in the conflagration, so there is fire in heaven and on earth.

There is a large controversy over 2 Peter 3:10c, which Bauckham does his best to sort out. We can only give his conclusion here: (1) *Heurethēsetai* being difficult is likely original. (2) Textual emendations or deletions are a last-ditch, desperate move, the tactic of a frustrated exegete. (3) Bauckham has provided a plausible explanation: the earth and human beings' works "will be found" out ("by God," as implied in a divine passive).[259] The point is that neither the earth nor human deeds will escape God's judgment (cf. *Pss. Sol.* 17:10).[260] They too will be found out and dealt with.[261] Perhaps here our author still has Psalm 90 in mind: "We are consumed by your anger. . . . You have set our iniquities before you, our secret sins in the light of your presence. All our days pass away under your wrath; we finish our years with a moan" (Ps 90:7-9).[262] Bo Reicke argues:

> The solar system and the great galaxies, even space-time relationships, will be abolished. . . . All elements which make up the physical world will be dissolved by heat and utterly melt away. It is a picture which in an astonishing degree corresponds to what might actually happen according to modern theories of the physical universe. In any case, the main point of it all is not the apocalyptic imagery which may or may not be literally fulfilled, but the moral implications of the parousia, to which Peter now turns his attention.[263]

This goes too far. Probably the author is talking about the dissolution of the heavenly bodies, involving stars falling to earth, and the fire then strips bare and exposes the earth but does not cause it to dissolve or disappear. It thus envisions some continuity with the new heaven and the new earth.

At **2 Peter 3:11** we begin to see a transition to more traditional eschatological paraenesis, for "as always in the New Testament the moral imperative follows the eschatological indicative."[264] Our author is coming full circle, readdressing some of the topics introduced in the exordium in 2 Peter 1:3-11 in preparation for the peroration.[265] No doubt Malachi 4:1 has somewhat influenced the lan-

---

258 Mayor, *Jude, 2 Peter,* p. 159.

259 Wolters, "Worldview and Textual Criticism in 2 Peter 3:10," pp. 405-13, thinks we have shorthand for "will be found genuine," which does not seem to comport with the idea of the burning up of things.

260 Danker, "II Peter 3.10 and *Psalms of Solomon* 17.10," pp. 82-86; Neyrey, *2 Peter, Jude,* p. 244.

261 Cf. Wenham, "'Being Found on the Last Day,'" pp. 477-79; Overstreet, "Study of 2 Peter 3.10-13," pp. 354-71.

262 Bauckham, *Jude, 2 Peter,* pp. 317-20.

263 Quoted in Green, *2 Peter,* pp. 138-39.

264 Ibid., p. 152.

265 See Watson, *Invention,* p. 134.

guage here, and even before this verse: "Surely the day is coming; it will burn like a furnace, all the arrogant and every evildoer will be stubble, and the day that is coming will set them on fire." In view of the dissolution of the heavenly bodies and the heavens themselves, Christians must be prepared to live a holy and godly life, lest they too undergo destruction. Quite clearly eschatology and its reality are seen as a sanction for ethical behavior. The two go together. Bad theology leads to bad practice. A proper view of the end leads to proper conduct till the end, or at least is more likely to do so than is cynicism. The plurals of the words for "devout" and "dedicated" are difficult to render in plain English. Our author is likely thinking of plural deeds of devotion and dedication.[266]

Second Peter 3:12 calls Christians to go on waiting but to realize that, because God can expand or contract the time till the end, their godly lives may even have the effect of hastening the end (cf. 2 Esd 4:38-39; Acts 3:19-20; *2 Clem.* 12.6—13.1; in the Jewish tradition there was the notion that God would send the Messiah or fulfill his promises for the end times sooner if Israel would truly repent or keep the law: *b. Sanh.* 97b, 98a).[267] In another age, Augustine conjectured that if all Christians remained celibate and chaste, God would have to return or else Christians would die out. He forgot that Christianity is mainly propagated by evangelism, not marriage!

The phrase "the coming of the Day of God" is odd (cf. only Rev 16:14; Jer 46:10). It is most unlikely that the author distinguished this from the Lord's Day. When that day comes, it will be the cause of the heavens being set on fire (cf. Mal 4:1 [3:19 LXX]) and the heavenly bodies melting (cf. Isa 34:4 LXX, variant reading: "All the powers of the heavens will melt"). We are talking about such extreme heat that none could survive unless God protects them. It is difficult to say how much of this our author intends to be taken literally and how much is simply eschatological and metaphorical language used to describe the very real and coming event of the parousia, which will involve real redemption and judgment.[268]

The language of new heaven and earth in **2 Peter 3:13** (cf. *1 En.* 72:1; Rev 21) makes it likely that our author believes in a real and physical transformation of the earth and its setting. Nevertheless, this is an earth-centered perspective. Yes, stars will fall; yes, the earth will burn; yes, the heavens surrounding the

---

[266]Horrell, *Peter and Jude,* p. 181.

[267]The verb *speudein* can mean to be zealous or exert oneself, but if it meant that, we would expect an object noun in the dative case, not the accusative as here, so surely the meaning "to hasten" is correct here. See Harrington, *Jude and 2 Peter,* p. 294.

[268]As Harrington, ibid., p. 292, says, our author promotes a linear, not cyclical, view of time and history, which is leading to a climax and conclusion.

earth will collapse: but even all this does not necessarily imply the destruction of the whole universe, just the part that needs to undergo judgment.[269] We are waiting for a new heaven and new earth. Here the vision of Isaiah lies in the background (Is 65:17-25; 66:15-16, 22-24). Our author envisions a time when God's very justice will finally be done on earth, when righteousness will find a home here on earth (cf. Gen 18:19; Lev 19:15; Ps 9:8; 11:7; Is 9:7; 11:4-5; Mt 5:6; Rom 14:17). There is certainly nothing here of a purely otherworldly piety or otherworldly resolution of all human problems. Our author stands with the earlier Christian witnesses in his eschatology. "After lengthy arguments with the heretics and vivid warnings of the fire next time, the writer turns in pastoral care toward those still clutching the promise of something better and asks that they match God's patience (vs. 9) with their own. Wait, he says; there will be a new time and place 'where righteousness is at home.'"[270] Thus our author has rounded off his final argument, ending on a positive note that could lead the audience to praise rather than more blaming, providing here a very smooth transition to his peroration, which begins in 2 Peter 3:14.[271]

2 PETER 3:14-18—PERORATIO AND CONCLUDING DOXOLOGY: FOREWARNED IS FOREARMED

> Look how Peter says that there is much to be admired in Paul's writings. Yet in his letters, Paul criticized Peter. Peter could have hardly said what he did if he had not read Paul, but when he read him we would have discovered criticism of himself in them. Thus the friend of truth was able to praise even the fact that he had been criticized, and he was happy to do so because he realized that he had been wrong. (Gregory the Great [*Lessons in Job* 2.6.9])[272]

> Note that Paul wrote to them not according to the wisdom which he possessed but according to the wisdom which was given to him specifically for that purpose. . . . Peter says this because he himself was overwhelmed by Paul's brilliance (Hilary of Arles [*Introductory Commentary on 2 Peter*])[273]

In any rhetorical discourse the peroration was of first importance as it brought the discourse to its rational and emotional conclusion. It was expected to include some repetition of previous main points, an appeal to the deeper

[269]The author seems to be advocating renovation in some form rather than absolute annihilation. See Schreiner, *1, 2 Peter, Jude,* p. 392; and Heide, "What Is New About the New Heaven and the New Earth?" pp. 37-56.
[270]Craddock, *First and Second Peter,* p. 121.
[271]See Meier, "2 Peter 3.8-18," pp. 65-70.
[272]PL 79:1100.
[273]PL Sup. 3:115-16.

emotions, and perhaps some amplification on a particular sticking point as well (Aristotle *Rhet.* 3.19.1419b.1; Cicero *Part. or.* 15.52-17.58; Quintilian *Inst.* 6.1). In a discourse that has literally been one appeal after another to apostolic authority (first to Peter, then to Jude, then to apostolic tradition about the parousia), it is no surprise that here in the peroration we have an appeal to one more apostolic authority: Paul. And indeed the appeal is undergirded by the suggestion that at least some of Paul's letters have become perhaps the first collected Christian Scriptures, to be set alongside all the Scriptures of the Old Testament. This is quite an amazing line of argument, and certainly one that did not transpire during the lifetime of Peter himself. It is possible that the false teachers that our author has had in his sights throughout this discourse may have been misusing Paul's letters. It is possible that our author is attempting here what Quintilian calls "the most attractive form of peroration," "when we have an opportunity of drawing some argument from our opponent's speech" (Quintilian *Inst.* 6.1.4). Thus, our author may be depriving the false teachers of their use of any apostolic material, including Paul's letters, to make their own case.

In an epideictic piece of oratory, and especially one in Asiatic form, we expect a considerable effort at *adfectus* (*affectus*), the appeal to the deeper emotions, and we are not disappointed here in 2 Peter 3:14-18. If the audience is to have that deep sense of wholeness or wellness, they must live into the future in a spotless and blameless way, and they must realize that those who distort the Scriptures and the apostolic tradition are heading for disaster. Thus the eschatological sanction card is played one more time to make sure that the emotional adherence of the audience to what they have already embraced is cemented for the foreseeable future. The audience must watch out as they journey forward lest they lose the secure footing that they currently have and not continue to grow in the knowledge and grace of God. The pathos of this appeal is apparent: our author is genuinely concerned about the possibility of apostasy, and he believes there is a real danger that the audience might not continue on the good path they have already been following. The pathos is heightened because the author believes that the outcome is not absolutely certain, and therefore it is crucial that the audience watch out, stand firm and go forward in their already chosen direction. They must not become like the ignorant and unstable false teachers have become. Rather, they must continue to grow in knowledge and in behavior that will glorify God and edify the audience itself. The difference between praiseworthy and blameworthy belief and behavior could hardly be clearer here at the end of the discourse.

The author also allows his own emotions to come into play, for he is evidently angry at the "unstable" who distort God's word. Quintilian says that if the accused is of dangerous character to the audience, then the rhetor must make quite apparent what the nature of the danger is in the peroration. "The appeal to fear . . . occupies a more prominent place in the peroration than in the exordium" (Quintilian *Inst.* 6.1.12-13). There is a God to be praised, a kingdom to be gained, a good journey to be completed, with an eternal outcome hanging in the balance, and unstable views of the Scriptures and values to be rejected and blamed: our author reminds his audience of all this in a brief and deft way. He knows that "it is in situations of danger [in this case spiritual danger] that the emotional appeal is most serviceable" (Quintilian *Inst.* 6.1.36). This "*peroratio* exhorts Christian behavior primarily within the context of the fear of being drawn away from such behavior by false teachers."[274]

As Watson points out, essentially what we have is the repetition of themes in 2 Peter 3:14-16, and the final emotional appeal in 2 Peter 3:17-18. Although it is mostly the final eschatological argument that is alluded to here in the recapitulation, the appeal to zeal touches base with the exordium itself, coming full circle (cf. 2 Pet 1:5-10 to 2 Pet 3:14-16; esp. 2 Pet 1:5 to 2 Pet 3:14; and 2 Pet 1:3 to 2 Pet 3:18);[275] and when the instability and distortions of "some" are mentioned, our author is revisiting the second main argument about the false teachers, where he modified the material from Jude. Here there is no noticeable allusion to the first argument, the testimony of Peter himself (2 Pet 1:12-21), which suggests that the main function of that argument was to establish the ethos and authority not only of Peter and the apostolic tradition in general, but also of this particular discourse. While 2 Peter 3:17 is intended to make the audience indignant at the blameworthy behavior of the false teachers, 2 Peter 3:17-18 serve as the *conquestio*, where "one recounts shameful, mean, and ignoble acts and what they have suffered or are likely to suffer that is unworthy of their age, race, former fortune, position or preferment" (Cicero *Inv.* 1.55.107). The audience has reached a good place in their spiritual journey; they must continue to grow in grace and knowledge and avoid the pitfalls of the false teachers, who themselves are falling into the Pit. They are reminded of the dawning of the eschatological day of judgment and redemption (2 Pet 3:18), which alludes back skillfully to 2 Peter 1:19 and 2 Peter 3:12. There really is no epistolary close here, but rather one drawn from Christian worship: a doxology.

> [3:14] *Therefore, beloved, while waiting for this, be eager to be found at peace (whole), without spot or blemish,* [15] *and look on the patience of our Lord (as) salvation, just as also our beloved brother Paul, according to the wisdom given him, wrote to you,*

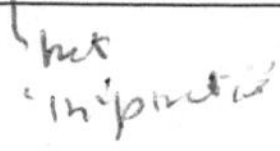

[274] Watson, *Invention*, p. 138.

[275] An inclusion; see Moo, *2 Peter, Jude*, p. 207.

[16]*as also in all (his) letters speaking in them about these things. In these (letters) are some things hard to understand, which the uninstructed and unstable distort as also they do the remaining (other) Scriptures, to their own destruction.* [17]*You, then, beloved, knowing this beforehand, be on guard lest the unprincipled leading you away to error cause you to lose your own stability;* [18]*but grow in grace and knowledge of our Lord and Savior, Jesus Christ. To him be glory even now and unto that day (of) which is eternity.*

Marking off this section from what precedes is the use once more of the term of endearment "Beloved." Yet as is appropriate, this peroration is closely linked to the final eschatological argument that has just preceded as well. The one aspect our author focuses on when he refers to the eschatological goal in 2 Peter 3:13 is that *dikaiosynē* (righteousness) will characterize that new dwelling place, and so we had better be living righteous lives now if we want to be part of that righteous realm. Thus, **2 Peter 3:14** follows naturally on 2 Peter 3:13 because the new heavens and earth will be a place of righteousness. While believers are waiting, therefore, they should be eager to be found at peace with God, experiencing *shalom,* wholeness, and the only way they can do that is to be found without spot or blemish (morally pure, like an acceptable sacrifice). Like various other discourses, such as Jude, this one ends with the vision of Christians as the clean sacrifices (being found without fault and blemish)[276] being offered to God in that final and consummate act of worship. This verse seems to be an echo of 1 Peter 1:19, which calls Christ *amōmos kai aspilos,* here using the same terms in reverse order.[277] This is the aural and content opposite of the false teachers, who were said to be *spiloi kai mōmoi* in 2 Peter 2:13. Ephesians 5:27 and Jude 24 provide partial parallels to the description of the believers here, though the image certainly is Old Testamental. However, in God's new community, Christian lives are the only sacrifices God requires (cf. Rom 12:1-2). **Second Peter 3:15a** exhorts believers to look on God's forbearance or patience not as a delay of salvation, but *as* their salvation because it gives them time for repentance, or else they will not be found "in that number."

Second Peter 3:15b begins the reference to Paul and his letters, which has caused so much speculation. It seems to me that here, especially at 2 Peter 3:16, Bauckham's whole argument about 2 Peter being a testament breaks

[276]Here again we have the language of "being found," and in this case the reference is to the eschatological inspection on judgment day, as was the case in the eschatological argument earlier in 2 Pet 3. The verb is also appropriate because of the sacrificial language here. The lamb would be closely inspected before being offered as a sacrifice. If it was found to be without blemish, then the sacrifice went forward.

[277]See Kelly, *Epistles of Peter*, p. 369.

down for several reasons: (1) The closing eschatological paraenesis here is customary in New Testament letters; it no more indicates a testament here than it does in James or elsewhere. (2) Our author is not trying to perpetuate a testament here or elsewhere in the letter when he is not quoting Peter's testimony.

Paul in **2 Peter 3:15b** is called "our beloved brother." Many all over the church greatly respected Paul. It is possible that Linus, or whoever wrote this letter, was indeed one who also knew Paul, as Peter did, and respected him greatly. This discourse, however, reflects no extensive knowledge of Paul's letters, but that may be contrary to his purpose here. He may know the letter that ended up in Rome (Romans) and have known Paul or at least have met him before his death). He also knows that Paul has written to some of these Christians whom he is addressing. Perhaps here the "our" is merely family language, meaning that all Christians are brothers and sisters. It may, however, imply a closer relationship to Paul on the part of our author than is sometimes thought. He speaks of Paul, who *wrote* to you (past tense), and also of all his letters (plural) being already written and known or known about by our author. This strongly suggests that our author is writing at a time after Paul's death, and it is quite difficult to explain this on the supposition that Peter wrote this entire document. Mayor notes: "At the same time the phrase *en pasais epistolais,* would be more naturally understood of a collection of letters made after St. Paul's death. If he were still living, we should rather have expected *tais allais epistolais*."[278] In theory, then, 2 Peter could have been written between 70 and 100, when we may posit that some of Paul's letters had already been collected, a process that likely began in earnest only after Paul died and the value of his letters to the whole church was recognized.

In **2 Peter 3:16** the present tense (Paul's letters *contain* things that are hard to understand [paraphrase]) is not a slip in the literary fiction: since 2 Peter 3:4 our author has simply been addressing his audience directly, though using Jewish apocalyptic material. Now he cites another authority whom he and his audience both respect. He does not try to hide that he is writing, not as Peter or as Paul's fellow apostle, but as himself, compiling apostolic authoritative testimony to back up his argument. This passage is not half so difficult if we do not try to impose the literary fiction of testament on this part of the letter, nor the literary fiction of a pseudepigraphon on our author's intention in composing the letter as a whole. Our author is a scribe, a compiler of sources: he does not see himself as original, much less as an author. Since he quotes Pe-

[278]Mayor, *Jude, 2 Peter,* p. 165.

ter's testimony, he gives the address of this letter as from Peter, which it is in part. The situation is somewhat analogous to Matthew's Gospel, where a Matthean source (special M) is used in addition to Mark and Q (other source[s] common to Matthew and Luke).

That "Paul wrote to you" *may* imply that the audience was alive, at least some of them, when Paul wrote, so that puts us at a time not extremely long after Paul's death. All in all, 2 Peter 3:15 indicates that we are dealing with a letter written after Peter and Paul's deaths, but not a pseudepigraphon or a testament so far as the letter as a whole is concerned. According to **2 Peter 3:16a** our author apparently knows that Paul also addresses the matters of eschatology and ethics and believes in a second coming for judgment. He reminds his audience that Paul wrote, and even wrote to them about such things. This is an especially effective tactic (1) if his audience greatly reveres Paul and some of them have some or one of his letters; and (2) if the opponents are quoting Paul to justify their immorality and perhaps also their realized or nonexistent eschatology. Our author is saying: "These ignorant teachers have it all wrong. Paul agrees with me on eschatology and ethics; check it out in all his letters."

In **2 Peter 3:15c-16a** our author says that Paul wrote and spoke "according to the wisdom given him." It was not on the basis of human wisdom: it was God-given wisdom. Paul is not to be dismissed as just another human opinion. Richard J. Bauckham is quite right that this is equivalent to saying that Paul is inspired. He spoke what words and wisdom God gave him (cf. Eccles 7:25; Mk 6:2; Acts 6:3, 10; 1 Cor 2:13; 12:8; Jas 1:5).[279] Paul knew himself to be dependent on God not only for his commission, but also for his gospel and wisdom (cf. Rom 12:3; 15:15). Here is perhaps another clue that our author knows Romans. In any case, we must see our author viewing Paul's inspiration as parallel to that of the Old Testament prophets mentioned in 2 Peter 1:20-21.

In **2 Peter 3:16d** our author ranks Paul's writings alongside the other Scriptures. *Hai graphai* (literally, "the writings") here surely must mean "Scriptures" because of the definite article, "the": "the other" or "remaining Scriptures." This also surely suggests that our author is writing at a time when Paul's letters have already begun to be ranked alongside the Old Testament itself, though we need not think of our author having or conceiving of an authoritative or closed canon of New Testament documents yet. The recognition of a document's inspiration and authority and truth content preceded the canonization of such letters, and we are at the former stage here. It appears, however, that our author does not limit the term "Scripture" to the Old Testament; indeed he

[279] Bauckham, *Jude, 2 Peter*, p. 329.

cannot be doing so since "the other" implies that Paul's letters are included.[280] By saying "other," what else would he include as Scripture? If citing of sources is an indication, he takes Jude to be Scripture, and it is quite likely that he sees apostolic material in general as Scripture, or perhaps better, as authoritative and inspired writings. Properly speaking, the term "Scripture" should be applied after canonization.

Our author has not directly cited *1 Enoch*, as Jude felt free to do. Is this perhaps because he does not see himself as one who has the authority to discern inspired writings? I suggest that this is correct; again it points to the fact that our author is writing as a rhetorically adept scribe, not as an author. His use of Jewish apocalyptic ideas is mainly based on the Old Testament and does not necessarily imply that he saw such material as inspired Scripture. Moffatt is right that the implication of what 2 Peter says about Paul's letters is that they are now treated as resources for the whole church, not just for particular congregations. They have in a way become "catholic" epistles.[281] Finally, "the other Scriptures" may include the Gospels or a Gospel, which covers ethical and eschatological matters. Possibly by now Mark's Gospel has been available, and since our author is likely from and in Rome, he can well know or know about it.[282] The Greek term *loipas* here means "the rest of the Scriptures," not "the Scriptures as well," much less "in the rest of the writings" in some broad generic sense.[283] Mayor is right to say: "If we had *hōs tas allas graphas* it might mean 'like the Scriptures also,' but if the writer made any broad distinction between Paul's epistles and Scripture, I think he must have said *kathaper autas tas graphas*. I incline to think that *graphai* is here used to denote any book read in the synagogue or congregation, including the letters of the Apostles (Col 4:16; 1 Thess 5:27) as well as the lessons from the Old Testament."[284]

In **2 Peter 3:16b** our author is also honest: he admits that there are some things in Paul's letters hard to understand (*dysnoētos;* cf. Diogenes Laertius *Lives* 9.13). This again points away from an author who is a pneumatic or sees himself as inspired to write this discourse. He is rather an editor and like most of us must wrestle with some parts of Paul's letters.[285] Watson, however, is correct that our author is not saying that Paul is obscure; instead, he is implying

[280]On the collection of Paul's letters, see Gamble, "Redaction of the Pauline Letters," pp. 403-18; Finegan, "Original Form of the Pauline Collection," pp. 85-86.
[281]Moffatt, *General Epistles,* p. 211.
[282]Bauckham, *Jude, 2 Peter,* p. 323.
[283]Moffatt, *General Epistles,* p. 212.
[284]Mayor, *Jude, 2 Peter,* p. 168.
[285]But see Schreiner, *1, 2 Peter, Jude,* pp. 397-98.

that correct interpretation of Paul comes in light of his own interpretation as well as apostolic tradition.[286] According to **2 Peter 3:16c**, the false teachers have been distorting or twisting some of these things (perhaps Paul's teaching on freedom from the law in Galatians) to their own advantage. Here a graphic word is used, *streblousin,* which literally has the sense of "to twist" or "torture" or even "to dislocate human limbs on a rack."[287] In other words, this is no slight misinterpretation we are talking about here, but a clear distortion of the text's meaning. Our author calls these men uninstructed: they had at best a superficial knowledge of Paul and had not really studied his letters. Not surprisingly, superficiality leads to instability. The word *astēriktos* literally refers to one who is without a staff and so is unsupported.[288] It contrasts nicely with the rare word in 2 Peter 3:17, *stērigmos* (only here in the NT), which refers to having a secure position. The false ones need a crash course in Pauline theology before they crash and burn. It is implied that they have used Paul, and perhaps also it is implied that they respect him, as does the audience of this letter, but they need to study him more. This appeal should lead the audience to reread their Pauline letters. Finally, Daniel J. Harrington is right to say that the phrase "all his letters" leaves the impression of a considerable collection of letters, not just one or two. With this remark we are surely well after the time of Paul's death, especially since now Paul's letters are circulating throughout the church as a whole.[289]

Unfortunately, says **2 Peter 3:16d**, these false teachers also distorted "the other sacred writings" as well, the end result being these teachers' destruction on judgment day. Here is a strong warning: It is not a matter of indifference how we handle Scripture. We must study it carefully and not twist it out of its context or distort its truth. Doing the latter badly can lead to heresy and even to a loss of final salvation. Too often Christians have but a superficial knowledge of Scripture, and this inevitably leads to wrong thinking, wrong attitudes, wrong behavior. The only alternative is diligent, thorough study of the sacred writings. We are not to be like the false teachers, who were uninstructed and willfully ignorant of the things of God.

Second Peter 3:17-18 brings this discourse to a close. The position of "you" in **2 Peter 3:17** is emphatic. While these false teachers are going on to destruction, "you," the audience, needs to be on guard. The audience is being fore-

[286]Watson, *Invention,* p. 137.
[287]Hillyer, *1 and 2 Peter,* p. 224.
[288]Ibid., p. 224.
[289]Harrington, *Jude and 2 Peter,* p. 295.

warned[290] and therefore forearmed by Paul's letter(s) and by apostolic teaching (in 1 Peter and Jude); they have been warned beforehand of the fate of such people, and forewarned should be forearmed. In context *proginōskontes* need not imply a return to the testament fiction; it just reminds the audience that Paul and others have warned them beforehand about such teachers and teachings. They must be on guard lest they be led astray into error, apostasy and finally destruction.

Second Peter 3:18 urges the audience to grow in the "grace and knowledge" of Jesus Christ. It is possible that Christ is seen as the source of both "grace" and "knowledge" here, or that Christ is the source of the "grace" but the object of the "knowledge." Or one could separate "grace" from "knowledge" and say that only the latter has to do with Christ here. I tend to think that the first of these possibilities is meant here (Christ as the source of both), because we have just heard that Paul's source of wisdom was from above.[291]

The discourse then finishes with a peroration that concludes with a stern warning, somewhat like what we find in 1 John, though here it is followed by a closing doxology. This doxology, unlike many in the New Testament (see only 2 Tim 4:18; cf. Rev 1:5-6), is to Christ, which confirms what we have already seen from 2 Peter 1: our author believes that Christ is divine or part of the Godhead and thus worthy of worship and praise, since only God should be praised in this way. Indeed he is the Lord and Savior of all humankind. As Craddock says, when it comes to Christology, the focus of this discourse is quite different from 1 Peter, and I urge that this is because our author is offering here an epideictic discourse focusing on the things that are now true, even about Christ, unlike the focus of 1 Peter, which is deliberative rhetoric. The "Christ of 2 Peter . . . is not the ethical example in whose steps we walk. He is not the suffering Christ who shows us how to take abuse without retaliating. He is not the Christ of the cross, bearing our sins. He is the ascended, exalted Christ who, in God's good time, will return to end the reign of evil and usher in the new age 'where righteousness is at home.'"[292]

Notice finally that the closing phrase is not "forever" but rather "to the day of eternity" (cf. Sir 18:10). This comports well with the reference to the eternal kingdom in 2 Peter 1:11.[293] The day of eternity is the day when Christ returns,

---

[290]Some take "knowing this beforehand" as a falling back into the genre of a testament; however, a living author is now warning the current audience beforehand about present and coming false teachers, rather than Peter himself as a voice from the past.
[291]See Schreiner, *1, 2 Peter, Jude,* p. 401.
[292]Craddock, *First and Second Peter,* p. 123.
[293]See Perkins, *First and Second Peter,* p. 194.

judgment and redemption happen and the kingdom is ushered in on earth as it is in heaven, once and for all. There is no diminution of early Christian eschatological hope or fervor in the heart and discourse of our author, whatever may have been the case with the false teachers. Our author has actually shown how Peter, Jude, Paul and our writer himself stand together and in harmony on the apostolic beliefs and behaviors appropriate in early Christianity.[294] Second Peter stands as a worthy addition to the canon, reflecting the original belief and piety of the earliest Christians and carrying forward the apostolic witness to the next generation. As John Meier ably says, there is some irony to the fact that the history of the New Testament canon, which began with Paul correcting Peter (in Gal 2:11-21), ends with our author speaking for Peter and correcting misinterpretations of Paul. We have indeed come full circle.[295]

A CLOSER LOOK

Theologizing out of the Apostolic Tradition for the Postapostolic Age

In a telling remark made around A.D. 115, Polycarp in reflecting on Paul's letters says of the man: "Neither I, nor anyone like me can keep up with the wisdom of the blessed and glorious Paul" (Pol. *Phil.* 3). Polycarp is clearly aware of the intellectual distance between himself and apostolic figures like Paul. But this selfsame attitude is already being reflected in a nascent form in 2 Peter 3, where the author candidly admits that some of Paul's thoughts are hard to comprehend and properly interpreted. It is this sense of distance from apostolic persons who had been especially gifted with divine wisdom that is so very evident in 2 Peter: it effects the very way our author does theology. It is not for him to forge out creatively in new directions. Rather, his task is to edit, interpret, amplify, highlight, cite the apostolic tradition. He operates as a teacher and a scribe or scholar, not as one of the original apostles. His assumption indeed is that the original apostles, whether it be Peter, Jude or Paul, whether it be representatives of Jewish Christianity or Gentile Christian, whether it be members of Jesus' family, the original Twelve or the architect of the Gentile mission—all stand together in embracing the apostolic vision, which is christological and eschatological to the core, and always has belief intertwined with behavior in the form of the call to holiness of both heart and life. Our author can speak of "our brother Paul" and thus reflects his view of the ultimate unity of Peter and Paul on the essentials of

[294]See Horrell, *Peter and Jude*, p. 186.
[295]Meier, "2 Peter 3.8-18," pp. 65-70.

the faith and between himself and these two apostles as well.

But our author is also quite aware that one must not only walk a clear line to honor apostolic orthodoxy, but also walk a fine one. G. K. Chesterton once put it this way: "Orthodoxy . . . is like walking along a narrow ridge, almost like a knife-edge. One step to either side was a step to disaster. Jesus is God and man; God is love and holiness; Christianity is grace and morality; the Christian lives in this world and in the world of eternity. Overstress either side of these great truths, and at once destructive heresy emerges."[296] The concern for apostolic orthodoxy and orthopraxy is one of the telling features of 2 Peter, and thus it is not a surprise that a clear conception of heresy begins to emerge as well, since these things are mirror images of each other. The use of purity language (spotless and without blemish) while essentially ethical in focus, nonetheless comports with this sort of theologizing. The author is drawing boundary lines in terms of belief and behavior, and clearly the false teachers are out of bounds on both counts.[297] Few discourses in the New Testament make clearer the connection between bad theology and bad ethics and vice versa.

Within the framework of Jewish Christian eschatology, our author seeks to preserve and pass on the theological legacy he has inherited. This involves a theology of creation, fall, flood (judgment), redemption, final judgment, new heaven and new earth. He speaks to all of this cycle with the possible exception of the fall, but its reality is implied in the stress on the need for redemption. Especially clear is his understanding of the goodness of creation, and thus redemption is viewed as ultimately involving creation, even if after a final conflagration. What punctuates this theology is a belief not only in divine beginnings by means of a word spoken by God, but also divine intervention for both judgment and redemption along the way to the end of human history.

A theology of creation certainly implies a theology of a Creator (2 Peter 3:5), the Maker and Remaker of heaven and earth.[298] Not only does Genesis figure into our author's theologizing about God, but also Isaiah 65—66, which declares that God intends for things to end well, with a new heaven and new earth. God's last word is not judgment, but rather redemption and a new beginning. Equally interesting is our author's discussion about God and time based on Psalm 90:4, which leads to an affirmation that God's timing for the End is determined by God's compassion and mercy. This does not cause the author to suggest that the parousia will come gradually, or at some distant time in the future. Rather, our author still affirms the sudden inbreak-

[296]Quoted in Green, *2 Peter,* p. 160.
[297]See Neyrey, *2 Peter, Jude,* pp. 247-49.
[298]See Martin, *Theology of the Letters of James, Peter and Jude*, p. 153.

ing of the return of Christ like a thief in the night, a theme we find in the teaching of Jesus and Paul and the book of Revelation as well. Our author is not really an innovator: he repeats what the apostles who came before him have said. It is also true that, as Martin says, our author does not mention the future millennium we find in texts like Revelation 20:4-6. This does not mean that he rules it out, but what he sees happening at some juncture after the return of Christ is a conflagration, which thereafter leads to a new heaven and new earth.[299]

Yet it is not just fallen humans and especially false teachers who have to answer to God's final inquisition and judgment; it is also God's angels, and in particular the fallen ones described in Genesis 6:1-4. Especially interesting in 2 Peter 2 is the way our author handles the Jude material. Not only does he interject the positive examples of Noah and Lot into Jude's doom-and-gloom sayings; he also deletes the extracanonical citations from other early Jewish literature, all the while depending on extracanonical ideas about Lot being righteous and Noah being a preacher of righteousness. What sort of theologizing is this? My answer is that our author wants to stick to the Old Testament and the apostolic tradition, and part of that early Jewish apostolic tradition involved looking for positive paradigms in Old Testament history. More to the point, he wants this material to speak to a broader and later audience than Jude's audience. If we ask how the audience of 2 Peter would make sense of the story of the wicked angels in lockdown in Tartarus, the answer is that even for Gentiles who do not know the Jude or 1 Peter materials, they may well have known about the Titans in Tartarus, the lowest level of Hades. In other words, here we have a small clue perhaps about the increasingly Gentile populace in the church as a whole. One could call 2 Peter 2 a rendering of Jude for a more Hellenized audience, who are not immersed in or perhaps even aware of arcane early Jewish lore not found in the Old Testament.

Despite the view of some scholars, it is not true that the Christology is hard to find in this brief discourse. It seems probable that Jesus is indeed called "our God and Savior"' from the very outset of this discourse (2 Pet 1:1). This beginning is striking because clearly our author's favorite christological phrase is "our Lord and Savior, Jesus Christ" (1:11; 3:18; cf. 2:20; 3:2). In this phrase Christ seems to be treated as part of Jesus' name (we do not have "the Christ" here) whereas the titles put front and center are both terms used in the Greco-Roman world for gods, and indeed of the emperor himself. Jesus is "our" God and "our" Lord and "our" Savior, in distinction from the gods and lords and saviors of others outside the community. Thus Christology becomes part of the

[299]See ibid., pp. 154-55.

boundary-defining language for the postapostolic community being addressed here (cf. 1 Cor 8:4-6). Here is one of those various places where there is a similarity between 2 Peter and the Pastoral Epistles, for it is only in the Pastorals where Jesus is regularly called "the/our Savior" (2 Tim 1:10; Tit 1:4; 2:13; 3:6).[300] But we should not make too much of these parallels, as Gilmour has rightly noted, since they do not reflect a literary relationship between the Pastorals and 2 Peter, unlike the case with Jude and 2 Peter.[301] What these documents do share in common, however, is a deliberate use of more Hellenistic-friendly and Gentile-friendly language to convey one's message, which again suggests something about the majority of the audience of this material.

With regard to what our author wants us most to know about Jesus, it is that according to the Petrine tradition he has already been glorified, which was a foreshadowing of his coming in divine glory in the future: the transfiguration is a parousia preview. The force of this is not only that Peter himself provides a witness for both of the comings of Jesus, past and future, but also that Peter becomes the prime witness to the sonship of Jesus, indeed a witness to the fact that God personally confirmed his sonship in the presence of Peter and other witnesses. Here salvation history is juxtaposed against cleverly devised myths. Our author will have none of attempts to dehistoricize Christology or Christ. In other words, no one could have more insider knowledge of what was really the case about Jesus' identity than the apostle Peter, and the judicious use of the Petrine fragment here sets up the theological argument against the false teachers. They are not merely standing against our author, but also against Peter himself, against Jude, against Paul, against the apostolic tradition. As Martin points out, Christ's kingdom is both present (2 Pet 1:11, but see the exposition of that verse earlier) and future (2 Pet 3:12-13). Christ's past and

[300]I am unpersuaded by the argument that though Jesus is called God in these texts, the term "God" is used in a looser sense to mean something like "partaker in the divine nature," or even like certain pagan notions of divinity, which could include the living emperor, for example. It is true to say that our author is a monotheist who is able to distinguish Jesus from God the Father, and at the same time say that Christ also is God. See esp. Callan, "Christology of 2 Peter," pp. 253-63; and idem, "Soteriology of 2 Peter," pp. 549-59. Because our author's conceptuality of God and Christ is thoroughly Jewish throughout this discourse, I am unpersuaded that "God" is used more loosely in 2 Pet 1—even though when speaking of virtues or human beings, he is able to speak in a more Hellenized way that Gentiles would understand. We are far from Philo in 2 Peter in terms of the use of Greek philosophical ideas and other Greco-Roman concepts. Our author distinguishes between Christ, who is called God and Savior, and humans, who are merely partakers of (someone else's) divine nature in some sense. In regard to soteriology, Callan has some helpful insights, and it is probably right to say that our author focuses on the fact that God does not desire any *Christian* to be lost or commit apostasy, which is why this discourse warns against such a thing, believing it to be possible.

[301]Gilmour, *Significance of Parallels*, pp. 125-34.

future work involves both judgment and redemption. It is thus unfair to say that "if 2 Peter has a Christology at all, it is undeveloped, and inchoate."[302] In such a brief discourse, we should not expect a full christological treatise, especially considering the hortatory and ethical focus of this discourse. Second Peter is doing theology largely in the service of ethics, which is no surprise in an epideictic discourse. One talks about the Deity in order to encourage people to behave in certain ways. Nor is it entirely adequate to say that the focus needs to be on God since our author is doing theodicy, providing a rationale for why final judgment has not happened. What our author has to say about final judgment and the Day of the Lord has everything to do with Christology since it is Christ who is returning and bringing in that judgment, and not Yahweh.[303] Our author's theologizing is traditional, christological and eschatological—all three.

Martin is quite right that our author shows some adaptability in framing his message for a largely Hellenistic world around him, and it is fair to say he is not venturesome in his theologizing. He is trying to faithfully adapt the apostolic tradition for a new generation, not to give it an extreme makeover, or transform it in his own image and imagination. But I do not think it is fair to say: "2 Peter represents a Christianity that is on the road to becoming tradition-bound, authoritarian, and inward looking. The next steps will be along the road to fossilization and fixation, with no room to change or to receive new light. 2 Peter, in our estimate, is not there, but its form of Christianity is potentially threatening and isolationist."[304] This view is too indebted to the older views of Ernst Käsemann and others who held that 2 Peter is serving up early Catholicism for the second century, and thus reflects a great fall from the pristine grace of Paul, for example. Our author is a scribe and tradent. His brief is to convey the apostolic tradition to a new generation, adapting its language somewhat to the audience while remaining faithful to orthodoxy. Frankly, since there is more ethicizing than theologizing in this discourse, we do not really know much about our author's potential as a creative theological thinker. He was not trying to speak in his own voice, but to allow the voice of God, of Jesus, of Peter, of Jude and of Paul to continue to echo in the ears of a new generation. This is no small thing, and it does not deserve to be dubbed fossilization. Then is he inculcating an isolationist sect? This is reading too much into the fact that his particular focus is on the problem of false teachers across the church. There is still a concern about the public witness, but it is not as pronounced as in 1 Peter, and more to the point, it is not the focus

[302]Martin, *Theology of the Letters of James, Peter, and Jude*, p. 160.
[303]Against Neyrey, "Form and Background," *JBL* 99, no. 3 (1980): 430-31.
[304]Martin, *Theology of the Letters of James, Peter, and Jude*, p. 163.

of this discourse. Second Peter must be judged on the basis of what it is trying to accomplish, not on the basis of what we might like it to say or speak to.

Evaluated fairly then, 2 Peter helped the church cross the bridge from the apostolic to the postapostolic era without leaving the apostolic witness behind. This alone is a great accomplishment, but in addition our author provides us with a rich perspective on the parousia, both in its connection with our behavior and "hastening" of the great day, and in its connection with God's compassion on sinners. Furthermore, it helps us to see God's compassion on Christians who need to repent—"for God desires that none of *you* should perish," which is to say, none should commit apostasy and suffer the eternal consequences. Eschatology and ethics work hand in glove in this discourse, and as such it sounds a note that Paul himself would have owned and endorsed. For all this we should be thankful that so much could be accomplished in three brief chapters.

BRIDGING THE HORIZONS

Certainly one of the important questions that 2 Peter raises for us is the role of apostolic tradition in the life of the church today. In the modern age of many books in print, we face the danger of assuming some "right" of individual interpretation of texts. Craddock puts it this way: "When I can sit alone with my Bible on my lap, I can easily be seduced into becoming my own church, and I might even cease to join the assembly that provided the Scripture and that continually seeks to hear aright the Word of God."[305] The possession of individual and personal Bibles has been a great blessing in so many ways, but in an age of rampant individualism, there is a danger of assuming that the Bible belongs to us individually, and that each is free to interpret it as one likes, as suits us. Contrast this with what Peter actually says about the Old Testament prophets: "Nothing they said was a matter of their own private interpretation." Even they had to submit to the divine word and simply pass it along, rather than give it their own personal spin. This reminds us that we must submit to the Word of God, not try to make it submit to our own rationales and justifications and interpretations. I often tell my students that they must beware of whittling off the hard edges of the biblical text, or explaining them away, because it is precisely the bits offending us that may show us areas of our lives least in accord with God's will for us.

Another crucial question that 2 Peter raises in an acute form is what we do with the fact that the parousia did not turn out to be imminent for the first

[305] Craddock, *First and Second Peter,* p. 108.

generation of Christians, even though it was a consummation for which they devoutly wished. For the twenty-first-century church, sometimes this question has been answered by replacing a first-century eschatology with a modern dispensational one that bifurcates things into an invisible coming of Christ for the rapture, followed by a visible second coming. Unfortunately for this view, the author of 2 Peter knows nothing of such parsing of the second coming into two parts.[306]

In other parts of the church, the second coming is still affirmed, but it is honored more in the breach than in the observance of it or with a living hope of it. Craddock puts the matter aptly: "Some tenacious believers hold on to the expectation, but even they have replaced the cardboard sign hand-lettered 'Jesus is coming soon' with one made of concrete and steel. The words are there but the conviction is gone."[307] What this assumes, however, is that there is indeed in the New Testament an element of calculation and not just expectation when it comes to the second coming. I disagree. Nowhere in the New Testament do we have a statement like "Jesus will come back within forty years after his ascension." The most one can get out of texts like Mark 13 is that various of the messianic woes or preliminary eschatological tribulations would happen during the first generation of Christ's followers. And so they did, leading to the fall of the temple in A.D. 70, exactly forty years after the death of Jesus. But as for the cosmic signs and second coming, all that that early apocalyptic discourse teaches us is that those events would happen at some unspecified time "after those days." We do not have a recipe for exact calculation of the second coming here. But this raises another point.

Too often scholars read the views of the scoffers as the views of the faithful in 2 Peter. They assume that early Christians are stressing out about the "delay" of the parousia or even have concluded that it is not coming at all since it did not come during the first generation. While I certainly do not want to deny that some early Christians likely thought such a thing, it is always a major mistake, from a rhetorical point of view, to assume that the view of the adversaries is in fact also the view of many of the faithful. This is a practice called mirror-reading, and it is dangerous in various respects. We assume that what our author is denying is what the audience is affirming. But this goes counter to our author's rhetorical approach here, which is simply to reassure the audience that what they have long believed about the parousia is still true. The argument in 2 Peter

[306]See Ben Witherington III, *The Problem with Evangelical Theology* (Waco: Baylor University Press, 2004).

[307]Craddock, *First and Second Peter*, p. 119.

3 does not read like an attempt at dissuasion from a false belief held by the audience. Rather, in epideictic fashion, our author is reaffirming and strengthening views and values already held by the audience.

What should we make of the fact that our author tells us in 2 Peter 1:3-4 that God gives us both everything we need to live a godly life and indeed also gives us the knowledge and the power such that we are partakers in the divine nature, which at a minimum means that we partake of the gift of eternal life? Is more meant here? I think the answer to this is yes in several respects. First, I stress that our author does not agree with the traditional Lutheran misreading of Pauline anthropology, which suggests that Romans 7 is a description of the Christian life. In short, he would not agree that Christians are still in the bondage of sin. To the contrary, they now have all the knowledge and power they need to live a godly and upright life. Sin is no longer able to make them an offer they cannot refuse. This does not mean that the Christian has become divinized or become "god in one's own little world." It means simply that the believer has power over conscious sin, and it involves the fact that one has godly knowledge such that one can know the difference between true and false belief and right and wrong behavior. In other words, our author believes in victorious Christian living, not defeatist Christian living. He believes that "greater is he who is in you" (1 Jn 4:4) than the external (or even internal) forces of temptation. Of course our author assumes that one must constantly depend on God day by day for power, insight and direction. But there is still more.

Both at the beginning and the end of this discourse, our author stresses the importance of having knowledge, the full knowledge of God. Although he does not think that this is the only important thing for a Christian to have, it is one of those important things. Moral and theological discernment are severely impaired in a Christian life not characterized by a deep knowledge of God. While some of this is heart knowledge, our author is also referring to head knowledge. And he actually believes that right thinking, right believing, right knowing of God as well as right behaving are essential to salvation. This is perfectly clear in our author's critique of the false teachers who once were orthodox Christians but have strayed into the ways of apostasy. Salvation for our author is not a done deal at conversion. Rather, our author stress that salvation has several tenses to it, several episodes, including conversion in the past and final salvation in the future. Between those two stages of salvation, there is a present possibility of apostasy: moral and intellectual. This is precisely what this discourse is warning real Christians against, lest they go the way of the false teachers.

Nevertheless, our author does not specify that there is a certain quantity of religious knowledge that one must have to be saved. For him it is more a matter of whom you know, rather than how much you know. Nevertheless, he is one of the New Testament authors prepared to speak about the saving knowledge of God in Christ. It thus is no accident that on one hand he seriously warns his audience that God desires for all of them to make it to the finish line and receive final salvation and enter the kingdom (which is not an inevitable result for a Christian); and on the other hand, as the discourse closes, he urges them that they need to keep growing in grace and the knowledge of our Lord and Savior.

How does one do that? Our author has an answer implicit on every page of this discourse: "Learn, embrace, imbibe the apostolic testimony that I am passing along to you." In my view this is one of the great contributions of this discourse to the canon. At the end of the apostolic era, we have a clarion call that we must embrace; we must make the apostolic witness our own, just as we see our author modeling in 2 Peter as he takes up and in his own language, style and way conveys this legacy to his audience. Here we have a model of how we too may take up and convey the apostolic witness to yet another new generation. We should be grateful that we have at least one model of this in the canon. It helps us with our entire hermeneutical approach to material that we are some two thousand years distant from in time, and light years away from in culture.

One of the things about 2 Peter that has made so many Protestants uncomfortable is its profoundly hortatory and ethical focus. Ever since the Lutheran Reformation, Protestants have tended to look down their noses at discourses that were mainly or merely dealing with ethics, and not with the lofty subject of theology, "the queen of the sciences." This has plagued the reading of James, and it blights the reading of 2 Peter as well. Though I would be the last person to denigrate theology, I must say that the habit of undervaluing ethics is a reflection of a bad theology. If your theology is that you will be saved to the uttermost, be granted final salvation purely by grace without having to live a moral or holy life after conversion, then you have badly misunderstood what even Paul has to say about grace and salvation and holiness. Both Jesus and Paul would have been appalled at such a notion, and so would be our author of 2 Peter. And this brings us to the issue of *dikaiosynē* in 2 Peter. It has a moral tone to it and is rightly translated either "justice" or "moral righteousness." It is not talking about forensic righteousness, a concept that we do sometimes find in Paul.[308] It is not talking about the righteousness of Christ imputed to the believer.

This certainly is one of the reasons scholars like Ernst Käsemann had such trouble with a discourse like 2 Peter. It seemed to him as a drastic fall from the

[308]On which see Ben Witherington III and Darlene Hyatt, *Paul's Letter to the Romans* (Grand Rapids: Eerdmans, 2004).

pristine heights of Pauline theology about salvation by grace alone, through the imputed righteousness of Christ. What such folks fail to realize or at least do not want to accept is that while it is true that Paul talks about being set right, or given initial right standing with God by grace through faith, and it is also right to say that Christians need grace and faith every step of the way on the journey to final salvation—nevertheless, it is simply not the case that the behavior of Christians cannot effect the final outcome of such a journey into the kingdom. While our author would not want to say that Christians are saved *by* their own godly behavior (which behavior after all is only possible by drawing on the grace of God), he certainly does want to say that they will not ultimately be saved *without* godly behavior, where there is time and opportunity so to behave. There does loom the real possibility of Christians committing apostasy, however remote in the case of most loyal Christians.

Thus one needs to say that when we have a mostly hortatory discourse like 2 Peter, we must understand that, when it comes to salvation, this is because godly living is just as important as godly knowledge. Behavior after conversion is just as important as belief when it comes to salvation. As Wesley used to say, you can be as orthodox as the devil (for the devil knows everything that is true about Jesus and believes it to be true) and still not obtain final salvation. Ethics should not be seen as a footnote or a mere appendix (which can readily be taken out and not missed) to theology in the New Testament thought world. Shall we ignore remarks of Jesus like "Unless your righteousness [not Christ's righteousness, yours] exceeds that of the scribes and Pharisees, you shall not enter the kingdom of God" (Mt 5:20)? It is Jesus who is saying this to his own disciples—not to outsiders!

While I realize that we must be careful not to neglect the great truth that salvation is by grace through faith, *that very faith* includes more than just right belief; it also involves faithful living after conversion. This is what our author in 2 Peter wishes to stress, however offensive this may be to some Christians then and now. Right standing with God is a gift, and holiness is a gift, but this gift must be unwrapped and used and exercised each and every day in the Christian life, "making every effort" lest we go some route such as the false teachers took, committing or becoming in danger of committing apostasy. In other words, our author is as ethically serious as he is theologically serious about the apostolic legacy, and so must we be as well. Listen, for example, to how our author speaks about the way that our character and behavior (our ethics) affect what we know of God and how effective we can be for God: "Make every effort to add to your faith goodness, and to goodness knowledge, and to knowledge self-control, and to self-control perseverance, and to perseverance godliness, and to godliness, mutual affection, and to mutual affection, real love. *For if you possess these qualities in increasing measure, they will keep you from being ineffective and unproductive* in your knowledge of our Lord Jesus Christ" (2 Pet 1:5-8). Character and behavior counts, just as right belief does. We need to stop trivializing the ethics of the New Testament as if ethics were of secondary importance.

A word of caution is in order, however, when dealing with epideictic rhetoric such as we find in 2 Peter. This is the rhetoric of dramatic hyperbole. So, for example, one has to weigh how much of what the author says is polemical or for dramatic effect and how much should be taken literally. For example, how seriously should we take the idea that the false teachers were in the way of righteousness and had escaped the corruption of the world by knowing Christ, but then have turned back to their old sinful ways (2 Pet 2:20-22)? How seriously should we take the author when he says we are already partakers in the divine nature? How seriously should we take our author when he suggests that Christians, by good repentant behavior, can hasten the Day of the Lord (2 Pet 3)? My answer to this is that the hyperbole does not come in the basic theological and ethical ideas here: it comes in the dramatic metaphors and proverbs used to describe it, as in the proverb about the dog returning to its vomit. I doubt that our author is encouraging us to call people "dogs." The idea is that the false teachers' behavior is so revolting that one must use a revolting image to warn off the audience from behaving like that. In other words, when reading epideictic rhetoric, "these things call for discernment," and "there are some things hard to understand that the unstable distort" (cf. 2 Pet 3:3, 16).

The subject of myth versus history also comes up in this discourse, not only in the testimony of Peter, but also in 2 Peter 2. Our author believes that there is a historical foundation and bedrock to the Christian faith, which must not be compromised or trivialized by treating it as if it were cleverly devised myths. This is not because there is no mythological language used in the New Testament. Of course there is, as in the dragon imagery used in Revelation 12. However, that is a very different matter than saying that the stories about the life of Jesus are myths, which our author instantly repudiates. In this letter the "knowledge of God" is not, as in later Gnostic documents, some esoteric insider knowledge about aeons or Demiurges or the hidden nature of reality, which only the elite can obtain. On the contrary, the knowledge of God in Christ was conveyed through a historical experience (the transfiguration) and passed on to us by Peter's eyewitness testimony. God himself said of Jesus, "He is my Beloved Son." Knowledge, including full knowledge of God, includes but is not limited to knowledge of the historical facts and life of Jesus on which the Christian faith is founded. Our author is neither a docetist nor a Gnostic, nor would he see such persons as genuine Christians, any more than the author of 1-3 John would. In a postmodern world these truths need to be especially emphasized. We cannot get closer to God by getting further and further away from the historical knowledge of Jesus. It is not just about our experience of God; it is also about our knowledge of God in Christ, including our knowledge of the historical foundations of the faith, without which there would have been no Christian movement in the first century.

There is a robust theology of the word of God in 2 Peter, which brought creation into being and indeed brings judgment into history as well, according to our author. Our author is fully in accord with Jewish theology about God creating all things and judging all things in the past and in the future. He affirms the goodness of creation and re-creation at the eschatological end of things. There thus is an arc to the narrative of God's relationship with humankind: it has a beginning, a middle and an end, just as the physical universe does. Creation and creature are bound up together, being born, living and dying. "Life and death upon one tether, and running beautiful together."[309] Our author is not focusing on heavenly compensation for earthly disappointment. His focus is not on heaven or the other world, but it is eschatologically focused on the afterlife when Jesus returns, the dead are raised, final judgment happens and we enter the kingdom of God on earth, as it is in heaven. Our author may be the last writer of the New Testament era, so far as documents which made it into the canon, but he still maintains the same early eschatological vision of the future held by our earliest New Testament writer: Paul. And so the story of creation and flood are not told as stories in themselves, but as part of the larger drama of redemption, which is heading for a big bang climax just as it had a big bang beginning.

It is telling about our own era that while people are often prepared to entertain the notion that creation had a beginning, they have a much harder time accepting that there will be a dramatic conclusion in which justice will be done and righteousness and love and truth will prevail. The cynicism of our age is not unlike the cynicism of the false teachers in 2 Peter, and for the same reasons: "Where is the promise of his coming?" they ask. And I must say that they have a right to ask such a question, especially when so many crazy Christians have turned into theological weather forecasters in our time. What predictions of the timing of the second coming all have in common is that they, throughout two thousand years of church history, have all been wrong. But our author is right to insist that we should continue to have great expectations for the return of

[309] A line from a poem by Robert Coffin titled "Crystal Moment."

Christ without giving way to grandiose calculations.

Calculation involves a failure of faith. It involves the arrogance of thinking one knows even more than Jesus knew while he was on this earth, who said "of that day or hour no one knows" (Mk 13:32). The way our author fires up expectation without encouraging calculation is by using vivid images to dramatically depict what is yet to come when Christ returns, while at the same time using Psalm 90:4 to remind us that it is all a matter of God's timing, and he is not on the same watch as we are. Thus he both affirms that the "thief" is still coming suddenly at some juncture while also insisting that we don't know when. A sudden coming, even a possibly imminent coming, does not necessarily mean a "soon coming." Both divine and human factors are in play, says our author, including God's patient mercy in giving people time to repent. Thus our author preserves the careful New Testament balance of firing up expectations while snuffing out calculations. This inspires hope without ceasing to require faith and trust in God. As I have said before, God reveals enough of the future to give us hope, but not so much that we do not have to have faith and trust in God. Calculation is both a failure of nerve and of faith. It is an attempt at manipulation, to take God's Word into our own hands and force it to give us precise answers on subjects that God has decided not to give precise information on. Patience and perseverance are Christian virtues inculcated in 2 Peter. Calculation and human manipulation are not.

Finally, it is hard not to gather the impression that our author is excited about the Christian life, which in various ways can be said to partake of God's own glory, at least by way of reflection of the divine light. The notion that we can be conformed to God's glorious image is indeed a breathtaking one, and we should not sell this birthright for a mess of pottage suggesting that the Christian life is all about ethically falling short of the glory of God. It is not just about that, even though it does often involve that. Our author is optimistic about the effects of God's grace on the human character. He even believes that by grace one can grow in character and in knowledge of God. He believes that even now we can in some measure participate in the divine nature, in the sense that we already have the gift of everlasting life, a foretaste of glory divine. If a person cannot become excited about being all that we could be by fully reflecting God's image, then one is a Christian without a pulse, who has failed to listen to the New Testament promises about our life and lifestyle, promises like "No temptation has overcome you which is not common to humanity, . . . such that with the temptation God can provide a way of escape" (1 Cor 10:13). There can indeed be victory over sin in the Christian life. There can indeed be a growing reflection of the divine glory and nature in a human life if one will allow the Spirit to work in one's life. Our author believes God's yes in our life is greater than sin and death's no. It is not just that he thinks, "You ought to live holy and godly lives as you look forward to the Day" (2 Pet 3:11-12). He also believes that by the grace of God, Christians can do so.

It is this optimism of grace (while being perfectly aware of all the flaws of human nature that must be overcome) that characterizes the New Testament authors from both first to last, from Paul to 2 Peter. They believe that God's power is greater than the scope of our sins or our frailties. This is the good news the early Christians heralded throughout the Roman Empire, that a person can be converted, sanctified, saved to the uttermost, partaker of the divine nature in part now and in full when Christ returns, and even that a believer can know and be assured that one has been and is being saved. Destruction will not have the last word: instead, new creation will have the last word. Christ has not left us bereft or as orphans in this world.

What the author of 2 Peter says we "ought to do" in regard to living godly lives, he also believes that by grace we can do. As Wesley once said, All the commandments of God are but covered promises. If God says, "Thou shalt be holy," God means not only that we must or ought to be holy; God also means that we indeed "shall be so." But only by grace. In this, Wesley is following Augustine of Hippo, who in his famous remark said, "Give what you command, Lord, and command what you will" (Augustine *Conf.* 10.29). The author of 2 Peter believes that God has both given and continues to give such liberation to his people, and therefore even at the climax of the New Testament era we continue to hear the strong and insistent call to live godly lives in this world, in this lifetime, until the kingdom comes. Ethics is not merely a mirror of one's theology; it also is the living out and fulfillment of one's theology, and the attitude of the believer must always be this: if all of theology is of grace, then all of ethics is gratitude. Grace is what motivates Christian behavior, but it is also what enables it. If one believes and lives by this grace, then works righteousness is an attitude that can never develop, and a person could never delude oneself into thinking one was engaged in a program of self-salvation. It is just that God has chosen not to save a person without one's also "making every effort." Theology and ethics should never have been divorced or radically separated in New Testament studies. I hope to say much more about their "more perfect union" in the not too distant future.

FINAL REFLECTIONS: LETTERS AND HOMILIES FROM THE LAST THIRD OF THE FIRST CENTURY A.D.

Second Peter brings us to the climax and end of our study of letters and homilies in the New Testament, which has taken us through some eleven of the twenty-seven New Testament documents, or a bit over a third of the New Testament itself. I have reserved until this point one of the surprises that a reader discovers if one studies 2 Peter as the latest or nearly the latest (with the possible exception of Revelation) New Testament document. It is this: the church can be addressed as a whole, as Jew and Gentile united in Christ. Earlier in our three volumes, we have seen that some of these documents are likely addressed to congregations that were overwhelmingly Gentile Christian (such as the Pastorals), and some to congregations overwhelmingly Jewish Christian (such as James, Jude, Hebrews).

But with 2 Peter we have taken a step forward and are closer to the second-century church, where in the person of figures like Ignatius, the church as a whole must be addressed, whether the congregations originally were more Jewish or Gentile Christian, more Pauline or more Petrine in character. Second Peter not merely shows us that this process of consolidation was already going on in the first century; it also shows us that the social networks were such that we have *no canonical evidence* of any great resistance to this consolidation of the Christian movement. To be sure, we could point out evidence of groups like the Ebionites and perhaps others who did resist this consolidation, but they were by no means in the mainstream of the early apostolic Christian movement anymore than 2 Peter's false teachers or the later Gnostics were. There indeed was an apostolic orthodoxy and orthopraxy that shaped the entire Christian movement from Paul and Peter to Linus and Clement, such that even the false teachers and "heretics" bore witness to this orthodoxy and orthopraxy by the very way they reacted to things like apostolic eschatology.

This means that somewhere in time in the 80s and early 90s, as the last of the apostolic eyewitnesses died out, the consolidating process was beginning, which is not yet reflected in 1—3 John or even the Pastoral Epistles. We frankly do not know how this began, but it does look as though after the demise of Jerusalem in A.D. 70, there was an impetus for Christians to pull their act together, especially having been branded a superstition during Claudius's and then Nero's times. Likewise, there was impetus for early Judaism to pull its act together at Jabneh (Yavne, Jamnia) after A.D. 70. But if 2 Peter's connections with Peter are any clue, and if there is any cogency in the suggestion that perhaps Linus is responsible for this apostolic potpourri we call 2 Peter, then it looks as though the initiative for this consolidation comes from the Roman church. This is not a surprise since this is where the great apostolic Gentile and Jewish missionary leaders Paul and Peter finished their lifework.

What were to be the social obstacles to consolidation of the Christian movement? The answer is right in front of us in 2 Peter. It would be teachers and prophetic figures who no longer were kept in check or in line by living apostles. They began to go their own way theologically and ethically. And the dilemma for someone like the author of 2 Peter is that the false teachers could always say: "Why should we listen to you? You are not an eyewitness or an apostle. You are just another authority figure like us, and we too have the Holy Spirit." Our author's response and way of establishing ethos and authority is by citing and amplifying and drawing on the given apostolic testimony and tradition from the past, in much the same way a Protestant today would see the final authority as lying in the Bible itself. It is no small thing that our author, perhaps for the very first time, ranks Paul's letters with the Old Testament Scriptures themselves as sacred and inspired documents, foundational documents. Increasingly the issue was to be foundational documents and the relying on them. We can see this, for instance, in *1 Clement,* where the author is not merely enriched by Paul's 1 Corinthians but in fact draws on it in much the same way that our author draws on Jude and Peter's testimony. Or we can see it in the *Didache,* where the author is repeatedly drawing on material from the Matthean stream of the Jesus tradition. In my view, 2 Peter needs to be compared not just with Jude or 1 Peter or even the Pastorals. In terms of its modus operandi in handling the apostolic tradition, it should be compared to contemporary Christian documents from the end of the first century: *1 Clement* and perhaps *2 Clement*, the *Epistle of Barnabas*, the *Didache.* These latter two documents seem to have come out of predominantly Jewish Christian settings, whereas 2 Peter, like at least *1 Clement,* comes out of a mixed church that has a majority of Gentiles and reflects that ethos. Is it an accident that the consolidation movement begins from Rome?

Did the consolidation Paul was longing for, where he hoped the Gentile Christians would treat the Jewish Christians in Rome better, embracing them (see Rom 12—16),[310] happen in the 70s-90s in "the Eternal City," in the wake of Nero's wrath? It would seem the answer to this question is yes. And so the consolidation came after the devastations of Nero's wrath, which certainly was later than Paul and Peter might have wanted, too late for them to see it consummated, but nonetheless better late than never. Thus I am suggesting that the Roman church members managed to put their own house in order (or their own catacombs in order) during the Flavian period (69-96), and they were largely left alone under the reign of Vespasian and Titus, but not, alas, during the reign of megalomaniac Domitian (81-96).

I suggest that it was precisely the rise of Domitian that gave impetus to the

[310]See Witherington and Hyatt, *Letter to the Romans.*

church in Rome to try to help the rest of the movement become more united across the empire. We see the first attempts at this in 2 Peter. The handwriting was on the wall: there would be more persecutions. We see that beginning to be played out in Revelation, written at about the same time as 2 Peter. But the strategy of the author of 2 Peter is grander than that of John of Patmos, who must content himself with strengthening his several churches in Asia Minor. Our author of 2 Peter thinks that church leaders must do the same for the entire movement. And here is where I suggest that 2 Peter was not the only vehicle for this consolidation of the movement. I suggest that other documents in the Petrine tradition were being circulated more widely to help facilitate this end: Mark's Gospel and 1 Peter itself. One of the reasons for sending out these documents is that they could be equally useful in addressing Jewish as well as Gentile Christians. They had a more universal character in language, style, and even to some degree in content. If we want to understand the ascendancy of Peter and not Paul in the Western church, we must trace its roots back to what the Roman church did to consolidate the faithful communities in the wake of growing hostility from the Roman government. The vehicles used to accomplish the consolidation were coming mainly from the Petrine tradition. The Pauline letters had already been circulating for a good number of years, even as a collection, but they in themselves could not effect the consolidation of the apostolic movement, especially if there was to be a concerted effort to include all the various Jewish Christian groups within the fold. Thus the church had to draw on Peter and his legacy, for he was the one bridge figure who had one foot in the ministry of Jesus itself and one foot in the early church: he himself by the power of the Holy Spirit had been responsible for both some Gentiles and many Jews coming to faith in Christ. Paul's legacy was largely for the rising majority of Gentile Christians, but there was a danger that the Jewish roots would become buried, neglected, left behind.

Our author, the writer of 2 Peter, did not want the Jewish legacy lost any more than the historical Peter as a missionary to Jews had wanted that. How could church leaders send forward the legacy of those who had ministered largely to Jews, people like Peter and Jude, all the while realizing that the church was becoming increasingly Gentile and was in danger of losing touch with its Jewish roots? Our author's answer was to draw from that deep well and spread out the early Jewish Christian water across the entire landscape of early Christianity. It was a daring move, and it seems to have helped to make the church's transition into the postapostolic era easier. First Peter could be used to speak to the issue of suffering and persecution. Mark could help in this regard as well with his apocalyptically oriented Gospel, while also grounding the audience in the original foundational story of Jesus. And 2 Peter could help with the eschatological and ethical consolidation of the movement, all the while reaffirming the church's ongoing high Christology. Most of this is generally conjecture, but the test of any good historical hypothesis is its explanatory power. My hypothesis not only explains why a document like 2 Peter was crucial in the transitional phase of the Christian movement into the postapostolic era; it also gives glimpses of how the consolidation of the movement in terms of orthodoxy, orthopraxy and indeed social connections may have taken place. Paul and his letters were prophetic and challenging. Galatians is not the kind of document that would help the church build a consensus or forge a consolidation. Second Peter, however, is a horse of a different color: a blending of old and new, and various apostolic strains. But there is more to the story.

The Gospel of Matthew became the runaway most popular of all Gospels in the second century A.D. How did this happen when it is the most Jewish of Gospels and probably was written mainly for Jewish Christians in Galilee or Antioch?[311] My suggestion is this: leaders like Linus in Rome collected evidence of the Jewish Christian heritage in documents like James, Jude, Hebrews, and certainly Matthew, and then had them copied and distributed widely. We know with reasonable certainty that by about A.D. 125 there was already a collection of the four earliest Gospels, headed by Matthew, circulating in codex form through church. Who initiated this? It seems most unlikely to me that it was Jewish Christians in Galilee, Antioch or Pella. For one thing, we must remember that the Bar Kokhba revolt brought chaos and turmoil to that whole region during the early stages of the second century. The forceful suppression of that revolt led to even Jerusalem being turned into a pagan city: Aelia Capitolina (A.D. 135). It seems likely to me, then, that Linus and others in the church in Rome had called in their markers, had asked Christians to bring the documents to Rome, and now they were sending out a variety of foundational source documents for all Christians to read, writings originally addressed to particular audiences. The author of 2 Peter not merely knows of a collection of Paul's letters; he also knows at least some of what is in them, or he could never have said that some things in Paul's letters are hard to understand.

But most remarkably, our author is prepared to rank Paul's letters right up there not just with the other apostolic documents but also with the inspired Old Testament Scriptures themselves. This too is a consolidating rhetorical tactic. The Pauline and Petrine and other churches must band together. The Roman church must aid and abet this movement of consolidation. How would they accomplish this? They would copy and send out a full spectrum of apostolic doc-

[311]See Witherington, *Gospel of Matthew*.

uments, even the controversial Pauline ones. What we see in this is a profound belief that the apostolic testimony is just as inspired and prophetic as the Old Testament itself. It is just as much the word of God as the Old Testament itself. The living word of God in apostolic Christian form, as well as its written residue, is normative for all these churches and must be passed along as such. But there is a further corollary as well: the author of 2 Peter does not feel free to speak in his own voice in a document that is actually an anthology of apostolic materials. He can look back at the early eyewitnesses as apostles and writers of inspired documents that can be called the word of God, but his own composition only has this quality because it is a compilation of earlier apostolic materials. He was not to go on and write the Gospel according to Linus. His job was to preserve, protect, copy and transmit the earlier apostolic witness. The fact that 2 Peter finally found a place toward the end of the canon shows that the church recognized that it faithfully passed on apostolic tradition.

In his thought-provoking study, Father Denis Farkasfalvy makes some interesting remarks about 2 Peter that can further our discussion at this juncture.[312] To an even greater extent than we have done in this study, he meticulously demonstrates the composite nature of 2 Peter. One of the points he makes in telling fashion is that the later documents of the New Testament period reflect the fact that in the church the death of the apostles became a problem with theological and ecclesiological dimensions, which texts such as John 21:18-23 and *1 Clement* 44 demonstrate, and so does 2 Peter.[313] He is quite right about this, and right to see 2 Peter as in part a response to this situation of absent apostles, which made the challenge of false teachers all the worse. Second Peter sets something of a precedent in calling the church to apostolic remembrance, pointing to the need not to dwell in the past but to draw on and be faithful to the apostolic tradition of the past. Our author responds to the end of the apostolic era not merely by collecting documents from the past, but also by composing one that reminds the audience of the apostolic heritage and also maintains that the great apostolic leaders stood together on essential issues like eschatology and Christology. He feels that there is a need in the church to indicate that they stood together on such things. "The author is convinced that his understanding of Peter and Paul is correct; he also believes that Peter and Paul as apostles of the Lord who were divinely instructed, must be in agreement with each other."[314] The net effect of this document, as it looks back to the apostles and

[312]Farkasfalvy, "Ecclesial Setting of Pseudepigraphy," pp. 3-29.
[313]Ibid., p. 21.
[314]Ibid., p. 23.

does not presume to speak on its own authority, is that it has an orientation and "employs devices that make new [pseudonymous] apostolic products lose their credibility."[315] He understands that as the apostles were dying off, there was a growing importance to both the remaining living or oral testimony and increasingly the written memory and testimony of these persons (cf. *1 Clem.* 13.1; 46.7-8; 62.2-3; Pol. *Phil.* 2.3). "Thus we might observe that Second Peter promotes the closure of the canon in two senses: (1) It condenses and explicates, at least in its intention, the doctrine contained in documents already established as normative in the Church. (2) It *inserts itself among these writings in a way that blocks the addition of further documents of a similar (Petrine) claim.*"[316]

In short—and here I go beyond Denis Farkasfalvy, who does not see this inference—by offering the last testimony of Peter from just before his death, the author of 2 Peter seeks to present us with the last words of the Petrine tradition, not to add further posthumous words in Peter's name that do not go back to Peter. Farkasfalvy is right, however, that we must see the ecumenical value of 2 Peter, in its attempt to affirm the various streams of earlier apostolic tradition and use them together to deal with the false teachers. He does not choose sides between Peter and Paul or even against Jude. Rather, he sees these witnesses as in harmony and standing together, and even more to the point, he sees himself as in harmony with them and fairly representing them. "Second Peter has the distinction of recognizing a wider scope of Christian traditions with a commitment to integrating them into one treasury of 'remembrance' sealed by the authority of the same Lord. . . . Second Peter [as a whole] neither imitates the style of First Peter, nor does it manifest a preoccupation to lessen Paul's authority by subordinating it to that of Peter. Second Peter's special merit is its decidedly inclusive thrust."[317] All the voices in the apostolic choir ought to be allowed to sing and make their contribution without rivalry or hostile takeovers, in our author's view. Second Peter is a document that gives the lie to the old thesis of Ferdinand Christian Baur that there were, and were perceived to be, irreconcilable differences between the Petrine and Pauline traditions, the more Jewish and the more Gentile Christian traditions, and between their respective advocates. No indeed: even though Linus wishes to present us with more Petrine material, Paul is warmly affirmed as "our beloved brother Paul." This document, which is not pseudonymous, was actually to aid in setting up criteria against pseudepigrapha.

[315]Ibid.

[316]Ibid, p. 24, emphasis added.

[317]Ibid., p. 27.

The signal sent out by 2 Peter appears to have been clearly picked up in the second century. Thus we have Bishop Serapion in that century stressing, "Brothers, we accept Peter and the other apostles as Christ himself, but pseudepigrapha under their names we routinely reject" (quoted in Eusebius *Hist. eccl.* 6.12.3). Or again the Muratorian Canon, the ending of which attests to its second-century provenance,[318] tells us that the letters to the Laodiceans and Alexandrians were rejected because of "Pauli nomine fictae," which is the equivalent of the term "pseudepigrapha." But would a document like 2 Peter, published after the death of Peter, be seen as a pseudepigraphon? To judge from what Tertullian says, the answer would be no: he stresses "it is allowable that that which pupils publish should be regarded as their master's work" (Tertullian *Marc.* 4.5). In other words, if the document is published in Peter's name, then there needs to be a real connection between the "author" and Peter, and he needs to be conveying things he learned from Peter or that came from Peter. A composite document like 2 Peter, with a Petrine testimony included, would qualify under this criterion.

In these volumes we have talked about the differences and also the overlap between letters, sermons and rhetorical discourses. Here it is time to draw together some of the things we have learned from these studies. In the first place, we have learned that it is time to stop talking about some of these documents being letters: 1 John is certainly not a letter in any sense of the word. It has no epistolary features, whether compared to other early Jewish or Greco-Roman letters. Second, we have a whole batch of New Testament documents that have only minimal epistolary features at either the beginning or the end of the document. Hebrews has no epistolary opening, but it does have something of an epistolary closing. The important thing to recognize about this is that the audience who heard this discourse called Hebrews would never have known that it was a letter at all before they reached the end of the document. This is important because in an oral and aural culture, documents, which would be read aloud, needed to send genre signals up front, not just at the end. Hebrews is not a letter: it is a lengthy Jewish Christian sermon with an epistolary close because the author is sending it from a remote location and cannot make personal remarks in person.

This contrasts quite nicely with 2-3 John, which are the documents in the New Testament most like ancient letters. They are short, succinct, purpose-

---

[318]The word *nuperrim* (*e temporibus nostris in urbe roma*), "recently," implies a clear chronology that this document was composed within about 50 years after Pius, the brother of Hermas, was the bishop in Rome. See ibid., p. 29 and n. 50.

driven, and they have epistolary features. James is a homily that does have an epistolary opening, but as a circular letter its content is not like the ad hoc letters of Paul written to specific congregations with specific problems. James, like Peter in 1 Peter, is dealing with more global issues and problems, not those that plagued just one church. First Peter does indeed have epistolary features at its beginning and end, but the vast majority of the document is not busily conforming itself to epistolary structures. Rather, it follows rhetorical structures in its outline, arrangement of material and way it sets up a thesis statement, pursues arguments and then draws conclusions in a peroration. This general rhetorical structure is the most prevalent pattern we find in the vast majority of the so called letters of the New Testament. If we want to put the emphasis where it actually lies, it would be better to talk about the discourses or homilies of the New Testament that sometimes do and sometimes do not have some epistolary features.

What about the Pastoral Epistles? They are the only "personal" discourses/letters in the New Testament, for even Philemon is addressed to the church in his house as well as to him. But as Luke Johnson has shown, basically we do not have ordinary letters in the Pastorals: they are mandate letters, from a superior giving instructions and mandates to a subordinate. And even in the case of these more personal letters, one can say that they are as much or more shaped by rhetorical conventions than by epistolary ones. I want to reiterate here what was said in the first volume of this series. Rhetoric was the dominant and most pervasive literary paradigm into which epistolary conventions had to fit themselves. Letter writing of the sort we find in the New Testament—letters that read more like treatises or essays on some subject—stood in a relatively new tradition that had risen to importance in the time of Cicero and thereafter. When scholars like Pseudo-Libanius later sat down to formalize epistolary theory, they were always cognizant that they lived in a rhetoric-saturated environment. In short, epistolary analysis of the New Testament should take a back seat to rhetorical analysis of such documents since they are mostly, and for most of their substance, actually rhetorical discourses of some sort set in an epistolary framework, because they could not be orally delivered in person. This conclusion includes the Pastoral Epistles.

Jude may well be the most sectarian Jewish Christian document in the entire canon. It is a brief letter, as its beginning indicates, but it is even more an impassioned sermon with some rhetorical features as well, and it ends with a liturgical form, the doxology, which indicates that it was probably meant to be orally delivered as a sermon in a worship service. The same can certainly also be said about 2 Peter, which has no epistolary close either; instead, it has the ethos and character of an epideictic polemic about blameworthy and praiseworthy behavior.

First Peter is a powerful meditation on suffering and persecution in deliberative rhetorical form. It does indeed have an epistolary opening and closing, but in between the structure is rhetorical. I would just add that when one actually analyzes the so-called thanksgiving periods (passages) in the New Testament, one discovers that they are very little like the health wishes in secular letters. It would be better to say that Christians have substituted for the health (farewell) wish either prayers or eulogies, which suited the worship setting of the discourse's oral delivery and would have sounded more like an exordium and thanksgiving prayer than a pagan health wish.

We have also recognized that the designation "body middle" tells us nothing about the form or the content of the material we find in these documents, and that material *covers the vast majority of these documents.* There was no ancient literary form called "body middle"! It is the rhetorical conventions that dictate how the middle of these documents are structured, not epistolary ones, and this is hardly a surprise since these are "oral texts," texts operating in and for a largely oral culture. More often than not they are surrogates for oral communication and have been framed according to these oral and rhetorical conventions, so that they may be orally delivered by a surrogate. In the case of 1 Peter, that apparently was Silvanus. If it is true that form follows function, then we should hardly be surprised that these oral documents largely follow the forms of oral communication: rhetoric, the ancient art of persuasion.

Time after time in this study we have pointed out the numerous oral and rhetorical devices we find in these discourses, devices that only really work when heard. It is precisely because we do not read these documents out loud in the original Greek today that we miss so much of the oral and rhetorical skill that these documents display. Indeed, most of the ornament of these documents is entirely lost by silent reading, much less reading them in English translation. Something becomes lost not only in translation but also in silent reading. We are a text-bound culture, where speeches are often viewed as secondary, ephemeral, here today and gone tomorrow, boring, tedious and less substantial than texts. The ancients, however, preferred the living voice, the living word of God. It is time to respect these texts more, and to do our best to study them as products of an oral culture, not a text-driven culture. The "letters" and homilies of the New Testament were meant to supplement, indeed even supply scripts for, the oral performance of the good news. This should come as no surprise since Christianity was an energetic evangelistic movement and its writings reflect the ancient art of sermonizing and persuasion.

I want to say something more about the issue of epistolary pseudepigrapha. I have pointed out that our categories are impoverished if the only two slots we have for 2 Peter are a letter written by Peter or a letter written using the pseudonym Peter, an epistolary pseudepigraphon. The problem with this limitation is that there are other options, not the least of which is the one I proposed for 2 Peter: a composite discourse drawing on a variety of sources, the most well known of which is by Peter, the leader of the Twelve and the apostle to Jews. I drew an analogy with the Gospel of Matthew. This latter document is a composite one that draws on Mark and other sources, one of which is called special M and appears to go back to Matthew himself. This is why that Gospel is called the Gospel of Matthew. In antiquity a document could be named after its most famous contributor, as sometimes happens today when there is a volume of collected essays. Clearly, a composite document that includes one or more genuine sources coming from the named author is not simply a pseudonymous document. It is not merely a document that pretends or appears to be by the named author; instead, the named author is a contributor whether knowingly or posthumously. In this case it is the latter. I propose that we need, then, to broaden our categories, and there is one further reason to do so as well.

Since these are oral documents, sermons or more formal rhetorical discourses sometimes set in an epistolary framework, we should seek for the usual rules when copying and passing on a sermon or such a discourse. With regard to Christian sermons, it is indeed striking that the two most obvious examples in the New Testament, 1 John and Hebrews, are *anonymous*. The names of the persons who actually wrote these homilies are not mentioned. In 2 Peter we have an inscribed author in the epistolary prescript, but the actual framer of this composite discourse, a homiletical polemic, is anonymous. In this case it is probably by design because it is a sermon borrowed from another person's discourses, and at least one of them needed to be credited: the first one cited. I suggest that the same thing happens in Matthew: Matthew 1—2 is by Matthew; it is not Markan material. The document is named after the first main contributor. One could also pursue the issue of what the rhetorical conventions were about using other people's rhetoric or discourses without attribution as well. Certainly the practice was known: indeed, Quintilian complains about his discourses being used at times without attribution.[319] This in turn suggests that for him, the normal ethical thing to do was to mention the source of the material. Our author of 2 Peter is certainly an ethical person, indeed a very conservative one. It follows from all this that we would expect him to credit not himself but his source or at least one of them

[319]See my *Letters and Homilies for Hellenized Christians,* 1:23-38.

when he drew together his composite epideictic discourse. This seems to have been the minimum and normal expected ethical requirement for borrowed material, and the author of 2 Peter has met it. In other words, whether one is evaluating 2 Peter according to the ancient conventions of a letter, a homily or a rhetorical discourse, it still is not a pseudonymous document.

Thus there are no pseudonymous documents in the New Testament if even 2 Peter is not one.

Several of the discourses in our three-volume work come to us from the Pauline circle, in particular the Pastoral Epistles and probably Hebrews. The rest come from elsewhere, but as both James and 2 Peter show, they are well aware of the sort of things Paul said, and indeed of the false teachers' and others' distortions of things said by Paul. As we have seen, these documents are mostly addressed to Jewish Christians, those evangelized by the likes of James, Jude, Peter and perhaps Apollos. The only exceptions to this would be the Pastoral Epistles, which are for largely Gentile contexts, though Timothy himself is Jewish. The Johannine Epistles and probably 1 Peter are, like all the documents in the second volume of our study, written primarily to Jewish Christians.

It is unfortunate that these documents were relegated to the trunk end of the canon, later called General or Catholic Epistles, and seen as second rate by many well into modernity. Indeed, this is a stigma that still plagues the study of these documents. What they bear witness to, as we stressed in the conclusion to the second volume, is that there was a vibrant ongoing group of mostly Jewish Christian churches all over the empire well into the waning stages of the first century and beyond. It was not inappropriate, then, that those who came from these Jewish Christian circles in Rome were those who stepped forward to help consolidate the movement involving more and more Gentiles. The original Jewish Christian legacy must not be lost, whether it had originally been disseminated by Paul and his coworkers largely to Gentiles, or it had been disseminated by Peter, James, Jude and their coworkers mainly to Jews. It is the Jewishness of all these documents, whether addressed to more or less Hellenized Christians, which makes them stand out from Greco-Roman literature, and certainly their Christianity likewise makes them distinct from such literature. None of these documents was likely written by non-Jews, *except possibly 2 Peter*, if it is by Linus, and also it would appear that Luke was the person mainly responsible for writing down the Pastorals for Paul.

What do these documents teach us about how to study the New Testament? They remind us that the past is indeed like a foreign country, and we should not expect documents from the past to meet all our modern expectations or desires. We must study them in their original contexts the best we can; those authors and their contexts cannot now come to us. We must respect the historical givenness of these materials if we are ever to hear how these documents were and are the living word of God for them and for us.

Second, it is time for rhetorical studies to become more primary and epistolary analysis more secondary when it comes to the understanding of the character and structure of these documents. This is not because there are no epistolary features in these documents. There are, and they are used rather flexibly at the beginning and/or end of some of these documents. But if the goal is to explain the form and content of most of these documents, then rhetoric needs to be a more major tool for analyzing them.

Third, the skill in the use of Greco-Roman rhetoric displayed in these documents ranges from rather rudimentary (e.g., Jude) to extremely adept (Hebrews). But none of them, and I do mean none of them, lack reflection of knowledge or use of ancient rhetoric. This is not a surprise since rhetoric was a staple part of education throughout the empire and including as Jewish a place as Jerusalem or the Jewish districts of Alexandria. Those who wanted to be effective communicators in Greek had best have some rhetorical skill. And those who wanted to persuade people to adopt a whole new religion had better have not only good arguments, but also know how to assemble and effectively deliver them. We are used to categories like theology and ethics, but what is overarching about all the material examined in these volumes is that they are acts of persuasion, rhetorically adept homilies or sermons or discourses or instructions and mandates. They are always tendentious, they are always arguing or urging a particular case and point of view, and none of these documents reads like a modern technical theological or ethical textbook. They are far more akin to preaching than they are to textbooks. And this leads to a warning.

Scholars like to think of those that they admire as being scholarly like themselves, and having the same sorts of scholarly interests. But I doubt that this does justice to any of the authors of the New Testament. However intellectually gifted they were, however inspired by the wisdom that comes from above, they always had evangelizing and discipling aims in what they wrote. They were always preaching for a verdict and were in no sense armchair scholars interested in arcane lore or in merely scratching their intellectual itches. Even the author of 2 Peter, who is more of a scribe (which in some cases was the ancient equivalent of a literate scholar of earlier literature), has very practical and pragmatic and pastoral aims in what he writes. He is not interested in a debate about the timing of the second coming as an intellectual exercise. He desperately wants his audience to avoid spiritual danger that can come with embracing bad theology and its bad ethical consequences. All of this material comes to us in the service of very specific practical and Christian and pastoral and evangelistic aims.

In a sense this will come as a relief to current pastors and laypeople. This material was written by and for people just like themselves in that regard. It was written by and for the churches, to be used in worship and instruction, and as such there is continuity with modern teaching and sermonizing in church contexts. None of these documents are evangelistic tracts to be handed out: they are in-house material. They are the ancient equivalent of Sunday school and worship resources. They are not the ancient equivalent of doctoral dissertations!

What is my point? Am I saying that scholars should stop studying these documents? Certainly not. But we need to recognize their character, and indeed the character of the early Christian missionary movement. Our authors apparently did indeed believe "vox populi, vox Dei" in a different kind of way than when that phrase was first promulgated. They believed that the voice of God, the living word of God, should be conveyed in the language of the people of the day, a language that most anyone who knew Greek could appreciate and understand. It needed to use all the tools of persuasion that could be mustered in Greek if people were going to be convinced of the truth of an odd story about a crucified manual worker from Galilee, whom God raised from the dead and declared to be his unique only begotten Son, and indeed to be Lord and Savior of all.

This is not to suggest that Koine Greek is all we find in the New Testament. Certainly not. We have seen that we have plenty of Asiatic Greek as well, but that too was the language of the people, especially those in Asia, which was in so many ways the cradle of Christianity, both Petrine and Pauline. Listening to rhetoricians was one of the great spectator sports of antiquity, ranking up there with watching gladiatorial contests. In fact, at many of the Greek-styled games, there also were oratorical contests, the ancient equivalent of spelling bees! Nero, not surprisingly, once won the poetry contest at the games in Corinth. The more I have studied the oral culture of the New Testament era, the more profoundly I have become convinced of the oral and rhetorical nature of these New Testament documents. In antiquity as today, Christians had their favorite preachers. Here, then, in part of the New Testament we find some of the early illustrious sermons and discourses of early Christianity. They may at first appear dull, abrupt, too polemical on the first silent read, but they come to life when they are read out loud and then proclaimed.

The sermons and discourses have now become the sacred texts and resources for new sermons and discourses and teaching lessons. The proclamations have become the basis for more proclamations. I have to believe that the authors of the so-called New Testament "letters" would have been very pleased with this, whether we are talking about Paul, Peter, James, Jude, Apollos or even Linus. After all, they were all homileticians. So in closing I offer a new suggestion. For missionary-minded literate early Christians who wrote these documents, "divinity" or theologizing was not the queen of the sciences: it was rather the rhetorically adept proclamation of the good news, which deserved that title of "good news." So to those who read this last of my commentaries, I leave you with a singular exhortation: Preach it, brother and sister, preach it!

Index of Authors

Index of Ancient Sources

Callan, Terrance D.

The Chiastic... of II Pe... Rel

II Peter

Bib 82 252-63

549-59

- Available (US)
- October (UK)
- Hardback
- $39.95 (UK £26.99)
- 9780664221386
- 328 pages
- World rights

THE NEW TESTAMENT LIBRARY

I & II Peter and Jude

A Commentary

Lewis R. Donelson

LEVEL: Seminary and graduate

COURSES: Petrine Epistles

The letters of 1 and 2 Peter and of Jude come from a time in Christian history about which we know little; thus they represent rare voices from a crucial time in Christianity's development. And the picture of early Christianity suggested by these letters is a fascinating one.

In them, Christianity seems to exist as an intersection of readings of the Old Testament, stories and traditions about Jesus, and the demands of living in the Roman world and the still-emerging church. Donelson's illuminating commentaries show that each letter reflects those forces in its own way. Viewed collectively, these documents portray communities deep in conflict, both with outsiders and with insiders. However, the letters also portray communities full not only of enormous theological resources but theological creativity as well.

Traditionally the letters of 1 Peter, 2 Peter, and Jude have been grouped together, because they have typically been seen as coming from similar situations in early Christian history and out of similar theological traditions. Donelson's interpretation deems 2 Peter's dependence on Jude to be so great that, in this commentary, Jude is considered before 2 Peter, reversing their canonical order.

Lewis R. Donelson is Ruth A. Campbell Professor of New Testament Studies at Austin Presbyterian Theological Seminary in Texas. His books include *From Hebrews to Revelation* and *Colossians, Ephesians, First and Second Timothy, and Titus.*

SEXUALITY

IN THE NEW

TESTAMENT

UNDERSTANDING THE KEY TEXTS

WILLIAM LOADER

Sexuality in the New Testament

Understanding the Key Texts

William Loader

LEVEL: College and seminary

COURSES: New Testament Ethics, Sexual Ethics

Available (US)
Paper
$19.95 (UK NA)
9780664231613
176 pages
World rights, excluding UK

Loader looks at hotly contested New Testament passages on sexuality and offers a fair and balanced treatment of what scholars say about them. He also offers an analysis of interpreters' views and demonstrates how texts may be interpreted specifically to support a preformed opinion. Written in straightforward, nontechnical language, this is the ideal classroom text.

William Loader, FAHA, is Professor Emeritus at Murdoch University, Perth, Australia. He is currently a Professorial Research Fellow of the Australian Research Council engaged in research on attitudes toward sexuality in Judaism and Christianity. He is the author of *Sexuality and the Jesus Tradition*.

"William Loader brings an honest and authoritative voice to the discussion of what the New Testament says about human sexuality. He invites his readers to join in a serious engagement with the scriptural texts in their social and historical context and [undertake] the challenge of wrestling with how those texts should be read today."

—Judith Lieu, Lady Margaret's Professor of Divinity, University of Cambridge

"Loader has brought together sources from the ancient world and opinions from

74 On "Goodbye" = "God be w[ith] ye"

354 [illegible] anesthetic [illegible]

* p17 – on early Chr. history – the characters of Peter (Jewish) (James, I II Peter, Hebrews, Jude) I II III John
Paul (Mediator) 1204

29-30 III The Diaspora Jews – more liberal – "eating with Gentiles in pagan temples" cf also I Cor. 8–10
Rom. Paul – the guilds – & Priscilla & Aquila

v63 on "apostles in [illegible]" III the Part of the baptism

155 on "following" Xst

188 Then the Creed: "descended into Hell" – 400 AD

191 foreskin – "unclean" 193 [illegible] – baptism

191 Jordan – & the flood 206/216 [illegible] in I Pet

239 the Devil 215 Persecution & Decius

240, 254 The Stole Earth & Satan (Rev) 228 On church officers – elder –
254 the Bauble 228 Shepherd & Pastor (Rev)
225 "Clergy" [illegible]

Sheol 238

247 on the Qn. of Hebrews
" or John Mark

15 ~~Absalom~~

353 deluge cataclysm

195 enthymeme " "

~~Robert E. Booth~~, 398

Robot ~~Ctr.~~ Security 399

399 Jerusalem – Temple ~~x~~ ~~cult~~ 40 ~~2~~ 274
after x's death

394 "

Zeus in Dan. ~~W.~~ p 398
on E

~~Ti~~

~~Acts 2~~ ~~X~~ Luke

123 Acts 2

406 I Cor. – Peter
Paul ~~vs.~~ Christian

136 II P. 1:1

409 The Acts 15 ~~Paul/Peter~~ argument

88 Isa 53

57 on ~~Hooch~~

272 on ~~Ephesians~~ "
~~9~~ II P.

191 ~~on food~~

399 " quote in my paper

411 Hebrews
416 ~~Bel sermon~~

417

~~213 Isa 11:2~~

241 Eph ~~56~~

77 On ~~Asiatic~~ rhetoric

3~~4~~ ~~kerygma~~

326 Post ~~Eventum~~

~~Vox Populi~~
~~Vox Dei~~ 417

P. ~~"Sermon"~~

402 "big bang"

also ~~II P.~~

412 ~~416~~ ~~sermon~~

412 ~~tithes~~

398 Rm 4 / 2 ~~ages~~ ~~realized~~

155 Isa 53

329–30 why did ~~Peter~~ Peter

Mk 9:5–6 "booth" as ~~tabernacle~~

374 ~~Mt 6~~ – The ~~Good~~ ~~people~~

~~270~~ 290 ~~Prov. Ecc.~~ – Solomon's

272 on ~~Ephesians~~ Ephesians

208 on John 13–17 – ~~"Beloved disciple"~~ – edited

323 ~~Gen~~ 1–2

398 ~~Gen 6~~

406 ~~Matthew~~

411 II ~~John~~ *

178 ~~Acts~~ *